PITIRIM A. SOROKIN IN REVIEW

THE AMERICAN SOCIOLOGICAL FORUM

PITIRIM A. SOROKIN IN REVIEW

Edited by PHILIP J. ALLEN

DUKE UNIVERSITY PRESS   Durham, N. C. 1963

301.082
AL5p

© 1963, Duke University Press

Library of Congress Catalogue Card Number 63-7634
Cambridge University Press, London N.W. 1, England

50,256

July, 1965

This book is published with the assistance
of a grant to the Duke University Press
by the Ford Foundation

Printed in the United States of America
by the Seeman Printery, Inc., Durham, N. C.

Biographic Sketches of Contributors

Othmar F. Anderle, Director of the Institut für Theoretische Geschichte in Salzburg, Austria, is Secretary-General of the International Society for the Comparative Study of Civilizations. He has published numerous volumes and journal articles in cultural morphology and the philosophy of history.

Bernard Barber, Professor of Sociology at Barnard College, Columbia University, previously taught at Harvard University and at Smith College. His major publications and professional interests lie in the sociology of science and social stratification. He is best known, perhaps, for his volume *Social Stratification.* He is on the Council for Atomic Age Studies.

Gösta Carlsson, Head of the Sociology Department at the University of Lund (Sweden), previously taught at the University of Stockholm. His major research interests lie in methodology, history of sociology, public opinion, and social stratification. Among his publications are *Dimensions of Behavior* (Lund, 1949); *Social-psykologisk metod* (Stockholm, 1949); and *Social Mobility and Class Structure* (Lund, 1958).

F. Richard Cowell has just retired from a lifetime of public service with the British government. Up to his retirement he was Secretary of the United Kingdom National Commission for UNESCO, a post he had held since UNESCO's foundation in 1946. He has been invested by H. M. Queen Elizabeth II with the Order of "Companion of the Most Distinguished Order of Saint Michael and Saint George" (C.M.G.), the first investiture of Queen Elizabeth after she ascended the throne. His major publications include *Cicero and the Roman Republic* (1948 and 1956); *Everyday Life in Ancient Rome* (1961); *History, Civilization and Culture: An Intro-*

duction to the Historical and Social Philosophy of Pitirim A. Sorokin (1952); and *Culture in Private and Public Life* (1959).

Joseph B. Ford, Professor of Sociology and Chairman of the Department at San Fernando Valley State College in Los Angeles, California, has taught at several universities here and abroad. He has published numerous articles in professional journals (American and other), and he is now writing a volume with C. C. Zimmerman on *The Sociology of Change,* to be published by Ronald Press.

Corrado Gini, President of the International Institute of Sociology, is a most prodigious scholar, whose publications span a half-century. He was Professor of Statistics at a number of Italian universities before going to the University of Rome, where he was successively Dean of the School of Statistics (1928-35) and Dean of the Faculty of Statistical, Demographic, and Actuarial Sciences (1935-54). He has been President of the Italian Society of Genetics and Eugenics (1924), the Italian Sociological Society (1937), the Italian Society of Statistics (1941), and the 14th International Congress of Sociology (1950). He was a member of the League of Nations Committee of Statistical Experts (1930-37), and he has filled numerous other important offices in Italy and elsewhere. Among his many publications are *Il sesso dal punto di vista statistico* (*Sex from the Statistical Standpoint,* 1908); *I fattori demografici dell'evoluzione delle nazioni* (a publication which Sorokin says influenced him greatly while he was yet an undergraduate student); *Il neo-organicismo* (1927); *The Cyclical Rise and Fall of Population* (1930); *La dinamica della popolazione* (*Dynamics of Population,* 1932); and many other volumes and journal articles.

Alex Inkeles is Professor of Sociology at Harvard University and Director of Studies in Social Relations at the Russian Research Center. He is author of *Public Opinion in Soviet Russia,* and co-author of *How the Soviet System Works* and *The Soviet Citizen.* He has published numerous articles in various professional journals in areas of his major research interests: the interrelations of personality and social structure.

David R. Mace is Executive Director of the American Association of Marriage Counselors and President of the National Council on Family Relations. He has taught at Drew University and at the School of Medicine of the University of Pennsylvania. Since 1953 he has been Chairman of the International Commission on Marriage Guidance, set up by the International Union of Family Organizations (headquarters in Paris), Consultative Body of UNESCO. He has helped to develop marriage guidance services in South Africa, West Africa, East Asia, Australia, New Zealand, India, and Ceylon. He has probably written more articles on marriage than any other writer in the world, having had regularly serialized columns in numerous newspapers and magazines in England, Australia, New Zealand, South Africa, and the United States. His published books include *Does Sex Morality Matter?*, *Marriage Counselling*, *Marriage Crisis*, *Hebrew Marriage*, *Whom God Hath Joined*, *Marriage: The Art of Lasting Love*, *Success in Marriage*, *Youth Looks Toward Marriage*, and *Marriage: East and West* (with Mrs. David R. Mace). In 1960 he visited the Soviet Union to collect material for a forthcoming book on Soviet family life. His contribution to the present volume draws perceptively upon such material.

Lucio Mendieta y Núñez has been Chief of Mexico's Department of Population of the Bureau of Anthropology; Director, *Revista Politica Social;* Director of the Institute of Social Investigations of the University Nacional de Mexico (since 1939); Director of the *Revista Mexicana de Sociologia* (since 1939); member of the Mexican-U. S. Institute of Cultural Relations; and President of the Instituto Mexicano de Derecho Agrario. He has written many volumes, among them: *Las Poblaciones indeginas de America ante el derecho actual* (1935), *La Universidad creadora y otros ensayos* (1936), *Valor economia y social de las poblaciones indeginas de Mexico* (1936), *La Economia del indio* (1938), *La Habitacione indegina* (1938), *El problema agrario de Mexico* (4th ed., 1940), *La Administracion publica en Mexico* (1942).

Robert K. Merton, Professor of Sociology and Chairman of the Department at Columbia University, has directed, advised, and/or served on many boards, foundations, councils, etc., and was President of the American Sociological Society (1957). Among his numerous publications are *Science, Technology and Society in 17th Century England* (1938), *Mass Persuasion* (1946), *Social Theory and Social Structure* (1949 and 1957); he is co-author of *The Focussed Interview* (1952 and 1956), and *Freedom to Read* (1957). He has also been contributor to and co-editor of *Continuities in Social Research* (1950), *Social Policy and Social Research in Federal Housing* (1951), *Reader in Bureaucracy* (1952), *The Student Physician* (1957), *Sociology Today* (1959), and *Contemporary Social Problems* (1961).

Mary E. Moore, Instructor in Psychology and Psychiatry at the University of Pennsylvania, has collaborated with Matilda White Riley on several methodological papers, notably in the area of dyadic relationships. Currently she is associated with a research project investigating the social and psychological correlates of obesity.

Kanailal M. Munshi, attorney, philosopher, writer, and educator, has served as a public servant in India in numerous capacities: Home Minister, Government of Bombay; Member of the Constituent Assembly and Drafting Committee; Member of Parliament (1947-52); Agent-General for the Government of India (1947-48); Minister of Food and Agriculture (1950-52); Executive Chairman of the Indian Law Institute; and Advocate of the Supreme Court of India. He was an associate of Mahatma Gandhi, and he has published over fifty books on India's life, history, philosophy, art, literature, and contemporary affairs.

Matilda White Riley, Professor of Sociology at Rutgers University, also teaches in the Graduate School at New York University. She has for many years been active in the affairs of the American Sociological Association, serving as its Executive Officer from 1949 to 1960. She has held both research and teaching appointments at Harvard. During the war she served as Chief Consultant to the War Production Board and has continued to advise on federal programs. She is the author of several books and many articles in the field of sociology.

T. Lynn Smith, Research Professor of Sociology and chairman of the Department at the University of Florida, has taught at and headed the sociology departments of Louisiana State University (1931-47) and Vanderbilt University where, in addition, he was Director of the Institute of Brazilian Studies (1947-49). He has been with the U. S. Department of State (1942-46), assigned to embassies in Rio de Janeiro, Bogota, and San Salvador. He has served as Visiting Professor at numerous universities in the United States and abroad, and he has lectured extensively abroad under the auspices of the U. S. Department of State. Among his publications are *The Sociology of Rural Life* (1940, 1947, and 1953), *Population Analysis* (1948), *Brazil: People and Institutions* (1946 and 1954); *Rural Sociology: A Trend Report* (1957), *Fundamentals of Population Study* (1960).

Nicholas S. Timasheff is Professor Emeritus of Sociology at Fordham University. He taught at the Polytechnic Institute at St. Petersburg, Russia, at the University of Prague, and at Harvard University before going to Fordham in 1940. He also was a member of the Institute of Slavic Studies and Franco-Russian Institute of Political and Social Science, in Paris (1927-36). Among his publications are *Criminology, Introduction to the Sociology of Law, The Great Retreat, The Law of Soviet Russia, Sociological Theory: Its Nature and Growth.*

Arnold J. Toynbee, British historian and philosopher of history, was a Fellow and tutor at Balliol College (1912-15); member of the staff of Political Intelligence, Department of Foreign Office (1918); member of the Middle Eastern section of the British Delegation to the Peace Conference; Professor of Byzantine and Modern Greek Language, Literature and History at London University (1919-24); Director of Studies of the Royal Institute of International Affairs (1925-55); Research Professor of History at the London School of Economics (1925-55); and has occupied many other positions of importance in England. Among his numerous publications are *Nationality and the War* (1915), *The Western Question in Greece and Turkey* (1922), *A Survey of International Affairs* (with V. M. Boulter, 1924), *A Journey to China* (1931), *A Study of History* (12 volumes, 1934-61), *Civilization on Trial* (1948), *The World and the West* (1953), *An Historian's Approach to Re-*

ligion (1956), *Christianity Among the Religions of the World* (1958), *East to West: A Journey Around the World* (1958), *Hellenism* (1959).

Alexandre Vexliard, now Professor of Psychology and Pedagogy at the University of Ankara, Turkey, has been Director of Technical Colleges at Avignon and Clermont-Ferrand (1942-47) and has taught Applied Psychology at the University of Clermont-Ferrand. He was Attaché des Recherches at the National Scientific Research Center in France (1948-53); and psychologist at the French International Labor Office in Geneva. His many publications include *Le Clochard, Etude de Psychologie Sociale, Introduction à la Sociologie du Vagabondage,* and over one hundred articles in various professional journals dealing with psychology, sociology, history, and other fields.

Translators

Lia Beretta, who helped to translate Corrado Gini's essay, is Assistant Professor of Modern Foreign Languages at Mary Washington College of the University of Virginia.

Marion A. Greene, who helped to translate Alexandre Vexliard's essay, is Associate Professor of Modern Foreign Languages at Mary Washington College of the University of Virginia.

Edwin H. Jones, who helped to translate Alexandre Vexliard's essay, is Associate Professor of Modern Foreign Languages at Mary Washington College of the University of Virginia.

Kurt F. Leidecker, who translated Othmar F. Anderle's essay, is Professor of Philosophy at Mary Washington College of the University of Virginia.

Clifton B. McIntosh, who helped to translate Lucio Mendieta y Núñez's essay, is Associate Professor of Modern Foreign Languages at Mary Washington College of the University of Virginia.

T. Lynn Smith, who has already been identified as one of the contributors, helped to translate the above-mentioned Mendieta y Núñez essay from the Spanish. In correspondence with him, he has asked that credit be given to *W. Kennedy Upham* and *Fabio Barbosa da Silva,* two of his associates at the University of Florida.

General Foreword

The American Sociological Forum is a continuing project with two major aims: (1) a critical assessment of the writings of unusually creative behavioral scientists, and (2) a critical examination and analysis, from divergent disciplinary approaches, of contemporary social problems which are widely recognized as most pressing.

As Professor Arnold J. Toynbee states elsewhere in the present volume:

The blinkers that have been inserted between the so-called disciplines into which the study of human affairs has been arbitrarily partitioned are as much against the interests of mankind as any political iron-curtain is. In the Atomic Age that has now overtaken us, it is a good deed to provoke people, if one cannot entice them, to cross these perverse man-made barriers. If the trans-frontier traffic becomes brisk enough, the barriers will gradually be worn down, and to get rid of them is one of the present vital interests of the human race. In the Atomic Age, as we know, the choice confronting us is "one world or none." Sorokin has overridden the conventional barriers between the "disciplines." He has taken human affairs as a whole, and has studied them from any promising angle by any promising method. Perhaps this is the greatest of his many services to mankind's common cause.

To fulfil its first aim the Forum intends, from time to time, to publish a volume on a social scientist—sociologist, social-psychologist, cultural anthropologist, or other—whose publications, having evoked widespread interest and reaction, call for serious assessment by competent contemporaries. Together with such assessment, each volume will include: (*a*) a sociological autobiography that endeavors to bring to light important factors and events in the life-history of the scholar under review, which may provide an insight into his major motivations and achievements, and (*b*) a carefully deliberated reply to the assessment by the scholar being evaluated.

To fulfil its second aim, the Forum will attempt, from time to time, to analyze what may be considered major social problems and issues in the social sciences, by way of confronting diverging or conflicting social analysts with each other, encouraging them to communicate within and across disciplinary lines. The long-range aim is a cross-fertilization of ideas, as well as an optimum utilization of human energy and resources for a more comprehensive attack upon pressing problems themselves, with a minimum wastage of such human energy and resources, which is sometimes found in unilateral approaches, or in segmental approaches that cancel out each other's efforts.

                                                                    P.J.A.

Editor's Introduction

The idea of The American Sociological Forum was conceived in an intellectual climate of mild exasperation at Northwestern University during the years 1938-40. It resulted from a multiplicity of influences converging from graduate courses taken in diverse fields: sociology, social psychology, scientific methodology, statistics, philosophy, ethics, and others. Taking some of these courses simultaneously, I experienced the enlightening amazement of the student who is on the receiving end of lectures delivered by professors who are oblivious of each other and whose intellectual operations are often carried on within mutually exclusive frames of reference. Gradually I became painfully aware of the reciprocal intransigence and mutual unintelligibility of some specialists digging in different academic fields and, on occasion, of subspecialists working in the same field.

It is well known that specialization is almost invariably accompanied by a corresponding differentiation of the specialist from his fellows in other academic disciplines. Even within each discipline, when subspecialists have emerged and established themselves, they have tended to promote a further differentiating process. It is precisely the differentiation accompanying specialization that gradually and nearly imperceptibly tends to mold and shape attitudes, to redirect emotions, and to slant a point of view to fit a given frame of reference, one that is internalized as part of the psychological structuring apparatus of individual specialists. Often, after specialists have been molded, shaped, and polished over according to specifications of a given set of Ph.D. requirements of a particular discipline, they seem to exhibit a trained incapacity to communicate effectively with specialists from other disciplines.

This difficulty in communication between specialists from different disciplines assumed, in time, the proportions of a large enough problem, in my judgment, to merit special examination and analysis. It was my reading of Karl Manheim's *Ideology and Utopia,* which deals with the sociology of knowledge—a field, as I later learned, which had been systematically explored by Sorokin—that enabled me more clearly to see and understand the nature of the problem.

I tried to explore various facets of this problem with individual professors, but in vain. Each seemed to be psychologically entrenched within a particular frame of reference and he could not be easily dislodged. I noted, too, the contempt with which some philosophers viewed psychologists and sociologists, and the cultivated indifference toward philosophers with which the behavioral scientists responded.

In 1939 Professor Edward Alsworth Ross came to teach at Northwestern University, and I happily enrolled in two of his courses. Ross's impatience with philosophers, found in many of his publications, showed up repeatedly in the classroom. But it was couched in a magnanimity so characteristic of Ross that it was usually well received, even by graduate students with major commitments to philosophy.

I found Professor Ross delightfully stimulating in the classroom. As one of the founders of sociology and social psychology in America, he had a perspective that no other living sociologist possessed. But it was in personal consultations on my thesis project that he proved most helpful.

At one of these individual conferences one day, I ventured to broach to him my idea of a sociological forum in which divergent views on a particular problem could be expressed by competent scholars, sociologists, and others from different disciplines. To my pleasant surprise, Professor Ross responded with hearty approval. He agreed that there was plenty of room for any device that aimed to promote a "meeting of minds" and reduce the amount of "talking past each other."

Meanwhile, in the spring of 1940, I made the acquaintance of Professor Paul Arthur Schilpp of Northwestern's philosophy department. We talked about various matters of common interest. In the course of our conversation, I mentioned my discussions with E. A. Ross on the idea of some sociological forum. Professor Schilpp hastened to point out that, not only had he himself encountered a problem among philosophers similar to the one then of concern to me, but that he had actually embarked upon a venture that aimed to meet it for philosophers, by way of his recently established "Library of Living Philosophers," which had just published its first volume on *The Philosophy of John Dewey.*

In Professor Schilpp, at long last, I found a man with whom it seemed possible to communicate fruitfully. We were so concordant in views exchanged on problems we discussed that, then and there, at this first meeting, Professor Schilpp invited me to become his assistant in "The Library of Living Philosophers," as soon as his present assistant secured his degree, in June. I pointed out to Professor Schilpp that my major interests were in sociology, and he replied that I could continue working toward my Ph.D. in sociology, while I assisted him in his "Library." I promptly accepted.

My association with Professor Schilpp, during 1940-41, was most profitable to me. More than once, as we worked together, sharing the same office, he urged me to go out and do for sociologists what he was doing for philosophers.[1] Originally, my idea, as broached to Professor E. A. Ross, had been one that involved identifying and defining problem areas; then, inviting scholars to examine and analyze a given problem from different disciplinary approaches; next, submitting the analytical papers to a third scholar, preferably one who had managed to tuck away "two disciplines under one skull," for his assessment; this would then be submitted to the original scholars for their reactions to this assessment and to each other's analyses; and these, finally, were to be followed by the assessor's concluding remarks. This, it seemed to me, could become a grand dialogue, a delightful and enlightening forum.

My work with Professor Schilpp, in time, persuaded me that his own approach—that of taking one outstanding scholar, having his writings criticized by various contemporaries, and then providing him an opportunity to answer their criticisms—had great merit.[2]

[1] Professor Schilpp continued to urge me to be sure to start a "library" in sociology while, at the same time, he urged another graduate student of his, whose primary interests were in theology, to go out and start such a "library" in theology. The other graduate student, Charles Kegley, finally acted upon this suggestion and started his theology series, calling it "The Library of Living Theology" (of which volume I was on *The Theology of Paul Tillich*, 1952, and volume II was on *The Theology of Reinhold Niebuhr*, 1956, both published by Macmillan).

[2] Professor Schilpp launched his "Library of Living Philosophers" series in 1939, with the publication of *The Philosophy of John Dewey.* He proposed to clarify issues in philosophy by publishing "at more or less regular intervals a volume on each of the greater among the world's living philosophers." Each volume would

Indeed, the sociological forum could be launched in this form, it seemed to me, although scholars participating would have to be selected from diverse disciplines to achieve the primary goal I had earlier visualized.

While the core of the idea of The American Sociological Forum, therefore, was conceived before I met Professor Schilpp, in classes I had with Ernest R. Mowrer, Arthur J. Todd, Irl G. Whitchurch, Murray Leiffer, and E. A. Ross, the idea underwent considerable change as a consequence of my fruitful association with Professor Schilpp. This present volume of the Forum series shows configurations that clearly reflect my profitable association with Professor Schilpp.

As the idea of the Forum took shape, I began to think seriously of enlisting the co-operation of Professor E. A. Ross, to try to persuade him to be the first subject for analysis and assessment in the Forum. Not only was he a controversial figure, academically, but his numerous influential publications fully justified his selection. In the next few months, therefore, I undertook to work out a tentative outline for a volume on Ross. When I completed this, I submitted it to Ross and then waited for his reply.

To my pleasant surprise, Professor Ross responded with delight, not to say enthusiasm. That first tentative table of contents contained the names of nineteen potential contributors each of whom was to assess a special area of his own demonstrated competence, to which Ross had made a widely recognized contribution. The first tentative list of contributors included Arthur J. Todd, Ernest R. Mowrer (both of whom had consented to participate), P. A. Sorokin, and others. After several rounds of correspondence with Professor Ross, he wrote:

As to your projected volume, the chief thing I can say is that it's just too good to come true. Such a volume should satisfy any thinker's demands. . . . If you got one-third of the nineteen men you seek to interest to

---

contain: (1) "critical articles written by leading exponents and opponents of the philosopher's thought"; (2) a reply by the philosopher being criticized; (3) "an intellectual autobiography" or biography of the philosopher; and (4) an up-to-date bibliography of his writings. The widespread acclaim accorded to the volumes published by Professor Schilpp in his "Library" speaks eloquently for the value of this series to the world's philosophers. I desire, here, merely to acknowledge my own debt to my very dear friend, Paul Arthur Schilpp, for all I learned from him throughout my pleasant association with him at Northwestern University, and for his constant encouragement.

"come across" I should be more than tickled. So all I can say: If you receive fair encouragement, you can count on me to do everything that might help to make the book a success.

Meanwhile, at the 1940 annual meeting of the American Sociological Society, Professor P. A. Sorokin delivered a major address, which evoked heated responses from a number present. Sorokin undertook to criticize adversely efforts of some sociologists to emulate the natural sciences. After Sorokin's paper, Professor Ross and others arose on the conference floor to take issue with Sorokin. This, to me, all the more dramatized the need for a sociological forum such as I had visualized: one that encouraged systematically planned confrontation of persons with divergent opinions and points of view.

Some days after the meeting, I wrote to Professor Sorokin, commenting upon his address, and he replied: "I hope in my forthcoming volume four of *Dynamics* to be able to substantiate most of the statements put in my paper dogmatically." In my letter to Sorokin I had expressed the hope that we might meet in person, sometime, to discuss a project I had in mind. I had wanted to discuss, not only his participation in the Ross volume, but also the tentative volume I had planned on Sorokin himself.

Unfortunately, this meeting never materialized; for shortly thereafter, the war in Europe began to assume world-wide proportions, threatening to involve the United States. Sometime after this country's entry into the war, I was commissioned an officer in the Air Force and I did not return to civilian life until 1946. Meanwhile, Professor Ross had aged so greatly that I abandoned most reluctantly the idea of the volume on him, since its success required his very active and vigorous participation.

Subsequent events, academic and other, since that time, so usurped my time and energy that I continued to postpone implementation of the Forum idea. It was not until the fall of 1958, when Professor Sorokin was invited to lecture on our campus, through The Richmond Area University Center,[3] that I outlined the present volume to him and secured his consent to participate in the venture. He encouraged me to go ahead, promising every co-

[3] I hereby wish to acknowledge with gratitude the modest financial support provided by The Richmond Area University Center for the typing of the present volume manuscript.

operation he could give to help make the volume a success. So I undertook to launch the Forum series. The present volume, at long last, is the fruition of an idea nearly a quarter of a century in gestation, and I am grateful to Professor Sorokin and all the distinguished contributors for its realization.

Of all those who early agreed to participate in this volume, only Howard Becker, then President of the American Sociological Association, was prevented by his untimely death from carrying out his commitment. His death was a great loss, not only to those of us working upon this volume, but to the American Sociological Association and the rest of the sociological world.

Professor Sorokin has given of his time and energy most generously, co-operating in ways far beyond reasonable expectation, for which I am profoundly grateful. The publication date of this volume so closely coincides with Professor Sorokin's seventy-fourth birthday, January 21, that he may well consider it a grand birthday present from his professional colleagues over the world.

I am indebted to many others, far more than can be named here. Mention should be made of the publishers of Professor Sorokin's various works for giving their generous consent to quote. I am grateful to Miss Marguerite L. Carder, Reference Librarian at my institution; to Mr. Ashbel Brice, Director of the Duke University Press, for valuable counsel; and to the competent staff of the Duke University Press for their painstaking co-operation in preparing the manuscript for publication. Finally, I wish to acknowledge my debt to my wife, Dorothy Wiley Allen, for her untiring assistance, patience, and perseverance at all stages of this project, from beginning to end.

PHILIP J. ALLEN

Mary Washington College
  of the University of Virginia

Contents

Part One

SOCIOLOGY OF MY MENTAL LIFE

Pitirim A. Sorokin

Part Two

SOROKIN IN REVIEW

Part Three

REPLY TO MY CRITICS

Pitirim A. Sorokin

Part One

SOCIOLOGY OF MY MENTAL LIFE

Pitirim A. Sorokin

I. Preliminary Remarks

One of the main tasks of so-called sociology of knowledge (*Wissensoziologie*) is a study of the factors which condition the essential contents, configurations, and transformations of the mental life of an individual or of a group: their language, scientific ideas, religious and other beliefs, philosophical views, moral and legal convictions, aesthetic tastes, political and economic ideologies, social aspirations, and their set of values in general. The sociology of knowledge or, more exactly, the sociology of mental life tries to answer the basic questions of how and why the mental life of any given individual or of a group happens to be such as it is and how and why it often changes in the course of the individual's or group's life, and why the mental life of various persons or collectivities is often quite different.

The sociology of mental life endeavors to elucidate these problems through a study of the mentalities of vast cultures and societies (macrosociology of mental life) and through that of the mental life of a given individual (microsociology of mental life). My *Social and Cultural Dynamics* investigates these problems on a macrosociological scale. This present essay deals with them on a microsociological scale in an attempted exploration of my own mental life.

There are several reasons for use of autobiographical, instead of biographical, material for such a study. First, one knows his mental life, its contents, motivations, continuity, and change more fully and directly than that of any other individual. Second, through one's direct, unmediated experience one knows many motivations and changes in his mental life which remain hidden from all outside biographers and investigators; as a rule they have at their disposal only a few fragmentary records about the behavior and inner experience of the individual studied, and even these dead fragments are often interpreted by them in quite different ways. Like Leibnitz's monad, the mind or the soul of every person still remains either closed or only partially open for the inspection of outsiders (except, perhaps, the most intimate friends and the closest relatives). Third, in the late afternoon of my life I am simply curious to find out why my mental life has run its actual (and not a different) course and, especially, why my sociological theories and other "mental productions" have assumed the character they actually have. I have a personal interest in understanding the reasons and factors that determined the course of my mental life and, especially, the character of my sociological theories and other "mental productions."

Side by side with these advantages, the autobiographical material has, of course, its serious drawbacks. But if and when a scholar tries to be honest with himself and with others, when he does not have any special reason to falsify his life records, and when he is on guard against ever-present dangers of "justification," "rationalization," and "beautification" of himself and of his mental life, the advantages of using the autobiographical material appear to be greater than the disadvantages.

After these remarks, I can pass on to a sociological account of my mental life—if not my whole mental life (which is impossible in a short essay), at least some limited areas of it. I shall attempt an analysis of the discernible factors responsible for the topics of my main studies, for the character of my theories and "philosophies," and for the main changes these "mental productions" have undergone in the course of my life.

II. *Early Years*

I was born January 21, 1889, and lived up to the age of eleven among the Komi people, one of the Ugro-Finnish ethnic groups, in the North of Russia. My Russian father was an itinerant "master of gilding, silvering, and ikon-making" (as his guild certificate testified). How and for what reasons he moved from the Russian city Velikiy Ustiug to the Komi region (a distance of more than three hundred miles) and remained there up to his death, I do not know. One of the possible reasons was that among the Komi people he probably found more work than among the Russian population. My mother was a Komi peasant daughter. The only thing I remember about her is the scene of her death—which occurred when I was about three years old. This scene is my earliest memory and it marks my birth into a conscious, remembered life. Of my life before this event I remember nothing. (This personal experience is one of the reasons why I regard various "dianetic" and psychoanalytical theories of an alleged remembrance by the human organism of everything, especially of the birth trauma and various sex experiences, as a mere fancy not supported by any real evidence.) From my father, relatives, and neighbors I heard that my mother was, though illiterate, a beautiful, intelligent, and very fine person.

Of my father I had and still have two different images. In his sober stretch (lasting for weeks and even months) he was a wonderful man, loving and helping his sons in any way he could, friendly to all neighbors, industrious and honest in his work, and to the end of his life faithful to our dead mother. "Christ has risen!" was his habitual way of saying "How do you do?" or "Goodbye." Unfortunately the stretches of soberness alternated with those of drunkenness, sometimes up to the state of delirium tremens. In his drunken state he was a pitiful figure; he could not care for us nor help us; he was depressed, irritable, and, once in a while, somewhat violent in his treatment of us. In one moment of such violence he beat my older brother and, with a hammer blow, he cut my upper lip, which remained slightly misshapen for many years.

Immediately after this event my older brother and I decided to separate from our father, and we started our own independent way of earning a living. One year later father died in a distant village. Because of the undeveloped means of communication it was weeks before we learned about his death. Despite father's alcoholism, the image of a sober, tender, and wonderful father overwhelmingly prevailed while we were living together and it still prevails in my memory up to the present time. Even in his drunken state he had nothing in common with the Freudian image of a tyrant-father, insensitive and cruel to his children. With the exception of the alcoholic periods which were considerably shorter and less frequent than his sober periods, our family—father, older brother, and myself (my younger brother was taken by our aunt and did not live with us)—was a good and harmonious team bound together by warm, mutual love, community of joy and suffering, and by a modestly creative work.

This deep mutual attachment continued in my relationship with my older brother and, later on, with my younger one. Each of us was intensely concerned with what was happening to the others; and this devotion and love continued to the end of my brothers' lives (both perished in the struggle with the Communist regime).

After our separation from our father, my brother and I moved, earning our living, from village to village for about one year, until we came to a small Russian town, Yarensk (about a thousand population). There we found plenty of work: painting the spire, the domes, and the outside and inside walls of the main cathedral, and silvering and gilding the cathedral's ikons and other cult objects. There, when we were painting the spire of the cathedral we were almost blown down (from the great height of the building) by a sudden storm and were saved from a fatal fall by a strong rope that withstood the assaults of the ferocious squalls. This town, Yarensk, introduced me to the urban world. I was then about eleven and my brother about fifteen years old.

After a few months of successful work in this town, we moved back into the Komi region and for several months continued our work there until, surprisingly for both of us, I found myself enrolled in an advanced grade school, described later on. This enrolment separated me from my brother for the nine months of the school year and, after two years, divided the course of our lives along quite different paths. During these two or three years of our living together my brother's leadership and care were truly vital for my survival and growth. Otherwise we were a real brotherly team, each being "the keeper and guardian of the other." Later on, during the Communist revolution, when the Communists hunted me and put a price on my head, to be captured dead or alive, my younger brother helped me many times at the risk of his own freedom and his very life. My illiterate aunt and her husband likewise most kindly treated me as their own son during my early years when frequently I lived with them in a hamlet, Rymia. Their place was my real "home" when there was no other home.

These lines sketch my family background. Among other things they show that I had in my early (and also later) life abundance of a true, pure, and warm love granted to me by my family, relatives, and many others.

III. External Course of My Life

Before proceeding with this analysis of my mental development it is necessary to outline the external history of my life. Without such a background it is hardly possible to deal intelligently with the problems of my autobiographical microsociology. The subsequent lines give the main landmarks of my life-course.

Eventfulness has possibly been the most significant feature of my life-adventure. In a span of seventy-three years I have passed through several cultural atmospheres: pastoral-hunter's culture of the Komi; first the agricultural, then the urban culture of Russia and Europe; and, finally, the megalopolitan, technological culture of the United States. Starting my life as a son of a poor itinerant artisan and peasant mother, I have subsequently been a farmhand, itinerant artisan, factory worker, clerk, teacher, conductor of a choir, revolutionary, political prisoner, journalist, student, editor of a metropolitan paper, member of Kerensky's cabinet, an exile, professor at Russian, Czech, and American universities, and a scholar of an international reputation.

No less eventful has been the range of my life-experience. Besides joys and sorrows, successes and failures of normal human life, I have lived through six imprisonments; and I have had the unforgettable experience of being condemned to death and, daily during six weeks, expecting execution by a Communist firing squad. I know what it means to be damned; to be banished, and to lose one's brothers and friends in a political struggle; but also, in a modest degree, I have experienced the blissful grace of a creative work.

These life-experiences have taught me more than the innumerable books I have read and the lectures to which I have listened.

As I stated earlier, my brother and I separated from my father, following one of his violent eruptions while he was under the influence of alcohol; and, not long thereafter, I became "independent" and penniless, but free to chart my own life-course, earning my living as best I could. Subsequently, I was a student at a teachers college; I was arrested and imprisoned four months before graduation because of my political activities in 1906; and then, I became a starving and hunted revolutionary, and a student of a night school, of the Psycho-Neurological Institute, and of the University of St. Petersburg. Two more imprisonments gave me a first-hand experience in criminology and penology—the field of my graduate study and then of my first professorship. Besides several papers, in my junior year I published my first volume on crime.

With the explosion of the Russian Revolution I became one of the founders of the Russian Peasant Soviet (dispersed by the Communists), editor of a metropolitan paper, *The Will of the People,* member of the Council of the Russian Republic, a secretary to Prime Minister Kerensky, and a leading member of the Russian Constituent Assembly (dispersed by the Communist Government). From the beginning of the Revolution I vigorously fought Lenin, Trotsky, Kamenev, and other Communist leaders. For this reason I was arrested on January 3, 1918, and imprisoned for four months in the Russian Bastille, the Fortress of Peter and Paul.

Released, I resumed my struggle against the Communists, and I was one of the group which engineered the overthrow of the Communist Government in Archangel in 1918. In October, 1918, I was again arrested and condemned to death by the Communist Government of Vologda Province. After six weeks of waiting to be shot, by Lenin's order I was freed and returned to my academic activity at the University of St. Petersburg. There I became the founder, first professor, and chairman of the department of sociology. During the years 1920-22 I published five volumes in law and sociology. In 1922 I was arrested and, finally, banished by the Soviet Government.[1] A few days after my arrival in Berlin

---

[1] These personal experiences are responsible for drawing my attention to the fact that an overwhelming majority (roughly about 80 per cent) of the great and distinguished social thinkers, beginning with Confucius, Socrates, Plato, and Aristotle and ending with Marx, and Lenin—not to mention several eminent social scientists who were imprisoned, banished, and executed at the hands of the Communist or Nazi governments—had similar experiences as "subversives." If I

my good friend, President Masaryk, invited me to be a guest of Czechoslovakia. I stayed there for some nine months. Having received invitations from the universities of Illinois and Wisconsin to lecture there on the Russian Revolution, in November, 1923, I came to the United States and in 1924 was offered a professorship by the University of Minnesota. After six years of happy work there I was invited to be the first professor and chairman of the sociology department at Harvard University. After 1930 (in which year I became a naturalized American citizen) I lived and worked in this great university until my retirement in 1959.

In 1948 Mr. Eli Lilly and the Lilly Endowment kindly offered $120,000 for my studies on how to make human beings less selfish and more creative. This generous offer led to the establishment of the Harvard Research Center in Creative Altruism in 1949, which I directed until my retirement, after which it became affiliated with the American Academy of Arts and Sciences.

During my lifetime in America, I have published, besides many scientific papers, some thirty substantial volumes. Most of these volumes have been translated into many languages: *Contemporary Sociological Theories* into eleven major languages of mankind; *The Crisis of Our Age* into eight; other volumes into a lesser number of languages. All in all, so far, there have been about forty-two translations of my published volumes.

This voluminous output of books and articles is due mainly to my deep enjoyment of research and writing. They have served me as the best way of self-realization and of release of my creative propensities, as the most fruitful form of mental and moral growth, and as the purest mode of joyful recreation. Through frustrations and failures inherent, to some extent, in this sort of activity, they have enriched my sense of reality and deepened my perception of the tragic aspects of life. For all these reasons I preferred this sort of creative work to other forms of recreation and spontaneously indulged in it at almost any opportunity I had.

The orderly way of my life in the United States, undisturbed by political and other troubles, and the exceptionally favorable conditions for scientific work offered by the American universities also notably helped in such "paper-wasting" activity. Though my

---

cannot be similar to these thinkers in their great achievements I am satisfied with being similar to them in the small matters.

load of teaching and administrative work (at Harvard) was fairly heavy, it still left a great deal of free time for study and writing. I usually did and still do this sort of work in the early morning hours before going to the office and then in the evening hours when free from other engagements. Practically all my writing and study I have done at home and not in my office.

These lines do not mean that I have neglected the *dolce far niente* of loafing, or the pleasures of various forms of recreation. Following the old precept of Lao-Tse that "doing nothing is better than being busy doing nothing" I have idled away plenty of time and rested from my mental work by attending symphony concerts and art expositions; by reading literary masterpieces; by camping, fishing, and mountain climbing; and, for the last twenty-five years, by laboring over my azalea-rhododendron-lilac-rose garden, which is visited by many thousands each season, which has earned me a gold medal from the Massachusetts Horticultural Society, and which was starred by full-page color photographs in several national magazines. I have also frequently enjoyed convivial meetings with a limited circle of close friends among whom it has been my good fortune to have several distinguished thinkers, artists, and other leaders of our time.

All this shows that I have fully enjoyed loafing, rest, and the finest forms of recreation that renew, enrich, and ennoble human life and turn it into a grand, meaningful, creative, and effervescent adventure.

To finish this brief sketch of my life I must mention that in 1917, during the Revolution, I was happily married to Dr. Helen Baratyn-skaya, cytologist-researcher in her own right. She has published a number of her studies in botanical and other biological journals and is still continuing her research. For the forty-five years of our married life we seem to have had, as yet, neither time nor sufficient reason for divorce or separation. We have two sons: Dr. Peter P. Sorokin, research physicist with IBM, and Dr. Sergei P. Sorokin, instructor and research associate at Harvard Medical School. Both have already published a number of papers in their fields and both are vigorously continuing their scientific work. Some of our friends nicknamed the Sorokin family "a little Sorokin university" with its own mathematician-physicist, two biologists, and one inter-loper-philosopher, sociologist, psychologist, and jack-of-all-trades.

Finally, at the age of seventy-three, I am not quite senile, as yet: my health is rather good for my age, I am still "wasting plenty of paper," and I find myself about as busy with my scientific and other activities as I was during my earlier years. Whether the factor of heredity is responsible (though my mother and father died in their thirties and forties) or, as I am inclined to believe, the factor of not having too many vices and not pretending to have many virtues, and especially the factor of pursuing in my life the real and great values, rather than short-lived *pseudo*-values—whatever is responsible for the delay of my senility, I do not know exactly. Possibly all of these factors have played their role in this matter, particularly the last two.

IV. Visible Factors of My Early Mental Life

As a general rule, the contents of the unintegrated and yet-unfilled mind of a child are largely determined by the contents of the mental life of persons and groups among whom the child is born and reared, and with whom he interacts. To a large extent this rule happens to be correct in my case. The character of the *mental life* of my early *sociocultural* milieu shaped most of the contents of my early mentality.

A. My native and learned languages. Since I was born and reared amidst the Komi people, speaking the Komi and the Russian languages, these languages have spontaneously, without any purposive intention on my part, become my native languages. At a later period of my life, again spontaneously, even contrary to my wishes, and exclusively because of lack of practice (caused indirectly by social and cultural factors), I largely forgot the Komi, and my Russian language was somewhat impaired. (These facts, by the way, show the fallacy of the prevalent contentions that all our mental and overt actions are purposive and have invariably some goal.) At a later stage of my life I learned the Latin, the French, the English, and, to a lesser extent, the German and Slavic languages. In these cases, however, I learned them intentionally. They did not enter my mental equipment spontaneously as in the case of "the native" languages, but were learned purposefully through rational determination and a great deal of labor. Knowledge of these languages was the necessary condition for enrolment as a student in a Russian university, for doing scientific work, for obtaining an academic position, and for earning my living as a university professor and scholar in Russia as well as, after my banishment, in the United States.

B. *Early religious and other beliefs.* Since the religion of the Komi people was the Russian Orthodox religion, supplemented by the survivals of pagan beliefs, these beliefs and their rituals spontaneously became my religious beliefs and ritual practices. Their imprint upon my mind was greatly reinforced through the *occupational* work of my father in which, together with my elder brother, I participated during my boyhood. This work of painting, silvering, gilding, and ikon-making was done mainly for churches of various villages. A large portion of our time we spent in, around, or on church buildings, painting them, and making, silvering, and gilding their cult objects. In this work we naturally met, talked, and interacted with the village clergy. In brief, in my boyhood years this religious climate was one of the main atmospheres in which I lived, worked, and formed my early beliefs, rituals, moral standards, and other values. Its influence was so strong that, after reading several old volumes on the *Lives of the Saints,* I tried to become an ascetic-hermit and many times retired for fasting and praying into the solitude of the nearby forest. This religious and moral climate served also as a stimulus and outlet for the development of my creative propensities.

Participation in church singing made me a popular singer at the church services and, later on, a conductor of church choirs; participation in the occupational work of our family made me the best craftsman-designer, painter, and ikon-maker in our family team; learning by heart all the prayers and psalms of religious services and the main religious beliefs, I became a good preacher-teacher at the neighborly gatherings of peasants during the long winter evenings. The splendor of religious ritual, the beautiful landscape of the countryside viewed from the top of church buildings, especially on clear, sunny days, these and hundreds of other situations enriched my mental life—emotionally, intellectually, aesthetically, and morally. Despite a low material standard of living, my early life was rich in joy and sorrow, in adventure and experience.

C. Early schooling. I do not remember exactly how, when, and where I learned the three R's of elementary school education. The nomadic sort of life of moving from village to village, with a temporary stay in the villages where we found some work, prevented me from regular attendance of, and graduation from, an elementary school. In these nomadic conditions I could only sporadically attend, for a few days or weeks, the schools of the villages where we were staying. The earliest of my teachers was merely a literate peasant woman who taught in her house the beginnings of the three R's to a few boys of the hamlet where my illiterate peasant aunt lived. In that "school" I received my first—and the greatest of all—prizes for my excellence in learning. The prize was the paper-wrapping of a single piece of hard candy. I still vividly remember the yellow-green picture of a pear depicted on the wrapping and all the joyful pride with which I accepted it, showed it to my aunt, and then carefully fixed it on the wall of my aunt's log house, near the ikons. None of the diplomas, prizes, and honors granted to me at a later period of my life by various great institutions of learning has elated me as much as this simple prize.

Somehow or other in this erratic way I acquired elementary school knowledge, and I greatly increased it by voracious reading of all sorts of books which I could get in the villages of the Komi, by the instruction of my father and elder brother, by talks with the village intelligentsia—teachers, clergy, clerks, and medical practitioners—and by conversations with wise, though often illiterate, peasants. Our nomadic life (our "social mobility") also contributed a great deal to my life-experience and knowledge in the way of meeting ever-new people, situations, and challenges in different villages in which we stayed and worked.

As a result of this sort of education I did not have any difficulty in being admitted to a higher kind of school (corresponding to American grades eight, nine, and ten) opening in the village of Gam when my brother and I happened to be working in that village. The day of the entrance examination in the new school was an important event in the life of the village. A large part of the villagers, including the boys aspiring to become the school's pupils, attended the public "show" of the entrance examinations. As one of the curious onlookers I attended also, with no intention of taking part in the tests. After listening to the test questions and finding them easy, I spontaneously volunteered to be examined also. I passed the tests with flying colors, was enrolled in the school and given a scholarship of five rubles ($2.50), which paid for board and meals in the school's dormitory for the whole academic year. (How fantastic this sounds in the range of present prices and scholarships!) In this entirely incidental way my regular school education began in this advanced grade school.

This was the first step of a number along an educational path that led me to the university and professorship as my main life work. Five teachers of the school, headed by the local priest, were very good men and excellent educators. Its library and other modest facilities were notably better than those of the elementary schools. Most of its students were capable boys, sound in body, mind, and moral conduct. The total atmosphere of the school was mentally stimulating, emotionally happy, and philosophically idealistic. As I happened to be the brightest student I was given the scholarship of five rubles for each of three years of the school curriculum. These five rubles paid for my room and board during nine months of each year. During the remaining three months I earned my living by carrying on my previous occupational work in company with my brother, and by helping my peasant uncle and aunt in their farm work.

These three years notably increased my knowledge, enriched my cultural equipment, awakened my creative propensities, and tangibly integrated my *Weltanschauung*. It was an idealistic world view in which God and nature, truth, goodness and beauty, religion, science, art and ethics were all somehow united in harmonious relationship with each other. No sharp conflict and no inner contradiction between these values marred, as yet, my peace of mind. Despite several sorrows and painful experiences inevitable in human life (the death of my father and peasant uncle, the growing alcoholic proclivity of my brother, my pneumonia, and other unwelcome events), the world appeared as a marvelous place in which to live and strive for its great values.

I did not foresee then that in the near future this harmonious and secure world view would be severely shattered by revolt and reassessment of its values. Obviously impressed by my mental brightness, teachers of the school and the higher educational authorities of the county and province strongly advised me to continue my education in a denominational teachers college in Kostroma province of Russia. In addition, they helped me to procure a scholarship there to take care of my very modest needs for subsistence. It was, then, my coincidental attendance of an exciting community event and my fortuitous participation in the examination at the school that tangibly conditioned my subsequent educational course that led to a university studentship, a professorship, and a fairly distinguished scholarship as my main life work.

D. Early moral, aesthetic, political, and economic mentality. My ideas, tastes, and convictions in these fields were also determined mainly by those of the Komi people and those which I learned from my father, teachers, clergy, and playmates, from doing my occupational work, and from the books I read. The morality and mores of the Komi peasant communities were well integrated around the precepts similar to those of the Ten Commandments and of mutual help. The houses of the peasants did not have any locks because there were no thieves. Serious crimes occurred very rarely, if at all; even misdemeanors were negligible. People largely practiced the moral precepts they preached. Mutual aid likewise was a sort of daily routine permeating the whole life of the community. Moral norms themselves were regarded as God-given, unconditionally binding, and obligatory for all. The same was true for the common law of the peasants. Living in this sort of a moral community I naturally absorbed its moral norms as well as its mores. The same can be said of my aesthetic tastes and preferences. My world of beauty was made up, first, of the beautiful world of nature: pure big rivers and lakes, not yet contaminated by industrial and urban pollutions; endless forests extending for hundreds of miles; flowery meadows and fields surrounding each village; vast expanses of pure snow in the winters; mainly blue and sunny sky with brilliant stars at night; and other scenes of an unspoiled nature in which the villages and hamlets were mere specks lost in an ocean of such geographic grandeur. It indelibly impressed me for the rest of my life and conditioned my mild dislike of big cities and industrialized surroundings. The life of wild animals of this environment was another realm of my aesthetic experience. Swimming in pure rivers, fishing in silvery streams and lakes, observing the animal life and ever-changing natural scenery, walking, and working amidst this kind of nature well satisfied a large portion of my aesthetic cravings.

Another part of my aesthetic world was a man-made world of fine arts of the Komi and Russian agricultural and hunter communities. My musical tastes were formed by the beautiful folk music of the region which was not, as yet, invaded by the vulgar—urban and commercial—crooning, jazz, and noise-making (Russian *chastushki*). In this region were still preserved the old folk songs of the Russian and the Ugro-Finnish peoples. From this and other adjacent regions they were collected by the eminent Russian scholars and composers: Rimsky-Korsakoff, Musorgski, Tchaikovsky, Kastalsky, and others. This explains why at a later age when, for the first time, I heard the music of these composers and also of Bach, Handel, Haydn, Mozart, or Beethoven, many of their tunes and melodies appeared to me quite familiar: I had heard them in childhood from the Komi and Russian peasant women and men who ordinarily sang collectively during their community work, at fishing or harvesting, or at their communal festivities and important events in their lives, like weddings and funerals. Religious music of the churches was another type of music which strongly conditioned my musical tastes. It was the "traditional" music of the Russian churches, including the early Russian plain chant (Kievsky and Znamensky chants), and once in a while the simple religious compositions of eminent Russian composers like Bortniansky, Lvov, Archangelsky, Kastalsky, Tchaikovsky, and others. Though the Komi and Russian churches did not have great choirs or soloists, nevertheless, the above-mentioned forms of Russian religious music, being beautiful and great in their own way and performed in a church with my active participation as a soloist, or one of the singers, or a conductor of a little choir, indelibly impressed me and tangibly conditioned my musical tastes for the rest of my life. I still enjoy such music and often play many records of it on my hi-fi phonograph.

My *literary* education began with the folk tales, folk poems, fairy tales, and heroic poems of the Komi and of the adjacent Russian folk. This rich and imaginative folk literature was supplemented by the literature of the great Russian writers: Pushkin, Gogol, Tolstoi, and others of whom I learned in school and from books I read. Even in the most elementary schools of the region pupils were taught a great deal of this literature and learned by heart a large number of poems of the great poets. The folk literature and the classics both represented genuinely fine literature, free from the vulgarity and ugliness of comic and "yellow" commercial publications of the urban-industrial centers. This accounts for my subsequent life-long aversion to all varieties of "pulp literature," commercial "best-sellers," and "yellow journalism."

My occupational work of painting ikons and other designs, of making "sculptured"—copper and silver—covers for ikons, and my living in the atmosphere of churches, with their frescoes, ikons, and many other—often beautiful—ritual objects, developed my sense of line, color, and form, and conditioned my subsequent interest in painting, sculpture, and architecture, and my aesthetic preference in these fine arts.

Peasant folk dances, festivals, pageants, and ceremonial rituals replete with color, simple elegance, and quiet drama were another formative source of my aesthetic tastes.

As to the formation of my *political* and *economic* views, "politics" and "economics," in their narrow sense, did not preoccupy my mind in my early life. The Komi and the Russian population of this region had never known slavery nor serfdom and democratically managed their local—political and economic—affairs by way of direct self-government of the village community similar to the German *Gemeinschaft* or to the Russian *"mir," obschina*. Village communities had their land in common possession, equitably distributed and redistributed among the individual peasant families (according to their size and increase or decrease in the course of time). A *Gemeinschaft*-spirit of mutual aid was still vigorous and manifested itself in many forms, including many activities collectively entered into by the whole village community. These conditions prevented development of notable inequalities and sharp—economic, political, and social—stratification within the village populations. There were neither notably rich, privileged, and "superior," nor particularly poor, disenfranchised, and "inferior" strata. Even the sexes were essentially equal in status. As a result, there was no real "class struggle," and there were no crystallized political parties with vested class interests. The power of the county elective authorities (*zemstvo*) consisted mainly in building schools, medical centers, and other educational and cultural institutions. Very limited also was the control of the central, Tsarist government. Among the many ethnic groups of Russia, the Komi group was one of the most literate and most democratic nationalities.

Growing in these political and economic conditions I naturally absorbed the spirit of equalitarian independence, self-reliance, and mutual aid. Though my economic conditions were nearer to those of the poor than of the rich peasants and though now and then I did not have enough food, warm shelter, clothing, and other necessities of life, nevertheless, I did not have strong resentment against these conditions nor, except in a few short-lived instances, did I feel lonely, unhappy, and depressed. The life I enjoyed seemed to be wonderful, meaningful, and full of exciting adventures and boundless hope. I was a member of a peasant community at peace with the world, fellow men, and myself.

Such, in black and white, were the visible factors of my early mental life. All in all the outlined social and cultural conditions (often viewed by urbanized and "civilized" scholars as "primitive" and "backward") were essentially sound and rich in variety and fulness of life experience. Taken as a whole, they were less monotonous than social and cultural conditions of big cities, especially of city slums, and more favorable for vital mental and moral development than the environment of megalopolitan and industrial centers.

V. Invisible and Dark Factors of My Early Mental Life

The preceding pages outline the visible factors that shaped my early mental life (up to about the age of fourteen years). These factors consist mainly in the character of the *mental life* of the people—individuals and groups—among whom I lived and with whom I interacted face to face. An additional factor was the character of the *mental currents* (beliefs, knowledge, standards, and values) with which I came in contact indirectly—through books read, pictures seen, music heard, and through other means of communication. These two factors, plus the geographic conditions of my early years, seem to account for a large portion of my early mental equipment but hardly for the whole of it.

They hardly account, for instance, for my becoming a voracious reader and developing an insatiable curiosity to know many things, while 99 per cent of the boys of this region (especially my elder brother) who lived under similar conditions and breathed the same atmosphere of the mental life of the people, did not develop these tendencies. And why did these boys and both of my brothers absorb from the *total* mental culture of these communities ideas, values, and forms of conduct essentially different from those absorbed by me? What were the reasons for these differences? And why was I the brightest pupil in all the schools attended at that period of my life? And why, at the age of fourteen, was my mental equipment probably richer and my mental perspective wider than those of boys of the region? And why, in the advanced grade school, did I become a leader a few times in "overthrowing the tyranny" of the profoundly disliked school's housekeeper and cook (by emptying a pail of water on her) and by this "revolutionary" action bring into the open her misdeeds and take upon myself the punishment for this "outrageous" conduct (unanimously approved by the pupils and tacitly approved by the teachers), and in several other non-scholastic actions? And why, when my views were different from those of nearly all the pupils, did I not hesitate to oppose them, despite my loss of popularity with them? (This sort of "bullheadedness" on my part I began to show fairly early.) These and other questions occur to me now.

These differences from the boys of the same communities and from my brothers can hardly be explained by the mental environment because it was about the same for me, for my brothers, and for the other boys. If anything, the rank and file of the other boys had a better family, and better economic and other social conditions than my own. (My mother died when I was about three years old; my father—a very good man when sober—became a chronic alcoholic as I earlier indicated and, in his search for a job, was often away from "home," though frequently there was no "home" in a good sense of the word.)

Most of the scholars would probably try to explain these differences by the factor of heredity. But such an explanation would
only replace the unknown X by the no-better-known Y. First, so
far as I know my genealogy (which does not go, however, beyond
a knowledge of my father, mother, brothers, aunts, uncles, and
grandmother), my relatives, parents, and grandparents did not distinguish themselves by any particular achievement, except, perhaps,
my illiterate uncle. Knowing nothing about human anatomy, he
nevertheless successfully treated dislocated joints. By a simple
manipulation of such dislocated joints he performed this operation
in a shorter, simpler, and better way than the local medical personnel. He never charged any of his patients for this service and he
never boasted of his "God-given" ability. However, being an uncle
through his marriage to a sister of my mother, he was not one of my
ancestors. Second, today's biology has not learned, as yet, what
kind of germ cells nor which of their chromosomes are bearers of
a "fortunate" or "unfortunate" heredity, nor with what kind of
heredity this or that individual is endowed. For this reason in most
of the "hereditary" interpretations of personality characteristics the
"hereditarians" do not deduce or predict these characteristics from
their knowledge of the specific traits of the paternal germ cell of
the individual, but postulate the quality of his unknown hereditary
endowment from the known characteristics of the individual. If
the individual has distinguished himself by a notable creative
achievement, they conclude that he had a fortunate heredity; if he
has not distinguished himself in any way, his heredity is assumed to
have been average or poor. Obviously, such a conjecture is purely
speculative and unproven. It is in no way better than a hypothesis
of a "creative grace" or "uncreative curse" visited upon the person,
or his "good or bad luck," or "favorable or unfavorable chance." It
is possible that each of these factors plays some role in determining
the life course or mental equipment of the individual; but at our
present poor knowledge of their role, they remain a purely residual
guess. They can be left at this point of this essay.

VI. *First Crisis and Its Visible Factors*

After my graduation from the advanced grade school in 1904
at the age of fourteen, I enrolled in the Khrenovo Teachers School.

It was a denominational establishment controlled by the Holy Synod of the Russian Orthodox Church. It trained teachers for denominational elementary schools. Situated near the parish church in the village, its campus was near several textile factories not far from the city of Kineshma and other sizable industrial centers. I found myself in a new, more "civilized" environment and among people notably different from those I had known before. The three-year curriculum of the school was much more advanced, the students and teachers were better qualified, and the library and other facilities of the school were better than those of the elementary and grade schools I had attended. The outsiders whom I met there represented a wide diversity of ideas, standards, and values: peasants, factory hands, clerks and administrators, government officials, the intelligentsia of the region—teachers, priests, doctors, writers, newspapermen, leaders of co-operative organizations, representatives of various political parties, the "Social-Revolutionaries," "Social-Democrats" (Mensheviks and Bolsheviks), the "Anarchists," the "Monarchists," the local leaders of various liberal and conservative political organizations—these outsiders acquainted me with a multitude of new ideas, standards, and values. This new milieu, new people, and especially my intensive reading of hitherto unknown books, journals, and newspapers rapidly broadened my mental horizon and enriched my mental equipment. Their concerted impact was greatly reinforced by the Russian-Japanese War of 1904 and especially by the brewing revolutionary storm that was rapidly spreading over the whole of Russia and that resulted in the revolution of 1905 and subsequent years.

The total impact of all these factors was so powerful that within about two years after my enrolment at this school, most of my previous religious, philosophical, political, economic and social ideologies collapsed and were replaced by new views and values. My previous religiosity gave way to a semi-atheistic rejection of the theologies and rituals of the Russian Orthodox religion. Compulsory attendance of church services and the obligatory courses in dogmatic theology, imposed by the school, notably stimulated this revolt. Its place was largely taken by "scientific theories of evolution" and a "natural science philosophy." My preceding acceptance of the Tsarist monarchial regime and "the capitalist" economy was replaced by the republican, democratic, and socialist standpoint. Previous political indifference gave way to a revolutionary zeal. I became an enthusiastic missionary of the anti-Tsarist revolution and the leader of the Social-Revolutionary party in the school and adjacent region. In contrast to the Social Democrats, the Social-Revolutionary party claimed to be the party of all—peasant, industrial, and intellectual—labor classes. In contrast with the Marxian social-democratic materialism and economic interpretation of man and history, the philosophy and sociology of the Social-Revolutionary party was much more idealistic or integralistic. It emphasized strongly the role of creative ideas, voluntary efforts, the "struggle for individuality" vs. "struggle for existence," and the importance of non-economic factors in determining social processes and human conduct. My previous *Weltanschauung* was much more congenial to this kind of ideology than to the "proletarian," "materialistic," "economic" ideology of Marxian social-democracy. This congeniality explains why I chose the Social-Revolutionary but not the Social-Democratic party and why throughout my subsequent life I have never been "infected" by most of the Marxian ideologies.

Having been transformed into an ardent Social-Revolutionary, I began to spread the gospel of the revolution among the students, the factory workers, and the peasants of nearby villages.

On the eve of Christmas, 1906, at one of my regular meetings with a group of peasants, I was arrested, together with my fellow-revolutionist, and jailed in the prison of the city of Kineshma. There I met other political prisoners among whom there were several notable Social-Revolutionaries and Social-Democrats. Together we soon turned the prison into the safest place for keeping the revolutionary literature. The prison guards volunteered to serve as our messengers, and the warden offered his office, with its telephone and other facilities, for our use. During some five months of my imprisonment, the political prisoners had daily discussions of philosophical, social, and politico-economic problems. These discussions, plus my reading of the works of Marx, Mikhailovsky, Lavrov, Plekhanov, Lenin, Kropotkin, and Tolstoi, as well as those of Darwin, Hegel, and other evolutionists and philosophers, acquainted me fairly well with some of the basic works of the revolutionary thinkers, and of a few philosophers and scientists.

In these five months I probably learned a great deal more than I could learn in a semester in the Teachers School. In the prison I also met daily and conversed with many of the criminals: murderers, thieves, burglars, rapists, and other unfortunate "deviants." These meetings and conversations introduced me to the world of crime and criminals. They were largely responsible for the topic of my first book, *Crime and Punishment, Service and Reward* (published in 1913) and for my choice of criminology and penology—or more exactly of criminal, penal, and constitutional law—as the field of my first specialization at the University of St. Petersburg. (Here again "the existential," personal experiences seem to account for this rivulet in my mental life.)

After five months of imprisonment I was released, subject to "open surveillance of police," to whom I had to report regularly about my domicile, any change of my address, and about my activities. Since I was discharged from the school, I decided to become a sort of an underground "professional revolutionary," going from factory to factory and from village to village to spread the gospel of the revolution and organize revolutionary "cells" and groups. Often hungry, cold, shelterless, and dirty (because nobody paid for this "professional work"), constantly hunted by the law and occasionally at mass meetings becoming the target for barking guns of attacking Cossacks and police, I carried on this "missionary activity" in contact with a few other revolutionaries for about three months. Towards the end of this period, my health and nervous system became impaired, my energy was greatly depleted, and my arrest appeared to be imminent.

These circumstances forced me to flee from this region to the region of the Komi, where my revolutionary activities were, as yet, unknown. I returned to the little farm of my peasant aunt in the small hamlet of Rymia, where I had stayed before many times. There for two months I helped my aunt with harvesting and farm work and regained my vitality and peace of mind. Having no prospects for either interesting employment or for continuation of my education in the Komi region, in the fall of 1907 I moved to St. Petersburg. Thus one big chapter of my life ended and a new chapter began.

Some of the factors of this crisis in my mental life are fairly obvious. They are the new mental currents and values, the new people, and the new environment I met and largely absorbed in the Teachers School and its region. Especially important was "the spirit of revolution" that was sweeping over the whole of Russia, with its ideologies, values, and aspirations. My previous idealistic *Weltanschauung* accounts somewhat for my choice of the Social-Revolutionary and not Social-Democratic party and ideology. My contacts and talks with the ordinary criminals as I earlier indicated largely account for my first book and specialization in the field of criminology and penology. These tangible factors consisted, however, not so much in a change of my *social position, group-structure, and class-affiliation* (as many sociologists of knowledge claim) as in different mental currents and cultural values I encountered and learned from books and people, in this new environment and in the all-pervading storm of the Revolution of 1905-6. Nor was my "mental revolution" a consequence of some grudge against, and frustration by, the Teachers School. Until my arrest I was treated very well by the teachers, administration, and students, and I had no grudge against the school or local authorities. For these reasons the visible factors of the sharp mutation of my mentality had to be the new ideas, values, and aspirations I had learned and my own selection and development of these in the inner workings of my mind. This hypothesis accounts for a large part of the discussed crisis of my mentality. It partly explains also why in my later works, particularly in my *Social and Cultural Dynamics,* I took for the basic factor of social, cultural, and personality change the cultural-mental factor, and not the social factor of structural composition of groups and social classes. As we shall see further on, the configurations of cultural-mental systems and social structural systems neither coincide with each other nor change simultaneously in time and space.

Although they may account a great deal for the crises, the indicated visible factors leave, however, a number of dark points unexplained. Why, for instance, did not many of my fellow-students in the school experience a similar "mutation" of their mentality, though their background and social affiliations were similar to my own? Why, among those who underwent a change in their mental life, did not an overwhelming majority become the active missionaries of the revolutionary gospel rather than continue the prescribed routine life of the school? Why did I involve myself in the

dangerous and most exacting activities of an itinerant missionary of
the revolution and continue these activities until my health and
peace of mind were seriously impaired?   There were neither economic incentives, nor other sensate advantages such as power, popularity, respect, security, and sensate comfort, to be gained from such
involvement.   And yet, like many other apostles of the revolution,
I was "driven" by some powerful force (often termed "call of duty"
or "moral imperative") into this sort of activity; and this kind of
"foolish," "unprofitable," and highly risky involvement has been repeated several times in later periods of my life.

These and similar "whys" give an idea of the dark points in the
explanation of the dynamics of my own, as well as of many others'
mental life.   These points suggest that human beings and their
mental life are something much more complex and intangible than
most of the "economic," or "instinctive," or Freudian, or other popular theories indicate.   This sort of experience and behavior, repeated later on several times in my life, may be partly responsible
for my "integral theory" of human personality, cognition, creativity,
and of social and cultural processes, developed in my later works.
This integral theory shows the one-sidedness of all "simplistic"
theories of man and of the sociocultural world and the extreme
complexity of their "superorganic" nature and of the man-made
sociocultural world.   According to this theory, man and his man-
made sociocultural world are "the fields" of manifestation and operation, not only of physical and vital energies, but also of the higher
energies of the rational, conscious thought, and especially of the
highest "super-rational" energy of creative genius different from
the rational and vital energies.

VII. *Post-Crisis Integration of My Mental Life*

I arrived in St. Petersburg practically penniless.   To keep my
body and soul together, I had to obtain some job at once.   A helping-
hand to the janitor of an apartment house, a factory worker, a clerk,
a tutor to the boys of mainly middle-class families, an occasional
writer of articles in provincial papers—these were my jobs during
my first two years in St. Petersburg.   The earnings hardly met my
elementary needs but somehow they kept me alive.   In subsequent

years I earned my living by more remunerative tutoring and writing for various periodicals, by a secretarial and research assistantship to such an eminent scholar and statesman as Professor M. M. Kovalevsky, by the scholarship granted to me by the University of St. Petersburg, and after 1914-15, as a lecturer of the Psycho-Neurological Institute and *Privatdocent* of the University of St. Petersburg.

Anxious to continue my education, very soon after my arrival in the capital of Russia in 1907 I was permitted to attend one of the good night schools (Tcherniaevskie kursy), which I did for two years. During these two years I prepared myself and successfully passed, in the spring of 1909, a rather stiff "examination of maturity"—the equivalent of the examination for the whole eight years of the Russian high school (gymnasium). Passing this examination entitled me to enrol at the newly opened Psycho-Neurological Institute in 1909, and at the University of St. Petersburg in 1910. Graduated with the highest honors from the university, I was "retained by the university for preparation to professorship" in criminal and administrative law. (At that time there were no sociology courses in the university's curriculum.) In 1916 I successfully met all the requirements for and had conferred upon me, by the university, the degree of "the magister of criminal and administrative law"; and in 1920 I received my degree of Doctor of Sociology from the same university. Sociology was introduced into the curriculum of the university in 1918.

Such, in brief, was the course of my group and social class affiliations during this period of 1907-16 (up to the eve of the Revolution of 1917 and subsequent years).

As to the course of my mental and cultural life during these years, its main trends consisted in an intensive absorption of the immortal cultural values in music and literature, in painting and sculpture, in architecture and drama, and in enrichment, development, and integration of the *Weltanschauung* ushered in by the crisis. Fairly soon after my arrival in St. Petersburg, I became acquainted with several Russian leaders in literature, music, painting, and the theater. Through attendance of, and participation in, various literary and artistic groups, and philosophical, ethical and cultural societies; through visiting various museums, concerts, and plays; and through personal study, I became fairly well oriented in these cultural fields. Continuation of my revolutionary activities had led me to two new imprisonments in 1911 and 1913 and well acquainted me with political leaders of the Social-Revolutionary, the Social-Democratic, the Constitutional-Democratic, the Anarchist, the Monarchist, and other parties. My co-operation in revolutionary and in scientific work in the seminars of the university with several Social-Revolutionary and Social-Democratic students who eventually became leaders in the Kerensky and the Communist governments resulted in our mutual close friendship. When in 1918 I was condemned to death, this friendship with the Bolshevik students saved me from execution by the Communist firing squad. (When Karakhan, Piatakov, and others learned about the sentence of death passed upon me by Veliky Oustiyg Communist Cheka, they went to Lenin and demanded from him an immediate cancellation of the sentence and my release from prison. Lenin did precisely that and simultaneously published his first complimentary article about me in *Pravda*. Later on he published three uncomplimentary articles about me, calling me "the foremost ideologist of reaction," "the defender of slavery and serfdom," "our implacable enemy," and so on.)

This active political work firmly grounded me in the field of political science and practical politics. Finally through meeting the stiff requirements of the curriculums of the night school, of the Psycho-Neurological Institute, and of the university, I acquired a substantial knowledge of philosophy, and of mathematical, physical, biological, and psycho-social sciences. This knowledge was notably increased by my intensive study of the basic problems in these disciplines and in sociology, social philosophy, and philosophy of history, the disciplines in which I had become deeply interested already in the Teachers School.

Thus, during these years of 1907-16 I succeeded in enriching notably my cultural and scientific equipment and—what is more important—in integrating its parts into one fairly consistent system. Philosophically, this system was a variation of an empirical neo-positivism or critical realism, based on logical and empirical scientific methods. Politically, it was a variety of socialistic ideology, founded upon the ethics of co-operation, mutual aid, and freedom. My sociological views represented a sort of synthesis of Comtean-Spencerian sociology of evolution-progress, corrected and

supplemented by the theories of Russian scholars such as Mik-
hailovsky, Lavrov, De Roberty, Petrajitsky, Kovalevsky, Rostovtzeff,
Pavlov, Tolstoi, Dostoievsky, and Jakov, and by the theories of
Durkheim, Simmel, Weber, Stammler, Pareto, Marx, and other
Western scholars, to mention but a few names. All in all, it was an
optimistic *Weltanschauung*, fairly similar to the prevalent "World
View" of the Russian and Western thinkers of the pre-castastrophic
decade of the twentieth century.

My scientific and semi-popular papers and my volume on *Crime
and Punishment,* published in the years of 1911-16, reflect various
aspects of this *Weltanschauung.* These publications and then my
active participation in various seminars, scientific, philosophical,
and political conferences and, finally, my course of lectures on sociology given in the Psycho-Neurological Institute earned me the
reputation of a talented scholar, notable political figure, and eloquent speaker and writer. My name became fairly well known in
Russian intellectual circles, among various peasant-labor groups,
and among Tsarist officials and police. Such, in brief, were the main
changes in my mental life of this period.

VIII. *New Crisis and New Reintegration*

Already, World War I had started to make some fissures in my
optimistic *Weltanschauung* and in my conception of the historical
process as progress. The revolution of 1917 enormously enlarged
these fissures and eventually broke this world outlook, with its system of values and its "progressive," rational-positivistic sociology.
Instead of the increasingly enlightened and morally ennobled humanity, these historical events unchained in man "the worst of the
beasts" and displayed on the historical stage, side by side with
the noble and wise minority, the gigantic masses of irrational human
animals blindly murdering each other, indiscriminately destroying
all cherished values and, led by shortsighted and cynical "leaders,"
"overthrowing" creative achievements of human genius. This unexpected world-wide explosion of the forces of ignorance, inhumani-
ty, and death in the supposedly civilized and enlightened humanity
of the twentieth century, forced me, as it did many others, to re-
examine sternly my "sweet and cheerful" views of man, society,

culture, and values, all moving, according to these views, harmoniously from ignorance to wisdom and science, from barbarism to magnificent civilization, from the "theological" to the "positive" stage, from tyranny to freedom, from poverty to unlimited prosperity, from ugliness to ever-finer beauty, from animality to noblest humanity and morality.

This re-examination was fostered also by my personal experiences during the years of 1917-22. My book *Leaves from a Russian Diary* gives a detailed account of these experiences. Since the beginning of the Revolution, I wholeheartedly dedicated myself to the revolutionary reconstruction as one of the leaders of the Social-Revolutionary party, as an editor of the party's papers, *Delo naroda* and *Volia naroda*, as a member of the Council of the Russian Republic, as one of the organizers of the all-Russian Peasant Soviet, as a member of Kerensky's cabinet, and as a notable professor of the University of St. Petersburg. For many years, fighting for the basic reconstruction of Russia (and other countries), I never believed that this reconstruction could be successfully made by the blind and destructive violence of masses led by unscrupulous leaders using all means—good and evil—for realization of their purposes. Guidance by available scientific knowledge and by the binding power of universal and perennial moral norms appeared to me as the necessary conditions for a fruitful and painless reconstruction. These convictions were responsible for my revolt against the early—cynical, ignorant, and inhuman—policies of the Communist party and government (now largely replaced by constructive ones), against the beastly and destructive violence of its followers, as well as of its opponents, and against the "abomination of desolation" wrought by these forces during the first five years of the Communist revolution. There was too much hate, hypocrisy, blindness, sadistic destruction, and mass-murder to leave my "cheerfully progressive" views intact. These "existential conditions" and the trying, personal experiences of these years started a re-examination of my *Weltanschauung* and a reappraisal of my values. This reconstruction of my views, values, and my very "self" proceeded slowly during the five years I lived in Communist Russia and then, after my banishment, in Europe and the United States.

To the end of the 1920's this painful and, at the same time, blissful process of reintegration continued and gradually matured into its essential features. It resulted in what I now call the Integral system of philosophy, sociology, psychology, ethics, and values. My volumes: *Sociology of Revolution, Contemporary Sociological Theories, Social Mobility,* and *Principles of Rural-Urban Sociology,* published in the years 1925-29, already are marked by the features of this reintegration, sufficiently advanced but not quite completed as yet. My *Social and Cultural Dynamics* (1937-41), *The Crisis of Our Age* (1941), *Man and Society in Calamity* (1942), *Society, Culture, and Personality* (1947), *Reconstruction of Humanity* (1948), *The Ways and Power of Love* (1954), and *Fads and Foibles of Modern Sociology* (1956), not to mention other books published in the period of 1930-61, are the fruits of a more or less matured reintegration. Writing these volumes, I have been quite aware that in many essential traits my reintegration theories have sharply deviated from the prevalent theories of American and European sociologists, historians, and psychologists.

For this reason, I expected a strong opposition to my "integralist" views on the part of the psychosocial scholars who, before World War II, did not pass through the crucial experiences of the great revolution and World War I. However, the expectation of a severe opposition and other unpleasant consequences of my "deviant"—integralist—standpoint did not, for a moment, make me hesitate to publish these volumes. My usual "bullheadedness" (mentioned before), and my deepest conviction that a supreme duty of a scholar is "to tell the truth" as he sees it, regardless of any and all consequences, are probably responsible for a lack of hesitation, on my part, in challenging the prevalent theories in my later volumes. The expected opposition and some of the adverse "existential" consequences have come, indeed.

But with these negative results have also come many positive reactions. Somewhat surprisingly for me, my "integralist" views and theories have found an enthusiastic response on the part of sociologists, psychologists, philosophers, religious leaders, and eminent thinkers throughout the world. My volumes have been translated into all major languages of humanity; and my "deviant" theories have been widely discussed and have already a considerable literature in the form of books about my books, Ph.D. theses, hundreds of scientific articles, and special chapters in the textbooks of sociology and in the history of social thought, not to mention thousands of popular write-ups about them. And as time goes on, my "yarns" seem to be paid increasing rather than decreasing attention throughout the world. Personally I am gratified by both—positive and negative—reactions to my "mental productions."

Other "existential" conditions of my life, at this age of seventy-three years, are also satisfactory: my health is rather good for my age; I am still fairly vigorously continuing my studies, writing, lecturing, and enjoying recreational activities; there is no scarcity of invitations for lecturing and counseling on the part of American and foreign universities and learned institutions, and even on the part of several governments.

So, in spite of routine tribulations of human life, these existential conditions permit me to be at peace with the world, with my fellow-men, and with myself, notwithstanding the most turbulent state in which mankind finds itself at the present time. However, this peace does not hinder me from taking a humble, but active, part in the paramount tasks of our age: the prevention of a new threatening world catastrophe and the building of a new, nobler, and more creative order in the human universe.

IX. Conclusions

The preceding brief sketch of the existential and mental factors underlying the main topics of my studies and the character of my "yarns" can be summed up as follows:

a. The existential fact of being born and reared among peasants and remaining in deep sympathy with rural people—with their way of life, culture, and values—largely accounts for my studying these problems and, in co-operation with C. C. Zimmerman and C. J. Galpin, publishing *The Principles of Rural-Urban Sociology* and three-volumes of the *Systematic Source Book in Rural Sociology*. The same existential factors, processed, tested, and enriched by the existing scientific knowledge in this field, explain most of my theories and conclusions embodied in these volumes.

b. Since my life has been a sort of continuous "wayfaring" through most different occupational, social, economic, cultural, political, and ethnic positions and group-affiliations, this—vertical and horizontal—mobility possibly accounts for the concentration of my studies upon the dynamic aspects of personal, social, and cultural phenomena and for the comparatively less attention given to their static and structural aspects. My *Social Mobility, Social and Cultural Dynamics, Sociology of Revolution, Man and Society in Calamity, American Sex Revolution,* and *Reconstruction of Humanity* deal mainly with the how and why of the change and with the uniformities in the change of these phenomena. Their structural analysis is not neglected, but it is reduced to the minimum necessary for a detailed analysis of their dynamics.

c. Since I actively participated in and directly observed two world wars and two revolutions, with their disastrous results— great famines, devastating epidemics, and other calamities—it is comprehensible why these phenomena attracted my attention and became the topics of my investigations published in my *Sociology of Revolution, Man and Society in Calamity,* in the third volume of my *Dynamics,* in a number of chapters of my *Society, Culture and Personality,* and in a substantial volume, *Influence of Hunger upon Human Behavior and Sociocultural Processes* (destroyed by the Soviet government in the process of printing).

d. Having been imprisoned three times by the Tsarist government and three times by the Communist government, and having come in contact inside prisons, not only with political prisoners but also with non-political criminals, I naturally became interested in the phenomena of crime, criminals, and punishment. This existential condition explains the topic of my first substantial volume, *Crime and Punishment, Heroic Service and Reward.* The same condition accounts also for my first professorial specialization in criminology and penology. I would have preferred to specialize in sociology, but before the revolution, sociology was not taught in Russian universities and could not, therefore, be chosen as a field of professorial specialization.

e. Since my early boyhood, being incessantly confronted with a multitude of human problems, beginning with the problem of procuring means of subsistence and ending with those of "peaceful co-existence" with the ever-changing persons and groups whom I met in my wayfaring life—and experiencing and observing in this mobile life most different situations, persons, groups, values, and events—I could not help becoming interested in human beings and in social and cultural problems, as well as in the how and why of their emergence. My "wayfaring" life itself incessantly challenged and demanded from me some intelligent answers to questions concerning these problems. This sort of continuous "challenge and response" (in the terms of A. J. Toynbee) stimulated my interest in the social, psychological, and humanistic disciplines and was tangibly responsible for my choice of sociology as the main field of my study and professorship.

f. During the two world wars and two revolutions, I lived amidst and observed a gigantic explosion of human bestiality and hateful destructiveness of demoralized individuals and groups. Exploding in their raw, unembellished form or being masked by highfalutin— "Patriotic," "Socialist," "Communist," "Conservative," "Liberal," "Democratic," "Religious," and other—beautifying ideologies, these forces uprooted anything and destroyed anybody that stood in their way. Their catastrophic effects induced me to undertake a systematic study, on the one hand, of the role of a selfish, individual and collective "struggle for existence," violence, hatred, and cruelty and, on the other hand, of the role of the opposite forces of unselfish love, sympathy, mutual aid, and heroic sacrifice in human behavior and in sociocultural processes. As a result of my personal encounters with these "hate-powered" forces and of my study of their nature, sources, and effects, I became a convinced opponent of these forces in all their destructive manifestations in the forms of wars, bloody revolutions, and violent strife, and a firm proponent of the opposite forces of sympathy, mutual aid, and unselfish love. These circumstances prepared a general ground for the subsequent establishment of the Harvard Research Center in Creative Altruism and for continuation of my studies published in the volumes: *The Reconstruction of Humanity, The Ways and Power of Love, Forms and Techniques of Altruistic and Spiritual Growth, Altruistic Love,* and *Explorations in Altruistic Love and Behavior.*

However, this general ground alone might not have been sufficient for realization of these tasks. A decisive role in these matters was played by another unexpected factor—by the generous offer of some $120,000 by Eli Lilly and the Lilly Endowment for financial assistance in my studies in this field. This offer was made entirely on their own initiative, without any request or even any previous meeting with Eli Lilly and the members of the Lilly Endowment on my part. This totally unexpected grant, initiated by an eminent industrialist, civic, and cultural leader, and scholar-archeologist, has played the role of the Aristotelian "effective" cause in the establishment of the Center and publication of some twelve volumes of its research.

g. Since I came out of the lowest peasant-labor stratum and had a full share of hardships and disenfranchisement common to such strata, I naturally identified myself with these classes and eventually became disrespectful toward *the incapable* privileged, rich, and ruling groups. This attitude engendered my opposition to their arrogant domination and to many injustices perpetrated by such persons and groups. This opposition, in its turn, led me to several collisions with the Tsarist government, and to ensuing imprisonments and other penalties imposed upon me. These circumstances are tangibly responsible for my "revolutionism" and eventually for my political position of a "conservative, Christian anarchist" (in Henry Adams' term). This critical attitude toward all *uncreative and irresponsible ruling groups* has been reinforced by my subsequent studies of these groups. It has remained such, up to the present time, toward all pseudo-aristocracies and all incapable and demoralized governments—autocratic and democratic, monarchic and republican, communistic and capitalistic. Besides many pages devoted to this topic in my volumes, these attitudes and views find their clear expression in my and W. Lunden's recent volume, *Power and Morality.*

Summary Remarks. The preceding existential and intellectual factors account, to a tangible extent, for the *main topics* of my studies and publications. These factors make somewhat comprehensible why these and not different problems attracted my curiosily and led me to a substantial investigation of these phenomena. In this "conditioning" of my theories, the role of the existential factors consisted in arousing my curiosity and interest in their what, how, and why, and possibly in suggesting rather rough, unverified, and untested answers to these questions. The role of "intellectual" factors has consisted in taking over the aroused curiosity, or the specific what, how, and why, engendered by the existential factors, and in trying to investigate these problems as systematically and thoroughly as I could, until my curiosity was quenched and these questions were more or less satisfactorily answered. So much for *the factors underlying the main topics of my studies.*

As to the factors underlying the *character of my theories*—why I accepted or constructed the theories presented in my volumes and rejected many others different from these—an adequate answer to this question is very difficult and hardly possible within the limits of this essay. The general reason for acceptance or rejection, or construction of my own theories, has been that, on the basis of my study of the investigated problem, the theories sponsored or constructed by me appeared to me more adequate and true than all the other competing theories. In all my studies, this criterion has been the only reason and motive for acceptance or construction of my theories, and no other motives or reasons have ever played any part in this matter. Unswervingly following the categorical imperative, to "find and to tell the truth" regardless of any consequences, I did not hesitate to repudiate even some of my own theories when subsequently I found out, or was apprised by critics, of their inadequacy or errors. For the same reason I have not hesitated to attack many a prevalent and "generally accepted" theory, if and when it appeared to me fallacious or inadequate. The old adage *Amico Plato sed veritas amicissima,* is another formula faithfully followed by me in all my studies.

The existential factors of my faithfulness to this categorical imperative or, in my critics' terms, of "Sorokin's idiosyncrasies," and "Sorokin's bullheadedness and deviationism," lie probably in several important and persistent facts of my life course. Forced to be "independent" and "free" to survive as well as I could at the age of ten, since this early age I have had to cope with the hard realities of life, beginning with the procuring of my means of subsistence and continuing with the never-ending task of a satisfactory co-adjustment to the ever-changing persons and groups, mores and morals, beliefs and values, through which I passed in my wayfaring life. Such a stern school of life either breaks its pupils or makes them self-reliant and independent. Sternly disciplined for many years in this sort of school, I became, to a notable degree, a self-reliant, independent, now and then nonconformist individual who in his search for truth does not accept any authority, any theory, any belief, or any value until it is tested and verified by all the relevant evidence available.

An unusually wide range of my life experiences and dealings with most different persons and groups, and of my exposure to most different cultural climates probably has been instrumental in directing my attention not only to their differences but especially to their *similarities and uniformities*. Such sorts of existential conditions, reinforced by a substantial study of the respective phenomena, explain, to a tangible degree, the somewhat broad and encyclopedic character of some of my theories and concentration in my research upon a discovery and formulation of the structural and dynamic *uniformities* in the phenomena studied.

The same stern school of life with its severe discipline favored also a development of logical consistency and scientific discipline of my analytical thought manifest in many of my volumes and culminating in my efforts at a construction of consistent systems of integral philosophy, sociology, and psychology; of an integral system of reality, cognition, creativity, and of values—all based upon the same basic axioms and all mutually consistent with each other.

At the present time this *Integral Weltanschauung* has just about matured.[1] It serves me—and I hope it may serve others of my fellow-men—as a firm, ideological, axiological, and existential foundation for my peace-of-mind and integrity of self and for my guidance through the devastating-regenerating, epochal hurricane sweeping over the human universe today.

[1] For a brief exposition of this *Weltanschauung*, see my articles, "This Is My Faith," in S. C. Cole, ed., *This Is My Faith* (New York: Harper, 1956); "Integralism Is My Philosophy," in Whit Burnett, ed., *This Is My Philosophy* (New York: Harper, 1957); "Quest for Integral System of Sociology," in *Memoire du XIXe Congrès International de Sociologie*, Vol. I (Mexico, D.F.), 1960; "Three Basic Trends of Our Time," in *Akten des XVIII Kongress des Institut International Sociologie* (Meisenheim/Glan), 1960.

Part Two

SOROKIN IN REVIEW

Joseph B. Ford

Arnold J. Toynbee

Othmar F. Anderle

Gösta Carlsson

David R. Mace

Alexandre Vexliard

T. Lynn Smith

Matilda White Riley and Mary E. Moore

Alex Inkeles

Nicholas S. Timasheff

F. Richard Cowell

Kanailal M. Munshi

Corrado Gini

Lucio Mendieta y Núñez

Robert K. Merton and Bernard Barber

Sorokin as Philosopher

Joseph B. Ford

I. *Is Sorokin a Philosopher?*

Sociologists have condemned him for being "philosophic." Yet philosophers have taken little note of his work. Sorokin himself has what he calls a "philosophy." "*Integralism,*" he says, "is my philosophy."[1]

What is a philosophy? And what is a philosopher? It may be easier to establish what Sorokin is, and what integralism is, than to answer these two questions to the satisfaction of everyone. Social scientists, in our day, have tended to use the term "philosophic" or terms linked to it in a deprecatory sense, especially when applied to members of their own fraternity. Vivid illustrations of this negative use of terms linked to philosophy can be found in discussions of Sorokin in major sociological journals. His *Social and Cultural Dynamics* was characterized by reviewers as a "metaphysical quest" (*American Journal of Sociology*) or placed in the realm of "mists of intuition" (*Social Forces*). Sorokin's works are full of the very empirical data highly valued by anti-philosophic critics. However, critics buttress their case with references to Sorokin's critique of "extreme sensate empiricism," and slight the masses of facts collected by him and his assistants in their roles as empirical sociologists.

The characterization of "philosophical," "metaphysical," or the like seems to have had for these critics little specific content save as something outside the pale of science. The limited attention his writings have attracted among philosophers has been largely critical. His writings are, as he himself clearly recognizes, out of sym-

[1] P. A. Sorokin, "Integralism is My Philosophy," in Whit Burnett, ed., *This is My Philosophy* (New York: Harper & Bros., 1957), pp. 180-89.

pathy with most of the prevailing trends in philosophy. One of the few philosophers to deal at length with Sorokin attacks him for his "neglect of modern philosophy."[2] Thus, from both sides comes condemnation of Sorokin's efforts to link the problems of sociology with broader ones in the area of traditional philosophy. Yet it is clear that labeling Sorokin a philosopher and his work *philosophic* is not wholly in error. To make sense of the statement, however, it is necessary to clarify the use of the term "philosophic" and to dispense with the contemptuous connotations of his sociological critics and the more restricted sense of the term preferred by many philosophers today.

Here, we propose to discuss briefly the relevance of Sorokin's works in such traditional branches of philosophy as logic, ethics, epistemology, aesthetics, and the philosophy of history and of science. We shall then turn to a fuller presentation of Sorokin's "integralism." Finally, we shall analyze some basic philosophic issues raised in his work.

Sorokin's knowledge of the history of philosophic thought is especially evident in his work on *Contemporary Sociological Theories*. Paradoxically, this work devotes far more attention to the history of thought than many works on social theory not using the rubric "contemporary." In addition, Sorokin includes logical analysis of the relationship of premises and evidence to conclusion throughout, citing instances of the traditional fallacies, violations of "laws of thought," etc. He treats metaphysical and epistemological issues, where relevant, to an extent seldom found in the writings of social scientists. Among his other writings, *Social Philosophies of an Age of Crisis* deals most directly with issues of traditional philosophic concern.

Ethical problems, of course, are the main focus of his later writings. These deal with the "reconstruction of humanity" and the vast range of issues linked to the general topic of "altruism."

In his *Sociocultural Causality, Space, Time,* Sorokin comes more closely to grips with fundamental problems of the philosophy

---

[2] John A. Irving, *Science and Values* (Toronto: Ryerson, 1952), p. 123. Chap. xi is devoted to an attack on Sorokin's work, particularly his *Reconstruction of Humanity*. Irving confuses some of Sorokin's basic terminology, such as in his reversal of the meaning of "ideational" and "idealistic." Other philosophers demonstrate a more careful reading in their critiques (e.g., Daya Krishna in his "Sorokin and the Problem of Knowledge," *Indian Journal of Philosophy*, I, No. 3 [April 1960] 175-83).

of science, already analyzed in his *Dynamics*. A full coverage of the philosophic implications of his work would require a considerable discussion of this work and its major topics. The same would hold true of his detailed discussion of the problems of the sociology of knowledge and of the philosophy of history, which are the topics for other chapters in this volume. We shall therefore limit our detailed treatment here to the "integralist philosophy" which is, in one sense, the basis for Sorokin's views on all these other topics, and in another the outcome of them. In any event, it is so intertwined with the other aspects that we shall necessarily assume some acquaintance with them while holding to the central topic of integralism. Sorokin is, indeed, one of the few who fulfil the injunction by his critic Irving that the issues of philosophy and social science should be treated *in conjuncture*.[3]

II. Sorokin's Integralism

Sorokin's "integralist philosophy" bears an intimate relationship with his analysis of the why of super-rhythms in historic social change. In this analysis the principles of *immanent change* and of *limited possibilities* play crucial roles. His earliest full-scale presentation of his "integralist philosophy" emerges in the latter chapters of his *Dynamics* from his treatment of these two principles in their empirical setting. While they are covered more fully in other chapters of this volume, it is necessary to review them briefly here because of their relevance to Sorokin's philosophy. For it is in the insufficiency of the philosophic premises of each of the major super-systems of culture that Sorokin finds the fundamental explanation of the limits and the eventual decline of each major supersystem.

It may serve us well to note, first, how the concept of *integration* itself plays a key role in Sorokin's empirical studies of social systems. While constantly aware of the presence of cultural congeries and imperfectly integrated systems, he focuses on the role of a "system of meanings" as it is "objectified" and "socialized" or "grounded" in empirical sociocultural reality. This is for him a key to the *unity* and hence the *intelligibility* of sociocultural phenomena.

[3] Irving, *op. cit.*, p. 124.

After presenting a wide variety of evidence, Sorokin states this proposition in clear and categorical form:

Among cultural phenomena there hardly exists any pure causal relationship or any pure causal system "unmarried" to the meaningful relationships and systems and based entirely upon inherent—physical, chemical, and biological—properties of the vehicles. Any sociocultural system is at the same time meaningful, and its "causativeness" is based upon the system of meanings it incorporates.[4]

Again, while congeries of meanings and empirically integrated meanings are always present in every empirically grounded system, nonetheless, the most general criterion of a system of meaning is *"a logical compatibility and specific dependence or interdependence of each meaning-element upon the other meanings-elements, of the meanings-elements upon the whole system and of the system upon the elements."*

This specific dependence, he asserts, is either *"logical dependence or interdependence* for all the propositions and systems of propositions that have a form of judgment," or else "aesthetic dependence or interdependence for all the *art meanings or values—* expressive of consistency and consensus or harmony—which represents a kind of aesthetic logic different from the logic of verbal propositions."[5]

The analysis of empirical sociocultural systems is enormously complicated by the different forms in which logical and aesthetic dependence and interdependence manifest themselves in theories of science, articulated norms of law, creeds of religion, principles of political and economic organization, theories and judgments of art, etc. Yet all of these are only part of the picture. Sorokin continually stresses the "infinitely manifold and inexhaustible" nature of "true reality." He states that logically consistent meanings give only "one-rational-aspect of this reality," and that *the task of the social scientist is enormously more complex than that of the "natural scientist, who has to deal with and study only one (the causal) aspect of his phenomena,"* as well as that of the *"pure philosopher, who deals only with the realm of the pure meanings."*[6]

[4] *Dynamics*, IV, 39.
[5] *Ibid.*, IV, 21. The matter of the role of aesthetic interdependence, and its relationship to logical consistency, is one of many questions we cannot treat fully here.
[6] *Ibid.*, IV, 67-68.

While Sorokin proceeds then to discuss how empirical socio-cultural systems function and change in important parts as a whole and in "togetherness," he analyzes in considerable detail and depth the "conditions of the optimum integration of empirical socio-cultural systems."[7] Through all this analysis he notes the elements of *congeries* again and again. Here, however, it is necessary only to indicate his constant use of the concept of *integration* in one form or another as a criterion and also as an index of what is "optimal" and in some cases even "ideal." Many critics have missed this reiterated stress on the chaos and congeries alongside the unified elements in concrete social reality. Hence, they have rushed forth to battle Sorokin on a point where he made his position quite clear. He certainly has immunized himself against the charge that he has neglected the discordant and unintegrated elements in culture; yet he has made *integration* the keystone of his system.

In his careful analysis of the principle of immanent change he makes this even clearer. For example, he states the proposition that:

Other conditions being equal (including the milieu), in the social and cultural systems of the same kind, the greater and better is their integration, the greater is their self-determination (and autonomy from the environment) in molding their own destiny. . . . Such is probably the most important condition of the amount of self-determination of the system, in unfolding its potentiality during its life career.[8]

Thus, integration becomes the clue to the autonomy of a system, which makes possible its margin of self-determination.

Among corollaries of his major propositions, Sorokin states that "other conditions being equal, *the highest amount of self-determination belongs to those social and cultural systems which are most perfectly integrated, causally and meaningfully.*"[9] This greater amount of integration has, of course, its corollaries in the greater "causal interdependence" of the components of the system and the most "solidary" and "consistent" relations of the human agents. These, clearly, are variations on the theme of integration, and the terms are near synonyms for it in their own contexts.

Sorokin acknowledges that between perfectly integrated and un-integrated systems there are many "intermediate systems." Nonetheless, the crux of his analysis is the *degree of integration.*

[7] *Ibid.,* IV, 68 ff.   [8] *Ibid.,* IV, 610.
[9] *Ibid.,* IV, 611.

In this connection he notes that "eclectic pseudo-systems of philosophy come and go, but that *consistent* systems (such as idealism and materialism, eternalism and temporalism, realism and nominalism, unified systems of religious beliefs and ethical teachings) tend to persist and may remain dominant for centuries." Indeed, he adds:

Even when they are on the decline, they still exist and are distinguishable; and . . . dominant (see Volumes One and Two). It is not incidental that, whether it be in the history of philosophy, art, ethical systems, scientific theories, religions, or law—in all such histories very little can be found about innumerable eclectic theories which existed, and still exist. The bulk of the histories deal with only the more or less perfectly integrated systems of philosophy of the great "integrating minds," or with the integrated systems of art, ethics, science, or religion. The greater the integration of the system, the more space is given to it, and the longer it persists, and often the greater the influence it exerts upon the destiny not only of its own but other cultural systems of mankind.[10]

As with philosophies, so is it with social systems. Unintegrated armies, states, families, or business organizations invariably lose out and are short-lived in comparison with integrated ones. Integration is the key. Sorokin adds a word of caution, that is, use of the term *integration* "should not be mixed with fashionable terms." By these, he means popular terms like "progressiveness," "plasticity," and "adjustment." A system may be well or poorly integrated, yet have these characteristics or not. Integration is far more basic.[11]

This may suffice to show Sorokin's repeated use and emphasis of the concept of integration both in his empirical analysis of social systems and in his theoretical explanation of them. From this treatment emerge the conclusions of his "integralist" philosophic viewpoint.

Sorokin reviews the predecessors of his own integralist philosophy and makes no claims of complete novelty for it. Among the various forerunners, one may particularly note the influence of Aristotle's ideas.[12] In noting the parallels between Aristotle's and Sorokin's thought one should not neglect the fact that Sorokin makes reference to numerous other predecessors of his own use of the principles of Immanence and Limits and, hence, explicitly and im-

[10] *Ibid.*, IV, 613.   [11] *Ibid.*, IV, 613-14.
[12] For example, note Sorokin's own statements and citations as on pp. 603, 636, 640-41 and elsewhere in Vol. IV of *Dynamics*.

plicitly, parts of his integralist philosophy. These references include numerous examples from Chinese and Hindu thought, as well as from Western thinkers from ancient to modern times.

Sorokin's sociological analysis focuses on the main *integrated* forms of culture. He repeats for emphasis that "the number of the unintegrated forms of culture is much larger, practically unlimited, if we keep in mind all the variation of diverse congeries, accidental traits, and unrelated systems."[13] Unintegrated and eclectic or mixed combinations of culture elements are thus not subject to the principles of limits, but the main integrated forms are.

Sorokin highlights the limited possibilities of integrated forms. He states that in regard to the nature of "true reality—the main premise of each of these integrated forms"—the number of possible answers is limited to five fundamental solutions: first, the ideational premise that "true reality" is suprasensory; second, the "sensate" one, that it is sensory; third, the idealistic premise that it has both aspects inseparable from one another; fourth, the skeptical premise, that it is unknown and unknowable; and fifth, that it is "known only in its phenomenal aspect, while in its transcendental aspect (if it has such an aspect) it is unknowable (the premise of Hume-Kant's Criticism and Agnosticism)." Sorokin maintains that "there exists hardly any solution of this problem essentially different from these five possibilities."[14]

Sorokin is keenly aware of the myriad subtypes of each of these five types of main premises. For example, the idealistic philosophy may appear in such diverse forms as those of Plato, Plotinus, Saint Augustine, and Hegel, and sensate premises may differ greatly, as in Lucretius, La Mettrie, Holbach, and Marx. These differences, however, are secondary and do not affect the main characteristics.

Of these five main types, the fourth and fifth are viewed by Sorokin as "negative" ones and "can hardly serve as a basis for a long existing integrated culture." Hence, only the three main forms, with the other two as subsystems, "cannot help being repeated in the integrated cultures that continue to exist after the first run of all the three or five fundamental forms." He concludes: "Hence repetition of these forms; hence our super-rhythm in the history of the cultures studied."[15]

[13] *Ibid.*, IV, 738.   [14] *Ibid.*
[15] *Ibid.*, IV, 739.

From this it is clear that Sorokin finds the main key to socio-cultural change in the *philosophical* premises of integrated culture forms. This becomes even clearer as he proceeds to discuss "systems of truth." For Sorokin, there are and can be only five or six "main integrated systems of truth." These are those based on (1) faith, (2) reason, (3) the senses, (4) their idealistic synthesis, and (5) an "integrated sceptical and agnostic, or critical system." The rest would be "merely an eclectic mixture of these systems." Since these are all the logical possibilities, it is of course "inevitable—logically and factually—that these systems should recur in any long-existing culture (in time) or in various cultures (in space)." Sorokin applies the same to the main styles of art, ethics, and social, economic, political, and other relationships. All of these are treated as "sub-systems in our super-system and as such live and change together." Thus, it is their "total coordinate recurrence" that accounts for the "recurrence of the Ideational, Idealistic, and Sensate phases in the life process of our super-system."[16]

There is some ambiguity here in that Sorokin includes the "systems of truth" and of "true reality" as "sub-systems," but he makes it clear as he proceeds that at the basis of each form of integrated culture lies, as its major premise, its *system of truth and reality*. "It is this premise," he adds, "that, to use W. I. Thomas' term, 'defines the situation' for the rest of the related compartments of each of these forms of culture."[17]

This makes it clear that, for Sorokin, the philosophic premises are the basic key to the integration of a culture. It is the inadequacy of each of the main systems of truth and reality that constitutes the most important "reason for the super-rhythm of ideational-idealistic-sensate forms of culture." It is from this standpoint that Sorokin investigates the possibilities of truth and falsity in each of these philosophical premises, and it is from this that he develops his own "integralist" solution.

He holds that the various compartments of culture articulate the three major systems of truth and reality, and that if one of these systems were entirely true, then, the other two would be "entirely or mainly false." Hence, with this assumption he states that one true system of reality and its corresponding culture form would be able to "exist and dominate forever without any fear or possibility of

---

[16] *Ibid.*, IV, 739-40.   [17] *Ibid.*, IV, 741.

being dislodged by the false system." An entirely false system could hardly dislodge an entirely true system, nor can "complete ignorance overthrow complete knowledge." A completely true system would continue forever; yet, a completely false system could hardly dominate for any length of time and "still less recur" because no society could endure in "complete ignorance and error." Human beings must know what is eatable and what is not, and if they do not have this and other minimal knowledge they will perish. This minimum of "true knowledge" must have been present in each of the three main systems of truth and reality, and if any of the three were absolutely false, it could not have dominated for centuries nor have had the capacity to recur.[18]

Since each of the main systems has, in fact, shown a capacity to endure over a period of time, and to recur several times in Greco-Roman, Western, and other cultures, we may reasonably conclude that "the *super-rhythm studied seems to be possible only under the conditions that each of the three main systems of truth and reality—and the corresponding form of culture—is partly true and partly false, partly adequate and partly inadequate.*"[19]

Each of the three principal forms of truth, thus, contains a "vital part" that enables human beings to adapt to their cosmic, social, and organic milieu and to serve as a "foundation for their social life and culture." On the other hand, each system has its invalidities and these are likely to develop further as the system achieves a monopolistic dominance. Thus, each newly dominant system "undergoes again the same tragedy and sooner or later is replaced by its rival; and so these *corsi* and *ricorsi* must go on, and have been going on."[20]

Under this third assumption, the recurrence of the super-rhythm becomes "not only comprehensible but logically and factually inevitable." This is the "deeper reason" for the why of the super-rhythm.[21]

Sorokin states that the validity of this reasoning is "almost axiomatic" provided that it can be shown that "each of the three main systems of truth and reality is indeed neither wholly false, nor wholly true, but contains a part of truth and a part of error; and that with an increase of domination of each system its part of

[18] *Ibid.*, IV, 741-42.
[20] *Ibid.*, IV, 743.
[19] *Ibid.*, IV, 742.
[21] *Ibid.*

truth decreases while the part of error increases."[22] That each of these systems of truth is indeed "not the whole truth and nothing but the truth" is for Sorokin "almost evident." For if the partisans of any one system had the absolute truth, they would be in his words "the omniscient God." There would also be the assumption that "true reality is exhaustible and finite" and this assumption is also impossible. On the other hand, the assumption that each of the main systems of truth is entirely false is likewise unacceptable.[23]

A certain circularity and vein of pragmatism appear to be present here. The integrated systems of truth prove themselves in their success and survival. One finds also creative, consistent thought in the great theological, or philosophical, or scientific systems that are elaborated, once the major premises are accepted. These great systems are the "best and finest examples of human consistent thought—the standards for logic and refined thinking." Whether or not one agrees with Augustine, Aquinas, Kant or Plato, Newton or Darwin, one has to grant to these philosophical and scientific systems and to other great systems, the "humanly possible superlative coherency of thought."[24]

However, Sorokin is aware of the dangers of circular reasoning, and wishes to avoid any merely pragmatic test of truth. The partial truth of each major integrated system is assured, but Sorokin notes that even with the sensate empirical method he has followed in his *Dynamics*, the evidence is strong that extreme sensate philosophic systems (such as materialism and radical forms of empiricism) are relatively weak, even by the pragmatic tests of success and survival. He notes that his figures, over the recorded history of Western culture, show religious and idealistic rationalism so far to be the "most powerful system of truth" among competing epistemologies, and that in the metaphysical area, all forms of idealism (used in the traditional rather than the Sorokinian sense) have proved (in his "weighted indices") about four times as prevalent as all types of materialism. This may, then, be interpreted as "an indication that, all in all, a certain predominance of Idealism over Materialism is necessary for the continued existence of human culture and society and that a balance of the Mixed-Idealistic-Ma-

---

[22] *Ibid.*   [23] *Ibid.*, IV, 745.
[24] *Ibid.*, IV, 746.

terialistic systems is still more indispensable than pure, other-worldly Ideationalism and Idealism."[25]

Despite some ambiguity here (as in the very same sentence Sorokin switches to using the term idealism in his own special sense), this offers nonetheless a strong argument, on sensate grounds, that sensate systems of truth are less viable. With respect to extreme forms such as materialism, and especially mechanistic materialism, he believes the argument is even more conclusive, since these are shown to be at all times "relatively insignificant" and at no time in twenty-five hundred years have they been "monopolistic or clearly dominant." It seems, thus, that "a considerable proportion of idealism is a prime requisite for the durable existence of society." This implication is reinforced by evidence that the "tide of materialism . . . almost always occurred before or during crises, hard times, social disintegration, demoralization, and other phenomena of this kind."[26]

Thus, while Sorokin affirms the minimal elements of validity in all main systems of truth, it appears at the end that—even by the sensate pragmatic test—idealism in metaphysics and rationalism in epistemology prove strongest, and that a certain predominance of these may be indicated, even in a pragmatic prescription for the future of humanity.

III. The Theory of Integralism

From this argument emerges Sorokin's "integral theory of truth and reality." This theory incorporates what he deems to be the partial truths of each of the main scientific and philosophic systems. He stresses that this "integral truth is not identical with any of the three forms of truth but embraces all of them." It is "nearer to the absolute truth than any one-sided truth of one of these three forms." Using all the sources of intuition, reason, and the senses, this "integral three-dimensional truth . . . is a nearer approach to the infinite metalogical reality of the *coincidentia oppositorum* than the purely sensory, or purely rational, or purely intuitional reality, given by one of the systems of truth and reality."[27]

[25] *Ibid.*, II, 55 and 200-201. [26] *Ibid.*, II, 201.
[27] *Ibid.*, IV, 762-63.

This integral system allows for the truths of the senses, which give us the empirico-sensory aspect; the truth of reason for the "rational aspect"; and the truth of faith for the "super-rational aspect." The three-dimensional theory gives us more adequate knowledge of the whole, as well as a more valid picture of each part. Here again Sorokin's stress on the concept of integration as such looms as a key to the knowledge of reality. For he underscores the statement that *each of these systems of truth separated from the rest becomes less valid or more fallacious, even within the specific field of its own competence.*[28] Yet, again, it is not in any mixed form, or mixture as such, but in the degree of integration that one must seek the clue.

Many have criticized Sorokin for putting too much stress on the "truth of faith" as contrasted with the sources of truth in the senses and in reason. However, he justifies his more detailed and emphatic treatment of the "truth of faith" on the basis that it has been neglected in the modern sensate period, whereas the empirical and rational sources have been recognized and treated more adequately. Therefore, he makes an extended presentation of the reasons for accepting the sources of the "truth of faith," known under such diverse names as "intuition," "inspiration," "revelation," and the like.

Sorokin prefers to use a residual definition of intuition along the lines of K. W. Wild's definition: "Intuition is an immediate awareness by a subject of some particular entity without such aid from the senses or from reason as would account for that awareness."[29]

Without doubt, in Sorokin's view, there is such an "intuitive method and immediate intuitive awareness on which reason and all other forms of knowing are dependent." Sorokin summarizes his arguments for accepting some form of intuition as follows:

First of all, for the reason that some kind of intuition is at the very basis of the validity of the systems of truth of reason and of the senses. *Second,* because intuition, as distinct from discursive dialectic and sensory experience, has been one of the most important and fruitful "starters" of an enormous number of the most important scientific, mathematical and philosophical discoveries and technological inventions. *Third,* because a variety of the religious and mystic intuition has been

[28] *Ibid.,* IV, 763.
[29] K. W. Wild, *Intuition* (London: Cambridge University Press, 1938), p. 226.

the main source and the main force for the creation of the greatest artistic, religious, and ethical systems of culture. *Fourth,* because there is a sufficiently large body of the testimonies of the great thinkers, creators of religion, of art values, of science, demonstrating the reality, the functioning, and the power of this source of truth.[30]

Sorokin also stresses that the role of intuition is "recognized or clearly implied in the epistemology of the most different currents of philosophical and scientific thought"—as in the "Kantian and neo-Kantian use of *a priori* categories of mind" and in such varying theories as those of Bergson, Croce, Jung, Whitehead, and Spinoza (as analyzed in detail by Wild), to which list Sorokin adds "almost all the great philosophers: Plato, Aristotle, Plotinus, St. Augustine, all the Church Fathers, all the Scholastics from Erigena to St. Thomas and Nicolas of Cusa, Descartes, T. Hobbes; all the mystics, and so on."[31]

Sorokin includes many nineteenth- and twentieth-century thinkers, thus bringing a paradoxical element into his discussion, inasmuch as he asserts that intuition has been neglected in the extreme sensate philosophies of modern times. He notes that "even such pillars of the empirical method as John Stuart Mill state that 'the truths known by intuition are the original premises from which all others are inferred.'" This paradox, however, may not be a real inconsistency. He is here stressing the recognition *even* by extreme empiricists and rationalists of the ultimate basis of new knowledge in something akin to intuition. In the articulation of their detailed theories, intuition may still play a minor role. Moreover, his criticism is directed mainly against the "poorly informed pseudo-empiricist" who rejects intuitive methods *in toto,* whereas "the intuitive method of cognition has differed from the purely sensory or rational and is acknowledged by an enormous number of thinkers and by most of the currents of scientific and philosophic thought."[32]

Sorokin particularly highlights the role of intuition in all forms of creativeness both in science and in art and notes that "any genuine creation is a real cognition as any real discovery is a creation." From this he concludes that the "truth of faith, derived from and

[30] *Dynamics,* IV, 747.
[31] *Ibid.,* IV, 750. He adds: "See their names in the Appendix to Chapter One of Volume Two of *Dynamics;* all the names listed there under Mysticism, Criticism; and the greater part of the names under Rationalism, Fideism; and some of the names under Empiricism belong to the explicit partisans of intuition."
[32] *Ibid.,* IV, 751.

based upon intuition, is the genuine truth as much as the truth of the senses and of reason" and that "it is especially indispensable in the apprehension of those aspects of the true reality which are inaccessible to the senses and to reason." Here again the intimate relationship of his integralist philosophy to his sociology of knowledge is apparent, for he states:

This explains why the truth of faith has been able to dominate for centuries, and why the super-rational religions have been eternal concomitants of the development of human culture. If the truth of faith (and intuition as its source) were entirely false, such a fact could not be. In the light of the above statement, the important and often indispensable role played by intuition in the cognition of true reality explains the perennial fact of the immortality of religion and arts, and the domination of the truth of faith over long periods; and this immortality of supersensory religion and super-rational arts and ethics and the domination of the truth of faith for long periods corroborates the important role of intuition as the source of truth, knowledge and creativeness.[33]

Finally, Sorokin highlights again the point that the integral theory of truth cannot be reduced to any of the three forms of truth, but it embraces all of them. He stresses, again, the infinite and inexhaustible manifoldness of reality and cites the ideas of many mystical philosophers to illustrate how the ultimate nature of reality is beyond our ken—how, in his favorite citation from Nicolas of Cusa, it is always a *coincidentia oppositorum* (reconciliation of opposites).

More than any contemporary social scientist, and probably as much as any contemporary philosopher (and even more than adherents of currently popular schools of philosophy), Sorokin affirms the crucial role of the major philosophic premises of a culture in the total articulation and, indeed, in the very quality of continued existence of the society and the culture. Not only does the main philosophic premise "define the situation"; it defines the future, the very potentiality of survival. In the current sociocultural crisis, he sees the only hope in a new integralist philosophy which can and must become the basis for a new integralist culture.

Integration, the key concept in his empirical and theoretical analysis, becomes also on this level the key to the solution—to salvation for humanity. This is, in essence, what Sorokin means by his philosophy of *integralism*.

[33] *Ibid.*, IV, 761.

IV. Evaluation of Sorokin's Integralism

How shall we evaluate Sorokin's integralism as a philosophy?

Sorokin's catholicity of interest leads him to treat almost every branch of philosophy. Metaphysics, epistemology, ethics, and the philosophies of history are central concerns. Yet no problem is excluded in his broad study of man and society. Aesthetics, for example, is involved, as is the philosophy of science. All of these would be relevant in a full-scale evaluation of his integralism. Here, it will be possible to make only briefest mention of some of the crucial issues raised by him in connection with philosophy in general and then to deal a bit more fully with his special contributions. These involve chiefly the relations of social theory with epistemology and with ethics.

A. Crucial philosophic issues: General. Sorokin's work is important for philosophy precisely because he has raised and faced crucial philosophic issues while the majority of his sociological colleagues have been content to ignore or sidestep them, making often gross and even grotesque philosophic assumptions. One of Sorokin's great accomplishments has been to demonstrate the inescapable presence of these issues in the scientific as well as philosophic consideration of man and society.

What follows is illustrative. No treatment of this length could be either exhaustive in scope or adequate in detail. But the examples may afford some vision of the diversity and range of the linkages between empirical social research and philosophy, as these become visible in the work of this eminent scholar.

i. The integralist system of truth, as proposed by Sorokin, bears a close resemblance to what he calls the idealistic system. Indeed, in his more recent statements, he tends to equate the two.[34] Yet for over twenty-five hundred years the idealistic system of truth has proved, according to Sorokin's own quantitative studies, the *least* stable of the three main systems of truth. It may be that these idealistic systems of the Golden Age in Greece and of the thirteenth to the fifteenth centuries in Europe were imperfect efforts to approximate

[34] "A Quest for an Integral System of Sociology," in *Memoire du XIXe Congrès International de Sociologie* (Mexico, D.F., 1960).

an integral system. It may be, on the other hand, that the conflicting tendencies in them may have led to an early decline and
fall, whereas the one-sided ideational and sensate systems prevailed
for longer periods. This question is intrinsic to Sorokin's analysis
in the sense that it rests on the assumption that the system of truth
plays a crucial role in sociocultural dynamics, and that the duration
of the several main systems is adequately evidenced in his empirical
studies. As the "main integrated systems" are said to demonstrate
their superiority to the mixed forms by their very success and survival, it would seem that the same tests might well be applied to
comparisons among these systems themselves. This question of
empirical social science is also a question of philosophy. For
Sorokin (as for Hegel and Schiller before him): *Die Weltgeschichte
ist das Weltgericht*[35] (world history is the world court). It is interesting that, in the interim between the publication of the
Dynamics and Sorokin's more recent statements, some have identified Sorokin more closely with the ideational position.

ii. The opposition in the premises of the ideational and sensate
systems of truth—and the difficulties in their integration—leads in
turn to a more basic question: the relationship of the philosophic
premises and the sociocultural results or consequents of these
premises. Sorokin states that the fundamental laws of logic retain
their validity in all systems and are in this sense "absolute and continue to be absolute."[36] This has broader significance as well, but
here it indicates a possible ambivalence within the Sorokinian argument itself. It appears that the consequent developments in ethics,
law, technology, and other sociocultural areas are logically and
meaningfully related to the premises—not always perfectly, but
with a strain of some sort toward logical consistency. This has
implications whose full analysis is more for the sociology than
the philosophy of knowledge.[37] There, empirically as well as
logically, is raised the problem of the incompatibility of the
consequences as a necessary entailment of the opposition of the
premises. How, then, can we hope for a successful integration on

[35] A favorite quotation of Sorokin, in recent works. Cf. *ibid.* and *Fads and
Foibles, passim.*

[36] *Dynamics,* II, 208 n.

[37] Editor's note: See the Merton-Barber essay on "Sorokin's Sociology of Knowledge" in this volume.

the level of sociocultural events? Sorokin suggests that the integration on the level of ultimate reality involves a reconciliation of opposites. But can this reconciliation succeed in a working social
system? Evidence to date would seem negative.

iii. Along with this goes the problem of the link between logico-
meaningful values, especially "the major philosophic premises, and
material vehicles, and actual human events." In his analysis of
Northrop, Sorokin holds that his own system involves something
akin to what Northrop calls "epistemic correlations." Sorokin's own
system is based upon a "triple epistemic correlation," as opposed to
Northrop's double one.[38] At times this seems to rest on a problematical construction of Northrop's terms. Still there is considerable
convergence between Northrop and Sorokin in general. Sorokin's
extension of Northrop's "epistemic correlations" may have a legitimacy and a profound value, both sociological and philosophical.
But the issue raised here is one which involves considerably more
than the interpretation made by Sorokin in his commentary on
Northrop. It involves a fundamental epistemological and empirical issue, inherent in Sorokin's own work, as to the connection of
the fundamental values and the empirical consequents. This may
well be in an "epistemic correlation." If so, the key to integration
would be on the level of the *episteme* ("knowledge" or "thought").
This could be true integration, but not of separable and co-equal
"sources." Reason would still be the charioteer, after Plato's
analogy.

iv. Along with his effort at an empirical underpinning of his
version of integrating sources of knowledge goes this even more
daring effort to transcend them all in what seems to him the only
logically justified explanation of their partiality and their inadequacy. Thus, without his version of the "meta," Sorokin's system is
incomplete and—in his sense at least—not integral.

The most serious problem of all in Sorokin's metaphysics—and
there are many that we cannot discuss here—lies in his view of the
metarational and *metalogical* nature of "*ultimate reality*." Sorokin
continually speaks of the infinitude, the uniting of contraries, the
inexhaustibility and perfection of this "true total reality." Integral-

[38] Sorokin, *Social Philosophies of an Age of Crisis*, p. 248

ism, he insists, "views the total reality as the infinite X of number-less qualities and quantities: spiritual and material, momentary and eternal, ever-changing and unchangeable, personal and superper-sonal, temporal and timeless, spatial and spaceless, one and many, the littlest [of] the little, and the greatest [of] the great."[39] He is even led to paeans of praise of the "highest center" as the "Infinite Creative X that passes all human understanding." It is in connec-tion with it that he often cites leading mystics and their terms for it as the *"mysterium tremendum et fascinosum"* (tremendous and fascinating mystery) and *"coincidentia oppositorum."*[40]

Sorokin, indeed, argues that in essence all philosophers agree with his point in that they admit that the ultimates are beyond their grasp. He claims that "practically all the philosophical currents of thought" recognize the inexhaustibility and the infinitude of infinitudes of true reality. Skepticism does this with its explicit declaration that we cannot know reality. Criticism does it with its Kantian conception of the impossibility of adequate knowledge of things in themselves. Others like idealism and materialism, posi-tivism and empiricism, mysticism and fideism, do the same in "their respective contentions of the inexhaustibility of their true reality," as does contemporary phenomenologism (of Husserl and others) in its own way. In brief, he concludes that "there is hardly any serious scientist or philosopher or religious thinker who claims that the true reality—the world of God—is exhaustible and finite, and is already fully known."[41] It is in this very quest of integration at a higher level that other problems arise for Sorokin's integralism.

There arises here the matter of consistency of the empirical and rational methods used throughout Sorokin's work with this postulate that the true nature of reality is beyond *all* rational or empirical knowledge. Certainly few of the philosophers and scien-tists, cited as in agreement on the unknowability of the ultimate, would agree with Sorokin in adopting the mystics' terminology for describing that "ultimate reality."

One possibility would be to separate Sorokin's metarationalism from his integralism and discard the former to retain the latter. Maquet seeks to demonstrate the separability of integralism as a

---

[39] In Burnett, *op. cit.*, p. 180.   [40] *Ibid.*
[41] *Dynamics*, IV, 745.

"scientific theory" from integralism as a "gnosiology" (theory of knowledge).[42] But either of these proposals would rob the integralist philosophy of its integration. Hence they would take away its quintessence.

Maquet admits the consistency of Sorokin's integralism with his metaphysics. That is, the infinite nature of ultimate reality may be beyond knowing by any of the main sources. Yet, because of its very inexhaustibility, each one of the three sources could not help hitting it at some point. Maquet, however, believes that one could hold to a non-integralist philosophy of knowledge also consistently with Sorokin's positive sociology, including his sociology of knowledge. He does this by showing how a sensate and ideational philosopher, each from his own perspective, could simultaneously admit Sorokin's positive sociology while affirming that only his own sensate or ideational theory of knowledge was true.[43]

Maquet's error in his otherwise splendid logic is that he fails to note the most salient fact of all: the very point and power of Sorokin's integralism is that it offers an explanation of *how* each of these two opposed philosophies could lead to an adequate understanding of a *part* of the whole. Such a part would be the subject matter of positive sociology, including Sorokin's own. But the understanding of the "true total reality" calls for more than any of the three sources could afford. Hence, the very *raison d'être* of the integralist philosophy.

But the deficiency in Maquet's criticism does not remedy all defects in the topic of critical analysis. These defects may include the very vocabulary of analysis, which Maquet adopts in part in his criticism. One need not be a logical positivist or semanticist to question the adoption of the mystical vocabulary of Pseudo-Dionysius, Scotus Erigena, Meister Eckhart, and Nicolas of Cusa. If God is, as Scotus taught, not even a What, the vocabulary for representing our belief in him may indeed be beyond all comprehensible expressions—and indeed beyond *all* understanding as claimed by Scotus and others. If so, we are left with the "source"—another sometime and ambiguous word—of faith. And is faith, in all its appeal and all its own frequent ambiguity, an adequate source of knowledge? Especially of that which cannot be known? In

[42] J. J. Maquet, *The Sociology of Knowledge* (Boston: Beacon Press, 1951), p. 217.

[43] *Ibid.*, pp. 216-23.

Sorokin's positive sociology of knowledge it is not, but must always be supplemented with other sources.

Sorokin himself recognizes, in some measure, that his metarational views are based primarily on faith and not integrated wholly with his integralist system of sociology or even with his integralist theory of knowledge insofar as this is indissolubly bound to this positive empirical study. In response to a theological critic,[44] he replied that belief in the role of Divine Providence, or the Divine intervention in historical processes, is "logically possible," and that "as a believer I, perhaps, share it, though incapable of seeing it often clearly." But all that is a "matter of belief" and based necessarily on "the standpoint of pure truth of faith." Whereas, as he goes on to note, he has been himself engaged in studying sociocultural phenomena "from the standpoint of the truth of reason and the senses" and not "exclusively or mainly" from the "standpoint of this truth of faith."[45] While he is writing here on a question of the unilinearity of history, his reply would apply generally as well.

The philosopher Wheelwright, in *The Burning Fountain*, suggests that the language of science is a "steno-language," and hence incapable of formulating with precise logic what may be expressed in what he calls "depth language." While by no means entirely novel, this distinction is of interest in that it is made in the course of a study in the "language of symbolism" by a modern philosopher —in an inquiry that is "partly ontological, partly semantic." This is relevant to other considerations of Sorokin's terminology but we can hardly pursue the issue here.

To be sure, a proposition derived from faith might have confirmation from other sources, but in this case Sorokin does not appear to assert that it has. He expresses considerable doubt regarding philosophies that seek to trace the course of God's hand in the empirical data of history. Indeed, he seeks to refute the uniformity, overt or hidden, that such guidance would imply. He criticizes "eschatological" theories of history as "speculations rather than scientific conceptions." In his analysis of the theodicy of Toynbee, he applies the same principles.[46]

[44] John La Farge, "A Critique of Progress," *America*, LVII, No. 26 (Sept. 25, 1937), 597.

[45] *Contemporary Sociological Theories*, p. 739.

[46] *Social Philosophies*, pp. 113-20 and chap xii; also in *Pattern of the Past*, pp. 99-126.

If these principles of criticism are applied in turn to Sorokin's own reliance here on faith, how will the Sorokinian version of metarationalism stand up? To be sure, faith can be confirmed (and hence integrated) with reason and sensory experience. But in this case such confirmation is denied, even as a possibility. For "in its inexhaustible plentitude the total reality is inaccessible to the finite human mind."[47] Each of the modes of knowing can grasp some main aspect, but it seems that we know its unity, its infinitude, its perfection, by faith and faith alone. Or do we "know" it at all?

How are these seeming contradictions reconciled?

One powerful argument may be that it is only the integralist theory that makes their contrariness explicable, and that even the partial and relative pragmatic success of each of the three types of major philosophical premise cannot be understood consistently in any other light. Sorokin sometimes seems to accord to the principles of logical consistency an absoluteness that he denies to the truths of the senses and in his positive sociology of knowledge even to the truths of faith and intuition. But there his use of the term "absolute" is somewhat different from its use as a quality of the Infinite Creative X. The laws of logic are valid in all systems of truth and, in this sense, these laws are "absolute" for Sorokin, as already noted.[48] But this must be a different sort of absolute quality from that which is by its nature beyond all logic—hence *metalogical* in the strictly literal sense.

Krishna senses this same difficulty in the *form* of integration that Sorokin seeks in his conception of ultimate reality. He also presents a vigorous argument that "the empirical-rational field of knowledge crosses the classificatory categories of ideational and sensate culture and that it is *only* with respect to it that a *cross-cultural, developmental, integral system of cognition is even possible.*"[49]

One may see here the problem of the relation of the metarational metaphysics to the positive sociology of Sorokin—and its remarkable convergence with Northrop's insightful cross-cultural philosophic studies. Further than this we cannot go. Complexities of the relationship of these issues to metaphysics are so immense

---

[47] Burnett, *op. cit.,* p. 180.
[48] *Dynamics,* II, 208, cited above.
[49] Krishna, *op. cit.,* p. 184.

that in a recent publication Moschetti devotes a substantial portion of his work, *L'Unita Come Categoria,* to just one of them.[50]

The fact that Sorokin's work does raise philosophic questions that go well beyond the above-mentioned problem highlights its significance. It may also be the reason that, as Krishna puts it, "most thinkers seem to be afraid of coming to terms with it," and that one finds a "general evasion of the issues raised by this outstanding work" (i.e., the *Dynamics* alone) "which combines the encyclopedic exhaustiveness of the data with a self-consciousness about methodology that is rarely met with among sociological thinkers."[51]

Unlike virtually all other social scientists of his era, Pitirim Sorokin has presented an explicit, far-reaching system of philosophy. Indeed, more so than many philosophers who would restrict the field, he has developed theories with implications in such diverse branches of philosophy as ontology and ethics, gnosiology and the philosophy of history. Nor has he hesitated to take up whatever has seemed to him relevant. As a result, his inquiries have embraced many usual and quite a few unusual problems in these branches of philosophy. His catholic interests, along with his integralism, have led him to find some element of value, not only in the orthodoxies, but also in the heterodoxies of each epoch—and not only in the rationally and empirically oriented systems, such as his own sociological system is in the aggregate, but also in wideranging mysticisms of the Orient and Occident, whose conception of "ultimate reality" he seems finally to credit and accept himself in his metarational metaphysics.

With this catholicity, he has combined incisive critiques of nearly all major viewpoints, save the metarational mysticisms, whose satisfactory integration with the rest of his philosophy we have expressed some reasons for doubting. Likewise, however, we must doubt the radical excision of this part from the rest of Sorokin's system, or indeed even the separation of the integralist philosophy from his "positive sociology" and his sociology of knowledge as proposed by Maquet. His sociology of knowledge seems satisfactorily integrated with his integralist philosophy, although they are not mutually indispensable, whereas the former, the metarational

[50] Andrea M. Moschetti, *L'Unita Come Categoria* (Milano: Marzorati, 1959). A substantial part of Volume II considers the relation of Sorokin's work to one major philosophic problem, as indicated in the title: *Unity as a Category.*

[51] Krishna, *op. cit.,* p. 175.

element, seems less satisfactorily integrated and, to our mind, not at all "proved" by the rational or the "common agreement" of scientific and philosophic "currents" on the seeming unknowability of much that is unknown at any given juncture and, *perhaps,* for all time.

To follow out all the problems raised by Sorokin's presentation would be, in the end, to discuss all the relevant problems of philosophy. While these would well merit such discussion, it must be left for a longer work.

B. *Epistemological and ethical issues.* This mention of some of the gamut of issues relevant to Sorokin's work hardly does justice, therefore, either to the work or the issues. But in the brief compass of this treatment, it seems wisest to devote more attention, in this closing section, to the great positive contribution of Sorokin's integralism to the social sciences and to the re-establishment—or perhaps the establishment for the first time on a sound and lasting basis—of the ineluctable connections of social theory with the philosophy of knowledge, on the one hand, and the philosophy of value on the other.

With respect to the former—the issues of epistemology and gnosiology—little additional comment is needed. The positive presentation and the issues raised even by Sorokin's critics attest to the fact that he has shown much of sociology and social theory to be what Winch has aptly dubbed "misbegotten epistemology."[52]

Whatever criticism philosophers, on their part, may bring to bear on Sorokin's own theory of knowledge, most would agree, if they inspected his works closely, that he has demonstrated the relevance of the issues of social science to these issues traditionally linked to the sphere of philosophy. The sociologists who have tried to show their irrelevancy have only revealed a superficial under-standing of their own philosophic presuppositions and considerable ignorance of what they purport to treat as irrelevant. If one were to try to frame it in syllogistic form, their argument has run, in effect: All that is unknown to us is irrelevant to the study of man in

[52] Peter Winch, *The Idea of a Social Science* (London: Routledge and Kegan, 1958), p. 43. It would be relevant—if space permitted—to illustrate in detail how other social scientists became entangled unawares in epistemological questions. Winch does this in part.

society. These issues are unknown to us. Hence, they are irrelevant to the study of man in society.

Sorokin himself summarizes the sterile position of these apostles of irrelevancy most succinctly and correctly:

As to the revolt against "armchair philosophy" in sociology, here again a sociologist can reject a specific brand of philosophy as a wrong philosophy but no sociologist can dismiss philosophy qua philosophy from sociology and sociological research. The very nature of psycho-social, cultural and value-problems cannot be properly defined and analyzed without some philosophical—epistemological, ontological, and phenomenological—presuppositions.[53]

The relevance of the questions of logic and epistemology is palpable in all science, but especially so in a science of man. For here the "problem of knowledge" is involved in both the knower and the known. The differentiating core of the subject matter is the presence of *meaning*. The sociocultural level has as its distinguishing characteristic the presence of meaningful components in one form or another—the existence of evaluative interaction in the groupings of this most intelligent and productive of primates. Sorokin's role in clarifying the problem of meanings and values in human interaction has been, perhaps, his greatest contribution to social science, both in its theoretical and empirical reaches. It certainly has been a signal contribution to the philosophy of social science in bringing the science itself *home* to its philosophic base, and *homeward*—at the very least—in the evaluation of its object of inquiry, and, through this, in its structure, its method, and its referential principles.

Parallel, at least, with the summons to epistemological sense is Sorokin's contribution to ethics—or to the philosophy as well as sociology of value. Here we cannot enter into a discussion of even the meaning—much less the full history and implications—of these terms. But ethics has always dealt with the concepts of value in one form or another: the Good, the Ought, the Right. A cardinal principle of sociology, on the other hand, has been their partial or total exclusion, or their redefinition in a form that would make them the proper object of "science." Thus, when sociologists have used explicit value-concepts, they have often tried, quite literally, to strip them of their *value*.

[53] "A Quest for an Integral System of Sociology."

Yet value—or its synonyms—cannot be eliminated in the study of man and society. Major sociologists from Comte to date have tried to account for the role of values in many different ways, usually through the substitution of other terms: consensus, solidarity, concord, ideals, valuations, even Greek and Latin translations, as if somehow the problem of value could thereby be eliminated. Documentation of this is the subject for a volume—or volumes.

One salient example may suffice here. Sumner tells how he himself was tempted to use the Greek *ethica* in place of "mores" and "folkways," but like Mill's suggestion of "ethology," it seemed too unfamiliar. However, "morals" as used in modern languages is, according to him, "an impossible and unreal category." He then proceeds to devote the body of his writings to the detailed study of that which he declares "has no existence and can have none."[54] But by calling factual morals "mores" he presumes to have solved all sociological and philosophical issues!

All great social thinkers have had to deal with the problems of value, and hence with the concepts of value. Sociologists, however, in common with most other modern social scientists, have tried to eliminate the problem of value, in fact, by treating values as so-called facts. What they have meant has been, almost always, that there is *no relationship* between the philosophic concern with the concepts of value and the sociological concern with the factual results of such "value judgments" as people do actually make. Indeed, the idea has been that to study one, the other must be excluded wholly from consideration.

Usually, in addition, it is implied, if not expressed as with Sumner, that the whole of the moral philosopher's concern is an unreal and impossible category. Sometimes this is modified to permit the scientist, as citizen, to have value judgments, but these are purely individual matters and not part of his role in society as a scientist. They may, to be sure, be part of his other role as citizen, and this other role can be studied by him as a scientist. Presumably he may thereby become a better citizen and a better scientist, but that is a value judgment in the category of the "unreal" and "impossible"—certainly beyond the pale of science. The whole matter has become a buzzing confusion, and we cannot

[54] W. G. Sumner, *Folkways* (Boston: Ginn and Co., 1906), p. 37 and Preface, p. iii.

even attempt a solution here. But this very confusion may help us to appreciate the contribution of Sorokin.

We have already noted that, whatever the faults of their subalterns, great thinkers in the social sciences have been forced to recognize and deal with the problem of value, even if obliquely. How, then, is Sorokin's contribution distinctive? On several counts, his work stands forth.

First, Sorokin has recognized the role of values and meanings *directly*. He has not tried to redefine them as something else, or reduce them to something less than they are, or change them to something different from that which marks them as what they are. He has sought to make the social *intelligible* by perceptive analysis of the elements that are immanent in it that make it meaningful and susceptible to the type of understanding that, in one form or another, important social thinkers have sought.[55]

Second, he has held to consistent concepts of "meaning" and "value" on a sociocultural level, and yet has urged and demonstrated their use in widely varying empirical fields. He has thus blended his discernment of this philosophic purport with an equally incisive insight into their empirical connections and applications. In this sense, he has given real content to the "triple epistemic correlation" claimed for his system, despite his somewhat variant usage of the terminology.

Both in his theory and his research, Sorokin has pointed a way to one possible solution of the problem of the objectivity of value. Not that some other sociologists (Durkheim, for example) have not glimpsed this to some extent, but hardly so explicitly or with the same attention to the whole gamut of relevant issues. Sorokin finds the objective element in value through its infusion with the "sociocultural" in a way that helps make possible the study of values as such, as well as their effects. This again opens a subject too vast to treat here, but it should be noted that philosophers may

[55] It would take a lengthy work to give full evidence of the importance of the *direct* (as against an indirect, oblique, or otherwise garbled and deficient) treatment of values qua values. The present writer has a work of this sort under way. Another work, with Professor C. C. Zimmerman, *The Sociology of Change*, includes this theme as an important collateral issue (to be published by Ronald Press). From a philosophic point of vantage, Winch analyzes some of the confusions in sociology and social psychology (as well as much philosophy) on this score, especially in the treatment of language.

find a valuable "lead" in this phase of his work. A few indeed have already done so.[56]

Third, he has started with the clear-cut recognition of the relevance of philosophic problems at every stage of scientific analysis of the *socius* (group-member) and of society, and has held to this principle throughout immense researches and copious writings, even though this has led him into spheres far removed from those of colleagues with more limited horizons. Most social scientists have not wanted to be led to "think vastly"—and sometimes, indeed, not to think at all of other than their own circumscribed range of Lilliputian facts. Only a few have given even lip service to the intimate and ubiquitous ties of social theory and philosophy.

Fourth, Sorokin has exploited his tremendous knowledge of the historic social theories as well as the empirical studies of the day to demonstrate to value-free and meaning-free scholastics in social science that their paths are variously blind or circular, and their hopes of avoiding the crucial issues are illusory. Many ears are tone-deaf to any philosophic message, but when combined with this scientific erudition, such profound advice as that of Sorokin is bound to have an enormous impact. To slight his scientific work would rob the science of society of much that is precious, but to dismiss the ineluctable philosophic questions that he has raised would be to beggar the science utterly.

Fifth, like many another notable thinker before him, Sorokin has sought a practical outcome in action for his theories of value. Many may criticize his investigations of altruism, reported in his later writings. Even more may scoff at his hopes for "creative altruism" in the "reconstruction of humanity." But few would doubt today the depth and seriousness of the "crisis of our age," as so many did when his earlier works used this phrase. In a relatively short time, Sorokin asserts, "these 'loony' forecastings have come to pass."[57] Perhaps, after a nuclear war or two, even some of the critics may not view it as so "loony" to seek to study and develop further the "production, accumulation and actualization" of "creative altruism." Other terms might be used. Comte's "consensus

---

[56] Moschetti, *op. cit.*, pp. 107 ff. Moschetti considers Sorokin's work highly significant in this regard. He criticizes him mainly for going too far and not recognizing always with equal clarity the role of the "personal" in the "sociocultural."

[57] Burnett, *op. cit.*, p. 187.

universalis" might be more readily accepted by some scholars. But social solidarity on a universal scale may now have become a prerequisite of survival, and indeed it was Comte himself who later came to concentrate on "altruism." Perhaps these "loony" investigations, with all their faults, may prove more important than the highly efficient studies of trivia made by those who have raked Sorokin so roundly for his attention to the production and distribution of "higher values."

One cannot help thinking that the purely anti-philosophic criticism of Sorokin will dissipate itself with the dust of the critics themselves. Sorokin's works aim to deal with significant scientific and philosophic questions *in conjuncture*. Whatever their relative successes and shortcomings, these works are likely to be read and prized anew by succeeding generations of scholars in the science of society—and other "lovers of wisdom" under whatever passport.

Sorokin's Philosophy of History

Arnold J. Toynbee

The extent to which a culture is integrated is one of the most important of the questions that Professor Sorokin has examined. Some other scholars may dispute his findings on this point (judiciously balanced though these findings are). But nobody could deny that Sorokin's own intellectual interests are integrated—and not just his intellectual interests either. He has lived through shattering events: two world wars in one life time; two revolutions in one year of Russian history. And, being human, he has had deep feelings about these experiences, as well as creative intuitions and ideas (creative in the sense of revealing meanings in a multitude of sociocultural phenomena).

To parody a dictum of Gibbon, the philosopher of history owes something to Kerensky's private secretary. Sorokin himself has recorded, in a moving and illuminating passage,[1] the effect on him of the unexpected and brutal disappointment, in his early manhood, of the liberal expectations in which he had been brought up. What overtook him in 1914-17 set his mind searching; it has never stopped; his life-long intellectual quest has been the consequence of a series of personal experiences. His interest in social and cultural dynamics cannot be disengaged, on the critic's dissecting table, from his interest in the current flow of human affairs. Nor, again, can his analytical and comparative study of human affairs be disengaged from his study of the phenomena by which he tests his hypotheses. He is a historian as well as a sociologist, and a participant as well as a spectator.

This makes it impossible for Sorokin's appraisers to portion out Sorokin's living personality among half a dozen separate "disci-

[1] *Social and Cultural Dynamics,* I, ix.

plines," and then each get to work on dissecting his own allotted morsel. One cannot attempt a serious critique of Sorokin if one does not take him as a whole. I therefore make no apology to my fellow-appraisers for trespassing on their preserves—and they are welcome to trespass on mine, if I have one—though, as I see it, the term "philosophy of history" cannot be construed as having any meaning short of a study of the totality of human affairs.

Curiosity and versatility are distinctive characteristics of pioneers. Sorokin is a pioneer, and a recognition of this truth about him is a necessary first step toward trying to appraise and appreciate his work. He is a pioneer even in the geographical sense. He comes from the northern fringes of the present-day Oikoumene—not from northern North America, but from northern Russia. His inborn ability and enterprise have conspired with the chances and changes of human life to precipitate him into the cauldron in which mankind is brewing its destiny. He has seen life first in Petrograd at boiling point; and then, at a more equable temperature, at Cambridge. Perhaps (this is only a guess), life in the world cities has made a more vivid impression on him than it might have made if he had been born and reared in one of them.

But it is, of course, as an intellectual pioneer that Sorokin has made his mark on the history of thought about human affairs. A pioneer condemns himself to be corrected and surpassed. This fate is on the pioneer's own head, because in the intellectual field, at any rate, one need not be a pioneer unless one chooses. At least, one need not report one's findings and thereby draw fire (and Sorokin has, fortunately, reported his findings circumstantially). A pioneer's sketch map will be corrected by his less enterprising successors, the surveyors; his trail will be progressively straightened out, underpinned, surfaced, and double-tracked; his axe's blaze marks on tree trunks will be replaced by neon signs. All these improvements will overtake his pathfinding work; and, the quicker they do, the more eloquent will be their testimony to his achievement. Later generations do not spend time and energy on improving pioneer trails that lead nowhere. The trail on which they work is always one that has proved its value; and, in all their subsequent improvements on it, there is one thing that they cannot do to its discoverer. They cannot supersede him. Even when his work has been completely overlaid, it will still remain invisibly on the map. Daniel Boone's trail, for instance, still lives today in the radar beam that a pilot gratefully follows in navigating his plane from Washington, D. C., to St. Louis.

It is not possible for Sorokin or his contemporaries to foresee exactly how his pioneer work is going to be appraised in each successive future generation; but it seems safe to predict that his creative intuitions and thoughts will have entered into the main stream of thought in his field, and also that they will continue to hold their place there. Sorokin's successors may not endorse his ideas, but they will still have to take account of them. The mental traffic will still pass along the route that he has been the first to hew out.

This point can be illustrated by considering the prospects of one of his most characteristic methods of work; his honest-minded determination to express his findings in statistical form, and his adventurous eagerness to conquer, for his statistical approach, fields of inquiry in which this approach is so difficult that no one, perhaps, before him has dared to attempt it here.

The safety zone for statisticians is the field of economics and other kinds of practical activity in which human beings, in large numbers, each take action individually, and this repeatedly. This gives the statisticians the needful enormous quantities of instances to play with; and in this field, for the last 150 years and more, they have been as busy as bees refining their procedures and complicating them by employing the latest and most abstruse mathematical devices. Armed from head to foot in this high-powered professional panoply, they had been standing poised to fall upon any outsider who might have the temerity to try to open up wider territories with simpler tools; and Sorokin has provided the professional censors in the field of statistics with a magnificent target. The four volumes of his *Social and Cultural Dynamics*, which are his principal work up to date, are sown generously—one might say, almost recklessly—thick with statistical tables and figures, and a majority of these are concerned with subjects that most of the conventional statisticians have fought shy of.

In dealing statistically with war,[2] Sorokin is still perhaps within the safety zone. He has at his disposal numerical information about frequencies of wars and about magnitudes of armies and of

[2] In Vol. III, Part II.

casualties which he can bring into comparison with magnitudes of populations. In passing on to internal disturbances,[3] he is near the fringe; the figures at his disposal in this zone are already more fuzzy. But, after that, he strikes out boldly into regions that, in the professional statisticians' eyes, have been, and still are, impenetrable wildernesses. Here are a few samples: Volume II, Table 29: "Indicators of the Fluctuation of the Influence of Ethical Systems and Mentality by 20-year periods, 580 B.C.–A.D. 1920"; Volume II, Figure 14: "Movement of Singularism, Universalism, and Mystic Unity"; Volume III, Table 54: "Geometric Averages for Historical Persons"; Volume I, Table 31: "Fluctuation of Types of *Genre*"; Volume I, Figure 7: "The Spiritual and Sensual in Art, by Countries"; Volume III, Figure 1: "Extensity of Interaction"; Volume IV, Tables 1-18: "Geometrical Averages of Creative Pulsation of Various Subsystems of Culture in Time," based on "all the names of historical persons mentioned in the *Encyclopaedia Britannica* (the ninth edition) for each specified period of fifty years, in each of ten specified fields of culture"; Volume III, Table 54: "Geometric Averages for Historical Persons Engaged in Religious and Business Activity included in the *Encyclopaedia Britannica.*"

This last-cited table, which is the grand finale of Sorokin's first batch of three volumes, and also the colossal set of 18 tables in Volume IV, will make a conventional savant's flesh creep and a conventional statistician's hair stand on end. What a place to go to for samples! And, then, what a way of sampling! Meanwhile, Sorokin's fellow prisoners in the dock will be chuckling with amusement and cooing with delight, for they can see what has happened and what is bound to follow. What has happened is that Sorokin has seized the initiative; what is bound to follow is that his furious specialist pursuers will come pounding after him into fields that they would perhaps never have trodden except in hot pursuit of a heretic. Laboriously, they will pick perhaps as much as 90 per cent of Sorokin's findings to pieces. But Sorokin will come out strategically victorious from any number of tactical defeats. It will have been he, not his pursuers, to whom the credit will have been due for this involuntary but nonetheless fruitful broadening of the conventional statisticians' horizon; and the result will have been a solid gain for one of mankind's common causes: the drive to increase

[3] *Ibid.*, Part III.

human knowledge and understanding. This intellectual service far outweighs Sorokin's statistical errors (if he has made some, and, no doubt, he will have). The loss, if there is any, is his; and the gain is everyone's. Pioneer Sorokin will (let me say this again) have provoked the stay-at-home specialists into extending the scope of their thorough-going operations into regions into which they might never have ventured if Sorokin had not provocatively led them on.

Sorokin himself has made a spirited and telling defense of his decision to present his findings in the form of figures.

> . . . there is scarcely any historical work . . . where, explicitly or implicitly, quantitative judgments are not given in verbal form. What historians of ideas, human thought, science, religion, art styles, political systems, or economic processes do not use quantitative expressions like the following: "the period was marked by an *increase* of riots, revolts, and disorders," "the period was marked by a *decline* of idealism and religion," "Kant was one of the *greatest* philosophers," "It was an epoch of the *rise and triumph* of materialism, nominalism, the Gothic style, or socialistic doctrine," and so on? . . .
>
> The above quotations and thousands of other statements of historians and social scientists are quantitative and also *verbal quantitative*. The procedure used here [in Sorokin's own work] is *numerical quantitative*. The first makes quantitative statements but in an indefinite verbal form without the use of figures or numerical indicators. The second describes the quantitative change with the help of figures. Which method is preferable?[4]

Sorokin's own use of his chosen "numerical quantitative" method of presentation is one of the most distinctive, as well as controversial, features of his work. I admire, as I have said, his boldness in his use of it. At the same time, I do think that, on occasions, it plays him false. Volume IV, Tables 1-18, already cited, seems to me to be a case in point. Here he is using statistics, extracted from the *Encyclopaedia Britannica,* for the purpose of trying to refute the thesis that in some provinces of human activity (e.g., science and technology) achievements are cumulative, whereas in others (e.g., poetry and philosophy) they are not. Sorokin is, of course, too good a workman not to be aware of the technical pitfalls besetting the path of any statistician who seeks to use an encyclopedia as a quarry for statistical material.[5] He is on his guard against these

[4] *Dynamics*, II, 21-22.
[5] See, for instance, *Dynamics*, IV, 326 n. 3; 363 n. 15; and 365.

pitfalls, and he makes due allowance for them. On the other hand, he does not allow for the possibility that the statistical method itself may be inadequate for dealing with his opponents' point. His statistics tell him that, in all fields, "the number of the historical persons and of the achievements, respectively, systematically grows in the course of time," and that "in this respect there is no difference between the fields of culture: they are all accumulative."[6] The scholars against whom Sorokin is here breaking a statistical lance would not, I am sure, contest these statistical findings of his. They would agree that the human race produces more poets, as well as more physicists, as time goes on. The point that they are making is one about the respective relations of a present-day poet and a present-day scientist with a predecessor of his in, say, the sixteenth century. The present-day physicist's work will have superseded the sixteenth-century physicist's work and will have made it obsolete and out of date, because a physicist begins where his predecessor left off, and stands upon his predecessor's shoulders. On the other hand, a poet's relation to his predecessor is not the same. He, too, of course, may have been greatly influenced by his predecessor's work, but, nevertheless, the poet, unlike the physicist, is not able to start where his predecessor left off; he has to start all over again from the ground up, and therefore he is not bound to surpass his predecessor—as the physicist is bound to surpass his, even if the earlier of the two physicists has been the greater genius. By contrast, in the field of poetry, Tennyson may be a better poet than Milton, and Milton a better one than Shakespeare; but it is equally possible for him to be not so good a one. Sheer posteriority does not give to the poet the decisive superiority that it does give to the physicist. As far as I can see, this point is not met by Sorokin's statistical approach to it. I should like to have Sorokin's comments on that.

The use of statistics is one of Sorokin's methods. Another of his methods has been mentioned already. He brings them to earth by testing them on the phenomena, and he does this, too, at his peril. His surveys of instances will be impugned because no survey of phenomena can ever be exhaustive. His selection of instances will then be impugned on the ground that it is arbitrary and tendentious. Yet it is both more honest and more instructive to test

[6] *Ibid.*, IV, 351.

one's hypotheses, even though all such tests are inevitably imperfect, than it is to enunciate them oracularly, as Spengler does, and to leave it at that. Sorokin's heuristic method of testing his hypotheses is as characteristic and as controversial as is his use of statistics. Yet, important though these and other methods of his are, they are not, of course, of such importance as the substance of his work is for an appraisal of this work's value.

When we turn our attention to the substance, we run into a practical difficulty. There are few aspects of human affairs with which Sorokin does not deal—and this in concrete detail. In a short critique one must pick out for consideration what seem to be the key topics in Sorokin's comprehensive system. Perhaps we shall not go far wrong if we concentrate our attention on the following: Sorokin's discussion of the extent to which a culture is integrated; his theory of change; his identification of three cultural "super-systems" (ways of feeling, thought, expression, conduct, or, in short, ways of life) through which the historic cultures have been integrated, insofar as they have been; his vision of the alternation of these three ways of life with each other in time and his explanation of this; and his conception of the relations between types of culture and types of personality.

Before entering into this brief examination of some of Sorokin's leading ideas, I will mention one virtue of his—a cardinal one—that runs through all his work. He refrains from pushing his ideas to extremes. He allows for the likelihood that the principles, patterns, and rhythms that he finds in sociocultural phenomena have limits to their validity and to their currency. He does not maintain that they cover the whole field and explain everything in it.

This moderation is not due to any lack of conviction. He believes whole-heartedly in the reality of his rhythms as far as they go, and in the applicability of his principles within their limits. Woe to the critic who ventures to challenge the validity of Sorokin's tenets within the limits that Sorokin himself has set for these. The critic who fires one shot into this sensitive target area is likely to draw a broadside from Sorokin in return. The one point in which Sorokin is, in fact, immoderate is his confidence that, within his own self-demarcated limits, he himself is 100 per cent right and any opponent of his is 100 per cent wrong. In a scholar with a different character and temperament, this self-assurance, and this militant assertion of it, might seem offensive; but in Sorokin they do not. I think this is because Sorokin's zeal is for his work, as distinct from himself. There is nothing personal about it.

As for his moderation in the claims that he makes for his ideas, his practice here is, I should guess, not so much a reflection of his temperament as a conscious application of one of his principles. In his belief, it is of the essence of sociocultural phenomena that they have limits; and this principle is fundamental in his theory of change and rhythm. It gives him, as we shall see, an explanation of the rhythmical recurrence of his three cultural "supersystems"— a recurrence that he detects in the histories of the Greco-Roman and Western civilizations.

Sorokin opens his whole inquiry by examining the forms and problems of culture integration and the methods of their study.[7] Are cultures integrated wholes? Or are they mere unintegrated congeries? Sorokin does not adopt either of these two extreme opposite accounts of a culture's structure or lack of structure. He distinguishes among four basic types of interrelations of culture elements: spatial or mechanical adjacency; association due to an external factor (e.g., climate or race); causal or functional integration; and internal or logico-meaningful unity.

Sorokin maintains convincingly, against some of his critics, that the meaning of the term "meaning" is "clear to anyone who has mind and thought," and that this is also one of those ultimate ideas that are not clarified by attempts to define them in terms of something other than themselves.[8] A system of meaning, as Sorokin sees it, *"is a logical compatibility and specific dependence or interdependence of each meaning-element upon other meanings-elements, of the meanings-elements upon the whole system, and of the system upon the elements."*[9] Alternatively to being logical, the dependence and interdependence may be aesthetic or expressive.[10] When a system of meanings is "objectified," it turns into a causal system as well.[11]

Causal interdependence in empirical cultural systems is due to the interdependence of the meanings of the system that stands behind the vehicles and agents and unites them into one interdependent whole.[12]

[7] *Dynamics*, I, Part I, chap. i.   [8] *Ibid.*, IV, 12 n. 10.
[9] *Ibid.*, IV, 21.   [10] *Ibid.*, IV, 22.
[11] *Ibid.*, IV, 34.   [12] *Ibid.*, IV, 35; cf. 18-19.

In Sorokin's view, the causal and logico-meaningful unifications are the central forms of culture integration, and, of these two, the logico-meaningful form is the higher.[13] We merely take note of the existence of functional or causal relations; we understand the inwardness of logico-meaningful relations.

Meaningful and logical integration by definition can only exist where there is mind and meaning. It cannot exist outside of the realm, though elsewhere there may be causal, external, or spatial unities.[14]

The meaningful components of sociocultural phenomena make them fundamentally different from physicochemical and biological phenomena and call for a logico-meaningful method profoundly different from the pure causal or pure probabilistic method of the natural sciences.[15]

Since the highest values and complexes of values in any great culture belong to the class of the logico-meaningful unities, *this level gives it its sociocultural* and *logico-meaningful individuality; its specific style; its physiognomy and personality.*[16]

Before declaring a given culture nonlogical or alogical, one has to experiment with as many principles as will fit any of the relevant facts at all . . . .

As a matter of fact, if no cultures are completely integrated logically, hardly any are absolutely alogical or nonlogical. Therefore, with the proper efforts, a principle can be found that unifies at least a small part of the components of any culture.[17]

Any logically, or even just functionally, integrated system has, in Sorokin's view,[18] a certain degree of autonomy and inherent self-regulation. This measure of autonomy gives it some measure of choice or selection in its encounters with external agents and objects. The system's destiny is determined more by its own nature and by the relationship between its parts than it is by external circumstances; and it is no true explanation of it to profess to explain it in terms of external conditions.

Even such seemingly special problems as that of the juridical person enter as an organic component into an integrated culture and live and change as such a culture changes. . . . The rise and decline of the main conceptions in the field are . . . incomprehensible without considering them in the light of the much larger perspective and much broader and more embracing "variable"—the culture—of which it is a part.[19]

---

[13] *Ibid.*, I, 18-21.
[15] *Ibid.*, IV, vii-viii; cf. 4 n. 1.
[17] *Ibid.*, I, 36-37, with n. 45.
[19] *Ibid.*, II, 336.

[14] *Ibid.*, I, 28.
[16] *Ibid.*, I, 29.
[18] *Ibid.*, I, 50-51.

Since, however, we virtually never meet with a perfect case of either an absolutely unintegrated or a perfectly integrated cultural complex, Sorokin rejects the thesis that, in any of the historic cultures, "any change in any component of a given cultural configuration functionally or logically effects all the other components and therefore the whole of the given culture."[20]

In each compartment of culture there is a limited autonomy of functions and changes from those in the other compartments; and within each compartment many a secondary change occurs without any tangible connection with either the changes in the whole type of culture or in any of its other compartments.[21]

The economic connection is rather loose as compared with the correlation of the other culture processes with one another. *Art and science, science and religion, ethical systems and law, law and religion and art— these and other especially "ideological" compartments of culture are interrelated and change in much closer unison than do, for instance, economic conditions and art, economic conditions and science, economic conditions and criminal codes, economic conditions and any other compartment of culture.*[22]

On the crucial question of the relations between the various elements in the "total culture" of any one of the historic human societies, Sorokin's position is a middle one. He holds, as has been noted, that this total culture is neither a completely integrated whole nor a mere heap or dump ("congeries") of utterly unrelated and mutually irrelevant particulars.[23] The distinction between what is integrated and what is not is of capital importance in Sorokin's thought, and he has coined terms of his own—"systems" and "congeries"—to describe sets of things that are integrated and unintegrated respectively.[24] If challenged to declare whether the difference between "congeries" and "systems" is, in his view, absolute and unbridged, I guess that Sorokin would say that it is not. At any rate, he holds that "homogeneity" and "heterogeneity" are relative, not absolute, concepts;[25] and he declares explicitly that "the transition from a pure congeries to the most highly unified systems of meanings is gradual."[26] *"Between these types stand the intermediate systems, which are neither congeries nor*

[20] *Ibid.*, I, 48.   [21] *Ibid.*, II, 467 n. 148.
[22] *Ibid.*, III, 254.
[23] See further *ibid.*, IV, 102-5, 132-37, 142, 152 n. 6, 195-96.
[24] See, for example, *ibid.*, IV, 3.   [25] See further *ibid.*, IV, 9.
[26] *Ibid.*, IV, 31.

perfectly integrated systems."[27] One of Sorokin's guiding principles, as we have already noticed, is to refrain from pushing anything—even one of his own fundamental tenets—to extremes. It is, indeed, one of his tenets that no rule and no distinction is absolutely or universally valid. All the same, it is notoriously difficult to live up to this principle when one is using key concepts as instruments in intricate mental operations. In the course of being used, they have a way of becoming more sharply cut and more rigid than their maker and user intends them to be. This has, I think, happened to some extent in the case of Sorokin's distinction between "congeries" and "systems." I suspect that, in the empirical world of phenomena, these two poles are really linked by a series of intermediate terms—as Sorokin himself recognizes.

All the same, the total culture of any society, at any moment of its existence, is, as Sorokin sees it, "*a coexistence of a multitude of various systems plus various single congeries that exist partly as heterogeneous elements in many a system, partly as congeries outside of the systems.*"[28] By a system Sorokin means a meaningful configuration within some one particular province of cultural activity. He finds that there are five main systems, in this meaning of the word, which, among them, cover the whole field of culture more or less completely; namely language, science, religion, fine arts, ethics.[29] This description of a society's total culture calls up in my mind a picture of five towers rising out of a rubbish-heap. Each tower has, admittedly, an architectural structure of its own. More than that, the five buildings are co-ordinated to some extent in a common architectural plan.[30] But they have nothing in common with any of the rubbish, and no scrap of the rubbish has anything in common with any other scrap.

This description of the picture is, however, incomplete. It leaves out the light, without which the picture could not be seen at all. And the light brings out the architectural unity of the five buildings. It plays on the buildings continuously, but it alternates in a series of three phases which have recurred in a constant order in the serial history of the Greco-Roman and the Western civilization to date. The phases of the lighting change from time to time, but, in one respect, the effect of the light on the picture is the same

---

[27] *Ibid.*, IV, 612.
[29] *Ibid.*, IV, 110-20.
[28] See further *ibid.*, IV, 97.
[30] *Ibid.*, IV, 120-24.

in all phases.   In all phases the light brings out the structural unity of the architectural elements in the landscape.

The picture, thus completed, of the total culture of a society, and of the relations, or lack of relations, among the elements of which it consists, has been derived by Sorokin from the study of a single civilization, the Greco-Roman, taken together with a particular one of its successors, the Western. The series that these two episodes of history constitute, in conjunction, extends in time over about twenty-five fairly well documented centuries.   These 2,500 years or so of Greco-Roman and Western history are the quarry from which Sorokin has drawn most of his statistical material.   He has, in fact, used this Greco-Roman-Western series as what the physical scientists call a "model."[31]   He finds "somewhat similar rhythms" in the histories of several other cultures (e.g., the Hindu, the Chinese, the Islamic).[32]   At the same time, he declares explicitly: "I do not claim anywhere in my work that I regard it [this rhythm] as universal, applicable to all cultures and for all times";[33]   "I do not think the sequence observed in the history of the Western Society is universal or uniform for all societies and at all times."[34] What I have called the three different lights that play successively upon the cultural landscape are, in Sorokin's terminology, "super-systems."   They are his three alternative and alternating ways of life—the "ideational," the "idealistic," and the "sensate,"[35] each of

---

[31] A more obvious model would have been the Greco-Roman-Byzantine series—more obvious because the Byzantine, not the Western, Christian civilization was the Greco-Roman-civilization's principal heir.   It is understandable that, nevertheless, the Greco-Roman-Western series should have been seized upon by Western students of human affairs when they required a "model" (e.g. by Vico, Spengler, me, and Philip Bagby in succession).   It is more surprising that Sorokin should have followed suit to Vico, considering that Sorokin is, by origin, not a Westerner, but an heir of the Byzantine civilization in virtue of being a Russian by birth and upbringing.

[32] Ibid., IV, 425 and 737.

[33] Ibid., IV, 425; cf. 432 n. 86.

[34] Ibid., III, 131, reaffirmed in IV, 770 (see the whole of pp. 770-73).

[35] The coining of new technical terms, such as these three, is, no doubt, the lesser evil if none of the familiar current terms exactly fits the categories that have formed themselves in the intellectual explorer's mind.   At the same time, new terms are an impediment to the mental communication between a writer and his readers.   Would any of the pairs "other-worldly-minded" and "this-worldly-minded," "spiritual-minded" and "materialistic-minded," "credulous-minded" and "skeptical-minded," "living by faith" and "living by reason," have met Sorokin's needs? Presumably Sorokin himself will reply that he felt compelled to coin a new terminology of his own because his meaning was not either precisely or comprehensively expressed by any that was already in use.   But it is one thing to strike coins and another to put them into circulation; and unfortunately these particular three coins

which embraces all the five main human cultural activities. Each of the three supersystems *"cuts across all these five and their many derivative systems, and unites into one supersystem (Ideational, or Idealistic or Sensate or mixed) all the big five and an enormous number of derivative systems."*[36] Sorokin *"does not contend that each or all of the three [super] systems embraces all the phenomena of culture, or even all the parts of the main five and of many derivative systems."*[37] Moreover, *"practically, in any culture of any period, none of these three [super] systems exists monopolistically without the coexistence, as a minor or equal stream, of the other systems."*[38] And *"the subsystems and sub-subsystems that make each of these supersystems are not equally closely integrated with one another and with the whole supersystem."*[39] As for the miserable congeries that lie strewn round the sub-subsystems' feet, it goes without saying that these remain in outer darkness. "Even in regard to valid uniformities one should not exaggerate either their rigidity, their universality, or their unexceptionableness."[40] It will be seen that Sorokin's conclusions are moderate and cautious. At the same time, Sorokin does claim[41] a high "cognitive value" for "tidal embracing rhythms," and particularly for his own ideational-idealistic-sensate rhythm. It is consistent with this view of his that, when he comes to the practical question of choosing the portions of his field of inquiry to which he is to direct most of his attention and efforts, Sorokin concentrates on those relations that are of the most highly integrated type. Confronted with relations of the less highly integrated kinds (including even the causal or functional kind), a human mind cannot, as we have seen, in Sorokin's opinion, do much with them beyond taking note of their existence. In practice, it is only insofar as a culture does have an inner "logico-meaningful" unity that it becomes eligible for being dealt with by Sorokin's mental operations.

As Sorokin sees it, the largest units of meaningfulness are his

---

of Sorokin's are cumbrous—like English "florins" as compared with American "quarters." Moreover, one of the three—the "idealistic" type of culture—may be as difficult for an outsider to distinguish from the "ideational" type, when he is visiting Sorokin-land, as he finds it, when he is visiting Britain, to distinguish between a "florin" and a "half-crown." By "idealistic" Sorokin means, he tells us (I, 68), "a balanced synthesis of both pure types."

[36] *Ibid.*, IV, 138.
[37] *Ibid.*, IV, 141.
[38] *Ibid.*
[39] *Ibid.*
[40] *Ibid.*, IV, 198.
[41] *Ibid.*, IV, 423.

three alternative and alternating supersystems. He denies—and this vehemently—that the total culture of historic society is meaningful in its totality.[42]   In particular, he denies that a culture has a dominant penchant that is characteristic of it throughout its geographical domain and from beginning to end of its history.[43]   He rejects Spengler's characterization of the individuality of each different culture, and he blames me for following Spengler in practicing this exercise of the intuitive imagination.   Here Sorokin is in a minority.   (This does not, of course, in itself prove him wrong.) Most critics of Spengler's work have praised his *Physiognomik* as being a brilliant achievement of his intuitive genius; and most critics of my work (including so eminent a one as A. L. Kroeber) have censured me for being remiss in exploring the characteristic qualitative configurations of cultures, and for concentrating too much on the pattern of the events in the histories of the societies on which the cultures are borne.

In the field of the fine arts, at any rate, it seems difficult to deny that cultures have distinctive individualities which display themselves in a culture's artistic products of whatever place and date. A layman, visiting a museum, is aware of the qualitative kinship of all the works of art in, say, the Greco-Roman room with each other, and of their qualitative difference from all the works of art in, say, the Egyptian or the Chinese room.   In opposition to this, Sorokin would, if I interpret him right, maintain that Greek works created in the ideational phase of Greek history have less affinity with Greek works expressing the sensate phase than they have with Western, Chinese, Hindu, or Islamic works created in the ideational phases of these different cultures.   If this is in truth Sorokin's view, it seems paradoxical.   It would be interesting if he would take up this point and discuss it in his own contribution to the present volume.

It is not for nothing that Sorokin calls his treatise *Dynamics*. When he has brought his three main ways of life, or types of culture-mentality on to his stage, he spends only one chapter of fifty pages[44] on giving still-life illustrations of them.   Nearly two-fifths of Volume I and practically the wholes of Volumes II and III are occupied with the tracing of fluctuations in the flow of history

[42] See, for instance, *ibid.*, IV, 80 n. 22; 87 n. 25; 104 n. 4; 150 n. 4.
[43] *Ibid.*, IV, 373 n. 21.   [44] *Ibid.*, I, Part I, chap. iii.

in which now this, now that, way of life, alias supersystem, is predominant. He begins with the fluctuation of ideational, idealistic, and sensate forms of art, and goes on to examine successively the fluctuation of the same three standard ideologies in systems of truth and knowledge, ethical and juridical culture-mentality, systems of social relationships, war in intergroup relationships, and internal disturbances in intragroup relationships. In beginning operations in the province of art, he shows flair; for art is undoubtedly the most sensitive indicator of the changes in a culture and of the limits of its prevalence in both time and space.

A study of human affairs in movement is certainly more fruitful, because more realistic, than any attempt to study them in an imaginary condition of rest.[45] One of Sorokin's finest intuitions and most fruitful principles is his thesis that change is of the essence of sociocultural as well as all other kinds of empirical phenomena,[46] and that, accordingly, change needs no explanation. What would require explaining would be the absence of change, if this could ever actually be detected. In sociocultural human affairs, change, as Sorokin sees it, is immanent[47] and this means that it is at least partly autonomous,[48] even though it is incomplete.

"The change is an immanent consequence of the system's being a going concern. Its functioning makes change inevitable."[49] Sorokin believes in a "principle of immanent generation of consequences"[50] (the Indian concept of *Karma*?); a "principle of immanent self-determination of the system's destiny";[51] and "immanent self-determination as synthesis of determinism and indeterminism."[52] "Immanent self-determination is equivalent to indeterminism."[53] But, as usual, Sorokin does not press his thesis to extremes. He also believes in a "principle of differential degrees of self-determination and dependence for various sociocultural systems."[54] *"The very existence of the external conditions of a system makes its life career not absolutely predetermined at the moment of the emergence of the system."*[55] The degree of self-determina-

[45] See *ibid.*, IV, 677-81.
[46] *Ibid.*, IV, 587 and 667.
[47] *Ibid.*, IV, 590-92 and 655-66.
[48] *Ibid.*, IV, 532 and 542.
[49] *Ibid.*, IV, 593.
[50] *Ibid.*, IV, 600-602.
[51] *Ibid.*, IV, 602-4.
[52] *Ibid.*, IV, 604-5.
[53] *Ibid.*
[54] *Ibid.*, IV, 605-10.
[55] *Ibid.*, IV, 606.

tion varies as between different cases.[56]   It varies with the degree
of integration.[57]

All the same, the contrast drawn by Sorokin between "immanentist" and "externalist" explanations of change is sharp, and
he himself comes down emphatically on the immanentist side.   It is
true that explanations of change as being produced by the impact
of some external force confront one with an awkward choice.
Either one has to admit an infinite regress of external forces, each
moved by another force external to itself, or else one has to assume
the existence of an unmoved prime mover.   Yet, when the antithesis between "immanentism" and "externalism" is approached
from an epistemological point of view, this pair of concepts looks
like a necessity of thought rather than like a confrontation between
a right and a wrong way of thinking.   Each of the two concepts is,
surely, valid in a particular perspective.   When we are looking at
something as a whole, the changes that take place in it necessarily
appear to be immanent.   But as soon as we try to explain the
process of change, we find ourselves having to dissect the changing
whole into two forces, one of which is being acted on by the other.
To talk the Hegelian language which Sorokin justly admires, we can
take note of the immanent change through which Thesis Number
One turns into Thesis Number Two.   But, to explain the change of
which we have taken note, we have to see in Thesis Number Two
a synthesis produced by the impact on Thesis Number One of an
antithesis.   This antithesis has been latent in Thesis Number One
from the start, but it has to become overt and distinct in order to
become actual and operative.   Sorokin explicitly rejects the explanation of psychosociocultural change as being a response to a stimulus.[58]   Yet if one is unwilling to explain change in some such terms,
one may find oneself compelled to renounce any attempt to explain
it at all.

Sorokin concentrates his attention on rhythmic change—meaning
by "rhythm" a series of recurrences that are uniform in character
without necessarily being of equal duration.[59]   One, at least—and
this the queen—of Sorokin's three supersystems cannot be studied
at all without recognizing that it is not merely subject to rhythmic
fluctuation but is actually a product of it.

[56] *Ibid.*, IV, 608.   [57] *Ibid.*, IV, 610.
[58] *Ibid.*, IV, 589.   [59] *Ibid.*, IV, 390.

A special combination of cultural circumstances is necessary, namely, the beginning of the decline of an Ideational mentality, so that the Idealistic mentality may come to the front as a transition to a newly ascending Sensate mentality.[60]

It is an important feature of Sorokin's system—at any rate as this is exemplified in the Greco-Roman-Western series—that the idealistic mentality is not also given scope by the inverse transition from a sensate phase of culture to an ideational one. In the province of art, in this series, a transition from sensate to ideational inspires, according to Sorokin, not an art of the serene, harmonious, sublime, idealistic kind, but something incongruous and freakish.[61]

Fluctuation is a form of recurrence, and Sorokin is convinced that some measure and some form of recurrence is intrinsic to human affairs.[62] One of his most vigorous and compelling pieces of argument is his polemic[63] against historians who believe that every historical event is unique and is in no sense ever repeated. Here he is perhaps unjust to the historians as a tribe. "Explicitly and implicitly," he declares, "the assumption [of uniqueness] is shared by so many 'classic historians' that it is needless to give references."[64] These "classic historians" are surely no more than one school that happens to be prevalent in our time—and this only in the Western World. There is no reason to think that their predominance, even in the West, will be long-lasting. The "uniqueness" school may have a short life even here, where the influence of the Israelite one-way-street view of history has been so powerful. Recurrence was always taken for granted by historians in Ancient Greece, in India, and in China.

The fluctuations that Sorokin finds in the flow of human affairs have distinctive properties. They are characterized by punctuation and pulsation. *"Any punctuation of a process is always the result of a change of one or more of its directions and their senses."*[65] In exploring this rhythm Sorokin is as cautious and balanced as he is when he is exploring the extent of cultural integration. He finds no evidence for mechanical periodicity in the sense of recurrence in chronological cycles of uniform duration.

[60] *Ibid.*, I, 143.
[61] *Ibid.*, I, 321, 364-68, and 505. But see also *ibid.*, III, 131, quoted above.
[62] *Ibid.*, IV, 421.   [63] *Ibid.*
[64] *Ibid.*, I, 167 n. 15.   [65] *Ibid.*, I, 174.

Rising and falling tides of any one of the main currents have occurred within very different spans of time. . . . To insist upon the recurrence of any uniform mechanical periodicity in these crescendos and
diminuendos is to impose upon reality a uniformity which it does not
possess. History repeats itself, but its themes recur in variations ever
new—with changes not only in content but also in rhythm and tempo.
As a great artist, history provides creative, not monotonously mechanical,
variations.[66]

The most general pattern of the sociocultural change is that of
incessantly varying recurrent processes.[67]

Thus, as Sorokin sees human affairs, their fluctuations display no
chronological regularity. They do, however, display "immanent
self-regulation."

In the sociocultural life and sociomental processes there seems to be
present some factor which, in the long run, does not permit any single
or extreme current to absorb all the other systems for any length of time
and thus to narrow the richness and many-colored completeness of truth.
Sooner or later the prejudices and limitations of any single current call
forth ever-increasing criticism and result in the reappearance of its rivals,
their growth, and the overthrow of the dominant current.[68]

Here Sorokin, with the aid of his "model" episode of history (the
Greco-Roman-Western series), has arrived independently (so I
guess) at a concept that has played a key part in the systems of
notable predecessors of his in at least three different cultural milieux,
none of which has been either Western or Russian. "Immanent
self-regulation" of alternations of recurrent states: this is how
Empedocles accounted for his alternations between states of the
Universe in which love and hate are respectively in the ascendant.
In the Chinese *Weltanschauung*, as in that of Empedocles, this is
the master rhythm in the flow of phenomena. The Chinese use,
not Empedocles' names of two emotions, but the two labels "Yin"
and "Yang," which, being more technical and more abstract, have
the advantage of being more widely applicable.

The immanent self-regulation which is the mode of working
of the alternating fluctuations of Yin and Yang has been taken by
Chinese historians as being the key to the pattern of human history
as the Chinese have experienced it. In human history, seen with
Chinese eyes, the regulator is a mandate given by Heaven to a

[66] *Ibid.*, II, 201-2.   [67] *Ibid.*, IV, 731.
[68] *Ibid.*, II, 53-54.

dynasty. This mandate is not a blank check or an unlimited credit; it is expendable; and human nature on the throne will be certain to expend it. Some dynasties have been longer lived than others, but none of them has been everlasting up to date. At some stage, Heaven's mandate to each successive dynasty has been exhausted, and then this particular dynasty has been supplanted by a successor. This newcomer, not having been in power till now, has, *ex hypothesi,* not yet had time to be demoralized, as its predecessors have all been—not yet—but it can be predicted at the start that one day its turn, too, will come.

A corresponding explanation of the successive rises and falls of a series of dynasties was found by the North African Muslim historian and philosopher of history Ibn Khaldun in the fourteenth century of the Christian Era. The cement of empires, as Ibn Khaldun saw it, is *asabiyah* (an Arabic word that may be translated *"esprit de corps," "public spirit," "social solidarity"*). This virtue is a monopoly of the nomadic peoples. Therefore only nomads ever have been, or ever can be, empire-builders. But a virtue that is bred in the tent is lost in the palace. Therefore, each successive nomad-built empire is ephemeral. It is no sooner established than it is doomed to be supplanted, sooner or later, by another nomad-built empire, doomed to be supplanted in its turn.

These identical accounts of the workings of the fluctuations of human affairs must have been arrived at independently by Empedocles in fifth-century-B.C Sicily, by Ibn Khaldun in fourteenth-century-A.D. Algeria, and by the Chinese at the opposite end of the Old World. My guess (as I have said) is that Sorokin's presentation of it in twentieth-century North America is a fourth instance of an original discovery of the idea. I am not, of course, meaning to imply that Sorokin has been unaware of these predecessors of his. One of Sorokin's virtues is that he puts his own ideas to test. He does this in a thoroughgoing way. And in Volume IV there is a whole chapter (Chapter XIII) on "The Principles of Immanent Change in the History of Social Thought and in Contemporary Research." Here Sorokin surveys not only his Chinese and Islamic predecessors, but his Greek and Western predecessors, too. And he rightly feels fortified by their consensus with each other and with Sorokin himself. But his knowledge of these predecessors is not incompatible with his having made the same discovery independently; and, if Sorokin did arrive at the idea independently, its discovery at least four times over suggests that there is likely to be something in it. It would be imprudent and presumptuous not to take it seriously and not to test it for oneself by applying it to the phenomena—without prejudice, of course, to one's eventual conclusions about it. As it happens, I myself had learnt it from Empedocles and had then come across it in its Chinese version before meeting with it in Sorokin's work. This consensus between minds with very different cultural backgrounds is surely most impressive.

One merit that Sorokin's version of the theory of immanent self-regulation shares with the Chinese version is its elasticity. In his application of it to the study of the fluctuation of systems of truth, Sorokin incidentally criticizes both Hegel's dialectical formula (thesis-antithesis-synthesis) and Herbert Spencer's "increasing differentiation" formula, not for being untrue to reality as far as they go, but for being too rigid and too narrow to cover all the phenomena.[69] I find myself in agreement with Sorokin in thinking that the Yin-Yang formula does enable one to marshal the phenomena in some kind of order over a wider range.

In studying the transitions from one of his three ways of life or supersystems of culture to another in the province of art, Sorokin makes an observation which would appear to be correct, and which, if correct, is important in itself and is also valid in other provinces of human activity as well.

He points out that the difference between "ideational" (i.e., non-naturalistic) art and "visual" (i.e., naturalistic) art is not that between the presence and the absence of artistic skill, maturity of technique, and progress in art and in aesthetic genius.[70] Nor is it the difference between ancient and modern, considering that the most ancient art known to us—that of the Later Palaeolithic cave-dwellers—is naturalistic to a high degree, much more so, in fact, than the art of the subsequent Neolithic and Bronze ages.[71] He goes on[72] to point out that there is no evidence that the change of artistic style in the Greco-Roman World toward the close of the third century of the Christian Era—a change from sensate to idea-

[69] See *ibid.*, II, 203-4. Sorokin's account of Hegel's philosophy in IV, 630-35, is generously appreciative.

[70] *Ibid.*, I, 269.   [71] *Ibid.*, I, 270-71.

[72] *Ibid.*, I, 309-11.

tional—was due to loss of technical ability. As Sorokin sees it, it was due to a deliberate abandonment of a sensate artistic objective in pursuit of an ideational one. In other words, it was a transfer of love and allegiance, not a decline and fall of technical skill—though it was a reaction to a decline and fall of the creativity of the sensate way of life in the Greco-Roman bout with this. Sorokin gives a convincing explanation of such a deliberate revolution in the values and the aims of art when he is discussing the history of Western art in the modern age.[73]   In art, sensatism, carried to extremes, ends in a blind alley.   When "the whole of Reality has been reduced by visualism to the mere passing impression, to the momentary appearance, the reality amounts to mere illusion and mirage, to self-deceit and dreaming."   And thus, "paradoxically, Visualism and Sensatism, pushed to their limits," come "to self-destruction."[74]   Sorokin pursues this point in Volume IV.[75]

The deliberate revolution in the province of art in the Greco-Roman world in the age of the Roman Empire had its counterpart, as Sorokin observes, in an equally deliberate contemporary revolution in the province of thought and belief.   In that world in that age, people abandoned rationalism for faith, and made the change with open eyes and with enthusiasm.[76]

Sorokin is not content simply to detect "the super-rhythm of ideational-idealistic-sensate phases in the Graeco-Roman and Western systems of culture."[77]   He inquires into the reason, or reasons, for this phenomenon, and he suggests two of these.   One follows from his principle that the possibilities of change are limited,[78] and that therefore any sociocultural process is bound to repeat itself if it does not come to an end before it has run through the whole gamut of its alternative possibilities.   "The recurrence is sufficiently accounted for by the principle of the limited possibilities of the main *integrated forms of culture*."[79]   He finds a second, and a deeper, reason in the inadequacy of each of the main systems of truth and reality.[80]   Each of the three supersystems is partly inadequate and also partly false.   And Sorokin postulates[81] that,

[73] *Ibid.*, I, 361-64.
[75] *Ibid.*, IV, 314-17.
[77] *Ibid.*, IV, 737.
[79] *Ibid.*, IV, 738.
[81] *Ibid.*, IV, 743.

[74] *Ibid.*, I, 362.
[76] *Ibid.*, II, 78-88.
[78] *Ibid.*, IV, 701-11.
[80] *Ibid.*, IV, 741-46.

"when such a system of truth and reality ascends, grows, and becomes more and more monopolistically dominant, its false part
tends to grow, while its valid part tends to decrease . . . . In this
way the dominant system prepares its own downfall and paves the
way for ascendance and domination of one of the rival systems. . . .
The new dominant system undergoes again the same tragedy."

This reads like a version of the Ancient Greek and Biblical
belief that success brings with it a temptation to succumb to pride,
and that pride leads to a fall. Certainly this can happen, and has in
fact happened innumerable times over. But is it bound to happen?
Is the temptation intrinsically irresistible? If it can be resisted,
and has been, then success is not inevitably fatal, and the challenge
that success presents would not account for a downfall that, in
Sorokin's vision of history, follows each time and follows inevitably.
This postulated inevitability seems to be at variance with Sorokin's
belief in a sociocultural system's power of partial self-determination. I should like to hear more from him on this point. It touches
the heart of his *Weltanschauung*.

Sorokin's vision of the past workings of these tides in the affairs
of men has given him an instrument for taking the bearings of the
Western civilization in our day.[82] What is more, it has given him
the spirit to peer into the future without flinching and at the same
time without losing hope. "Western society and culture seem to
have entered the stage of transition from an overripe sensate to a
coming ideational form. The transitory period already is, and will
continue to be, painful, cruel and bloody. . . . Beyond the grim
transitory period there loom, not the decline and end of Western
culture, but the magnificent peaks of a new ideational society."
The chapter that is thus summarized by Sorokin himself is labeled
"Postscript," and it was written, presumably, not long before the
publication of the first three volumes of *Social and Cultural Dynamics* in 1937. Sorokin's interwar expectations were, of course,
confirmed by the outbreak of World War II, and on this point he
found nothing to change when he published Volume IV in 1941.
His diagnosis has also been borne out by what has happened since
then, and my guess is that he would not be in a hurry today to alter
what he wrote twenty-five and twenty-one years ago. At this
moment, mankind is still living in tribulation and apprehension, as

[82] See *ibid.*, III, Part Four, chap. xvi; IV, Part Three, chap. xvii.

it was in the 1930's and '40's, but in the 1960's the gloom is shot through with rays of faith and hope which, in Sorokin's terms, portend the dawn of a new ideational age.

When Sorokin comes to consider the relationship between types of culture (alias supersystems or ways of life) and types of personality and behavior,[83] his finding is that,

When the essentials of each type of culture are understood, and the nature of an historical culture complex is diagnosed in terms of these types, then the peculiar personality of its members becomes comprehensible. Their multifarious traits, mores, mental patterns, and contents, hitherto unrelated and fragmentary, now appear intelligibly ordered into a single, meaningful *Gestalt*. For this reason, a study of these major culture types, their distribution in time and space, their alternation and change, is at the same time a genuine social psychology of human personality in its structural, as well as its dynamic, aspects.[84]

In the later chapter in which he works this thesis out and puts it to the test of application to the phenomena, Sorokin shows some of his customary caution. Here he begins by pointing out that the relationship between the dominant type of culture and actual conduct cannot be expected to be as close as that between the dominant type of culture and the mentality of the persons that live in it. "However different from each other are the Ideational and Sensate cultures, the societies that are the bearers of such cultures have of necessity a general fund of similar activities"[85]—particularly the acts necessary for the satisfaction of the elementary biological needs. However, in a looser fashion the relationship between type of culture and type of conduct does exist and is measurable—and Sorokin intrepidly sets out to verify this thesis by testing it on four sets of relevant data. His four tests are the frequency of the ideational and sensate types of personality among all historical persons as listed in the *Encyclopaedia Britannica* by fifty-year periods from 950 B.C. to A.D. 1849; among all the Roman Catholic popes from A.D. 42 to A.D. 1937; among the French, Russian, Hapsburg, and English sovereigns; and, fourthly, the proportion of historical persons who became historical through religious and through business activities respectively from 900 B.C. to A.D. 1849.

These four sets of tests are perhaps the least convincing of any

[83] *Ibid.*, I, 68, and III, Part Four, chap. xv.
[84] *Ibid.*, I, 68.   [85] *Ibid.*, III, 511.

in the whole book; and, in my judgment (I give this with diffidence), they do not warrant the following unusually extreme conclusion that Sorokin draws from them.

In an integrated Ideational or Sensate society, not only the dominant mentality becomes correspondingly Ideational or Sensate, but the actual *behavior* also becomes Ideational or Sensate, in whatever field it acts and, what is more important, even in the *field of activities closely related to the satisfaction of the urgent biological needs.*[86]

Most students of human affairs will agree with Sorokin that all human beings take color in some degree from their cultural milieu. "Great" men and women, as well as the common run of mankind, are unmistakably "children of their age"—and also of their local society and its culture. This is true even of the most deliberate and self-conscious revolutionaries. Ikhnaton, for instance, challenged and assailed some of the key points of the Ancient Egyptian cultural heritage. He would not have been what he was or have done what he did or have failed to do what he failed to do if the accident of birth had cast his lot in contemporary Babylonia or in seventeenth-century-A.D. France. His Egyptian milieu was too much for him. All the same, his controversial personality made an indelible mark on the subsequent history of the civilization that had repudiated him.

Has not Sorokin gone astray in presenting the interplay between a society and the human beings whose mutual relations constitute that society as being virtually a one-way current of influence? Surely the influence is really reciprocal. The social milieu into which a human being is born determines, no doubt, the scope of his opportunity—expanding this if his character happens to be in harmony with his ancestral culture, and conversely contracting his scope if he and his ancestral culture happen to be at loggerheads. But it is surely also true that each human being's character has a reciprocal effect on the development of his society's cultural tradi-tion. A human being does not live and die without modifying this tradition at least to an infinitesimal degree—and this however ob-scure, weak, or incompetent he may be. Sorokin himself recognizes that the human agents of a sociocultural system are one of its three constituent elements,[87] and that human beings play, at the

[86] *Ibid.*, III, 528-29. The italics in the passage quoted above are Sorokin's own, not mine.
[87] *Ibid.*, IV, 45.

very least, the part of the poles that carry a number of different networks of communications-wires (telegraphic, telephonic, etc.).[88] We have already noticed Sorokin's insistence that cultural change, when it comes, is the result of deliberate choice, and in human affairs there are no choosers except men, women, and children. Civilizations and cultures cannot make choices. Unlike men and women, institutions are not persons. So, who does make those historically momentous choices that produce the fluctuations in the stream of culture—giving the ascendancy now to this type of culture or way of life and now to that? If this is not the work of human beings, how are we to account for it?

On this point we can cite Sorokin as a witness against himself. We have already noticed, and endorse, his finding that the periodical changes-over from one way of life or type of culture to another are the result of conscious and deliberate acts of choice. Let us take the pertinent case of the artistic and intellectual revolutions in the Greco-Roman World in the early centuries of the Christian Era—a case which Sorokin has cited as one of his examples. When we probe this case to discover how the conscious and deliberate revolution actually came about, we find, in concrete historical terms, that a growing number of people became bored and disillusioned with the fag end of the Hellenic cultural tradition, while at the same time a growing number were thrilled by, and fell in love with, the style of contemporary Oriental art and the spirit of contemporary Oriental religion. When the rebels had grown to be a sufficiently numerous and powerful minority to be able to carry the more passive majority along with them, the long-since impending revolution became an accomplished fact. This translation of Sorokin's finding into terms of the feelings and actions of men and women is in line with the explanation of the successive rises and falls of dynasties, as this series of fluctuations is analyzed by the Chinese dynastic historians and by Ibn Khaldun.

A sociological analysis of the formula "immanent self-regulation" makes it evident, so it seems to me, that this formula (like so many other fruitful formulae) is a poetical simile, and that it should not be taken *au pied de la lettre*. A cultural rhythm cannot be self-regulating literally. A rhythm does not possess a self to do the job. The selves that actually do the regulating are the real selves of

[88] *Ibid.*, IV, 11, 52, 98-101, 131.

human beings. The self-regulation is immanent in the cultural rhythm in the sense that, while the abandonment of one type of culture and adoption of another type is the work, not of a rhythm or a culture, but of human beings, these particular human beings are not outsiders. They themselves are participants in the particular network of social relationships whose cultural style or configuration is being transformed by their action. This is one sense in which a cultural revolution is self-regulating in the different sense that, when any fashion—artistic, philosophical, whatever it may be—is carried to extremes, or is merely served up repeatedly *ad nauseam*, it is apt to provoke a revolt among its human victims, whereas, conversely, *omne ignotum pro magnifico*. The new art, new religion, or new dynasty starts its career with a credit; and, though its credit, too, is expendable, as its predecessor's credit has proved to have been, the new king, too, can look forward to enjoying a period of grace before the inevitable eventual discredit overtakes him in his turn.

When Sorokin has read these last few paragraphs of mine (and I understand that he has undertaken to read all our critiques and to reply), I suspect that his first impulse may be to reach for his thunderbolt. He has provided himself with a formidable one, all ready for hurling: it is the giant footnote 9 on page 69 of *Dynamics*, Volume I. Here we read that objectors who maintain "that only human beings with a developed nervous system can have mentality . . . demonstrate—what was logically inevitable—their inability to understand the realistic-universalistic language of the Idealistic-Ideational culture, and show themselves flesh and bone of the Sensate culture." Unmerciful heavens, what a warhead! But please, Jupiter Tonature, stay your hand. No intellectual activity is so barren as intellectual warfare, and you, Sorokin, are self-dedicated to the scholar's proper talk of helping to increase mankind's knowledge and understanding. This cannot be done by fighting, but it can be done—and done most fruitfully—by discussion. The purpose of the present book is to set going a discussion of this fruitful kind. The nature of the relation between cultures and human beings is perhaps one of the questions that Sorokin might be invited to reconsider in his coming colloquy with the present appraisers of his work. My old school's motto, "Manners makyth Man," is not, I believe, the last word on this topic.

I have tried to carry out my assignment in this volume: that is, to sketch and discuss Sorokin's philosophy of history. In attempting, this, I hope I shall not have embroiled him with some of my fellow historians. If a historian of the now prevalent school happens to pick this volume up and to run his finger down the table of contents, he will not find anything in any of the chapter headings to excite his ire. Sociology, demography, psychology, cultural morphology, philosophy: as he reads the entries under these heads, the historian on the war-path will mutter "not my subject" and will read on without his hackles rising. But the chapter-heading—mine—that associates Sorokin's name with the word "history," and this with the word "philosophy," is likely, I fear, to draw fire. And this fire might become furious if the militant historian were impulsively to take *sortes Sorokinianae*, and, opening one of the volumes of *Dynamics* at a venture, were to happen, by ill luck, to hit Volume II at page 299 and then grimly read on. What is a historian of the would-be factual school going to say to Sorokin's indictment of "fact-finding"?[89]

The nemesis of the fact-finders: they find usually only such facts as are already well-known; their study of these is often but a "painful elaboration of the obvious." They rarely find *new relevant* facts. . . . This leads to a progressive narrowing of the mental vistas.[90]

This is not the only passage in which Sorokin indicts "the 'strainers at gnats': the Lilliputian fact-finders."[91] As Sorokin sees them, "the philistine 'matter-of-fact' researchers and scholars are often very proud to be just 'plain fact-finders,'" but one cannot think without bringing general principles into play; and the "fact-finders" are none the better for having contrived to be unaware of what their own general principles are.[92] The plea that this indictment is deserved will merely magnify the enormity of Sorokin's offense in the defendants' eyes. Fur, I fear, will fly.

However, if a chapter on Sorokin's philosophy of history does expose Sorokin to attack, the personal inconvenience to him will perhaps be compensated by the gain for the cause of knowledge; for the indignant historians cannot pursue Sorokin out of history into the philosophy of history without themselves trespassing healthily beyond their own self-imposed bounds. The blinkers that

[89] *Ibid.*, II, 299-304.
[91] *Ibid.*, IV, 421.
[90] *Ibid.*, II, 301.
[92] *Ibid.*, IV, 658, 659, 662.

have been inserted between the so-called disciplines into which the study of human affairs has been arbitrarily partitioned are as much against the interests of mankind as any political iron curtain is. In the Atomic Age that has now overtaken us, it is a good deed to provoke people, if one cannot entice them, to cross these perverse man-made barriers. If the trans-frontier traffic becomes brisk enough, the barriers will gradually be worn down, and to get rid of them is one of the present vital interests of the human race. In the Atomic Age, as we know, the choice confronting us is "one world or none." Sorokin has overriden the conventional barriers between the "disciplines." He has taken human affairs as a whole, and has studied them from any promising angle by any promising method. Perhaps this is the greatest of his many services to mankind's common cause.

Sorokin and Cultural Morphology[1]

Othmar F. Anderle

The experience of an inner crisis and, what is more, the lethal
threat to which the Western World has been exposed since the end
of World War II, have caused the maturing of an awareness among
the peoples of the Occident that they form a community with a
destiny, that they belong to a single people which, by and large,
has a destiny. The expression of this unity has been discovered
in the concept of civilization (*Hochkultur*) which, since Spengler's
Decline of the West, has been on everybody's tongue and has become replete with content. Since then, the Western World has
thought of its life and existence as a civilization, that is, as one
civilization among others, for it is aware, at the same time, that
there are, or have existed, several such civilizations.

Let us express it differently. The concept of civilization has
become, for us, a dominant historico-sociocultural category similar
to the earlier concept of nation, which was the predominant historico-sociocultural category some time ago. "Thinking in terms of
civilizations" has supplanted "thinking in terms of nations," as I
formulated it some years ago.[2] This has become apparent also in
science, where the emphasis has been shifted from peoples and
nations to more comprehensive structures and processes in civilizations. Today, problems connected with this shifting meaning are
everywhere in the forefront of research. Sorokin himself is one
of the most impressive exponents.

In this new kind of cultural research, whose subject is not so
much *civilization* as such, but *civilizations*, the purpose is no longer
primarily finding out *what* has happened, i.e., fact-finding, but *how*

[1] Translated from the German by Kurt F. Leidecker.
[2] Othmar F. Anderle, "The Revolution in the World-View of History," *Diogenes*,
No. 9 (1955), p. 44.

things happened—determining the laws which govern an occurrence. Occasionally we have the uncomfortable feeling of gross
dissatisfaction over knowing "more and more about less and less,"
that is, we become dissatisfied with the belief that if we know
enough about the "trees," we shall then know more about the
"forest."[3] We venture to express the hope, however, that with
knowledge of those laws that govern the processes of how things
happen, we shall also gain a method for overcoming the crisis of
our age and of the civilization of which we are a part. At the very
least, we expect to learn where the path leads us and what, above
all, is left for us to strive for meaningfully.

Since Spengler, we have called the science which deals with
what is formal in the structural aspects of cultural phenomena,
"cultural morphology." This term was, however, not introduced by
Spengler, but by Leo Frobenius.[4] Today Spengler is looked upon
as the classical cultural morphologist. To be sure, in a certain
sense he is that, as I shall presently explain. As far as the subject
itself is concerned, there have been cultural morphologists long
before Spengler. They go back to Giambattista Vico, the Neapoli-
tan philosopher of history of the early eighteenth century,[5] and since
Spengler their lineage is uninterrupted.

Sorokin, too, belongs to this lineage; it does not matter whether
or not he acknowledges it. For even if we cannot, perhaps, look
upon him as a cultural morphologist in the narrower, holistic sense
(see below), he is, nevertheless, quite certainly one in the wider
sense, in which cultural morphology is defined as the science of
historico-sociocultural phenomena (shapes and processes) in their
formal aspects. The *how*, and not the *why*, stands in the foreground for him also. He, too, seeks to fathom its rules and laws,
and no one can deny that he has made very substantial contributions to its explorations.

In the future it will be equally impossible to do work in cultural

[3] Arnold J. Toynbee, A *Study of History: What the Book Is For, How the Book
Took Shape* (London, 1954).   Also Gerhard Ritter, "Gegenwartige Lage und
Zukunftsaufgaben deutscher Geschichtswissenschaft," *Historische Zeitschrift*, CLXX
(1959), 5, and Geoffrey Barraclough, "The Larger View of History," *The Times
Literary Supplement* (London), VI (Jan., 1956), Special Supplement: "Historical
Writing," II.

[4] Leo Frobenius, *Der Ursprung der afrikanischen Kulturen* (Berlin, 1896).

[5] Cf. Othmar F. Anderle, "Giambattista Vico als Vorlaufer einer morphologischen
Geschichtsbetrachtung," *Die Welt als Geschichte*, XVI (1956), 85-97.

morphology without reference to Sorokin as it now is without reference to Spengler and Toynbee, who are frequently cited in this connection. However, the circle of those who know of Sorokin's significance for cultural morphology must be considerably enlarged. Americans who are generally well acquainted with Sorokin —although primarily as a sociologist—must focus more upon his cultural morphology, which is less well known by them. Continental Europeans—by whom he is known primarily within narrower professional circles—must, in turn, become acquainted with Sorokin as a whole.

In order to describe Sorokin's relationship to cultural morphology and appreciate his contribution to this science, it is necessary to go somewhat into the details of its peculiar problems.

First of all, we have to distinguish between cultural morphology in the wider sense as a science dealing with the formal character (or the forms) of historico-sociocultural processes in general such as Frobenius, Koneczny, and perhaps Sorokin also understood it, and cultural morphology in the narrower sense as a science of structured cultural wholes, a concept developed by Vico, Danilevski, and Spengler, and basically also by Toynbee. The peculiar problems we have referred to are connected with this latter view.

Let us state that a "morphological" treatment of historico-sociocultural unities presupposes a knowledge of their material. This is a condition which, to be sure, is relatively easily fulfilled in simpler complexes, but becomes increasingly more difficult the greater their scope. For, in this case, a factor appears which F. A. Hayek has characterized as "the dilemma of specialization," that is, the impossibility for the historian to be at once exhaustive (depthwise) and comprehensive (extent-wise) while maintaining established scientific standards.[6]

It is, therefore, a question of the problems of integration in historical science[7] which consists in the difficulty, more precisely impossibility, of proceeding from the results of special investigation

[6] F. A. Hayek, "The Dilemma of Specialization," in *The State of the Social Sciences,* ed. Leonard C. White. (Chicago: University of Chicago Press, 1956), pp. 462-73. Concerning this dilemma, cf. Othmar F. Anderle, *Geschichtswissenschaft,* pp. 526 ff., *Integrationsproblem,* pp. 229 f., *Theoretische Geschichte,* pp. 12 f.

[7] Othmar F. Anderle, "Das Integrationsproblem in der Geschichtswissenschaft," *Schweizer Beitrage zur Allgemeinen Geschichte,* XV (1957), 209-48. Cf. also his *Geschichtswissenschaft,* pp. 501 ff.

to the more comprehensive complexes of history and societal and cultural life, retaining, all the while, the already mentioned methodological standard, that is, the norms established by the philosophical-critical method.

The reasons for this impossibility I have already expounded elsewhere.[8] Hence I would like to limit myself here to a brief resumé. They lie, basically, in the quantitative inexhaustibility of reality. For this inexhaustibility renders every additive or mechanical integration, be it ever so intensified even by teamwork and automation, illusory. Furthermore, we have to look for other reasons in the lack of uniformity and complexity of historico-sociocultural structures, for it is they that prohibit the application of inductive or even statistical methods in working with the concept of causality. Finally, the reasons for the above-mentioned impossibility may also be contingent upon the fact that in these structures we have super-additive ones. For in this case every additive integration must, from the very start, miss the historico-sociocultural complex we wish to grasp and reach into nothingness.

Most obvious, of course, is the following technical difficulty: the historian who is schooled in classical methods feels obligated by these very same methods to turn to the small, even minute, details, of the historical substratum. That means that he will have to *work* (if not to think) positivistically and nominalistically. At the same time, he has to specialize more and more; for the (quantitative) inexhaustibility of reality already mentioned of necessity leads him step by step further into the inexhaustible.[9] Thus, it is the resulting overspecialization which makes it impossible for the individual to work with greater complexes. For it is in every case only a certain quantum, that is, a quite definite yet limited sector of the historico-sociocultural reality, which we may treat thoroughly according to the precepts of philological, critical methods, working, at the same time, with originals, inspecting the sources, studying them critically, etc. The farther the historian penetrates in depth, the more meaningful his material becomes. But the deeper the hole, the smaller, of necessity, the area to which one must confine

---

[8] *Ibid.*

[9] With reference to this almost tragic fate of specialization, see especially A. J. Toynbee, "The Limitations of Historical Knowledge," in *The Times Literary Supplement* (London), VI (Jan., 1956), "Special Supplement Historical Writing," II.

himself; the sum total of his ability to work, however, remains the same.[10]

Now, it is precisely the large and very large complexes of historical existence and cultural and social life, however, which we must aim at. For it is they from which the decisive impulses proceed, but first and foremost the civilizations in which we, today, discern the most comprehensive historico-sociocultural structures of mankind as such. Primarily, it is a complete understanding of the material structures which we presuppose in a cultural morphology as a formal theory of culture. It would by no means suffice in cultural morphology to be an expert in one or the other of these civilizations. For as a science of the formal aspects of these structures, it presupposes a *comparative* study and, hence, a knowledge of several of these civilizations, if not all of them. That, however, is humanly impossible within the framework of the philological, critical method and the scientific standards that should be adhered to. The whole lifetime of a scholar is needed to be an Egyptologist or a Semitist "by profession." Nobody can, in all seriousness, be Egyptologist *and* Semitist, or Indologist *and* Sinologist, historian of antiquity *and* historian of modern times, at one and the same time. Much less can we speak of a person's truly scholarly knowledge of all, or even several, cultures, if such knowledge is to be based upon inspection of the sources, critical studies and knowledge of the sources, etc. Such knowledge would be and is possible only when dispensing with scientific standards, giving up the scrutiny of sources and working only with material at second-, third-, and fourth-hand, etc.—in brief, when making the transition from scientific to journalistic methods, such as the profession rightly rejects categorically.[11]

Cultural morphology, however, to state it again, is possible only on the basis of an actual knowledge of the civilizations and all other somehow relevant historico-sociocultural complexes. It presupposes a solution of the historiographic problem of integration and remains problematic so long as such a solution is not found. This

---

[10] Whoever expects to surmount this difficulty by teamwork and automation is unaware of the inexhaustibility of reality *in principle* which I have already mentioned, let alone all other objections against every kind of summative integration. Cf. above.

[11] One should consult on this issue what the professional literature says regarding the enterprise of Toynbee in integration, who, distressed by the dilemma of specialization, dared to pursue unorthodox ways: Othmar F. Anderle, "Die Toynbee-Kritik," *Saeculum*, IX (1958), 189-259. On Toynbee's method, see also his *Das Universalhistorische System A. J. Toynbees* (Frankfurt M. Wien, 1955).

is the fundamental difficulty; this is the reason why cultural morphology, still "young" as a science, must be taken seriously. This,
too, is the reason why historians by profession are so reticent in regard to it and why so few of them are prepared to incorporate
"morphological" problems into their program. As things stand
now, cultural morphology seems to be possible only on a journal-
istic-dilettante basis. Hence, every serious historian is afraid to
occupy himself with it.

Nevertheless, a useful solution of the historiographic problem of
integration, and with it that of a scientific cultural morphology,
has come into view in the meantime. To be sure, the solution has
come from the quarter which has placed the greatest obstacle in
the path of an additive integration. I am referring to a consideration of the possibility that in historico-sociocultural phenomena, we
are at least also dealing with super-additive holistic structures, a
possibility which, in the present state of our knowledge, we have
to take into account seriously.

Parenthetically we must add that the existence of such structures is a relatively recent discovery.[12] In German, we call them
Ganzheiten (wholes), whereby we understand, in the technical use
of the term, very precise, non-homogeneous units of any substratum
whatever which are more or less clearly distinguishable from their
surroundings, are more or less abundantly articulated and logically,
as well as ontologically, antecedent to the members or parts which
are discernible in the wholes.[13] This discovery was made about
the turn of the century, approximately simultaneously in psychology
(by Christian von Ehrenfels, on the one hand, and Felix Krueger, on
the other) and in biology (by Hans Driesch).

As a result, in both sciences, scientists changed over from the

[12] More strictly speaking, the rediscovery for science. For, first of all, the whole
Middle Ages operated with the greatest matter-of-factness with the idea of such
structures; indeed, one looked upon the universe itself in scholasticism as nothing
else but a hierarchically articulated totality. Furthermore, the naïve experience of
the world never ceased presupposing "wholes" and behaved in knowledge and action
accordingly. For the history of the holistic concept, see Othmar F. Anderle, "Die
Ganzheitstheorie, ein historisch-systematischer Ueberblick," *Zeitschrift fur Ganzheitsforschung*, Neue Folge, IV (1960), 2-18.

[13] Supersummativity is being designated as the First Ehrenfels Criterion, systematic unity as the Kohler Criterion, articulation and graduation as the First and
Second Volkelt Criterion. To these must be added the Second Ehrenfels Criterion
of Transposability, the Aristotelian Metathesis Criterion (non-interchangeability of
parts), the Criterion of Interdependence, and others.

meristicsynthetic ("from parts to complexes") method alone in use until then, to the holistic-analytic method ("from the whole to the parts"). Psychology developed in this manner into modern holistic psychology (Krueger, Wellek, Metzger, Wertheimer, Koffka, Köhler, Katz, Lewin, *et al.*), and biology into modern holistic biology (Driesch, von Bertalanffy, Troll, Portmann, Meyer-Abich, *et al.*). Other sciences, such as economics (the Viennese School of Spann and Heinrich) followed suit, and even philosophy began to occupy itself with the concept of the whole and to parallel the special holistic theories of the sciences with general holistic theories concerning the problem of "the whole" in general (Spann, Friedmann, Burkamp).[14]

Decisive in this development was the discovery made simultaneously with the uncovering of the actual existence of holistic structures, that such structures and processes would have to be understood, by no means additively, nor somehow meristically-synthetically "by starting with the parts," but, although complex, immediately as such, and in their totality and with their specific holistic characteristics.[15] We should, thus, say that these wholes may as well be static or simultaneous as well as dynamic or successive. This new discovery was of the greatest significance epistemologically as well as methodologically, for it has permitted us to *start* with the complexes to be understood, *instead of steering toward them* as a result of the procedure. Only from such a position can our holistic-analytic method be developed. It consists in our forming, first of all, an image of the whole of the structure or process under investigation in its most general properties, thus "cursorily testing" the "material" or "substratum" of the whole in question. Thereupon, we must endeavor to lay bare the structure,

[14] Concerning the inner unity of this movement and its significance for *Weltanschauung*, as well as its prehistory which reaches back into the Middle Ages, see Othmar F. Anderle, *Ganzheitstheorie*, pp. 2 ff. and 15, as well as the same authors, "Die Monadologie O. W. Leibnitz-Modellfall einer allgemeinen Ganzheitstheorie in nuce," *Zeitschrift fur Ganzheitsforschung*, IV (1960).

[15] We owe this discovery to Christian von Ehrenfels, the discoverer of the "qualitites of configuration," the most primitive wholes in the field of the psychology of perception. The so-called Berlin School of Gestaltpsychologie (Wertheimer, Koffka, Köhler, and others) later deserved much credit for developing Ehrenfels' discovery in the direction of epistemology. Cf. also Othmar F. Anderle, "Christian von Ehrenfels und das Problem einer wissenschaftlichen Kulturmorphologie," in *Gestalthaftes Sehen. Festgabe zum 100. Geburtstag Ch. v. Ehrenfels*, ed. F. Weinhandl (Darmstadt, 1960).

penetrating step by step, while isolating successively the substructures, thus clarifying the totality of the structure and making it understandable. This we continue to the point at which we arrive at the substratum where partial structures may no longer be ascertained.[16]

Since the holistic-analytic method may be, or must be, applied where structural wholes are present, it offers concomitantly a solution for the problem of historiography, and hence the problem of scientific, cultural morphology, even though it incorporates one grave difficulty. This consists in the fact that, here, too, we shall find we are dealing with wholes, that is, structures and processes corresponding to the holistic criteria mentioned above.

A solution of the problem of historiographic integration and the successful completion of a program of a scientific cultural morphology is possible upon the presupposition that holistic structures can be demonstrated to exist also in the field of history, as well as in the life of society and civilization. It can be accomplished by applying henceforth to the historical and cultural sciences, as we have done to psychology and biology in the past, the holistic-analytic method together with the whole theoretical apparatus of holistics, which consists of concepts, insights, and types of methods developed and correspondingly adopted by modern holistic psychology, holistic biology, and holistic philosophy.

So far so good, someone might say. But is such a presupposition correct? *Does* historical and cultural science have to do with phenomena, that is, structures and processes of the kind described, with *wholes,* to be exact?

Here we enter upon a complexity of problems in which Sorokin has something fundamental to say and which, in general, is of the greatest significance, not only for science, but for our entire attitude regarding historico-sociocultural reality. Ultimately and finally, it is a question, is it not, as to whether history in its totality or in its parts is an open or a closed process. In other words, is anything and everything possible in history at all times and does it depend

[16] From a book on general and cultural morphology now in preparation. What was indicated was merely the principle of the method. Even though it has already been applied in psychology and biology for nearly half a century and has a prehistory of a thousand years, it still leaves many questions unanswered which only the future will clarify. The principle as such can, however, be looked upon as established to the same extent as the justification of its application, provided that holistic structures are under investigation.

merely on chance or upon the free decisions of man? Or again, are certain limiting conditions given, conditions which impart to what happens direction and character on the whole, even though in individual cases they may leave us with a great number of possible alternatives? If the latter is the case, then, *not* everything is possible at any and all times, and it is *not* up to man's initiative to guide the development in this manner or in that direction. In this case, the decisions, insofar as we draw within our purview only the meaningful ones, are dependent on the frame of reference which limits their number, or, more precisely, renders meaningful only certain ones; but from the very outset, all others are condemned to failure.

If conditions in history were, indeed, such, then everything would naturally be dependent upon comprehending the established framework or the structural order of the sociocultural totality enveloping us. Only on the basis of such knowledge, then, would meaningful decision become possible. Let us assume the case that we of the Occident and in the twentieth century are, as Sorokin believes, in process of moving through a dying, "sensate" culture, which is necessarily to be followed by an "ideational" phase. It would then be nonsensical to cling most mightily, with the one hand, to the dwindling sensate values and to resist, with the other, the germinating ideational tendencies. Rather, it would make sense to do the opposite, for in the former case, one would swim against the current and be destined to suffer shipwreck. In the latter case, by swimming with the current, one's success would be assured. The same would be true if we were standing in the midst of a life cycle of a particular culture as imagined by Spengler, let us say, at the threshold of the "Caesarian" initial phase. It would be meaningless were we to fight for, let us say, the ideal of a democratic nationalism. We should rather do our utmost to bring about the sociocultural complex of Caesarism as quickly and painlessly as possible.[17]

[17] Of what practical consequences scientific insights are may be evident from the following reflection: Let us assume that the Western World is a civilization in Spengler's sense, to be sure at the threshold of its "Roman period," and, furthermore, that the Slavic East ("Russia") represents—as was likewise Spengler's view—a civilization which is beginning to flower and which, though new and homogeneous for the rest with the Occident, is at the end of its primitive stage (the phase of "first imperialism"), then the relationships between these two world-historical organisms can only be, even in view of the geopolitical situation in Europe, that of

As concerns the problem of a holistic structuralization of history we can, first of all, assume as indisputable that civilization as such, that is, Civilization capitalized and as a mere abstraction, cannot be a whole and thus is to be eliminated as a topic for morphological treatment. To be sure, the connection between a morphological treatment and a holistic structure is only a mediate one, for morphological treatment does not necessarily presuppose totality. And, is it not true that one should also investigate non-holistic structures as to their formal characteristics? Yet, since it turns out that one can engage in research in cultural morphology only if and where the problem of integration is soluble—this being the case, however, only in wholes—it seems commendable to make a virtue out of necessity and limit the concept of a "morphological" point of view right from the start to holistic structures,[18] as is to an extent already customary in biology.[19] This point of view was actually already in the making since Spengler's writings and the influence he exerted, only it has not yet been carried through consistently, a circumstance leading to many an obscurity.

A particular civilization, thus, is as such not subject to a holistic cultural morphology. With this as criterion, quite a number of students of civilizations must be excluded from being cultural morphologists in the strict sense, among them Frobenius and Koneczny. Sorokin who, by the way, is close to Koneczny without knowing it, escapes this danger, only by virtue of the way in which he places his concrete cultural systems into the foreground.

As a further category we have the cultures which have been called *Hochkulturen* since Spengler. The emphasis shifted to them,

---

an enmity to the death. That is to say, only the disappearance of the one could guarantee the future of the other, and the politicians would have to draw the consequence. But what about it if even only one of the two assumptions were not correct and "Russia" were not a civilization in and by itself but, as, e.g., Toynbee seems to believe occasionally, a part of the Western World which has split off for a time by way of the withdrawal-and-return from the main body of civilization in order to find by its own methods a solution of the great problem of humanity, and, after finding the solution, will return again to the main body? Every conflict between East and West would, then, be suicidal; every war would be a fratricidal one, and "coexistence" should, then, be the watchword at all cost.

[18] In the future, "morphological" will therefore mean: *Related to the informal configuration of holistic structures.* Perhaps we should, when misunderstanding is to be feared, speak of a "holistic morphology" even in face of the danger of being redundant.

[19] In the so-called Neo-idealistic Biology (Radl, Naef, Troll, Meyer-Abich, Rufner, and others), as well as previously in the biology of Goethe's time.

as everyone knows, under the influence of the transition from "thinking in terms of nations" to the modern "thinking in terms of civilizations," which may be traced back to the first appearance of Spengler's *Decline of the West* (1918).[20]　Hence one can say without exaggeration that civilizations with their complicated problems are at all events in the foreground of contemporary research.

Now, are civilizations holistic structures or not?　Do they satisfy the criteria of being a whole as established by Ehrenfels, Köhler, and Sander-Volkelt?　Do they possess the characteristic of systematic unity, of being distinct from their environment, of non-homogeneity, of internal articulation, of interdependence of their parts, of supersummation, of logical and ontological priority of the whole over its parts, of having the ability to be transposed?　Since they represent processes, are they, as such, unique or open at their ends? As they develop, are they determined as to number, kind, or duration of their phases, or are they not so determined?　Are the occurrences within the civilizations free or are they subject to a limiting order which determines their how?

As is well-known, Spengler answered all these problems in favor of the holistic conception, with the categorical verdict "Civilizations are organisms."　In fact, however, he did not know anything about the modern holistic theory which, in his day, was only in its first stages.　Vico, Vollgraff, Lassaulx, Danilevsky, Ligeti, and Schubart are of the same opinion, whereas Toynbee, while noting a *de facto* cyclical development, does not otherwise press the view that civilizations are principally open processes.[21]

Sorokin roundly disputes the holistic nature of civilizations. The problem is treated by him in a very clear manner in *Social Philosophies* (1950), in which we find a condensation of the theories he developed in *Social and Cultural Dynamics* and in *Society, Culture, and Personality*.　In 1950, he wrote:

I have already indicated that even the *total culture* of a single individual, as the smallest possible "culture-area," is not entirely integrated and represents a dominant system . . . that co-exists with many minor systems and a multitude of congeries, partly neutral, partly contradictory to the dominant system or to one another.　If such is the structure of the

[20] See above.　Even the self-experience of the Western World as a culture, i.e., as a community of destiny, which goes back to the lethal threat of this culture emanating from without, took part in it.

[21] Cf. Othmar F. Anderle: *Das Universalhistorische System A. J. Toynbees.*

total culture of an individual or of the smallest culture area, then the immense and infinitely diverse universe of the *total culture* of Egypt or India, the West or China, consisting of many billions of cultural phenomena, is certainly not, and cannot be, completely integrated into one causal or meaningful-causal system.   Assuredly it represents the co-existence of a multitude of cultural systems, of a supersystem. . . , and congeries that are partly mutually consistent, partly meaningfully indifferent, and partly contradictory.   The whole field of all the cultural phenomena of each of these "cultures," "types," or "civilizations" is a sort of dumping ground where billions of diverse cultural phenomena are thrown together.   Only a part of these is causally and causally-meaningfully united with other parts; another part is made up of mere congeries or semi-congeries "tied together" only by spatial proximity or by indirect causal ties.   They are not interdependent: a part of these can change without any change taking place in other items in the dumping ground.[22]

We should make this observation regarding Sorokin.   The world of socio-cultural phenomena he defines as *"the totality of the 'immaterial' meanings-values-norms, not objectified as yet through the material vehicles but known to humanity; the totality of already objectified meanings-values-norms with all their vehicles; finally, the totality of mindful individuals and groups—past and present."*[23] In this world he distinguishes the following kinds of correlations (forms of interconnection): *congeries,* consisting of phenomena connected by chance which have nothing to do with each other and whose only connecting link is spatial contiguity; *causal unity or systems* in which a direct causal connection exists between the individual phenomena; *meaningful systems* in which the individual phenomena form a meaningful connection; and *causal-meaningful systems or unities* in which a system of meaningful contents has become objectified through material carriers and does not merely occur as a thought system but also as a behavioristic and material system causally integrated within.[24]   The coming about of this last-mentioned system is explained by Sorokin in this fashion, that "when diverse persons, material objects, or energies become agents and vehicles of the same system of meanings, the component of the meanings throws a causal net over all such persons and vehicles

---

[22] Sorokin: *Social Philosophies of an Age of Crisis* (Boston: Beacon Press, 1950), pp. 209 f.

[23] *Ibid.,* p. 189.

[24] *Ibid.,* pp. 192-97; cf. *Dynamics,* I, chap. i, and IV, chaps. i-xiii; *Society, Culture and Personality,* chaps. xvii and xviii.

and introduces a causal dependence where it would otherwise not have existed."[25]

In the total culture of a people these congeries and systems are represented in all magnitudes, from the smallest, which often comprise only two elements, up to the largest, i.e., the main cultural systems and cultural supersystems. Generally speaking, the latter represent the most comprehensive, complicated systems of a socio-cultural kind in existence. Sorokin names three in this category: first, the *ideational* complex system whose ideology rests upon the basic assumption that the ultimate true value-reality is a super-sensory and super-rational divine principle with respect to which the sensate as every other reality and value is a Fata Morgana-like mirage or, at best, an infinitely inferior and adumbrated fictitious reality and sham value. Secondly, there is the *idealistic* complex system which, to be sure, also recognizes this supersensuous and super-rational principle as an ultimate value-reality, but permits us to approach it, though at a distance only, be it under the aspect of rationality, or under that of the sensate, or under that of the super-rational-supersensuous, in which latter case the ideal is looked upon as a union of all three aspects. Thirdly, there is the *sensate* complex system whose basic assumption is that "the ultimate, true reality-value is *sensory*. Beyond it there is no other reality nor any other non-sensory value."[26]

Finally, it is of special significance that Sorokin distinguishes all these cultural systems, beginning with the congeries, very carefully from the social systems or organized groups. A cultural system of whatever kind can, to be sure, coincide theoretically with a certain social system, but in actuality this occurs, according to Sorokin, practically never. The reason is, first, that the cultural systems, especially the most comprehensive ones among them are, as a rule, distributed over many, if not all social systems of mankind, and, secondly, that the total culture of an organized group, like that of even an individual, consists never of a single cultural system but of a multitude of smaller or larger cultural systems which are

[25] *Social Philosophies*, p. 196.
[26] *Social Philosophies*, p. 199. The conception of these three supersystems and the tracing of the cultural change resting upon their development for almost all phases of sociocultural life and the entire history of the Western World from Homer to the present (with instructive reference to Asia Minor, India, and China), especially in the four volumes of the *Dynamics*, represent the main achievement of Sorokin as a cultural morphologist.

partly in harmony with each other, but may partly also be contradictory. Moreover, the total culture consists of many congeries of
different kinds.[27]

It is clear that, on the basis of such presuppositions, Sorokin must
arrive at quite different ideas of the nature of civilizations than, let
us say, Danilevsky, Spengler or Toynbee. However, what specific
arguments has he brought up against the holistic structure of
civilizations?

First and foremost he *simply asserts* the non-holistic nature of
these structures or processes: "The immense and infinitely diverse
universe of the *total culture* of Egypt or India, the West or China,
consisting of many billions of cultural phenomena, *is certainly not,
and cannot be, completely integrated into one causal or meaningful-
causal system. Assuredly, it represents the co-existence of a multitude of cultural systems. . . .*[28]

Next, Sorokin thinks that none of the "cyclists" or representatives
of a holistic cultural conception (Danilevsky, Spengler, and Toynbee are meant) is in a position to indicate any major premise or
ultimate principle unfolding in the complete cultural phenomena of
Egypt, Babylonia, and the others. Even Spengler's *"Ursymbole"*
(primary symbols), he maintains, explain only a few of the many
systems and millions of congeries of which the civilizations in question are composed, and "serve rather poorly," because Spengler's
examples are "very remote, unconvincing and artificial."[29]

Furthermore, we read that the interdependence of the individual
cultural elements insisted upon by the "cyclists" does not exist at all.
The reference here is especially to Toynbee's passage in Study III,
p. 380, where it is stated that cultures are not wholes whose parts
are all interconnected and influence each other mutually.

Civilizations, thus, are not causal systems in Sorokin's language.
Toynbee himself allegedly furnished proof to the contrary of this
assertion on several occasions.[30]

[27] *Ibid.*, pp. 202 f; cf. *Dynamics*, IV, chap. iii; and *Society, Culture and Personality*, chaps. xvii-xx.
[28] *Social Philosophies*, p. 209; cf. above. Italics are mine.
[29] *Ibid.*, pp. 210 ff. Nevertheless, Sorokin is ready to accept Spengler's
"Ursymbol" as a local general denominator for a certain variant of one of his
supersystems, such as the Egyptian, Indian, etc. "This reconciliation does not,
however," Sorokin emphasizes toward the end of the presentation of his point of
view, "mean that Spengler's prime symbols can and do unify the total culture of
his civilizations" (p. 212).
[30] Sorokin's term "causal system" is somewhat confusing in this connection. It

These two arguments must, in conjunction with the previously mentioned somewhat dogmatic assertion, suffice to put the conclusion on a firm basis so that the "sum of the foregoing reasons is sufficient basis for the conclusion that the Danilevsky-Spengler-Toynbee type, High Culture, or civilization is neither a causal, nor a meaningful, nor a causal-meaningful system, but rather a *cultural field where a multitude of vast and small cultural systems and congeries—partly mutually harmonious, partly neutral, partly contradictory—co-exist.*"[31]

To further buttress his thesis Sorokin then says that the advocates of cycles among the cultural morphologists are by no means so agreed among themselves as to the identification of their civilizations as we would expect if these civilizations were such well-defined unities as they say. Sorokin, furthermore, asserts that Toynbee's "operative criterion" of civilizations being "intelligible fields of historical study" fails completely in practice and, finally, that the same advocates of cycles mix up cultural and social systems and even here manifest the crassest inconsequences.[32]

The occasion of this volume gives me a chance to remove Sorokin's objections. First of all, if we do not pay attention to the last argument nor to the arbitrary assertion made at the beginning, I cannot be of the opinion that even the totality of the objections he has raised is sufficient to demonstrate the non-integration of civilizations. Especially with regard to the value of Spengler's *Ursymbol,* one can think far differently from Sorokin. Moreover, it cannot be the task of an *Ursymbol* to explain every trait of a civilization, large or small, essential or unessential. What Spengler meant by this concept was apparently what the modern holistic theory calls the "quality of wholeness" or the "quality of configuration" of a very general nature. Qualities of such a nature first of all lend color to the complex as a whole. In general, such qualities come to the fore in shades more or less variegated exactly in the same way as does the individuality of a person. Although always

---

designates, as Sorokin expressly explains, only a connection of the type "if A eventually (and in a certain manner) changes, then also B changes (in a certain manner)." With that he has not stipulated yet a causality in the sense of a *causa efficiens;* change of A must, therefore, by no means yet be the cause of B because B's change is connected with it. The term "causality" is, for "cyclists," simply too narrow a description of the relationships of holistic interdependence.

[31] *Social Philosophies,* p. 213.
[32] *Ibid.,* pp. 214 ff.

present they are by no means expressed in every behavioral act with the same force. As everyone has experienced, at times he is more "himself" while at other times he is less "himself." That is to say, although our actions originate deep down in our personality, the circumstances, also, must be considered, and their resistance plays an important role. And, finally, the failure of Spengler's *Ursymbol* to function at times does not constitute an argument against the *Ursymbol*, for it is quite intelligible that on a particular occasion better and more productive qualities of wholeness of this kind may be discovered than on some other occasion.

The second objection also lets the matter appear more simple than it is. Here, too, in the interdependence maintained by the "cyclists" and denied by Sorokin (causal dependence is, as we have already remarked above, not the correct word), we are dealing in the analysis with a concept of holistic theory which one cannot reduce to the terse formula: "Whenever A, then B." The structure of a whole is much more flexible and elastic than the rigid schematisms taken from the world of causal mechanics are able to convey. The apparent exceptions which Toynbee allegedly must admit are, therefore, not contrary to the validity of the principle, and we would need a much more detailed investigation in order to arrive at a valid judgment concerning the existence or nonexistence of holistic relationships of interdependence within civilizations.

As concerns the lack of agreement between individual civilizations, it is easily explained by virtue of the fact that we, as individuals, live on another plane than civilizations as a whole. We see and experience normally only one another, but not the structures of which we are a part. Even the social life of a village and the citizenry of a city are abstract structures which are very difficult to imagine as such, structures which we can really picture to ourselves only in the shape of bodily assembled villagers or citizens. To a still higher degree, this is true of such social bodies as peoples and nations in which, let us say, parts or symbols represent the whole and thus bring them into view. If in this case the drawing of limits, and hence an identification, is not always simple and often is, in fact, an act of arbitrariness, no one will be surprised if still greater difficulties obstruct the identification of civilizations. These are the difficulties or obstructions the "trees" comprise in our attempt to identify the "forest," which they make up, in the analogy where trees and forest represent individual persons and civilization. By the way, we should not pay too much attention to such extremes as Toynbee cites in connection with this problem. One is almost tempted to say that concerning the existence of a Western, a Classical, an Egyptian, an Indian, a Chinese, a Middle-American, and a Peruvian civilization, there has been sufficient agreement for quite a long time. Whatever is still problematic rests upon the fact that cultural morphology is still a young science whose categories and concepts have not yet been worked out clearly enough.

The character of theoretical wholeness is shared also by the "operative criterion" of Toynbee, the "intelligible field of historical study," as I have repeatedly pointed out,[33] and it is shared to a very special degree. All the more, we have to guard against applying it mechanically, as is done in Sorokin's presupposition and that of many others whose criticism resembles his.

Let us admit that our definition has been insufficient and has, therefore, left the door open for misunderstanding. If Toynbee had been better informed about the holistic theory, he would surely have given the "operative criterion" another formulation. But the way it was intended expresses nothing else but the challenge to investigate world-historical complexes (which, I would say, are under suspicion of harboring wholes) as to the somewhat crude criterion of systematic unity and the Second Sander-Volkelt Criterion of distinctness from the environment. This, of course, belongs to the most elementary operations of a holistic cultural morphology. To be sure, carrying out such operations presupposes an exact knowledge of their special presuppositions and a training in holistic theory such as hardly a single cultural morphologist possessed at that time. It requires an eye for what is essential and whole, playing into the intuitive and irrational. Furthermore, the application of this procedure carries the unavoidable methodological scope of every mode of holistic study within itself in that a certain image of the complex structure to be identified by the delimitation must be presupposed.[34]

Again, it cannot be denied that the delineation of a civilization,

[33] Othmar F. Anderle, *Das Universalhistorische System A. J. Toynbees;* Anderle, "Arnold Tonbee und die Problematik der geschichtlichen Sinndeutung," *Die Welt als Geschichte*, XX (1960); Anderle, "Die Ganzheitstheorie," p. 10.

[34] I intend to go into this difficult problem in my book *Ganzheitsforschung und Kulturwissenschaft*: I. *General Morphology*, II. *Cultural Morphology*.

the segregation of what is "native" and what is "foreign," belongs to the most difficult tasks of a holistic, theoretical view. Exactly the same problem is met when we submit the individuality of a single human being to scrutiny. We require, as it were, a special organ to sense the psychic vibrations. At all events, we are dealing here with meaningful holistic connections and hence with qualities, not with quantities. Only he who keeps this in mind can do justice to Toynbee's postulate and apply the criterion of the "intelligible field" successfully. In acknowledging this we have also stated that a wrong use of the criterion does not constitute an argument against it nor against the wholeness of the civilizations defined by it.

Before answering the objection that the theorists who believe in cycles have confused the cultural with the social systems, I would like to clarify my position. The accusation is made that the confusion is brought about by an extreme disregard for logic, from which alone we are to deduce the fact that civilizations are not wholes.

The alleged disregard for logic, as such, we must admit. However, it is not to be traced to a heterogeneity of the social systems in question, as Sorokin maintains, but to the inadequacy of the sociological categories utilized in establishing the relations. The Greeks, the Romans, and the Egyptians of antiquity were as little a "nation" as are "the" Hindus or "the" Chinese at the present time. If we use the term "nation" in the exact, specifically Western, sense, then, the groups referred to do not even consist of such "nations," for their substructures are of a different kind in every case.[35] By exact and specifically Western, we mean "nation" in the sense of a blood-related group of people who possess a common cultural tradition, are politically unified, are confined to a certain area on the surface of the globe, and represent essentially a specific type of civilization which overshadows them. The social groups corresponding to the "cyclical" cultural systems are by no means heterogeneous. We only still lack a common name for them. It is our categories which are insufficient and misleading; hence an argument against the wholeness of civilizations cannot be deduced from them.

[35] Cf. Spengler's polemics against the indiscriminate application of the concept of nation (*Decline of the West*, II), his own concept of "nation of magical style" (*ibid.*), as well as the corresponding term of consensus or *idjima* in Toynbee (cf. Anderle, *Das Universalhistorische System A. J. Toynbees*).

Sorokin's reservations, which we have treated thus far against a holistic comprehension of civilization as put forth by the "cyclists" he mentions, are not so serious as the objection that the "cyclists" confuse, in general, "cultural systems" and "social systems."

As already alluded to, at the basis of this confusion lies the fact that Sorokin himself distinguishes rigorously between both kinds of systems and, at least in practice, does not even wish to admit their overlapping. Hence we encounter a basic position which is well worth our careful consideration. Is it, in general, permissible to distinguish so rigorously between cultural and social systems, as does Sorokin, and to treat both as factors occurring completely independently and variable in and by themselves?

I would like to venture certain objections.

To be sure, no one is able to deny that there are, in actuality, what Sorokin calls "cultural systems," and that they are certainly separate and distinct from social systems. For instance, Plato's philosophy is something that existed even after the death of Plato and exists even today, and a person may decide for himself whether he wants to accept it or not.

Somewhat more problematical is the culture of the Renaissance. True, someone in the middle of the twentieth century could conceive the crazy notion of leading a life in the style of Bartolomeo Colleoni or Leonardo da Vinci. But apart from the difficulties which a transformed environment would offer, it would amount, would it not, to toying with a mask, being a stage actor to oneself and to others. I am afraid that our scholar, who is otherwise so perceptive, may have failed to discern in his treatment the difference between living (better: functioning) and dead cultural systems. But it is especially this difference which seems to me to be significant. A cultural system is "living" if and so long as its vehicle—be it an individual or a social system—is alive, has created and developed it, has animated it, and uses it as an expression of himself or itself. Cultural systems of this type change with the carriers; they are in every respect dependent on them and form a unity with them. Nevertheless, they do not always perish with them, not under all circumstances and not completely. They leave behind in their objectifications (e.g., the book *Politeia,* traces of the life of Bartolomeo Colleoni which is fixable historically; or the pictures, drawings, and journals of Leonardo) points of contact on the basis of which they may be reconstructed as possibilities. Over the centuries and millennia, these possibilities may be realized by other persons and systems or societies.

But what is the significance of all this? A mere option? Only under certain circumstances; that is to say, only if the cultural system concerned is accepted more or less mechanically, without particular meaning, submitted to unwillingly as to external coercion, as we submit to many things, like the student who unwillingly submits to an examination in order to get an "education." Such cultural systems or congeries are, however, in these cases more or less irrelevant to the psychic equipment of the persons and groups in question. We can call relevant only the independently existing, self-created cultural system through which one's own life courses and which, as such, perishes *per definitionem* with the carrier. That does not mean that every "functioning" cultural system is in each and every sense a novel or original creation of him who supports it. As a "going concern" as well as an expression of this individual or that individuality of a single person or a social group it is a new and original creation. However, as to its material content it is *a possibility* as a rule, and new only to a lesser degree. The greater part of what we as individuals and as groups realize in life we see and experience as a possibility in front of our eyes and subsequently we put it into operation. The decisive element in all this is, however, the manner in which the "alien elements" are being incorporated into one's "own" being, how they are being assimilated. And it is an assimilation we are dealing with unless the "alien elements" remain meaningless "congeries," accretions to the organism of our own cultural system, such as the shells on the dwelling of the hermit crab.

Thus, the "alien element" in the form of given, "inanimate" cultural systems or their traces remains either alien, in which case it is meaningless, or it is utilized as a structural element in our own cultural system. In the latter case it is being assimilated, transformed, and subjected to the new meaning. What it originally was now becomes meaningless, that is, so far as the new cultural system is concerned. When Sorokin views all cultural systems from the point of view of transferability, he can only lay hold of the inanimate ones among them which are really no longer genuine systems, but only possibilities of such, in other words, thought structures which must first be awakened to life. But this can be brought about only by incorporating them into a living cultural system, which is, however, never accomplished without a more or less thoroughgoing change in meaning and transformation. The significance of the old systems is limited to being structural material. What is important is not what they themselves are in the way of possibilities, but what they become in the new union. Thus, the emphasis must be put fully on live, "functioning" cultural systems, which, in turn, may not be viewed apart from the people supporting them, not even social systems.

The objection which Sorokin raises against his "cyclists," that they do not distinguish between cultural and social systems and fail to note that both never coincide, is thus likewise open to dispute and cannot very well be utilized as an argument against the holistic nature of civilizations. On the contrary, the rigorous distinction of cultural systems and social systems is untenable in this formulation, especially when we are considering genuine, that is, living, functioning cultural systems.[36]

Obviously, there is a connection between the failure to recognize the inseparable unity of cultural systems and those supporting cultural systems, on the one hand, and the fact that Sorokin is unwilling to concede holistics to the total culture, beginning with the individual and particularly with respect to the social body as a whole, on the other. Does he not state expressly "that even the total culture of a single individual . . . is not entirely integrated and represents a dominant system . . . that co-exists with many minor systems and a multitude of congeries"? Even the "dominant system" may be lacking, as with eclectics, and he even uses this as an argument a fortiori against the holistic nature of civilization.[37]

All this is absolutely incapable of being brought into harmony with modern holistic psychology and corresponds, at most, to the psychic habitus of schizophrenic types. Personality, insofar as it is not sick, meaning psychotic, is described by modern holistic

---

[36] The eminent author seems not to have escaped entirely the danger of a certain conceptual realism, as is the case also in Dilthey (there are probably relationships here; consider, for instance, the meaningful and structural connections in Dilthey!), with the "Polish Toynbee," F. Koneczny, as well as with Northrop and Kroeber, to whom Sorokin characteristically and admittedly feels essentially a greater relationship than to the "cyclists," Danilevsky, Spengler, and Toynbee. See *Social Philosophies,* pp. 244-66 *passim.*

[37] *Op. Cit.,* p. 209. Cf. above.

psychology positively as a well-integrated whole in the strictest sense of the word, distinct from its surroundings, unified into a system, articulate, interdependent, supersummative, governed centrally, self-regulative, fitted with assimilatory and regenerative powers, holistically determined in its developmental process, "stylistically" determined, "a form, die-cast but alive and developing."[38]

Naturally, within the framework of such an integrated system there are also congeries. I have already made provisions for that. Furthermore, not everything is thoroughly integrated. There are differences in rank with respect to significance within the system and applied to the system; but these are minor matters. Decisive for personality is and remains the integrated relatedness, for this determines all subsidiary elements as well.

If, in view of what we know about modern psychology dealing with personality and characterology, it may be regarded as settled that individuals are integrated holistically in their psychic-spiritual make-up, insofar as they are normal, then, we have knocked the foundation from under Sorokin's conclusion as to the non-integratedness of civilizations. More than that, we could even turn the tables. We know today, and Sorokin himself started with the fact, that a considerable number of human social structures (especially the significant ones among them), in brief, all those structures which Sorokin includes under the expression of "social systems" or "organized groups," are, *as social structures,* interpreted holistically and hence represent, as it were, individuals of a higher order.[39] Is it, then, not natural to say that their psychic-spiritual world and concurrently its "total culture," are likewise integrated holistically in the same manner as that of individuals?

To be sure, Sorokin categorically asserts the contrary. However, can he prove it? This might be difficult, even methodologically, as he would have to prove it purely on the strength of non-presence, and all would depend on the logicality of the arguments he advances, which are, moreover, almost wholly of an indirect nature. Furthermore, there are abundant indications which point unmistakably to the fact that even social systems (if they are genuine

[38] Cf. Albert Wellek: *Person, Personlichkeit und Charakter* (Meisenheim a. Glan) and the literature cited there, as well as Ph. Lersch, *Aufban der Person* (1951) and E. Rothacker, *Die Schichten der Personlichkeit* (1952). Also E. Spranger, *Lebensformen* (1950) and the writings of Freud, Adler, and Jung.
[39] *Social Philosophies,* p. 202.

systems!) are integrated holistically up to the stage of civilizations so far as their psychic-spiritual habitus is concerned, hence in their total culture. To be sure, there are the limitations of the graduated intensity of integration and loosely joined congeries which we admit in the case of single individuals. It would require a separate volume to enumerate all these indications beginning with the results of social psychology, and particularly group psychology, up to those we meet in modern cultural morphology in most of its variations.

Especially from the last-mentioned discipline we do obtain, on the whole, an impressive picture of the external, as well as internal, solidarity of civilizations and, to be sure, not only as structures, but also as processes, which in reality they are. However much the theories of Vico, Vollgraff, Lasaulx, Danilevsky, Spengler, and all the rest diverge from one another in detail, they nevertheless agree in that their civilizations appear as entities of a special kind. Even Toynbee, who geared his whole life's work toward proving the *openness* of the processes of civilizations, cannot help himself presenting their factual compactness. Sorokin himself experiences the same thing. For even though his conception of three supersystems threatens to obscure the picture, the local characters of these systems nevertheless meet us, especially in his presentations, in a grandiose unity and thus reinforce our impression that every civilization is a seamless, integrated system in which everything is related to everything else and, in the last analysis, expresses a single basic thought or, better still, a single entity.[40]

To this must be added, to a lesser degree, the single results and, to a greater degree, the total impressions we get from special humanistic disciplines. Classical antiquity, Egyptology, Babylonian studies, Indology, Sinology, American studies, and even Orientalistics which, to a large extent, denies the subject we are talking about, whether or not we desire it, all bring to mind the unity and compactness, peculiarity and individuality, in a word the holistic nature of the cultures under consideration. This is peculiarly the case also in view of our own occidental culture where we are even more readily exposed to the danger of not seeing the forest because

[40] For this purpose one should visualize the enormous amount of data which have been gathered from practically all fields of material as well as non-material culture in the four volumes of *Dynamics*. There is no more impressive and, at the same time, more exact proof for the truth of Comte's "consensus" than this one!

of the trees. If, here, we have first and foremost the humanistic and art historians spearheading the movement of giving us a comprehension of what is "Western," there are still political historians from whose expositions the integrated nexus of the Western world comes clearly but unintentionally to the fore.[41]

I shall not be so foolhardy as to say that the holistic nature of civilizations which Sorokin denies is thus already proved. However, I entertain the hope of having shown that it is at least justified to work with such a conception as a heuristic hypothesis. But this is sufficient to render a scientific cultural morphology possible, again, only as a working hypothesis, in that, as I have shown, such a cultural morphology stands or falls with the solution of the historiographic problem of integration. Such a solution is, however, possible only for holistic structures and when we apply the theoretical mode of viewing things holistically.

So far as Sorokin's position with regard to cultural morphology is concerned, we may therefore gather that, in denying the holistic nature of civilizations, he cannot at least officially be a cultural morphologist in the narrower sense of holistic cultural morphology pursued on holistic theories. That does not preclude, however, his centering his whole thinking and writing upon the exploration of laws and rules and on the formal structural relations, if not in individual civilizations as such, at least in cultural process in general. He is thus comparable to Koneczny, Northrop, Kroeber, and others who must likewise be designated as *cultural morphologists in the wider sense.* As such he was, evidently, not dependent on a solution of the historiographic problem of integration, but was able to work meristically, or inductively and statistically. This he did, indeed. In this manner he has presented us with an abundance of insights into the nature of social and cultural dynamics and elevated the general morphology of culture to a position which it did not have before him.

Similarly he has unwittingly contributed materially to a holistic

[41] In the first place, I am thinking of the presentation of the European system of states in the book by Wolfgang Windelband, *Die auswärtige Politik der Grossmachte in der Neuzeit 1494-1938* (Essen, 1938). The author, a member of the classical German School of historians, was as far removed from cultural morphology as is possible and had no inkling of the holistic theory. Nevertheless, without noticing or knowing it he drew a picture of the system of states as could not have been more "holistic" in the strictest sense of the theory. *Exact* proofs of the holistic nature of a civilization are given here such as only the professional science is able to furnish.

morphology of civilizations (note the minuscule at the beginning of the word!). This he accomplished above all as we have already noted by proving, as it were, experimentally in his careful, thorough investigations made with natural science exactitude, what the "genially" operating holistic morphologists merely asserted on the basis of a more or less venturesome intuition. In this realm belongs the fact already mentioned of a "consensus," the spiritual harmony of all cultural phenomena of a period whose inductive-statistic proof will always appear to me to be the most admirable accomplishment of Sorokin's *Dynamics*. Likewise the "ideational," "idealistic," and "sensate" attitudes, as such, which, Sorokin himself observes in his analysis, agree to a very large extent with the phases of growth, maturity, and decline, advocated by Danilevsky, Spengler, and Toynbee, as well as with the ascetic-messianic, "harmonic," and "heroic-Promethean" cultures of Schubart, and with the "barbarous religions," "medieval and Renaissance" and "humanistic-worldly" types of Berdyaev.[42]

"What Danilevsky, Spengler and Toynbee call a period or phase in the life-cycle of a civilization, the others call a type or a form of a cultural supersystem. What the first three authors consider as the succession of the phases in the life-course of the same civilization, the others view mainly as a succession of different prototypes of supersystems of culture. Thus the real disagreement between the two groups of writers is considerably less than appears on the surface."[43] Sorokin sees in this a confirmation of his own view, and not without a certain justification. I myself, representing as I do a holistic cultural morphology, would prefer to see in it rather a confirmation of "cyclical" suggestions.

Sorokin is inclined to interpret the phases of the "cyclists" as local specialties of his, Northrop's, Kroeber's, and other general types. The emphasis lies here on the "general type"; even the appearance and disappearance of the phases is being traced back to the inner dynamics of the "super-system" as such.[44] This inner dynamics is being explained in the Hegelian dialectic manner: "The change is . . . immanent in any socio-cultural system, inherent

[42] *Social Philosophies*, p. 295.
[43] *Ibid.*, p. 294.
[44] See the magnificent Part IX of the new one-volume edition of *Dynamics* of 1957, corresponding to the end of the last volume of the four-volume original edition of 1937-1941 (pp. 630-704).

in it, and inalienable from it. It bears in itself the seeds of its change." *"By virtue of the principles of immanent change, each of the three integrated forms, or phases, of the ideational, idealistic and sensate super-systems cannot help changing; rising, growing, existing full-blooded for some time, and then declining."*

Decisive in all this is the principle of limited possibilities: *"if not for all, then at least for an enormous number of sociocultural systems in process, the number of fundamental possibilities as to ever new fundamental turns in direction, essentially new forms, patterns and appearances the system can assume is limited and bounded."*[45] Since the same principle also holds true for the totality of cultural supersystems, in which case it states that, corresponding to the three possible positive answers to the question as to the nature of the ultimate value reality—the ideational, idealistic, and sensate—three and only three forms of an integrated culture are possible, these three systems *must* follow each other.

This as it were logical coercion is reinforced by the lack of satisfaction which these systems ultimately hold for us. For we long for final truth and reality, whereas the systems named are "partially true, partially false, partially adequate, partially inadequate." Disappointed in one, people turn to one of the other systems without ever being able to break the circle of "limited possibilities."

The empirically observed sequence—ideational-idealistic-sensate, or sensate-ideational-sensate, which, according to Sorokin is, however, not compulsory—Sorokin explains purely dialectically as a "veering around." In the overripe stage of sensate culture, man himself is brought to his senses by the tragic consequences of his own stupidity and is led into the opposite extreme of the ideational attitude, whereupon normally follows a state of tranquility which manifests itself in the state of equilibrium and harmony of an idealistic culture.[46]

Nevertheless, one can again turn the tables and perceive in the rhythm of Sorokin's supersystems the abstract formulation of a general biological law, a sort of typology of cultural development in which the emphasis might lie on concrete developments in the shape of civilization. Sorokin's "ideational" type would then, in-

---

[45] *Dynamics* (1957), pp. 633, 676, 654.
[46] *Ibid.*, pp. 681, 697 f.

deed, be simply the type of an early period; the idealistic one simply that of a period of maturity; the sensate one simply that of the final period, and it would be easy to show how excellently Sorokin's characterizations correspond to these developmental phases.

In a very special sense, this is true in view of Sorokin's sensate culture, for which, quite obviously, our time served him as a model although our age is made intelligible through the concept of a sensate supersystem. In cases where Sorokin appears as an analytic thinker and critic of contemporary culture and, especially, as the keen and incorruptible diagnostician of its pathological features, the borderline between his general cultural morphology and that of a holistic cultural morphology related to concrete cultural wholes is completely obliterated. His description of the final stage of the "sensate" culture of the West-European and American world since about the middle of the nineteenth century (see the corresponding periods in his *Dynamics*)[47] is in itself a piece of cultural pathology par excellence, and as such a brilliant achievement of genuine, even though unintentional, cultural morphology in the narrower, holistic sense. For, with unexcelled powers of penetration, Sorokin here has described what happens when a civilization falls apart.

Sorokin may, nay, surely will, reject this compliment in order not to allow himself to serve as agent for a type of interpretation he rejects. Nonetheless, he should not be too sure of himself, for no one can know what "cunning reason" has in store for him. Apart from that, it will not detract from his fame; it can only augment it.

[47] See especially the soul-searching chapter, "The Crisis of Our Age," in *Dynamics* (1957), pp. 622-28, as well as the last (42nd) chapter, "The Twilight of Our Sensate Culture and Beyond," pp. 699-704. Still stronger accents are found in the book *S.O.S.—The Meaning of Our Crisis,* in view of whose vehement attacks upon the responsible bearers of our sensate culture one cannot wonder enough what measure of self-criticism American society tolerates.

Sorokin's Theory of Social Mobility

Gösta Carlsson

I. Some General Remarks

This is a report on a book rather than on the man who wrote it. Our subject is Sorokin's *Social Mobility*,[1] not his thoughts on social stratification and mobility in general, and very little attention will be paid to his other works. His mobility book is a justly famous one, a classic in the field, and one of Sorokin's major contributions to sociological learning and research. It is big enough, well over five hundred pages, to permit the author to develop his argument at some length if he thinks it necessary. By all accounts this work and the theory presented in it should be able to stand by itself in the sense that it can be understood and evaluated independently of later corrections and additions.

What follows, therefore, is the result mainly of a reflective re-reading of *Social Mobility*. Now, when a study made some years ago is evaluated, either one of two standards can be applied. We can ask whether the author improved on the job done by others before him. Or we can judge him by the standard of present-day knowledge. Do the problems our author chose to investigate still seem important? Were his methods adequate as we understand them, and do his conclusions appear as firmly established now as they might have appeared then? To follow this second road is less fair to the man we are criticizing, but promises more interesting results. For in this manner we may discover, not only that the particular study we are examining is in some respects inferior to

[1] First published under this title in 1927 (New York: Harper). Reprinted as *Social and Cultural Mobility* (Glencoe, Ill.: Free Press, 1959), with chap. v from Volume IV of *Social and Cultural Dynamics* added. Page numbers are identical in the two editions.

what is being done today, but also that it is superior in other respects. That is to say, we have not only added to our store of methods and ideas in the meantime, but we have also lost something. And this would surely be a finding of some consequence. Accordingly, the following discussion of Sorokin's theory will be more concerned with its relation to the questions that worry us today than with its place in the intellectual tradition of stratification research.

A brief description of Sorokin's work is needed to start us off; naturally, we shall have to come back to many points later on. First of all, it is as much a theory of social organization in general as a study of mobility. It deals with vertical mobility, which occurs in a social space defined chiefly by three dimensions or principal forms of stratification: the economic, the political, and the occupational. Mobility consists in individuals or groups of individuals moving from one stratum to another, up or down. We learn about the various aspects of such mobility: its frequency, the qualities of those who go up as compared with those who remain in their station of life, or go down the ladder of hierarchically ordered strata, and the changes in the rate of mobility in history.

But the book also discusses this question: How great are the differences between the strata between which men may move? Every organized group is stratified,[2] stratification is a natural phenomenon, and rights and privileges are always unequally shared between and among members of the group. But there may be more or less of this inequality, and the distribution of the population between the strata varies from one historical epoch to the next, though there is no steady drift either toward more or less equality. In short, there are two major themes in Sorokin's analysis, and both are treated with a wealth of data, drawn from every period of recorded history, and as often as not in the shape of statistics.

There was nothing new in this concern with social differences and with the struggle between individuals or groups for a better position in society. It was a prominent topic in the writings of the first generation of American sociologists,[3] not to mention many European sources. Nor were statistical inquiries into these matters

---

[2] *Social and Cultural Mobility,* pp. 12-15.
[3] Cf. Charles H. Page, *Class and American Sociology* (New York: Dial Press, 1940), pp. 249-54.

lacking, as is shown by the many references in Sorokin's book. But there remained the task of bringing together in a common frame speculation on the nature and mission of social classes, and their future, on the one hand, and the perhaps all-too empirical studies of income distribution, or occupational mobility on the other. And this is what Sorokin has to offer: a survey of data and problems which is both analytic and systematic. Of the heritage from his predecessors he retained a strong interest in the long-term historical changes in stratification or mobility and in the nature of the class system in pre-industrial society.

Much of the terminology is still with us. We speak of vertical mobility and strata, and often the same dimensions are used—the political, the economic, and the occupational one. Strictly speaking, we should perhaps call the third the honor or prestige rather than the occupational dimension. Indeed, it may be questioned whether occupation can ever be called a stratification variable in quite the same sense as income, power, prestige, or even education; in stratification research occupation is mostly used as a convenient pointer to these other variables, or as a means of holding them constant.[4] But on this issue there is little to distinguish Sorokin from the sociologists now active in the field; whatever difficulties his terminology may lead into we seem neither much better nor much worse off in this respect, though we have undoubtedly gained in technical experience.

What we have now lost is some of the historical perspective; for better or worse, sociology has become more concerned with the industrialized (or industrializing) society and less with other epochs. This brings us to the question of the validity of Sorokin's historical generalizations, and their importance for the study of stratification in modern society.

II. The Argument from History

To Sorokin, the real point in the history of stratification and mobility is the very lack of a goal or direction of the historical process. His examination of every important form of social in-

[4] Cf. Gösta Carlsson, *Social Mobility and Class Structure* (Lund: Gleerup, 1958), pp. 44-45.

equality ends on this note. For instance, neither the general prosperity of the society as a whole, nor the gap between rich and poor, is steadily increasing or decreasing. To be sure, there are fluctuations in both respects, a period of increasing inequality is followed by a period of lessening differences. In the long run these fluctuations turn out to be goalless; the historical process should be likened to a man who is "circling in various directions without any definite goal or point of arrival."[5] And this is equally true of vertical social mobility. Though our own society has become a highly mobile one since the eighteenth century, this does not mean that there is a permanent trend towards increased mobility.[6]

This, compressed into a few words, is Sorokin's cyclical theory of class and mobility. Of the many questions that may be raised in this connection only two will be taken up here. First, what part does this historical law, or alleged law, play in Sorokin's theory as a whole? Second, is it true as a description of recent changes of Western society, and as a forecast for the future?

On the first point, it can be said that history furnishes the laboratory in which theoretical deductions and inferences based on abstract reasoning can be tested. Sorokin very properly attacks his target, the full understanding of stratification and the structure of society, from two directions. Given certain elementary facts of human nature and life in groups, certain things appear to follow as necessary, or at least very probable, consequences. About this kind of analysis much more will be said presently. Here, it is sufficient to observe that the results thus reached have to be verified, for we could, after all, be mistaken about human nature and the rules of group life. Reasoning, based on psychological and sociological premises, leads Sorokin to expect that social inequality should be a universal phenomenon, something which is never entirely missing, never developed beyond a certain limit. The precise nature of the argument need not detain us just now; but it is clear that our trust in the conclusion will depend on the demonstration that the historical facts bear it out. And this is what Sorokin is trying to show.

It follows that we shall be doing less than full justice to Sorokin's views on stratification and social mobility in Western society if we

[5] *Social and Cultural Mobility*, p. 62.
[6] *Ibid.*, p. 409.

assume them to be only a crude generalization or "extrapolation" from history. At the same time, there is no doubt that the element of historical generalization plays an important role, and this brings us to the second question, namely: How far can valid inferences be drawn from past to present or future social conditions?[7] It is beyond the scope of this essay, and the competence of its author, to determine how true the pictures are that Sorokin draws of the social, political, and economic conditions in various Western and Oriental societies. Even if the historical facts were well established, the question remains: How confident can we be in generalizing from them to the future, or in using them for the diagnosis of our own society? And the answer seems to be that we cannot feel any confidence at all in such inferences. For if anything is true of modern Western society, it is that it is radically different from its forerunners in almost every important respect. Its machinery of production and degree of economic development is unequaled. It is a society where everyone can buy and read newspapers, or listen to the radio, and thus become aware of social and political goals. It is also a society where government is by consent, at least in the nominal sense that there are general elections in which everyone has the right to vote.[8]

The failure, as it seems, to take fully into the account the industrialization of Western society and all its consequences is one of the chief defects of Sorokin's analyses. It may still be true that social inequality is necessary, and that the difference between the poor and the rich, or the humble and the exalted, will continue to fluctuate and grow large at times. Should history repeat itself, it will be for reasons that are different in many ways, and in the difference lies much of the interest. If this line of thinking is correct, we learn from history that we cannot learn from history. At any rate, it does not seem possible to use pre-industrial and industrial societies, side by side, as so many equally relevant negative or positive instances to some law or principle.

Sorokin's treatment of economic inequality may serve as an example. He finds evidence of both increasing differences during certain periods and a leveling of such differences at other times,

[7] For an example of the prominent role of the argument from history, see *Social and Cultural Mobility*, p. 153.

[8] Cf. S. M. Lipset and R. Bendix, *Social Mobility in Industrial Society* (Berkeley and Los Angeles: University of California Press, 1959), p. 4.

though they never disappear completely. An important distinction is drawn with respect to these opposing tendencies. The "natural direction" of change is that of increasing differences, more inequality. "In a similar way, within a social group numerous and as yet unknown forces in a 'natural' way tend to increase economic stratification, unless there is an intervention of opposite forces acting as a check." Sorokin admits that these interventions are also natural, but he holds that they work "convulsively and spasmodically, and manifest themselves clearly only from time to time. Being always marked by a special effort to stop the natural process of stratification, they remind us of the artificiality of the cutting of permanently growing hair."[9] A series of historical illustrations further clarify this distinction.

Now, whatever may be the truth of this theory as applied to pre-industrial systems, it does not seem valid for industrial society. In the latter we find a process of leveling of income differences at work, and the most remarkable feature of this process is its continuous and automatic operation. Most classes profit from the development of the economic machinery, but particularly those at the bottom of the income scale, so that the gap between bottom and top is lessened. And this effect does not seem to be something imposed from without, so to speak, by means of legislation and welfare measures. It appears in countries with different political systems and with varying emphasis on social legislation. Even in Sweden, with its "semi-socialistic" political and economic system, and rather close approximation to the idea of the welfare state, it has been estimated that only a minor part of the leveling is due to the taxation and welfare measures and the major part to other forces.[10] Indeed, the observation that countries that are well developed economically have more economic equality than less developed countries has recently been promoted to a kind of law.

The moral of all this is not so much that Sorokin was wrong about economic stratification in modern society. It is rather that the industrial system of production sets free forces which are quite different from those found in traditional society and which may tend to bridge the gap between strata with respect to material standard

[9] *Social and Cultural Mobility*, pp. 46-47.
[10] R. Bentzel, *Inkomstfördelningen i Sverige* (Stockholm: Industrins utredningsinstitut, 1953) ("Income Distribution in Sweden"; in Swedish with summary in English, pp. 211-18).

and life-chances. Still, there might be a limit to this process; a minimum of inequality may be a necessary trait of any organized group or society. By this we are brought back to the second of Sorokin's two main types of arguments.

III. The Argument from Function

Whatever may be their general reaction to Sorokin's work, today readers will at least feel at home with his discussion of the fundamental causes or reasons behind social stratification. This appears to be an example of functional analysis which is so important in present-day sociological theory. It is true that Sorokin has expressed serious doubts about the soundness of the functional school of thought in one of his later books[11] and, therefore, presumably cares little to be referred to it himself. But the paradox may be more apparent than real as the label in question can be and actually is applied to sociologists of rather varied theoretical orientations. In fact, functionalists are often quite dissatisfied with the methods and results of other functionalists. It is therefore important to note both where he agrees and where he disagrees with current interpretations of social class and mobility.

First, about the agreement, which is, indeed, striking. If we take the well-known article on social stratification and its functions by Davis and Moore[12] as a representative specimen of more recent thinking on the subject, we find much of their argument offered by Sorokin some twenty years earlier. Inequality is a universal attribute of societies because it is a necessary attribute. Every organized group is stratified; otherwise it cannot survive. The permanent and invariable bases of occupational stratification are, first, the importance of an occupation for the survival of the group as a whole, and second, the degree of intelligence required in it.[13] And what he has to say about economic inequality can be interpreted in a similar way: Either we have a "flat" distribution of income and wealth

[11] Sorokin, *Society, Culture and Personality* (New York: Harper, 1947), pp. 338-39.

[12] K. Davis and W. E. Moore, "Some Principles of Stratification," *American Sociological Review,* X (1945), 242-49. There are hardly any references to other works in this article, and none to Sorokin's mobility theory.

[13] *Social and Cultural Mobility,* pp. 100-101.

and a poor society, or greater inequality and a more prosperous society.[14]

With social mobility, as contrasted to stratification, the case is not so simple. Under favorable circumstances individuals move up, remain on the same level, or move down on the social hierarchy, according to their talent, so that each one is able to do his work properly. If the "testing mechanism" fails, society as a whole suffers and may perish.[15] But a high rate of vertical mobility is followed by symptoms of *anomie,* and also by the "burning out" of the supply of intelligence and of leadership qualities by reason of the low fertility of the strata into which the talented are promoted.[16]

So far Sorokin may be open to the criticism he himself has directed against functional analysis, namely, that it is teleological rather than causal. But there are other elements in his theory, and in particular the idea of an equilibrium governed by laws, which are more tangibly causal. From time to time the distance between bottom and top becomes too great, he says, or too small, and the situation, therefore, is highly unstable. Eventually there is a readjustment; the degree and forms of social inequality are shifted back to the vaguely defined middle range of what is tolerable and more stable. The story about class relations, as told by Sorokin, is not always an edifying one, but there is a moral in it. The powerful and dominating groups will try to cheat and oppress the underdog; insincerity and cynicism are necessary qualities for many types of social climbing,[17] and compulsion or lies may be needed to keep power. One consolation is that a bit of brain is needed for all this, and even the underprivileged groups may therefore reap the fruits of able leadership. But more important, in this connection, is the idea of redress through reform or revolution. When the disproportion of privileges exceeds a certain limit, those who have been cheated and oppressed will revolt.[18]

Put another way, there is a minimum a social order must do for each one within it. There are basic human needs which those in control neglect at their peril. And men have to learn by painful experience that too much equality will also leave those needs unsatisfied. Human nature may be plastic, and many desires are the

---

[14] *Ibid.,* p. 59.
[16] *Ibid.,* p. 496.
[18] *Ibid.,* pp. 92-93, 113-14.

[15] *Ibid.,* p. 182.
[17] *Ibid.,* p. 309.

product of a social environment, but at the very least the requirements for physical survival put a limit to such variations, and quite
possibly some psychological needs can be added to those for food,
drink, and shelter as universal. If this is so, "constraining factors"
will act on institutions. A certain piece of the social structure
cannot be changed without the change affecting other parts, or
perhaps even the whole structure.

All this is a part of Sorokin's explanation of social class and
mobility. It is a kind of functionalism, no doubt, which might be
called the "individual variant" for simplicity's sake. It is all a little
speculative, and not a method that is likely to lead to clear and
indisputable results when applied to concrete situations. But
there appears to be little in it which is completely mystical or un-
intelligible, and the teleological element can be removed.

Unfortunately, this is not the whole story. There is also the
"social variant" of functionalism to which some passages in Sorokin's
work point, and which is very much at the forefront in contemporary theory. And with this variant, we are in far deeper trouble.
Here, a social institution, or some similar phenomenon, is explained
or understood by pointing to its contribution to the survival of the
group or society. The elimination of teleology is, here, a much
harder task, if possible at all. Not the least difficult is to say what
exactly is meant by the survival of a society, beyond the physical
survival of its members. If Aristotle is to be believed, as long as
there are human beings they will form some sort of society. And
society (or culture) is always dying and at the same time renewing
itself. This point has been forcibly put by Myrdal, who holds that
the concepts of function and equilibrium more often than not serve
as instruments of conservative teleology.[19] Regarding the concept
of mores, which he puts in the same category, he observes: "It
conceals what is most important in our society: the changes, the
conflicts, the absence of static equilibrium, the lability of all relations even when they are temporarily, though perhaps for decades,
held at standstill."

Now, functional analysis probably belongs to those topics which
should be discussed either at great length or not at all, and it might
therefore be just as well to leave it here. What has been said above

[19] G. Myrdal, *Value in Social Theory*, ed. P. Streeton (London: Routledge &
Kegan, Paul, 1958), pp. 79, 151.

is not likely to convert anyone from belief to disbelief in the method. There are, however, one or two allied questions that deserve a few remarks. One concerns the relation between the two variants of functional analysis here distinguished. They are, of course, often used side by side; it is not easy to say where one type ends and the other begins. But in Sorokin's case it may be asked how far the social variant can be harmonized with other elements in his theory. The more one stresses the sudden and violent death of a social order as a recurring event, caused by the inability of this order to satisfy human needs, the more doubt is cast upon social stratification as an integrating force.

Be this as it may, later sociologists are hardly in a position to attack Sorokin's approach as fundamentally unsound, since so much of their own speculation on stratification and mobility follows the same track. And the part of the theory which has been criticized here as particularly questionable, the so-called social variant of functionalism, is the part which seems to have the strongest appeal in current thinking.

While functional analysis, in a restricted sense of the term, may not impress everyone as a promising venture, there is also a wider sense in which we are all functionalists. It is our business as sociologists to study the interdependence between different parts of the social structure. It would be rash to assume that everything is related to everything else; but at least some important institutions or conditions of group life do not occur independently of each other. This is not necessarily the same thing as determining part-whole relations, and cannot be covered by the formula "contributions to the stability and survival of society." But it is an important task in itself and particularly so in the field of social stratification. For instance, what is the relation between the forms of social inequality and social mobility?

IV. The Quantitative Study of Mobility

It is the purely technical side of stratification and mobility research that has developed most rapidly since the publication of *Social Mobility*, and it is accordingly here that one would expect Sorokin to be least up to date. With vertical social mobility, the question is clearly not whether there is any, but how much there is; and whether it is higher in some countries than in others. Before sociologists can answer such questions they cannot test more ambitious theories.

More precisely, there are two problems involved in the measurement of social mobility. One is how to get reliable information about social status and changes of status for the right segments of the population, so that the results are accurate and can be generalized within known and not too narrow limits. The other problem is the selection of the appropriate formulas for the computation of an index of mobility, and the interpretation of such indices.

On the whole, more progress has been made with regard to the first problem than the second. Hence, the mobility data reported by Sorokin do not meet modern standards; they are often based on samples which are not representative of the general population or any major part of it. Criticisms on these points should, however, be tempered by two considerations. For one thing, Sorokin is perfectly aware that his results should be regarded as preliminary and are not to be trusted too much. He had to use what was available in the 1920's; a firmer basis could not be laid before the methods of statistical sampling and field work had been improved. And we still lack much of the information needed for a comparative and analytic study of mobility. Not until the 1950's did more reliable national mobility estimates appear. Even now we are far from sure of how to handle the errors caused by faulty data and how to get comparability between different studies.

As to the second problem, the choice of a statistical index of mobility, or several indices, the situation is a little more confused. Sorokin's procedure is a straightforward one; he uses simple percentage figures to determine mobility or recruitment of classes. That this index is not always suitable is quite clear; the values will depend on the numerical size of the different strata or classes. Unfortunately, it is not easy to find a remedy which meets with general approval by specialists in the field. In later years, another index of mobility (or immobility) has been widely used, namely, the departure of observed recruitment figures from those expected on the hypothesis of "perfect mobility," that is, statistical independence between the two attributes studied: for instance, the status of the father and that of the son. But this index has disadvantages, too, and some sociologists prefer to do much the same type of computations as Sorokin, and try to keep the status or occupational distributions as nearly identical as possible when they are studying mobility in different countries.[20]

This may seem like a purely statistical point, and not very important as such. But it illustrates a difficulty which is met quite frequently. Sociologists run into trouble with their mobility measures because too many such measures can be invented, and different indices may not support the same conclusion. Judged by the percentage of sons of laborers who become white-collar employees, the rate of mobility is perhaps increasing, but when a perfect-mobility index is computed, the rate may appear stationary, or even decreasing. There is little to be gained by appeal to the intuitive or common-sense notion of mobility, for this is too vague and fluctuating. It is rather the function of theory to guide empirical research in this matter by indicating what indices are relevant for what purposes. So far, sociologists have not solved this problem; even with the identical data, they may therefore arrive at different conclusions.

One aspect of this question should be particularly observed in connection with Sorokin's theory of mobility. There are principally two components of vertical social mobility. One is the "reshuffling" of people; there is a stream going up the ladder, and perhaps an equally big stream going down. This will be called the "distributive" component of mobility. But there is also a "demand and supply" component; it can happen that a great number of men coming from lower strata will find a place somewhere in the middle range because more jobs and positions in this middle range are created and have to be filled. In many societies, and certainly in ours, both components are needed to explain social mobility. A complete theory must therefore do justice to both, but mobility indices may be designed to isolate either component and assess its strength.

With Sorokin it is definitely the distributive component that is the center of attention. For this reason competition and conflict are favored themes in his analysis, and little use is made

[20] This is the case in S. M. Lipset and R. Bendix, *op cit.*, pp. 17-38. For an extensive discussion of this problem, see K. Svalastoga, *Prestige, Class and Mobility* (Copenhagen: Gyldendal, 1959), pp. 285-99.

of the idea of society moving as a whole along the income, power, or prestige dimensions. Sorokin's discussion of the influence of social change on mobility is characteristic; what he notices is, in main, the effects on the chances of a given group *relative* to other groups.[21]

By this we come back to an objection raised earlier, that he neglects the consequences of an expanding economy for the chances and aspirations of different social strata. Now, it may still be true that social status should be treated strictly as something relative, or at least that it can be so treated for some purposes. According to this view, if some middle-class occupations become much more frequent, then their value is also diminishing at the same rate. The sum of all mobility in society is zero, whether it is group or individual mobility; by definition, there is no such thing as society as a whole moving up or down. This view is not likely to contain the whole truth, but it may, nevertheless, be worth the effort to construct an index of mobility that corresponds to it. The subject is too technical to go into here, but it seems clear that this measure will have to be something more complex than the simple percentages describing the flow between classes or occupational categories.

As it is, little is to be gained by detailed comparisons between Sorokin's estimates of vertical mobility and more recent figures. But it may still be relevant to ask if modern sociologists agree with Sorokin in their general diagnosis and in the broad trends they find. To this question, it is hard to give a definite answer, for on the most important point, the change of mobility rates, no clear picture emerges in either case. We have seen that Sorokin's long-term perspective is one of fluctuations without a steady trend upwards or downwards. Within a limited period the rate may be rising or declining, and he thinks that mobility has been increasing in Western society in the period after the Industrial Revolution, though he professes no certainty on the point.[22]

After Sorokin sociologists have by no means been of one mind as to the changes in the rate of mobility. Not a few have held that mobility is diminishing and that class barriers, to that extent, are becoming more effective; but this, as well as the opposite belief,

[21] *Social and Cultural Mobility*, pp. 366-68.
[22] *Ibid.*, p. 424.

was long supported by inferences rather than by direct quantitative evidence.[23]

It would be too much to say that the mobility studies carried out in several countries in the 1950's have settled the issue once and for all. Modern sampling and interviewing methods may give a faithful picture of the present state of things, but how far they can be trusted to reveal past conditions is another matter. When the inquiry is to be extended beyond the nearest decades, the difficulties mount. What data there are tend to show that the mobility rate has been rather stable, neither generally increasing nor decreasing during this century.[24]

The situation is much the same when we come to the other main type of comparative mobility analysis, that between countries. In the light of modern studies such differences, if they exist at all, are much less impressive than might have been expected.[25] Here again, no high degree of precision can be claimed for the results; errors are hard to avoid and can both conceal real and create spurious differences. Most probably, the order of magnitude of the real variation between industrialized countries is no greater than that of the errors caused by insufficient information or faulty classification.[26] As the social and economic differences between countries increase, promising better contrasts, so mostly do errors of measurement.

The tentative conclusion reached above on the basis of later studies does not appear to be different from Sorokin's views. In his presentation of mobility data from various countries, the impression of similarity dominates, and he remarks specifically on the exaggerated belief in American mobility and European immobility.[27] On the point last mentioned, he was able to explode a common misconception almost amounting to a myth.

V. The Limits of Mobility

Though his main interest is social mobility, Sorokin uses a considerable part of his book to discuss stratification and its changes.

---

[23] G. Carlsson, *Social Mobility and Class Structure*, pp. 105-13.
[24] Cf. S. M. Lipset and R. Bendix, *op. cit.*, pp. 33-38.
[25] *Ibid.*, pp. 17-38. [26] Carlsson, *op. cit.*, pp. 114-20.
[27] *Social and Cultural Mobility*, pp. 414-57, 461 n.

This, of course, is almost inevitable; the two topics cannot be separated. Mobility and stratification are related by definition; in the extreme and perhaps never realized case of complete equality, there is no problem of mobility, and we would tend to regard a society with no mobility at all—an equally rare case—as highly stratified because of that fact. But between these improbable extremes there is the great middle range with some degree of inequality, and some, but no perfect, mobility. Here, the relation between the two things becomes an empirical and, therefore, more interesting question. How are changes in the degree of stratification related to changes in the rate of mobility?

Though Sorokin's work contains references to this question, and much that has a bearing on it, there is no detailed discussion of it. In both popular thinking and sociological analysis, it is usually taken for granted that there is a direct relation between the extent and frequency of mobility, on the one hand, and the degree of stratification, on the other. A high rate of mobility is accepted as a sign that class barriers generally are low, and that no great social distance separates different strata.

Sorokin repeatedly warns his readers not to equate mobility and equality; the high and possibly increasing rate of mobility in Western society should not lead us to the illusion that stratification is disappearing. Theoretically at least, a society can have a very intensive and general mobility, although it is highly stratified.[28]

At other times, however, he is more apt to stress the connection between the two. He points to the important effects of mobility on the psychological atmosphere of a society. For instance, mobility will weaken the bases for class solidarity and class antagonism. Because men frequently move from one stratum or class to another, there will be more communication between classes, more of common feelings, and less hostility.[29] It is, therefore, among those who have been stationary, neither climbed nor descended the ladder, that we shall expect a "class psychology," and even in Western society this is no small proportion.[30] Sorokin may be right in saying that modern Western society is, essentially—that is, when we look at the distribution of income, power, and prestige—no less stratified than many earlier societies. However, modern man certainly ap-

[28] *Ibid.*, pp. 137-38, 381.   [29] *Ibid.*, pp. 438-39.
[30] *Ibid.*

pears much less willing to emphasize social inequality in daily life. There is no generally accepted "social order" in the old sense. Class and status distinctions are covered by a kind of protective layer of hazy distinctions; there is also some reluctance to accept the idea of stratification and social inequality at all.[31] Perhaps this should be passed as mere "speech reactions" in Sorokin's terminology, or a product of wishful thinking. Yet a widely accepted mode of thinking, or shall we say a shared lack of perception, is a social reality in its own right, and it is not without its further consequences. Besides, both political democracy and the leveling of income differences show victories for the idea of equality that are more than symbolic.

The phrase, "protective layer," used above for the uncertainty about class and status relations, may need some clarification. What is being protected? In the first place, the feelings of those who are placed on the lower rungs of the status ladder, but thereby also the system of stratification itself. Because they no longer have unpleasant social facts rubbed into their faces, the underprivileged are less apt to question the existing order, or revolt against it. Ours is a system of social inequality which may be more durable because it is less harsh and more blurred in outline than previous systems.

Here vertical mobility comes into the picture again. Though a high rate of mobility may have the effect previously discussed of diminishing some of the gaps between classes, it may also tend to conserve the system and ultimately even create inequality. The myths and rationalizations defending a caste-like society—that it is ordained by God, or part of a natural and eternal order of things— have probably never entirely convinced those who lacked opportunity in this society, and their dissatisfaction was a constant threat against the system. As a contrast, take, instead, a society with a high rate of vertical mobility, where young people will rise according to their ability, unhampered by legal or financial barriers and helped by a school system which selects the gifted, irrespective of social origin, for an advanced education, and holds down the less gifted regardless of the status of their parents. Such a state of things has not been realized anywhere; but in many places it serves

[31] Cf. T. H. Marshall, "General Survey of Changes in Social Stratification in the Twentieth Century," *Transactions of the Third World Congress of Sociology* (London: International Sociological Association, 1956), III, 1-17.

as an ideal to be approached as nearly as possible. What would be the social and psychological consequences of its full attainment?

A number of interesting, if sometimes depressing, hypotheses or conjectures come to one's mind. Vertical mobility, although high according to the assumptions, would not necessarily be unlimited or "perfect" in the statistical sense, for intelligence presumably would be quite important in the selection for higher education, and intelligence is inherited to some extent. One would expect most of the mobility to be between generations rather than within one. That is to say, the fate of a young man or woman would be decided relatively early, with his or her entry into a certain educational program, and the subsequent career would only slightly modify the class-position reached. Relatively few would be able to by-pass the school system as an instrument of selection and promotion by moving from a low- to a high-status job as adults.

This society, utopian or nightmarish according to one's taste, would be highly stratified in several important respects. There would be marked differences in intelligence and some in cultural background between the classes; selective education would see to that. The groups at the bottom of the scale would no longer have the consolation that society distributes its rewards unfairly, for what can be fairer than giving everyone a chance to prove his native ability and go ahead as far as it permits him?

There is no need to pursue this line of thinking any further; other and more able writers have done so. It may well be that the assumptions have been unrealistic and the conclusions wrongly drawn. There are certainly counteracting forces at work, some of which have just been mentioned. It could be argued that the "function" of schools and education has been misunderstood; that it is (or should be) to provide future citizens with a cultural basis common to all segments of society, not to create differences or even serve as an instrument of social selection. But there is no doubt that a place must be found somewhere in the educational system for the selective function, and that schools, as Sorokin puts it, contribute to the "aristocratization of society."[32]

The only certain conclusion is the usual one, that these questions have to be gone into more carefully. What seems to be

---

[32] *Social and Cultural Mobility,* p. 190.

needed to guide our thinking and research is a kind of *disciplined speculation* where the most reasonable assumptions and the best data available are put in, and the consequences examined. The nature and working of the school system will require a much more detailed and technical examination than it received in Sorokin's hands; with more young people getting a higher education, it becomes more important to study this aspect of the mobility problem. It will also be necessary to take up such a difficult question as the relative importance of nature and nurture for variations in intelligence or other abilities, a question Sorokin did not neglect but one with which most of his successors are reluctant to grapple.

With these and many other tasks before us, the study of social mobility is likely to be broken up into a number of specialties, and it is much to be feared that the writings of the various experts will seem obscure and dull to a wider circle of readers. Worse still, the essential unity of subject may get lost in the process, so that no one is any longer able to see how the various pieces can be fitted together to form a meaningful picture. If the prospects are such, there is a constant need for thinkers as bold and independent as Sorokin, and with his ability to grasp an immense number of facts and get sense and order out of them.

Sorokin's Theories on Sex and Society

David R. Mace

I gladly respond to the invitation to discuss Professor Sorokin's sexual philosophy, because I have long admired him as a pioneer and a prophet. I propose in this discussion to confine myself exclusively to the thesis he has developed in *The American Sex Revolution*. I shall use the first person singular in making my comments; and, for convenience and I trust without appearing to be disrespectful, I shall refer to him simply as Sorokin, without title or other prefix.

Let me begin with a little of my own background. For some twenty-five years I have taken a keen interest in questions of sexual, marital, and family behavior, approaching the subject from the standpoints of sociology, of psychology, and of religion. One of my early discoveries in this field was the challenging hypothesis of J. D. Unwin's *Sex and Culture,* which deeply influenced my thinking. Some years after I had read this book I was working at Cambridge on a doctoral thesis on the origins of the Christian sex ethic, and I discovered to my surprise and delight that my supervisor, Professor Stanley Cook, had also guided Unwin in his researches. Thus I learned much of the man to whose earlier work Sorokin has paid so high a tribute. Unwin's untimely death had by that time terminated a career of great promise; but I was so eager to follow his thought as far as it had progressed that I obtained permission from his family to go through some of his unpublished writings. In 1942, in England, I wrote a small and unpretentious book entitled *Does Sex Morality Matter?* which was largely the result of Unwin's influence.

The appearance of *The American Sex Revolution* was therefore, for me, a most welcome event. I was delighted that a social philosopher of such outstanding distinction as Sorokin had allied himself, unequivocally and emphatically, with the general view that the pattern of sexual behavior which a culture adopts has a deep and decisive effect upon its upward or downward movement; and that he had further accepted the specific assertion of Unwin that the standard of "absolute monogamy" appeared, in the light of the testimony of human history, to create the best conditions for cultural expansion.

This thesis had previously been stated as a general conclusion worthy of attention. What Sorokin did was, first, to endorse it, and then to apply it fearlessly to the culture of the country of his adoption. This was a courageous step to take; for in the light of the data which he adduced, it compelled him to accept the role of a harbinger of doom. The book does, indeed, convey the atmosphere of grave concern and urgent warning that we find in the writings of some of the Old Testament prophets.

It will be clear, from these personal observations, that I am in very substantial agreement with the fundamental position which Sorokin adopted in this book. If my comments were merely laudatory, however, the purpose of this exchange, as I understand it, would be defeated. I therefore propose to address myself to some criticisms, comments, and questions that emerge from a careful rereading of the book.

I begin with criticisms, and I have three to make: the volume lacks documentation, it tends to weaken some of its arguments by overstating them, and it sometimes adopts a denunciatory attitude which fails to make reasonable allowance for the other side of the argument.

The first criticism can be quickly stated. The book is without references, bibliography, or index. The preface explains that this policy was adopted because the volume grew out of an article in the popular press, and was intended as non-technical for "the intelligent lay-reader." I consider that this was an unfortunate decision. The book contains many challenging and controversial statements. I believe the intelligent lay reader likes to know that facts presented to him can be verified if he wishes to investigate them further. Readers of this volume are expected to be able to understand quotations in Latin and German. Readers of that caliber expect, and deserve, references to the sources of statements used as the basis of arguments which they may naturally be inclined to challenge.

Secondly, I feel that from time to time Sorokin presses a convincing case too far. Let me offer some illustrations.

Sorokin frequently seeks to show how sexual anarchy and familial degeneration cause all manner of social ills. He blames them for "the endless conflicts of our time," which though strong language I am ready to accept. But in the next sentence he elaborates this in terms of "the present wars of everyone against everyone else."[1] This is going too far. We are not all at war with one another, and never have been. Even in this era of violence, most of us, for most of the time, have nurtured only peaceable sentiments toward the rest of mankind.

Elsewhere[2] Sorokin seeks to establish that mental disorders arise in periods of sexual anarchy. Quoting figures that indicate rising incidences of the former in the United States since 1880, he acknowledges that these increases "can in part be accounted for by the more adequate and accurate diagnosis of mental illness." However, on the succeeding page[3] he tries to establish a connection between "the spread of licentiousness and the multiplication of mental disorders" in Ancient Greece and Rome, in Ancient Egypt, and in the cultures of Babylonia and Assyria. If data on mental illness in the United States of America in the past eighty years must be treated with reserve (and I agree that they must) how could any corresponding information from these ancient civilizations be relied upon? Evidence of this kind seems to me to be so flimsy that it renders a disservice to the argument it is intended to support.

Again, in establishing a relationship between an "exceptionally high rate of mental disorders" and "promiscuity and excess in sexual behavior," Sorokin quotes as illustrations "Bohemian artists, musicians, and writers."[4] What he is attempting to do is to establish a causal relationship between persons of Bohemian propensities and licentious behavior, which is not easy to do. However, whether he achieves this or not, he does imply quite emphatically that the Bohemians *are* sexually loose in their behavior. Yet later, in support of a different thesis, namely that creative potential is not dependent on "sex diversions,"[5] he declares that "the sex adventures

---

[1] Pitirim A. Sorokin, *The American Sex Revolution*, p. 12.
[2] *Ibid.*, p. 66.   [3] *Ibid.*, p. 67.
[4] *Ibid.*, p. 68.   [5] *Ibid.*, p. 69.

of the Bohemians have been exaggerated. . . . Actually, there remains little more than myth concerning the excessive sexuality of the Bohemians."[6]

Now it is reasonable to suggest that there may be legitimate differences of opinion as to whether the Bohemians are or are not given to sexual excesses. What is not reasonable, however, is for the same writer to paint them black in support of one argument, and then later present them, duly whitewashed, in support of another!

These are illustrations of a tendency I detect in Sorokin to allow himself, under the influence of the enthusiasm generated in him by the cause he is espousing, to carry his argument further than prudence would dictate. It is, I believe, a very common human failing, from which we all suffer to some degree. Nevertheless, I believe we have the obligation, as scholars and scientific investigators, to correct each other, in all charity, when we find such tendencies manifesting themselves. A sound argument does not need such tenuous support.

Thirdly, I find myself disturbed by Sorokin's tendency to denounce. Up to a point, this is legitimate. It is a proper concomitant of crusading zeal, and I would not wish to see the arrows of good rhetoric blunted to the extent that they could not strike their target. Therefore I accept Sorokin's use, in describing sexual misdemeanors and their consequences, of such colorful words as "sham," "muck," "trash," "cancer," "sewers," and the like. I can chuckle over his description of the Freudian man as "a sort of libido-bag filled with all kinds of sex perversions and incestuous and deadly conflicts."[7]

However, while barbs are permissible, stings are not. In the passage just quoted, an earlier part of the same sentence refers to the Freudian ideologies as being "responsible for an utterly debased concept of the human being."[8]

This either means that the view of man which Freud held was itself utterly debased, or that others used his writings to elaborate such a view, and that Freud must be blamed for this. I believe that neither position is tenable. Sigmund Freud may have been mistaken in his conclusions; but he surely was not malicious

[6] *Ibid.*, p. 70.   [7] *Ibid.*, p. 163.
[8] *Ibid.*

in his intentions. He may have been a fool; but he was not a knave. Freud was exploring dark and mysterious territory, which any explorer in quest of the truth may do. The ultimate verdict of history may be that his findings were false—as Newton's particle theory of light proved to be false. But if so, this would not indict him, nor bring him personally under judgment, even if his hypothesis had regrettably been employed for evil purposes or with evil consequences.

I am not defending Freud's doctrines, which Sorokin is entitled to attack with the utmost vigor. I am, however, defending Freud himself, because I feel that the attack on his doctrines becomes an attack on himself. For example, in one passage Sorokin says: "In these fantastic yarns Freud utterly distorted the meaning of the Greek myths and the essence of human culture."[9] This conveys an impression of Freud deliberately doing something dishonest. The passage may be ambiguous, and could mean that Freud's theories led, without intention on his part, to misrepresentation. But a passage which could indict the integrity of another scholar should not be allowed to contain ambiguity. Disagreement—even strong disagreement—with each other is valid. Denunciation of each other is not.

A similar attack is launched on Kinsey and his associates. Sorokin says: "In recent works like Dr. Kinsey's volumes, no proof of the validity of his statistics is given. The authors did not subject their interviewees to thorough examination of any kind. . . ."[10]

These are sweeping statements—particularly when they are addressed to lay readers, who lack the resources to investigate their truth. What is meant by the validity of a statistic? The phrase is not easy to define precisely. Kinsey's figures were certainly not fictitious. They were what they purported to be—data descriptive of the sexual behavior of the persons interviewed. It is difficult to determine what kind of "proof" could have been supplied that was in fact withheld. Clearly, the names and addresses of the persons concerned could not have been given. The nature of the investigations was such that this would have constituted a breach of confidence. Beyond this information, I can think of nothing else of material significance that was in fact withheld.

Again, what kind of "thorough examination" should have been

_____

[9] *Ibid.*, p. 162.   [10] *Ibid.*, p. 57.

added to the investigation procedure? I myself happen to be one of those who submitted themselves for interview by Kinsey. For an hour I was asked questions about my sex life that went far beyond anything I have ever been asked before or since. The questions were asked in a detached, scientific manner that was entirely inoffensive. Afterwards, in a discussion lasting two hours, Kinsey convinced me that it would have been very difficult for me to misrepresent the facts and that if he had suspected me of doing so he would have rejected my return. I tried, unsuccessfully, to think of any data, essential to Kinsey's study, that he had not secured from me.

As I reread Sorokin's statement in the light of these facts, I feel again the sting of personal denunciation. In the same passage Sorokin declares of the Kinsey group: ". . . nor did they sample a sufficiently wide range of people to validate their conclusions."[11] This is a statement he is entirely justified in making. It is a legitimate criticism of the study. But I feel that the earlier statements constitute not criticism of the study, so much as denunciation of those who undertook it. They leave an impression that Kinsey was irresponsible, as the attack on Freud leaves the impression that he was malicious.

The same denunciatory note is encountered in Sorokin's analysis of the family disintegration of our era. He speaks of "the growing inability of married couples to adjust to one another"[12] as the cause of "an ever greater difficulty in mutual adaptation of the members of all other social groups." With this reasoning I have no quarrel. I am sure he is right. But in his analysis of the causes of their troubles in marital adjustment, Sorokin seems to censure the couples themselves. He speaks of "the higher standard of living demanded by today's Americans, especially the women," the "inflated egoism that is incapable of bearing the shortcomings of the other partner," the "lack of genuine all-giving and all-forgiving love."[13]

What this conveys to my mind is that the married couples of today are responsible for creating their own troubles because they demand luxuries, lack forbearance, and are not loving enough. Since the emphasis here is on "today's Americans," the implication seems to be that yesterday's Americans, had they lived today,

---

[11] *Ibid.*
[13] *Ibid.*   [12] *Ibid.*, p. 10.

would have done better. In short, today's Americans are being compared unfavorably with yesterday's, and denounced because they are found wanting. This is how I interpret references to "a progressive decline of 'parental instinct,' or more exactly, of parental attachment, love, and care for offspring";[14] "this withering of the strongest form of inter-human sympathy and care";[15] and Sorokin's conclusion that, of the causes for marital maladjustment he himself cites, "inflated egoism" is the one most likely to explain the facts.[16]

I doubt whether Sorokin, if pressed on the point, would contend that the Americans of yesterday, if they had happened to live today, would have acted very differently from the members of the present generation. As I see it, the family disturbances of our time are not due to excessive egoism or unwillingness to be loving, but to the fact that under the stresses and strains of a vast cultural transition men and women find the management of family relationships far more difficult than was the case in the recent past. The traditional family institution has taken a heavy beating as a result of such influences as greatly increased social mobility, the social and economic emancipation of women, the chaos created by two world wars, the prevailing sense of insecurity, and many other factors which are listed in every volume on family sociology. In my clinical experience in dealing with marital problems, I have not found much reason to judge the men and women concerned, but rather to pity them. Frequently I am amazed at the tenacity with which, amid constant discouragement, they continue to be unselfish and loving and forgiving.

Who, then, is to blame? I would find it hard to answer that question. But whether it can be accurately answered or not, I do not believe that any useful purpose is served by pointing an accusing finger at the married couples who are failing in their relationship to each other or in their relationship to their children.

In short, our scholarly analyses of social and cultural pathology should be as scrupulously careful in passing judgment as is any court of law. In politics and elsewhere, personal invective is accepted as part of the stock in trade of all interchange which expresses disagreement. Many distinguished scholars have not hesitated to use denunciation to make their points. I am nevertheless

[14] *Ibid.*, p. 11.   [15] *Ibid.*
[16] *Ibid.*, p. 10.

contending that this weapon does not belong in the armory of true scholarship; and insofar as I seem to detect a denunciatory note in some of Sorokin's passages, my admiration for him is somewhat diminished in consequence.

I now pass from criticism to comment. I wish to discuss, somewhat further than he does, some of the issues he has raised.

Sorokin's thesis is that irregularities of sexual behavior are personally and socially deleterious. In general, I am in agreement with him. The libertine, the profligate, the fornicator, the adulterer, the seducer: these are, in consequence of their sexual acts, disturbers and destroyers of the health and security of the body social. The interests of family and community alike are best served by adherence to the traditional standards of chastity and fidelity which have, in their highest periods of achievement, characterized the great human cultures.

What exactly is it, however, that happens when these standards of behavior are departed from? It is clear to me that there is a degradation of character and integrity, a lowering of the respect and sense of worth accorded to other persons as these become objects of personal gratification, rather than partners in the altruistic enterprise of building a family. It is equally clear that the attainment of such gratification involves, again and again, recourse to dishonesty and subterfuge, and the engendering of cupidity and jealousy and deadly rivalry; and that such sentiments and practices, once accepted as part of the commerce of human relations, become poisonous sources of infection in the life of any human community.

Where I encounter some difficulty, however, is in trying to determine how this is related to the physical consequences of sexual acts. Most custodians of the traditional pattern of sexual behavior place considerable emphasis upon the concept of "excess"; and Sorokin follows the usual pattern in this respect. Referring to the Kinsey team he says: "In the light of today's medical knowledge, their claims, especially in regard to the supposed harmlessness of over-indulgence, are fallacious. The existing body of evidence points clearly to the fact that excessive sexual activity, particularly when it is illicit, has markedly deleterious effects."[17]

This is one of the points at which I find the lack of documentation particularly exasperating. Where is this body of medical evi-

[17] *Ibid.*, p. 57.

dence? I can only say that I have been unable to find it. I have discussed this matter with a number of medical sexologists, and ranged widely, though not very systematically, through the literature on the subject. The conclusion at which I have arrived is the opposite of that to which Sorokin's studies have led him.

Let me make myself quite clear. Sorokin talks of sexual overindulgence, but does not define what he means. What I have been given to understand by medical authorities is that the sexual apparatus, like most other bodily organs or groups of organs, has its own built-in safeguards against overuse that might result in damage. Repeated use of the sexual function, both in men and in women, simply leads to fatigue and a consequent cessation of operating faculty. This creates the necessity for rest, which soon leads to the complete recovery of functional capacity. As Dr. Clifford Allen, a distinguished British sexologist, once expressed it to me in a conversation: "Sexual capacity cannot be damaged through use."

Nor have I encountered reliable evidence that any other area of physical or emotional health suffers damage as a result of sexual functioning, as such, to the limit of capacity. Temporary fatigue, from which rest brings complete recovery, appears to be the only consequence. Of course, concomitant factors, such as the use of physical violence to excite sensation, or accompanying emotional conflict because what is done is erroneously *believed* to be harmful, may alter the reckoning. But that is not the question under discussion. What I am considering is whether or not physical damage can result from the exercise of the sexual function to the limit of capacity. I believe the answer to be that it cannot.

The way in which Sorokin phrases his statement leads me to suspect that he is himself confusing the issue at this point. The clause "particularly when it is illicit" is, I think, significant. What difference can there be, physically, between licit and illicit sexual functioning? The body knows nothing of what is moral or immoral. It may of course be influenced, and quite profoundly, by the mind. But to the body as such, all that matters is stimulus and response. It continues to respond to any stimulus that excites it sexually until its capacity to respond is exhausted, when it ceases to recognize further stimulus until it has recovered from its fatigue.

Whence, then, has the widespread belief come that "excessive" sexual activity is physically harmful? I think I can furnish the answer. Sorokin, in his continued discussion of this subject, goes on to say: "Each sexual act involves an expenditure of vital physiological forces. When this becomes too frequent, the organism as a whole begins to wither, and the profligate goes into physical decline."[18] This idea is very widely held. Yet I have never found reliable scientific evidence to support it.

I should like to press the matter further, and ask just what are these "vital physiological forces" that are expended in the sexual act? Answers I have received to this question always refer to the seminal fluid in the male. Indeed, I have never encountered the use of this kind of statement in reference to female sexual activity. Yet all libertines are not of the masculine sex.

The male seminal fluid features frequently in folklore, and has been the subject of many scientifically unexamined beliefs and attitudes. The view of most of the ancient cultures was that a seminal emission was in itself, or after admixture with the menstrual blood of the female, a potential child. Nothing was, of course, known of sperm and ovum, which belong to the era of the microscope.

It was quite natural that this mysterious fluid, the seed of new life, should become the object of awe and reverence. And it is logical enough that it should, in view of that association, have been endued with magical powers. Thought along these lines did not have to travel far to reach the point at which loss of this fluid, through irregular or excessive sexual activity, was regarded as weakening or dangerous to the man concerned. I have found such ideas widely current in Oriental culture,[19] where loss of seminal fluid is identified with loss of a man's strength and vitality. Gandhi accepted this view without question. Even in marriage, he declared that sexual intercourse for any purpose other than procreation was "criminal waste of precious energy." Speaking of the "vital fluid," he says: "A substance that is capable of producing such a wonderful being as man cannot but, when properly conserved, be transmitted into matchless energy and strength."[20]

There is both poetic beauty and religious reverence expressed

[18] *Ibid.*, p. 58.
[19] See David and Vera Mace, *Marriage: East and West* (Garden City, N. Y.: Doubleday, 1960), pp. 92-94.
[20] M. K. Gandhi, *Self-Restraint versus Self-Indulgence* (Ahmedabad: Navajivan Publishing House, 1947), p. 111.

in this idea. But I have been unable to find scientific evidence to support it. There are married couples who, year in and year out, enjoy sexual activity with a high degree of frequency—probably greater frequency than many a libertine finds possible—without apparent detriment to their health or their happiness. I would consider it both unjust and inaccurate to describe these married couples as "sex gluttons"—the phrase Sorokin uses to describe his libertines. They simply have hearty sexual appetites, and find both pleasure and enrichment in satisfying them. Perhaps they would be equally happy, or even more happy, if they practiced moderation. That, however, is not the point. The point is that, if Sorokin is right, they are damaging their physical health and shortening their lives. This I doubt. And because I doubt it, I believe that in defending sex morality we must be prepared to give up the argument that physical excess can, of itself, lead to bodily harm or deterioration.

This is not intended as a challenge to Sorokin's argument, well supported by incontrovertible data, that saints and ascetics are healthier and live longer than those who enjoy the fleshpots. It is an assertion that what determines the difference between the two groups is not their relatively low and high participation in sexual activity, but other concomitant factors that go with the ascetic and the libertine patterns of living. If Sorokin wishes to contest this assertion, he must adduce objective, scientific proof from medical authorities to support his position.

Now let me take up another question that disturbs me. While there is no doubt in my mind that transgressions against our traditional sex morality cause great harm to human society, I believe that harm also results from going to the other extreme. Sorokin makes only the most cursory references to this, and I think this can lead to a one-sided picture.

In his book Sorokin makes it quite clear that he is not arguing for complete sexual continence on a widespread scale. This, he says, would obviously lead to the extinction of the human race. Besides, he points out, the majority of men and women could not practice such restraint without "a rising tide of psychoneuroses and other mental diseases, severe physical illness, and depressive moods, tensions, and conflicts."[21] He therefore concludes that "universal

---

[21] *The American Sex Revolution*, p. 121.

continence cannot and should not be suggested for most people, but should be the rule only for the giants of spirituality and moral genius."[22]

This is eminently sound. But unfortunately it is not the whole picture. Sorokin is rightly concerned about current American society because, among its values, it gives a prominent place to what he calls "the glorification of Marilyn Monroe."[23] A swing toward asceticism would, for such a society, be a welcome move in the right direction. But we need to remember that a society can swing so far in the right direction that it begins to move in another wrong direction. It is not edifying for us to see many of our fellows glorifying Marilyn Monroe. But neither would we wish to see them glorifying Simon Stylites. Either pattern is unhealthy. And either pattern is possible.

In short, our difficult task is to steer a course between Scylla and Charybdis. To this fact, as far as I am aware, Sorokin makes no reference at all in the volume under discussion.

Human societies that practice strict chastity and fidelity do undoubtedly produce creative energy. But they often produce also some undesirable side effects. The austerities of the giants of spirituality and the "athletes of God" may do them personally nothing but good. But when these austerities become the models for men of lower spiritual stature or of less single-minded motivation, the results may be far from edifying. The behavior of many of the early Christian ascetics, the hermits and the spiritual exhibitionists and the desert fathers, furnishes choice material for acid comment in Gibbon's *Decline and Fall of the Roman Empire*. The fanatical zeal behind many religious persecutions can be traced to a vicious and punitive obsession resulting from world-denying austerity run riot. The cold and indifferent aloofness of the "unco guid," as Robert Burns knew in Scotland, the sadistic brutality of New England as portrayed in Nathaniel Hawthorne's *The Scarlet Letter*, the Puritan's pathological destruction of everything that symbolized beauty: these are but a few illustrations of the other side of the coin. A few days of living in such an atmosphere might soon make the benevolent indulgences of our easy-going amorality seem a much more comfortable climate.

[22] *Ibid.*
[23] *Ibid.*, p. 139.

There is more to be said on this topic. Unwin established the fact that sexually restrained cultures built up vast reserves of creative energy. But what did they do with this surging power? Without doubt, much that they did helped to further human progress. But one of the ways in which this happened was through mounting aggressiveness which impelled the societies concerned into conquest and colonization. "There occurred," Sorokin comments naïvely, "a vigorous expansion of these societies, accompanied by an astounding ability to defend themselves against their enemies."[24]

If these dynamic cultures had been content to defend themselves against their enemies, we might have little cause for complaint. But surely it is true that, throughout most of human history, these expansionist societies have been predatory societies, constantly harassing the weak and the peace-loving. The cultures that have practiced "absolute monogamy" have been mainly the patriarchal cultures; and it is they that have possessed the earth, often by ruthless conquest, driving the more easy-going, and morally looser, peoples to take refuge in relatively inaccessible mountains and islands. I have often wondered whether it was more than coincidence that the most rigidly patriarchal societies in Europe and Asia respectively—Germany and Japan—happened to be the aggressors who plunged mankind into World War II. I should be disposed to question whether Sorokin's contention that the morally decadent countries started our major wars can be substantiated. Would it not be more true to say that it was the morally strict expansionist societies that developed predatory impulses and fell upon the weak and decadent to despoil them?

What I am trying to say is that, sound as Sorokin's argument is, it presents only one side of a complex question. How are we to maintain a balance between the two extremes? Human history, so far, presents us with a melancholy record of constant oscillation from excessive ethical rigidity to excessive ethical laxity and back again—a constantly swinging pendulum that seemingly has been unable to settle at the dead center. Must our human cultures continue to pursue this erratic course, like a man riding a bicycle along the top of a narrow wall, and alternately falling off to one side and to the other? Is the whole structure of human society too

[24] *Ibid.*, p. 112.

unstable to attain, and then to maintain, any kind of healthy equilibrium?

These are questions which go far beyond the scope of this one book of Sorokin's. Yet they are questions which logically arise out of reflection upon the book's message.

I turn, finally, to two questions I wish to ask Sorokin. One is about the future of the Soviet Union; the other about the future of the United States.

Sorokin makes a number of references to Russian society—both pre- and post-Revolutionary—in his book. He says, ". . . an increase of sexual licentiousness occurred in the upper and to some extent the middle strata of Russian society before the Revolution of 1917,"[25] and suggests that this aided the final collapse of the aristocracy. He also refers to the "period of Sex anarchy" that followed the Revolution, adding that "roughly from 1918 to 1926, the institutions of marriage and the family were virtually destroyed within a large portion of the urban population, and greatly weakened throughout the whole Russian nation."[26] Later he refers again to this, saying that "during the first stage of the Revolution, its leaders deliberately attempted to destroy marriage and the family."[27]

However, what is not in doubt is that, during the forty-three years that have now elapsed, the Soviets have moved fairly steadily toward the establishment of a relatively strict standard of sexual behavior. Having recently spent a period of time in the Soviet Union with the express purpose of examining this situation, I would entirely concur in Sorokin's view that "Soviet Russia today has a more monogamic, stable, and Victorian family and marriage life than most of the Western countries."[28]

Indeed, my recent experiences in Russia were, again and again, reactivated in my mind as I read Sorokin's book. This was particularly true of the final chapter in which he outlines the cultural environment in which he considers young people should ideally live.

The control of sex impulses can be notably assisted by a continuous exposure of the youths to the noble patterns of total love among their parents and friends, and to the moving ethos of such creativity and love in the literature they read, in the grand music they hear, in the pictures,

[25] Ibid., pp. 101-2. [26] Ibid., p. 102.
[27] Ibid., p. 113. [28] Ibid., p. 115.

plays, movies, television they see, and in the total environment in which they live and act. Control of sex drive is also tangibly helped by the non-exposure of growing youths to all the conditioned and unconditioned sex stimuli of sex impulses in sham literature, in newspapers which colorfully describe sex scandals and crimes, in the "music" of crooners, jazzers, and rock 'n rollers, in sexy dancing and radio-movies-television plays, in sham-scientific books, lectures and discussions, in the debauched sex behavior of all sorts of people.[29]

If this be the setting likely to foster the goal of high cultural creativity, it appears to be more nearly achieved under the current Soviet neo-Puritanism than in most other Western countries I have visited. Throughout extensive travels in the Soviet Union, I found a complete absence of sexually stimulating material in newspapers, magazines, and books; on stage and screen; on radio and T.V. I found a strong and widespread insistence upon premarital chastity and marital fidelity, with many indications that these restraints are, in fact, generally accepted by the great majority of the people. I found an almost total absence of prostitution and evidence of a steadily falling divorce rate; a high regard for the seriousness of marriage and for the nobility of parenthood. In sum, I found in the Soviet Union something very like a practical demonstration of the precise principles and practices which Sorokin advocates as the necessary conditions of progress "from sex anarchy to the sane sex order."[30] Moreover, there were convincing indications that in the Soviet Union these principles and practices are steadily gaining ground; while in the Western lands generally the trends seem to be decisively in the opposite direction.

If Sorokin's thesis is correct, therefore, it would appear that the Soviet Union is, at present, in a phase of vigorous cultural expansion comparable to that which occurred in the powerful and influential societies which assumed a dominant influence during earlier eras of history. I should like to ask Sorokin, as a historian and social philosopher, to comment on this possibility and on its implications for the second half of the present century.

Finally, I should like to ask a somewhat similar question about the future of the United States.

One of the reviews of Sorokin's book, written in 1957, makes this comment: "The detailed discussion of what to do is perhaps inevitably inadequate, after the brilliant and overwhelming descrip-

[29] *Ibid.*, p. 160.   [30] *Ibid.*, p. 153, chapter title.

tion of the present situation."[31]   In short, in his application of Unwin's thesis to the United States of America, Sorokin has proved to be a superb diagnostician but a disappointing prognostician.

I agree. The prescription given for the patient's recovery is three-fold: ". . . first, the changes in the mind, heart and behavior of our men and women; second, the changes in various compartments of our culture; third, the modification of our basic institutions. All three types are equally necessary for a successful reconstruction of our sexual life and of the larger sociocultural order conditioned by it."[32]   When we examine what these proposals imply, it is as though the consulting physician instructed the anxious relatives to arrange for a completely new mental attitude in the patient, for the rehabilitation of several of his organs, and for some reconstruction of his anatomy. Having given these directions, the specialist bows and, with a sweep of his coat-tails, is gone.

What the relatives want to know is, "Doctor, will he recover?" To this unspoken question Sorokin gives no answer. It is this question, however, to which I should like to beg the favor of a reply. If, as I suspect, the verdict is going to be discouraging, I nevertheless want to know the truth.

Why do I suspect a discouraging verdict? Because I see little sign that what Sorokin considers to be necessary will be carried out. "The transformation discussed can be achieved . . . for an ever-increasing number of our fellow men and women, if they earnestly undertake their own transfiguration."[33]   This is evident. But do Americans today, in the area of their sexual behavior, show any sign of earnest zeal to undertake their own transfiguration?

What appears all too evident is that the present trends are being pursued with a reckless disregard for consequences. In recent years strong presumptive evidence has come to light, and has been widely publicized, linking cigarette smoking with lung cancer. Has this led to a reduction in cigarette smoking? Not at all. Indeed, I believe the consumption of cigarettes is now higher than ever.

Similarly, warnings go unheeded in the sexual sphere. The first two volumes of the Kinsey reports created a sensation, and became best-sellers. Why? Because they announced, with scientific

[31] *Family Living*, XVII, No. 4, 2.
[32] *The American Sex Revolution*, p. 153.
[33] *Ibid.*, p. 176.

objectivity that was taken for permissiveness and even encouragement, that sexual licentiousness was more widespread than had been commonly supposed. This intelligence was eagerly devoured, widely publicized, and avidly discussed. When the third volume of the Kinsey studies appeared, however, it was almost completely ignored. Indeed, many people are not yet aware that a third volume has appeared. Why? Because this volume contained disturbing evidence of the appalling slaughter of unborn children that has resulted from the increase in sexual freedom which the earlier volumes had announced. That, at least, is my interpretation of the otherwise inexplicable failure of the third report to arouse any significant public interest. The fact that nearly everyone is breaking the moral code is welcome news. The reminder that breaking the moral code leads to tragic consequences is news that no one wishes to hear.

What have been the trends in sexual behavior in the United States since Sorokin's volume first appeared in 1957? Illegitimacy has increased. Venereal disease has shown a disconcerting upturn, especially among early teen-agers. Pornographic literature has poured from the presses in mounting volume. "Frank" novels, "realistic" films, "daring" magazine articles, and provocative advertising have stepped up the barrage of sexual stimuli to which the inhabitants of this country are now almost incessantly subjected. It is only when one leaves the West for a time, to live on the other side of the Iron Curtain, and then returns, that one becomes vividly aware of the fetid atmosphere in which our citizens are continually living. All that Sorokin has described, now intensified, and more besides—this is the state of the Union, sexually speaking, five years after the grave warnings of "The American Sexual Revolution" were sounded.

Sorokin did not predict otherwise. "For a long time, however," he concedes, "there will be a large portion of human beings who cannot or will not abandon the region of the sexual sewers."[34] What he did not venture to suggest was that the crowds around the sewers would grow bigger than ever before, and that more and more sewers would be opened up for their morbid entertainment.

One of the hopeful aspects of the situation to which Sorokin

[34] *Ibid.*

draws attention is the operation of what he calls "the law of polarization"—a principle which he expounds in these terms:

When a society experiences some frustration or calamity or emergency, the bulk of its members, who in normal conditions are neither too saintly nor too sinful, tend to split and polarize, some becoming more religious, more moral and saintly, while the others become more irreligious, more cynical, sensual, and criminal. In this way the ethically mediocre majority of the normal times moves toward the opposite poles of religious and moral ennoblement and degradation.[35]

Sorokin claims that this process of polarization has taken place in the United States in the field of sex, marriage, and the family. He speaks of a section of the population which "has ennobled their sex-marriage-and-family life and elevated it to the level of the total love outlined above. The positively polarized men and women of our own country are now greatly concerned with these matters; and with a great responsibility they control their thoughts, words and deeds."[36]

I fail to recognize this picture in the United States at the present time; and unfortunately, Sorokin gives no clues to the identity of this group, except to concede that it is much smaller than the negatively polarized majority. Indeed, while I recognize the operation of this law of polarization, and can think of several instances of its operation, it does not seem applicable to the American sexual situation which Sorokin is discussing.

In the first place, I do not believe that the American people in general have the slightest idea that, touching its standards of sexual behavior, this country is in a condition that remotely resembles "frustration or calamity or emergency." It is hard to find any individual, or group of individuals, who have communicated the idea that they are "greatly concerned with these matters," and who with any persistence have made such a concern widely felt. Sorokin himself refers to the half-hearted or hypocritical way in which sexual licentiousness is challenged. He speaks of "spasmodic drives against 'vice' "[37] which have no real sustaining zeal behind them and come to naught; of pseudo-reformers whose public righteousness is belied by their private acquiescence in the system. In short, he laments the lack in our society of the kind of strong,

[35] *Ibid.*, p. 183.   [36] *Ibid.*, p. 184.
[37] *Ibid.*, p. 185.

courageous, ardent reformers who might be expected to arise in a true process of positive polarization.

I contend, therefore, that the polarization process of which Sorokin speaks has not, in fact, taken place. I suspect that it would take a reformer combining the qualities and zeal of Francis of Assisi and John Wesley to awaken the American people out of their present moral torpor and to bring about a changed climate in which "the ordinary citizen refuses to buy and read the contaminating publications, to attend erotic shows, plays, and movies, to patronize joints, to vote for libertine politicians, to listen to sexy music."[38] Can Sorokin really see the ordinary American citizen behaving like this in the foreseeable future?

It is on this improbable note that the book closes. "If a considerable and ever-increasing part of our women and men follow this path in their thoughts, words, and deeds, the infection discussed will rapidly diminish until its ugly scales, rashes, and sores disappear from the cultural and social world in which we live."[39] In other words, if the patient will proceed to do what he is manifestly incapable of doing, his recovery is assured.

I think it is very understandable that Sorokin should end his essay on a positive note. Every writer wishes to leave a good impression on his readers, to leave some hope in their hearts as he bids them farewell. The compassionate physician, having completed his examination, does not meet the anxious eyes of the patient and declare, "Your malady is mortal. The end is no more than a matter of time." A little subterfuge, a softening of the blow, some note of reassurance, however tentative, is in order, in addressing the patient.

But in the case conference, later, with the door closed and only the consulting physicians present, more candor may, and must, be employed. As men set apart to study human society, to read the signs of the times in the light of the testimony of history, to face the truth honestly and fearlessly, we are permitted no evasion. As I try, in that spirit, to grasp the significance of what Sorokin has to say in *The American Sex Revolution*, it is that American society, as judged by the present condition of its sexual life and by the likely future outcome of the trends now in evidence, has passed its zenith and is in a state of cultural decline. When I apply the same tests

[38] *Ibid.*
[39] *Ibid.*, p. 186.

to the Soviet Union, it gives every manifestation of being a society in the full tide of cultural growth and expansion.

The implications of this are as unpleasant to contemplate as they are difficult to evade. I see three possible positions that could be adopted. First, we might say that Sorokin's thesis is not true, or only partially true; that there are other factors which must be weighed on the other side, and which could tip the balance. Second, we could recognize that, despite the logic of Sorokin's argument, human culture is far too complex to be predictable, and that some unexpected factor (such as the collapse of the Soviet political system) will probably change the world picture. Third, we could acknowledge that it is probably true that a fundamental shift in the cultural orientation will bring Western supremacy to an end, and that we must face the inevitable like heroes.

It would interest me very much to have Sorokin's comments on these reflections which are prompted by a careful attempt to grasp the implications of his thesis on sex and society.

Sorokin's Psychological Theories[1]

Alexandre Vexliard

All the published works of Pitirim A. Sorokin are full of original ideas and profound psychological analyses. It is not easy, therefore, to select a limited number of specific concepts and ideas of his for assessment in this area. His psychological theories are expressed, not only in such specialized works as *The Ways and Power of Love,* but also in writings where the author shows himself to be essentially a sociologist, a historian, or a philosopher of history.

In the present chapter, before proceeding to a choice, we will limit ourselves to an analysis which is completely devoid of some points which seem to us particularly representative of Sorokin's psychological theories. This choice is rather arbitrary and we regret the necessity of having to sacrifice certain important ideas developed by Sorokin in this field. In addition to certain original investigations by Sorokin, who has founded the Research Center in Creative Altruism, we are grateful to him, also, for having elucidated numerous points in the history of psychology, as well as in various phases of its current development.

The present analysis will be divided into six parts: (I) A bird's-eye view of Sorokin's psychological theories; (II) the structure of personality, according to Sorokin;[2] (III) the influence of cultures upon the structuring of personality, mentality, and behavior; (IV) methods of study and transformation of personality; (V) criticisms of contemporary psychology; and (VI) responses to certain of these criticisms.[3]

[1] Translated from the French by Edwin H. Jones, Marion A. Greene, and Philip J. Allen.

[2] We will not repeat after the title of each paragraph "in Sorokin's sociological theory" or "according to Sorokin."

[3] To lighten this text, I shall avoid most transitional phrases and paragraphs, among the various sections and paragraphs. I beg the reader's indulgence for this.

I. A Bird's-Eye View of Sorokin's Psychological Theories

We will first present a fundamental difference between Sorokin's positive theories and his criticisms of psychology, as well as certain reflections on his "normative" or "moralizing" attitude.

A. Positive theories and criticisms of psychology. As a guide for the reader, it should be said that Sorokin's main points in psychology, the positive and constructive ones, are found in *The Ways and Power of Love*, while his criticisms of contemporary psychology are systematically presented in his *Fads and Foibles in Modern Sociology*, particularly in Chapters III, IV, and V. In my judgment, this work concerns psychology as much as it does sociology.

One will also find Sorokin's psychological theories in publications the titles themselves of which are significant: *Time Budgets of Human Behavior; Society, Culture and Personality; Altruistic Love: A Study of American Good Neighbors and Christian Saints; Exploration in Altruistic Love and Behavior: A Symposium; Forms and Techniques of Altruistic and Spiritual Growth: A Symposium;* and *The American Sex Revolution.* As I have stated, however, one finds important psychological ideas in all of Sorokin's works, even those devoted, in principle, to other themes, particularly *S.O.S.: The Meaning of Our Crisis* and, especially, in his major work, *Social and Cultural Dynamics.*[4] Let us examine one aspect of Sorokin's work in particular which merits close examination and analysis: the relation between Sorokin's positive investigations and his normative inclinations.

Sorokin's normative attitude is relatively absent from his major works, which are largely sociological and historical in character. On the other hand, it is very apparent in all his psychological works. As a sociologist, Sorokin observes and describes facts and events, demonstrating their relationships, their coherence or incoherence, and draws from them certain ideas and theories, sticking close to his observations. As a psychologist, however, especially when he handles techniques of transformation of the personality, for example, his normative and moralizing tendencies are evident.

[4] My quotations are taken from the revised and abridged one-volume edition, 1957.

Sorokin's research in this field clearly undertakes to discover the various methods that promise to increase in man the potential of altruism, creativity, and love. One may well object, here, that such preoccupations are foreign to science and the scientific spirit which, after all, is characterized by objectivity and impartiality, where observation and experimentation must remain indifferent to distinctions between good and evil.

We now find ourselves in a classical field of discussion about general ideas, which doesn't seem to have any place here. As in the case of Sorokin's psychological theories, the normative point of view appears here in an obvious fashion; and since the legitimacy of such a point of view can be argued, we should briefly examine this matter.

In reality, in spite of the unfavorable prejudice against normative tendencies that dominates the sciences in research, one will always find a background of practical preoccupations in the social sciences, as in the natural sciences. Without this motivation of practical considerations, it is improbable that the positive researches would have been undertaken. For example, is it purely fortuitous that psychologists, sociologists, and psychiatrists are becoming increasingly concerned with the problem of juvenile delinquency today?

Let us take another example which is seemingly separated from any normative preoccupation: Durkheim's ideas concerning the role of collective consciousness in the formation of concepts, abstractions, collective imperatives, and collective representations. Durkheim stoutly supported the idea of neutrality of the sciences. Indeed what could have been the normative substrata of these ideas? The fact is that, while showing the *collective* origin of general ideas and moral imperatives, which dominate the individual within the framework of society, Durkheim wished to prove equally the collective and therefore democratic character of the ideological forces which dominate the individual in the framework of society. If these forces do, in fact, proceed from the individual himself, it would then be just and proper that political power be claimed by everyone and be democratic, rather than *aristocratic* or *monarchic*. These ideas would then be injected into political discussions, as into theoretical, and would, in time, find their way into politics. Those who support monarchy and aristocracy in politics maintain, in effect, that all ideas that lead mankind forward have been produced exclusively by a few eminent persons who owed nothing to the "masses."[5]

Indeed, without normative motivations, Sorokin himself would not have sensed the need, nor even found the opportunity, to continue his research into the structure of personality, or into the techniques of its transformation. These prefatory notes may better prepare us to undertake to study Sorokin's psychological theories; so let us proceed to examine those concerning the structure of personality.

II. The Structure of Personality

As we have seen, Sorokin has undertaken research in psychology whose practical aim "is to find out the efficient ways of making persons more creative and altruistic." This is the reason why he has built up a theory "of the mental structure of human personality and of the energies generated in and operating through the human organism."[6] Without pretending to give an exhaustive definition of personality, he understands by this term, from the perspective of his investigations, "the total mentality plus conduct of the individual."[7]

Sorokin's personality theory is dominated by his historical and sociological views. For him there exists a relationship between the two variables: the character of the dominant culture and the characteristic conduct of persons living in its milieu.[8] This relationship, however, far from showing a one-to-one correspondence is, instead, quite variable. Some cultures show a closer relationship to mentalities of individuals than do others. Let us remember that Sorokin conceives three major types of culture which he calls sensate, ideational, and idealistic, as well as mixed cultures and non-inte-

---

[5] One might also compare normative preoccupations in the natural sciences, which are often overlooked. What is more "impartial" in appearance than astronomical research, concerning the origin of the position and movement of the stars? The great discoveries, here, have come by way of the development of maritime navigation. Hydrostatics began to develop at the moment when the great undertakings of cities in Italy gave rise to the problem of transporting water. In the nineteenth century the theoretical discoveries in thermodynamics were encouraged by the development of the steam engine. Examples of this kind are legion.

[6] *The Ways and Power of Love*, p. 84.

[7] *Social and Cultural Dynamics*, p. 608.

[8] *Ibid.*, p. 607.

grated cultures (pseudo-ideational, etc.)[9] corresponding to mentalities and, to a lesser degree, to the behavior of the individual, of a sensate type, ideational type, etc.

A. Sorokin's Typology. Sorokin criticizes contemporary theories which make personality merely a result of conflict between the conscious and unconscious, placing greater emphasis upon the unconscious. Sorokin himself distinguishes four levels of total personality, of mental life, and of behavior: (i) the biological unconscious; (ii) the biological conscious; (iii) the sociocultural conscious; and (iv) the supraconscious. In his theory of personality, Sorokin places emphasis upon the higher levels of mental structure, the supraconscious levels, in contrast to contemporary theories stressing the lower levels of unconscious energy. Let us examine these points.

i. *The biological unconscious* represents the inferior part, the animal, the instinctive, reflexological part of man's mental apparatus. It is this that contains within it the predisposition to different forms of excitation and inhibition of the human organism, as well as tendencies and activities having an automatic, instinctive character. These forces, which are qualitatively and quantitatively distributed unequally among individuals, determine basic differences, notably those between the sexes, age groups, and races. It is these that assure and protect animal life, without the participation of the ego or the "me." This total unconsciousness may be defined as "the undifferentiated total life energy of man's organism," or again, in terms of "*life* or *vital* force without any further differentiation and specification." The unconscious, thus defined, cannot be identified with the id of Freud. The latter, according to Sorokin, gives the id at least three definitions that are unilateral and, for the most part, incomplete.[10]

But above all, Sorokin does not admit, as do Freud and his disciples, that the higher psychic phenomena, the creative, conscious

[9] *Ibid.*, chaps. ii and iii, especially charts on pp. 37-39 and below p. 13 where the author distinguishes, besides the three chief types of culture, the mentalities peculiar to the following types of culture: Ascetic-Ideational; Active-Sensate; Active-Ideational; Passive-Sensate; Cynical-Sensate; Pseudo-Ideational.

[10] The criticisms of Freud and his school are scattered in the numerous works of Sorokin. On this particular point, see *The Ways and Power of Love*, pp. 85 ff.

and supraconscious, can be explained in terms of the sublimation of the lower, obscure, unconscious, instinctive forces. The man of genius is not necessarily a "neurotic"; the saint is not a "deviant"; sacrifice is not an expression of a masochistic tendency; and creative inspiration does not manifest the displacement of a complex. The enormous success of Freud's work cannot be explained, except within the framework of a materialistic, sensate civilization on its way to decay. Only in such a climate has this doctrine been able to emerge and prosper.

ii. *The biological conscious, or the bioconscious,* represents the second level of the human spirit, or of personality. At this level, the biological energy becomes conscious and controls bioconscious activities. Consciousness, here, concerns especially conflicts, tensions, obstacles, and difficulties of a biological nature: such as awareness of hunger or thirst, or concern with how "I must act as a man or as a woman," or with my being "too old or too young," and so on. With the bioconsciousness appear a series of *egos,* or biological roles: the sexual ego, nutritional ego, and others which, in their turn, can monopolize, for a time, the field of consciousness. Thus, in the course of a day and of a lifetime a succession of different egos dominates the individual.

As in the case of unconscious impulses, bioconscious energies are neither social nor antisocial by their very nature. But they can be found either in mutual harmony or in conflict among themselves. Moreover, these impulses can be satisfied in time through socially approved means, or, in certain conflicting cases leading to paths of antisocial actions, through socially disapproved means, or means disapproved by the sociocultural ego, the socioconscious.

iii. *The sociocultural conscious or socioconscious* comprises the third level above the bioconscious. The socioconscious is formed by way of interaction with others, by personal experiences in contact with others, by way of the collective life, its demands and recurrent testing. These collective and accumulated experiences are transmitted from individual to individual, from group to group, and from generation to generation. It is in this way that traditions, norms, moral values, philosophical and religious values, knowledge, artistic tastes, political attitudes, technological processes, institutional forms and, in a general way, sociocultural novelties are transmitted. As each individual belongs, simultaneously or successively, to a variety of sociocultural groups, some voluntary and others involuntary, he is assigned a variety of roles, activities, and egos, corresponding perceptibly in number and character to these various groups. Thus, in our societies, nearly all men possess one or more family egos (son, husband, father, etc.), a national, religious, or professional ego, which correspond to the diversity of roles in these different groups. Each of these egos is replete with its own values, its ideas, its volitions, and its feelings. Roles corresponding to these egos include, in their turn, definite forms consisting, for example, of attitudes which, at times, imply a particular language, a manner of being toward another person and, in certain cases, even special clothing. The composite of egos and sociocultural roles of an individual comprises a microcosm which reflects the social macrocosm in which the individual was born, was reared, lived, acted, and experienced the impact of his environment.

The harmony and integration of the different egos of an individual are usually achieved when the different groups to which he belongs are characterized by closely knit solidarity and co-operation. This harmony presupposes that the different groups suggest to their members similar goals to pursue, prescribe to them similar duties, and, in general, motivate them to think, feel, and act in similar ways. On the other hand, the different egos of the individual come into conflict when the groups in whose life he participates are more or less violently in conflict with each other. Such conflicts, for example, may appear among family, political, religious, and professional groups. Of course, there is an interaction and interdependence between the sociocultural macrocosm of society and the sociocultural part of the mentality of the individual. Every marked modification of the sociocultural universe is reflected in the structure of individual egos and, conversely, notable changes in ego structures among members of a group will have their impact upon the social groups of which they are a part.

One must emphasize, in short, that the unconscious and bioconscious structures of personality are influenced almost exclusively by biophysical factors. On the sociocultural level, the personality depends essentially upon the social and cultural universe in which it evolves.

iv. *The supraconscious level* represents the fourth and highest level of psychic activities, mental energies, and personality. It is the level of inspiration for spontaneity, originality, and creativity of genius. In the writings of all civilizations it is designated by numerous expressions, such as "the divine element in man," "the manifestation of divinity," "the sublime energy of Truth, Beauty, and Goodness," "creative genius."

Contemporary, positivistic psychology attempts to explain these superior forms of creativity as elaborations of and emanations from lower mental activity. In effect, it views these forms as "sublimation" of impulses whose origin is essentially instinctive. It is against such views that Sorokin battles vigorously. For him the supraconscious presents its own characteristic originality, irreducible to lower psychic functions and uniquely differentiated from them. With numerous examples to support him, he shows how the supraconscious manifests itself in most sublime creations and in most varied realms: mathematics, natural sciences, poetry, art, literature, technology, ethics, religion, philosophy, law, politics, economics, and, in general, in all realms of truth, beauty, and goodness, in which three forms of its manifestation it may be found to appear interchangeably.

The realm of the supraconscious is the object of the most profound and most original analyses of Sorokin.[11] It is on the level of the supraconscious that the great discoveries, fruitful intuitions, and the most important creations of the human spirit, which transcend the realms of sense and reason, are found. Sorokin produces a large number of witnesses, showing among other things: (i) the precocity of geniuses in numerous realms of spiritual creation; and (ii) the uncontrollable, spontaneous, instantaneous character of these immediate intuitions, independent of will and reason. In all these manifestations the subject feels himself led, inspired by a force outside himself: "One does not work, one listens; it is as if a stranger were speaking into one's ear," Alfred de Musset writes. Sorokin presents numerous pieces of evidence, not only from artists and poets, but also from mathematicians and scientists; not only from those of the West, but also from Muslim thinkers, from India and from China, all of whom express, in more or less picturesque terms, the same ideas concerning creative spontaneity. But even more,

[11] *Ways and Power of Love,* chap. vi, and *Fads and Foibles.*

the intuition of genius at the supraconscious level can manifest itself in scientific activity of individual scientists who, in everyday life, show themselves to be endowed with average or mediocre intelligence.

In the same way that the biological unconscious establishes a bond between man and the biophysical universe, so does the supraconscious, according to Sorokin, bind man to a cosmic supraconscious. But the types of personality are formed, largely, by the sociocultural environment in which the individuals evolve. Let us examine, therefore, the manner in which sociocultural forces exert their influence over the individual.

III. *Society and Personality*

In all his historico-sociological works, as well as in those devoted to psychological analyses, Sorokin insists on the reciprocal and ever-ongoing interaction between sociocultural systems, on the one hand, and the individual's mentality, personality, and behavior, on the other. For Sorokin, there is no existence of social phenomena, "of and by themselves" (as for the formal school of sociology); nor do social relations exist independently of mental phenomena. Likewise, human behavior cannot be separated from its social context. The realm of social relations must be studied as a phenomenon of fluctuations of mentality.[12]

It should be remembered that when Sorokin studies these interactions between mentalities of individuals and their sociocultural environment, he does so within a framework of his historico-sociological classification, which may be briefly recalled as: (A) Ideational culture (i. Ascetic ideationalism, ii. Active ideationalism); (B) Sensate culture (i. Active sensate, ii. Passive sensate, iii. Cynical sensate); (C) Mixed types of mentality and culture (i. Idealistic mixed type of integrated culture, ii. Pseudo-Ideational, mixed and non-integrated).[13]

These different types of culture, which Sorokin defines in a precise way, correspond perceptibly to different types of mentality in individuals. This does not mean, however, that the relation be-

[12] *Social and Cultural Dynamics* (1957), pp. 436-37.
[13] *Ibid.*, pp. 27-39 and, more generally, chaps. ii, iii, and xxxvi of this work.

tween the two variables—the dominant characteristics of the culture and the behavior of individuals living within it—is strictly unilinear and absolute. This relationship is more perceptible between culture and mentality than between culture and behavior. Although this relationship is not absolute, it exists, nevertheless. On the whole, one can say that the behavior, mentality, and personality of an individual living in an ideational society will be more ideational than will the behavior, mentality and personality of one living in a sensate society. In any case, the differences between these two bearers of different cultures will not be so great, perhaps, in behavior and personality, as in mentality. The latter includes, for Sorokin, ideas, opinions, convictions, beliefs, tastes, and scales of moral and aesthetic values.

There exist, then, forms of behavior and types of personality and mentality which correspond to the sociocultural idealistic, ideational, sensate, and mixed types (integrated or non-integrated), which are found with greater statistical frequency in their own types of culture. To support this view, Sorokin presents and analyzes a statistical table of historical characters who lived from the years 900 B.C to A.D. 1908, drawn from the *Encyclopaedia Britannica*, classifying them into three categories, ideational, sensate, and mixed, according to their overt behavior. Likewise, he examined and analyzed in the same statistical manner the characteristics of popes and of European monarchs.[14] Let us see, at this point, how Sorokin describes the types of mentality that correspond to his three types of culture.

A. *Ideational mentality.* Sorokin shows that the ideational mentality, which our materialistic, sensate civilization tends to consider exceptional, even abnormal, is actually widely scattered throughout history; it has dominated the lives of thousands of human beings. Indeed, this was the dominant mentality of civilizations in which such doctrines arose as Hinduism, Buddhism, Jainism, Taoism, Sufism, primitive Christianity, and even such sects, groups, or movements as Orphism, Gnosticism, Cynicism, and Stoicism. Sorokin distinguishes the ascetic-ideational mentality from the active-ideational mentality, and these from the idealistic and mixed types.

[14] *Social and Cultural Dynamics* (abridged), pp. 613, 616, 617, 619.

i. *Ascetic ideationalism.* Within the framework of this cultural form, ultimate reality is conceived as a spiritual one; the philosophy of being dominates that of becoming; needs are essentially spiritual; it is these that must be satisfied before others; and the way to succeed in life consists in as complete a mastery of the self as possible, especially mastery over material, sensate needs, and to be able to go as far as the complete modification, and even dissolution, of one's self, the social, psychological, and biological "me." The ideal goal to attain is entirely an internal one; the individual becomes detached as completely as possible from sensations and from contacts with the outer world and, with a nearly superhuman attitude of indifference, from all concerns with the outer world. Rejecting values that perish, he concerns himself only with imperishable, eternal values. The ideational mentality accepts only the truths of inner experience, those of divine inspiration, of mystic union, of revelation, of pure meditation, and of ecstacy. The supreme goal toward which one strives in all his actions is "union with the absolute," or some other expression indicating the same ideal. The periods of history dominated by these forms of mentality have been characterized by flights of religious, ethical, and theological thinking, on the one hand, and by a stagnation and even regression of the natural sciences and the study of material phenomena, on the other.

ii. *Active ideationalism.* On the cultural level, active ideationalism departs from the same premises as ascetic ideationalism, but it constitutes a deviation in the sense that it is an organized and institutionalized idealism, attracting to itself not merely select and limited numbers, but the masses, and for this reason it has a large number of followers. It tends not so much to master, nor to reduce, the number of material needs of individuals, as it does to transform the material world and, especially, the sociocultural world. It is oriented, then, toward a collective, psychological action in which the adept seek, not only to "save their own souls," but also to save those of other human beings. An entire organization, a hierarchy, an entire way of carrying on may arise today from the flight of a contemporary, spontaneous ascetic, grafting himself upon the social order. There develops, then, a whole system of rules, laws, rewards and punishments, promotions and demotions, which tend to reinforce the moral life of the community and those who seek to escape it. In such a conjuncture, "the salvation of one's own soul has at stake the salvation of other souls." The ideal of the transcendental life is filled more and more with temporal considerations of the empirical world, and this ideal is progressively stifled by the latter.

B. Sensate mentality and culture. Sensate mentality is familiar to us. The only reality for it is that presented by the senses. It does not admit of any suprasensible reality. Its philosophy is not that of being, but rather of becoming, of changing, of process, of evolution, of progress, of transformation, of movement, and of flux. Its goal is essentially physical and it seeks maximum satisfaction of material desires. The way of satisfying these desires is no longer that of inner transformation of human beings, but the transformation or exploitation of the external world. Sorokin distinguishes three subgroups of this mentality:

i. *Active sensate culture mentality.* This is a matter of an active "Epicureanism" which seeks to satisfy physical needs by the most efficient modification of the external environment, which uses for this purpose those physical, biological, and sociocultural techniques immediately available to it. There is a search for the maximum satisfaction of a great variety of material needs, for the control of sense reality, and for the development of the natural sciences and of techniques. Culture and individuals are dominated by relativism, hedonism, eudaemonism, utilitarianism, and the search for pleasures; while social prestige is based upon material wealth and the ethics of "enlightened selfishness."

ii. *Passive sensate culture mentality.* Passive "Epicureanism" is characterized by a parasitic exploitation of external reality. It is, therefore, neither an inner transformation of the ego, nor an efficient, constructive modification of the world external to the individual. The object, here, is maximum enjoyment of sensual pleasures. The frankest motto of this attitude, which knows numerous variations, is Horace's "carpe diem"; no real control is exercised over the self, or over the outer world. There is no integration at all, the attitude being both extroverted and introverted. There is no seeking for truth, except in that coming through the senses. As for moral values, only those of the senses count; and aesthetic values, which are merely sensual, veer toward the pathological.

iii. *Cynical sensate culture mentality.* Cynical "Epicureanism" is characterized by hypocrisy, of which Tartuffe is the prototype. Generally speaking, it is professed by rather limited groups; but it is very characteristic of certain cultures that encourage "courtesy," "flattery," and such other behavior as reflects "good breeding." Their goals are sensual, although they may hide these behind an idealistic mask. They are opportunistic and "follow the fashion." They exercise control only under the mask. They utilize the environment by a simple and merely external modification of the psychosocial traits of the individual who, in fact, does not change. Actually, the picture, here, is comparable to the preceding type.

C. Mixed types of mentality and culture. These are made up of various combinations of ideational and sensate cultures. Sorokin gives us two examples: the idealistic and the pseudo-ideational.

i. *Idealistic culture mentality.* This is the only type of mixed culture which is presented as logically and organically integrated. It represents a balanced combination made up of ideational and sensate elements, with a predominance of the former. Confucianism and certain periods of ancient Egypt provide us with historical examples. The culture-mentality of fifth-century-B.C. Greece and thirteenth-century-A.D. Europe are other examples of this type of mentality. Men with such a culture mentality endeavor to lead a "reasonable" existence, while they "render to God what belongs to God." They are good citizens of the "gentlemanly" type who are preoccupied with the needs of their bodies, without forgetting, in any case, the aspirations of the soul and its non-material values. In all areas, the individual seeks to maintain equanimity and balance between spiritual and material values. It should be understood that the appearance of this type of culture has been rare, and its duration short, but its influence has been relatively great.

ii. *Pseudo-ideational culture mentality.* This is a form of culture typically non-integrated, or a "subculture," to the extent that the term *culture* designates an integrated system. Here, the nature of reality is poorly defined, but it remains essentially sensate. Needs and goals are essentially physical, and the means of gratification imply no modification of oneself, neither by way of action upon the environment, nor by searching for pleasure, nor by hypocrisy. The individual resigns himself to undergo passively the privations imposed upon him from the outside, as much as he is physically able. The attitude is characterized by reduction of physical needs, as well as of spiritual needs, without involving the will, to the extent that the privations are imposed by external agents. It is a vague attitude, undifferentiated, passive, without controls and without choices in matters of ethics, art, and knowledge. Such, for example, has been the attitude of slaves living in particularly depressing conditions, of prisoners, and even of people oppressed by a tyrant. Under certain favorable conditions, men of this type easily glide toward a form of passive, active, or cynical "Epicureanism."

IV. Techniques of Transformation of Personality

Probably the most important and most original part of Sorokin's investigations in psychology comprise his studies of techniques that tend to transform personality and behavior, as well as individuals, groups, and societies. We have seen, above, that these studies were clearly undertaken within a normative perspective and that, in spite of certain traditions of the "scientific spirit," this point of view seems justified to us. To choose to sketch this area, particularly rich in the work of Sorokin, is uniquely difficult; for to summarize here, one risks deforming the thoughts of the author. It is not without apprehension, therefore, that I proceed to move into this area.

Leaning on his theory of the structure of personality, which I have briefly summarized above, Sorokin distinguishes: first, ways of transforming personality; and second, the techniques of transforming individuals and groups. Let us keep in mind, once again, that Sorokin has undertaken all of these analyses with a view to transforming personality in the direction of altruism and creativity. To a certain extent we shall make an abstraction of this normative point of view. However, to get a substantial view of this idea, we shall have to come back to it.

According to Sorokin, the transformation of man, in the sense of his becoming altruistic, can be achieved only through the maximum realization of his superior potentialities: supraconscious and conscious. Through mobilization of these superior energies, the individual succeeds in organizing, ordering, and controlling the inferior and unconscious forces and in using them, at the same time, as a means of vital and mental, as well as social, ennoblement. The transformation of the individual implies a triple action: (a) the reorganization of the different egos by placing them under the authority of a vigorous supraconscious and conscious, which are developed to the maximum; (b) the revision of all values and their subordination to the highest, creative values (love, truth, and beauty); (c) an affiliation of the individual with those groups which cultivate these positive values, and his break with those groups which appear egoistic and negative. This triple action must permit the elimination of the different egos and negative values in the individual consciousness, in the groups, and in the institutions of a given society.

What Sorokin means by the *ways* of transforming personality is, above all, an analysis of detailed biographies of individuals (such as well-known altruists, great and small), with a view to showing the correlation of their specific behavior with their standards of integration and creativity. To the degree that this correlation exists, one can deduce a method of individual and collective therapy for the formation of a "desirable" personality. As a result of such analyses, one will be able to study the psychological techniques, properly speaking, particularly those used by moral "geniuses," in their development of certain qualities.

A. The ways personality is formed.[15] Studying biographies and autobiographies of many altruists, Sorokin distinguishes five factors favorable to the specific development of their personality: (1) a biologically favorable heredity that is still designated by such terms as "creative grace," "spiritual grace," "genius," etc.; (2) a pressing need impelling one to a research, a new creation, or an invention or discovery, this need being capable of seizing an individual or whole

[15] We summarize in a few paragraphs here what is developed in detail in *The Ways and Power of Love*, a work of 552 pages, large format, of exceptional wealth and originality. Our exposition fails to give a skeleton of this work.

group; (3) the individual or group finding themselves at the cross-roads of different ideas, beliefs, and values, or in a stream that impels them toward new creations; (4) a certain freedom at social and cultural levels; and (5) a sort of "luck," for example, in the form of an event able to serve as a springboard for the development of the creative process.[16]

The essential process for the formation of a superior personality is that of self-identification with the supraconscious. The individual becomes progressively aware that his real *me* is neither his body, nor his unconscious, nor the bioconscious, nor the socioconscious, but rather the supraconscious, to which various names have been given: the Divine, the Absolute, the Soul of the World, the Spirit, Heaven, the Logos, Wisdom, Atman, or in a more personal way, God, Tao, Jen, Nirvana, Jehovah, Allah, Jesus, Osiris, etc., without mentioning other terms that figure in metaphysical abstractions ... (Supreme Essence, Eternal Fire, Nature, The Inexpressible), or psychological and ethical terms: genius, inspiration, voice of conscience, inner light, moral duty, categorical imperative, etc. Sorokin distinguishes three types of altruists, according to the formation of their personality. But what is said, here, about altruism and its formation, may be applied onto the majority of the important psychological and moral characteristics of individuals.

i. *"The early fortunate altruist,"* who shows himself to be such from the earliest years of his life. He owes this "fortune" to various factors, especially to his family environment. As examples of the latter, Sorokin cites a great number of Christian saints, Francis of Sales, John Woolman, Albert Schweitzer, and others.

ii. *The late-altruists,* whose life started within a framework of egos, values, and contradictory groups poorly integrated and dominated by egotistical and materialistic values. They are led, in the course of their lives, through some "precipitating" event, to modify their attitudes completely, to reconsider their identifications, and to reorganize their egos and their group affiliations. This comes about, generally, by way of inner crises of disintegration and reintegration, depressions, disillusionments, and hesitations, before they achieve identification with the supraconscious. Among the altruists

[16] *Society, Culture and Personality,* p. 540.

of this type Sorokin cites St. Paul, St. Augustine, St. Francis of Assisi, Buddha, Ignatius Loyola, Simone Weil, and others.

iii. *The "intermediate" type:* Here are those whose primary identifications are located between the two extreme types above, with variable influences, whether of a primitive environment, or of an ultimate existence. In this category may be found Gandhi, St. Theresa of Avila, St. Basile, and St. Theodosius.

While studying about thirty cases, Sorokin singles out, from the psychological point of view, those favorable conditions conducive to self-identification with the supraconscious in the cases of the three types of altruists he describes. He avoids less well-known factors, and doubtful or inadequate factors such as agape, divine grace, spiritual inheritance, and even geographic, somatic, or biological determinism. Among the factors he examined profoundly is the role of the family which, to him, seems to be the most efficient agent capable of developing a love for one's neighbor.[17] Of course, the family can act positively as well as negatively. In the latter case it is also possible for opposition to the family to end in a positive, altruistic identification. Other factors, such as the environment in general and good deeds of the past, may reinforce the action of the family.

Sorokin analyzes with great care the role of inner conflict within those who have been converted late, by pointing out the importance of the early stages that follow the "crisis," and that precipitate the transformation. An important role is played by the "rearrangement" of group affiliations. Among the processes of the transformation of the individual, the author describes: (*a*) the process of self-seclusion, in particular, such as that of hermits; (*b*) the solution of wandering pilgrims; (*c*) that of institutionalized groups that tend to educate individuals, such as convents and monasteries that observe, more or less strictly, rules of "brotherhoods"; he thus studies the psychological techniques of different religious orders, particularly those of St. Basile, St. Benedict, St. Francis, and St. Ignatius of Loyola; and (*d*) finally, he describes the possibility of leading a good life in the normal "world."

We have here been able merely to list, and these incompletely, the factors and process brought to light by Sorokin, which he

[17] *The Ways and Power of Love,* p. 197.

analyzes and illustrates with numerous facts while, at the same time, he points out the techniques that tend to make for the formation of the altruistic personality. The author then passes on to a study of the three unified systems of these techniques: *Yoga and its variants, the monastic system, and the system of altruistic education in secular communities or brotherhoods.*

B. The techniques for transformation of persons and groups. In order to create a method for effective transformation of individuals or groups, the prescription would have to be universal; the method must be adaptable to conditions under which human beings live; and such conditions are always complex. However, an avenue remains, namely, that of the three principles that may be adapted to particular conditions: (1) the self-identification of the individual with superior (altruistic) values; (2) a new hierarchization of egos and of values; and (3) a modification by way of group affiliations.

Sorokin lists twenty-six of these techniques, among which we shall cite: (1) the techniques intimately tied with the organism, whereby body movements and breathing regulation are utilized; (2) the use of conditioned reflexes; (3) the use of pressures of public opinion; (4) heroic examples; (5) use of unconscious forces by way of such techniques as socio-drama, psycho-drama and psychoanalysis; (6) the fine arts; (7) private and public prayer; (8) an examination of conscience; (9) private and public confession; (10) private and public vows; (11) meditation; and (12) the auxiliary techniques of silence, or repetition of short formulas, and of ecstasy, etc. Some of the twenty-six techniques which have been enumerated overlap in part, but each has its own unique importance.

After studying each of these techniques, and demonstrating their concrete character in different religions, sects, groups, and among individuals, Sorokin goes on to examine unified techniques, notably the Pantajali Yoga and other Yogas, as well as those in monastic systems and secular brotherhoods, particularly "the Society of Brothers." While we cannot describe in detail any of these techniques, which are altogether too often neglected by psychologists, we should at least mention a few points concerning monastic techniques, which may be closer to us.

In the first place, monastic life suggests a supreme *goal*: a union with God, the kingdom of God, the love of God. Entrance into such a society must evolve from a free decision which rejects certain values and leads the individual to dedicate himself to a life in the chosen society. The candidates for this life pass through a series of tests during a more or less lengthy novitiate. The candidate or novice must give evidence of humility and patience, he must endure insults without complaining, he must submit to strict discipline and obedience, and he must give up all wealth and personal possessions. He must give up all earthly ties (sometimes even his family and friends). The vows most often made are those of obedience (submitting to the will of a superior, "in the manner of a corpse," as the Jesuits demand), of poverty, of chastity and, finally, of humility. Around these virtues competition is established, which often carries numerous degrees: for example, twelve for humility, in the Order of St. Benedict. In all these areas concrete action is required, with extreme severity specified in great detail, particularly in the litanies, and in the "ladders" of the Order of St. Bernard. To facilitate the difficult attainment of these ends, one uses "supra-individual forces," those of the monastic community: individual and collective prayer, and work as a means of moral and spiritual education.

On the other hand, monastic life implies a continual "psycho-analysis," as well as an organized system of counsel and therapy for the soul. It is, primarily, a matter of the purification of souls by both private and public confession. It is a question of driving away the most intimate, evil desires, including those appearing in dreams (e.g., St. John Cassian's recommendations on dealing with sex dreams), by processes used to combat major vices and to avert self-immolating tendencies issuing from guilt over monastic misdeeds. The purification must be immediately undertaken by good deeds and prayers. The conscience is first examined and regulated in detail and afterwards acts of repentance and more or less solemn purification follow. Each monk chooses, or is given among his older peers, a spiritual father, a veritable "psychoanalyst," who is not only his confessor but also his spiritual guide. The rites of absolution and of communion have a psychological value which has not yet been sufficiently analyzed.

The value of these different techniques lies in the fact that they comprise a unified system capable of achieving a profound transformation in man. However, such systems can be adapted only to certain individuals and certain groups, a fact that explains the great number of orders and regulations in the same religion. These techniques show a profound understanding of the human psyche, and modern psychologists have only rediscovered similar devices. Some of these techniques, especially those concerned with the necessary, step-by-step *gradation* in education, seem to be little understood by today's practitioners. If such techniques appear, at first, too awesome and daring, they may be recast into more comprehensible and acceptable human terms, so that the great principles they embody may provide the inspiration and motivation to use them—something which would certainly be more difficult to do in the case of the Yoga system. For example, a system which is clearly an attenuation of the monastic system is that which is exercised by modern fraternities, particularly the "Free Brotherhoods."

Sorokin reproaches contemporary psychology, particularly, because of its lack of awareness of the profound knowledge of the human psyche which is revealed in the rules and regulations of the monastic life. Moreover, he attacks in a most telling manner the theoretical principles and practices of Freudian psychoanalysis on the one hand, and psychological testing methods on the other. Finally, he makes certain criticisms of the sciences of human behavior in general, criticisms which, for the most part, are valuable for the psychologist. Let us examine these four criticisms of Sorokin's, starting with the last one first.

V. Criticisms of Contemporary Psychology[18]

The criticisms that Sorokin hurls at modern psychology which, although often severe and sarcastic, are not lacking in humor, may be found scattered throughout his various works; but they are to be found set down in a most systematic manner in his *Fads and Foibles*

[18] Consult, among others, concerning these criticisms: *The Ways and Power of Love*, pp. 121, 383, 414-15, 420, 432, and *passim; The Crisis of Our Age*, pp. 93-94, 121, 244, 267, 312; *The American Sex Revolution, passim.*

in Modern Sociology and Related Sciences.[19]   In spite of its title, this work refers as much to psychology as it does to sociology, if not more so.   These criticisms may be grouped under three broad headings: (*A*) criticisms of the social sciences, including psychology; (*B*) methods of psychological testing; and (*C*) psychoanalysis and techniques derived from it.

We shall scarcely mention Sorokin's criticisms that refer to "The Wonderland of Social Atoms and Small Groups."[20]   As in the positive part of his works, Sorokin supports his thesis here with an enormous quantity of facts, quotations, and examples; for this reason, the comments here can give only a faint idea of it all.

A. **The criticism of the psycho-social sciences** which, at different points, is particularly aimed at psychology will be presented under six rubrics:

i. *Forgetfulness of the past,* which is a sort of amnesia, perhaps, causes psychologists, more than their colleagues in other disciplines, to be seized by "a giddiness of discovering."   Everything happens, so they think, as if their science had emerged from a void several decades ago at the very most.   They extend mutual congratulations to each other for what they have discovered, "for the first time in history," without suspecting that in the majority of areas they explore they have had at least some predecessors—some, very distant ones—and, in many cases, their "discoveries" concern facts which have been as well known and thoroughly studied in ancient times as in modern ones.   Thus, Sorokin cites fifteen authors, among the better known, for whom the unconscious could have been discovered "for the first time, by Freud."   Several examples of this type are given, drawn from various areas, such as anthropology, semantics, metalinguistics, and other studies that concern themselves with "basic personality," etc.   If this does not always show bad faith, it reveals at least a notorious lack of culture among contemporary "scientists."   In many of these discoveries, it is a matter that was known before; at other times only empty ideas which were known before are produced; and at still other times there is only an evidence of platitudes, set forth in a pretentious and pedantic language.

[19] In particular, chaps. iv, v, vi, x.   [20] *Ibid.,* chap. x.

ii. *The pseudo-scientific jargon* which is particularly flourishing in psychology merely continues the pretenses of originality. The lack of simple logic in "new discoveries" is apparently, then, concealed in "speech disorders." The common error in this jargon consists in the substitution of vague expressions for clear and intelligible terms, which vague expressions often acquire several definitions, equally inconsistent and obscure, under the pretext of scientific precision. Thus, one uses such terms as "adience" and "ambience" instead of "love" and "dislike," and "entropy" instead of "habit," etc.

iii. *Operationalism* is a philosophy adopted, for the most part, by the human sciences, particularly by psychology. Psychologists give "operational" definitions of "happiness in marriage," of "dynamic social forces," etc. Such a philosophy, already considered inadequate in the natural sciences from which they pretend to draw their inspiration, turns out clearly to be ridiculous upon being applied to the human sciences.

iv. *The quantophrenia* of utilizing pseudomathematical methods has produced a veritable "cult of numerology." Words are replaced by algebraic expressions, so to speak $(a, b, c, -x, y, z)$, and interhuman ties are represented by arithmetic signs $(+, -, \times, :, =)$, without the reader's knowing why the author has chosen such and such a sign instead of another. Such writers try to quantify matters that are given qualitatively through a process, which, clearly, is not legitimate. They buttress with statistics what, in fact, shows no resemblance to the facts studied. They establish correlations between facts which turn out to be unrelatable (congeries), etc. Sorokin is not at all reluctant to use mathematical and statistical methods in the human sciences, as his works abundantly show. But he insists that such methods be applied only in those areas where they are legitimately usable, "controllable," and not for procedures that turn out to resemble numerological "rites."

v. *The use of models borrowed from physics and from mechanics* has become also a kind of "grand cult." In mechanistic psychology, as in sociology, we use expressions such as "social distance," "social atom," "valence," "dimensions of social space," "cohesion" (for solidarity), "social entropy" (for political and economic freedom), social "mass," models borrowed from cybernetics, etc. All these forms of interpretation provide only very superficial analogies, which do nothing to increase our knowledge and which only needlessly obscure things.

vi. *The psychology of small groups and social atoms,* currently fashionable, is an object of especially vigorous attack by Sorokin. He criticizes the very notion of social atoms—borrowed from physics —in which the emotions simply play the role of forces of attraction and repulsion, without taking into account intellectual and volitional elements of human relations. The so-called small-groups studies, as he sees them, may deal with groups of two to six hundred members, who are wholly unaware that they constitute a group. In their works the "ideologists" of small groups do not seem to know what they are talking about, and they are totally unaware of their predecessors in this area. The complexity of the real problems, here, seems to combine *sancta simplicitas* with *sancta ignorantia.*

B. *Testomania and testocracy.* Under this very significant double rubric, Sorokin assails the psychological testing methods which, progressively, have been invading all areas of individual and social living. Thousands of tests have been devised and continue to appear daily. Sorokin classifies them into eighteen categories. The enormous influence acquired by these tests, he says, is due to the fact that we suppose that they are "scientific and infallible." But human nature, says Sorokin, is essentially changeable and unstable. He cites the cases of dozens of great men (Newton, Tolstoi, Vico, Aquinas, etc.) in areas in which they have revealed their genius, of whose studies the modern test makers have taken little note. He demonstrates the mechanics of the tests, and he shows the reasons for the insufficiency and inconsistency of the pseudo-mathematical methods of which they make use. Such criticisms are as valid for intelligence tests as they are for aptitude, personality, and projective tests.

Sorokin marshals technical arguments, showing methodological errors, and he emphasizes the fact that replies made to tests, or to questionnaires, may vary considerably with the same individual, according to the time and method of administering such tests, etc. In the same way he brings to light the errors of the statistical methods used, and he does this by citing psychological texts themselves. This type of test seems to him particularly disastrous, since it stifles potentialities and talents at the outset, by preventing their possible realization, and it damages society as a whole, since it permits poor social distribution of individuals into various social activities. Moreover, where such tests have a sound basis, Sorokin shows, particularly in the case of "projective tests," that they have already been used for centuries to test novices in convents, in the East as well as in the West.

C. *Psychoanalysis.* Freud and his disciples are the object of vigorous attacks by Sorokin. He is especially contemptuous of this school, because of its willingness to explain the superior, conscious, and supraconscious activities and creative genius of man as derived from his lowest, instinctive, "libidinal" drive, particularly the "sublimated" sexual instinct. We have noted above Sorokin's view concerning this matter: the superior creations of the mind cannot be explained in terms of inferior intellectual activities. It is even said (and Freud is not the only one saying this) that the sexual drive is closely related to creativity, not only in the artistic area, but also in all social activities.[21] With numerous examples to support him, Sorokin shows that, on the contrary, the creative activity of great artists has often dried up at the very time they succumbed to "their sexual unorthodoxy." In a general way, the idea which Freud derives from the unconscious is one that "makes out of it a grotesque fantasma, fallacious logically, wrong factually, ugly aesthetically, and demoralizing ethically."

VI. Answers to Certain Criticisms Made by Sorokin

We can only express regret and surprise that psychologists have not paid closer attention to those parts of Sorokin's works which deal positively with psychological matters. To his great credit, it must be said that he has given us an extremely penetrating analysis of the backgrounds of contemporary psychology. He has brought out into the open certain psychological methods and has provided us with a superior understanding of the

[21] *The American Sex Revolution*, pp. 69-70.

process whereby human beings are transformed.[22] It is truly re-grettable that all this wealth of psychological knowledge, sup-ported by centuries of experience, has not been more thoroughly investigated by psychologists. Sorokin, moreover, is the founder of the "Research Center in Creative Altruism," whose investigations and publications should be of primary interest to psychologists. In view of all this, as well as in view of what we have pointed out earlier, we are tremendously indebted to Pitirim A. Sorokin, who deserves our highest esteem.

At the same time, we cannot refrain from commenting upon the very severe criticisms that Sorokin makes of contemporary psychology. We can more or less agree with the essential point of his criticisms regarding certain matters: psychologists have, indeed, shown too much of a tendency to overlook the past and to glorify their own present "discoveries" in certain areas. Unfortunately, moreover, they are inclined to utilize useless neologisms; to mistake "concocted phrases" for "scientific discoveries"; to divert verbal ex-pressions from their usual clear meaning and to give them their own special meaning, thereby creating a pseudo-scientific jargon which does nothing but promote confusion in science where, already, there are enough other difficulties. As for operationalism itself, it can be considered a nebulous philosophic position, unadaptable to the conditions under which the psychologist works.

As for mathematical methods, their use is completely justifiable in psychology, especially where they may be adequately applied. But the invasion of mathematism, whereby pseudo-formulae re-place normal vocabulary, is a sore spot, indeed, which we should never cease to denounce. Psychology, in brief, has no need to look for its models in the physical sciences and in the mechanical area on the pretext that in these disciplines it may alight upon rigorous ideas worth emulating. Prediction, as Sorokin says, is not the only basic criterion of a science.

On the other hand, with regard to Sorokin's criticism of testing methods, certain of his positions seem to us somewhat extreme. In the first place, there is hardly a psychologist at the present time who claims that tests are "infallible." The results obtained from

[22] We should point out, however, that religious orders often turn to psychology to test and select their novices. We can believe that their traditional, as well as secular, methods are not always satisfactory.

tests administered to an individual are handled with infinite precautions. In practice, in any case, these results alone are not taken
as a basis for counseling, nor for a decision. Within the framework
of an examination, or of a psychological consultation, the tests do
not necessarily have a privileged place. They take place within
the setting where the subject, such as an amnesia victim, is interviewed (although the tests, perhaps, may guide the conversation).
Where young persons are concerned, parents or teachers will be
consulted, or sometimes a meeting (of parents, teachers, and children) is arranged. And from such a social investigation, scholarly
conclusions may be reached. The tests allow one either to confirm
what he already knows through material gathered elsewhere, or to
clarify certain ideas in the light of hitherto unforeseen possibilities
and correct them, usually in the subject's favor. A realistic orientation of the psychologist requires that he be aware of the tastes and
preferences of the individual, as well as tendencies and possibilities
for his self-realization. The test is only one of the objective instruments which permit precision in a number of cases where previously there was lack of precision and general chaos. Sorokin cites
a large number of geniuses whose achievements were unappreciated
by their contemporaries. But the testing method has not been devised for the selection of geniuses. The psychologist, more than
anyone else, knows only too well how "unstable and changeable"
a subject man is. He never makes a statement of greater or less
probable certainty, therefore, without taking infinite precautions.
Except when excessive, then, testing methods cannot be condemned
as "testomania" and "testocracy." On this point Sorokin should
certainly agree. Actually, these excesses do not come from psychology; they come from a public eager to have simple and definite
answers to vibrant, complex, and many-sided questions. It is such
a public that is responsible for the commercialization tendency in
psychology.

As for Sorokin's assessment of psychoanalysis, one may be justified in observing that Freud and his disciples have gone too far
in their attempt to explain the higher psychological levels of human
activity in terms of deviation, or in terms of sublimation of lower,
instinctive impulses; or to explain talent and genius in terms of
neurosis and psychosis, sado-masochistic tendencies, the Oedipus
complex, etc.

However, one must render unto Caesar what is Caesar's. For one thing, Freud's early works, as well as the works of his first disciples, show that such explanations were made in only exceptional cases. It was somewhat later that these explanations came to be applied more widely over the civilized world; for civilization, according to Freud, represses the most demanding biological needs of man. But beyond this, being a man of great learning, Freud himself fully acknowledged his indebtedness to predecessors; not only to Schopenhauer and E. von Hartmann, but also to authors of great myths and to famous authors of well-known tragedies (Sophocles and Shakespeare).

At the same time, Freud was well acquainted with the psychological role of religious rites and obligations. According to him, it is precisely because religious feeling has weakened that we have witnessed an epidemic of neuroses, and that the birth of psychoanalysis has become possible. His summary statement of this whole affair is a pure gem: "Formerly (in case of insurmountable difficulties) the individual took refuge in a monastery; today, he takes refuge in a neurosis." It remains true, nevertheless, that Freud and his disciples have pushed to excess the unsupportable propositions which, at the very most, can be found to be applicable to only a few sick individuals. The widespread dissemination of such a doctrine indeed does constitute an evil, which Sorokin denounces with force and not without humor.

Only a few more words will suffice to conclude this assessment. By presenting a "humanly" realistic gradation of mental structure and human personality, and by projecting into bold relief the psychological and moral role of creative love, Sorokin has given us a profound analysis of methods of investigation and transformation of human personality in religious groups, and he has demonstrated with precision and lucidity the complex mechanisms of interaction between the individual and the group. He has, in brief, given us a tremendous push forward through his great work emanating from the "Research Center in Creative Altruism."

By the novelty and originality of his views and by the great, exemplary power of his achievements, Sorokin's work is capable of bringing renewal and a vigorous forward thrust to the psychology of the future, which should become a human science, and no longer remain a simple appendix of biology, or a museum of monstrosities. Finally, he has provided us with an idea of the science of man and with a knowledge, in this area, which should permit us to act in a more brotherly fashion, in the highest human sense, and to become most adaptable in this world man has created.

Sorokin's Rural-Urban Principles

T. Lynn Smith

Professor P. A. Sorokin, more than any other man, has influenced the nature and content of the systematized body of knowledge that today is designated as rural sociology or the sociology of rural life. This will be readily apparent to anyone who will take the trouble to trace the development of this science in the United States; and it probably is even more true with respect to the scope, content, and method of rural sociology in other parts of the world. Such an achievement might well be a source of great satisfaction to a scholar who had devoted his entire life to the building of a scientific discipline, but it becomes all the more remarkable in view of the following facts. Although Sorokin, along with other noted sociologists such as William F. Ogburn, consistently used rural-urban comparisons as a fruitful way of securing meaningful understanding of social phenomena, for only three or four years of his long, productive career was the specific study of rural society his principal work; and probably never was rural sociological research included among the activities for which he was paid all or even a part of his salary. Furthermore, it is unlikely that the royalties he received from his now classic books in the field ever totaled more than a fraction of his own out-of-pocket expenses in connection with their production. His rewards were satisfaction with the successful personal execution of important tasks and that which comes to the great teacher who lives to see his own students, the students of his students, and even the third generation of his "intellectual descendants" constructively building upon the foundations he has laid.

I. The Setting: The University of Minnesota

Befriended by Professor E. C. Hayes of the University of Illinois and Professor E. A. Ross of the University of Wisconsin, Sorokin lectured briefly at these institutions following his arrival in the United States in November, 1923; and then, in 1924, he secured a position as professor of sociology at the University of Minnesota, where he remained until 1930, when he moved to Winchester, Massachusetts, and became chairman of Harvard University's new department of sociology. It was during these last four years at Minnesota and while he was carrying a full-time teaching load that Sorokin produced (in collaboration with Carle C. Zimmerman) the *Principles of Rural-Urban Sociology*[1] and (in collaboration with Zimmerman and Charles J. Galpin) the three-volume work *A Systematic Source Book in Rural Sociology*.[2] These are the now classic works which contain the systematic exposition of his principles of rural sociology. It also was during the last four years of his work at Minnesota and the early part of his career at Harvard that he stimulated so greatly and trained the small corps of highly selected graduate students which has had such a large hand in developing the scientific study of rural society.

According to E. C. Hayes, Sorokin's principal motive in coming to the United States was "to study the cultural and economic organizations of farmers" in this country during the years following his banishment from Soviet Russia and while he and other refugees were "preparing to take part in the reorganization of Russia when it is possible for them to return."[3] Even so, during his first four years in the United States the tasks connected with a full-time teaching load and the writing and publishing of *Leaves from a Russian Diary*,[4] *Sociology of Revolution*,[5] *Social Mobility*,[6] and *Contemporary Sociological Theories*[7] must have left him comparatively little time for concentrated study of rural society in the Midwest and other parts of the United States.

[1] New York: Henry Holt and Company, 1929.
[2] Minneapolis: University of Minnesota Press, 1930, 1931, and 1932.
[3] "Editor's Introduction" to Pitirim A. Sorokin, *The Sociology of Revolution* (Philadelphia and London; J. B. Lippincott Company, 1925), pp. vii-viii.
[4] New York: E. P. Dutton & Company, 1924.   [5] *Op. cit.*
[6] New York: Harper & Brothers, 1927.
[7] New York: Harper & Brothers, 1928.

While *Contemporary Sociological Theories* was in press (in 1927), Sorokin, collaborating with Carle C. Zimmerman, then assistant professor of sociology and rural sociology at the University of Minnesota, threw himself enthusiastically into the preparation of the manuscript of a systematic treatment of the field of rural sociology. When the present writer arrived in Minneapolis, in July, 1928, to begin graduate work in sociology, that manuscript was complete. However, "it was so long that it could not be published in one volume."[8] Fortunately for the development of rural sociology, though, at about this time Dr. Charles J. Galpin, then Chief of the Division of Population and Rural Life in the U. S. Department of Agriculture, sought to enlist the co-operation of Sorokin and Zimmerman in the preparation of a comprehensive three-volume source book for rural sociology. The expression "fortunately" is used because from daily personal contacts in the fall of 1928, the present writer knows that during the impasse which developed when the manuscript proved to be too voluminous, and the making of the arrangements for the *Source Book* taxing, Sorokin already was well along with the preparation of a volume on *The History of Social Thought*. As it was, though, Sorokin's primary attention was not diverted from a study of the sociology of rural life late in 1928, but continued through 1929 and 1930, or until the organization of the department of sociology at Harvard University and the beginning of work on *Social and Cultural Dynamics*[9] monopolized his time and attention.

II. Objectives

In the preface to their *Principles of Rural-Urban Sociology* Sorokin and Zimmerman stated specifically the five ways in which they sought to make their book different from existing texts in rural sociology, and since to a considerable degree these endeavors served to orient the future development of the field, they deserve specific mention. They are as follows:

First, it tries to be a rural *sociology* and not a mere collection of various data pertaining to aspects of rural life and rural communities. . . .

[8] Sorokin and Zimmerman, *op. cit.*, p. v.
[9] Four Volumes. New York: American Book Company, 1937-1941.

It is certain that we use such data extensively, but not, so to speak, for their own sake: they are taken and used in intercorrelations with other social phenomena and serve only as "bricks" for the construction of more complex, general and sociological formulae of functional relationships and interrelationships.

Second, the book does not try to "preach" and does not bother itself with any evaluations of what is good and bad in rural life. . . . Likewise, the book does not stress "the sympathetic attitude" of the authors regarding rural life. . . .

Third, the courses in rural sociology in this country (in other countries such courses hardly exist) have been dealing almost exclusively with American data and have not touched the data of other countries. This present book tries to base its conclusions on the existing data of almost all countries. . . .

Fourth, several problems which have already been well studied and in which the conclusions reached are relatively certain, are only briefly summarized. . . .

Fifth, for all those who like "all embracing, clearly cut, and sweeping generalizations," easy to remember and thrilling in their universality, simplicity, and "rectilinearity" this book may appear somewhat disappointing. . . . we are convinced that a scientific text is not a "detective story"; and that a student of any science must take some pains to learn it. . . . We are not writing a "best seller" but a scientific study.

Later, in the preface to *A Systematic Source Book in Rural Sociology*, Sorokin and Zimmerman, along with Galpin, were equally explicit in stating their determination to help make the discipline of rural sociology more comprehensive, more scientific, and less provincial. Note especially the following statements from the preamble to that classic work:

The editors have been moved by the following considerations: Human society throughout its history—its origins, forms, activities, processes, growth, evolution—has been so largely under the pressure of agricultural and rural forces that up to the present sociology as a science of society has virtually been the sociology of rural life. A world view of the sociology of rural life is important for the development of the science. . . . There is need that the content of rural sociology . . . should contain facts of indubitably sociological character. There is need in the textual organization of the facts of rural sociology for a resolutely scientific methodology. In the training of American rural sociologists there is need for a broad acquaintance with the rural sociological thought and theory of Europe and Asia. And, finally, in this era of American teaching, research, and extension of rural sociological facts and theory and in this period of experimental agrarian legislation, a systematic source book world-wide in scope is timely.

Of course there still lingers today, at a time when mankind already is well within the portals of the atomic age, much of the provincialism that Sorokin and his asociates were trying to replace. In 1962, as in 1930 when Sorokin, Zimmerman and Galpin surveyed the scene, many of the "textbooks in rural sociology in America are still quite provincial, not even being developed on the geographic basis of the entire country." Even so, however, the charge that contemporary sociology and sociologists are provincial, an accusation that since 1950 has come with disconcerting frequency from men in the related social science fields, is not entirely justified; and certainly it is much less valid with respect to rural sociology and sociologists specializing in the sociology of rural life than it is with reference to sociology and sociologists as a whole. In this connection, therefore, it is important to recall that more than any other man, Sorokin deliberately sought to enlarge the mental horizons of those working in the field and to promote the comparative studies of rural societies by those engaged professionally as rural sociologists.

III. Sorokin's Share in the Work

Because the two works in which Sorokin's principles of rural sociology appear both were prepared in collaboration with other authors, it is essential to identify specifically the portions of those books for which he personally was responsible. Fortunately this is easily done, because in the preface to the *Principles of Rural-Urban Sociology* and also in that to *A Systematic Source Book in Rural Sociology* the portions for which each author was responsible have been clearly identified. Thus of the twenty-seven chapters in the *Principles* the sixteen chapters written by Sorokin are as follows:

    I. Definition of Rural and Urban Sociology
   II. Definition of Rural and Urban Worlds
  IV. Bodily Differences between the Urban and Rural Populations
   V. Comparative Health of Rural and Urban Populations
  VI. Predominant Diseases of the City and the Country
 VII. Rural-Urban Suicides
VIII. Comparative Longevity, and Mortality of the Rural and Urban Populations

XIII. The Experience Worlds and Psychological Processes of the Rural-Urban Populations
XV. The Rural and Urban Family
XVI. Comparative Criminality, Immorality, and Intemperance
XVII. The Role of the City and the Country in Innovation, Disruption, and Preservation of the National Culture
XVIII. Rural-Urban Religious Culture, Beliefs, and Convictions
XX. Agricultural Classes and Political Regimes
XXI. Rural-Urban Arts and Esthetic Culture
XXII. Farmer-Peasant Attitudes of Individualism and Collectivism
XXVII. Retrospect, Present Situation, and Prospect.

In addition, he and Zimmerman jointly were responsible for three other chapters, namely:

III. The Status of the Farmer-Peasant Class Among Other Social Classes
XIV. Sources and Theories Concerning the Psycho-Social Traits of Farmers and Peasants
XIX. Political Culture, Attitudes, and Behavior of Rural Groups.

Even greater was Sorokin's part of the responsibility for the contents of the *Source Book,* as is stated explicitly in the following extract from its preface:

> It should be stated also that most of the introductions, selections and systematization of the material and, in general, the greater part of the work of the *Source Book* were done by Professor Pitirim Sorokin.

Elsewhere the present writer has attempted to sketch the nature of the original contributions made by Sorokin in the preparation of the *Source Book,* and in the interest of brevity these comments are reproduced here:

> [*The Source Book*] is in no sense a "scissors and paste job." It is true that liberal extracts are presented from the writings of great thinkers in all countries and all ages along with substantial parts from the contributions of twentieth-century sociologists. But most of these were translated into English and then they were presented only after the setting of each chapter was carefully prepared by original expositions giving the basic frame of reference, classifications, and discussion of variations in time and space. Nor are the topics limited to those treated earlier in the *Principles.* In Volume I, for example, Chapter I, with the introduction and the materials from ancient Oriental, Greek and Roman sources, went over ground previously untouched in rural sociological literature; and the same is true of Chapter II, devoted to a "History of rural sociology: four-

teenth to nineteenth centuries." Here, thanks to Sorokin's depth of knowledge of social thinkers of all ages, the ideas and theories of the great thinkers from Ibn Khaldun, to John Graunt, and to Alexander Hamilton came into the arena of rural sociological theory. Furthermore, except for Chapter III, which is largely a repetition of Chapter II of the *Principles*, all of Volume I is occupied with what then were new and challenging aspects of the subject matter of rural sociology. Chapter V, "The ecology of the rural habitat," and Chapter VI, "Differentiation of the rural population into cumulative communities and functional associations," opened up new and challenging vistas to the men then working in the field. Chapters VII and VIII, devoted to social stratification and social mobility, respectively, did much to make these highly important subjects integral parts of rural sociology, some years before they gained comparable status in general sociology or in urban sociology.

In Volume II, also, the portion of the work devoted to "Rural social organization in its institutional, functional, and cultural aspects," the chapters dealing with the family, education, social control, religious organization and culture, and aesthetic and recreational organization helped greatly to advance these aspects of the general field. Volume III closely follows the subject matter and outline of the *Principles*, although even here the additional wealth of material contributed greatly to understanding of differences between the physical traits and health of rural and urban populations, vital processes, intelligence and migration.

In its entirety, a careful study of the book is still a *must* for all those wishing to achieve professional competency in the field of rural sociology.[10]

IV. Significance for the Development of Rural Sociology

In the work just cited the present writer has attempted to assess the importance of the publication of *Principles of Rural-Urban Sociology* and *A Systematic Source Book in Rural Sociology* in the development of rural sociology as a scientific discipline.[11] There the work of building the new discipline was divided into four epochs or stages, as follows: the period of genesis, to 1920; a decade of progress, 1920-29; the period of maturation, 1930-45; and developments and trends, 1945-56. In this schema Sorokin's contribution to the development of the principles of rural sociology came as the

[10] T. Lynn Smith, "Rural Sociology: A Trend Report and Bibliography," *Current Sociology*, VI, No. 1 (1957), 42-43.

[11] *Ibid.*, pp. 1-75. See also, T. Lynn Smith, "La Sociologia Rural en los Estados Unidos de America y en Canada," *Revista Mexicana de Sociologia*, XX, No. 3 (1958), 817-42.

culmination to the work during the second period and a major stimulus to that in the third. The following paragraphs are the ones in which an attempt was made to place these fundamental contributions in perspective:

Finally, the decade 1920-29 was the one in which efforts at synthesis got underway in earnest. This difficult work began on a small scale with the preparation of Gillette's new book on *Rural Sociology*. It was advanced considerably when in 1926 Taylor published the first edition of his *Rural Sociology*, and with the appearance of the first edition of Sims' *Elements of Rural Sociology* in 1928. The culmination came in 1929 with the publication of *The Principles of Rural-Urban Sociology* by Sorokin and Zimmerman, followed within a few years by the appearance of the three volumes of the *Systematic Source Book in Rural Sociology* by Sorokin, Zimmerman, and Galpin. The work of preparing these books brought to bear upon the field of rural sociology, in a long concerted effort, the ingenuity of Sorokin and his vast knowledge of European society and sociology, and Zimmerman's genius, determination, drive and mastery of developments on the American scene. Rarely have such extraordinarily able representatives of two such diverse currents of thought been brought together to work intensively side by side for a period of five or six years. The result was the finest synthesis of the field of rural sociology achieved to date.

The years 1930 to about 1945 may be characterized as the ones in which the discipline of rural sociology came of age. During the first few years of this period, the difficult work of synthesis was the outstanding feature, the appearance of the *Systematic Source Book in Rural Sociology* being the chief event.[12]

These extracts, along with a few brief excerpts from the annotations in the bibliography, also adequately express the present writer's evaluation of the importance of Sorokin's contributions to rural sociology. Thus the annotation commenting upon the *Principles* opens with the following sentence: "This volume constitutes one of the principal landmarks in the development of rural sociology"; and that pertaining to the *Source Book* indicates that along with the work just mentioned, "this three-volume set represents the greatest work of synthesis as yet achieved in the field of rural sociology."[13]

After the appearance of Sorokin's *Contemporary Sociological Theories* in 1928 it was fairly easy for sociologists in the United States to gain a passing acquaintance with the works and ideas of

[12] Smith, "Rural Sociology," p. 12.
[13] *Ibid.*, pp. 32, 42.

those in other countries who had contributed most to theory and method in the scientific study of society. Nevertheless, for sociologists in general and rural sociologists in particular the manner in which Sorokin wove the principles developed by European sociologists into his own systematic exposition of the principles of rural sociology was of great utility. This alone advanced by several decades the date at which the tested results of scholarship in other lands would form an integral part of rural sociology in the United States. Prior to 1929 and the publication of the *Principles of Rural-Urban Sociology* rural sociologists in this country rivaled their fellows in other branches of sociology in the degree to which they were unaware of the writings and ideas of their fellows abroad. Prior to this date few of them gave evidence of being acquainted with the work of any of the following: Emile Durkheim, Frederic Le Play, Ferdinand Toennies, Leopold von Wiese, Ibn Khaldun, R. Livi, E. G. Ravenstein, James G. Frazer, Max Weber, John Graunt, A. Meitzen, Vilfredo Pareto, Frederic Seebohm, Max Sering, Werner Sombart, L. T. Hobhouse, and Edward Westermarck, to mention only some of the more important names. Indeed the books and other publications by rural sociologists gave little indication that they were familiar with the fundamental contributions made to the sociology of rural life by such noted U. S. sociologists as William F. Ogburn, Howard W. Odum, Florian Znaniecki, W. I. Thomas, and G. E. Howard. After Sorokin had drawn heavily on these and, to a lesser degree, upon the works of hundreds of others in his own great work of synthesis, however, several of those preparing the textbooks and other compendia dealing with rural sociology leaned heavily upon the original works of these scholars; and it is evident that this was not done merely by relying upon the summaries of their studies which are conveniently available in *Contemporary Sociological Theories* and other books.[14] In this way alone, Sorokin achieved one of his stated objectives and thus contributed immeasurably to the reduction of the provincialism that characterized rural sociology in the United States at the time he was banished from Soviet Russia.

[14] Note, for example, that one of the outstanding specialists in the sociology of rural life, Charles P. Loomis, is also the scholar who eventually was responsible for the translation and publication of Toennies' classic work. See *Community and Society (Gemeinschaft und Gesellschaft)*, translated and with an Introduction by Charles P. Loomis (East Lansing: Michigan State University Press, 1956).

Perhaps even more directly and immediately, however, was the effect of his own exposition and use in the *Principles of Rural-Urban Sociology* of principles and concepts hitherto entirely unknown to or understood only vaguely by sociologists of all varieties in the United States. Little purpose would be served by listing all of these.[15] It is essential to include, however, some of the items for whose formulation Sorokin himself was largely if not almost exclusively responsible. Among these are the concepts of *social space,* and *vertical* and *horizontal social mobility,* the difference in social mobility in rural and urban areas, and the factors responsible for these differences. Closely related are his concepts of *social stratification* and his definition of *social class,* which he set forth explicitly in his book entitled *Social Mobility* and used effectively in analyzing the basic differences between rural and urban society. Even the most abbreviated list also should include Sorokin's definition of the *social group,* his elaboration of the differences between *elementary* and *cumulative* groups, and the manner in which he employed these concepts in the *Source Book*[16] to promote understanding of the structure of rural society.

It also is essential to mention specifically some of the concepts and principles of other scholars which made their way into rural sociology in the United States largely as the result of Sorokin's work as an author and as a teacher. In this category come such items as Toennies' dichotomy of *gemeinschaft* and *gesellschaft,* Durkheim's *mechanistic* and *organic social solidarity,* Ravenstein's laws (of migration), and Livi's *law.*

Finally, in addition to the principles described in the following section, it is necessary to mention, even though briefly, some of the analyses presented by Sorokin in the two books under consideration in this chapter which still stand almost alone in the literature of rural sociology. They remain basic sources that must be consulted by anyone who desires understanding of the important matters they treat. Three of these are as follows: (1) the differences between the rural and urban social worlds analyzed and described in Chapter II of the *Principles;* (2) the history of rural sociology to the

[15] More to the point would be a series of doctoral dissertations on such topics as the following: "The Roles of Social Stratification and Related Concepts in Sociology in the United States before and after the Publication of Sorokin's *Social Mobility.*"

[16] Chap. vi.

nineteenth century, Chapters I and II of the *Source Book;* and (3) "the differentiation of the rural population into cumulative communities and functional associations" which makes up Chapter VI of the same indispensable work.

V. The Durability of Sorokin's Principles

Because Sorokin's principles of rural sociology represented the work of synthesis at its best, the generalizations of others that he adopted and wove into his own work and those he formulated personally have stood the test of time in a high degree. Indeed, the large majority of them still retain a validity that makes the *Principles* and the *Source Book,* as earlier indicated, recommended reading for anyone who would aspire to professional competence in the fields of rural and urban sociology. This point is emphasized by a brief consideration of some of the basic principles which he set forth in his chapters in the *Principles.*

A. *The psychosocial status of farmers.* The fundamental generalization on this subject, in a chapter whose authorship was shared with Zimmerman, is that the economic, occupational, and sociopolitical status of farmers is fundamentally different from that of any of the urban social classes. In some respects farmers have basic interests in common with urban managerial and capitalistic groups, whereas in other fundamental respects their sympathies and actions are more closely tied in with those of the workers. For this reason the hopes for any lasting political alliance between farmers and those who work with their hands in the cities, such as was envisioned by those trying to promote a "Farm-Labor party" in the Midwest at the time Sorokin was writing, are doomed for disappointment. Although such movements are not entirely dead, in the United States and abroad, they appear to enjoy even less support among farm groups and labor groups alike than was the case in 1929. Indeed, Sorokin's generalizations with respect to the psychosocial status of farmers seem to be fully valid today.

B. *Livi's Law.* During the first thirty years of the twentieth century much was written (and read) about the bodily differences between rural and urban populations. Many studies had seemed to show that rural people differed from those who lived in cities in stature, weight, pigmentation, and the shape of the head, and the selectivity of migration versus environment was vigorously debated as a possible explanation of the asserted differences. Sorokin himself set the problem as follows:

Are there some bodily differences between populations of the city and the country, taken as whole groups? If so, what are they? If so, to what are they due: to selection or environment or to both of these factors? Much has been written about the topic. And yet, the problem is still definitely unsettled.[17]

Then he proceeded to a detailed analysis of the findings of the specific studies and the interpretations that had been placed upon them. This involved the presentation of a host of theories, some applying only to the study of stature, or weight, or pigmentation, or the cephalic index, and others to two or more of these characteristics. Finally, he generalized the findings as follows:

... *we do not find any valid evidence that the cities attract particularly those who are tall, or heavy, or dark, or dolichocephalic, or with large size of heads and so on, or vice versa.* ... The fact of recruiting of city populations from more remote and different places than the population of the country, and the interpretation by R. Livi, explain the differences found much more satisfactorily than the hypothesis of "selectional selection." ... Correspondingly, the hypothesis formulated by many, but especially well demonstrated by R. Livi, remains the most important generalization in this field.[18]

As nearly as the present writer has been able to determine, Sorokin's use of Livi's principle here and in *Contemporary Sociological Theories*[19] is the first time this important key to an understanding of an immensely complicated sociological problem was made available to sociologists in this country. Moreover, in his classes Sorokin applied the same principle effectively in explaining cultural differences between city and country such as those in religious preferences and affiliations, and for both purposes Livi's Law continues to be of prime importance today as it was in 1929.[20] As a matter of fact the present writer is convinced that a familiarity with Livi's

---

[17] *Principles,* p. 101. [18] *Ibid.,* p. 142.
[19] P. 278.
[20] Cf. T. Lynn Smith, *The Sociology of Rural Life* (3rd ed.; New York: Harper & Brothers, 1953), pp. 87, 89.

Law and an elementary knowledge of the social ecology of cities would have prevented the revival of Lombrosian theories of crime which emanated from Harvard's Department of Anthropology a few years ago.

C. *The experience worlds of farmers.* Using procedures comparable to those employed to arrive at the conclusion that Livi's Law is the principle which explains the observed differences in the physical characteristics of rural and urban populations, Sorokin took stock of the evidence that had been accumulated with respect to the conscious events which make up the sum total of the experiences of those who reside in the country and those who live in the city. All of this, on the basis of his analysis, he then classified into "direct experience," or that a person gains for himself, and "indirect experience," or that not secured by face-to-face or personal contact with the phenomena. Next, he proceeded inductively to generalize that the experience world of the farmer tends to be made up in large measure of direct experience whereas that of the person who lives in a city is secured for the most part in indirect ways.

. . . in the field of indirect experience the superiority belongs to the urbanite; in the field of the direct experience it belongs to the farmer. The city dweller knows everything from indirect sources; his mental vistas are broad; he talks about and can talk about the most different things. . . . But all of this is known to him quite superficially and in a fragmentary manner. . . . The farmer's outlook, from the standpoint of indirect knowledge, is much narrower; he often does not know anything that is going on outside of his country or province. . . . Nevertheless, in the field of direct experience, the farmer's share is rather better than that of the average "proletarian" with his very narrow field of direct and substantial dealing with realities.[21]

Finally, he developed several corollaries from these propositions, including the following:

. . . *the farmer-peasant's mental luggage is more stable and less fluctuating than many attitudes and convictions of the city population, often based on an inadequate and overdeveloped indirect experience, which inadequacy makes many changes necessary in order to correct or to replace one attitude, opinion, or belief with another.*[22]

If valid, these generalizations certainly represent some of the most

[21] *Principles,* p. 289.   [22] *Ibid.,* p. 290.

important principles yet advanced in the study of the social psychology of rural life; and if not valid, in 1962 that fact remains to be demonstrated fully as much as was the case in 1930.

D. Rural-urban incidence of crime. Perhaps Sorokin's legal training and experience in Russia made him cautious about conclusions relating to comparative criminality of the rural and urban populations, but in any case he was far less certain in this respect than appears to have been true of many of his contemporaries. Exactly this reluctance to attribute great criminality to urban populations seems to have added durability to his principles. After a lengthy examination of the data he did conclude that the city crime rates "remain somewhat higher than in the country or among the agricultural population."[23] Then, in accounting for the differences, he first dismissed as of little consequence the economic and educational factors, admitted the possibility of selectivity of migrations between rural and urban areas, and attributed in a large measure the slightly higher crime rates in cities to differences in the rural-urban density of population, family and home life, psychosocial heterogeneity, and social mobility.

E. The city as the innovator and the country as the preserver of national culture. Sorokin saw in the city's demographic, social, and cultural heterogeneity the forces which make for change, and in the country's homogeneous and self-perpetuating population and social and cultural system the factors favorable to the retention of the established order. In brief the city is the innovator and the country the preserver of national culture.[24] The facts he marshaled to demonstrate this thesis seem to have been sufficient to establish its validity, and the principle remains at the service of sociologists today. The present writer himself has found it useful in a variety of situations, ranging from the endeavor to introduce college students to the city's role in social change[25] to an attempt to determine how mortality rates in Latin American cities compare with those in the rural districts.[26]

[23] *Ibid.,* p. 388.   [24] *Ibid.,* pp. 105, *passim.*
[25] See T. Lynn Smith and C. A. McMahan, *The Sociology of Urban Life* (New York: Dryden Press, 1951), pp. 781-89.
[26] T. Lynn Smith, "Diferencias Demográficas Rur-Urbanas en Latino-america,"

F. *The distinctive features of rural religious culture and expression.*
Among those who have sought to understand religious phenomena
as they are expressed in rural areas, Sorokin is distinguished by the
breadth as well as by the depth of his analysis. He devoted relatively little attention to the statistics of rural church membership,
data about programs and Sunday Schools, facts relating to minis-
ters' salaries, and similar features which figure prominently in
many rural sociological works, but concentrated upon five principal
ways in which he maintained the religious beliefs and practices of
rural people differed from those of urban residents. *First,* he drew
upon Livi's Law and stressed the importance of the "native" elements in religious forms and expressions of country people, in contrast with the features drawn from all parts of the world that are
found as part and parcel of the religious heritages of the heterogeneous masses who inhabit the cities. *Second,* as a result of the
interaction of the diverse elements found in the city, changes take
place, and these changes later on spread or are carried to the rural
districts. Rural people, though, have a tendency to cling firmly to
their old gods and forms of worship. In the case of the spread of
Christianity (from Rome), for example, the rural inhabitants of the
Italian Peninsula maintained their traditional religious culture so
tenaciously that their name (*pagan* from *paganus*) became synony-
mous with non-Christian, and a similar development took place in
the British Isles where the term *heathen* originally meant nothing
more than those who lived in the *heather*. *Third,* the agricultural
setting of rural religion gives its various expressions a "coloration"
quite different from that which surrounds the forms of worship in
the cities. *Fourth,* rural religious beliefs and practices are less deterministic, materialistic, and mechanistic than those that have
been influenced by an urban and industrial environment. *Fifth,*
rigidity, firmness, lack of relativism, and so forth, are characteristic
of rural religious doctrines and behavior, whereas skepticism, sophistication, relativism, and the like, are more characteristic of
urban beliefs and practices.

Instituto de Investigaciones Sociales, *Estudies Sociológicos* (*Sociología Urbana*)
(Mexico: Instituto de Investigaciones Sociales, 1956), II, 19-20.

G. *The nature of rural radicalism.* Because of his personal, intense interest in revolutions and revolutionary movements, Sorokin also delved deeply into the nature of rural radicalism and the relationship of the agricultural classes to political regimes of various types. Far from asserting that rural societies are always conservative and that rural populations tend to support the status quo, he indicated that at times rural society is radical to the extreme. This contrasts with the radicalism of the urban populations, though, in that it is more sporadic and less sustained, is less frequent and, when it does arise, it bursts like a thunderstorm. On the whole, socialistic and communistic tendencies gain little support among the farmers, and the agriculturists sometimes direct their activities against the laboring classes in the cities and at other times against the upper classes. Rural radicalism is centered about the possession and control of the land, and it is likely to erupt violently if situations arise in which the farmers are threatened with the loss of their farms and homes. As a result, as mentioned above, over thirty years ago Sorokin gave little chance of success to the efforts, then widespread in the area in which he was living, to establish a Farm-Labor political alliance or party; and the results since that time bear out the validity of his analysis.

VI. *Teacher and Teacher of Teachers*

From what has been said above, it should be evident that Sorokin's great influence upon the development of a sociology of rural life was achieved through the publication of the two monumental works, namely, the mislabeled *Principles of Rural-Urban Sociology*[27] and the *Source Book.* Of course the emphasis he gave to rural-urban comparisons and contrasts throughout his other books, at least one paper[28] reporting on a project completed in his seminar on rural sociology, and the paper on rural religious culture which he presented at the 1928 meetings of the American Sociological Society played some part in relating his name to the study of rural social phenomena. But in addition to his two fundamental

[27] Mislabeled because, as mentioned above, the authors state specifically in the preface that they had attempted to prepare a textbook in rural sociology.

[28] P. A. Sorokin, Carle C. Zimmerman, and others, "Farmer Leaders in the United States," *Social Forces*, VII, No. 1 (1928), 33-45.

books devoted specifically to synthesis in the field of rural sociology, his work as a teacher was the principal way in which his influence was exerted in the development of a science of rural society. This is not to say that any considerable amount of his effort was expended teaching courses which carried the label of "rural sociology." Indeed the bulk of his time at Minnesota was devoted to teaching courses and seminars in the fields of sociological theory, the history of social thought, social organization, the sociology of revolution, and population problems, and only a small fraction of his teaching load was accounted for by the seminar on rural sociology for which he and Zimmerman were responsible; and at Harvard he did not even have time for the rural sociology seminar. Nevertheless, the small, highly selected corps of graduate students who trained as sociologists under his inspiration and direction, and then devoted much of their own lives to building—upon the foundations he had laid—a sociology of rural life, represent the second important way in which Sorokin influenced decisively the nature and development of rural sociology as a scientific discipline. Among those who studied with Sorokin at Minnesota or Harvard, or both, and whose names figure prominently in the annals of rural sociology since 1928 are the following: C. Arnold Anderson, Otis Durant Duncan, Fred C. Frey, Homer L. Hitt, Paul H. Landis, Charles P. Loomis, Bryce Ryan, Edgar A. Schuler, T. Lynn Smith, Conrad Taeuber, and Nathan L. Whetten.

There appears to be a widespread belief, at home and abroad, that some of Sorokin's students and teaching assistants have not been inclined to give appropriate credit to their teacher for the ideas and materials that eventually appeared in their published works. Be this as it may, it should be noted that none of the men enumerated above has shown any reluctance to acknowledge his indebtedness, in professional matters, to Sorokin's inspiration as a teacher and to his published works, a fact that will be apparent to all who will take the trouble to examine the publications they have produced.[29] Furthermore, during the third of a century that has

[29] For illustrations of this point, see, for example, the rural sociology texts prepared by members of the group: Paul H. Landis, *Rural Life in Process* (New York: The McGraw-Hill Book Company, 1940 and 1948); Charles P. Loomis and J. Allan Beegle, *Rural Social Systems* (New York: Prentice-Hall, Inc., 1950); Charles P. Loomis and J. Allan Beegle, *Rural Sociology—The Strategy of Change* (Englewood Cliffs, N. J.: Prentice-Hall, Inc., 1957); and T. Lynn Smith, *The Sociology of Rural Life* (New York: Harper & Brothers, 1940, 1947, and 1953).

passed since Sorokin began work on the *Principles*, Sorokin's students themselves have trained considerable numbers of the men now prominent in rural sociology, and even those whose graduate work was directed by the students of his students are making significant contributions to the development of the sociology of rural life. All of this represents not a slavish copying or imitation, but earnest endeavor to test, modify, add to, and otherwise build upon in a scientific manner the principles of rural sociology formulated by Sorokin.

Sorokin's Use of Sociological Measurement[1]

Matilda White Riley and Mary E. Moore

How will the historian of the future assess Sorokin's attempts to classify and quantify sociocultural phenomena? Our prediction is that he will look upon this work as well ahead of its time. In essence, what Sorokin has attempted to do is: (1) focus on total systems as they change over the entire course of history, and (2) adapt the procedures of scientific research to these peculiarly sociological problems.

Thus, on the one hand, Sorokin's research materials reflect the erudition and sweep of European scholarship. His problems are formulated within the frame of his prodigious knowledge and critical understanding of world sociology. And the extensiveness of his objectives is indexed by the far-flung secondary analyses of *Social Mobility*[2] or *Rural-Urban Sociology*, and by the measurements in *Social and Cultural Dynamics* which are based, for example, on nearly a thousand wars, over sixteen hundred revolutions, many thousand works of arts, all the historical figures mentioned in the *Encyclopaedia Britannica*, and the like.

On the other hand, Sorokin has at his disposal in this remarkable undertaking an empirical research approach which most American social scientists of the time were applying only to short-run, small-scale phenomena, and which they were using without any special regard for the matching of technique to theory or for the special problems of sociological analysis. Few techniques were ready at hand which were appropriate to Sorokin's objectives.

[1] Robert K. Merton and John W. Riley, Jr., were kind enough to read an earlier version of this manuscript and to make valuable suggestions. This methodological analysis of Sorokin's work was facilitated through a program of research which is supported in part by a research grant, M-926, from the National Institute of Mental Health of the National Institutes of Health, Public Health Service.

[2] References are to the revised edition of 1959, *Social and Cultural Mobility*, (Glencoe, Ill.: The Free Press).

This imbalance between his objective and the methods available in the field of sociology to carry it out—an imbalance which was at once a burden and a challenge for Sorokin's research—has not yet been fully redressed.   While research sophistication has been steadily increasing, sociologists on the whole have been slow to develop either the interest or the background for systematic dynamic analysis of literate societies throughout their history.   Thus it may well be that Sorokin's work will reach its full impact only at some point in the future when these two lines of development converge.

As a means of hastening this impact, it seems worthwhile to pause now to consider his achievements from the viewpoint of mid-twentieth-century methodology.   This paper will, accordingly, be concerned with Sorokin's research itself, referring to his underlying theories and the results of his investigations only insofar as this is necessary to a discussion of the matching of his research to his theory.   This paper will deal primarily with his procedures for measuring (i.e., either classifying or quantifying) as a major focus of his methodological contributions.   It will select for scrutiny only a few examples from the broad array of his analyses—examples which are scattered, far from complete, of varying degrees of generality and importance.   These examples are selected in order to illustrate some of Sorokin's contributions to sociological research method, and some of the further methodological problems which are suggested or implied by his work.   Thus the formulations and assessments are not those which Sorokin himself has made, but those of the present-day sociologist who considers the important bearing of the work on the developing application of scientific measurement to sociological concepts.

I. Elements of Measurement

The framework for Sorokin's use of measurement—prototype of much current research—is suggested in the early statement by Sorokin and Zimmerman.[3]   From this statement may be abstracted a number of the elements in the measurement procedure as this is defined today.

[3] *Principles of Rural-Urban Sociology,* chap. ii.

a. The authors start by defining the fundamental "traits"—often referred to now as the *dimensions*—for the classification of societies.[4]

b. They then refer to "quantitative variations" along these dimensions. They point out, for example (as applied to rural-urban sociology), that "many differential characteristics of the rural and urban community would consist not so much in the presence of certain traits in rural, and their absence in urban communities, as much as in a quantitative increase or decrease of these characteristics or in their positive or negative correlation with 'rurality' or 'urbanity.' "[5]   As the modern methodologist might read this, they attempt to measure the *degree* to which a given group has a particular trait—or, more importantly, to locate the position of a given group in terms of an underlying dimension.

c. They explain further that all of these dimensions (or variables) are interrelated with one another, so that "societies and their differences are undescribable in terms of *one* characteristic, and require a definition which combines several typical traits."[6]   As they put it, "The first 'variable,' so to speak, carries the others with it."[7]   Therefore, they employ here, following Max Weber, the *typological* method.   This enables them to classify "a complex and an uninterrupted series of phenomena into a few types or classes. . . ."[8]   That is, in the language of contemporary methodology, they first locate societies, not merely on one dimension, but in a multidimensional property space, and then they focus on those cells within the space which are, to revert to their own phraseology, "typical and constant."[9]

d. Finally, they anticipate a question which is of much concern in modern measurement: that is, how can the assumptions of a particular measuring procedure be *tested*?   While they do not raise the question in this form, they do express concern that a compounding of multiple dimensions may become a "purely mechanical 'piling together' of various unrelated traits."   A scientific approach, they feel, must rest on "a logical unification of traits functionally correlated with one another."[10]

Each of these elements will be considered in further detail at appropriate points in the following discussions.

[4] *Ibid.*, p. 13.   [5] *Ibid.*, p. 14.
[6] *Ibid.*, p. 13.   [7] *Ibid.*, p. 57.
[8] *Ibid.*, p. 15.   [9] *Ibid.*, p. 57.
[10] *Ibid.*, p. 14.

II. Classification of Cases on Multiple Dimensions

Many of the measurements reported in *Dynamics* illustrate such a procedure, of continuing concern to the modern methodologist, of using sense data as indicants to classify cases on each of several dimensions which are later combined so as to represent the concept as a whole.[11] For example, in his measures of war and of internal disturbances[12]—both of which are taken to reflect the breakdown of crystallized systems of relationships—Sorokin (and his various collaborators) provide two examples of this approach. Since these represent two rather different attacks on what appear to be rather similar problems, an examination of them may prove methodologically instructive.

In both cases Sorokin decides to use multiple dimensions. As the important quantifiable aspects of the magnitude of wars, he selects the total strength of the army, the number of casualties, and the duration of the conflict. Each of these is measured simply by counting such ready-made units as persons or years involved.

In the case of internal disturbances, however, he specifies various dimensions which require quite different means of quantification in order to match his definition of the concept.[13] These are the extent and social importance of the area involved, the duration of the disturbance, the proportion of the population engaged, and the proportional intensity of the conflict (i.e., "the amount and sharpness of violence and the importance of effects").[14] Here his procedure is to construct numerical scales for the evaluation of each dimension of any given disturbance. On a scale 1 to 100, for example, some of the points designated along the dimension of the "social area" of the conflict, together with the numerical values assigned to these points, are:

1—disturbances of a local character in a rural county or similar limited area,

40—disturbances in several large provinces or in the whole capital city,

100—disturbances which involve the entire country.[15]

[11] The distinctions made here between the concept as a whole and its component dimensions are purely arbitrary and relative to the particular focus of research.

[12] *Dynamics,* III, Parts II and III.   [13] *Ibid.,* III, 387.

[14] *Ibid.,* III, 389. He also classifies disturbances on a nominal scale according to their objectives (see Appendix), but does not employ this in his analysis.

[15] *Ibid.,* III, 394.

Apart from the obvious problems of such arbitrary quantification,[16] these scales make the important attempt to approximate the distinctively social definitions of the several dimensions. Even the scale of duration of the conflict is apparently assumed to have social implications which are not strictly commensurate with the scale obtained by simply counting the number of years.

III. The Combining of Dimensions

After these relevant dimensions have been selected, defined, and measured, the two analyses continue to diverge.

A. The aggregation of dimensions. In the case of internal disturbances, Sorokin aggregates the dimensions to form an over-all index. Each disturbance receives a single total score which combines—as a geometric average, in this instance—its scale values on the several dimensions.[17]

Without considering the difficulties engendered by this process of weighting and averaging these dimensions, let us examine the utility of the outcome. The resultant over-all index has the great advantage, of course, of providing a *single measure of a complex phenomenon.* Thus, Sorokin can conveniently plot trends in the movement of disturbances over time and relate these to the transformations in the types of culture. Yet, the geometric average is merely one of many methods of combination by *fiat* which have in common the disadvantage that the roles of the individual dimensions may be lost within the total score. Thus, several disturbances with the same score may be produced by very different combinations of factors;[18] or two apparently similar trends might mean, in one case, a marked change in the social area involved, but, in the other case, a marked change in intensity and violence. Therefore, when the results for the total index are studied, little is learned about the trends for the separate dimensions,[19] and the relationships

[16] Sorokin tries out several sets of weights here and discusses some implications of their arbitrary character. *Ibid.,* III, 390 ff. See also *ibid.,* II, 21-23.

[17] *Ibid.,* III, 392.

[18] Sorokin himself was, of course, aware of such difficulties. See, e.g., his early discussion of an "aggregate index" in *Social Mobility,* p. 137.

[19] To be sure, the raw data are all presented in the Appendix to Volume III of

among them may be completely obscured. Nothing in the measurement process itself serves to confirm any hypotheses Sorokin may have had in advance about the nature of such relationships as they reflect his definitions of the concept under study.

B. *Relationships among dimensions.* In dealing with war Sorokin's use of multiple dimensions is entirely different. Instead of combining them into an over-all index, he uses each one as a separate measure, in much the same way as he used the combined index of internal disturbance.[20] On the one hand, this procedure fails to reduce the complexity of the several dimensions. The magnitude of war must be examined, not through one measure, but through all three.

On the other hand, this approach avoids some of the difficulties of the arbitrary aggregation of dimensions. Not only does it illuminate, rather than obscure, the contributions of the several dimensions, but it also facilitates analysis of the relationships among them. Thus, Sorokin studies separately, and compares trends for, the number of years with war in each period, the size of the armies employed, and the number of casualties.[21] In Europe, for example, he notes, not merely that army strength and casualties have increased in absolute numbers[22] since the twelfth century (except for a drop in the nineteenth), but also that the increase in the number of casualties is greater than the increase in the size of the armies. By expressing the casualties in each century as a proportion of the total army size, he is able to demonstrate a steady increase in the casualty rate.[23] In such fashion, by studying the relationships between dimensions, he uncovers additional information about the changing nature of wars: not only has the absolute size of armies been increasing, but the destructive power of armies of a given size has been increasing also. Thus, this measurement procedure, in contrast to the aggregate index, begins to meet an important ob-

---

Dynamics, and some analysis by countries is presented (pp. 476 ff.), but no measures are developed showing trends over time in the separate dimensions.

[20] *Dynamics,* Vol. III, chap. x.

[21] He recognizes a certain degree of necessary association between the last two. See *ibid.,* III, 289.

[22] His major conclusions are based upon further corrections of these figures in terms of population size.

[23] *Ibid.,* III, 337.

jective of modern measurement: i.e., the measurement process itself tends to *reflect the empirical patterning* among the dimensions, and thus helps the investigator to clarify the concept under study.

Such examples, which merely hint at the ingenuity of this research in utilizing available techniques and inventing new ones, point clearly to the need for an improved measuring procedure which combines dimensions, not as arbitrary aggregates, but as a reflection of the actual patterning among them. The examples foreshadow such later[24] developments as Guttman scaling, image scales, latent structure analysis, and similar attempts to handle the patterning of acts or attributes of a given system[25]—which avoid (in Sorokin's language) the study of variables "torn from" their system context.[26]

Finally, such models from Sorokin's work seem to call for procedures which will reflect, not only such patterns within a system at a single point in time,[27] but also its properties of immanent change,[28] "changes in togetherness,"[29] and development of inherent strains.[30] The *dynamic* character of the analysis, by adding an entire further dimension to the measures used in static (cross-section) studies, constitutes a highly important contribution, although it also passes on many problems to subsequent research. How, for example, can measures designed as relative to a sociocultural system at a *given* time be used to compare changes *over* time?[31] How can researchers carry further the aim of *Dynamics*

[24] To be sure, L. L. Thurstone published his "Multiple Factor Analysis" in 1931 (*Psychological Review*, XXXVIII, 406-27); and this procedure was being used as early as 1939 by such sociologists as Ernest W. Burgess and Leonard S. Cottrell, Jr., in *Predicting Success or Failure in Marriage* (New York: Prentice-Hall, 1939).

[25] See, e.g., Samuel A. Stouffer, *et al.*, *Measurement and Prediction* (Vol. IV of *Studies in Social Psychology in World War II*) (Princeton, N. J.: Princeton University Press, 1950); or, in regard to the study of social systems, Matilda White Riley, John W. Riley, Jr., and Jackson Toby, *Sociological Studies in Scale Analysis* (New Brunswick, N. J.: Rutgers University Press, 1954).

[26] *Society, Culture and Personality*, p. 689.

[27] *Dynamics*, III, 373 ff.

[28] *Ibid.*, IV, 587 ff.

[29] *Society, Culture and Personality*, p. 635.

[30] See the recent formulation by Wilbert E. Moore, "A Reconsideration of Theories of Social Change," *American Sociological Review*, XXV (1960), 810-18.

[31] See the discussion of the cultural differences among major premises, *Dynamics*, III, 62 ff., and the consequences implied for systematic comparisons. See also Hans Speier's criticism of the dynamic analysis of an economic index which is relative to a changing historical context, *American Sociological Review*, II (1937), 928.

to fit together the "infinitesimal fragments of an unknown picture"[32] as these are revealed over time?

IV. Concepts vs. Indicants

Fundamental to all such details of the measurement procedure itself is an underlying assumption about the relationship of research to theory. Much present-day work rests on a *conceptual model* of a social system and its properties which is clearly distinguished from the concrete groups and their observable acts and characteristics which are taken as *indicants* of these concepts. Sorokin was working at a time, however, when many sociologists were influenced by extreme forms of "raw empiricism"; when the data themselves were frequently the ultimate interest; and when an index was rarely, as Durkheim put it, seen primarily as representing the internal fact which escapes us. Many students of the reactions and attitudes of individuals had not yet hit upon such constructs as the "intervening variable"[33] or the "latent structure,"[34] which organize in conceptual or probabilistic terms the myriad sense data used in measurement.

Sorokin himself, whose critical work attacks the extreme tendencies of raw empiricism,[35] is explicitly seeking underlying properties which are "repeated in time and space."[36] He writes, for example: "Hidden behind the empirically different, seemingly unrelated fragments of the cultural complex lies an identity of meaning, which brings them together into consistent *styles*, typical *forms*, and significant *patterns*."[37] He wants to "establish conclusively the empirical value of our conceptions" by throwing light on the relationships among "countless fragments, traits, details, events, proc-

[32] Among the promising attempts to meet this challenge—whether or not it be called "functional" analysis—is the model for studying "goal-directed systems." See, e.g., Robert K. Merton, *Social Theory and Social Structure* (Glencoe, Ill.: The Free Press, 1957), chap. i, and Ernest Nagel, "A Formalization of Functionalism," in *Logic without Metaphysics* (Glencoe, Ill.: The Free Press, 1956).

[33] To be sure, Tolman himself had begun to define this construct in the early 1930's. See, e.g., his discussion in Edward C. Tolman, "The Determinism of Behavior at a Choice Point," *Psychological Review*, XLV (1938), 1-41.

[34] See, e.g., the chapters by Paul F. Lazarsfeld in Samuel A. Stouffer, *et al.*, *op. cit.*

[35] See *Fads and Foibles, passim.*

[36] *Society, Culture and Personality*, p. 7.

[37] *Dynamics*, I, 23.

esses" and ordering "their chaotic multitude into comprehensible general formulas."[38] Thus, he frequently refers to his figures, which are based on these diverse phenomena, as "approximate," "rough," "rude" indexes from which "inferences" may be drawn, "aimed not so much to measure as to indicate. . . ."[39] This loose relationship between the observed phenomena and the underlying meaning derives from his basic theory of pure meaning as employed by "human agents," and embodied in overt action and material objects as "vehicles." As he puts it:

Since any meaning may manifest itself through different vehicles and human agents, and since any vehicle or human agent may incorporate different meanings, their relationship is "polygamous" rather than "monogamous," loose rather than close.[40]

V. Groups vs. Action

Not only does Sorokin distinguish thus explicitly between concept and indicant, and define the loose relationship between the two; he further differentiates between the two types of indicants— (1) the vehicles and (2) the human agents—that are of continuing importance in sociological measurement. While the mid-twentieth-century sociologist may not use the term "vehicles," he still recognizes that, on the one hand, indicants must be found to reflect the nature of social *action* (or collective orientation, or the product of social action). On the other hand, a group measure must often refer to the *actors* themselves as they make up the group. Thus, in one aspect a measure might classify symphony orchestras, for example, according to the pattern of notes which they play (action); and in another aspect it might classify the same orchestras according to the organization of the players of the several instruments (actors).

Sorokin himself states of "cultural" and "social" phenomena that "technically they can be studied separately, and for the sake of analysis can be isolated from each other, as different aspects of the same one and indivisible 'sociocultural world.'"[41] And he formu-

---

[38] *Ibid.,* I, 195.
[39] *Ibid.,* II, 23; III, 228, 286; *Social Mobility,* p. 418.
[40] *Society, Culture and Personality,* p. 49.
[41] *Dynamics,* III, 3.

lates what he regards as the appropriate co-ordinates for classifying both vehicles and human agents.[42]

Examples of both aspects of measurement abound in Sorokin's research. An early illustration of the distinction is his proposed index of the vertical mobility rates of societies.[43] One dimension of this measure (its "intensiveness") is indexed by the number of social strata crossed by an individual in a given period of time—thus referring to the *action* of the individual (as a vehicle). The other dimension ("generality") is indexed by the number of individuals changing their social positions in a vertical direction—referring, that is, to the component *actors* (human agents) within the society.

Each of these aspects of measurement presents its own peculiar difficulties; and still more stubborn is the research problem in fitting the two back together in some appropriate way. Some further examples from Sorokin's work will illustrate the nature of such problems and point to some possible solutions.

VI. Measurement of the Component of Meaning

Sorokin uses vehicles—the various cultural phenomena or social actions which he selects as indicants of the first type—primarily to measure underlying meanings. Such measures continue to provide a highly valuable model for the sociologist today because they deal with values, norms, and the subjective states of the actor as these are relevant to the understanding of sociocultural systems.

Several devices are employed by Sorokin and his collaborators for measuring fluctuations in the forms of art, scientific discoveries, law, and other aspects of culture. Here the usual procedure (known to the modern scholar as "content analysis") uses one or more "judges" to classify the particular phenomena according to a set of definitions and rules. Forms of painting and sculpture,[44] for example, are rated on a number of dimensions, according to whether the content is predominantly religious or secular; the style is impressionistic, formal, naturalistic, expressionistic, or mixed; the char-

---

[42] *Sociocultural Causality*, pp. 122 ff.
[43] *Social and Cultural Mobility*, pp. 136-37.
[44] *Dynamics*, I, 369 ff.

acter or atmosphere of the work tends to be spiritual or sensual; and the like. Each of these dimensions is defined in advance, and each is, in turn, related to the basic categories of ideational, idealistic, and visual (sensate). In view of the "subjective nature" of many of these ratings, the same works of art are independently classified by scholars working in two different countries, and the ratings compared.[45]

These procedures may interest the modern scholar less for their technical details than as illustrations of Sorokin's approach to the study of meaning. Any special science must, according to Sorokin, modify the general method of science in conformity with the phenomena under study. And the peculiarly distinctive feature of the sociocultural, in contrast to the natural, sciences, lies in the component of meaning-value-norm.[46] Various studies of this component as reported in *Dynamics* illustrate an approach in which the investigator (or the several judges) acts as an *outside observer*. Indeed, the methodological notes on the study of the main systems of truth start by "assuming the position of a perfectly impartial observer, and taking the systems involved as the factual datum. . . ."[47] And a comment on the classification of crimes states that the analysis is "behavioristic," without reference to the intent or the state of mind of the criminal.[48]

In his discussions of this important approach, Sorokin distinguishes between this "logical reading" of meaning by an outside observer and a "psychological interpretation," which refers to the states of mind of the persons involved in a relationship.[49] The way a master feels toward his slave, for instance, might differ markedly from the outside investigator's view of this same relationship. Or the intent of the artist may be quite different from the social meaning of his creation. Although Sorokin says that "any social relationship has to be studied from both standpoints,"[50] his work suggests that the sociologist uses the "psychological interpretation" in a special way—that he maintains the system level of analysis, treating

[45] *Ibid.*, I, 372-73.
[46] *Society, Culture and Personality*, p. 18.
[47] *Dynamics*, II, 14-15.
[48] *Ibid.*, II, 535. Sorokin carries on a continuing struggle, of course, against the more extreme forms of behaviorism, emphasizing the central importance of his notion of "meaning." See, e.g., *Fads and Foibles, passim.*
[49] *Ibid.*, I, 57-61; III, 3-5.
[50] *Ibid.*, III, 4-5.

the actor's intent as a part of the social process rather than as a "cause" to explain social phenomena.[51]

At this level, some of his measures based on cultural phenomena might be interpreted as indicants of the actors' subjective states. On the one hand, as he points out, "most of the cultural phenomena represent the results of the activities of many individuals and groups, whose purposes and meanings may be different from one another. . . ."[52] In this sense, his measures of sets of mores, or of architectural structures, might be thought of as indices of the composite ideas of many actors. On the other hand, his measures of personal influence—as of prominent thinkers on their partisans— might be taken to reflect the subjective states of the persons to whom the meaning is transmitted. Thus interpreted, this phase of Sorokin's work appears to afford a challenging model for the study of such contemporary topics as mass communication and other "vehicles" of culture and social action.

VII. Combining Indicants of Action and Actor

The sociologist of today often seeks measures which will fit together the two types of indicants: those which refer to collective acts or attitudes and their underlying meaning, and those which refer to the actors as parts of the group.

Much present confusion over this problem has arisen because one major line of development in recent years has concentrated on measures of the *individual,* thus isolating for exclusive attention the component of actions and attitudes. And when this line of development is carried over to the group, it often leads to treatment of the group as an undifferentiated entity which is formally analogous to the individual.[53] Such a "sociologistic" treatment (to borrow Sorokin's term) might classify orchestral performances, first, ac-

[51] Sorokin's formulation of Durkheim's theory, for example, states that the cause of suicide is "the total character of the respective society and culture. . . . When the entire network of social relationships is well integrated . . . people feel themselves to be vital parts of the society to which they belong. . . ." *Society, Culture and Personality,* p. 12.

[52] *Dynamics,* I, 61.

[53] Cf. Matilda White Riley and Mary E. Moore, "Analysis of Two-Person Groups: Some Notes on Lazarsfeld's Formalization," paper delivered at the annual meetings of the American Sociological Association, 1959.

cording to the pattern of their notes (acts) and, second, according to the proportions of the members (actors) who play strings, woodwinds, brasses, or percussion instruments—all without any fitting together of actors and their respective acts, without taking cognizance of the orchestration involved.

Yet these sociologistic measures may fail to match the concept which the sociologist has in mind. He often wishes to represent the group, not as an undifferentiated entity, but as a system of parts. His hypothesis frequently takes a form which cannot be tested merely by counting the number of transients and the number of suicides in a group. Because of growing awareness of such problems, there is an urgent present search for *social system measures*—as distinguished in this sense from sociologistic measures. One solution which has been recently suggested lies in *identifying the actors* in respect to their contributions to the over-all pattern.[54] Such social system measures would indicate *which* members of the orchestra contribute *which* notes to the symphonic pattern. Their classification of groups according to the rates of transiency and of suicide would show also whether or not the *same* group members who are transients also commit suicide.[55]

Our re-analysis of Sorokin's research suggests that some portions of it anticipate exactly this kind of solution to the problem. For example, in his appraisal of the economic well-being of countries, he starts out by rating each society as a whole according to its changing prosperity. Then he goes beyond this to provide some further information: he also shows the prosperity ratings of each of the main *classes* within the society. As he says, "even though the country as a whole is on the upward trend, this does not mean, necessarily, that the economic situation of all its classes follows the same trend."[56] Thus he accounts for the over-all trend in terms of the trends for the various classes (clergy, nobility, etc.). That is, in our formulation, his group measure of prosperity identifies the various parts (classes) within the group with respect to their prosperity, and follows each of the parts through the over-all process.

[54] See the discussions in Riley, Riley, and Toby, *op. cit.*, Part III.

[55] Our notion of a "sociologistic fallacy," which refers to research dealing with groups, is not to be confused with Robinson's "ecological fallacy," where the focus of theoretical concern is the individual. For a recent related discussion, see Peter M. Blau, "Structural Effects," *American Sociological Review*, XXV (1960), 178-93.

[56] *Dynamics*, III, 230.

Sorokin's concern with classifying the group in terms of the circulation of subgroups or individuals within it dates back to his classic study of *Social Mobility*. Here he postulates "two opposite types of society: one in which all children (100 per cent) 'inherit' the occupational status of their father; another in which no child inherits it."[57] By assembling data from many sources he is able to show that the average index of transmission in present Western societies is much less than 100, indicating that "contemporary occupational groups are far from being rigid."[58] Seeking further for possible trends in this transmission index, Sorokin and his students collected new data from several hundred families covering occupational changes over four generations. Again the important methodological point, as we see it, is that the same parts of the system—in this instance, families—are *identified* in terms of the property under study (occupation) and followed through the analysis, in order to explicate the nature of the total social process. Because he uses this form of measurement, Sorokin is able to suggest that "within the same society there may be groups in which inheritance of occupation goes down, while within other groups it increases."[59]

To be sure, this form of analysis is suggested, rather than fully developed, in such examples from Sorokin's work. Although he was eminently concerned with the "group structure" of a population,[60] his practical research approach seems generally better suited for over-all characterizations of societies than for indicating how various subgroups contribute to these over-all characteristics.[61] On the one hand, he is often (unwillingly) forced to a "statistical approach"[62] in which individuals are merely counted—or, at best, aggregated after weighting for their "influence"; and, on the other hand, many of his analyses are not concerned with identifying which of these individuals may contribute differentially to the total pattern of action or of culture. Nevertheless, the few examples which we have

[57] *Social and Cultural Mobility*, p. 415.
[58] *Ibid.*, p. 419.
[59] *Ibid.*, p. 424. This analysis of groups is in some respects comparable to "panel analysis" which was later developed for study of individuals. Cf. Paul F. Lazarsfeld, Bernard Berelson, and Hazel Gaudet, *The People's Choice* (New York: Columbia University Press, 1948).
[60] See, e.g., his important discussion of the classification of groups in *Society, Culture and Personality*, pp. 296 ff.
[61] Robert K. Merton has pointed this out in *Social Theory and Social Structure*, p. 467.
[62] *Society, Culture and Personality*, p. 296.

selected seem sufficient to set the stage for a further methodological development which would allow systematic analysis of the connections between (1) various aspects of the culture and (2) identifiable groups, classes, or individuals within the society.[63]

VIII. Social System Tests

A central problem in measurement today concerns the possible procedures for testing the assumptions underlying the selection and use of certain sense data as indicants of the concept under study. Various tests in current use (paired comparisons, item analysis, Guttman scaling, and the like) are concerned with establishing the existence of patterns and consistencies in acts or attitudes (e.g., perceptions of objects or responses to test items).

In addition to this, however, sociologists often need procedures for uncovering the underlying structure of the group.[64] Measurements may, for instance, be based on reconnaissance activities of a large number of soldiers, or the avowed aspirations of a large number of adolescents. The question may then arise: Is there any underlying structure among these individuals? Are the soldiers acting together as members of squads? Have the adolescents influenced each other's aspirations through interaction as members of peer groups? That is, is there any basis (apart from direct observation of the process itself) for treating and interpreting these data as measures of *groups?*

One incipient approach to this problem is a present attempt to develop a new type of statistical test[65] for making inferences from observed phenomena to the underlying social system. The ultimate objective is to test some of the peculiarly sociological assumptions about the interaction and mutual expectations which characterize the social process.

Sorokin is also directly concerned—at a high level of generality—

[63] The chapter in this volume by Barber and Merton deals with this matter in further detail: e.g., see their Summary, point 4.

[64] See Riley, Riley, and Toby, *op. cit.*, pp. 210 ff.

[65] See, e.g., Richard Cohn, Frederick Mosteller, John W. Pratt, and Maurice Tatsuoka, "Maximizing the Probability that Adjacent Order Statistics of Samples from Several Populations Form Overlapping Intervals," *The Annals of Mathematical Statistics,* XXXI, No. 4 (Dec., 1960), 1095-1104.

with this kind of problem.[66]   The problem, as he states it, is to determine "whether a given set of cultural phenomena are parts of a single system or merely coexisting congeries."[67]   He establishes two criteria for such determination (apart from "synchronicity," which, according to Sorokin, "plays some part," and which other scholars today often find extremely helpful in such tests).   One criterion is the "meaningful, logico-aesthetic unity" which may be latent within a given science, for example, or a given set of social actions.   The other criterion is the "causal interdependence" in which the actors may, perhaps, influence each other through inter-action.[68]   The test for system then consists in ascertaining that both the meaningful consistency and the interdependence are inherent in the set of phenomena.   And here Sorokin suggests a "short-cut" method of *first* establishing the "meaningful relatedness between two or more phenomena," and only then going to the further re-search required to establish "factual contact between them."

IX. Limitations and Difficulties

This discussion has been concerned with the constructive aspects of Sorokin's research, not with its defects.   But the very magnitude of Sorokin's undertaking and the relative lack of technical sophisti-cation of the time meant that some shortcomings were inevitable. His methods have met with a storm of criticism in some quarters of the sociological fraternity, and, in other quarters, with what some-times appears as a studied neglect.

At the technical level, many of the difficulties which beset this work in the 1920's and 1930's are now solved.   If Sorokin were starting the research today, modern sampling methods and data processing techniques would be available to reduce the enormous volume of materials and the time required for their analysis.[69] Moreover, increasing sophistication concerning mathematical sta-tistics would eliminate much of Sorokin's experimentation and re-sulting confusion over what kind of statistical average to choose, or what set of weights to use in combining various dimensions.

[66] *Society, Culture and Personality*, pp. 635 ff.
[67] *Ibid.*, p. 637.   [68] *Ibid.*, pp. 146-48.
[69] The senior author of this paper, who worked on a few of the statistics for *Dynamics*, remembers doing all of the computations by hand!

At the broader methodological level, many of the basic difficulties facing Sorokin's research arise from the vastness of the design and from the attempt to adapt scientific method to peculiarly sociological questions.   Since his critics seem, in effect, to expect that he should overcome *all* the weaknesses of a composite Weber-Durkheim-LePlay, they are, by the exaggerated standard, often right.   It is certainly true that his method is only partially adequate to his research objectives.

Yet Sorokin himself, far from professing complete adequacy for the task, is one of his own best critics. After his thorough analysis of the work of others in *Contemporary Sociological Theories,* he is fully aware of many of the pitfalls.   Thus, he seems to set forth upon the stupendous task of avoiding as many of them as he can.   He writes that the study of war, for example, is "no more than a pioneer survey of an unknown country, made without perfect instruments and without perfect training for the task."[70]   Of the study of internal disturbances he says, "Anybody who attempts to tackle these problems meets difficulties at every step, and realizes the dangers possibly more fully and clearly than any critic."[71] Despite these patent difficulties, he proceeds anyway, as he says, for the sake of "my adventurous spirit" and the "welfare of science."[72]

The almost unparalleled extent of such difficulties is suggested by the author in various passages of the *Dynamics.*   For example: "We collected so many singularistic facts that at the present moment we are lost in their multitude; . . . we do not know what to do with them and still less do we know what they mean and what knowledge they contain.   Courageously we continue to compile them. . . ."[73]   Most researchers have run into similar difficulties. But not on this grand scale!

X. From the Observer's Viewpoint

In spite of the color and the pathos which such comments add to our inquiry, our objective in this paper has not been to deal with the psychological state of Pitirim A. Sorokin *qua* actor.   We have

[70] *Dynamics,* III, 288.   [71] *Ibid.,* III, 384.
[72] *Ibid.,* III, 271.   [73] *Ibid.,* II, 303.

rather attempted to play Sorokin to Sorokin's own data, to "grasp the hidden meaning" in the details of his work, to look for its "typical and constant" elements. That is, we have attempted to take the viewpoint of the observer.

Hence our effort has been to avoid even the methodological component of his polemics. His own research, together with such scholarly formulations as those in *Sociocultural Causality, Space, Time,* constitutes the best answer to his opponents. Through his own example he counters various aberrations and limitations of modern sociology with his emphasis on meaning, his use of imagination and reason as well as sense perception, his efforts to deal appropriately with systems in contrast to congeries. Yet, his zest for disputation often leads him to unfortunate overstatement. He tends to weaken his own powerful position by inveighing against friend and foe alike. Thus, for example, despite his avowed use of verbal materials (where these "do not disagree with real behavior")[74] in the study of subjective states of actors within the system, he nevertheless seems to condemn, as useless, all "speech reactions"—from answers to hypothetical poll questions,[75] or psychological test results,[76] to changes in knowledge or reported behavior following a mass communication[77] or the verbal interaction observed in small groups.[78] Similarly, notwithstanding his continuing concern with problems of measuring qualitative variables, he ridicules as "metrophrenia"[79] the solutions to these problems worked out by serious and competent scholars. His gratuitous attack on Guttman scaling, for example, serves only to demonstrate his fundamental misunderstanding of the meaning of scalability and his own failure to recognize the procedure as an important complement to his own work. Thus the reader can find passages in his critical writings which seem to support almost any standpoint—or its opposite!

If Sorokin avoids consistency (the hobgoblin of little minds)[80] in his polemical writings, he also escapes it through his discussions of the epistemological dilemma. Having defined three systems of truth, he sometimes denounces his own research as the product of a

[74] *Social and Cultural Mobility,* p. 17 n. See also *Fads,* p. 93, or the interesting use of verbal materials in prediction cited in *Fads,* p. 259.
[75] *Fads,* p. 146.   [76] *Ibid.,* p. 58.
[77] *Ibid.,* p. 181.   [78] *Ibid.,* p. 234.
[79] *Ibid.,* pp. 122-30.
[80] Editor's note: The full statement of Ralph Waldo Emerson is: "A *foolish* consistency is the hobgoblin of little minds."

sensate age in which the truth of the senses is largely predominant. Here, too, our aim has been to cut through the ambivalence implied in what he says, in order to focus on what he does.[81] We try to employ only those "speech reactions" which fit our observations of his research—like the following: "In this work [*Dynamics*], I am not engaged in the study of the sociocultural phenomena from the standpoint of this truth of faith exclusively or mainly. I am studying them from the standpoint of the truth of reason and senses."[82] As late as the volume on *Society, Culture and Personality*, he shows how "in essence the methods and referential principles of sociology are the same as those of science generally," using logical and deductive methods, moderately exploiting "intuitive insight (always checked by other methods)," and widely applying empirical observation, statistical analysis, case study, and even experiment.[83]

Thus, our reading of his works leads us to expect that sociology will continue to benefit from his methodological models, both through the problems which he has solved and the problems which he has either formulated or implied. We can, in fact, imagine that the sociologist of the future may well complain, much as a frustrated successor to Plato once did, "Whenever I go anywhere in my attempts, I meet Sorokin coming back." We dare say that our reading will differ from the present "psychological" reading of the actor himself, and we look forward to Professor Sorokin's reply to our comments.

[81] We have not dealt with any question as to how he, *qua* investigator, establishes criteria for the classification of meaning. At the same time, we are quite aware that our own attempt to play the observer role in this paper is affected by our personal perspectives!

[82] *Dynamics*, IV, 734.

[83] *Society, Culture and Personality*, p. 18.

Russia and the United States: A Problem in Comparative Sociology

Alex Inkeles

Professor Sorokin's volume on *Russia and the United States*[1] grew out of a series of lectures he gave during the early years of World War II. It is easy to understand, under the circumstances, that his chief aim was to assess the chances that the wartime allies would continue to enjoy peaceful, or even cordial, relations in the postwar period. In evaluating the book, therefore, we should keep in mind that he did not set out to present a systematic comparative analysis of the social structure of the two countries. Nevertheless, one of the assumptions with which Professor Sorokin approached his task of prediction was that "sociocultural similarities conduce toward peaceful relations between communities of men."[2] In order to estimate the future course of Soviet-American relations, therefore, he was led to examine the extent of sociocultural similarity between the United States and Soviet Russia. Indeed, he acknowledged that the possibility of reconciling the American way of life and its system of values with those of Soviet Communism posed a problem "so important that it cannot either be dodged or passed by."[3]

Professor Sorokin felt it was a "fallacy" to argue that "there is an irreconcilable conflict between the Soviet and American way of life."[4] Feeling as he did he understandably sought mainly for evidence of sociocultural similarity or congeniality between the social structure of the United States and that of the Soviet Union. His illustrations include instances of technological progress, eco-

[1] E. P. Dutton and Co., New York, 1944. Unless otherwise indicated, the page citations given in parentheses all refer to this first edition.
[2] P. 162.　　　　　　　　　　[3] *Ibid.*, p. 177.
[4] *Ibid.*, p. 209.

nomic growth, development of music and the arts. In the last hundred years these two countries, he argues, have become the "chief bearers of the torch of sociocultural creativeness." "Far from being polar antitheses," he concluded, "the two nations reveal a series of most striking similarities geopolitically, psychologically, culturally, and socially."[5]

As background for an evaluation of Professor Sorokin's analysis, I have drawn up a series of brief statements comparing and contrasting five of the major institutional realms of Soviet and American society: political structure, economy, social classes, family, and school. In those instances in which Professor Sorokin made relevant comments, particularly with regard to the polity and the economy, I have reported his assessment. I do not, however, focus my presentation directly on an evaluation of his position, reserving for a separate concluding section a fuller assessment of Professor Sorokin's contribution and its implications for students of comparative social structure.

I. Some Features of Social Structure in the U.S. and U.S.S.R.

A. Polity. Our era is characterized by the predominance of the centralized national state over the autonomy of the region and the diffuse power of the local community, both of which progressively lost their significance in the eighteenth and nineteenth centuries. Any comparison of the Soviet and American systems must, therefore, begin with a discussion of the nature of the state and its relation to the rest of the society. The contrasts here are understandably the most obvious, but they are none the less basic.

Despite Marx's emphasis on the primacy of economics, that is of the mode of production and productive relations, in determining the character of the social order, the distinctive contribution of Lenin and Stalin was to reverse the formula and to demonstrate the possibility of determining the economic system through control of the political power. This is the basic meaning of Stalin's affirmation that the Soviet revolution was made "from above," from those "commanding heights" of which Lenin spoke so often. The Soviet state did not spring full grown from the head of Marx; indeed, its

---

[5] *Ibid.*, p. 161.

development was never dreamed of by him, and if he had conceived it he would almost certainly have labeled it a bastard—no child of his. Credit for the conception must go to Lenin, but even he did no more than suggest its outlines and provide it the breath of life. The actual forging of the system was the work of a man initially as obscure and demeaned among the Bolshevik lords of creation as was Hephaestus among the Greek gods. While others busied themselves with oratory and stood on the front lines of the battle, Stalin quietly went about the unromantic work of fashioning an apparatus of control which in time carried him to the highest seat of power.

Almost from its very inception the Soviet Union has known only a one-party system in which all political power was concentrated.[6] Indeed, with the exception of a very few years this system has functioned as a one-man dictatorship. In any event no one will quarrel with the characterization if we say that it is a self-perpetuating oligarchy. The Communist party has never been a mass movement, certainly not in the sense that the trade unions or the Youth League are. It has for a long time numbered its members in the millions—most recently over seven million—yet, these have represented only between 2 and 4 per cent of the population. Although size, therefore, has not been an absolute barrier to its attainment, there has at no time been effective democratic control of the leadership. On the contrary, the rank and file of the membership has served mainly as the agent of those whom they nominally elect and control. Within the government, party members serve as a kind of special extra-governmental bureaucracy for enforcing the party's decisions and checking on their application. Among the people the party members serve as a source of exhortation and inspiration in the effort to mobilize the masses behind the party's program. Soviet leaders place great store on the semblance of legitimacy. They fear the label of "adventurers" in politics, which would be applicable to them by Leninist standards if they acted without the consent and support of the working masses who presumably define each historic moment for appropriate revolutionary action. Hence the solemn play which is periodically acted out, of

[6] There are several excellent standard works on the development and structure of the polity in Soviet society. Generally acknowledged as outstanding is Merle Fainsod, *How Russia is Ruled* (Cambridge, Mass.: Harvard University Press, 1953).

citizens voting for the Supreme Soviet and party members electing delegates to congresses of the Communist party. In all elections there is only one slate, which is officially designated, and for which one can only vote yes or no. In elections to the Supreme Soviet one is expected as a show of loyalty to disdain the available secret polling booth and to cast one's ballot openly and proudly for the officially sponsored candidates.

At every point this system is polar to that in those societies generally acknowledged to have democratic political systems. To qualify for inclusion in this group a country must have at least two political parties which are factually independent and autonomous. The concept of a loyal opposition must be accepted by the party in power, and it may not deny the opposition the reasonable opportunity to continue to work for its platform and the prospect of holding office in the future. This requires, as a minimum, that the group out of power have the freedom to hold political meetings and to propagandize for its program, to maintain an independent press and other organs of communication, and to criticize the policies of the government on all matters including the most fundamental.

In no respect are these conditions met in the Soviet Union. The legislatures of all the democratic regimes of the world are in more or less continuous session, engage in protracted debate, and produce legislation which clearly reflects the compromise of diverse interests and aspirations. Soviet legislative bodies, including the congresses of the Communist party, meet infrequently or even rarely, conclude all their momentous business in a matter of days, hear almost no discussion, let alone debate, and produce legislation which virtually without any alteration represents the precise wishes of the leaders who convened the legislative session to give approval to policies already selected.

Even within the Communist party itself the maintaining of a free minority is not possible, since such groups are labeled as impermissible factions intending to destroy the "monolithic unity" of the party. There is a nominal rule that public organizations such as the trade unions are allowed to publish newspapers, but their control is in fact in the hands of the ruling Communist party. Exercise of the rights of free speech and press are explicitly limited in the Constitution to those forms which are in accord with the interests of the proletariat, and these are, of course, in turn defined by the Communist party.[7]

A democratic system assumes the general recognition and firm institutionalization of definite limits on the powers of all governments, including the central government. The United States has no doubt gone much further in implementing this principle than the more centralized government of France and, indeed, exceeds England in this respect. Nevertheless, in all democratic systems such principles as the inviolability of the judiciary, the rights of the local community, the rights of security of person and of property, the autonomy of family and home reflect the general recognition, and legal implementation, of definite limits on the power of government. By contrast, we may note, in the words of Sorokin, "an almost unlimited and centralized regimentation of government is the heart of the Soviet system."[8] While endorsing Professor Sorokin's general characterization of the Soviet system in this respect, we yet cannot accept his reservation that this is not distinctive to the Soviet Union, nor his assertion that such regimentation developed there mainly in response to the emergency of revolution and war. On the contrary, it represents a typical feature of the conception of government in the Soviet Union. This is not to deny that as the regime has become stabilized or normalized, actions exceeding constitutional, legal, and moral and popular value limits have decreased in frequency and extremity. That there has been less need for repression does not mean that in principle the Soviet leaders accept the idea of legitimate limits on the freedom of action of the central authorities, or that in fact they would hesitate to take drastic action at home, as they did on the international front in Hungary, should the domestic situation require it.

Even if we acknowledge the profound differences in formal structure and in the regular practice of politics in the United States and the U.S.S.R., is it not correct that the direction of change in the two political systems is such as to make them ever more alike? C. Wright Mills, for example, argues that effective power in the United States has drifted into the hands of a self-perpetuating elite which cuts across government, industry, and the military and

[7] The system of control of means of communication, and the Communist theory underlying that control, are dealt with at length in Alex Inkeles, *Public Opinion in Soviet Russia* (Cambridge: Harvard University Press, 1956).

[8] Sorokin, *op. cit.*, p. 173.

which actually makes all of the important decisions affecting the fate of this country.[9] Numerous Sovietologists argue that the progressively entrenched vested interests of Soviet industrial management and military leaders severely limit the freedom of action of the Soviet political rulers. Does this suggest that each system is moving away from its polarized position toward some common middle ground? Perhaps, but the evidence on either side is far from compelling. If Mills were correct, it hardly seems likely that programs such as the Marshall Plan or the American aid program in India and Pakistan could have been launched. On the Soviet scene, we must recognize that an autonomous and powerful army would hardly have permitted the demotion of Zhukov or the demobilization of the Soviet ground forces, that a politically effective managerial elite would have demanded a larger role in shaping the decentralization of Soviet industry, that an even slightly effective political opposition would hardly have allowed, even in defeat, the exile of its leaders in the persons of Molotov, Kaganovich, and Bulganin.

The differences in the formal structure and the informally accepted rules of the game in Soviet and American politics have profound consequences in the capacity of each system to act, and especially to act on itself in order to effect adaptive change. The essence of the democratic system is that it permits the embodiment of diverse groups and their interests in competing political organizations and programs. The democratic process then becomes the slow, protracted, often inchoate development of compromise and adjustment between these interests in the gradual evolution of new programs and policies. This feature of democratic systems is almost entirely absent in Soviet society. This is not to say that the leaders need not reckon with any group. On the contrary it is evident that Soviet leaders, especially since the death of Stalin, weigh very carefully the effects of various actions on popular morale in general or in specific segments of the economy. They are especially concerned with morale as manifested in willingness and ability to produce or otherwise effectively to perform functions of importance to the state. This mode of influence, however, has little in common with the direct participation by workers, managers, farmers, or others, acting as interest groups in the process of public discussion and the exercise of influence through votes, funds, or

[9] C. Wright Mills, *The Power Elite* (New York: Oxford University Press, 1957).

appeals for public opinion support. It is very different indeed from direct action in strikes or non-violent defiance of law, as in the Negro fight for civil rights in southern United States.

One consequence of the suppression of such struggles is that there is always a clear and precisely identifiable national purpose in the Soviet Union, one defined by the only group with the right and the power to determine it. In the United States, by contrast, it is almost impossible to state a clear and commonly accepted national purpose, except the dubious principle of giving everyone a break sooner or later. This means that the Soviet system is characterized by enormous flexibility, by almost unlimited freedom of action, by exceptional capacity for adjustment of its internal organization to take account of changes in either its externally defined situation or the internal structure of the society. Since these changes can be made without full consultation, and certainly without effective opposition by the various interest groups in the society, the capacity of the Soviet system to adjust to changed circumstances, to adapt to developments arising from technological advance, or to reorganize more effectively to meet changed goals is virtually unprecedented in modern society. It certainly gives the Soviet system, for good or ill, an enormous advantage in competition with the governments of democratic societies, which must always consider the vital interests of major strata of the society as a matter of principle, and in fact are often unable to act at all effectively because of the resistance of entrenched local, parochial, class, and related interest groups.

B. Economy. It is one of those typical anomalies of history that the feature of the Soviet and American societies which in both Marxist theory and popular thinking most distinguish them is in fact far from being the most reliable indicator of the nature of the two systems. Professor Sorokin argues that in the United States the role of the modern corporation and that of government intervention in economic life have transformed the "classic capitalist system," while in the Soviet Union the principles of mass ownership have in fact not been fully implemented. We may agree with him that "in neither country do the real owners—the Russian people and the hundreds of thousands of shareholders in the United States

—manage what they theoretically own."[10]   He may even be right
in saying that "American capitalism and Russian Communism are
now little more than the ghosts of their former selves."[11]   Nevertheless, it is not very likely that anyone will mistake the one system
for the other.

Both the Soviet Union and the United States are outstanding
exponents and embodiments of modern industrialism, with its
glorification of mechanization and its fostering of large-scale production, rapid transportation, and vast urban complexes.   Production as an end in itself, the preoccupation with the making of things,
especially things which make other things, has in both countries
come to dominate the value system to a degree probably without
precedent in history.   Despite this similarity, the two systems remain profoundly different.   Corporate and state ownership are very
different forms which produce profoundly different consequences.
Not the least of these is the fact that the big corporation, however
much it may escape the control of its stockholders, may still be
regulated by the state, whereas in the government-owned establishment the interests of state and economic enterprise are fused.
Among the many consequences of this fusion is the vital fact that
the freedom to strike is generally denied the employees of state
enterprises, which in the Soviet Union means it is denied to everyone.

The outstanding characteristic of Soviet economic life is its
uniform pattern.   This contrasts sharply with the mixed nature of
the American economy, which involves government controls in
some areas, but not others.   Large corporations predominate in
some sectors while others, such as trade or newer industrial realms
like electronics, tend to be dominated by smaller business.   It is
rather striking to note, in this connection, that Professor Sorokin
says almost nothing of the role of planning.   Planning is after all a
distinctive feature of the Soviet economy; indeed, some would argue
it to be the chief distinction.   By contrast, in the United States
planning is almost completely absent, at least in the sense of a centralized, co-ordinated program backed by the power of the state.
This contrast was certainly less sharp when viewed from the wartime perspective from which Sorokin wrote, but it was certainly
evident even then.   In any event, since the war the American

[10] Sorokin, *op. cit.*, p. 202.   [11] *Ibid.*, p. 179.

economy has returned to its more characteristic low level of control, whereas planning persists in undiminished strength in the Soviet Union. The postwar decentralization of industrial administration under Khrushchev was not accompanied by any decrease in the importance of the centrally determined plans which the locally administered industries must follow.

Not only is the role of government in economic life profoundly different in the two systems, but so also is the part played by the mass of citizens. In their status as shareholders, Americans may be denied essential control over management, but they exercise profound, indeed almost absolute, control over industry in their role as consumers. By marked contrast the consumer has almost no significance in the Soviet industrial scene. Economic planning for preeminence in heavy industry, government allocation of materials and administration of prices have contributed to a chronic shortage of consumers' goods and to the high prices and poor quality of what has been available. The situation of the consumer has been bettered and continues to improve in the post-Stalin era, but he still plays a markedly different role in the structure of the Soviet economy from that he occupies in the United States.

One sector of the Soviet economy does more approximate the economic pattern appropriate to a mixed economy, namely agriculture. It is true that the State Farm, which is run on the same principles as a factory, has been of increasing importance, especially in the newly opened steppe regions. Nevertheless, the collective farm remains the overwhelmingly predominant form of agricultural, productive organization in the Soviet Union. Like the factory, the collective farm is subject to centralized planning and allocation of resources, and the greater part of its crop is purchased at fixed prices. Yet the collective farm is unlike the factory in that it runs on a modified profit-sharing basis. A part of its crop is sold in an open and only mildly regulated market. In addition the peasant has his own private economy alongside that of the collective, raising food on a family plot not only for his own consumption but for sale in the peasant market. We can by no means accept Professor Sorokin's version of the common misconception that the peasant collective farm is "merely a modernized form of an old national institution—the peasant 'mir' and 'obschina,' or a variety of workers' productive cooperative society known to all countries and greatly developed in pre-revolutionary Russia."[12]   But we must acknowledge the collective farm as the structural feature of Soviet society most approximating the principle of mixed economy which characterizes the United States and the democratic countries of Europe.

The similarities and differences in the nature of the respective economic systems generate characteristic similarities and differences in the responses of the typical occupational groups working within each.   This presents an interesting realm for sociological investigation, which Professor Sorokin has rather notably neglected. To a degree both management and labor in the United States and the Soviet Union work in a very similar institutional setting.   In both countries people work in large-scale units functioning bureaucratically under centralized but distant centers of control.   Each unit is expected to maximize the effective exploitation of the resources placed at its command.

A comparison of Soviet industrial managers with their counterparts in American industry, therefore, reveals a striking number of similarities in their response to their situation.   Professor Granick has called to our attention the conflicts of line and staff units, the conflict between loyalty to one's shop as against that to the plant or the economy at large, the low level of worker participation in programs to encourage innovation, and the circumventing of bureaucratic rules and regulations promulgated at the top and meant to be executed at the local level.[13]

In addition, the researches of the Harvard Project[14] revealed that workers and other occupational strata in the Soviet Union respond to their life situation in ways comparable to the response of the corresponding groups in the United States and other industrial countries.   For example, in both the Soviet Union and the United States the proportion enjoying job satisfaction is very high among professional and managerial personnel, and falls steadily as one descends the occupational ladder.   In both countries the upper white-collar group feels the most important qualities of a job are its

[12] Sorokin, op. cit., pp. 203-4.   For the definitive statement on the similarities and differences between the mir and the collective farm, see Lazar Volin, "The Peasant Household Under the Mir and the Kolkhoz in Modern Russian History," in The Cultural Approach to History, ed. Caroline F. Ware (New York: Columbia University Press, 1940).

[13] David Granick, The Red Executive (New York: Doubleday and Co., 1960).

[14] Alex Inkeles and Raymond A. Bauer, The Soviet Citizen (Cambridge: Harvard University Press, 1959).

intrinsic interest and the opportunities for self-expression it offers, whereas those lower in the occupational scale give more emphasis to pay and security.

Whether such similarities are significant or merely curious and unimportant is an issue which we cannot, unfortunately, enter into. Certainly such parallels should not be allowed to obscure persistent bases of structural differentiation. When discussing their occupational problems, American managers place labor relations and selling their product in a competitive market at the very forefront of their concern, whereas neither problem is ever mentioned spontaneously by Soviet managers. This difference in emphasis arises, of course, from the structural differences in the two economies. Under a system of planning, allocation of material, and high production goals, the Soviet manager's prime problems are to secure the materials to attain his output targets. Since trade unions are defined as adjuncts of the party in the task of mobilizing the workers and have no power to strike, labor relations hardly loom as a major problem to the Soviet manager. This means, equally, that the significance of the trade union to the worker in both countries is also profoundly different. The Soviet worker is not particularly conscious of his trade union. He does not look upon it as distinctively "his own" organization, and he certainly does not think of it as a militant force acting to advance the workers' interests. On each of these dimensions we should be obliged to place the American worker at the opposite pole. Differences of this order cannot be freely put aside for the sake of easy generalizations which suggest that the two systems have become so much alike that this overshadows the remaining contrasts.

C. Social classes. In our examination of the economic systems of the Soviet Union and the United States we stressed that certain similarities should not obscure the basic differences. In assessing the structure of stratification in the two societies we must reverse the emphasis and urge that certain differences between the two systems not be allowed to obscure the basic similarities.

True, the American "big capitalist" still exists, even though he exerts much less influence on the American scene. We must grant that there is no equivalent in the Soviet Union of the independent small businessman, a socially important if not numerous element in the American class structure. Soviet peasants form the largest class in that nation, and although there are some parallels between their situation and that of agricultural labor on large ranches, estates, and farms, there is no very precise equivalent in the United States. Yet in important respects the Soviet class structure is like that of the United States. As industrial countries, both have the familiar strata of administrative-professional elites; white-collar, skilled, ordinary and unskilled worker; and lower-level service personnel and farm labor in approximately that rank order of prestige and standing in the community. In both societies class position is predominantly determined by one's occupational position rather than on the basis of inherited characteristics, and one's occupational standing in turn rests largely on educational attainment or technical training. Both countries, therefore, qualify as open class societies characterized by substantial upward mobility. Under these conditions consciousness of class and interclass hostility tends to be modest and mild, the sense of opportunity for the capable and willing is strong. Manners are informal, relations between classes easy and natural, and the feeling of equality pervasive. These easy relations are greatly facilitated in the United States by the absence of a history of traditional legally enforced class distinctions. The equivalent force in Russian history was the sharp break in the class pattern introduced in the early period of the Soviet Revolution.

Comparable structures encourage comparable responses. Soviet citizens talk about their class structure in much the same way as Americans do about theirs—beginning with the high frequency of initial denials that there are any classes at all in their country. There are of course distinctive attributes. The role of the political elite is much wider and their domination of the status scene infinitely more marked and pervasive in the Soviet Union. But equalitarianism is deeply rooted in the values of both sets of people, as well as being institutionalized in both social structures. Indeed, there is probably no realm of social structure in which an American set down on the Soviet scene would feel more at home. Considering this fact it is rather striking that Professor Sorokin said almost nothing systematic about social stratification, classes, social mobility, and the like, since his thesis of increasing similarity of the

American and Soviet social structure receives considerable support in this area.

D. Family and character formation. One feature the United States and the Soviet Union certainly exhibit in common is considerable confusion about the role of the family in modern society. The United States of course has never had a national family policy. In the earlier years of the republic such an idea was unthinkable, and in any event unnecessary. By the time it became apparent to all that a policy was essential, no one could propose any which was meaningful and could be implemented. Everyone is, however, piously agreed that the family is the very foundation stone of society and must be aided in every way.

Initially the situation was quite different in the Soviet Union. Engels' writings had made it quite clear that the family was expected to wither away under Communism. After a number of rather foolish assaults on that doughty institution, it was the policy itself which withered away. Today in the Soviet Union as in the United States the family is defined as a pillar on which society rests. The family is called upon to shape the future by bringing up well-mannered, conscientious, courteous citizens who will not litter the streets, will work hard, and strive to succeed in life.

In either the Soviet Union or the United States it is very difficult, however, to ascertain just what one is supposed to do to bring about the beneficial results everyone expects from the family. The ineffectual pamphleteering by the Soviet Academy of Pedagogical Sciences and the women's magazines bears a striking resemblance to the message disseminated by the U.S. Children's Bureau and similar agencies in the U.S. Department of Health, Education, and Welfare. It cannot be said of either country that the government knows how to bring about the results it desires. In both cases it is evident that the government does not wish to become too directly involved in internal family affairs. Consequently in both countries there is much wailing and wringing of hands about juvenile delinquency and the less serious but more widespread failings of youth—disrespect for parents and general disregard for authority; shirking work, and other forms of irresponsibility, especially as regards money and property; emotional instability, volatility, and often explosive destructiveness. Since the character of youth is laid down in the internal relations of the family, and these are relatively inaccessible to the respective governments, effective countermeasures are not easily come by short of accepting full-time public responsibility for the rearing of children—something which no one is willing to attempt.

In an important degree each society has nothing but itself to blame, because in each the family is only responding to forces emanating from the larger society. Both systems stress the future rather than the past, and acclaim youth as the hope of the future. American and Soviet society value daring and initiative, which leads to the encouragement of aggressive self-assertion in the young, and in turn often encourages disdain for authority. In the Soviet Union, as in the United States, the obvious reason for success and the validation of it lies in amassing prestige and income, with which in turn one amasses consumption goods, which again fosters self-aggrandizement and a basic hedonism. Emphasis on the essential dignity of *every* person, and on the more radical belief in basic human equality, weakens respect for hierarchical, formally constituted authority.

The virtual disappearance of the extended family and the progressive depersonalization of the work setting in modern office and industry have encouraged people to concentrate their search for emotional satisfactions on the few members of the nuclear family unit and particularly on the children. Modern parents manifest deep fear of loss of the child's love—an interesting reversal of the classic training pattern in which emphasis was laid on the *child's* fear of the loss of parental love. Parents are therefore led to overindulge their children, which again contributes to producing in the young an exaggerated sense of their importance, and the expectation that they should be served and cared for without limit and without contributing their own efforts. The end result is often a person who secures rewards by effective use of his personality and by the manipulation of others rather than by effort and mastery over nature and materials.

These tendencies in the larger society are, perhaps theoretically, amenable to change. In most cases, however, they are part and parcel of the basic social structure of the two most modern, advanced, and "progressive" of nations. In many ways both countries depend on these qualities, which are functional to the system. How often are we told how important to the American economy it is that people so strongly want things, and so deeply wish to accumulate them without end? Although a passion for consumption goods cannot be so easily satisfied in the Soviet economy, the system depends heavily on the strength of the desire for increased earnings felt by manual, white-collar, and professional workers.

If the family cannot be relied on to inculcate in the young certain values important to society, it must seek to exert influence through other segments of the social structure which play a role in character formation and in shaping values. This is more readily accomplished in the Soviet Union. The greater and more intimate control over education exercised there by the central authorities (rather than by local school boards subject to parental influence) gives the government great leverage in using the primary school to indoctrinate children in the virtues of obedience, the values of group participation, the importance of co-operation, and a sense of obligation to the community. The more authoritarian structure of the school regime aids the regime's self-conscious effort to inculcate these ideas. Youth movements organized by the Communist party —the Pioneers enrol children from the age of ten to fourteen and the Komsomol which takes them from there—provide an additional source of training in social service and co-operative action. They also serve to inculcate the values of service, self-sacrifice, submission to group discipline, respect for authority, and orderliness. They try to teach the children the pleasure of sharing work and production rather than leisure and consumption.[15] The United States lacks comparable extra- or non-familial socializing agencies of this type, at least on a scale which would influence a large proportion of the youth and do so with an effectiveness greater than that of the Boy Scouts. This is one of the most serious deficiencies in the contemporary American social structure, and one of the decided disadvantages it suffers in long-term competition with the Soviet system.

[15] The role of the Communist youth organizations in socializing the young for life in Soviet society is dealt with at length in Allen Kassof, "The Soviet Youth Program: Socialization in a Totalitarian Society," unpublished Ph.D. dissertation, Department of Social Relations, Harvard University, 1960.

E. *Education (the school).* Until the Soviet regime came on the scene no other large country rivaled the United States in the extent to which the society as a whole had accepted and implemented the principle of universal free education, and not only at the elementary but also at the secondary and to some degree even at the university level. Although the "struggle" against illiteracy, as it was called in the U.S.S.R., was there waged more dramatically, and with greater propaganda effect, the underlying forces impelling this development were in both societies broadly similar. The dominant political ideology in both countries stressed the widespread and active participation of the citizen in the process of government and in the management of public affairs. In the United States this tradition can be traced back to Jeffersonian, certainly to Jacksonian, democracy, while in Russia it had its roots in the Zemstvo schools of the mid-nineteenth century, to which Sorokin calls our attention.[16] The Bolsheviks revived this tradition and vastly extended the principle of mass action. Such participation, however, required an educated and informed citizenry. Education for all was the indispensable precondition for the attainment of that state in which every cook would help to run the government and every worker at the bench would take his turn at record keeping and administration.

Lenin's hopes for mass participation in government were not to be realized, but the impetus to widespread education was preserved because literacy was deemed a necessary qualification for effective participation in the more complex labor processes of modern industry and for the growing ranks of white-collar employees who serviced it. The same need was felt in the United States. Perhaps a more important consideration, however, lies in the fact that both systems stressed the right of the individual to secure full personal development of his faculties and to win a position in society commensurate with his native talents—goals which could be attained only by individuals with access to educational opportunities.

Neither the Soviet Union nor the United States has quite fulfilled the goal of giving everyone all the education he is capable of absorbing. The United States, being in terms of gross national

[16] Professor Sorokin does not explicitly mention the schools, but he does discuss the role of the Zemstvo in local government and in supplying medical care. See pp. 75, 78, and 149.

product roughly twice as rich as the Soviet Union, does better in the proportion of young people it provides a college education, but even there as many as a third of the qualified high school graduates do not go on to college. More difficult to evaluate but probably more important than the failure to meet the quantitative demands for higher education are the changes in the conception of educational goals and the methods of their implementation.

Over the years Soviet education came progressively to be subordinated to training for vocational purposes, even at the higher levels, with less and less emphasis placed on general education as a means for personal rather than occupational or professional development. In the process an approach to curriculum and classroom atmosphere which had originally stressed freedom, initiative, and creativity was suborned to emphasize authority, obedience, and rote learning. On the American scene the popularization of education led to a general decline of standards and values, and at the college level to the demeaning of education through replacement of the conception of the liberally educated man by the image of college man as playboy.

Certainly, at their best both the Soviet and American educational systems are quite impressive. The Soviet Union does a remarkable job in training a steady and large supply of the teachers, doctors, engineers, technicians, and scientists needed by the nation, and the good students of the better American colleges can certainly qualify as men of broad culture and learning. At the average level and below, however, the Soviet educational system becomes a glorified trade school and the American college a never-never land in which the youth pass time in a prolongation of adolescence, acting out their own impulses and living out their parents' fantasies of the good life, before accepting adult responsibilities.

These differences are not merely happenstance, or cultural "accidents." They reflect important differences in the social structures in which the respective educational systems are embedded. The objectives of education in the Soviet Union are determined by the central political authorities, and the emphasis on technical and scientific training reflects both the primacy they assign to production and economic development and the fear and hostility to free and full exploration of philosophical, literary, and humanistic ideas which characterize the narrow dogmatism of the Soviet Marxist leadership. In the United States the local community has relatively complete autonomy over elementary and high school education. At the college level the importance of private money in both the support of educational institutions and the payment for the student's educational expenses permits the colleges to be relatively free of central control and dictation of the content of their curriculums. This, plus the absence of any clear and compelling national purpose in education to which most would adhere, fosters the extraordinary diversity and complexity of the American educational system. It also permits the degradation of education encountered in many schools and in parts of almost all American college student bodies.

II. Problems in Comparative Structural Analysis

No doubt there are important, often striking, similarities in Soviet and American social structure, and in some respect they may have followed parallel paths in the course of their development. In addition to those developed by Professor Sorokin, I have pointed to several others in the comparison of the two systems in the preceding section. Both nations are large-scale societies, composed of populations of diverse ethnic origins, sharing a diffuse secular culture. The United States and the Soviet Union are outstanding in their devotion to the maximization of industrial production through large-scale organization, the exploitation of science, and reliance on widespread popular education. In both countries physical and social mobility is taken for granted in an open class system which stresses equality, challenges tradition, and encourages individual and collective progress.

This list of similarities could be expanded to great length. The same is unfortunately true of the list of differences. Dictatorship, or at least one-party oligarchy, as against a multi-party democratic political system; state control and planning as opposed to corporate management and the dominance of the market; controlled communication and governmental dictation in art as against free expression and private pursuit of the arts. Here again the list could be expanded to greater length.

We are therefore faced with the same difficulty which sooner or later confronts all efforts at the systematic comparative analysis of social structure, namely that of combining or weighting similarities and differences to yield one composite judgment. Unfortunately, sociology does not provide any equivalent for such measures as gross national product, per capita income, or rate of growth of industrial output, which permit us to combine diverse economic factors into one common and standard measure. There is no unified scale to the metric with which we can reduce the similarities and differences in social structure, leaving us with a single score for the comparison of the Soviet Union and the United States.

Professor Sorokin stresses the fact of change. However wide apart their starting points, he says, the two systems are "now little more than the ghosts of their former selves."[17] Indeed, he argues that "economically and politically the two nations have been steadily converging toward a similar type of social organization and economy."[18] There are many who would challenge this assertion, especially as regards the political structure and the economic organization of the two countries. Yet, even if the two nations were moving closer together, the fact of convergence could be much less important than the nature of the differences which persisted. How can we then assess the relative significance of one or another similarity or difference between two social systems? Although he does not explicitly state them to be such, Professor Sorokin's study suggests implicitly two relevant tests or standards of judgment. One is a test in action, the other a judgment based on values.

The test in action is provided by the pattern of relations between the United States and the Soviet Union after World War II. In the first edition, published in 1944, Professor Sorokin at a number of points asserted quite vigorously a prediction about Soviet-American relations in the postwar period. Since the two nations were not separated by deep-seated value conflicts and were socioculturally "congenial," this was "bound to perpetuate [the] noble record of peace between the two nations, regardless of the personal whims of their rulers." Professor Sorokin went even further, to declare: "If and when these rulers become unwise and begin to commit one blunder after another, there may conceivably be some temporary differences and quarrels between the countries. But even these conflicts are bound to be minor and can hardly lead to an armed

---

[17] Sorokin, *op. cit.*, p. 179.   [18] *Ibid.*, p. 208.

conflict."[19]   At a later point he commented that the same forces making for similarity and congeniality of the two systems "presage still closer cooperation in the future—a welcome destiny, beneficial to both peoples and to the rest of mankind."[20]

We need not labor the point that the development of "cold war" relations after World War II, an unceasing arms race with indescribable powers of mass destruction, and actual armed conflict in Korea, all lead to the conclusion that Professor Sorokin's prediction of cordial relations was hardly borne out by subsequent events.   In the second edition of *Russia and the United States*,[21] which appeared in 1950, Professor Sorokin acknowledges these facts, and seeks to explain why, when "there was every apparent reason for the postwar continuation of American-Russian friendly relationships, and no apparent reason at all for the 'cold-war,'" the latter nevertheless suddenly replaced the previous co-operation of the two countries.[22]

In considering this change, Professor Sorokin argues that the popular explanation in terms of ideological, social, and economic differences is not adequate, because there are so many historic examples of cordial relations and alliances between the United States and other countries which were even more profoundly different from it than is the Soviet Union.   It is not appropriate to enter here into a discussion of the alternative explanation Professor Sorokin does offer.   We should note, however, that he has here shifted the basis of his argument.   In the first edition he did not restrict himself to saying that differences did not preclude understanding.   Rather, he mainly emphasized the similarities, and asserted that the two nations were "steadily converging toward a similar type of social organization and economy."[23]   Furthermore, he argued that it was above all these "similarities" and the "congeniality" of the two sociocultural systems which made for such good prospects for cordial relations.   We must conclude, therefore, either that the theory is inadequate and that similarity in social structure does not make for a greater probability of cordial relations, or that Professor Sorokin was incorrect in his assessment of the degree of congeniality between Soviet and American social structure.   It is, of course, possible that he was incorrect on both counts.

[19] *Ibid.*, p. 162.   [20] *Ibid.*, p. 209.
[21] London, Stevens and Sons, Ltd., 1950.   Page citations for the second edition refer to this source.
[22] *Ibid.*, p. 165.   [23] Sorokin, *op. cit.*, first edition, p. 208.

The test of values provides quite a different basis for dealing with the fact that social science provides no single standard scale on which any two nations may be placed, but rather always confronts us with a list of discrete similarities and differences. Clearly, the mere number of similarities and differences, however important, is unlikely to be decisive. The critical question will be the weight each of us assigns to one or another factor according to his own scheme of values. On this score Professor Sorokin makes his position quite explicit in the second edition. While acknowledging some important differences between the United States and the Soviet Union, he judged them to be unimportant relative to certain other overriding common values such as survival. In the face of this common interest he ruled that all other "seemingly conflicting values . . . are so insignificant that their 'incompatibility' amounts to no more than the 'incompatibility' of the advertisements for this or that brand of cigarettes, each claiming superiority over all other."[24]

We do not deny Professor Sorokin the right to his perspective, but we need not automatically accept it for ourselves. Professor Sorokin chooses to judge the Soviet Union and the United States from a great distance, an Olympian height. Yet, if we get sufficiently distant from the immediate and concrete, any two contemporary large-scale systems will seem basically alike, just as any two men, no matter how different in character and action, are alike as "men." No doubt there are similarities in the two societies as great industrial nations. Without question we can in each and for both point to flaws, defects, failures, denials of liberty, denigration of values, and the like. When we have completed such a tabulation, however, there remain certain stubborn facts with which we must reckon. Probably the most important are the differences in the freedom of political activity, the share people have in deciding their future, the opportunities for free expression of the spirit in art and religion, which in the United States are at a level comparing favorably with most periods in history, but which in the Soviet Union remain at a point very near the bottom in the experience of Western European society.

It is very difficult to believe that in the judgment of history the differences in the political structure of the Soviet Union and the United States, and in their role in the period following World War

[24] Sorokin, *op. cit.*, second edition, p. 176.

II, will be seen as inconsequential. It may be true, as Professor
Sorokin asserts, that in both societies "germs" of the "disease" represented by the disintegration of the sensate Western culture are
equally abundant and active. Although the germ may be the same,
and the illness equally advanced, this hardly makes the organism
infected the same. Many features of the Soviet system violate the
most profound principles of the liberal political tradition painstakingly built up in European culture over several hundred years.
With regard to these differences we cannot agree with Professor
Sorokin that "any sane person pays no attention to such incompatibilities."[25]

[25] *Ibid.*

Sorokin on Law, Revolution, War, and Social Calamities

N. S. Timasheff

I. Law

Sorokin is one of the very few contemporary sociologists ascribing to law a prominent position in the universe of sociocultural phenomena. For him law is one of the most important components of the cultural system, an essential mechanism in social organization, possibly the strongest single motive power in the operation of the personality system, and the very mechanism of orderly sociocultural change.

A. Law as a component of the cultural system. Law can be approached from several points of view. One may emphasize the legal norm, or rights and duties, or behavior as molded by law, or legal conviction. For Sorokin law is first of all a system of norms forming one of the major culture systems.

In the total culture system of an inhabited area, he says, we find five major culture systems. One of them is ethics, consisting of law and morals. This is an empiric generalization since, according to Sorokin, every organized group and its culture has a set of ethical values. In other words, every culture has a kind of division of the field of human actions and of other events into opposite classes: right-wrong; approved-disapproved; recommended-prohibited; sacred-sinful; moral-immoral; and lawful-unlawful. In this sense the ethical mentality (of which law is a part) is a universal and permanent component of any culture.[1]

Sorokin distinguishes law and morals as the two subsystems of

[1] *Social and Cultural Dynamics,* II, 523; III, 479; IV, 117.

the system ethics in the following way. By law, he says, is meant the totality of the imperative-attributive conviction of a given person or the totality of persons, i.e., two-sided convictions ascribing rights to one party and duties to another. In contradistinction to that, the purely moral rules are one-sided, only imperative (not attributive) rules which urge, recommend, and advise to do such and such, but do not ascribe to anybody the right to demand such action.[2]

These definitions exactly follow the theory of Sorokin's major source of inspiration in the field of law, the great Russo-Polish jurist Leon Petrazhitsky, whose classic works appeared in Russian in 1904 and 1906-7.[3] Indebtedness to Petrazhitsky in matters concerning law is gratefully acknowledged by Sorokin in both major works dealing with law.[4] As those of Petrazhitsky, Sorokin's definitions of law and morals, in contradistinction to his definition of ethics in general, are "imposed definitions."[5] They are definitions not arrived at by induction, but chosen because of their adequacy, or ability to serve in theory construction. This is approximately the same procedure as that used by Max Weber in constructing ideal types. Sorokin continues by saying: "In any organized group there is an 'official' code of law (and respectively of morals) which by the powerful part of the group is regarded as 'obligatory' for all its members, and as such is enforced. What generally is known as law represents only this 'official' subclass of the law and moral phenomena."[6]

This addition to the definition (also inspired by Petrazhitsky, but significantly modified by Sorokin) is extremely important when interpreting most of his statements about law. Relative to law in culture, it allows one to decipher the true meaning of propositions which otherwise could be termed as a sort of "legal imperialism." These propositions read as follows: The legal system "embraces the so-called *economic system* because the norms of law determine what it is ... what is the system of commercial relations ... what

[2] *Ibid.*, II, 526 n. 3.

[3] Now available in an abridged English translation, Leon Petrazhitsky, *Law and Morals* (Cambridge: Harvard University Press, 1955), with an introduction by the present writer.

[4] *Dynamics*, II, 526 n. 4; and *Society, Culture and Personality*, p. 71 n. 3.

[5] N. S. Timasheff, "Definitions in the Social Sciences," *American Journal of Sociology*, LII (1947), 8.

[6] *Dynamics*, II, 526 n. 3.

is wealth or economic value." Similarly the legal system embraces the "so-called political system, because [the latter] is determined by the norms of *the constitutional and administrative law.*" Law and morals embrace also almost all the norms of conduct which often are loosely covered by the terms mores, customs, and the like. Outside of law and morals there remain only the technical norms, i.e., purely utilitarian norms prescribing how to do this or that and devoid of any imperative-attributive urge, and finally, the norms of etiquette, fashion, religion, folkways, mores, custom, if and when the parties regard them neither imperative-attributive, nor imperative.[7]

From the statements above it appears that Sorokin is inclined to classify the norms or rules depending on the *meaning* ascribed to them by those whom they concern. This is in full accordance with his general treatment of culture. He identifies the "cultural aspect of the superorganic universe [with] meanings, values and norms . . . as they are objectified through overt actions and other vehicles in the empirical sociocultural universe."[8] Consequently, his general conception of norms and their relations to meanings and values is essential for the understanding of his sociological theory of law. In *Society, Culture and Personality,* where Sorokin has no opportunity to discuss *ex professo* norms, no definition of norms is offered.

In *Society, Culture and Personality,* Sorokin is inclined to identify the three terms and declares that "the terms, 'meaning,' 'value' and 'norm' will be used interchangeably to denote a general class of meaningful phenomena superimposed upon the biophysical properties of persons and objects."[9]

The identification of meanings (ideas), norms, and values is not felicitous. The three obviously form a triad of interrelated "terms," but each of them conveys a somewhat different emphasis.

Contrary to Petrazhitsky for whom norms were "phantasmata," projections of specific states of mind of the individuals who experienced attributive-imperative or purely imperative emotions, for Sorokin norms are real. "A law-norm is not a futile and lifeless figment of the imagination of jurists [as assumed by Petrazhitsky],

[7] *Ibid.,* IV, 117-19; *Society, Culture and Personality,* pp. 84-85.
[8] *Society, Culture and Personality,* p. 313.
[9] *Ibid.,* p. 47.

but a powerful living force in constant operation." We will unfold
the meaning of this statement when discussing the operation of
law-norms in personality systems.

B. Law and social organization. As has already been stated, law,
particularly the law-norm, plays the dominant part in Sorokin's discussion of social organization. The existence of interaction does not
mean as such that the interacting persons constitute an organized
system or group. (The two terms, as well as institution, are used
by him interchangeably.) The central trait of organized (group)
interaction is, for him, the presence in it of law-norms regulating and
controlling the conduct of the interacting persons.[10] These law-
norms must precisely define all the relevant actions-reactions of the
interacting individuals in their relationship toward one another, toward outsiders, and toward the world at large. Moreover, these
norms must be effective, obligatory, and, if need be, enforced by the
conduct of the interacting persons. Only if these conditions are
met, the totality of the interacting individuals forms an organized
group. In order that they be met, the group (which equals the
totality of interacting individuals) must possess a central set of
meanings and values somewhat consistent within itself. That central set forms the very reason for the interaction of the individuals
and is expressed in the law-norms just mentioned.

Organized interaction is, then, interaction regulated by law.
"*Law norms are the essence*—the skeleton, the heart and the soul—
of any organized group or institution."[11] In Sorokin's view such
interactions constitute the major and, by far, the more important
part of interaction going on in a society. To unorganized and disorganized interaction, as well as to interaction regulated by moral
(purely imperative) norms, he pays but little attention.

At first glance one may conclude that for Sorokin the field of
sociology almost coincides with the field of jurisprudence. But one
must immediately remember that, for Sorokin, law means a much
larger segment of social reality than for the overwhelming majority
of jurists and sociologists. In principle, law is the sum total of
imperative-attributive norms. Sorokin significantly contracts the
volume of phenomena to be considered legal as compared with

[10] *Ibid.*, p. 70.   [11] *Ibid.*, p. 77.

Petrazhitsky. Though not introducing the trait of enforceability into the definition of law-norms (which Petrazhitsky emphatically declined), Sorokin is inclined to pay attention mainly to norms which possess this trait. Following Petrazhitsky, Sorokin sometimes discusses "law-convictions" as a component of law; but if law-convictions are not enforced by the respective group, they do not perform the basic social function of law, that of organizing interaction, and therefore remain almost negligible. In consequence, Sorokin actually confines law to the sum total of norms which are both imperative-attributive and socially enforceable. This modification of Petrazhitsky's views still leaves Sorokin far beyond the conception of law prevalent among the jurists: enforcement by diffuse sanctions derived from the existence of social pressure approving specified conduct and disapproving the opposite one. This is, for Sorokin, sufficient to make a norm legal while *communis opinio* identifies the law with the sum total of norms enforced by the state.[12]

In the final account law becomes almost identical with social order understood as the sum total of socially enforceable norms of conduct which, as commonly assumed, depends on the effective internalization of norms by group members. Most commonly, similar propositions about social order are not further explored. It is one of Sorokin's contributions that, owing to his expansion of the commonly held conception of law, he transfers a large number of propositions found in jurisprudence (which equals general theory of law in European terminology), especially in Petrazhitsky's interpretation, into the field of custom, which has never been systematically explored by sociologists despite the brilliant beginning found in Sumner's *Folkways* (which is, however, anything but systematic). Here Sorokin's ideas meet and fructify another line of exploration going back to Linton's formulation of status as the sum total of rights and duties ascribed to the occupant of a social position.[13] Linton's proposition immediately poses before the sociologist the problem: What, sociologically speaking, is a right or a duty? Attempts, rather inconclusive, have been made in that direction by some members of the Upsala school in the sociology of law.[14]

[12] Sorokin briefly discusses the state theory of law and rejects it for many reasons. See *ibid.*, pp. 71-72.
[13] R. Linton, *A Study of Man* (New York: Appleton, 1936), p. 113.
[14] Cf. N. S. Timasheff, "Growth and Scope of Sociology of Law," in Howard

In the present writer's opinion, a large number of propositions about law-norms formulated by Sorokin could and should be incorporated into general sociology and the sociology of law. One, however, has to interpret these propositions as the construction of an ideal type of an organized group, rather than as propositions covering the infinite variety of configurations met in social reality. When Sorokin says that law-norms determine in detail the rights and duties of group members, that the norms generate "the official government" of the group with its legislative, executive, and judicial functions, etc., he leaves unanswered such questions as: What happens if, in a system of interaction, the rights and duties of members are not determined in detail? What happens if there is no official government? Obviously between the ideal type of an organized group as conceived by Sorokin and unorganized interaction there is a whole gamut of transitions.

C. Law and the personality system. Having emphasized the legal norms in his treatment of culture and of social organization, Sorokin approaches the treatment of law as operative in the personality systems, again emphasizing legal norms. His basic ideas on the subject are treated under the heading "Psychological characteristics of the law norms." These traits are singled out as: (1) an idea of a pattern of action demanded by the law-norms; (2) "normative motivation" behind the respective action; and (3) powerful emotional (affective and volitional) backing of the actions propelling us to realize unhesitatingly our rights and to fulfil unflinchingly our duty. Most important is the second of these traits. Our law actions (those actions depending on the impact of law-norms on the individual minds) are motivated in a specific way (which, however, stands also behind moral motivation) called "normative motivation." This term, taken over from Petrazhitsky, connotes a specific stimulant of action reducible to the image of the action patterns themselves. The normative motivation is different from the purposive and other motivations of human behavior. It is self-sufficient motivation in the sense that the deeply ingrafted norm is a perfectly sufficient motive for the person's compliance

Becker and Alvin Boskoff, eds., *Modern Sociological Theory: Continuity and Change* (New York: Dryden Press, 1957), 424-49.

with it. No other motive is necessary. It differs from purposive motivation because many law-actions take place without the idea of a future purpose, without any hedonistic, utilitarian, or other consideration. Normative motivation is also different from the "because of" type of motivation. (Petrazhitsky used the term causal motivation.) "Because of" actions do not have any definite norm or pattern. "They are devoid of the specific experience of normativeness and of ascription of right and duty which is typical of normative motivation."[15]

The theory of normative motivation just unfolded allows us to fill a gap in Sorokin's presentation of the concept of norm. We could define norms as those meanings (ideas) which are endowed with the capacity of eliciting normative motivation—which, for instance, is not true of a physical or metaphysical theory, provided that it is not supplemented by corollaries of an ethical nature.

While the theory just reported has been taken over by Sorokin from Petrazhitsky, he has given it a new meaning by incorporating it into his theory of culture. Law-norms form purely cultural systems, i.e., systems independent of whether they remain in the minds of their originators or are diffused. But they become sociocultural systems through the processes of objectification (i.e., expression in vehicles comprehensible to fellow men) and socialization (i.e., acceptance, or internalization by members of smaller or larger groups). In this way the law-norms become a motive power of human actions, especially interactions. Sorokin asserts that in the totality of actions those performed as a realization of our rights and duties occupy a larger place than any other kind of actions.[16]

The law-norms of different members of an interacting group may be and often are different, even contradictory. For such a group no stable or definite distribution of rights and duties is possible. This function of integration is performed by a set of law-norms that are obligatory for all the members of the group, i.e., official law. "Compulsory enforcement . . . can be accomplished only by an authoritative power agency capable of enforcing law and applying sanctions. . . . This authority . . . [is founded on] the law convictions of the members of the group (or their majority) which attribute to the government the right to govern, to legislate,

[15] *Society, Culture and Personality*, p. 78.
[16] *Ibid.*, pp. 56-57, 75-76.

to judge . . . , ascribing at the same time to the members of the group the duty to obey its orders."[17]

The official law of the state regulates the most important relationships of its members and groups. However, neither in the state nor in any large group does such an official law exhaust all the law-norms (and law convictions) possessed by the members. Side by side with the official law there always exist many norms of unofficial law supplementing, correcting, or even contradicting the norms of the official law of the group. Everyone, in the totality of his law-convictions, side by side with law-convictions identical with the norms of official law of the state, may have law-convictions partly supplementing the official law, partly contradicting it. In any group there is some contradiction between its official law and the unofficial norms of some of its members, though normally this discrepancy is not too great.

It seems to me that, at this place, Sorokin has wrongly identified unofficial law, i.e., the complex of imperative-attributive norms enforced not by the state, but by other social groups, and legal convictions of individuals which, if not socialized, cannot be considered as part of the sociocultural system "law." The confusion goes back to Petrazhitsky, whose reduction of law to mental state of individuals has been elsewhere overcome by Sorokin.

D. Law and sociocultural change. The discrepancy between official and unofficial law serves as the starting point of Sorokin's theory of the role of law in sociocultural change. Official law always lags behind unofficial law. When the discrepancy becomes considerable the official law is commonly changed in an orderly way by due process as provided in the official law itself. This orderly change is contrasted by Sorokin with revolutionary change, which is tantamount to the overthrow of the official law and its government. But so long as the change proceeds according to the official law of the group, it is legal and orderly, no matter how radical it may be, or how fast the tempo. Orderly change is possible only if, for the bulk of the members, the norms of official law have become their second nature, controlling their mentality and conduct; if the unofficial law convictions of the members do not sharply deviate or

[17] *Ibid.*, p. 78.

contradict the norms of official law; and finally, if the proportion of the members unimpregnated by the norms and uncontrolled by them is not too great.[18]

The maladjustment between official and unofficial law calls forth the phenomenon of crime or violation of official law by ideological or ordinary offenders. Still more important, in these phenomena one can perceive the deepest root of every revolution.

In addition to this rather sketchy treatment of the role of law in sociocultural change, Sorokin has submitted to empirical test a number of current propositions dealing with the development of law. This he has done by an unusual combination of the historical approach to the study of social phenomena and quantification. The questions which he has asked and answered are these: (1) Have there been definite trends in the scope of human actions so disapproved by society as to provoke penal sanctions? And (2) have there been definite trends in the change of the relative severity of eventual sanctions?

The task has been performed against the background of a painstaking study of the consecutive criminal codes of five major nations of continental Europe covering about 1,500 years of their development.[19] On the basis of a preliminary examination of the codes, a kind of "historical questionnaire" was prepared listing 104 types of actions which have been considered criminal, in all or some of the codes studied, in all or some historical stages of development. The penal sanctions were codified by reducing them to index numbers one to ten. Then, relative to each code, it was established: (1) which of the 104 types of actions were punishable, and (2) how intensive were the sanctions. Finally, relative to each nation the consecutive codes were compared to establish the extension or concentration of the scope of punishable actions and the ignorance or decrease of the severity of sanctions. The codes of the particular countries belonging to the same stage of historical development were compared along similar lines.

On the background of these findings, a number of generalizations could be drawn. Most important has been the establishment of the fact that, relative to the countries and periods studied, there

---

[18] *Ibid.,* pp. 79-82.
[19] This study has been carried out by Sorokin in co-operation with the present author.

was no unilinear trend, but a kind of wave fluctuation both with respect to the scope of punishable actions and to the severity of sanctions. The age of classic liberalism (the first half of the nineteenth century) proved to be least inclined to extend the scope of punishable actions, while the age of the greatest severity of punishment was not the Middle Ages, as commonly assumed, but the period immediately preceding the liberal period (sixteenth to eighteenth centuries). These and many other generalizations have been confronted by Sorokin with his general theory about the wave fluctuation of culture; but they can serve as well for the testing of other theories about the factors, the velocity, and the direction of sociocultural change. And, of course, they form a first-class contribution to the sociology of law.[20]

II. Revolution

A. The initial phase of the theory. In Sorokin's work the treatment of revolution is systematically connected with that of law. While law is considered as one of the main mechanisms of orderly change in social organization, revolution is the mechanism of disorderly change, i.e., change contrary to the rules of official law.

To the sociology of revolution, Sorokin has devoted the first sociological volume published by him in America (1925), but written in 1922-23, when he was in Czechoslovakia, immediately after his banishment from Russia. It naturally reflects the scientific position he occupied in his earlier (Russian) works. Society is interpreted in terms of reduction to the individuals and their behavior,[21] and the treatment of this behavior is tainted by behaviorism. Accordingly, the inner cause of a revolution is to be found in the repression of the main instincts of the majority of a society's

[20] At this place, I should like to divulge some facts showing to what an extent the gathering of facts for Sorokin's monumental work was free of influence by any preconceived idea. He asked me (I then resided in Paris) to collect for him data necessary to answer the two questions above and to find a way of quantifying them, without communicating his basic hypothesis about the pattern of culture fluctuation. I carried out this task and, communicating my results to Sorokin, expressed the fear that they probably could not be utilized in his work since they departed so drastically from commonly held views. Sorokin answered by cable "OK" and wrote an enthusiastic letter stating that the wave fluctuations found by me were in complete conformity with his own basic hypothesis.

[21] *The Sociology of Revolution*, p. 367.

members. These "instincts" (a term standing both for the innate and the conditioned reflexes) are the alimentary reflex, the reflex of individual and collective self-preservation, the sex reflex, the reflex of ownership, and that of self-expression. To cause a revolution, there must be an exceedingly strong repression of some of such instincts in a large number of persons. This general cause, however, must be supplemented by the impotence of the groups which stand for order.[22]

Although the discussion of the causation of revolution is relegated to the last chapter, the whole book may be conceived as a step-by-step preparation for the demonstration of the basic theorem. One by one Sorokin discusses "the perversion of human behavior," the transformation of speech reactions, the perversion of the relations concerning themselves with ownership, of sexual relations, of the actions and reactions of authority and subordination, and of the religious, moral, and aesthetic forms of conduct. There follows a study of the influence of revolution on the composition of the population, the structure of the social aggregate and the main social functions, political, economic, and spiritual. The author's aim is to offer a generalized image of revolution. He acknowledges, however, that he has amply used the experience of the abortive Russian revolution of 1905-6, and of the five years he spent in Russia after the revolution of 1917. He has supplemented that personal experience by extensive reading about other revolutions, especially the Paris Commune, the French revolutions of 1848 and 1789, the English Revolution and, to a minor extent, about major medieval outbursts, as well as revolutions in Rome, Greece, and ancient Egypt. Of course the historical events are treated only briefly and often by analogy with the Russian Revolution of 1917. The exposition often suffers from lack of a precise definition of the phenomenon called revolution. Sorokin explicitly states that he had no intention to add to all the existing definitions one more; but he does not select one of them and declare his adhesion to it.[23]

B. Definition of revolution. In later works, Sorokin has three times returned to the sociology of revolution, first in *Social and Cultural Dynamics*, Volume III, where 120 pages of text and 40

---

[22] *Ibid.*, pp. 369-71.   [23] *Ibid.*, pp. 8-9.

pages of an appendix are devoted to the topic; second, in *Man and Society in Calamity;* and, finally, in *Society, Culture and Personality,* where he has condensed and integrated his views on revolution. In these works Sorokin has entirely discarded the behavioristic approach and with it the explanation of revolution in terms of repressed instincts and conditioned reflexes. But many of the concrete data collected in *The Sociology of Revolution* have been salvaged by him and used in the more recent versions of the sociology of revolution.

In the last of these works just cited, he identifies revolutionary change with comparatively rapid and violent change of the obsolete official law of a group, or of institutions and values which this law represented. Using this definition in a set of propositions, he states that revolutionary change attacks not just one or a few norms of the official law, or a few minor values, but the entire body of the official law, or a substantial part of it and either all social institutions (including government) and the whole system of values protected by official law, or at least several fundamental institutions and values. He adds that revolutionary change involves the direct or indirect participation of a considerable part of the membership of the group, and that revolutionary change is always accompanied by the use of force or violence, either on a moderate scale, or in the form of civil war.

The definition thus elaborated serves as a starting point for the treatment of "uniformities in revolutionary change,"[24] but it does not cover Sorokin's major contribution to the topic offered in his *Dynamics,* where, in collaboration with me and S. S. Oldenburg, he surveyed 1,622 inner disturbances in ancient Greece and Rome and in the major European states from the sixth century up to 1925. On the basis of this study he drew important conclusions about the frequency of revolutions in the particular societies surveyed and in their totality; moreover, he sketched a theory of the causation of revolution entirely at variance with the one found in *The Sociology of Revolution.* But, in contradistinction to the general characterization of revolution offered in *Society, Culture and Personality,* he includes in his *Dynamics* "relatively small disorders" which could not be interpreted as "attacks on the entire body of official law or a

[24] First formulated in *The Sociology of Revolution* and reproduced in *Dynamics,* III, 487-95.

substantial part of it." Many of these smaller disturbances did not involve a considerable part of the membership of the group since he has included "palace revolutions," political plots, murders, and so on.[25]

Does this mean that Sorokin changed his conceptual scheme between 1937 and 1947? Perhaps not, since, in *Society, Culture and Personality*, he reproduces in brief form the findings of his empiric investigation published in 1937.[26]

Actually, Sorokin uses two concepts of revolution which will later be referred to as Definitions I and II. By Definition I he refers to a revolution in the meaning of inner disturbance of some importance, from which he has omitted "quite insignificant disorders," even though they may otherwise qualify by his criterion of appearance, or non-appearance, in the records of history,[27] in the standard works on the history of the countries concerned. By Definition II he refers to revolution in the sense of an attack upon a substantial part of the official law of the country and involving a significant proportion of the population. While the empiric study of the frequency and movement of revolutions deals with all the cases covered by Definition I, Sorokin's presentation of uniformities in revolutionary change deals only with cases covered by Definition II.

C. Quantification. Quantification has been essential for the formulation of a number of propositions about the frequency and movement of revolutionary disturbances. Such quantification has been carried out by assigning to each disturbance indicators expressing: (1) the proportional extent of the social area of disturbance, (2) the proportion of the population actively involved, (3) the duration of the disturbance, and (4) the proportional intensity of violence, in combination with the importance of the effects. These four indicators have been integrated by finding their geometrical average. For each country the general indicators thus arrived at were summed up for periods of 25 and 100 years. To trace a curve of the movement in the total area surveyed, different coefficients have been assigned to the countries considered, chang-

[25] *Dynamics*, III, 385 and 395.
[26] *Society, Culture and Personality*, pp. 482-87.
[27] *Dynamics*, III, 385.

ing in time depending upon the increase or decline of the country's importance, and the indicators thus modified have been summed up.

Sorokin's quantification of revolutionary phenomena has been much criticized, even ridiculed. He acknowledges that his procedure has been imperfect, but asserts that an imperfect numerical quantification is still better than vague verbal quantifications commonly used. This argument has been decisive in the mind of the author, who explicitly states that he is not an ardent quantitativist at all. In a delightful footnote Sorokin tells readers that the preliminary draft of his work was submitted by a prominent scholar to two critics whose names remained unknown to him, and that one of the critics found the findings absurd because they were contrary to all existing historical knowledge while the other one found them unnecessary because they were in full accordance with knowledge already existing![28]

The very findings of the quantitative study can be summarized as follows: (1) Inner disturbances are much more frequent than commonly assumed. This is probably the case because people more often than not think of revolution in terms of Definition II, not I. (2) The countries investigated differ but little as to the frequency and severity of disturbances, so that it is impossible to divide nations as relatively orderly or disorderly. (3) Most of the inner crises in the life process of a social body come and pass their acute stage within the period of a few weeks. (4) There is neither periodicity in revolutions nor a continuous trend toward "orderly progress" which would be expressed in the decrease of the frequency and intensity of revolutionary upsurges. (5) There is a slight tendency for inner disturbances to occur more frequently in a period of war and in years nearest to war years; but the tendency is slight. Even when wars are divided into successful and unsuccessful ones, the data do not show a particular association between unsuccessful wars and revolutions.

On the basis of these propositions, Sorokin reaches the following generalization: inner disturbances simply belong to the life process of a society, just as tensions and relaxations, sickness and health, crisis and repose incessantly alternate in the life process of an individual. Social disturbance is perhaps an immanent trait of sociocultural life itself and in this sense is inescapable. In particu-

[28] *Ibid.*, III, 401-2.

lar, the fact that the average duration of disturbances is closely similar in most of the countries permits one to conclude that the occurrence of disturbances seems to be controlled by forces and conditions which lie very deep, far below the specific cultural and other circumstances in which these countries differ markedly. Here probably we meet the fact of the immanent self-regulation of social processes which any thoughtful investigator often comes across. These statements are almost tantamount to the formulation of a theory of the immanent causation of revolutions, which is in full accordance with Sorokin's general views on the immanent character of sociocultural dynamics.[29]

He does not, however, stop at this point; instead, he makes an attempt to correlate the more or less frequent occurrence of revolutions with specific phases of the fluctuation of culture between the ideational and sensate poles. He does not assert that inner disturbances would reach their climax at the time when culture is sensate, still less when it is ideational. He states that, on the basis of data collected and projected on the general curves of culture fluctuations, disturbances have sometimes increased but sometimes decreased in periods either of blossoming or of decline. He makes, however, a distinction between disturbance analogous to tensions of childbirth and of healthy growth and disturbances accompanying illness or senility. Later on, he significantly refines his hypothesis and makes it more plausible. This he does in saying that, during periods when the existing culture, or the system of social relations, or both, undergo a rapid transformation, the internal disturbances increase; when they are strong and crystallized, disturbances tend to decrease and stand at a low level.[30] I myself believe that this formulation of the hypothesis much better fits the facts and possesses the quality of precision which the other formulation (dividing disturbances into those of growth or decline) lacks. Who shall decide whether a disturbance expressed growth or decline and how? The answer is especially difficult if one accepts Sorokin's general view on culture fluctuation which always means simultaneous increase of the sensate element and decrease of the ideational element, or vice versa. The second formulation seems also better to explain the alleged immanence of disturbances which appear as temporary but inevitable phases of the sociocultural process. In

[29] Ibid., III, 383, 479-80.   [30] Ibid., III, 494-99.

some places,[31] Sorokin seems to emphasize the increased frequency and intensity of disturbances in times of transition, thus contradicting his own statement that they appear both in periods of culture blossoming and culture transition: culture blossoming may be highly dynamic and may be accompanied by many, perhaps important, inner disturbances. Nearly all the great revolutions happened in such a sociocultural framework.

D. The latest phase of the theory. In *Society, Culture and Personality*, written ten years after the publication of the volume of *Social and Cultural Dynamics* dealing with war and revolution, Sorokin elaborated his theory of the causation of revolution and applied the ideas developed when writing *Social Causality, Time, Space*, and *Russia and the United States*. After eliminating the theory of multiple causation he says: "More fruitful seems to be the way of discovery of *the main, the necessary cause . . . with an indication of supplementary factors that facilitate or inhibit the effects of the main cause.*" He is fully aware of the objections of the logicians against such a formula, but believes that its investigational advantages are so great that the objections can be disregarded.[32]

The main cause is, in fact, the same as the one which served him in *Social and Cultural Dynamics* as background for the second formulation of the theory of the causation of revolution. "*The probability* of [internal] *peace varies directly with the integration of the systems of basic values and their mutual compatibility. When their integration . . . declines, especially suddenly and sharply, the chances for civil war increase.*"[33] He emphasizes that integration is not tantamount to homogeneity or identity. In a society like the American, citizens possess different religious, aesthetic, and political values; but their heterogeneity is not conducive to civil war. It is noteworthy that revolution appears in the formula only in the garb of civil war. This means that the theory of the causation of revolution, unfolded in *Society, Culture and Personality*, is adapted to Definition II only and does not cover minor disturbances.

The positive supplementary factors of revolution are listed ap-

[31] *Ibid.*, III, 505.
[32] *Society, Culture and Personality*, p. 507.
[33] *Ibid.*, pp. 507-8.

proximately as they appear in innumerable books and articles on the subject, without any elaboration or classification. Similarly are treated the supplementary negative conditions. Let us single out one of the particular negative factors because it relates Sorokin's theory of revolution to that of law: this is an "efficient and fair legislative apparatus promptly removing the discrepancy between the old official law and the new unofficial law convictions of the population."[34]

The theoretical propositions are then checked by using evidence collected in *Society, Culture and Personality,* supplemented by cursory references to other facts known from history or from current information. One of the most important corroborations is given by civil wars (revolutions) arising from a rapid and fundamental change in the basic values of one part of a given society while the other part does not undergo it or moves in the opposite direction. The data show that practically all the civil wars (revolutions) of the past have emerged from a sudden increase of contrasts in the major values. We should therefore expect the greatest magnitude of revolutions in the periods of radical transformation of a given society. Unfortunately, Sorokin relapses into the ambiguity found in *Social and Cultural Dynamics* when, again, he asserts that revolutions crowd particularly in periods of the blossoming and decline of a given nation.[35] It is very difficult to see what periods would not be covered by this formula and therefore remain relatively free of revolution (perhaps just periods of stagnation?).

E. Uniformities in revolutionary change. In addition to the quantitative study of the distribution of revolutions in time and space and to the theory of their causation, in *Society, Culture and Personality* Sorokin has made an attempt to formulate, on an empiric basis, a certain number of uniformities in the revolutionary change of society and culture.[36] Two generalizations may be conceived as the key to the whole treatment of the subject: first, "the cycle of revolution" and, second, "the law of polarization." The former is not Sorokin's invention, as he explicitly acknowledges. In nearly every revolution one may distinguish a destructive and a construc-

[34] *Ibid.,* p. 508.   [35] *Ibid.,* p. 510.
[36] Integrating and somewhat modifying statements found already in *The Sociology of Revolution* and *Man and Society in Calamity.*

tive phase. During the former the revolution destroys much of the old sociocultural order, usually not only obsolete and moribund institutions, but also many institutions and values which, were there no revolution, could have developed. During the second phase the revolution recedes and many vital institutions and values emerge.

The law of polarization is one of Sorokin's own contributions. In the course of a revolution the rather indifferent majority consisting of persons neither markedly social-minded, nor extremely antisocial, tends to split and is attracted by the two poles; therefore, a society emerges where the contrasts are more accentuated than in normal times. In the first phase, negative polarization prevails, while in the second the positive polarization increases. Sorokin had already formulated this law in *Sociology of Revolution* and then elaborated it in *Man and Society in Calamity*.

These remarks should be made: First, the generalizations are applicable to revolution in the meaning of Definition II only. A palace revolution, a coup d'état, even a revolution which meets almost no opposition (e.g., the July 1830 revolution in France) cannot be analyzed into the two phases, and no polarization obtains because of the lack of time. Second, the empiric verification is very difficult, perhaps impossible, because of the paucity of our knowledge about earlier revolutions.

These difficulties are still more conspicuous when Sorokin shifts to more detailed formulations of secondary uniformities. Revolution, he asserts, affects the birth, death, and marriage rates. It results in the breakdown of personality structure. Speech reactions and ideologies change, property relations are affected, sex behavior is liberated of many inhibitions, the productivity of labor declines, ethical and religious conduct is conspicuously dominated by the law of polarization, the entire integration and differentiation of the population is blurred, relative positions of many groups change, the distribution of persons depending on their capacities is replaced by distribution depending on loyalty to the victorious party, voluntary and especially involuntary migration of the population increases, economic life is disintegrated, political life becomes unsettled, and cultural life is badly shaken. Of course, the propositions above are asserted to be true during the first phase of the revolution, while during the second phase many disturbances caused by the revolution are taken care of.

What Sorokin has offered is a realistic and condensed description of the basic social and cultural processes obtaining during a revolution which, in his terminology, is called total, especially during the Communist revolution of which he has been a keen participant-observer. But the smaller disturbances and even some revolutions of the total type, such as the Fascist revolutions in Italy and Germany, have not displayed some of the traits mentioned by Sorokin (e.g., decline of the productivity of labor). Consequently, Sorokin's treatment of uniformities in revolutionary change is tantamount to the construction of an "ideal type" of a revolution, either total or approximating it, but not a realistic description of any inner disturbance. As such, it is valuable since it offers a frame of reference to be used when making a case study of any concrete inner disturbance. On the basis of such case studies, a new method of quantifying the intensity of a revolution could gradually emerge and then be applied to a recalculation of data used by Sorokin in his pioneer study of the 1,622 cases appearing in *Social and Cultural Dynamics*.

III. War

A. Definition and quantification. While, for Sorokin, revolution is an internal, or intragroup, disturbance manifesting the breakdown of crystallized relationships within the group, war is an external, or intergroup disturbance, also manifesting the breakdown of a crystallized system of relationships, but between groups, more especially states.[37] In *Social and Cultural Dynamics* war connotes, however, only the sharpest outbursts of violence resulting from such a breakdown. The empiric data compiled there are confined to interstate disturbances giving rise to overt violence.[38] However, some civil wars involving one state only are considered, such as the war with the Pretender in England and the Carlist wars in Spain. Included also are some colonial expeditions where the adversary of the European power was in the stage of rudimentary political

[37] Such is his standpoint in *Society, Culture and Personality*
[38] *Dynamics*, III, 26 and 263.

organization, or fights waged by an organized state against nomadic neighbors, such as Russia's wars with the Polovtsi.

In *Society, Culture and Personality,* war is, in principle, identified with an outburst of violence; most revolutions above the lowest level are treated as "civil wars," and even murder is considered as a specimen of interindividual war. But in actuality the discussion of the major phases of the sociology of war is confined to phenomena covered by the definition found in *Social and Cultural Dynamics,* namely, interstate disturbances resulting in sharp outbursts of violence.

The most important contribution of Sorokin to the sociology of war has definitely been the quantitative study of its fluctuation in time and space. The study was undertaken by him despite his awareness of the tremendous factual and logical difficulties. As he states, he had the choice between the answer "ignoramus" and the manipulation of data which, more often than not, were only estimates. Because of his "own curiosity," he chose the second alternative.

On the background of a careful study of historical material available (with the assistance of two outstanding Russian military historians), a list of nearly all the known wars of ancient Greece, Rome, England, Austria, Germany, France, the Netherlands, Spain, Italy, Russia, and Poland-Lithuania was compiled, containing 967 items. Relative to each war, its duration, the strength of the armies and the number of casualties were estimated. The strength of the armies and the casualties were related to the size of the population and thus the relative burden of each war was weighted.[39] The relative indicators were summed up, for each country, with respect to 25- and 100-year periods.

The comparison of indicators thus reached has served as background for inductive generalizations. As relative to revolution, the data are shown to be destructive of any "progressivism," i.e., of theories according to which the march of history could be interpreted as a gradual ascension of mankind to more and more progressive stages.[40] Any continuous trend as to the frequency and intensity of wars is lacking. The erratic fluctuations of these

[39] *Ibid.,* III, 264-83, 286-95.
[40] This statement is especially directed against Q. Wright, *The Causes of War and the Conditions of Peace* (London, 1935); cf. *Dynamics,* III, 264 n. 3.

magnitudes mean that in any society at any moment two sets of forces are incessantly working and struggling with each other. One set tends to create, magnify, and sharpen the antagonism of a given state with other states; the other set works for solidarity and peace. At one period the first set becomes dominant and leads to war; at another period the second becomes overwhelming; then, peace prevails.

Under what conditions do the forces of war, or, respectively, of peace, prevail? *"In the life history of nations,"* he says, *"the magnitude of war . . . tends to grow in the periods of expansion—political, social, cultural and territorial . . .—at least as frequently as in periods of decline,"*[41] perhaps even more. *"War tends to fall in periods of 'sinking' or decay of a given nation."*[42]

B. Theory of war causation.

The proposition above has been used by Sorokin to introduce a tentative theory of war causation, although he maintains that a systematic analysis of this problem is beyond the scope of *Social and Cultural Dynamics*.[43] He suggests an approach logically following from the definition of war as a breakdown of the organized relationship between states.

Such a breakdown, tantamount to the disruption of existing interstate equilibrium, is the absolute condition of the possibility of any war. War, then, appears to be a resultant of this breakdown. On the one hand, however, this proposition is a tautology, since the breakdown is included in the definition of war. On the other hand, it does not completely solve the question of war causation; there have been many cases of the breakdown of organized relationships not followed by war. Although rejecting as "blunder" any theory which chooses some variable as a real and main cause of war, Sorokin asserts that war is always caused, in addition to the "necessary condition," by a combination of secondary factors which vary from case to case.

Sorokin rejects the temptation of identifying the fluctuations of war with the dominance either of the ideational or of the sensate culture; neither the sensate nor the ideational culture is more belligerent than the other. But the periods of transition from "Ideational to Sensate culture," or vice versa, are *"periods of notable increase*

---

[41] *Ibid.*, III, 364.   [42] *Ibid.*

[43] *Ibid.*, III, 371.

of war activities and war magnitude," while crystallized and settled cultures of both types have been relatively peaceful. This proposition is qualified by another one: the transitional period within a group comes somewhat earlier than it is manifested outside of the group, i.e., in international relations. In other words, the transition in international relations lags behind the transition within the particular group. With that correction, Sorokin believed he had solved the problem of the relationship between war and culture fluctuation: "All in all, the movement of war by centuries agrees with the hypothesis," with possibly the exception of the third century B.C. in Rome.[44]

But the theory of war causation implied in *Social and Cultural Dynamics* was only a starting point. One year after the publication of the volume discussing it, Sorokin contributed an article containing a sketch of a theory which he calls "sociological" since it is correlated with some basic concepts of general sociology. "As sociologists we know that the state is a network of relationships and a system of culture values. We can deduce that each time when relationships between two or more states and the pertinent values become shattered, or muddled, or indefinite, such a change favors the chance of war."[45]

The later development of Sorokin's views on war causation has been somewhat affected by the appearance of an article by Leo Martin[46] where the author asserted that, in *Social and Cultural Dynamics* two incompatible theories about the relationship between war causation and culture fluctuation have been offered, one that war was more likely in periods of culture blossoming and another that war was more likely in periods of culture transition. Going back to Sorokin's data, Martin expressed his preference for the first hypothesis.

As a consequence, the next time Sorokin had the opportunity to discuss the problem of war causation, namely in *Russia and the United States* (1944), he modified the propositions stated in *Social and Cultural Dynamics* and in his article of 1938, which somewhat mitigated (but did not completely eliminate) the contradiction

[44] *Ibid.*, III, 375-79.

[45] "A Neglected Factor of War," *American Sociological Review*, III (1938), 475-86.

[46] Leo Martin, "The Problem of War Causation," *American Catholic Sociological Review*, III (1942).

noted by Martin. In *Russia and the United States* we read: *"The main cause of international peace is the presence in each of the interacting societies of a well integrated system of ultimate values"*[47] and the corresponding norms of conduct. This is somewhat surprising: two well-integrated societies may be bearers of two incompatible value systems which would make war between them likely. Sorokin is obviously aware of this fact since he says: "When within a given universe of societies the integration [of values] declines, especially suddenly and sharply, the chances for international war increase." Discussing "evidence of the validity of propositions,"[48] Sorokin consistently confronts the value systems of two or more societies and naturally comes to the conclusion that war and peace largely depend on the compatibility of the value systems. He correctly emphasizes that compatibility is not tantamount to similarity, homogeneity, and identity.

If it were so, we should expect the greatest magnitude of wars in periods of radical transformation of the main values of societies and, using data from *Social and Cultural Dynamics*, he is satisfied that this has been actually the case. It is noteworthy that the first hypothesis stated in that work (war is more likely in periods of culture blossoming, which obviously requires integration, and least likely in periods of decline) is lacking, as is also lacking the idea of the lag of periods of transition in international relations behind transition in particular groups.

In *Society, Culture and Personality*, the theory of war causation receives still another shape. Sorokin returns to the duality of propositions presented in *Social and Cultural Dynamics*, but now makes explicit: (1) that in the history of a nation, wars tend to multiply during periods of political, economic, and social growth and expansion, as well as during those of decline and decay; (2) that in the history of a given constellation of interacting nations, wars tend to increase during periods of acute transition and change occurring non-synchronously in the nations involved. It is explicitly stated that periods of transition from one fundamental type of culture to another are those in which wars attain their maximum.

Three questions may be asked here: (1) How could one distinguish war causation on the background of phenomena particular to each of the belligerents from war causation on the background of

[47] Pp. 215, 216.   [48] *Ibid.*, pp. 217-31.

"non-synchronous change" of value systems in two or more societies involved? (2) If war is at its maximum during periods of growth and expansion but also of decline and decay, what remains for peace periods? (3) The idealistic culture is, according to Sorokin, a very important (and likable) type of culture. But it appears only in periods of transition from ideational to sensate culture. Should we, then, consider idealistic culture as especially belligerent (which could perhaps be supported by Sorokin's data for the Golden Age of Greece, but not for the climax of the Middle Ages), or should we ascribe highest war frequency to periods of transition from ideational to idealistic and again from idealistic to sensate culture? The time limits of such transitions have, however, never been established by Sorokin with any precision, obviously because of the very nature of idealistic culture.

Later on, Sorokin returned to the problem of war causation in an article which appeared in Great Britain[49] and, in expanded form, in the British edition of *Russia and the United States*. The problem as posed in the title is that of the real causes of the Russo-American conflict. It gives the impression of a complete change of views of the author on the subject. He begins by asserting that any attempt to explain the conflict by enormous differences between the prevalent ideologies, the political, economic, and social institutions, and the basic cultural values of the United States and the Soviet Union is wrong. He asserts that similar differences existed between the value systems of the United States and of Tsarist Russia, prior to World War I, which exist now between the value system of the United States and of such countries as Turkey, Saudi Arabia, and Franco's Spain without provoking war. Then he restates his hypothesis on war causation by saying that wars (as well as revolutions) tend to emerge precisely in periods characterized by the disintegration of the dominant system of culture, especially of sensate culture, such as our culture is in our time. Consequently, wars (and conflicts preceding them) are particularly probable in our day. That the main conflict has centered in the United States and Russia is typical of "a world ruled by brute force assisted by hypocrisy. In such a world, small nations cannot afford to challenge the most powerful ones single-handed; only the most powerful

[49] "The Real Causes of the Russo-American Conflict," *World Affairs* (London), New Series, III (1949).

states, more or less equal in military might, dare to oppose each other." If, instead of Russia, France or Great Britain had emerged as the second great power, the conflict would be centered between the United States and one of them. On the other hand, the American-Russian conflict would have occurred even if Russia had been a Tsarist, democratic, or any other regime.

The departures from views expressed in the preceding works are three-fold: (1) the incompatibility of value systems is no longer declared to be "the main cause of war"; (2) periods of maximum belligerency are asserted to be synchronous with those of the disintegration of one of the basic types of culture, while the ideas of war causation in periods of culture blossoming, or in periods of non-synchronous evolution of value systems of different nations, have been put aside; (3) contrary to the explicit statement in *Social and Cultural Dynamics*, sensate culture is declared to be by far the most belligerent of all. But, perhaps, Sorokin could say that there is still no "hot war" between the United States and Russia. Consequently, his new propositions may be interpreted as covering conflicts below the level of war in the narrow meaning.

In my opinion the difficulties met by Sorokin in formulating a theory of war causation are the result of his attempt to correlate the fluctuation of belligerency with the fluctuation of culture style. Moreover, since the writing of *Russia and the United States,* he has anchored his general sociological theory on the concept of value without stating precisely what the term value means for him. Value may be understood: (1) as a more or less steady criterion of choice, in which sense, value is one of the high-level components of culture; (2) or as an object or a situation in which value in the first meaning is embodied. In the former meaning, the incompatibility of values is not particularly conducive to international conflicts, as is well shown by Sorokin in the article just quoted. On the other hand, far-reaching similarity of values does not prevent conflict and war as shown, for example, by France and Spain in the sixteenth and seventeenth centuries when they were continuously fighting each other, despite the fact that both nations were absolute monarchies, Catholic, and both ascribed high value to the possession of more territory. In the second meaning, value conflicts are often conducive to war. France and Spain ascribed particular value to the possession of the lands having formerly belonged to the

Dukes of Burgundy. Another instance would be the incompatible claims of Russia and Japan on Manchuria and Korea, prior to the Russo-Japanese war of 1904-5. Against the final version of Sorokin's theory of war causation, one could say that under neither idealistic nor ideational culture did a small state challenge a great power single-handed, and that we do not know enough about wars during periods of decay of ideational culture (preceding the rise of idealistic culture) to allow any comparison of the frequency of wars during these periods and in periods of decaying sensate culture. The main contribution of Sorokin's sociology of war seems to be the definitive destruction of arbitrary theories asserting a kind of pre-established periodicity in their occurrence, or a kind of evolutionary trend toward progress making wars rarer and less bloody.

C. *The impact of war.* Exactly as in his study of revolution, Sorokin's study of war contains a number of propositions on the impact, temporary or durable, of war on the societies involved. This topic is discussed in many chapters of *Man and Society in Calamity* and is systematically presented in *Society, Culture and Personality.* Most processes engendered by war are similar to those of revolution.[50] In particular, there is a phase of "conversion" and another of "reconversion," when peace returns. There are similar changes in vital processes. In mental life, war, like revolution, operates according to the law of polarization.

In the field of overt behavior, activities unrelated to war tend to disappear while those connected with war tend to increase. The law of polarization obtains also in overt behavior. There are changes in social differentiation and stratification. War effects a sharp increase in centralization and regimentation in the political field. In ethical and religious processes, one observes the polarization of the population into "sinners and saints." Important changes happen in the fields of science, technology, philosophy, and the fine arts. Of course, these processes run through the period of "conversion," whereas during "reconversion" the opposite processes obtain, resulting in "the restoration of equilibrium," an expression which Sorokin badly dislikes but which nevertheless well connotes the main social and cultural processes during the after-war periods.

[50] *Society, Culture and Personality,* pp. 499 ff.

In *Society, Culture and Personality,* the propositions above are presented dogmatically; but footnotes contain references to sets of chapters in *Man and Society in Calamity,* where "empirical verification" is offered.

IV. Social Calamities in General

Revolution and war are treated by Sorokin as inner and international disturbances, but also as social calamities, together with hunger (famine) and pestilence. In this way a class of social phenomena has been formed to which he has devoted a volume entitled *Man and Society in Calamity* (1942); there he occasionally mentions also flood and earthquake; surprisingly, he does not at all consider economic depression.

In that volume Sorokin's aim has been to formulate a set of sociological uniformities connected with social calamities. As indicated by the title, he begins by studying the impact of calamities on individual behavior, but then shifts to the study of their social implications, very much as he did relative to revolution in *The Sociology of Revolution.* He considers their impact on the vital processes, on vertical and horizontal social mobility, on political, economic, and social organization, and on the major phases of sociocultural life—religious, ethical, scientific, technological, as well as the fine arts and ideology.

Some phases are treated in more detail than the rest. This is the case with the impact of famine on human behavior, probably because, when still in Russia, he wrote a monograph on the subject, of which, however, no copy seems to have survived a kind of Bolshevik "book burning." When studying the impact of calamities on sociocultural life, he singles out two special cases, the Renaissance and the rise of Methodism. He mentions also as a good case the Russian Revolution, but devotes to it only a few lines, probably because he had already treated the subject in detail in the *Sociology of Revolution.* Everywhere he finds working the "law of polarization." Much historical material has been used, of course, taken over from secondary (but commonly reliable) sources. But often he says: "and similar things happened during other famines, pestilences, wars and revolutions," which is quite probable, but not empirically proved—because of lack of historical evidence.

Two major objections could be raised against Sorokin's treatment of social calamities in general. First, a precise unit of analysis has not been chosen. In some cases these units are of the same type as those used in his studies of the fluctuation of wars and revolutions. He speaks, for instance, of the European famines of 793, 868-69, 1005, and so forth.[51] In other cases he seems to cover long periods of consecutive or recurring calamities, such as the "long and protracted crisis of 2,000-1,000 B.C. in India."[52] Some of Sorokin's uniformities concern themselves with sociocultural change caused by acute outbreaks of social problems he is discussing; but others, i.e., change in basic ideologies, could be caused only by long periods of exposition of human societies to social calamities, perhaps of various types.

This leads us to the second objection: As has already been stated relative to revolution, a precise line of demarcation between rather insignificant cases and cases like long and bloody wars, total revolutions, famine or pestilence affecting large human masses, is lacking. This makes many "inductive generalizations" plausible relative to some cases of the four calamities, but dubious relative to the rest. That this is the case Sorokin seems to notice toward the very end of the volume, where he writes of the termination of calamities.[53] There he distinguishes wars and revolutions whose necessary and supplementary causes[54] were superficial and those where they were deep and formidable. In the former case the manifold changes predicated by him of calamities do not materialize; in the latter case they do obtain and may even result in the destruction of a society and its culture. *Mutatis mutandis,* the same is true of famine and pestilence. Consequently, the logical subject of propositions developed by Sorokin varies, and the class concept, "social calamity," shows up to be not quite appropriate to the formulation of "adequate theories."

It is possible that Sorokin has come to a similar conclusion since, in *Society, Culture and Personality,* he no longer uses the concept of social calamity and does not discuss famine and pestilence.

[51] *Man and Society in Calamity,* p. 67.
[52] *Ibid.,* p. 214.   [53] *Ibid.,* pp. 296-301.
[54] In the same meaning as in his article on "A Neglected Factor of War."

Probably the change of Sorokin's views on social causality, conspicuous when comparing the first three volumes of *Social and Cultural Dynamics* with the last (published four years later), has also contributed to their omission. The major cause of famine and pestilence (the biological phenomena of crop failure and of the increase of the mass and virulence of the germs of infectuous diseases) could no longer be treated along the same lines as purely man-provoked phenomena of war and revolution. Nevertheless, *Man and Society in Calamity* remains an important contribution, testifying to Sorokin's exceptional ability to grasp uniformities in seemingly heterogeneous phenomena, comparable only with that of Georg Simmel.

How Cowell of England Assesses Sorokin[1]

F. R. Cowell

A faithful account of Great Britain's assessment of Sorokin up to the year 1960 is more revealing as a comment upon the velocity of circulation of new ideas in contemporary sociology than as a considered national judgment upon the merits or demerits of his theories. Reputations in academic life seem to have at least one thing in common with national coinage systems in that ideas usually circulate more vigorously in the land in which they were minted than beyond its borders. Particularly is this true of international sociological speculations, many of which are rarely quoted on the British market.

To report, therefore, that the impact of Sorokin's theories upon British academic and sociological writings cannot so far be regarded as at all pronounced is to say something which might equally well be said of any, if not of most, other eminent contributors to the subject also. Not that overseas writers are ignored out of a spirit of narrow chauvinism; it is simply the fact that sociology itself does not flourish here, and that British contributions to sociology too often share a similar fate. A recent survey estimated the number of sociologists teaching in British Universities as "nearly forty, compared with 200 philosophers and perhaps 350 economists," and it gave the membership of the recently founded British Sociological Association as "500 or so."[2] In fact the initial impetus given in the United Kingdom to sociology after the middle of the nineteenth century, despite a more promising second start at the beginning of the present century, has not proved as fruitful as the pioneers had

[1] Editor's note: This title represents a slight modification of the essay title originally assigned to Mr. Cowell.

[2] Donald G. MacRae, in *The Twentieth Century*, CLXVII (May 1960), 440 and 473.

hoped. In the light of the figures just quoted, it would seem somewhat optimistic to believe that anything in the nature of a vigorous dialectic in sociology in the United Kingdom has yet begun. It is an impression confirmed by a reference to the British *Subject Index to Periodicals* and checked by the *International Index to Periodicals,* neither of which reveals any British discussion of Sorokin's contribution to sociology in the wide range of periodicals they index. Actually the situation was not as bad as this "nil return" seems to indicate.

When Professor Sorokin's books first began to appear, the only professional journal in which they might have been noticed, the *Sociological Review,* had lost its early impetus and the Sociological Institute, of which it was the main publication, was struggling along with inadequate support. The space it could spare for reviews was limited and not one of Sorokin's works was noticed in it. His name, however, was not unknown to readers of the *Review,* for already in 1932, in a paper on "Rural Sociology in the United States,"[3] Kaysenbrecht said of Sorokin that "his authority for such work cannot be contested." That topic has not so far aroused great interest in the different circumstances of rural England and there has been no further perceptible echo of this aspect of Sorokin's work.

Surprisingly the *Sociological Review* was also silent upon Sorokin's later and major works in the philosophy of history and the sociology of knowledge. Not only were they not reviewed but they were not even mentioned in the relatively few articles in the *Review* devoted to the philosophy of history. The leading British literary review has done better. *Social and Cultural Dynamics* was welcomed in the *Times Literary Supplement,* on March 26, 1938, by a review on page 198 which included appreciative comments such as the following:

The value of such co-operative labour can scarcely fail to appear at some point and the mere comprehensiveness of the volumes is spectacular. . . . The great care and the admirable statistical methods adopted by Professor Sorokin both in establishing his definitions and in fitting innumerable phenomena in the history of art, philosophy and social organization into his Platonic scheme of classification . . . and his hundreds of pages of statistics are among the most important though astonishing things in the work.

[3] XXIV (1932), 42-43.

This review refers, of course, to the first three volumes of *Social and Cultural Dynamics* which appeared in England, thanks to the enterprise of the well-known publishing house of George Allen and Unwin. Sir Stanley Unwin, the founder and head of the firm, in reply to an inquiry very kindly reported that he does not recall that a great deal of notice was given to the volumes apart from the *Times Literary Supplement* review quoted above. He also said that for a work of such importance, "the sales were negligible and we seldom if ever get any inquiries for the book." It was not, however, completely ignored by British sociologists, fewer though their numbers were then than they are today. A weighty assessment by the *doyen* of British sociologists, Professor Morris Ginsberg, appeared, not in the United Kingdom but in the *Zeitschrift für Sozialforschung*,[4] then a refugee publication. Concentrating upon Sorokin's basic classification by types of mentality as characterizing individuals, groups, and entire cultural systems and upon their development in accordance with a law of immanent causality, Professor Ginsberg described Sorokin's central thesis that social and cultural change is subject to fluctuations of varying amplitude showing, however, no consistent or regular trend, so that the idea of progress is unfounded historically. He also singled out as a central theme the fluctuations traced by Sorokin through his statistical studies of types of mentality of representative exponents and the numbers of their disciples and adherents, and also the fact the coherent cultural traits characterizing the cultural systems so revealed are not only empirically found but are functionally connected.

After briefly signalizing the central features in Sorokin's thought in this way, Professor Ginsberg offered four main critical reflections. In the first place he pointed out that "even if we grant the occurrence of fluctuations as a historical fact, it does not dispose of the problem of development," and he pertinently asked in support of this observation from the side of natural science, whether modern science is really as subject to erratic changes in fundamental points as Sorokin seems to think—adding that Sorokin's examples from biology and physics struck him as being insufficient to establish the position he had taken upon this question.

In the second place Professor Ginsberg doubted whether Sorokin had sufficiently weighed the difficulties inherent in any attempt to

⁴ VII (1938), 418-20.

relate general social mentality to the mentality of particular thinkers or leaders, especially in the sphere of ethics and practical life. He instanced the mode of conduct regarded as desirable by utilitarian philosophers as being no different from that advocated by idealists and as being far removed, therefore, from the crude, commercialized hedonism which Sorokin regards as characteristic of contemporary society. Even today, he thought, it cannot be held that utilitarian doctrines outweigh those of other schools either in their influence or importance.

Both these penetrating remarks recall Sorokin's own contention that a cultural system never wholly dies, so that those which succeed it can never be wholly pure. It would not seem that the classification of cultural types proposed by Sorokin would necessarily be overthrown on this account, or by the need to recognize more progress and less relativity in scientific knowledge in recent times than, perhaps, Sorokin allowed for in the first edition of *Social and Cultural Dynamics*. Similarly he could, and indeed does, hold that elements of ethical thought survive from one cultural system to another. Indeed, if there is to be any hope of transcending the relativity of all cultural values which would be the logical consequence of regarding Sorokin's three super-systems—ideational, idealistic, sensate—as self-contained "absolutes," it must be found in values or principles able to survive in each. Whatever may have been true of cultural super-systems in the past, the development of natural science should be particularly fruitful in this regard in the future. The modern hospital as a product of a sensate society is, perhaps, a symbol of such a likely lasting scientific achievement. The continuing vitality of principles, such as the Golden Rule, may also be found to support such a forecast from the side of ethical theory. In drawing attention to these perdurable principles, Professor Ginsberg seems to have made an important contribution. It is evidently one that he thinks that Sorokin might be able to accept, for he wrote, "if the extreme historical relativism adopted by Sorokin were consistently maintained, there would be no common standards for comparing different periods with one another and therefore no units of measurement. I suspect therefore that Sorokin is not as sceptical and relativistic as he pretends to be."

His two remaining comments would not seem to be likely to require more than some drafting changes in Sorokin's presentation, for Sorokin has in places anticipated Professor Ginsberg's contention that "the mere occurrence of fluctuations in the past offers no sufficient basis for prediction," but the success of some of his more startling predictions may have obscured his recognition of the basic correctness of Professor Ginsberg's logic. The final comment, that it is not clear how seriously Sorokin takes his own statistics, can largely be met by reference to Sorokin's own repeated disclaimer of infallibility and his reiterated pronouncement that the statistics and the deductions from them are put forward in the hope of stimulating others and so increasing knowledge, and not as ex-cathedra dogmas to be swallowed whole. Since Sorokin and his teams of researchers worked over the field, mechanical computers have been invented, and it does not seem too much to hope that his highly suggestive results achieved without the aid of these new devices could and should be reworked in the light of the refinements of a new generation of inventors.

In considering these early reactions to Sorokin's philosophy of history, it must be recalled that they were made before the publication of volume IV of *Social and Cultural Dynamics*, very few copies of which reached England for some years. It has never been republished in the United Kingdom, as were the first three volumes. When it appeared, in 1941, World War II was requiring a tremendous concentration of effort from all British citizens. There were not merely the physical and financial difficulties of importing American books, but British newspapers and periodicals were drastically reduced in size owing to paper shortages. Contributors were absent on war duty and the limited number of available printing works were made fewer by bomb destruction. A year or two after the war, the *Times Literary Supplement* returned to a general consideration of *Social and Cultural Dynamics*, including volume IV, in a front page article, "Man and Society."[5] Lengthy in relation to normal articles in that weekly newspaper, which in common with others was still suffering from paper shortages in the long aftermath of a disastrous war, the article attempted a general summary and commendation of the salient features of Sorokin's philosophy. While it is impossible to assess the impact of such a contribution, it was at least a full-dress survey of Sorokin's thought in the one literary publication seen by most people in the United Kingdom taking a

[5] Sept. 18, 1948, pp. 521-22.

serious interest in books and reading, among whom are the majority of the country's librarians and booksellers. It was not, however, merely a matter of record for it was directly responsible for provoking, thanks to the enterprise of the old-established publishing house of Messrs. A. & C. Black, a more extended study of Sorokin's philosophy of history by the writer of this essay. The book which resulted was called *History, Civilization and Culture, An Introduction to the Historical and Social Philosophy of Pitirim A. Sorokin.*[6] (It has since been reissued by Thames and Hudson in London.) Its purpose was to reduce the scale of Sorokin's four volumes by condensing the main trends of his thought, rather as Toynbee's ten volumes, *A Study of History,* have been summarized in two volumes by Somervell. Again it is impossible to estimate the degree of success achieved by the book in its main purpose of inducing greater study of Sorokin's own volumes. Unfortunately this short volume of mine seems to have been regarded less in this light than as a substitute for first-hand acquaintance with Sorokin's writings and for this reason, rather than from any pride of authorship, it will be necessary to give some account of its reception also. Fortunately it was not alone in the field, for Messrs. A. & C. Black republished in the United Kingdom Sorokin's *Social Philosophies in an Age of Crisis,* which *The Times Literary Supplement* described in a leading article on November 28, 1952 (p. 777), as "a fascinating conspectus of modern attempts to revive, in one form or another, the cyclical theory." This book was only indirectly a reflection of Sorokin's own approach to the problem, but it probably served to alert British readers to the dimensions of the task of interpreting history and to stimulate interest in it.

History, Civilization and Culture was noticed in *The Times Literary Supplement* on March 13, 1953 (p. 163), when it was remarked that "Professor Sorokin's ideas are obviously not easily absorbed but Mr. Cowell has resumed them very clearly and dispassionately. His book succeeds in being what it is called: an introduction to Professor Sorokin's philosophy." Unfortunately, I had not succeeded as well as I had hoped, for the review made what may be said to be the stock objection to Sorokin's work: "Since the statistics are based on questions chosen and judgements made by the Sorokin School itself, it is difficult to accept the claim that the

[6] Published in the United States by Beacon Press, Boston, 1952.

figures provide a better basis for the comprehension of history and civilization than anything previously available." This is a comment which recurs in later criticism and is so typical of the British approach that more must be said about it below. In a refreshingly candid and charming manner, Miss Veronica Wedgwood, the very well-known and deservedly popular historian, gave a more understandable reason for her doubts about philosophies of history in general. Her welcome for *History, Civilization and Culture* was all the more charitable for this reason.[7] Her words are of especial significance for they point to the real reason for the notorious apathy of the British public for work in this field. For she plainly declared that the skepticism with which she approached "the answers which have from time to time been put forward to elucidate the troubled course of history is at least in part the skepticism which resists the whole idea of elucidation." The reasons for such skepticism, she said, were the two insuperable obstacles to all philosophies of history, which are "the piecemeal and fragmentary character of all historical evidence and the essentially subjective approach of all historians." Here speaks what William James would have called the "tough-minded" British empirical approach, not merely towards Sorokin's views but, as in Miss Wedgwood's case, to the philosophy of history in general. Most historians in the British Isles would rally to the side of the late Sir Lewis Namier, who said to me in discussing such questions, that he was a microscopic and not a macroscopic historian. The sort of deflating remark with which he would welcome the larger philosophic view would be of the order of "how clever you must be to understand the book you have written," which is a view I once heard attributed to him—not, however, in relation to any effort of my own.

The British assessment of Sorokin must therefore be considered not merely in the light of the comments actually provoked by Sorokin's own work but within the context in which the philosophy of history is pursued in the British Isles. That there is a strong latent interest in the subject cannot be doubted, but before 1939 it cannot be said to have been an academic interest. It would, in fact, be difficult to name any prominent British historian since David Hume with any standing as a philosopher. Professor R. G. Collingwood, a philosopher turned historian, or perhaps arche-

[7] In *Time and Tide*, Aug. 16, 1952, p. 936.

ologist primarily, is the one possible example. Sheer genius in narration such as Macaulay's, or deep insight and a wise, sympathetic comprehension of the past such as F. W. Maitland's, are generally accepted very willingly as a more than adequate substitute for philosophic speculation about the course of history, however novel, arresting, and ingenious it may seem to be.

A plausible explanation of this British aversion to any philosphical approach seems very easily to be found in the simple fact that in England, unlike France for example, philosophy is not regarded as a suitable subject for even the higher forms of secondary and grammar schools. Apart from those trained in the *litterae humaniores* school at Oxford, most graduates of British universities can set themselves up as historians without gaining any notion of the place and importance of philosophical thought in the annals of human cultural activity or any sound grasp of the ideas of men such as Descartes, Locke, Leibniz, Hume, and Hegel. So it comes about that a great work such as Professor Toynbee's *Study of History* can gain wide popularity without exhibiting any interest in the nature, progress, and development of the philosophy of history as such. Indeed, in view of the absence of references to the leading protagonists of the subject from his *twelve*[8] volumes and the tone of the very occasional comments he makes upon some of them, Hegel for example, he might be said to have disavowed any concern with it.

There is nothing new in British distrust of generalizations in history. When in 1858 greatly daring Henry Thomas Buckle made his remarkable pioneer attempt to search for general ideas to explain the history of civilization in England, he was assailed with criticism, often vitriolic in intensity, from almost every writer of assured reputation in the country. While his serious and wholly praiseworthy effort to bring history, science, and sociology into some intelligible relationship was universally condemned, readers were still to be found for a great amount of the contemporary pseudo-scientific, pseudo-philosophical rubbish aptly described by Buckle's stout posthumous defender, John M. Robertson, as "a laurelling of philosophical incompetence by philosophical ignorance."[9] If a pessimist would say that Sorokin's fate is no happier than was Buckle's

[8] Volume XII of *A Study of History* is titled *Reconsiderations*, and it was published by Oxford University Press, 1961.

[9] In *Buckle and his Critics: A Study in Sociology* (1895), p. 471. This acute book deserves to be far more widely known.

a hundred years ago, he would not lack for supporting evidence. Nevertheless, there are signs in the present generation of the expansion of just that wider, more reflective consideration of the course of history for which Buckle pleaded in vain. It was a somewhat novel departure when, in 1931, Professor Butterfield drew attention to what he called "the whig interpretation of history." Many of those who were attracted and enlightened by it probably looked upon it as an exercise in answering the old question, *cui bono,* rather than as a pioneer effort in that "deduction of the categories" which history has so long lacked. It is all the more astonishing a deficiency because well over a hundred years have elapsed since Hegel in one of the more popular of his works, and one of the earliest to be translated into English and sold at a relatively low price, called attention to the fact that no historian worthy of the name writes without some orientation, some sense of values, some standards of judgment which are nothing if not philosophical in essence.[10]

The sociology of knowledge, seen against such a background, should hardly rate as the novelty it has been made to appear in the few years of its currency, but novelty it still is, and, despite Sorokin, who has done so much to stimulate its development, it can hardly yet be said to be exercising any very marked influence upon historical writing.

It has already been recorded that there was no discussion of Sorokin's views in the *Sociological Review.* They were also passed over in silence in two short studies in the series of *Oxford Classical and Philosophical Monographs,* the first of which was *The Nature of Historical Explanation,* by Mr. Patrick Gardiner, in 1952. It was followed, in 1957, by Professor William Dray's answer and commentary upon *Laws and Explanation in History.* Both volumes exhibit an equal lack of any apparent acquaintance with Sorokin's views, and for that matter with those of many other foreign contributions also, despite some reference to Spengler and Toynbee.

In 1954 Mr. Gardiner reviewed my book *History, Civilization and Culture in Philosophy* (XXIX, No. 108, Jan. 1954, pp. 81-82), two years after his own book had appeared. His ingrained skep-

---

[10] G. W. F. Hegel, *Philosophie der Geschichte* (1848), p. 15. "Auch der gewöhnliche und mittelmäszige Geschichtschreiber ... ist nicht passiv mit seinem Denken, und bringt seine Kategorien mit, und sieht durch sie das Vorhandene."

ticism about the possibility of scientific explanations in history probably accounts for the fact that his review consisted not of his own opinions but of a string of questions so framed, it would seem, as to invite answers discrediting Sorokin's views. The main positive critical suggestion, although that also hung upon a question, was that the apparent knowledge of the art, philosophy, religion, ethics, social organization, and so on, which Sorokin seeks to establish as characteristic of a cultural super-system, is to be dismissed as "a mere logical consequence of the definition of the super-system in question," so that "Sorokin's system ceases to be empirical and classificatory and becomes instead a metaphysical theory," endowing cultures with mysterious "real essences" and breeding uninformative "explanations" and "laws." Although somewhat tentatively put forward by Mr. Gardiner, this same fundamental objection, that Sorokin's work consists of a vast tautology, that his whole enormous apparatus of quantitative research merely "discovers" what he has all along assumed by his system of classifying the facts of cultural history, is basic to most of the criticism his historical philosophy has received in the United Kingdom, with the honorable exceptions of Professor Ginsberg and Miss Wedgwood.

It is difficult to believe that those who accuse Sorokin of falling in this way into one of the most obvious traps of the philosophical historian can have studied his works with any care. I should personally feel very guilty if, in my very condensed volume attempting to summarize Sorokin's theories, I had not faced and sought to anticipate and to deal with this objection. Indeed, I explicitly stated it, as on page 50 of *History, Civilization and Culture,* where I referred skeptics to Sorokin's own awareness and avoidance of a pitfall of which few could be better aware than he himself, the encyclopedic survey of *Contemporary Sociological Theories.*

It would almost seem as though the determination to discredit any attempts to "explain" history in any philosophic, general way prejudges the issue and blocks a truly scientific interest in views such as those of Sorokin. That Sorokin's concept of "logico-meaningful integration" and his statistical methodology should not be studied or carried forward in the generation after their formulation is a sad commentary upon current orientations in sociology in the United Kingdom. There has been no echo here of the discussion both have provoked in the United States, where they have been sharply attacked but in both cases cogently defended by Sorokin.[11] Such a comment may provoke the retort: "Why should Sorokin make the agenda for future inquiry?" And there would, indeed, be no argument against apathy, as there is against mere destructive criticism, particularly when it seems purveyed rather as a means of inflating the ego of the critic than in the true scientific spirit of trying to follow where the argument leads. The current refusal, or at least neglect to do so, may have the simple honest explanation which Samuel Johnson offered for his incorrect definition of "pastern" as the "knee" of a horse—"Ignorance, Madam, pure ignorance." For we cannot read everything and the philosophy of history, particularly in England, is not, as they say in America, everybody's "cup of tea."

What would be unfortunate would be to have the quest impeded by a species of false reasoning which might be expressed somewhat as follows:

All claims to be able to trace a structure of history are a priori and therefore valueless.

Sorokin seeks to trace a structure of history.

Therefore, Sorokin's views are a priori and valueless.

Unless freedom is won from this kind of *idée fixe*, it is difficult to see how any improvement in the ordering of historical knowledge is ever to be achieved. Refusal to see the need for any advance upon the rough and ready historical patterns and classificatory rubrics passed on from one generation to another, such as "Ancient, Medieval and Modern," the "Age of Reform," the "Age of Imperialism," and the like which, at present, do dubious duty in imposing some sketchy structure upon the historical continuum, does not advance the comprehension of history. Such rubrics cramp it within an ancient stereotype, or rather a somewhat ancient stereotype; for some of those in use probably owe their existence to the need for a harassed author, publisher, or even printer's reader to find a title for a chapter heading, and they are not hallowed by a very long tradition. They have, however, "caught on" to serve as one of those "categories" by which the past is viewed, which Hegel said historians bring with them, ready made for unquestioning use.

[11] See R. Bierstedt, *American Sociological Review*, II (1938), 813, and H. Hart, IV (1940), 635.

It is, of course, right that warnings against the misuse of bad "categories" should be clear and vehement. Such was the useful service performed by Sir Isaiah Berlin in a lecture upon a text furnished by Bernard Berenson protesting against the idea of the inevitability of events and the impotence of individual man in the grip of vast impersonal historical forces. This is not Sorokin's belief either and he is not mentioned in Sir Isaiah's text. Other philosophers of history are, however, and the references to them might incline a careless reader to assume that Sorokin would be equally vulnerable to Sir Isaiah's strictures. Although therefore there is no evidence that Sir Isaiah regards Sorokin as in any way incriminated, it may be permissible to quote from his book purely in order to illustrate the manner in which certain aspects of the philosophy of history have appeared in contemporary Britain. Says Sir Isaiah:

From the days of Herder and Saint-Simon, Hegel and Marx, to those of Spengler and Toynbee and their imitators, claims have been made, widely varying in degree of generality and confidence, to be able to trace a structure of history (always *a priori* for all protests to the contrary), to discover the one and only true pattern into which alone all facts will be found to fit. But this is not, and can never be, accepted by any serious historian who wishes to establish the truth as it is understood by the best critics of his time. . . . [They will] instinctively perceive that some kind of violence is being done to the facts, that the relation between evidence and interpretation is in some way abnormal; and this is so not because there is any doubt about the facts but because there is an obsessive pattern at work . . . for there is no historical thought properly speaking, save where facts are distinct not merely from fiction, but from theory and interpretation in a lesser or greater degree.[12]

It is not of course difficult, especially in the full context of his remarks, to realize that this somewhat vague language justly attacks certain inadequate philosophies of history, but at the same time it is not difficult either to see that it needs qualification in the light of Sorokin's achievement. Some bases for such qualification may be drawn from Sir Isaiah's book itself, for he earlier had recognized that history employs in its work of interpretation only the categories or concepts of common sense (p. 51), which is just what Hegel said, and he also acknowledged that "cultures possess patterns and ages

[12] Sir Isaiah Berlin, *Historical Inevitability* (London: Oxford University Press, 1955), pp. 69-70.

spirits" (p. 16). He may or may not accept Sorokin's description of the patterns to be discerned in the cultural life of the past, but he would not find Sorokin guilty of the mistake against which he chiefly inveighs, of endowing his cultural patterns—the ideational, idealistic, and sensate—with an independent vitality, of "re-ifying" them as ghostly beings from whose toils no man can escape. Yet, if Sorokin's patterns do not frighten Sir Isaiah—they may, of course—Sir Isaiah's word will make many others frightened of them, for he speaks of other abstract descriptive labels which have been used to describe the spirits of past ages such as "the Collectivist Spirit," "the Crisis of Faith," "Modern Man," or "the last stages of Capitalism," as "supernatural entities of great power" which constitute "a quasi-sociological mythology." He states quite clearly the reason for his alarm: "In a world where such monsters clash, individual human beings can have but little responsibility for what they do; the discovery of the new terrifying, impersonal forces may render life infinitely more dangerous."[13]

Now while everybody would be at one with Sir Isaiah in wishing to stand up for moral standards and for the maintenance of the idea of individual responsibility for individual actions, we are not authorized to declare that any sociological research which might have the effect of demonstrating that there are patterns in cultures and that there are "spirits of the ages" is, for that reason, taboo. One might just as well tell doctors in tropical Africa that they should not subject the river water to bacteriological examination for fear that they might discover the cause of bilharzia in it.

The urge to replace phantoms of the imagination, such as those condemned by Sir Isaiah, by some valid cause or explanatory principle remains, despite his denunciations. It is a very old impulse. "If we take away from history the discussion of why, how, and wherefore each thing was done and whether the result was what we should have reasonably expected, what is left," said Polybius two thousand years ago, "is a clever essay but not a lesson" (III, 31). What the lesson ought to be remains the mystery. That there can be no lesson has not yet convincingly been established. As Sir Isaiah's essay shows, men will seek for some general explanations and the tendency is increasingly to believe that "historical problems are largely influenced by what for a better name can be called the

[13] *Ibid.*, pp. 72-74.

climate or the spirit of the age."[14] "Cultures possess patterns" said Sir Isaiah a few years later, "and ages spirits." "Like rolling clouds in the sky the spirit of an age is never immobile but remains elusive and volatile," says Mr. Einstein. So elusive in fact that "to use the word 'climate' in order to describe the atmosphere of a period is something of a misnomer for what can neither be measured nor weighed by any recognized standard."[15] Such may still be said to be the orthodox view of historical change. Yet nearly ten years before Mr. Einstein wrote, Sorokin, whom he nowhere mentions, had taken up the challenge and published a major work in which he boldly faced the difficulties of finding standards and of weighing and measuring the facts upon which the idea that there have been changes must necessarily repose.

The point at issue is best illustrated by an example, by one out of the scores of examples in Sorokin's work. Confronted by the facts upon which the history of one aspect of cultural life is characterized, the phenomena of painting pictures, what is a historian of human culture to do? Two fairly representative collections alone totaled some 39,000 separate works of art. Is the historian to wander among them, gathering "impressions" from which wisdom about art history will automatically arise, rather as wine would run out of a huge mound of grapes as they were crushed under their own weight? Given the right sensitive soul, much might be gleaned that way, but the result would remain subjective, uncertain, and largely incommunicable, with a steadily diminishing influence upon later generations. Yet, if he is forbidden by Sir Isaiah Berlin to indulge in "theory and interpretation" it is difficult, in fact impossible, to hope for any contribution from the side of painting to the story of human cultural development which would have any pretension to verifiable objectivity. For better or worse, Sorokin sought to discover some order in this mass of facts. His purpose was to discover, by examining the content of each picture in these two collections, whether there had been any significant changes in the social character of art from one generation to another since the history of painting began. He did not undertake the work himself but was fortunate in having two independent research teams to do

[14] L. Einstein, *Historical Change* (Cambridge: Cambridge University Press, 1946), p. 123.
[15] *Ibid.*, pp. 125 and 123.

it for him. He was responsible for devising the twelve categories into which the investigators were asked to group their findings.

At this point English critics of Sorokin's work will at once jump in, as they have already done, with the damning remark: "There you are, you see, the whole thing is 'framed' in advance! He 'finds' what he has first injected into the inquiry and then tries to palm off the result as more 'scientific' than anything achieved by his predecessors." They certainly have not undertaken the mountain of labor recorded in Sorokin's volumes and they have not given the hostages to fortune and to their critics that he has. For he has set out clearly and precisely the questions he asked. The twelve points of the inquiry into the nature of paintings in two collections were: whether the subject was religious or secular; landscape, *genre* or portrait; of men or women; of royalty, aristocracy, bourgeois, or working class. The final heading, in which alone some risk of subjective bias might seem able to endanger the result, was that which required the investigators to report whether any paintings of the nude were ascetic, erotic, or neutral. But here the findings were checked by more than one observer.

It can hardly be denied that the result of such an inquiry is a collection of "facts," and facts, moreover, which it would be useful to have collected for more than the two collections inspected by Sorokin's investigators. It may, of course, be argued that Sorokin asked the wrong questions, that the answers to them cannot be regarded as significant for the social history of art and for the study of the development of human culture. But to sustain such criticisms, any critic respecting himself, his readers, and the subject of inquiry must surely offer some suggestion of what the correct questions would be which would be better able to advance knowledge. The alternative is to rest in the nebulous state of uncertainty depicted by Mr. Einstein, in which aesthetic satisfactions from the contemplation of rolling clouds, *tout lasse, tout passe,* must remain the sole compensation for our lack of knowledge. But if the facts collected by Sorokin are admitted to be facts, and it is difficult to see how that could be denied, then the critic who refuses to accept Sorokin's use of them still has to explain why they are irrelevant or incorrectly employed in the reasoning Sorokin bases upon them. After all, Sorokin puts forward his whole work as a series of hypotheses to be tested and criticized without concealing his sources or his methods, neither of which are as perfect as he could wish. If this is not a "scientific" method of trying to deal with the "facts" of history, what is the scientific method that is better? Is Sorokin's basis of collecting and analyzing facts really very different from, say, that of Linnaeus in classifying plants? The Linnaean system of handling the "facts of plant life" seems just as much tainted with "theory and interpretation" as is Sorokin's treatment of historical facts. It is not the only system by which plants may be and have been classified; neither does Sorokin claim that his method of cataloguing the facts of cultural life is the only road to historical knowledge. He has worked hard to make it what he believes to be a good road without so far having the satisfaction of seeing it put to the use it deserves. Perhaps the "climate of opinion of the age" is such that he cannot hope for a fair hearing, as some pregnant words by Professor Carl Becker suggest: "The essential quality of the modern climate of opinion is factual rather than rational." The word "factual" here is interpreted to exclude all efforts to "explain" anything as though all attempts to "explain" are suspected of being attempts to sway opinion in favor of some specious doctrine or program, for "no respectable historian any longer harbors ulterior motives; and one who should surreptitiously introduce the gloss of a transcendent interpretation into the human story would deserve to be called a philosopher and straightway lose his reputation as a scholar."[16] From such a charge Sorokin should be secure. If his work has any flavor of a transcendent interpretation, it is what emerges out of it rather than what he has put into it, in the sense that his discovery of cultural supersystems points to the existence of distinct and different value-systems at different epochs of human history to which men with difficulty can remain neutral, for they correspond to the tug of conflicting loyalties they may very likely feel within their own mental and behavioristic make-up.

The attempt to make a sample survey of one aspect of the facts of cultural history, that of painting, is but one out of many. Sorokin was able to organize teams of workers to undertake a great number of similar surveys in other fields. The biographical articles in the *Encyclopaedia Britannica* were worked through for data about literary characters and philosophers. The source may be ques-

[16] Carl L. Becker, *The Heavenly City of the Eighteenth-Century Philosophers* (New Haven: Yale University Press, 1932), pp. 27 and 18.

tioned—it was the ninth edition that was used. The form of the questionnaire may be challenged and errors of fact and interpretation might be alleged against some of the findings. There is, obviously, a margin of error in all such work. The question is whether that margin is significant, and if so how significant. Does it vitally affect Sorokin's findings and the interpretation he bases upon them? Until such questions are answered it would not be permissible for some hasty reader of, say, Sir Isaiah Berlin's essay on *Historical Inevitability*, to denounce Sorokin's suggested structure of history by repeating, "always *a priori* for all protests to the contrary."

The British reverence for pure facts is all the more strange in that, as Sorokin has pointed out, no great discoveries have been made by the pure grubbers after facts "distinct from theory and interpretation." The great names in British natural science and philosophy are those who brought theory and interpretation to bear upon the facts. Today, when the climate of opinion is factual to the virtual exclusion of rational argument, we need not be surprised if a kind of "mass-observation" larded with a few amusing anecdotes, often about the semi-literate, can pass muster as sociology, while credit can be won in philosophy from acute discussion about the meanings of words—an exercise contributing little more to the true study of philosophy than the solution of crossword puzzles does to the progress of literature. The most that an optimist can say to console us for the lack of a real sociology or philosophy is that such exercises are a temporary and necessary reaction against facile system-building on flimsy foundations which characterized too much of the sociological and philosophical speculations of the recent past. Even a pessimist could hardly contemplate the perpetuation of the present sterility with satisfaction. The plain man with no academic or other vested interests to worry about is more likely to give attention to those who, like Buckle, Spengler, and Toynbee, give him new ideas. Sorokin not merely does this on a vast scale, but his ideas emerge from a wealth of facts, systematically and scientifically collected, far in excess of those with which his predecessors illustrated their ideas. That the fact-loving British have not yet discovered what Sorokin has done for them in the way of amassing and analyzing facts is, as was said at the outset of this essay, a striking commentary upon the slow circulation of new ideas in sociology in the British Isles.

It would falsify the picture to leave the impression that the strongly marked pragmatic, practical, matter-of-fact qualities discernible in British thought determine the approach of every Briton to the riddle of the universe. If William of Ockham was one of their distant spiritual godfathers, the claims of Richard Rolle of Hampole to be another should not be overlooked; both are supposed to have died in the same year. Already there are signs of a change in the climate of opinion in the slow rise of a greater interest in the philosophy of history. Despite the pioneer work of Professor Flint in the nineteenth century, it can hardly be said to have been of marginal academic interest in Britain until Oakeshott and Croce stimulated Professor R. G. Collingwood to revivify it at Oxford before World War II, which Collingwood did not survive. Outside academic circles the discussion was more vigorous. Mr. Christopher Dawson in particular was already making contributions to it drawn from a wide reading which, however, as late as 1957, when his *Dynamics of World History* was published, surprisingly did not seem to include the works of Sorokin. Neither are they considered by Professor Butterfield, who has done much to arouse interest in the wider perspectives of history, nor by Professor Barraclough, whose *History in a Changing World,* of 1957, courageously called for "a new vision of the course of modern history." While he did not share their views, he commended both Spengler and Toynbee for "seeking to perform a serious function which other historians are increasingly neglecting" (p. 10).

It would not be difficult to multiply instances of the tendency to seek the wider vision, the more philosophic grasp of the enormously complicated range and mass of facts with which historians must grapple. Equally easy would be the multiplication of refusals to contemplate the very possibility of generalization, the obstinate determination to prefer the microscopic to the macroscopic point of view. Reflection upon the impasse this conflict has caused and the depressing failure of attempts to arouse interest in Sorokin's theories stimulates the effort to seek a new approach. One hopeful new development might well be the rise of the "sociology of knowledge" which has begun to claim some attention from the present generation, even in England, as a result of the work of the late Professor Karl Mannheim and, more recently, of Professor Stark.

The very powerful impetus which Sorokin's ideas have imparted to this study has not received in the United Kingdom the attention such ideas merit. Dr. Stark certainly has not ignored him, but I personally could wish that he had relied less on my very summary account of Sorokin's philosophy and more upon the works of Sorokin himself. Nevertheless, he says of Sorokin that "he is still essentially an all-round sociologist . . . it is only right and logical to regard him and his like as true sociologists of knowledge."[17] This is not the place to deal with Dr. Stark's important work in any detail, save only in his references to Sorokin, and especially his critical comments. They single out especially two main points. He considers the three main "cultural super-systems" proposed by Sorokin to be "far too wide to fit the culture-content of any concrete society."[18] The statistical basis for the classification is no more than "a very first and very distant approximation to the facts." As Dr. Stark points out, Sorokin himself so describes them. They are, however, an approximation and, within their limits, as accurate a measurement of a vast range of facts in fields hitherto assessed by the purely subjective impressions and the vaguest of "hunches." Dr. Stark would appear to believe that nothing more is possible. He writes:

Our criticism of Sorokin's experiment is not on matters of detail; it is one of principle. His whole procedure assumes *a radice* the possibility of quantifying what is qualitative. . . . A book, or a work of art is all quality, because it is all spirit. The unity of a culture consists in the stylistic similarities shown by its ingredients, not in their statistical identity. There is really nothing that can be counted, though there is a good deal that can be compared. It is to be feared that the sociology of knowledge will never be able to get much assistance from statistical techniques. Much though we may regret the fact, it will always have to rely heavily on the more cumbersome monographic and descriptive methods.[19]

There is a clash of opinion here which is clearly irreconcilable. It seems based upon an imperfect acquaintance with Sorokin's own writings. If we accept Dr. Stark's first point, that Sorokin's three supersystems in cultural history are "far too wide to fit the culture-content of any concrete society," it would seem to imply

[17] W. Stark, *The Sociology of Knowledge* (Glencoe, Ill.: The Free Press, 1958), p. 238.
[18] *Ibid.*, p. 280.   [19] *Ibid.*

that Sorokin's terms can be applied indifferently to any period of culture. This is a very hazardous proposition. By what stretch of language could fifth-century-B.C. Greece be called a predominantly sensate society? Or contemporary Manhattan, or Rome under the Empire, idealistic or ideational societies? Dr. Stark seems to think that Sorokin's is an "all or none" affair of sharply differentiated epochs in which everybody behaves alike. Yet Sorokin is careful to point out that this is just what he does not believe.

It is equally impossible to follow Dr. Stark in denying that quantitative notions have any place in cultural life. There is no question of trying to reduce all qualitative notions to quantitative ones, a process that Dr. Stark rightly likens to attempts to square the circle. The aim is to get, as far as it is possible to do so, clear and distinct ideas, instead of vague and fuzzy notions. Is it preferable to announce as an *ipse dixit* that "since the sixteenth century the proportion of religious music tends to decrease while that of secular music tends to increase" or to record, as Sorokin does, that "In the sixteenth century, the number of known musical works (those mentioned in the standard histories of music) were 44 per cent religious and 56 per cent secular [or that] in the nineteenth century religious compositions were only 21 per cent against 79 per cent of secular works"? Certainly this does not exhaust the matter; there is the question of quality or intensity which escapes enumeration. As Sorokin himself points out, the quality of some of the religious music of the nineteenth century had overtones which seem pronouncedly secular. But does this mean that the statistics are valueless and that we are just as well off with the vague statement of a tendency as with a precise statement of the actual facts of the situation insofar as we are able to discover them? Only those who have had no training in statistical or scientific techniques would say "yes" to such a question, and they should receive no aid and comfort from one concerned with the sociology of knowledge. I had, I thought, labored this very obvious consideration *ad nauseam* in my *History, Civilization and Culture*, saying, on page 86: "As was pointed out in Chapter One, and must be repeated elsewhere in this work, just as the refusal to be interested in the philosophy of history is itself a philosophical position, so the refusal to attempt to give greater precision and clarity to ideas about size, quantity and number, relying instead upon rough estimates or vague guesses, is also to make quantitative judgments although they will probably be crude, un-reliable and not very enlightening."[20]

The conclusion of this very general and sketchy survey of British reactions to Sorokin's thought must be that so far they have been insufficient and inadequate. My own condensed exposition and introduction to his ideas is the only such volume and it cannot be said to have had any very perceptible influence. His books are generally available in the larger public libraries, as far as one or two sample inquiries are typical. No serious student in the United Kingdom is likely to lack access to them through the National Central Library, provided that not many want what copies there are at the same time. Apart from one or two active centers, it does not appear that any very marked attention is given to Sorokin's theories in British universities at the undergraduate level, because philosophy and sociology are rarely taught to large numbers at that stage of academic life. Reflection upon this slow progress, in a study that seemed to me to offer great promise, led me to try an approach from another angle. The proposition that cultural ideas offer a valuable clue to historical development, which is central to Sorokin's philosophy of history, encounters the difficulty that there is no general agreement about the meaning of the word *culture*. Yet the word is being increasingly used in all manner of contexts; in anthropology and archeology it has been generally but vaguely used to a greater extent than it has in history. Explanations of the major changes registered in the annals of history have been sought in the last two or three hundred years by laying a varying emphasis upon such critical factors as environmental forces of geography, race, climate, food and diet, and economic possibilities. Great as such contributions are, it is plain that they cannot exhaust the matter. The religious interpretation of history, which they modified and to some extent replaced, has by no means been given up, as the work of Toynbee is not alone in demonstrating. Neither, of course, can it be, for religious ideas have always been a most powerful influence. So, however, have "secular," humanistic or cultural ideas and values. "Except in primitive life," said Lewis Einstein in

[20] Editor's note: Pressed by Franz Adler's criticism of Stark's negative attitude toward statistical methods and insufficient attention paid to Sorokin's works, Stark admitted: "Not that I have really rejected them. Do I not call Sorokin's 'a re-markable effort' . . . ? . . . he is a pioneer, a man who has opened a new chapter, not a man who has closed an old one." Stark's "Reply" in *Kyklos,* XII (1959), 223.

1946, "human action is neither automatic nor instinctive, and is nearly always receptive to the influence of ideas that may be near or remote, direct or indirect. We therefore associate the pressure for change with the influence of ideas." Sorokin may be said to have concentrated upon and greatly developed this line of approach which may, for short, be called the cultural approach. In trying to spell out the full implications of this approach, he has fulfilled a herculean task, and he has advanced the study of history, for, again to quote Mr. Einstein, "the historian's problem is to discover how far any changes whose consequences are registered by events have been influenced by ideas."

To discover whether ideas can be said to have developed in accordance with any sort of pattern and, if so, what that pattern or those patterns may be, and how they arise and decline, and whether they or some of them always endure from one age to another—such were the tasks which Sorokin set for himself. Regarding the matter as essentially the study of human "culture," since all matters of this sort must have some title or descriptive label, I tried in my book, *Culture in Private and Public Life*,[21] to sketch its range and dimensions and to provide a working definition or description of the idea of culture. It will be relevant to the climate of opinion in the United Kingdom in relation to such an inquiry, for it goes far to account for the neglect of Sorokin to record that one or two friends advised me not to undertake it. In the academic world, I was told, more than one scholar had said that he would not try to make any contribution to philosophical inquiry for at least ten years, for it would be too dangerous for his academic reputation to seek to go against the prevalent fashion, the fashion aptly described by Carl Becker as "factual and not rational." Such is the blighting effect of logical positivism and its aftermath. Not having any academic reputation to lose or any academic hopes to be blighted, and preferring to trust to what I rightly or wrongly consider to be the tradition of English letters, it seemed legitimate to try to follow where the argument led, in spite of the probably unpleasant consequences. They in any case would be nothing new. "Philosophy is such an impertinently litigious lady," said Newton in 1686, "that a man had as good be engaged in lawsuits as have anything to do with her." My book appeared in the summer of 1959 and it is too

[21] New York: Frederick A. Praeger, 1959.

early to say whether it will have the least effect in arousing greater interest in Sorokin's massive contribution, or in stimulating greater attention to the tremendous importance of the cultural side of the life of our times. As the subject of this essay is actually England's assessment of Sorokin, these personal details are of some relevance, for they show that at least one Englishman has been greatly influenced by reading his works. To such an avowal it is necessary to add that I have never had the pleasure of meeting Professor Sorokin and that the two books of mine to which I have alluded were both written and published without his prior knowledge and without any communication whatever from him upon their subject matter or treatment.

Litera scripta manet must be the ancient faith that sustains the expectation that the influence of Sorokin's work is only in its early stages and that much more will be heard of it when certain current academic fashions, personalities, and prejudices are less powerful than they seem to be at present. For there are promising signs that the long neglect of the philosophy of history is ending, even in England. In addition to several books on the subject, a useful journal, *History and Theory,* made its appearance in 1960. International in sponsorship and published in the Netherlands, it may be expected to carry the dialectic forward in a manner that has not been easy to achieve without a specialized periodical. The first issue opened with a powerful article by Sir Isaiah Berlin in which, although Sorokin is not mentioned, a series of critical points are set forth in Sir Isaiah's magisterial style with many of which it may be anticipated that Sorokin would be in substantial agreement.

When a future survey of sociological theory of this type is undertaken in the years to come, it will be seen that the cultural approach to history contributed by Sorokin inaugurated a new development in historical explanation by providing operational concepts for its achievement and by relegating to their proper and often subordinate sphere the military, political, racial, geographical, climatic, economic, and other canons of historical interpretation, all of which have had their enthusiastic supporters, yet all of which can now be seen to be but partial approximations to the truth, illuminating facets and aspects of mankind's past, but failing individually and collectively to point to the more fundamental ideas and valuations by which man creates his destiny and shapes his future. Despite all the imperfections in statement, inadequacies of thought, errors in enumeration and calculation of which Sorokin may be convicted, his great and enduring title to fame will rest unshakably upon his devotion to the search for truth, his fertility in striking out new lines of inquiry, his tireless energy in undertaking a mountainous labor, his optimism and his faith in the human spirit which early sustained him in imprisonment and under sentence of death and which has since seen him through and enabled him to survive neglect, rebuffs, and carping criticism in the fine tradition of all those by whom humane learning has been promoted, *cultores veritatis, fraudis inimici.*

How Munshi of India Assesses Sorokin[1]

K. M. Munshi

Professor Pitirim Sorokin is the pre-eminent social philosopher of our age. His studies embrace social institutions and ideals; religion and philosophy; instincts, urges, and aspirations; the flight of man through ages into the region of the Spirit in search of Truth, Beauty, and Love; and his ageless yearning for God. His conclusions are based on massive evidence collected with scrupulous care and marshaled with scientific precision.

Among living thinkers, Sorokin and Toynbee have spent their lives in studying the past and the present to find a pattern for the future. Toynbee's outlook and training are those of a historian, while Sorokin brings to his work on social philosophy a spiritual insight which was denied to Auguste Comte and an optimism that Spengler never had. Professor Sorokin's penetrating analysis of the social, moral, and political conditions in the modern world, particularly in Europe and America, discloses the trends which fully justify his two main conclusions based on undisputed data: first, that we are passing through a decadent age; and second, that we are on the threshold of a new and creative age, which will give free play to the moral and spiritual urges of man. The first conclusion is as devastating as the second one is heartening.

Some of Sorokin's works strike a deep chord in Indian hearts. When we read his books, we find Indian thought interpreted in terms of world movements. What to our seers was given through inspiration or intuition, we find expounded with scientific accuracy and thoroughness on the background of comparative studies in history, sociology, and religion. His outlook throughout is synthetic as of Indian seers. Today, when man is emerging from the present

[1] Editor's note: This title is a slight modification of the original one assigned to Dr. Munshi.

decadent order, he looks forward to an era of integrated culture based on universal moral order, or as Indian thinkers would term it *Dharma*, based on *Satvam, Shivam, Sundaram*—Truth, Love, Beauty.

One of the remarkable conclusions to which Sorokin comes after his study of society through the ages is that the belief that man is making a continuous progress, except in the narrow sense of technical progress, is historically unfounded. This was anticipated by ancient Indian thought when it divided individuals and societies into *daivi* and *asuri*—"rising Godward" and "falling demon-ward," or to use Sorokin's words, "ideal-ideational" and "sensate." Many of the passages in his works describing modern sensate culture appear to be an echo of the thought succinctly expressed in the Bhagavad-Gita. When describing men who are the creatures or the victims of their egoistic impulses fostered by the "falling demon-ward" culture, the Lord says:

> Such lost souls, with vision dim
> Like determined foes
> Come forth with cruel deeds to destroy the world.
> Quenchless are their longings.
> By fraud, conceit and lust,
> They live inspired and strive
> Deluded, grasping lies for truth,
> Bound to vows impure.
> Engrossed in ceaseless worries are they
> Till they die; satisfying their desires their only goal.
> Enmeshed by a hundred fetters of hope,
> Steeped in desire and wrath,
> They seek but to gather wealth
> By unjust means,
> Bent only on satisfying their lust.

> "See what I have secured today," they say,
> "On this is my mind set next,
> Already this much is mine;
> This much more shall be mine hereafter.
> This enemy have I slain today:
> Those others I shall slay anon.
> I am the lord: I enjoy as I like.
> Successful, strong, and happy am I.
> I am high born, wealthy—
> Who else is there like me?

I shall offer sacrifice;
I shall scatter gifts, rejoice."

Deluded by ignorance, maddened by fancies,
Caught fast in delusion, these men,
By sensual pleasures dragged,
Rush headlong into Hell.
Such cruel men of malice, most vile of men,
I hurl back again in other godless wombs.
Deluded fools these,
Birth after birth passing through godless wombs,
Never do they come unto me, son of Kunti!
They wend their way to the lowest of low estate.

The ancient Hindu thought again has a cyclical theory. According to it, whenever *adharma* or unrighteousness prevails, the society is destroyed and the rule of righteousness is re-established again. This basic thought acquires scientific validity in the works of Sorokin.

Sorokin is one of the very few Western thinkers who have appreciated the standpoint and technique of yoga. Speaking about the technique of yoga, in his book, *The Ways and Power of Love*, Sorokin says:

The system of the techniques of each yoga contains in itself some of the techniques of other Yogas. The integral Yoga of Sri Aurobindo (and also the various techniques practised by Ramakrishna) deliberately attempts to unite the main techniques of all the Yogas.[2]

In many respects, Sorokin's works provide a scientific background to the integral philosophy of Sri Aurobindo, the great Indian mystic and thinker, who has synthesized ancient and modern thought in India and elsewhere. Both, one by insight and the other by scientific study, stand against materialism and that brand of rationalism which denies to man a higher or a supra-conscious mind. Both of them, each in his own characteristic way, stand against the insectifying psychology of Freud. Both stand for an integrated approach to reality. The true reality and value, according to Sorokin, is "an infinite manifold; has sensory, super-sensory, rational and super-rational aspects, all harmoniously reflecting this infinity."

The altruism of Sorokin was emphasized in Indian thought as *paramartha*, "seeking other's welfare," and has the same goal as the

[2] P. 375.

integral yoga of Sri Aurobindo, viz., the total transformation of man and society to be achieved by overcoming the conflicts in individual and collective life and releasing creative energy.

Like Indian seers, Sorokin holds the view that genuine creativeness demands "something more than the operation of our conscious egos." It can be realized only by developing the inspiration or intuition of the superconscious, in Sanskrit called *prajna,* by developing which, as Patanjali, the ancient author of the classic textbook Yoga Sutra, puts it, all things are seen in "their real meaning and significance."

With regard to the imperative need of developing the forces of the superconscious, which Indian seers emphasize, Sorokin says:

If the as yet largely unknown "fission forces" of the superconscious are revealed and fully exploited, they can become the most decisive agency of man's self-control, as well as of the control of others and of all the known and unknown forms of the inorganic, organic, and conscious energies in man and the universe. Their neglect by sensate science has been one of the chief reasons for its failure in the fields discussed. What is needed is a concentration of humanity's efforts on unlocking the secrets of the superconscious as the realm of the most powerful, most creative, and most ennobling forces in the entire universe. The more man becomes an instrument of the superconscious, the more creative, wiser, and nobler he grows; the more easily he controls himself and his unconscious and egoistic conscious energies, the more he comes to resemble God, as the supreme ideal. In the superconscious lies our main hope, the road to humanity's "promised land" of peace, wisdom, beauty, and goodness.[3]

Referring to the technique of evoking the superconscious followed by seers in all lands, Sorokin summarizes the position, as follows:

As a preliminary condition for obtaining control of the unconscious and conscious by the superconscious and for unlocking the forces of the superconscious, they unanimously demand the liberation of a person from all forms of egoism and the development of a love for the Absolute, for all living beings, for the whole universe, in its negative aspect of not causing pain to anybody by thought, word, or deed, and in its positive aspect of unselfish service, devotion, and help to and sacrifice for others.

The same is true of the systems of all the great mystics, stoics, ascetics, and other true followers of these systems. *They all unanimously say*

[3] P. A. Sorokin, *Reconstruction of Humanity* (Bhavan's Book University Series), pp. 185-86.

that the practice of kindness and love is one of the best therapies for curing many mental disorders; for the elimination of sorrow, loneliness, and unhappiness; for the mitigation of hatred and other anti-social tendencies; and, above all, for the ennoblement of human personality, for release in man of his creative forces, and for the attainment of union with God and peace with oneself, others, and the universe.[4]

After a comprehensive survey of religious thought and practice, Sorokin establishes the scientific value of the goal of human effort as envisaged by the Bhagavad-Gita. In that Lord's Song, Sri Krishna, the Lord, says:

Integrated in yoga, the man who has realized himself sees the Supreme Self abiding in all things and all things in Him. To Him, all things are equal.

He who thus sees Me everywhere, and sees everything in Me, is never separated from Me, nor I from him. With all his powers fully integrated, he worships Me as dwelling in all created things.

Both Toynbee and Sorokin agree in the view that humanity cannot survive without the religious spirit born of faith. Even Jung, after a clinical experience of thirty years and of many hundreds of patients in his *Modern Man in Search of a Soul*, comes to the same conclusion that men in modern times are unhappy because of want of faith. Those alone are happy, who are rooted in supreme faith. Thus we have been seeking light, though the light was there all the time.

Rightly, therefore, Sorokin comes to the conclusion that the older world religions need not be replaced, for their "intuitions and conceptions are essentially valid and supremely edifying." That confirms the attitude of Indian thought towards all religions. "Whatsoever the form," Sri Krishna says, "in which the devotee desires to worship with faith, that faith I strengthen in him."

Sorokin's solution for human ills, among other things, is for the individual to escape "religious shells" and revitalize his own religious spirit by developing a vital sense of the living presence of God and by transforming overt conduct in the direction of practicing what he preaches. This is the age-old concept of *ishvar pranidhana*, surrender unto God, and *Satya*, the unity of thought, word, and deed.

Indian religious philosophy and literature are replete with

[4] *Ibid.*, pp. 202-203. Italics by the author.

bhakti, love in the sense of agape described as God's way to man
—or rather God Himself. We have in India practical textbooks like
Narada's *Bhakti-sutra,* devotional epics like the *Bhagvata,* and
hymns of saints and mystics which have uplifted millions for
centuries.

Such form of devotion is described, preached, and practiced in
most religions. But, for the first time in modern thought, Sorokin,
as a result of modern research carried on with scientific precision
and thoroughness, describes, analyzes, and illustrates all the aspects and techniques of love, in his monumental work, *The Ways
and Power of Love,* and makes it the basis for transforming individual and collective life.

Thus, all aspects of life, conduct, urges, and aspirations are
passed in review and co-ordinated in Sorokin's works to produce a
system of social and psychological reconstruction, which the seers
of every country stood for and which alone can lead man out of the
sorry mess which he has made of his life in modern times.

How Gini of Italy Assesses Sorokin[1]

Corrado Gini

I had to decline the invitation to write on "How Italy Assesses Sorokin," because no scientific market has yet been activated for sociology in Italy to exchange ideas, through which one can arrive at a clear position of various authors' valuations. In a poor nation like Italy, the nearly complete absence of university chairs of sociology does not offer sociologists a scientific career for research in this area. Sociologists, therefore, are quite rare here, and one can scarcely find more than one or two in a university center, and often none at all, although self-styled sociologists are numerous—men who, with good will but with meager preparation, discuss sociological questions in a way that often has very little to do with the science.

Instead, I have willingly accepted this opportunity to write my own personal impressions concerning the scientific character of Sorokin. This will turn out to be a much easier task, since it is not many years ago that I had occasion to demonstrate my appreciation for his important publications.[2] Indeed, it will be an even more welcome undertaking, especially since that recent appreciation will remove any doubt that my judgment today might have the character of an apologia arising from the circumstances of this present volume. Without having read all the prodigious works of Sorokin, the first of which were published in Russian, I think I have read enough; and what I have read, together with my personal acquaintance with Sorokin, enables me to form an adequate idea concerning the position he occupies in contemporary science.

[1] Translated from the Italian by Philip J. Allen and Lia Beretta, with subsequent corrections made by Professor Gini.

[2] See "Recenti trattati generali e speciali de Sociologia," *Genus*, IX, Nos. 1-4 (1950-52) *passim*.

Professor P. A. Sorokin is a unique personality as a scientist and, without doubt, an eminent one. It is not possible for one to understand his scientific characteristics without taking into account his life history. Born in 1889, in humble conditions in a Russian village, he has been able to lift himself through sheer force of character and power of mind. Experiencing a highly mobile life, or rather a turbulent one, as he himself has indicated, often involved in political events of his native country, he rose to a first-rank scientific position. Such personal experiences, by his own admission, have contributed more to his scientific achievement than the lectures he attended, or even his prodigious readings.[3]

In short, he is self-taught; and if not a revolutionary, he is certainly a non-conformist, with all the virtues and faults that inevitably accompany such a role. These faults, if not completely corrected, have been tempered by his varied experiences in different environments and by his wide and varied education in the social sciences, to which his knowledge of many foreign languages has greatly contributed.

He may be characterized by independence of thought and a tendency to assume a clear position in every problem, which can give timid souls—who are in the majority—an impression of intransigence; a conspicuously constructive imagination with a tendency to build systems of a wide-ranging character, accompanied by an actualizing attitude, thanks to his knowledge of ancient and modern sociological literature that ranges over many countries, as well as to the collaboration which he has secured from many of his followers attracted by his outstanding personality; a sensitivity—peculiar to political temperaments—to current social problems, and in dealing with them, an objectivity which, if not perfect, is certainly superior to that found among politicians. These are his principal qualities, and they are not often found in one and the same person.

His education in the physical and biological sciences does not always seem to be up to the level of his education in the social sciences. This may be due to the short-cut taken in his secondary studies. He started school at fourteen and, after attending a provincial boarding school for three years, we find him taking psy-

[3] See the passage of a letter of Sorokin's, of Aug. 1959, to the publisher of *Campus World*, Inc., of Los Angeles, reproduced in the biography of Sorokin written by Carlos A. Echanove, *Sociologues d'aujorud'hui* (Comite' organisateur du XIX Congrès International de Sociologie, Mexico, 1960), pp. 111-12.

chology for two years in night school, after which he went to the Psycho-neurological Institute and then to the University of St. Petersburg. Here, after a normal academic sequence of five years, he graduated in criminology, after he had already been teaching it for one year as a *privat dozent*.

His publications started early. The earliest I know is his *Crime and Punishment*, published in 1914, which was very likely an outgrowth of the criminology course he taught, a work which confines itself to a specialized area of sociology. Although Sorokin started producing general treatises very early, in 1919, he never lost sight of arguments concerning the specialized fields of sociology (such as revolution, social mobility, rural-urban sociology, contemporary crises, and sexual revolutions). Better known as a writer in sociological theory, he never has, however, neglected special areas for empirical research; and some of his works following such lines of study as *Social Mobility* and *The Crisis of Our Age* have had international success. As far as I know, he has never been a field worker, nor has he ever extended his research to preliterate societies. His activity has covered so many fields that one cannot blame him for not having covered these too. But as we shall see, this fact has not been without influence upon his concept of sociology.

The work on social theory which gave him international fame was his *Contemporary Sociological Theories*. There were other comparable works, of course, that had appeared earlier—among other praiseworthy ones, in Italy, that by Squillace—and he naturally availed himself of these. But his treatment by far surpasses the others, in orderly arrangement and comprehensiveness, as well as by virtue of number of authors considered. Useful to sociologists of all nations as a valuable source of information, and for its contribution in systematizing the field of sociology, it represented a milestone in the progress of the science in the United States of America, placing scholars of that country, who up to that time had had access chiefly to Anglo-Saxon writers, abreast of contributions made by sociologists elsewhere. It is clear that after more than three decades the work needs to be better integrated and brought up-to-date. But the author can hardly be expected to do this; and if he did, it is doubtful that he could improve its essential quality. The achievement of works such as this represents a synthesis of one who has reached the fulness of personal preparation and it carries the imprint of the entire personality of the author, which cannot be recast. Such works are a significant milestone for their time. Others may come along in the future. But such an achievement requires exceptional education and labor. It is not easy today to foresee who has equally adequate abilities.

However, the work of Sorokin which is most impressive for its vastness of conception and for the amount of labor its execution required, it seems to me, is the four-volume work on *Social and Cultural Dynamics*, the fourth volume of which is a recapitulation and synthesis of the others.

All of Sorokin's theories, not only from the dynamic point of view, but also from the structural point of view, are synthesized in his volume *Society, Culture and Personality*, which aims to give a definitive picture of his thought. The synthesis seems to be complete. When closely examined, however, lacunae and inconsistencies may be discovered among the various parts of this work. But these seem to be inevitable in a work so massive, the gathering of whose materials very probably had to be intrusted to various collaborators. I have pointed out some of these, particularly those that concerned Italian sociologists.[4]

He who knows the difficulty of obtaining reliable and complete information, which is greater for the past than for the present, is doubtful of the reliability of the results of such historical research which aims to present for all the countries and for twenty-four centuries the development and fluctuations of the fundamental systems (theological, idealistic, and empirical) of human mental activity, not only described in words, but also numerically expressed and graphically presented.

Certainly, one can appeal to the principle of compensation of accidental errors (mutual cancellation of errors of opposite senses) when large masses of cases are considered. But besides accidental errors, one wonders whether personal inclinations, particularly in the selection of the material utilized, could not have affected the collaborators. One certainly must make an allowance for the weight of influence exercised by the director in co-ordinating the work. But in the end one cannot be sure of how much reliance he can place upon such figures. I think they must be viewed not as actual, accurate measures, but as indices not unaffected by coefficients of

[4] Cf. "Recenti trattati," p. 227.

uncertainty and inevitably influenced by criteria of choice and elaboration of material that present a suggestive and authoritative
scheme of the evolution of human philosophical thinking. But even
if one cannot trust it completely and exempt himself from prudent
controls, it must be considered as the synthesis of an enormous undertaking achieved under the direction of a scholar of exceptional
learning. Certainly, it has some value, even if such value may be
viewed by some as not proportionate to the labor expended. If
so, our gratitude to such a man who undertook so enormous a labor
should be even greater, especially since, as far as I know, it is the
only attempt ever made at a quantitative synthesis of such vastness;
and it is not easy to see who today would be equal to repeating this
feat.

From the structural point of view, Sorokin conceives society as
a composite of interdependent individuals who, by means of certain
vehicles, create, use, communicate, and exchange the meanings of
things. Sociology studies the sociocultural phenomena, understood
as direct or indirect products of human mental interaction.

No doubt Sorokin gives us an organic treatment of such an interaction, worthy of greatest consideration. Nevertheless, the question remains whether this conception of society and of sociology
is not too restricted, when compared with current conceptions.
Actually, we give a larger meaning to the words "society" and
"sociology." We speak of society every time there is a group of
individuals permanently interdependent that presents mechanisms
of self-preservation and self-equilibration. We speak, therefore,
of animal societies, even if the relations among the component parts
are considered—rightly or wrongly—as being determined only by
instinct. We speak of preliterate societies, even if—rightly or
wrongly—we think that rational factors remain secondary to the
influence of instinct, tradition, and habit. What is the advantage of
restricting the meaning of the word "society" to only one part of
those groups which are usually designated by it? If we do this, it
will be necessary to invent another word to designate those groups
which today are designated by the word "society," and which
certainly have some characteristics in common, precisely defined
and well studied, whereas the distinction between rational action
and instinctive or habitual and traditional action is far from free
of uncertainty.

Even in the most advanced human societies, then, the functioning is determined by factors which consist, not only in a relation of psychological or mental nature,[5] but also by physical, physiological, and demographic factors which intervene; and these latter not only intervene as vehicles of communication among individuals, but they exercise a direct influence over them. Who, if not the sociologist, should study the influence on society exerted by climatic and orographic factors, by age composition of populations, and by the physical resistance of its members? The necessity of considering these factors forces itself upon us and, if I am not in error, in spite of his definition, it has forced itself also upon Sorokin.

Actually, after giving the definition indicated, Sorokin speaks of animals that have complex societies; he speaks of a cosmosociology and a biosociology which would not fall under his definition but which, at the same time, he calls sociology. In the face of such expressions, it would seem justifiable for sociology, as he now understands it, to be called *Homosociology,* a term which he seems to have used at one time.[6] But if one excludes instinctive behavior from the field of sociology, one will come to exclude not only animal societies, but primitive societies as well, according to a widely accepted idea which maintains that the latter's behavior is determined by instinct, tradition, and habit, more than it is by reason.

However effective his treatment of sociology in his recent writings, Sorokin refers essentially to problems that concern advanced societies, a theme which, on the other hand—needless to say—touches us more directly and therefore is of very particular interest. In *Contemporary Sociological Theories,* however, when announcing the objective of sociology, next to studies of relations among various classes of social phenomena he placed those of relations between social and non-social (geographic, biological, etc.) phenomena. These latter hardly enter into the actual definition which he gives to sociology. Thus, if from many points of view his later writings represent a progress beyond *Contemporary Sociological Theories,* no progress seems to me to have been attained in the definition of the field of research reserved to sociology.

I know less—and because of this I do not hazard to judge—the constructive activity of Sorokin in his Research Center in Creative

[5] See *Society, Culture and Personality,* p. 4, text and note.
[6] See the above-cited biography of Sorokin, p. 113.

Altruism, founded by him at Harvard University through a donation of the Lilly Foundation and, I suppose, in response to a program suggested by it. Clearly, one cannot help but be gratified over the strengthening of altruism; but as a scientist, I maintain that moral goals are foreign to science, although probably there never has been a scientist, nor is there one now, nor is there any likelihood of there ever being one, who can completely ignore such moral goals.

In his numerous treatises, coming into contact with theories of many sociologists, past and present, Sorokin—in keeping with his decisive character, which is averse to compromises—can be said to have taken a clear position as he has confronted each of them, so that his creative activity has been matched by a nonetheless vivacious, critical activity. In this, two parts may be distinguished: one which concerns single theories and another which concerns comprehensive tendencies and general methods of research. In assessing single theories, Sorokin's contributions, especially in his earlier publications, remain clearly inferior to his creative ones.

Various circumstances very probably converged to account for this. In the first place, there is the immensity of the field cultivated and the consequent necessity of having to resort at times to selections and summaries of material made by students with a culture much inferior to his. Moreover, one cannot overlook the fact that he who reads and writes so much, over so long a period of time, does not always turn out to remember completely all which he has read and written (as I have occasionally discovered with myself), no matter how well endowed he may be with a strong memory.

In commenting with the appreciation it merits upon the volume *Society, Culture and Personality*, I had pointed out certain discrepancies among its various sections, particularly in what concerns certain Italian works, which are mentioned in certain chapters and ignored elsewhere in the same volume. The same bibliographic citations appear differently, here and there, leading one to suspect that the preparation of the material was given over to different persons. I notice also how the contributions of modern Italian sociologists to the study of the causes of war are not remembered; and it is not clear whether or not the theory of neo-organicism[7] was known to the author.

Having had occasion, in the preparation of this essay, again to

[7] See "Recenti trattati," p. 227.

consult *Contemporary Sociological Theories*, I have noted that the theory of neo-organicism which, at the time of its publication, had just been advanced, was duly pointed out,[8] as well as the Italian contribution to the study of the causes of war to which a long discussion was dedicated.[9] After the passage of two decades, this seemed to have been forgotten by Sorokin, just at the moment when the specialists in the subject fully recognized and exploited the material.[10]

Sorokin's own character, alien to compromise, although it may be admirable—as I myself consider it—does not make the understanding of the points of view of others any easier and in this shortcoming, from my point of view, he likewise reflects the defective training in secondary studies which usually inculcate some fundamental notions of science into the minds of students and teach them to define concepts on which scientific constructions are based with precision.

One is surprised at the lack of comprehension of the concept of equilibrium, a fulcrum of physical sciences and of economics, which requires no defense here. In the discussions of organicism, one is struck not only by the disregard of the recent theory of neo-organicism, but also by the absence of a precise concept of organism. Consequently, while Sorokin contests its application to human society, he gives a definition of such society which comes back to it, so that, in recent sociological publications, he has come to be classified among the organicists.[11]

In Sorokin's discussions, concise and precise definitions are generally lacking;[12] and if this be a defect which today is common among the masses of sociologists, it is no less unbecoming to an author like Sorokin who has risen so high above the mass. He partly remedies this by resorting to a double, triple, and even quadruple-hyphenation of adjectives (socio-cultural, anthropo-racial, psycho-

[8] See *Contemporary Sociological Theories*, p. 196 n. 1.
[9] *Ibid.*, pp. 384-88.
[10] See the review of Quincy Wright, *The Study of War*, 3rd ed., 1944 in the above-cited "Recenti trattati," pp. 238-39.
[11] See Don Martindale, *The Nature and Types of Sociological Theory* (Boston: Houghton Mifflin Co., 1960), pp. 115 ff. He is mentioned in the same sense by M. Marotta, in "Organicismo e Neo-organicismo," in *Sociologia*, 1959.
[12] One therefore can never be too sure how to interpret exactly the thinking of Sorokin, who at times presents various *nuances* from one passage to another. This is the case, as we have hinted, with the concepts of society and sociology, for example.

sociologistic, bio-social, cosmo-bio-social, empirico-sensory, meaningful-causal, Upper-Urban-Civilized-Male groups, Ideational-Idealistic-Sensate rhythms), which surround the concept he utilizes like
a grand halo, or holy smoke screen. This constitutes one of the
personal characteristics of his style. But one who is accustomed to
the precise language of the exact sciences remains only half satisfied.

Contemporary Sociological Theories, notwithstanding its importance in developing and systematizing sociology, as I have acknowledged, is weakened by the sometimes detailed discussions of the
theories under consideration on account of an imperfect comprehension of what can be expected of a theory.

His criticism, in general, rests upon the observation that the
theory considered does not explain all of the facts. But a scientific
theory is not able to, nor should it, explain all of the facts. If it
undertook to account for all of the facts, it would no longer be a
theory but a simple description of facts devoid of scientific value.
Theory represents, by definition, a scheme which, in the facts, emphasizes certain constants that are of particular interest, deliberately
disregarding other facts which are deemed secondary with respect
to the scope of research. Because of this, it is possible to construct
equally justifiable multiple theories from the same facts, theories
which are not mutually exclusive but complementary at times and
between which it will be advisable to choose according to the
objectives of the investigation.

Thus, it is proper, for example, for the evolution of human
society to have a geographic theory, an economic theory, a demographic theory, a psychological theory, a cultural one, and so on.
Nor is it to be precluded that others may be of some use, such as
mechanical and biological theories. Indeed, it is not to be disputed
that human society, in addition to physical and biological factors,
results from cultural factors which are different from physical and
biological ones, but precisely because it results from a convergence
of these various groups of factors, it is misleading to consider exclusively, or predominantly, cultural factors. Given the impossibility of constructing a theory which takes into account all of the
facts at one time, a useful contribution may be expected also from
those theories which express physical and biological constants
inherent in human societies. It is like the geologist who studies
mountains. He must not limit his examination of the mountain to

the part which rises above the surrounding plane, but he must also study the substratum of the mountain below the level of the plane, which can enlighten him on its origin, as well as on the characteristics of the elevated parts.

We are dealing here with a fundamental concept that, ordinarily, is not sufficiently emphasized. The majority of criticisms of sociological schools that are in conflict with each other, and whose conflict occupies so large a part of their discussions, are derived, to a great extent, from the lack of understanding of what can be expected of a theory.

It is well to recognize, then, that Sorokin's thinking on this point has undergone considerable evolution. Thus, in *Society, Culture and Personality* we are told that the logical procedure of the various schools (economic, technological, biological, etc.) consists in assuming a factor as the independent variable, studying its relations (and even interrelations, says Sorokin, but then the factor can no longer be considered an independent variable)[13] to other classes of factors. Rather than a shortcoming, this procedure comprises, however, a necessity in scientific research. As a matter of fact, the configuration of a system which intends to take all of the facts into account, as well as their interdependence, is destined to remain only on paper; at most it may be useful in providing an adequate idea of the complexity of social phenomenology (as has been the case in economics with respect to the configuration of systems of general equilibrium). But when one passes to more basic research into fundamental phenomena, one is compelled to limit himself to a consideration of one or a few factors at a time, considering the others as secondary, if not accidental as far as the aim of the research being conducted is concerned.

The statistician understands perfectly well how social phenomena may be studied usefully, from one or several points of view, since in the impossibility of considering the quantitative manifestations as a function of all the multiple variables, it is customary to consider them as a function of one or of a few variables, without intending, by this, to deny the importance of the others.[14] Thus, in studying the phenomenon of prolificity, the number of offspring

[13] See *Society, Culture and Personality*, pp. 28-29. The thinking of Sorokin can be even closer to mine, in what is said on p. 24.

[14] Cf. "Recenti trattati," p. 229.

are related successively to the age of the mother, the age of the father, the duration of the marriage, the economic conditions of the family, the occupation of the family head, race, climate and, if possible, simultaneously, to two or three or even four of these factors, without ever claiming, in so doing, to explain all the differences which are encountered in the prolificity of various ethnic groups and even less of single families, and without any thought of finding the results unsatisfactory because they do not furnish us such explanations.

I do not mean, in all this, that all the critical activity of Sorokin that has been devoted to a demolition or downgrading of the theories of others has been without foundation or value. But certainly of much higher caliber and greater value is that devoted to a more comprehensive assessment of the general trends of modern sociologists. A recent volume in particular, *Fads and Foibles in Modern Sociology and Related Sciences,* effectively denounces some of the crazes and weak points of recent sociology, particularly in America, sometimes exaggerating, but often with substantial foundation. I have particularly called the attention of the statisticians[15] to the two chapters entitled "Quantophrenia," where Sorokin criticizes the cult of numerosity, the cult of mathematical formulae without a substantial content, mathematical models, and certain statistical methods.[16] Although reservations are necessary at certain points, these do not nullify the great merit of this book. And this can be repeated for all the scientific production of Sorokin.

The criticisms I have already written[17] could be multiplied; but these do not take away the value of Sorokin's monumental work. One finds himself precisely in the presence of a monument which in its details presents a thousand defects, but which in its entirety is undeniably magnificent. The value of a scientific piece of work, like that of a work of art, must be judged essentially in terms of its contribution and worth, and not in terms of its defects. In the perspective of time the defects will vanish while the positive

[15] Editor's note: One of Dr. Gini's professional specialties is statistics. He has served as Professor of Statistics at a number of universities, as Dean of the School (then Faculty) of Statistics at the University of Rome, as president of a number of scientific societies of Italy, including the Italian Society of Statistics, and in other important capacities; and his publications, in number and variety, can truly be called prodigious.

[16] See the review published in *Genus,* XII (1956), pp. 273-74.

[17] See the review previously cited above, "Recenti trattati," p. 232.

values will remain; and that of Sorokin will remain as an achievement that will bring honor upon modern sociology. One is reminded of the Temple of Angkor Wat which, for the person with an eye accustomed to the rigorous canons of Greek statuary and to the architectonic masterpieces offered by Indian mausoleums, by Gothic cathedrals, by the Cathedrals of Florence and Siena, by mosques of Selim and of Soliman, presents ample reason for dissatisfaction, but which leaves one, in the end, with an impression of imposing grandeur.

I should like to include another consideration here. I have sometimes heard Sorokin spoken of by his American colleagues as a "lone wolf," in the sense—I believe—of a scholar who works alone and outside the prevailing currents. It is possible that this corresponds to their wish that he be left to work alone, not so much because of the nature of his theories, as because of his authoritarian intransigence in sustaining them, and possibly, too, because of his major stature which makes his colleagues feel uncomfortable in his presence. But I believe, in any case, that it would be most fortunate if, in modern sociology, there were many more similar "lone wolves," particularly in America, where a slavish conformity which extinguishes scientific initiative now seems to dominate.

For progress in vegetable and animal species, selective breeders have adopted the procedure of isolating subjects which are distinguished by particular characteristics and breeding "pure lines" with these. From the crossing of diverse pure lines, they then obtain the formation of new varieties. Among these, then, the selection fixes the best respondents. Thus it is well, I believe, that scholars of worth work in isolation, each moving in his own personal direction. Their contributions, then, even though unilateral, may be selected, integrated, and fused, and it is out of such results that tremendous progress in science is often made.

A Latin-American Assessment[1]

Lucio Mendieta y Núñez

Latin Americans' knowledge of North American sociology is very deficient. This may be credited to the language barrier, which comprises only a minor obstacle in conducting trade relations, but which is a very serious one indeed in matters concerning science and culture in general; for although there is no commercial establishment or hotel of average importance where English is not spoken, the cultured people here who master English are relatively few.

The teaching of foreign languages in the great majority of schools and universities of Latin America is very deficient, and students' interest in such languages seems to be declining. This phenomenon may be easily explained. As late as the beginning of the twentieth century, the learning of medicine, law, architecture, engineering, etc., occurred by way of texts written in French, and the student knew he was required to understand the French language with sufficient precision to understand the texts.

Not long thereafter, however, professors in the majority of Latin American countries began to write their own texts for use by their students. Sometimes such texts have been issued in mimeographed editions; at others they have been printed by publishing houses. Students prefer them to foreign texts, first, because they are the authorized versions approved by professors for their classes, and second, because they are written in Spanish.

But even when a student studies the English and French languages in universities or secondary schools for at least two years, he has neither persons with whom to practice such languages in his

[1] Translated from the Spanish by Clifton B. McIntosh, T. Lynn Smith, W. Kennedy Upham, and Fabio Barbosa da Silva.

daily life, nor adequate books to read in these languages. Under such conditions he soon forgets nearly all of what he learned about these languages and he loses all interest in foreign scientific literature which is not translated into Spanish.

The only foreign authors saved from this fate in Latin America are those whose prestige and reputation have succeeded in passing over and beyond the frontiers of their respective countries, and whose books have been translated and published in other languages. This is the case with the renowned Russo-American sociologist, P. A. Sorokin, whose works have been translated into French, German, Italian, Portuguese, Russian, Czech, Rumanian, Norwegian, Yugoslavian, Swedish, Hindi, Urdu, Turkish, Chinese, Japanese, and Spanish.

A number of Sorokin's sociological studies have been translated into Spanish and published in Latin America. Among these are his classic volume, *Social Mobility*, as well as *The American Sex Revolution, Society, Culture and Personality*, and *The Crisis of Our Age*. In addition, his *Estructura Mental y Energias del Hombre* has been published by the Institute of Social Research of the National University of Mexico. Thanks to these and other of the extensive works of Sorokin which have been translated into Spanish, young Latin American students of the social sciences are beginning to know Sorokin first-hand, supplementing thereby their earlier knowledge of him indirectly transmitted to them through texts and teachings of eminent Latin American sociologists. Indeed, there is no author of books on sociology or qualified professor of the subject in any of the universities of Latin America who is not familiar with the work of Sorokin and who has not been decisively influenced by it.

The object of this brief essay is to point out Sorokin's influence upon Latin American sociological thinking. To achieve this purpose, it seemed best to me to inquire directly among outstanding sociologists throughout Latin America and get their personal critical assessments of Sorokin. Accordingly, I have written each of them for an appraisal, and it is their replies which I am going to present at this time, following an order in their presentation which has nothing whatever to do with their merit. I admire them all.

Oscar Alvarez Andrews, the distinguished Chilean sociologist, expresses with sincerity the impact that Sorokin's writings had on his thinking, after he himself had tried to grasp the essentials of sociology through numerous other authors.

"It is easy," he says, "to understand that, coming from so many diverse and even conflicting sources, my sociological ideas lacked unity and precision. There were two criticisms I heard made of sociology that were especially bothersome to me: (1) that it was a theoretical science, vague and useless, the brain child of positivism and, therefore, paradoxical as it may seem, as abstract as positivism itself; and (2) that each ideological tendency had 'its own' sociology (Marxist sociology, Christian sociology, etc.)—or, in brief, that sociology was an appendix, a kind of combat weapon, for each ideological current.

"In 1927 one of Sorokin's early works, *System of Sociology*, was the first to reach my hands. It was like a revelation to me. For the first time, I gained a real insight into the nature of sociology. The reading of Sorokin convinced me that: (1) sociology is a definite, autonomous science, and, although related to other sciences, it is not dependent upon any particular one of them exclusively; (2) sociology is above and beyond all ideological tendencies; and (3) it has a strictly objective basis while, at the same time, it has common roots with all manifestations of art, of science, of industry, and of the spirit."

Doctor Alvarez Andrews has read and studied all the available sociological productions by Sorokin. "Thanks to the *Revista Mexicana de Sociologia*, which I have received and read since 1942," he adds, "I have become acquainted with various works of the sociologist from Harvard—works of extraordinary interest—which have only confirmed the esteem which I have formed for his personality."

"The achievement of Sorokin," he continues, "has been gigantic. In the short courses at the University of Chile and in the sociological congresses where, year after year, we professors of sociology in Chile and other American countries meet with those from other continents, it has been my opportunity to discuss Sorokin at times. On such occasions, there has been general agreement among those present in singling out Sorokin as one of the great teachers and leaders of contemporary sociology in both North and South America."

Alvarez Andrews notes several fundamental characteristics of Sorokin's sociological works: (1) a didactic method—his expositions are always objective, and the clarity and precision with which he focuses upon each problem are notable; (2) his impartiality—Sorokin is perfectly neutral in the exposition of all his ideas; (3) the inexhaustible wealth and variety of proofs; and (4) the exactness of his sociological position.

"For Sorokin, sociology is not a moral or normative science in the sense that it prescribes what ought to be or ought not to be. Rather, it merely studies the phenomena which 'are,' foregoing any ethical evaluation of them." Sorokin, Alvarez Andrews justly concludes, "has contributed to the placement of sociology in a position of universal prestige. He has broadened the horizons of hundreds of sociologists, and he has contributed more than anyone else to the extension of both sociology and culture—a high social culture which, through his readers and followers, has greatly influenced professors and students alike."

Alfredo Poviña, the brilliant Argentine sociologist, has produced a noteworthy article on "Sorokin's Sociological System," in which he gives evidence of having examined exhaustively some of Sorokin's theories and has provided us with a compact summary.

"Sociological theory," he says, "is based upon an analysis of the concepts and principles of the discipline. Sorokin begins by placing sociology in its proper place in the classification of the sciences. Within the scheme of Cournot, Windelband, and Rickert, it belongs to the group of generalizing sciences, because it studies what is constant and, therefore, repeated in space and time.

"The subject matter of sociology differs from other social sciences which study only a particular kind of social phenomena. Economics, for example, studies economic behavior and institutions; political science studies political behavior and institutions, etc. Sociology, however, studies the elements that all kinds of social phenomena have in common. Such common elements comprise the field of general sociology.

"Alongside general sociology, there are specialized sociologies which confine their study to traits and relations common, not to all social phenomena, but only to a particular class of phenomena.

"An example of specialized sociology is the one to which Sorokin contributed with his studies on the sociology of revolution, where he used a vast amount of material and took as his point of departure the Russian Revolution and included in his analysis a substantial amount of other material.

"For Sorokin," says Poviña, "all revolution is a change in the behavior of the population, on the one hand, and in its psychology, ideology, aspirations, and evaluations, on the other. It means a change in the biological composition of the population and in its reproductive and selective processes. It brings about a deformation in the structure of a society and a change in the fundamental social processes."

Perhaps, Sorokin's greatest masterpiece is his *Social Mobility*, in which, according to Poviña, Sorokin presents a complete theory, beginning with a study of social stratification, which is the differentiation of a population into social classes hierarchically superimposed. But even in a stratified society there is change in position: there is horizontal mobility, or change in location on the same level, and vertical mobility (ascent or descent), or passage of the individual from one social class to another. The effects of social mobility are to be seen in the racial composition of a population, in human psychology and behavior, and in the processes of social organization.

Poviña admires the works of Sorokin—those in rural sociology of which he was co-author, as well as those he wrote alone. Poviña appreciates Sorokin's speculations concerning the philosophy of culture and of contemporary history, and he goes on to comment upon Sorokin's numerous other works. "In a critical review of his sociological ideas," says Poviña, "one must say, in the first place, that Sorokin is a fertile and genuinely original thinker. I view him as the most hard-working and systematic sociologist in the contemporary scientific world." Sorokin, he says, is not only a sociologist, but a philosopher of history as well.

"As for the sociological system of Sorokin," he adds, after giving a schematic judgment of his philosophy, "it presents all the details befitting an orderly, coherent, scientific system, based upon precise criteria of objectivity, impartiality, and non-evaluation. It is a totality of generalizing studies, realistic and empirical, which fits well into the larger domain of sociological science.

"Finally," he writes, "Sorokin's system is a sociological relational structure, empirical in type and content, with a culturalist tendency which comprises a decided forward movement in contemporary, systematic sociology."

The eminent Brazilian sociologist, Pinto Ferreira, provides us with a clear, critical assessment of Sorokin and his works. "There is no denying," he affirms, "the profound contribution of Professor P. A. Sorokin to sociology. A social thinker of tremendous stature, endowed with a rich and extensive culture, as well as with a lively sense of social reality, Sorokin presents his concepts of sociology in fascinating ways that have far-reaching consequences. The person revealed in such writings is not only a social scientist; he is also a stylist who writes with clarity and simplicity even upon themes that are essentially complex."

Ferreira believes that a number of Sorokin's books "will turn out to be classics. Assessing Sorokin's work as a whole, one can hardly fail to recognize his contributions to sociology. He broadened and pushed back its horizons; he discovered new perspectives and discussed fresh problems, suggestive and original in character. His contemporaries cannot fail to recognize his genius. Like all human works, Sorokin's has its lights and its shadows. His studies on mobility and social stratification are classics. With his talent and creative imagination, he created a new nomenclature. Professor Sorokin, in brief, richly merits the well-earned respect of his contemporaries."

Eduardo Santa, one of the talented and dedicated young sociologists from Colombia, considers it difficult "from any point of view to give in a few words a critical assessment of the scientific works of one like P. A. Sorokin, who is justly and deservedly recognized as one of the outstanding leaders in contemporary sociology."

Says Santa, "Sorokin is, above all, an honest and independent thinker, whose research activities are characterized by tenacity and vigor, and who is clearly motivated by a great desire to discover the truth. He is a social theorist who candidly announces his discoveries and fearlessly affirms his insights, without regard to carping criticism of those ready to excommunicate him, when the truth he reveals turns out to be a clear X-ray of our time, as it often is.

"It seems that crisis has, in a way, been guiding his thinking and that he has reflected upon its nature, observing it from many points of view, in order to see clearly its magnitude and the multiplicity of forms it assumes.

"All of Sorokin's theories," Santa says, "are deeply rooted in reality; hence, his eagerness to demonstrate statistically many of his theses." In a brief biographical sketch of Sorokin, Santa points out that, after numerous trips over the world, Sorokin has ever returned to his professorial parapet, from which he has resumed his barrage of criticisms, aimed at shabby aspects of contemporary civilization.

"Sorokin's observations and theories," he concludes, "grow in timeliness, day by day, for contemporary thinkers the world over, and his observations concerning rural sociology are opportune and immensely profitable, to Latin Americans in particular."

Mario Lins, a young Brazilian sociologist of great stature, who has cultivated new sociological regions with unusual brilliance, joins the grand chorus of those who admire Sorokin by saying: "The work of Sorokin marks him as one of those truly great in present-day sociological thinking. Sorokin has based his system upon an exceedingly vast erudition linked with an extraordinary capacity to master the complex themes he approaches. He is one of the few sociologists who, knowing various languages, is capable of assimilating sociological ideas at their primary sources."

In his brief study on Sorokin, Mario Lins singles out one of Sorokin's masterly contributions to sociology—the concept of social space. "Social phenomena," he says, commenting upon Sorokin's works, "do not appear in a vacuum, but they depend upon certain conditions which are relatively constant in space and time. Such phenomena develop within a social space which is not to be confused with geometric, physical, or biological space.

"Sorokin attempts to show with considerable effort that an identification of social space with other types of space will not provide us with a real understanding of sociocultural phenomena.

"For Sorokin, social space possesses three planes or fundamental aspects: (1) the level of meanings, which is non-material, without space or time; (2) the level of vehicles, which is material (physical-chemical and biological), through which the meaning appears and materializes; and (3) the level of human agents, by means of which operations of the meanings are carried out.

"In spite of any limitations that one might place upon it, the work of Sorokin," says Mario Lins, "constitutes, without doubt, a vigorous attempt to integrate various aspects of sociological theory, through a rigorously logical conceptual framework, which yields promising perspectives for a better understanding of sociocultural phenomena."

One of the most serious and highly esteemed sociologists of Latin America, Dr. Roberto MacLeán y Estenós, present Peruvian Ambassador at UNESCO, provides us with a few biographical notes on Sorokin, and with a penetrating analysis of some of his work.

"I knew him and had close relations with him," he says, "on the occasion of the celebration of the XVIII Congress of the International Institute of Sociology, in September of 1958, in the German city of Nuremberg (so full of history and so laden with tragic memories, the very pinnacle and tomb of Nazism). Sorokin was then sixty-nine years of age, although he looked younger. He was one of the attractions of that international convocation, which included other illustrious sociologists."

MacLeán y Estenós analyzes the work of Sorokin, pointing out how incontestably correct Sorokin is on many points. But when referring to *Contemporary Sociological Theories,* published in 1928, he maintains that although Sorokin certainly "sketched the panorama of the contemporary sociological movement during the last half century with master strokes, he sinned by omission. He ignored the whole Latin-American sociological movement, as if Latin America did not exist in the contemporary world and as if the New Continent began in Canada and ended at the Rio Grande. His was, therefore, an intellectual symphony, masterly in its tones, but unfinished.

"Since no man is a prophet in his own country," concludes the illustrious Peruvian sociologist, "and the United States is the second fatherland of Sorokin, those there who consider him a sociologist of 'stratosphere mentality' are not few; he is a scholar who, they say, because he always has his head in the clouds, doesn't look or worry about where he puts his feet. This confession," he says, "Sorokin himself made to me personally in Nuremberg, Germany, in 1958. And he added:

" 'Those good people fall just a little short of saying that I am crazy and, in all probability, without my having learned of it, they have already said it. The fact is that they don't always like the truths I tell them—truths that I have a duty to tell them because this is the reason for my being a teacher.' And so it is. And that is a truth, indeed: that Sorokin is a teacher—an authentic teacher —whose work will endure in the changing perspectives of time."

I had already listened to criticisms that some North American sociologists had made to me verbally when, before knowing Sorokin, I asked their opinion of his personality. They were generous in their praises, but noted that "recently" he has abandoned the purely scientific field of sociology to plunge into the misleading roads of the reformer and idealist.

This is not the first case of a sociologist who, at the end of this glorious road, feels the desire to open new paths of redemption for humanity. The same was true of the brilliant Auguste Comte, who, after his *Course of Positive Philosophy* and after his sociology (which he at first called "social physics," to underline its strictly scientific character), rose to the greatest heights of idealism in his *System of Positive Polity*.

But while the work of Auguste Comte, in this respect, is purely speculative, and while his "Religion of Humanity" remains no more than a passing image in the history of social thought, it is different in Sorokin's case. For in the philosophical creation of Sorokin, as the Brazilian writer, J. Guilherme de Aragao says, "the structural aspect of his concept—in other words, the theory of the cyclical succession of cultures that characterizes the historic process—promises to remain incorporated as a basic concept in the philosophy of history."

This is how Aragao summarizes the central thought of Sorokin's much discussed volume, *The Crisis of Our Age*: "In order to justify the thesis of the generalized crisis of our time, Sorokin points out three types of culture: ideational, idealistic, and sensate, which succeed each other in the historic process. The most recent recurrence of these three types of culture has its beginning in the Middle Ages, when the ideational type of culture prevailed; then there was a movement from the twelfth to the fifteenth centuries toward the idealistic and, finally, with the Renaissance, into the sensate, which has continued with growing intensity to the present time. The crisis of our time is linked to the extreme sensate phase of culture through which we are passing. It is a crisis in the fine arts; in systems of truth, of morality, of law, of the family; in systems of government, of economic organization, of liberty, and of international relations.

"In its movement from the absolute to the relative, humanity reached the climax in the eighteenth and nineteenth centuries, and then it entered into crisis. Its path, in the realm of spirit, has been like a lofty current flowing downward toward its lowest point. In this respect," according to Aragao, "Sorokin reaches a level homologous to that of Berdyaev when the latter affirms that the 'new man,' the modern man, wishes to be author and regulator of life without help from on high, indifferent to divine sanctions, uprooting himself from the religious center to which he had been fastened during the Middle Ages; homologous to that of Maritain, in his *Religion and Culture,* and finally, to that of P. Leonel Foranca, in *A Crise do Mundo Moderno* (*The Crisis of the Modern World*).

"But even so, Sorokin provides us with a most up-to-date view which tends to depict the present moment of history as a special phase of historical transition, affirming that a fundamental aspect of sensate culture is, itself, declining and giving way to another emerging form."

To me, Sorokin's theory seems similar to other cyclical theories of the development of humanity expounded by various thinkers, from Plato to Auguste Comte and other modern ones cited by Aragao. However, in the case of the author of *The Crisis of Our Age,* we do not have a mere, imaginative speculation, but a logical concept based on abundant historical material.

But it is in his work *Reconstruction of Humanity* that Sorokin seems to go beyond the frontiers of science and to plunge into paths that are purely romantic. Nevertheless, on no occasion does he depart from the methodology of science: a realistic research and a rigorous system of investigation and reasoning.

Dr. Roberto Agramonte, the celebrated Cuban sociologist, has admirably summarized the essence of the above-mentioned work as follows:

"Sorokin's fundamental thesis set forth in his *Reconstruction of Humanity* maintains that human salvation lies only in increasing altruism in both individuals and social groups. That is the only motive force for interpersonal harmony. He extols creative love, the paradigm of which is found in the Sermon on the Mount. About this creative love we know very little, but it represents, nonetheless, a tremendous power, if only we knew how to disseminate it widely. It is the highest form of energy and one with the greatest therapeutic possibility. Our own capacity to produce it is but a drop in the sea. But governments, great organizations, and even powerful intellectuals seem to have in mind only the promotion of wars and the invention of means for the destruction of mankind by man.

"Sorokin, in the Research Center in Creative Altruism which he founded at Harvard, made investigations of that unknown and vital theme, studying in his 1950 *Symposium* the multidimensional universe of love as forms of eros and agape.

"Consequently, he does not treat it as a mere philosophical speculation, a dream or a utopia, as some of Sorokin's critics think, but as a genuine scientific investigation which begins as a hypothesis to be verified.

"With his collaborators," says Agramonte, "the brilliant sociologist studied the whole range from the mathematical theory of egoism and altruism to the psychology of love and hate, including the psychotherapeutic aspects of altruism, encephalographic aspects of abnormal, homicidal, and amicable personalities, problems of labor harmony, and other areas. He comes to the conclusion that this vast problem—one of the most important to humanity—has not been thoroughly studied by modern science and therefore the word 'love' does not appear in the majority of textbooks about psychology, anthropology, or sociology."

These fragmentary judgments are an eloquent sample of the influence which Sorokin has had upon Latin-American sociologists. Nevertheless, as I said at the beginning, it is only a sample, because I have limited myself to soliciting opinions from only a few of the most noted sociologists in Latin America, not from all sociologists, nor even from others as eminent as those included because the compilation of a greater number of statements would have surpassed by far the prudent limits of a single essay.

Now it behooves me also to say a few words regarding the famous teacher Sorokin, not because I pretend to belong in the same category with the other authors I have mentioned, but because I assumed the task of promoting the inquiry among them, because of my admiration for Sorokin, and because I consider him worthy of my homage.

My admiration was born of the knowledge of his work, which I consider that of a genius. In it I have learned what sociology really is, and how sociological questions ought to be investigated and studied; also I have seen the clarity and simplicity of his exposition, his analytical method, his logical rigor, and his decision not to evade problems, all of which lead to complete understanding of social reality.

It is clear that having learned all this from the books of Sorokin does not mean that I consider myself clothed with his creative qualities, for these are not acquired by reading; they are an innate gift, coming from on high. But having admired them in Sorokin gives me the deep satisfaction, the priceless benefit of understanding and loving sociology.

I had my first contact with the thought of Sorokin in his book *Contemporary Sociological Theories,* in the French translation published by Payot, and I was, of course, captivated by the systematic clarity of his exposition. There I caught a grand vision of sociology and I received the universal spirit which has shaped it from remote times until it has been brought by brilliant minds to its present efflorescence.

More recently I have been able to know other of his works which I regularly have come to use as inestimable guides and supports in my modest works, especially his *Social and Cultural Dynamics* and the monumental *Society, Culture and Personality,* through which I can now understand completely and share in the accurate judgments made concerning the work and personality of Sorokin by many true luminaries of world thought.

It is to this that Agramonte referred when he said: "Right after the publication of *Social and Cultural Dynamics,* Frank Wright classified him in the highest rank of sociologists; F. R. Cowell saw in his structure a new basis for the study of society; Hans Kohn thought that even those who were in disagreement with his judgments and predictions would nevertheless find themselves impressed by the profundity and clarity of his investigations. The great Polish sociologist F. Znaniecki considered Sorokin's system to be the only complete and consistent effort directed toward integrating all the special sciences in a general theory of culture; even more, he considered it superior to all the philosophies of culture developed by his predecessors, including Hegel, Comte, Spencer, Pareto, Toynbee, and others. F. Dyhman states that the publication of his monumental *Dynamics* indicates a climax in the history of social thought. Karl T. Compton asserts that, unlike many philosophies of history which have taken conscience as a central point in their theoretical development, Sorokin's system has been constructed on a base of inductions from facts; therefore it is free from the influence of prejudices and preferences; moreover, this great work helps us to understand clearly the situation of man and his circumstance in our time.   L. Duchesne welcomes his enormous erudition and the preparatory investigation which he undertook in order to perform his work: the brilliant logic of his deduction, the originality of his mind, and the ardor and willingness of his enthusiastic spirit.   In fact, with Sorokin we understand just what our civilization is, and how it came to be as it is through its beliefs, its directions, and its personalities.   Leopold von Wiese, finally, asserts that if we compare the great work of Sorokin with the constructions of Comte, Spencer, Pareto, and Spengler, the latter give the impression of being arbitrary and imaginative."

After such remarkable appraisals and the brilliant opinions from Latin American sociologists who answered my inquiry, it is impossible to add more without repeating judgments already made by others, which point out that Sorokin, without doubt, is clearly distinguished as one of the greatest sociologists of our time.

Lately my admiration for Dr. Sorokin has increased to personal affection; because from him I have received stimulating appreciations of my initial sociological essays, and to him I owe the possibility of having seen an early version of one of them about "The Social Classes," published in the *American Sociological Review*. This fact changed my mind from an early idea that North American sociologists lacked esteem for their Latin-American colleagues; for soon after the essay had been published, I was surprised to see my small work quoted in later articles in that and other journals and in textbooks of sociology.   Thus, I came to the conclusion that the only reason Latin-American sociologists seem to have been ignored by North American scholars is the language barrier referred to at the beginning of this essay, and not a lack of respect.   Hence, I have made efforts, so far in vain, to have UNESCO publish a journal, or at least an annual, with articles by Latin-American sociologists translated into other languages, and those by European and North American scholars rendered into Spanish.   In that way we could have a solid bond of spiritual union between and among world people which would be fruitful and profitable to us all.

My affectionate esteem for Sorokin grew through our correspondence, and it became greater when, on the occasion of the 19th Congress of the International Institute of Sociology in Mexico at the end of August and the beginning of September, 1960, I had the opportunity and honor to associate with him. I expected a man conscious of his importance, as would seem fitting for so prolific an author—one who was preceded by international fame and one who had received honors and praises given only to few persons in the world; but instead of that I met a man unaffected even to the point of showing humility in his manner. He and his wife, a distinguished biologist, are a North American middle-class couple, entirely without pretense. He is affable and most cordial in his bearing, without any affectation. I heard his lecture in the National School of Political and Social Sciences, and found that on the speaker's platform he is a charming lecturer, a teacher—simply a teacher—not even a professor with grandiloquent voice and theatrical gestures—who communicates to his students not only his knowledge but his own sociological, philosophical, and humanistic truth, full of optimism and hope.

Sorokin, an undeniable scholar, has lately oriented his efforts in an idealistic direction, based on his prior admirable works in research, analysis, and study of social reality. This direction, however debatable it may be, ennobles Sorokin and presents him as a great heart and an inspired mind at the service of humanity.

Sorokin's Formulations in the Sociology of Science

Robert K. Merton and Bernard Barber

From the beginning we must abandon the attempt to put into short compass all the wide-ranging, diversified, and developing observations in the sociology of science set forth by Pitirim Sorokin. Any such effort would be the work of a sizable book, not of a short essay. For his contributions to the sociology of science engage almost every other major part of his empirically connected sociological theory. To try to trace out each component in his sociology of science—or, more generally, in his sociology of knowledge—would mean to touch upon every other aspect of his voluminous works and this, even were it within our powers, would lead to an intolerable and presumptuous duplication of much found elsewhere in this volume. In place of a systematic treatment of Sorokin's contributions to the sociology of science, therefore, we shall substitute some observations that bear upon their most significant and sometimes thorny aspects. In place of the many details that enter into his sociology of science, we shall put the more general formulations that encompass these details, knowing that this means the exclusion of issues that in a more thorough examination would have to be taken up substantially. And finally, in place of tracking down the development of Sorokin's ideas about the sociology of science as these emerged over the course of almost half a century, we shall deal primarily with his later ideas, particularly as these were set forth in his *Social and Cultural Dynamics*. In short, this is only an essay toward a critical understanding of Sorokin's work in the sociology of science; it is not a comprehensive and methical analysis of that work.

As though this were not enough of a limitation, we must confess to another. We find it difficult, not to say impossible, to achieve a sufficient sense of historical distance from a scholar of our time and a scholar, moreover, who has been the teacher of us both. But here Sorokin himself has come to our rescue. And the respect in which he has done so is itself almost an essay in the micro-sociology of science, showing how the social structure of a university affects the relations between a professor and his students and so affects the transmission of knowledge. As every reader of this volume now knows, Sorokin first began to make his imprint upon American sociology shortly after he took up his first post in the United States at the University of Minnesota. But it was especially after he was brought to Harvard to found the department of sociology there that this emphatic, straight-spoken, and *urgent* man began to influence the thinking of substantial numbers of students. In order to understand the character of this influence, we should try the thought-experiment of imagining that Sorokin had gone not to Harvard but to some other important university—in Europe. He would have held "the chair of sociology" in that university. He would have had a number of assistants as well as students who, in accord with the cultural expectations of docility, would have become his disciples, echoing his words and thoughts almost as though they were their own. But in the American scheme of things academic, and particularly in a university such as Harvard, the social structure and the culturally defined patterns of expectations were of course quite otherwise. The authority-structure of the department was pluralistic rather than strongly centralized. There was not only *the* occupant of The Chair but other members of the faculty who had equal access to students. Nor was there an unchallenged norm of obedient agreement with the major professor. This structural situation meant that, at Harvard, many graduate students in sociology were apt to become anything but disciples. Moreover, Sorokin's own personality and role-behavior reinforced this tendency toward independence of mind among his students. They tended to adopt the same critical stance toward aspects of Sorokin's work as he, in the capacity of a role-model, was taking toward the work of others, both contemporary and bygone. All this meant that the structurally defined role of Sorokin was primarily that of alerting students to intellectual alternatives rather than that of imprinting the particulars of his own theory upon them. And all this, we conjecture, helps explain how it is that Sorokin's students have not hesitated to differ with him when, rightly or wrongly, they did not see matters just as he did. In adopting this sometimes timorous but socially supported position of criticism, they were helped in no small measure by the prototype of Sorokin's own behavior, when he was persuaded that other scholars had erred. This, then, is no occasion for exhibiting alumnal piety in public but rather an occasion for applying to Sorokin's work the same critical standards that he has applied to the work of others. It is primarily an essay in criticism rather than an essay in exposition.

I. Sorokin's Sociology of Science: The Central Position

Sorokin has explicitly adopted an idealistic and emanationist theory of the sociology of science. Unlike the theories of a Marx or a Mannheim, which seek primarily to account for the character and limits of knowledge obtaining in a particular society in terms of its social structure, Sorokin's theory tries to derive every aspect of knowledge from underlying "culture mentalities."[1] So prominent is this aspect of Sorokin's theory that it has been variously noted by every commentator upon his work. In somewhat restricted terms, for example, it has been observed by Maquet, a thoroughly sympathetic critic, that in Sorokin's theory the "independent variable is the intellectual position in regard to ultimate reality and ultimate value. . . . The three premises of culture are nothing else but philosophic positions."[2] This statement, as we shall soon see, places far too restrictive an interpretation upon the theory. By Sorokin's own testimony, much more is contained in his concept of types of culture than can be aptly described as the philosophic position basic to it. Nevertheless, Maquet does take hold of the essential fact that each of the types of culture discriminated by Sorokin has its distinctive ontological orientation. This has also been noted, to cite only one other commentator on Sorokin, by Stark, who observes that "It is essential for the understanding of the whole theory to

[1] Robert K. Merton, Social Theory and Social Structure (rev. ed.; Glencoe, Ill.: The Free Press, 1957), p. 466.

[2] Jacques Maquet, The Sociology of Knowledge (Boston: Beacon Press, 1951), pp. 135, 187.

realize that it considers the ontological convictions prevailing at a given time not so much as culture contents but rather as culture-premises, from which the culture proceeds and emanates as a whole."[3]

What, then, is the character of the "culture mentalities" that are variously expressed in distinctive kinds of (claims to) knowledge and how do these mentalities differ? To answer this question in detail would be only to echo several of the papers elsewhere in this volume. But enough must be said here to reidentify the core of Sorokin's conceptions. There are then two "pure types" of culture mentalities, which differ fundamentally in what is taken to be the nature of ultimate reality and value. The first is the ideational, which conceives of reality as "non-material, ever-lasting Being," which defines human needs as primarily spiritual and seeks the satisfaction of these needs through "self-imposed minimization or elimination of most physical needs."[4] The ideational culture adopts the "truth of faith." At the other extreme is the sensate mentality, which limits reality to what can be perceived through the senses. Concerned primarily with physical needs, this culture calls for satisfaction of these needs, not through modification of self, but through modification of the external world. It is oriented to the "truth of senses." Intermediate to these two is a "mixed type" of culture mentality, the idealistic, which represents a kind of balance of the foregoing types. It is oriented toward a "truth of reason." From these three types of mentalities—the major premises of each kind of culture—Sorokin derives their distinctive systems of truth and knowledge.

We shall have something more to say about the meanings, both expressed and implicit, of the idea that these culture premises are basic to distinctive kinds of knowledge developing within each kind of sociocultural system. For the moment, however, we need note only that Sorokin takes a great array of somewhat more specific types of knowledge as *dependent* upon these cultural premises. These include such dependent "variables" as the fundamental categories of causality, time, space, and number; basic philosophical conceptions such as idealism-materialism, eternalism-temporalism,

[3] W. Stark, *The Sociology of Knowledge* (Glencoe, Ill.: The Free Press, 1958), p. 226.
[4] *Dynamics*, I, 72-73.

realism-conceptualism-nominalism; various conceptions of cosmic, biological, and sociocultural processes, as expressed, for example, in notions of mechanism or vitalism in biology; the rate of scientific advance; the prevailing kinds of moral philosophy; and to take just one other, the various kinds of criminal law.

Sorokin himself best summarizes the brooding omnipresence of the three principal types of culture:

Each has its own mentality; its own system of truth and knowledge; its own philosophy and *Weltanschauung;* its own type of religion and standards of "holiness"; its own system of right and wrong; its own forms of art and literature; its own mores, laws, code of conduct; its own predominant forms of *social relationships;* its own economic and political organization; and, finally, its own type of *human personality,* with a peculiar mentality and conduct.[5]

In short, more than the forms of "knowledge" alone are dependent upon the premises underlying each type of sociocultural system. The forms of social structure and the kinds of prevailing personality also share this condition of dependence. Every sphere of culture, social structure, and personality is seen as emanating from the fundamental orientations characteristic of each of the three kinds of sociocultural systems.

As we shall also see in due course, Sorokin considers that particular theories of science as well as the rate of scientific advance are dependent upon these underlying cultural premises. Here we need note only the first of the puzzles presented in Sorokin's conception, which, so far as we can see, he does not solve for us. How can he escape from the self-contained emanationism of the theoretical position he adopts? For it would appear tautological to say, as Sorokin does, that "in a Sensate society and culture the Sensate system of truth based upon the testimony of the organs of senses has to be dominant."[6] For, sensate *mentality*—that abstraction which Sorokin makes ontologically basic to the culture—has already been *defined* as one conceiving of "reality as only that which is presented to the sense organs."[7] In this case, as in other comparable cases, Sorokin seems to vacillate between treating his types of culture-mentality as a defined concept or as an empirically testable hypothesis. This is the first of several questions

  [5] *Ibid.,* I, 67.   [6] *Ibid.,* II, 5.
  [7] *Ibid.,* I, 73.

which it would be useful to have Sorokin examine anew and clarify for future reference.

By way of introduction, then, we see that Sorokin's sociology of science, and by extension, his sociology of knowledge, is idealistic and emanationist. In this respect it differs fundamentally from the materialistic conception of Marx, which focuses on the intellectual perspectives generated by the position of thinkers in the class structure of their time, just as it differs from the quasi-Marxist conceptions of Mannheim, which extend Marx's notion of the structural bases of thought. It is this contrast, presumably, that led Maquet to conclude that "since Sorokin's independent variable is the intellectual position in regard to ultimate reality and ultimate value, his sociology will have a very idealistic character (in the current sense of the word. . . 'ideas rule the world'). . . ."[8]

This can be put somewhat differently without altering the basic point, but directing attention to some of its further implications. In one of his many books published after the *Social and Cultural Dynamics,* Sorokin addressed himself to the tripartite distinction of culture, social structure, and personality as abstracted aspects of all human action. This can be seen from the title of the book: *Society, Culture and Personality.* Although he attends to all three aspects, even in his earlier work, it is plain that in his sociology of science Sorokin asserts the dominance of culture over the other two aspects of social structure and personality. It is being asserted, apparently, that deep-rooted cultural assumptions override any variation in social structure and in diverse types of personality, producing a basic uniformity of outlook that is characteristic of men living in a particular kind of culture. Cultural mentality is regarded as fundamental; social structure and personality as producing, at most, minor variations on culturally embedded themes.

There is much to be said for this position, *providing* that it is not allowed to become a barely disguised tautology. To the extent that men in a particular society do in fact share the same fundamental assumptions about a reality significant to them, to the extent that they share much the same values, they will indeed tend to express this in their behavior and in their works. But the extent to which they do share these orientations and values is of course a question of fact, rather than an assumption of concept. It is a

[8] Maquet, *op. cit.,* p. 135.

matter for inquiry, not a matter of conviction, to find out how far this obtains in different cultures. In short, a major problem of inquiry is to find out how far there obtains a consensus of outlook and to explain the differences that are found to exist among men living in the "same" culture. Sorokin has addressed himself to this question, but only in part. His data, as we shall now see, demonstrate substantial variability *within* each particular type of culture, but Sorokin's theoretical commitments and preferences are such that he does not go on to examine some of the implications of this variability in order to extend and refine his theory of the sociology of science. In a word, it is being said that Sorokin has confined himself to a first approximation—to be sure, a vast and comprehensive one—but one which sets excessive limits to a sociology of science that must attend also to the bases of the considerable variability of scientific outlook within the same culture. The different conceptions set forth within the same culture, it is being suggested, need not be merely minor variations on a major theme; some of these variations are precisely those that lead to basic developments in thought and science. Committed to the first approximation—to the focus on dominant tendencies within a culture—Sorokin largely shuts himself out from *analyzing* those variations which often make for the advancement of cumulative knowledge—that which is recognized as authentic knowledge in cultures that otherwise differ in many respects.

This statement is a large claim. At the least, it must be elaborated if we are to assess the limitations as well as the contributions of Sorokin's sociology of knowledge in general, and of his sociology of science in particular.

II. Macro- and Microsociological Perspectives on Knowledge

Sorokin's theory of sociocultural systems is offered as a partial description and analysis of the whole vast sweep of Greco-Roman and Western societies—with something more than a casual orientation to Eastern societies—during the last three thousand years or so. The theory may fairly be described as a macrosociological perspective.[9] It attends to the gross rather than the microscopic

[9] For a comparison of the macrosociology and microsociology of knowledge, see Stark, *op. cit.*, pp. 19-37; also Maquet, *op. cit.*, *passim*.

features of each society and culture under view. The centuries-long periods of culture described as ideational, idealistic, or sensate, for example, are characterized in terms of their dominant traits. Discriminations within each culture are largely excluded by the very scope of the conception. This exclusion, we must realize, is imposed by the theoretical commitment, not by the external reality. Concretely, it means, for example, that for Sorokin the last four or five hundred years in the West comprise a single sociocultural type dominated by a sensate culture-mentality. All the substantial variations of science and knowledge generally that are to be found in this period are, under Sorokin's comprehensive scheme of analysis, regarded as expressions of one fundamental orientation toward reality.

Now, first approximations in approaches to social reality have a way of concealing, deep within them, basic commitments to values. For what is singled out as *fundamental* is what the observer takes to be that which "really matters." And in the same obvious sense, the variations that are excluded from notice by the observer's conception are thereby regarded as inconsequential for what the observer regards as significant. So it is that by characterizing the entire period as sensate, Sorokin does not direct his analytical attention to the differing kinds of scientific work that are to be found in that uniformly sensate period. This is a perspective which, precisely because it is macroscopic, throws together, for all pertinent purposes, the work of a Galileo, Kepler, and Newton, on the one hand, and the work of a Rutherford, Einstein, and, shall we say, Yang and Lee, on the other. It thus excludes from analysis the great differences that, for many human and intellectual purposes, are to be found in the science of the sixteenth or seventeenth century and the twentieth. It is a gross approximation that threatens to usurp the attention of those who have reason to regard the variability *within* the macroscopic sensate period as also fundamental.

These remarks may be enough to raise the second question that, in our view, needs to be dealt with by Sorokin in re-examining his sociology of knowledge and of science. What components of his theory will help us to account for the variability of thought within the societies and eras which Sorokin assigns to one or another of his sociocultural types? Has Sorokin imposed excessive limits upon his theory by a commitment to a kind of macroscopic analysis that excludes from detailed investigation the very questions which many would consider central?

In one restricted sense, Sorokin does address himself to this problem. He observes, for example, that the failure of the sensate "system of truth" (empiricism) to monopolize our sensate culture testifies to the fact that the culture is not "fully integrated." But this would seem to surrender inquiry into the bases of those very differences of thought with which our contemporary world is concerned. On the Sorokinian theory, how does one account for these differences? The same question applies to other categories and principles of knowledge with which he deals on the plane of macrosociology. He finds, for example, that in present-day sensate culture, "materialism" is less prevalent than "idealism," and that "temporalism" and "eternalism" are almost equally current, as are "realism" and "nominalism," "singularism" and "universalism." And now we come again to the decisive (and we repeat, self-imposed) limitation of Sorokin's theory: since, by his own testimony, these diverse doctrines exist within the same culture, how can the general characterization of the culture as "sensate" help us to explain why some thinkers subscribe to one mode of thought, and others to another?

The essential point is that Sorokin's theory does not lead us to explore variations of thought *within* a society or culture, for he looks to the "dominant" themes of the culture and imputes these to the culture as a whole.[10] Quite apart from the *differences* of intellectual outlook of different classes and groups, contemporary society, for example, is regarded by Sorokin as an integral example of sensate culture. On its own major premises, Sorokin's theory is primarily suited to characterize cultures in the large, not to analyze the connections between various positions in the social structure and the styles and content of thought which are distinctive of them.[11]

That the macrosociological level of analysis excludes from atten-

---

[10] So far as we can see, on only one occasion does Sorokin relate the internal differentiation of a society to any aspect of the types of thought obtaining in that society. This he does tangentially when he contrasts the tendency of the "clergy and religious landed aristocracy to become the leading and organizing classes in the Ideational, and the capitalistic bourgeoisie, intelligentsia, professionals, and secular officials in the Senate culture. . . ." *Dynamics*, III, 250. See also his account of the diffusion of culture among the social classes, IV, 221 ff.

[11] Cf. Merton, *op. cit.*, pp. 466-67.

tion problems which are of import in understanding varied developments within a culture has been noticed by several critics of Sorokin's work. The anthropologist, Alexander Goldenweiser, soon picked up the issue but stated it so extravagantly as to convert a sound observation into a self-defeating exaggeration, saying that "the meshes of his [Sorokin's] net are spread so wide that all [?] that counts in history slips right through it."[12]   And essentially the same point is made by Maquet about differing social and political systems when he notes that "some differences which are significant from a microscopic point of view are neglected. Thus, communism, capitalism, fascism are subsumable under the same category of sensate culture . . . the use of conceptual tools like the three premises of culture will let a rather large number of differences very important in regard to a narrower frame of reference escape."[13]

Inspecting the course of science through Sorokin's macrosociological lens is apt to blur specific developments in science rather than to bring them into sharp focus. For example, in his account of how culture-mentalities affect the foci of attention in science—a problem important in its own right—Sorokin observes: ". . . the scientists of Ideational culture would be more *interested* in the study of spiritual, mental, and psychological *phenomena*. . . . Scientists of Sensate culture would probably be more *interested* in the purely material *phenomena* . . ."[14] (italics inserted). The *comparative* degrees of interest in these two broad classes of phenomena at any one time need not be put in question. But it does divert us from considering the import of the fact that an immense interest has in recent generations developed in the sciences of human behavior which are concerned with "spiritual, mental, and psychological phenomena." Paraphrasing Derek Price's estimate of physical scientists, we have only to remember that more than 90 per cent of all social and behavioral scientists that have ever lived are still alive. This great interest in the scientific investigation of man and his works is a historical fact that requires interpretation by the sociology of science, but it is not one readily explained by Sorokin's macrosociological conceptions.

[12] "Sociologos," *Journal of Social Philosophy*, July 1938, p. 353, cited in *Dynamics*, IV, 291 n.
[13] Maquet, *op. cit.*, p. 199.   [14] *Dynamics*, II, 13.

In emphasizing this general point, we should prefer not to be misunderstood. It is not being said that Sorokin's macrosociology of science is *theoretically incompatible* with the more detailed analysis of varying developments of thought and science within each of his major types of culture. It is not a matter of theoretical inconsistency but rather a matter of the kinds of inquiry in the sociology of science that tend to be emphasized and those that tend to be neglected in the macrosociological perspective. That is what we mean by saying that, in this respect, Sorokin's theory is a first approximation. It can be and, we argue, should be complemented by intensive inquiries into the connections between types of scientific work by men variously located in the social structure of a particular society.

Much the same issue is involved in Sorokin's treatment of long-run and short-run fluctuations in the modes of thought prevailing in one or another sphere of culture. Sorokin is of course primarily interested in the long-run fluctuations of culture-mentalities which he regards as fundamental to all the rest. But he does attend—for example, in Chaper XII of the second volume of the *Dynamics*—to short-run changes in such scientific theories as atomism, vitalism, and mechanism in biology, abiogenesis, and corpuscular and wave theories of light, going on to note that "across the ever-recurring alternation of these theories, short-time fluctuations may also be perceived. . . ."[15] But these short-run variations do not engage Sorokin's interest; he makes no effort to investigate their social and cultural sources. More specifically, he observes, "The situation in regard to mechanistic and vitalistic conceptions in the present century appears to be one of armed conflict. Both conceptions seem to be existing side by side and both seem to be flourishing."[16] Again, Sorokin does not consider it part of his theoretical commitment to examine the social and cultural conditions under which these opposed biological theories are found in a state of armed coexistence. Yet this would plainly be a major problem for the microsociology of science.

[15] *Ibid.*, II, 446.
[16] *Ibid.*, II, 454.

III. Cultural Determinism and the Relative Autonomy of Subsystems

Up to this point we have treated Sorokin's general theoretical position in its more extreme and emphatically reiterated form. This position holds that the three types of "culture-mentalities" alone determine the form, substance, and development of knowledge in general and of science in particular. It is compactly expressed, for example, in Sorokin's assertion that "Scientific theory thus is but an opinion made 'creditable' and 'fashionable' by the type of the prevalent culture."[17]   That theories in science which are not acknowledged as valid by a substantial part of the community of scientists form no significant part of the science of the time is of course the case. But this is a far cry from concluding that scientific theory is *nothing but* a matter of accreditation and fashion. If this were so, it would negate a principal fact about the history of science, the *accumulation* of certified knowledge, albeit an accumulation that proceeds at uneven rates. Whatever else may be disputed, we can scarcely deny that there exists a greater stock of scientific knowledge today than in the past. There is more here than a mere matter of belief and fashion.

In point of fact, Sorokin does not confine himself to the extreme position that holds the development of science to be wholly determined by the prevailing culture-mentality. Instead, he introduces two qualifications, the one emphasized as an integral part of his theory and the other treated casually and only in passing. The first qualification assigns a margin of autonomy or independence to each subsystem in a culture, especially the subsystem of disciplined thought and science; the second briefly acknowledges that a differentiated social structure as well as the dominant culture-mentality affects the development of knowledge. Both qualifications, and particularly the first of these, are essential to a sound reading of Sorokin's theory.

Possibly because Sorokin himself so often emphasizes the dependence of everything in a sociocultural system upon its "cultural premises," critics of his work understandably take him to subscribe to a doctrine of rigid cultural determinism. The dominant emphasis overshadows the basic restriction upon this doctrine expressly intro-

[17] *Ibid.*, II, 455.

duced in the first chapter of his *Dynamics,* where each subsystem of a sociocultural system is seen as having a degree of autonomy or independence. Put most generally,

The autonomy of any system means . . . the existence of some margin of choice or selection on its part with regard to the infinitely great number of varying external agents and objects which may influence it. It will ingest some of these and not others. . . . [O]ne of the most important "determinators" of the functioning and course of any system lies within the system itself, is inherent in it. In this sense any inwardly integrated system is an autonomous self-regulating, self-directing, or, if one prefers, "equilibrated" unity. . . . This is one of the specific aspects of the larger principle which may be called "immanent self-regulation and self-direction."[18]

The problem then becomes one of developing a theory adequate to account for the different "margins" of autonomy possessed by various kinds of institutions and other subsystems. So far as we can see, this is another gap—in our accounting, the third gap—in Sorokin's theory as it now stands. Apart from the roughly ascertainable *fact* that particular institutions have a smaller or greater measure of independence of their social and cultural environments, there seems nothing *in the theory* to help us anticipate how this will turn out for various kinds of institutional spheres in various kinds of sociocultural systems.

With regard to this problem, Sorokin would seem to hold a position formally (not of course substantively) like that adopted by Marx and Engels. In view of Sorokin's well-known opposition to Marxist theory, this statement may at first seem to be implausible, not to say extravagant. Yet when theorists are confronted with the same problem, they not infrequently converge in their formal analysis of it, however much they may differ in their substantive conclusions. And this, it seems to us, is the case with Marx and Sorokin in their treatment of the relative autonomy of institutional spheres within society. Consider only these few parallelisms of formal analysis.

Just as Sorokin in the main makes his culture-mentalities the effective determinant of what develops in a sociocultural system, so, of course, Marx makes the "relations of production" the "real foundation" which "determines the general character of the social,

[18] *Ibid.,* I, 50-51.

political and intellectual processes of life."[19] Substantively, Marx and Sorokin could not be farther apart: Marx adopts a "materialistic" position in the sense of the social relations of production largely determining the superstructure of ideas;[20] Sorokin adopts an "idealistic" position in which the underlying premises and cultural mentality largely determine the general character of the society and culture, including its social relations. But both agree on the formal position of positing *primary* social or cultural determinants that nevertheless leave room for some degree of independence in the spheres of thought and knowledge.

Just as Sorokin postulates some measure of autonomy for social and cultural subsystems, so does the alter ego of Marx as, for example, when he attributes a degree of autonomy to law. Thus, Engels writes:

As soon as the new division of labor which creates professional lawyers becomes necessary, another new and *independent* sphere is opened up which, for all its general dependence on production and trade, has its own capacity for reacting upon these spheres as well. In a modern state, law must not only correspond to the general economic position and be its expression, but must also be an expression which is *consistent in itself*, and which does not, owing to inner contradictions, look glaringly inconsistent. And in order to achieve this, the faithful reflection of economic conditions is more and more infringed upon. All the more so the more rarely it happens that a code of law is the blunt, unmitigated, unadulterated expression of the domination of a class—this in itself would already offend the "expression of justice."[21] [Italics inserted.]

In the Marxist view, if this is true of law, closely connected with economic processes, it is all the more true of other spheres in the "ideological superstructure." Philosophy, religion, and science are in particular constrained by the pre-existing stock of knowledge and belief, and are only indirectly and ultimately influenced by economic factors.[22]

Political, juridical, philosophical, religious, literary, artistic, etc. develop-

[19] Karl Marx, *A Contribution to the Critique of Political Economy* (Chicago, 1904), pp. 11-12.

[20] As a reminder, we have only to read the sentence that follows the passage quoted from Marx in the text overhead: "It is not the consciousness of men that determines their [social] existence, but, on the contrary, their social existence determines their consciousness."

[21] Friedrich Engels, "Letters . . . ," in Karl Marx, *Selected Works* (Moscow, 1936), I, 385.

[22] *Ibid.*, I, 386.

ment is based on economic development. But all these react upon one another and also upon the economic base. It is not that the economic position is the *cause and alone active,* while everything else only has a passive effect. There is, rather, interaction on the basis of the economic necessity, which *ultimately* always asserts itself.[23] [Italics inserted.]

As we have seen, Sorokin puts all this more generally in his concept of the autonomy of logically or functionally unified systems. And he applies the concept, among other cases, specifically to the institutional sphere of science in these words:

. . . it is not claimed that all scientific theories show, or must show such a connection [with the underlying cultural premises]; many of them can fluctuate independently of our main variables, within their limited sphere of autonomy and the immediate mental atmosphere of their compartment.... Due to the *Principle of Autonomy* of any really integrated system, each of the integrated currents of culture mentality studied should be expected to have some margin of this autonomy....[24]

Thus, just as Marx-Engels regard the *pressure toward internal consistency* within each institutional sphere as a source of its comparative independence of the social relations of production which are the "ultimate" determinant, so Sorokin regards the *integration* of a subsystem as a source of its comparative independence of culture-mentality as the "ultimate" determinant. The difference of theory is substantive rather than formal.

This brings us back, then, to the third problem of Sorokin's theory to which we have alluded: How does the theory deal with the comparative degrees of autonomy characteristic of different institutional subsystems in a society? Is the measure of autonomy the same for them all—for religion and law, for science and philosophy? Or is there a theoretical basis for assuming that the degree of autonomy characteristically differs for these subsystems? To raise the question is one thing; to supply a satisfactory answer is quite another. When we suggest that the Sorokinian theory seems to provide no answer, we consider this rather as an identifiable and instructive gap than as an observation that undercuts the basis of the theory. The following loose formulation by Engels provides only a suggested clue to the solution, rather than the solution itself:

The further the particular sphere which we are investigating is removed from the economic sphere and approaches that of pure abstract ideology,

---

[23] *Ibid.,* I, 392.   [24] *Dynamics,* II, 474-75.

the more shall we find it exhibiting accidents [i.e., deviations from "the expected"] in its development, the more will its curve run in zig-zag.[25]

This suggestion still leaves open the difficult question of how to find out the "distance" of each institutional sphere from the economic sphere. But if Engels left the problem unresolved, so, too, it seems, does Sorokin.

That this is so is further suggested by Sorokin's passing observations on the independent functions of science in any sociocultural system. After pointing out that a society like the United States has a "highly integrated and differentiated system of science," while primitive societies have "little developed" systems of science,[26] he notes: "But in some form science will be found as a system in any culture area, because [note the functional assumption] any social group, as long as it lives, must have and does have a minimum of knowledge of the world that surrounds it, of the phenomena and objects that are important for its survival and existence. No group entirely devoid of any knowledge can exist and survive for any length of time."[27] It is not the functional assumption of some indispensable minimum of authentic knowledge that concerns us here; rather, it is that this assumption ascribes an independent function to "science" in every society, so that we see Sorokin once again implying that science is not merely the reflection of the culture-mentality but has its own functional basis as well.

After this extended discussion of the principle of autonomy of subsystems in Sorokin's theory and of the unfilled gap in that theory, we may turn for a moment to the second of his restrictions on the cultural determination of science. This must be brief, not because we consider it unimportant, but because, as we have intimated in the foregoing section, Sorokin has elected to give it only fleeting attention in his own work. This restriction upon the determination of thought by the general culture-mentality deals with the connections between the internal differentiation of the social structure and the character of the diversified thought that obtains in the society. It deals, in the language of the foregoing section,

[25] Engels, *op. cit.*, p. 393.

[26] As Sorokin informs us, he uses the term "science" as a shorthand expression for science-and-technology. In this passage he is evidently concerned with the low technology of everyday life in non-literate societies rather than with science, strictly speaking.

[27] *Dynamics*, IV, 111.

with problems in the microsociology of science rather than its macrosociology.

Symptomatically enough, Sorokin touches upon this only in a long footnote. Moreover, the note is not in his *Dynamics* where he most fully develops his sociology of knowledge and science but in his later general introduction to sociology, *Society, Culture and Personality*. Only there, in discussing what he describes as the "non-logicity" of ideas, does Sorokin remark of Mannheim's analysis:

He rightly looks for the cause in the group affiliations of a person; but ... his theory remains vague, and in many respects incorrect. Meanwhile the real reasons for non-logicity are at hand. They are the nature of one's group affiliations and one's cultural affiliations.... Unfortunately how our social affiliations influence our logic and judgments is still but little known. The so-called "sociology of knowledge" has hardly reached a clear formulation of this problem.[28]

In short, Sorokin here acknowledges the saliency of the problem of how, within the same culture, differences in social status and group affiliations affect the nature of non-logical sentiments, of logical thought, and, presumably, of scientific inquiry. No good purpose would be served in discussing Sorokin's appraisal of the current state of the sociology of knowledge, particularly since we are agreed that singularly little empirical inquiry has been developed in this field of enduring intellectual interest. What is pertinent is, not so much the appraisal of work left undone, but the *theoretical* issue that such inquiry, advocated by Sorokin, presupposes the probability of distinct lines of thought that will differ according to the social status and group affiliations of men of science and of the intellect generally. For this implies a conception of the sociology of knowledge which allows for significant variability in the ideas and knowledge developed *within* a particular culture—variability that results from social differentiation—and so supports our interpretation that Sorokin's macrosociology of knowledge does not deny in principle the pertinence of socially differentiated sources of knowledge. This, then, indicates once again the theoretical receptivity on the part of Sorokin, although he has chosen not to pursue this tack for himself, to the notion that the broad cultural mentality does not fully

[28] *Society, Culture and Personality*, pp. 352-53 n.

determine the character of knowledge but allows for significant and socially patterned variations in that knowledge.

Thus, if we take account of Sorokin's two basic qualifications to the determination of science and other knowledge by the prevailing culture-mentality, we find that his theoretical position is not as far removed as it would seem from that adopted by other sociologists of science. His theory sets us the empirical task of trying to ferret out the ways in which culture and social structure affect the development of knowledge, allowing some measure of independence to the requirements internal to each branch of knowledge and science. The appearance of this volume of papers affords an opportunity for Sorokin to set out his present thinking on this question central to the sociology of knowledge. It will then be possible to decide whether Maquet is correct, or merely vague, in his conclusion that "For Sorokin, it is certain that the existential factor [i.e., the social structure] is the least important. . . . He considers that the premises of culture are really the most important factors [*sic*] for the determination of mental productions. . . . We can say that in reality [for Sorokin] the cultural premise truly exercises a predominant influence."[29] Whatever else can legitimately be said of Sorokin's theory, it cannot be described as a theory of "factors," of great, middling, or slight "importance." When Sorokin undertakes to translate Maquet's fuzzy expressions—such as "least important" and "most important factors"—into ideas that are definite enough to bear inspection, we shall be the better able to appreciate his current position on the place, in his theory, of the socially patterned distribution of types of knowledge that is found within each kind of culture.

IV. Empirical Research: Quantitative Indicators in the Sociology of Science

Thus far we have attended to certain components of Sorokin's macrosociological theory of science, singling out those which give rise to theoretical issues that would profit from further clarification. In doing so, we have raised three questions about puzzles that persist in Sorokin's theory: first, how the theory escapes from an

[29] Maquet, *op. cit.*, p. 202.

emanationist position which postulates underlying culture-mentalities that seem to include, in their definition, what is later said to be an expression of these mentalities; second, and to our mind, basically, how the theory accounts for the socially patterned distributions, within a particular type of culture, of diverse modes of thought that do not correspond to the prevailing tendencies; third and correlatively, how the theory deals with the comparative degrees of autonomy characteristic of various subsystems within a sociocultural system, so that it can treat the extent of observed autonomy not simply as an empirical given but as theoretically explainable.

But since Sorokin's is an empirically connected theory, rather than one presented as a set of abstractions remote from systematically assembled data, we have now to turn to selected aspects of his empirical inquiries in the sociology of science. And here the most striking feature of Sorokin's work is the creation of massive accumulations of social and cultural statistics, designed to serve as basic empirical indicators of underlying changes in the rate and character of social and cultural changes. Surely more than any other single scholar dealing with problems in the sociology of knowledge, Sorokin has in effect heeded the maxim of the French social historian, Georges Lefebvre, "Il faut compter."

As one of us has had occasion to note before, "Studies in historical sociology have only begun to quarry the rich ore available in comprehensive collections of biographies and other historical evidence. Although statistical analysis of such materials cannot stand in place of detailed qualitative analysis of the historical evidence, they afford a *systematic* basis for new findings and, often, for correction of received assumptions. . . . The most extensive use of such statistical analysis is found in Sorokin's *Dynamics*."[30]

When we speak of Sorokin's "creation" of these social and cultural statistics, we do so advisedly. For, unlike the operations of governmental bureaus of the census, there are few kinds of social bookkeeping that systematically record evidence on the kinds of intellectual developments with which Sorokin's theory requires him to concern himself. (Statistics of patents for inventions in the modern period and data on the numbers of books published in

---

[30] Merton, *op. cit.*, p. 599 n. On a far less extensive scale, the use of quantitative indicators in the sociology of science will be found in R. K. Merton, *Science, Technology and Society in Seventeenth-Century England* and in Nicholas Hans, *New Trends in Education in the Eighteenth Century.*

various fields practically exhaust all that is readily available on these subjects.) And so, in spite of Sorokin's remarkably ambivalent attitude toward the use of sociological statistics, he found himself required, by the implications of his own theory, to assemble statistics that would testify to the degree of integration empirically found in each of his theoretically constructed types of culture.

By assembling these statistics, Sorokin boldly confronted the problem of how to find out the *extent* to which cultures are in fact integrated. Despite his vitriolic comments on the statisticians of our sensate age, he recognized that to deal with the extent of integration implies some statistical measure. Accordingly, for the field of knowledge, he developed numerical indexes of writings and authors in each time and place, had these coded and classified in appropriate categories, and thus assessed the comparative frequency and inferred influence of various systems of thought.

In the sociology of science, for example, the data cover the period from 3500 B.C. to the twentieth century, being based upon counts from such standard sources as Darmstädter's *Handbuch zur Geschichte der Naturwissenschaften und der Technik,* F. H. Garrison's *Introduction to the History of Medicine,* and the ninth edition of the *Encyclopaedia Britannica.* Counts such as these provide the basis for empirical confirmation of the theoretically derived proposition that "The rate of scientific development tends to become slow, stationary, even regressive in Ideational cultures . . . becoming rapid and growing apace in Sensate cultures. . . ."[31]

There is neither need nor space to report the limitations of his quantitative indicators as these are set out by Sorokin.[32] In any event, he concludes that, whatever their limitations, the indicators provide a valid and reliable measure of fluctuations in the rate of scientific discovery and technological invention as well as of other intellectual and artistic expressions of the culture. That is why he is prepared to assert that "Not only do the first principles and categories of human thought fluctuate, but also most of the scientific theories of a more or less general nature."[33] Plainly, he bases his empirical conclusions very largely upon these cultural statistics.

In view of the basic part played by these statistics in his soci-

[31] *Dynamics,* II, 125. All of chap. iii is devoted to the presentation of such evidence.
[32] *Ibid.,* pp. 125-31.   [33] *Ibid.,* p. 439.

ology of knowledge, Sorokin adopts a curiously ambivalent attitude toward them. This can be seen in his approval of the remark by Robert E. Park that his statistics are merely a concession to the prevailing sensate mentality and that "if they want 'em, let 'em have 'em."[34] Park's facetious remark need not be allowed to obscure the symptomatic nature of Sorokin's response. It is indicative, we believe, of Sorokin's fundamental ambivalence toward criteria of scientific validity, an ambivalence deriving from his effort to cope with quite disparate "systems of truth." In view of the vast effort that went into compiling the cultural statistics that underlie Sorokin's work in the sociology of science, it would not only be facetious but thoroughly irresponsible to conclude that these systematic data were merely trappings considered necessary to "convince the vulgar." The fact is that Sorokin's empirical descriptions are very largely based on these statistics. They are essential to his argument. To remove them would not be to remove a façade, leaving the essential structure of his theory intact; it would be to undercut his macrosociological theory of science and to leave it suspended in the thin air of unrestrained speculation.

This, then, leads to another, the fourth, question and this one two-pronged, which the dialogue of this book may help answer. In view of Sorokin's ambivalence toward social and cultural statistics, about which we shall have more to say, we must ask: What is his current and perhaps consolidated position with regard to the place of such statistics in sociological inquiry, primarily in the sociology of science and, by implication, in other branches of sociology as well? Further, how does his discussion of this question help clarify his position on the criteria of scientific truth which he adopts: does he regard systematic evidence of the kind caught up in his statistics as merely a mode of communication to his scientific compeers in a sensate culture or as a substantial basis both for confirming and developing his theory?

It is these cultural statistics, moreover, that serve to highlight once again two of the principal questions that we consider still unresolved in Sorokin's sociology of knowledge: the question of how the theory accounts for observed variations in the modes of knowledge within a culture and the question of accounting for the distribution of these differences among various groups and strata in

[34] *Sociocultural Causality, Space, Time,* p. 95 n.

the social structure. Take just one case in point. Sorokin describes empiricism as "the typically sensate system of truth." The last five centuries, and more particularly the last century, represent "sensate culture *par excellence!*"[35] Yet even in this flood tide of sensate culture, Sorokin's statistical indices show only some 53 per cent of influential writings to be characterized by "empiricism." Furthermore, in the earlier centuries of this sensate culture, from the late sixteenth to the mid-eighteenth, the indices of empiricism are consistently *lower* than the indices for rationalism (which, in the theory, is associated with an idealistic rather than a sensate culture). The statistical indicators, then, show that the notion of a "prevailing" system of truth needs to be greatly qualified, if it is to cover both the situations in which it represents a bare statistical "majority" and even a statistically indicated minority in the writings of a period.

Even more is implied by Sorokin's statistics. For the main purpose of our observations is not to raise the question of the extent to which Sorokin's conclusions coincide with his statistical data: it is not to ask why the sixteenth and seventeenth centuries are said to have a predominantly "sensate system of truth" in the light of these data. Rather, the purpose is to suggest that, even on Sorokin's own premises, the general characterizations of historical cultures as sensate, idealistic, or ideational constitute only a first step in the analysis, a step which must be followed by further detailed analyses of deviations from the central tendencies of the culture. Once Sorokin has properly introduced the notion of the *extent* to which historical cultures are in fact integrated, he cannot, in all theoretical conscience, treat the existence of types of knowledge which differ from the dominant tendencies as evidence of a mere "congeries" or as a merely accidental fact. It is as much a problem of the sociology of science to account for these substantial "deviations" from the central tendency as to account for these tendencies themselves. And for this, we suggest yet again, it is necessary to develop a theory of the socio-structural bases of thought in a fashion that a cultural-emanationist theory does not permit.

Apart from these theoretical implications, Sorokin's statistics presented in his *Dynamics* afford an occasion for exploring further the intellectual grounds of his ambivalence toward social and

[35] *Dynamics*, II, 51.

cultural statistics altogether. As is well known, Sorokin devotes a considerable portion of his book *Fads and Foibles in Modern Sociology* to an attack on "quantophrenia" or an uncritical devotion to faulty statistics. That quantitative methods in sociology can be, and have been, abused is surely not in question, any more than that qualitative methods, based on ill-devised and ill-confirmed impressions, can be and have been abused. And surely, no sober man will declare himself in favor of faulty craftsmanship, unsound assumptions, and mistaken inferences. The question is therefore not one of identifying this or that case of a fallacy in quantitative analysis in sociology but, rather, one of setting out the criteria and limits of sound quantitative analysis. And since so much of Sorokin's work in the sociology of science is pervaded by empirically grounded statistics, this question becomes thoroughly germane to our discussion.

What, then, are Sorokin's criteria for the appropriate use of social and cultural statistics?* We find it decidedly easier to raise the question than to answer it. Indeed, we raise the question in the hope that Sorokin will seize upon the dialogue constituting this book as an occasion for giving his pointed and definite answer to it. This becomes all the more pertinent when we find that some authors are prepared to adopt an even more extreme perspective on social and cultural statistics than Sorokin's own. Werner Stark, for example, says of Sorokin's *Dynamics* that

our criticism . . . is one of principle. His whole procedure assumes *a radice* the possibility of quantifying what is qualitative, and this is almost like supposing it is possible to square the circle. A book, or a work of art, is all quality [n. b.], because it is all spirit. . . . It is to be feared that the sociology of knowledge will never be able to get much assistance from statistical techniques. Much as we may regret the fact, it will always have to rely heavily on the more cumbersome monographic and descriptive methods.[36]

The issue is even more stark than Stark apparently supposes. For everyone in his senses would agree that what is "inherently" and "exclusively qualitative" cannot, by definition, be quantified. It is really asking too much to ask us to reject a strict tautology. But when we get down to cases, the crucial question, of course, is

---

* For an excellent and intensive examination of the answer to this question implicit in Sorokin's work, see the paper by Riley and Moore in this volume.—ED.

[36] Stark, *op. cit.,* p. 280.

begged by such an affirmation; the question is precisely one of establishing criteria of what is irrefragably qualitative and of what, in some aspect and degree, can be reasonably and usefully quantified. And since, in our opinion, Sorokin has wisely and justifiably counted *aspects* of complex works of science and art, it would be helpful to have him clarify the sense in which he found these to be quantifiable.

Sorokin's restatement of his position on the issue of such quantification would be particularly instructive in view of what he has said about the issue in his *Fads and Foibles*. At one place in that work, for example, he declares that

only through direct empathy, co-living and intuition of the psychosocial states can one grasp the essential nature and differences . . . of religious, scientific, aesthetic, ethical, legal, economic, technological, and other cultural value-systems and their subsystems. Without the direct living experience of these cultural values, they will remain *terra incognita* for our outside observer and statistical analyst. . . . These methods are useless in understanding the nature and difference between, say, Plato's and Kant's systems of philosophy, between the ethics of the Sermon on the Mount and the ethics of hate, between Euclidean and Lobachevskian geometry and between different systems of ideas generally. Only after successfully accomplishing the mysterious inner act of "understanding" each system of ideas or values, can one classify them into adequate classes, putting into one class all the identical ideas, and putting into different classes different ideas or values. Only after that, can one count them, if they are countable, and perform other operations of a mathematical or statistical nature, if they are possible. Otherwise, all observations and statistical operations are doomed to be meaningless, fruitless, and fallacious simulacra of real knowledge.[37]

It would no doubt be generally agreed that a proper understanding of cultural content is required for it to be validly classified so that specimens in each class can then be counted. The vast compilations and counts of such data in the *Dynamics* testify that Sorokin also thinks this can be done. But is it not too stringent a criterion to require a "direct living experience of the cultural values" in order for them to be classified and counted? Some substantial knowledge about the materials in hand is of course necessary but this would seem to fall far short of the extreme requirement exacted by Sorokin. We cannot assume that all of Sorokin's research associates and assistants had a "direct living experience" of the many

[37] *Fads and Foibles,* pp. 160-61.

thousands of scientific discoveries, technological inventions, philosophical doctrines, and art objects which they classified and counted in order to provide an empirical test of Sorokin's ideas. It is certain that one of his research assistants, R. K. Merton, had no such demanding experience of the almost thirteen thousand discoveries and inventions he computed on the basis of the Darmstädter *Handbuch,* just as it is probable that J. W. Boldyreff, another of his assistants, had no such experience of the thousands of scholars, scientists, artists, statesmen, etc., mentioned in the ninth edition of the *Encyclopaedia Britannica,* who were classified and assigned weights on the basis of the amount of space devoted to them in the *Encyclopaedia.*

Nevertheless, there is internal evidence that these counts were not vitiated by limited knowledge (though, we suggest, knowledge enough for the purpose in hand). For independent classifications and counts of different but theoretically related materials produced much the same empirical results. As Sorokin reports for one such case dealing with data on the "empirical system of truth (of senses)" and data on the rate of scientific discovery:

The items and the sources were entirely different and the computations were made by different persons who were not aware of the work of the other computers. (Professors Lossky and Lapshin had no knowledge of my study, and Dr. Merton, who made the computation of the scientific discoveries, was unaware not only of my study but also of the computations made by Professors Lossky and Lapshin.) Under the circumstances, the agreement between the curve of the scientific discoveries and inventions and the curve of the fluctuations of the influence of the system of truth of senses is particularly strong evidence that the results obtained in both cases are neither incidental nor misleading.[38]

In a word, the quantification of cultural contents cannot, need not, and is not intended to reproduce the entire complex whole of each item entering into the computation. Only selected aspects and attributes are classified and counted. And for this purpose, full, detailed, and empathic understanding of each cultural item is not, apparently, required. It would therefore be instructive to have Sorokin redirect his attention to the seeming discrepancy between the actual practice employed in quantifying cultural items in the *Dynamics* and the far more demanding criteria for such quantifica-

[38] *Dynamics,* II, 20.

tion proposed in the *Fads and Foibles.* What Sorokin actually *does* in the one case seems to us more compelling than what he *says* in the other. In making this observation, we only adopt and adapt the sage advice of Albert Einstein: "If you want to find out anything from the theoretical physicists about the methods they use, I advise you to stick closely to one principle: don't listen to their words, fix your attention on their deeds."[39]

All this allows us to note that not the least advance in sociology during the last century or so is reflected in the growing recognition that even crude quantitative data can serve the intellectual purpose of enabling the sociologist to reject or to modify his initial hypotheses when they are in fact defective. To see this change in outlook we have only to contrast the encyclopedic effects of a Comte with those of a Sorokin. Comte handles scattered facts gingerly and infrequently, as though they were unfamiliar and even dangerous things; he does not think of so assembling systematic arrays of data that they could, in principle, put his intuitive or reasoned guesses to the test of empirical reality. Sorokin drenches us in quantitative facts—for example, in the *Dynamics,* but not only there —and thus provides both himself and his readers with the occasion for matching theoretical expectations and empirical data. This practice would seem particularly required when scholars turn to the sociological drama of large-scale changes in the cultures and social structures that make up the framework of world history. For entirely qualitative claims to facts prove to be excessively pliable, easily bent to fit the requirements of a comprehensive theory. But if it is to be more than a dogma, a theory must state the empirical observations that will be taken to disprove it or, at least, to require its substantial revision. Independently collected, systematic and quantitative data supply the most demanding test called for by such an empirically-connected theory. And that Sorokin also thinks this to be the case seems implied by the way in which he has gone about his task of conducting empirical inquiries in the sociology of science.

V. Relativism and the Criteria of Scientific Truth

We have alluded, once or twice, to the problem confronted by Sorokin of locating his own work in one or another of the "systems

[39] *The World as I See It* (New York, 1934), p. 30.

of truth" which he makes distinctive of each of his three major types of culture. What criteria of truth does he employ in setting about his own work? Is he a thoroughgoing relativist, regarding scientific truth as *nothing but* a matter of satisfying the different criteria that obtain in each particular type of culture? Does he consider each system of truth just as compelling (or as arbitrary) as the next? Does he see himself as a creature of contemporary sensate culture, subject to contemporary criteria of scientific truth, or has he found an Archimedean point to stand upon, which enables him to move beyond these criteria? If so, what is this point and how does he assure himself and his prevalently sensate readers that it is an effective and justifiable one? In short, how does Sorokin try to escape the relativistic impasse?

This barrage of questions—at bottom, they of course comprise only one question—is something more than a matter of rhetoric. We are genuinely puzzled and unable to identify, with any assurance, the position taken by Sorokin on this matter. Our confusion is further confounded by what seems to be Sorokin's indecisive and possibly changing conception of science in today's sensate culture. We recall his statement that "In a Sensate society and culture, the Sensate system of truth based upon the testimony of the organs of senses has to be dominant."[40] But, it turns out, this statement is only a gross approximation. For reason enters into the system as well. The sensate method of validation requires "Mainly the reference to the testimony of the organs of senses. . . , supplemented by logical reasoning, especially in the form of mathematical reasoning. But even the well-reasoned theory remains in the stage of pure hypothesis, unproved until it is tested by the sensory facts; and it is unhesitatingly rejected if these 'facts' contradict it."[41] And, for our immediate purposes, finally, he writes that the sensate system of scientific truth "possesses some of the elements of the rationalistic system of truth in various forms; in the forms of the laws of logic which are obligatory for scientists and which are hardly mere results of the sensory experience; in that of deductions, which are incorporated in the queen of these sciences, mathematics; of many conceptual elements in the form of the fundamental concepts and principles of the sciences; and in several other forms"[42]

[40] *Dynamics*, II, 5.   [41] *Ibid.*, p. 9.
[42] *Ibid.*, p. 11 n.

With this statement Sorokin seems to have returned, from a distant point of departure, close to the position which, except for turns of language, is that generally adopted by working scientists in our time. Intuition, hunch, and guess may, and often do, originate ideas, but they do not provide a sufficient basis for choosing among ideas. Logical analysis and abstract reasoning interlock with empirical inquiry and it is only when the results of these two prove consistent that contemporary scientists consider them to be an authentic part of validated scientific knowledge. However much Sorokin may on occasion seem to take joy in the system of truth described as characteristic of an idealistic culture, he nevertheless *practices* under the rules of a sensate system. That, we suppose, is what lies behind his footnoted remark: ". . . however surprised a contemporary partisan of scientism may be at my impartiality in 'observing and ascribing' the existence of various systems of truth. . . , he has to countenance it because they are empirical facts witnessed by the testimony of our organs of senses, as will be demonstrated further. In other words, in my study I shall intentionally follow the 'empirical system of truth' which must be convincing to such a partisan of 'scientism.' "[43]

Here Sorokin says that he adopts as criteria for his own work that complex of rational discourse and empirical data which is characteristic of a sensate science. But he implies that he does so only as a *façon de parler*. Yet this reply-in-advance to our question seems facile rather than adequate. Does it mean that Sorokin as a social scientist is truly prepared to abandon empirical tests of his ideas? that he is ready to propose characterizations of historical societies and cultures which are at odds with the empirical evidence he has assembled? We suspect not. The composite of reason and ordered experience seems to us precisely what Sorokin in fact employs as a guide to his own inquiry and as a measure of the acceptability of the results of the inquiry. Intuition, scriptures, chance experiences, dreams, or whatever may be the psychological source of an idea. (Remember only Kekulé's dream and intuited imagery of the benzene ring which converted the idea of the mere number of atoms in a molecule into the structural idea of their being arranged in a pattern resulting from the valences of different kinds of atoms.) But whatever the source, the idea itself must be explored

[43] *Ibid.*, pp. 11-12 n.

in terms of its implications and these implications then examined in terms of how far they hold empirically.

To put the issue directly and so to afford Sorokin an occasion in this dialogue for further clarifying his position, we suggest that, whatever asides may be tucked away in footnotes, Sorokin adopts, in the course of his inquiries in the sociology of science, a thorough-going commitment to the combined criteria of internal consistency and empirical observation that are the mark of scientific work in our sensate age.

Sorokin's image of sensate science notwithstanding, the fact is that concepts and rules of reasoning are no mere props in modern science. They are as indispensable as the testimony of the senses. We call only one witness, although many more are waiting in the corridors of today's science:

Our experience hitherto justifies us in believing that nature is the realiza-tion of the simplest conceivable mathematical ideas. I am convinced that we can discover by means of purely mathematical constructions the concepts and the laws connecting them with each other, which furnish the key to the understanding of natural phenomena. Experience may suggest the appropriate mathematical concepts, but they most certainly cannot be deduced from it. Experience remains, of course, the sole criterion of the physical utility of a mathematical construction. But the creative principle resides in mathematics. In a certain sense, therefore, I hold it true that pure thought can grasp reality, as the ancients dreamed.

This is not the voice of the thirteenth-century Robert Grosseteste speaking; it is the voice of the decidedly twentieth-century Albert Einstein.[44]

Moreover, as the history of science during the last centuries testifies, not only can empirical data challenge established concepts and theories, but concepts and theories often challenge the super-ficial testimony of the senses. It is a familiar part of everyday practice in science to reject misleading empirical impressions when these run counter to theories that have themselves been firmly em-bedded in scientific thought. Any sharp separation of reason and empirical data in contemporary science must therefore distort much of the operative reality. Work in the scientific laboratory rests upon both, with one or the other raising questions that must be resolved by a congruence between them. Only then is there

[44] Einstein, *op. cit.*, pp. 36-37.

a reasonable prospect that an idea or a finding will enter permanently into the repertory of science. And this sensate conception of science, we suggest, is basic to Sorokin's own work, his incidental disclaimers notwithstanding. This, at least, is a sixth puzzle which Sorokin might helpfully unravel in his part of the dialogue.

VI. *The Cumulation of Scientific Knowledge*

The issue we have just identified leads us directly to still another question about Sorokin's theory of social and cultural dynamics, this one cutting deeply enough to isolate, for a moment, his sociology of science from the rest of his theory. The fact that it is an issue hoary with age does not make it any the less in point. We refer, as the caption of this section implies, to the particular sense in which science, as distinct from other spheres of culture, tends to be accumulative. In our view, this raises a question, deeply imbedded in Sorokin's theory of culture change, that requires him to consolidate his role as sociological historian and as sociological theorist.

As sociological theorist, and on his own accounting, Sorokin has identified two full cycles of ideational-idealistic-and-sensate phases in Greco-Roman and Western cultures. He sees a third sensate phase beginning roughly in the fifteenth [or early sixteenth—Ed.] century. In his vocabulary of abstract types of culture, one ideational phase in history is much like the other; one idealistic phase is much like the next; and one sensate phase is much like the rest. For these are described and analyzed in terms of general categories and criteria, in the light of which they seem to be "of the same kind."

As sociological historian, however, Sorokin must reckon with quite another question. Whatever his theory may identify as similar *kinds* of culture phases, there remains the historical question of the extent to which prior cultural products accumulate and become the possession of men living in a later period of the same or differing cultural type. The cycles of cultural change do not start anew. Particularly with regard to science, each succeeding historical phase makes use of antecedent knowledge on which it builds. In this more nearly concrete, historical sense, the sensate phase of the last centuries is *not*, of course, identical with the sensate phase of the preceding cycles. The phases are *alike*, in terms of the abstract categories employed by Sorokin, else they would not be classified as sensate. But they differ—and science remains our test case of this—in that some of the cultural products of the past are available to those living in the later phase. Science did not start anew in the sensate phase, said to begin early in the sixteenth century; as historians of science periodically remind us, it built upon the selective accumulation of what had gone before.

All this seems evident enough. Yet, possibly because Sorokin is adamantean in his rejection of a unilinear doctrine of cultural change, he tends to neglect the *implications* of selective cultural accumulation[45] for his theory. It is this accumulation and its consequences that distinguish the sensate culture of the twentieth century from the sensate culture of, say, the Hellenistic period. To describe both periods as sensate is justified only abstractly but not historically. For the accumulation of scientific and technological knowledge makes a difference that can make a very great difference to men living in the later of these sensate phases. To say that the thesis of a unilinear accumulation of knowledge cannot qualify as historical truth is one thing. But to ignore selective accumulation of knowledge is quite another. (To put it vulgarly, the Hellenistic Greeks did not have a body of knowledge about quantum mechanics or a technology of spacecraft; or to scramble legend and history, Icarus really cannot be equated with the astronauts Gagarin and Glenn.)

What we have been saying raises two related questions about Sorokin's macrosociology of science. These are questions about what he is prepared to take as significant similarities and what as significant differences in the scientific knowledge found in historical eras of the same abstract type.

The first question comes to the fore when we examine again his observations on short-run fluctuations of particular scientific theories in various periods.[46] He summarizes his judgment in these words:

---

[45] That is to say, Sorokin amply recognizes the fact but does not draw the possible implications of the fact for his theory. Thus: "The trend for the last four centuries has been for empiricism to rise steadily until, at the beginning of the twentieth century, it reached a unique, unprecedented [n. b.] level. . . . There was also a unique and unprecedented multiplication . . . of important discoveries and inventions in the sciences. Thus we truly live in the age of the truth of senses, of a magnitude, depth, and brilliancy hardly witnessed in other cultures and periods" (*Dynamics*, II, 113).

[46] *Ibid.*, II, chap. xii.

". . . as far as mere oscillation is concerned, there probably has been no scientific theory which has not undergone it, and, like a fashion, now has been heralded as the last word of science, and now has fallen into disrepute."[47] This judgment leads us to ask in what sense recurrent sets of ideas constitute one and the same theory that now finds general acceptance and later, rejection, only to be accepted again, still later. To consider one of the instances cited by Sorokin as a case of fluctuations in a theory, in what sense is present-day "atomistic theory" to be taken as the same as "atomistic theory" in ancient Greece? Similarities are there, of course, but also, obvious and significant differences. And it is these accumulative differences in what is on the surface the same kind of scientific theory that constitute an advance in science. To attend only to the formal similarity is to jettison the historically significant differences that enable present-day atomic theory to deal with problems in science that could not, of course, even be dreamt of by the Greeks. Or take the case of fluctuations in the long history of "the theory" of biological evolution which has been so often traced. Darwin's was not just another version of evolution; it differed from what had gone before by beginning to specify the processes through which the evolution of species took place. Again, to identify Darwin's or later evolutionary theory with ancient versions is to ignore that aspect of the development of science that leads to an enlarged scientific knowledge: selective accumulation. To attend only to similarities between early and later versions of a theory is to become subject to adumbrationism, "the practice of claiming to find dim anticipations of current scientific discoveries in older, and preferably, ancient, work by the expedient of excessively liberal interpretations of what is being said now and of what was said then."[48] This is a practice that can only stir up anew the obsolete quarrel between the ancients and the moderns.

The second question raised by Sorokin's relative neglect of the selective accumulation of scientific knowledge has to do with his diagnosis of the present condition of science and his forecast for its immediate future. Knowing Sorokin's sentiments about sensate

[47] Ibid., II, 467.
[48] Robert K. Merton, "Singletons and Multiples in Scientific Discovery: A Chapter in the Sociology of Science," Proceedings of the American Philosophical Society, CV, 5 (1961), 470-86.

culture, we can anticipate that his picture of the present state of science will be a gloomy one, and he does not disappoint us:

One can turn to any field of science now and find first of all a multitude of different theories and sometimes even opposite hypotheses fighting one another for "recognition" as true theory. Such an opulence of contradictions and mutual criticism does not permit any certitude, especially concerning the most important principles, and therefore fosters more and more uncertainty. . . . If such a situation continues—and empiricism, as long as it is dominant, cannot help continuing it—the incertitude will increase. . . . The boundary lines between knowledge and nonknowledge thus are bound to become less and less clear. . . . In such circumstances the truth of senses can easily give way to a truth of faith. In other words, neither doubt, nor uncertainty, nor changeability of the scientific theories can be pushed too far without destroying science itself and its truth. Contemporary science has already possibly gone too far in that direction and therefore is already exposed to danger.[49]

This is strong language. It is the prophetic utterance of a sociological Jeremiah. But, on *that* account, it is not to be lightly dismissed. No one who sat in Sorokin's classes during the 1930's is apt to forget his annual impassioned lecture announcing that one day men of science would create the possibility of destroying all that lives on the earth and that when that day comes, some of these men will be curious to see what really happens when the button is pressed.[50]

From this apocalyptic vision, we return to Sorokin's forecast of a decline in science. This raises again the question of how his theory takes account of the cross-cultural accumulation of scientific knowledge. When Western society largely turned its back on science—in Sorokin's overview, from the third to the eleventh centuries—it turned from a comparatively small stock of accumulated knowledge.[51] It is vastly different in our own sensate age.

[49] *Dynamics*, II, 119-20.

[50] In less passionate prose than he employed in his lecture, Sorokin wrote in 1937: "Suppose someone should discover a simple but terrific explosive which could easily destroy a considerable part of our planet. Scientifically, it would be the greatest discovery, but socially the most dangerous for the very existence of mankind, because out of 1,800,000,000 human beings there certainly would be a few individuals who, being 'scientifically minded,' would like to test the explosive and as a result would destroy our planet. Such an explosion would be a great triumph of science. . . . This half-fantastic example shows that there must be limitations of science imposed by the reasons which are outside it, and these reasons usually come from the truth of faith and that of reason" (*Dynamics*, II, 20).

[51] A. C. Crombie, *Augustine to Galileo: The History of Science A.D. 400-1650* (London, 1952), chaps. i-iv.

We are the legatees and initiators of an incomparably greater body of scientific knowledge and of an associated technology not as easily put to one side. To base a prediction on the two preceding cycles of culture would seem hazardous at best; to predict the decline of science in our world means to discount the immensely greater store of science that has accumulated since the last sensate phase and so to treat it as though it were of a piece with the limited scientific knowledge of ancient Rome.

Nor is it evident that confidence in science as a source of knowledge shows signs of diminishing. True, we find expressions of hostility toward science, largely because of the social consequences of some of the technology it has made possible. Science is seen as originating those engines of human destruction which may plunge our civilization into everlasting night and confusion. But there is little of that alienation from science which Sorokin believes to be immanent in the very development of contemporary science. The tonicity of scientists themselves seems more aptly expressed by C. P. Snow when, speaking of what happened in science during two decades at Cambridge University, he says: "I was privileged to have a ringside view of one of the most wonderful creative periods in all physics."[52] He then goes on to describe "a much louder voice, that of another archetypal figure, Rutherford, trumpeting: 'This is the heroic age of science! This is the Elizabethan age!' "[53] And finally, he expresses his conviction that this is a revolutionary time for science, a time in which to take joy in science:

About two years ago, he writes, one of the most astonishing experiments in the whole history of science was brought off. . . . I mean the experiment at Columbia by Yang and Lee. It is an experiment of the greatest beauty and originality, but the result is so startling that one forgets how beautiful the experiment is. It makes us think once again about some of the fundamentals of the physical world. Intuition, common sense—they are neatly stood on their heads. The result is usually known as the contradiction of parity.[54]

That each such advance in science enlarges our awareness of how little is still known is a judgment that has been endlessly reiterated by scientists, particularly the greatest among them.[55] But

[52] C. P. Snow, *The Two Cultures and the Scientific Revolution*, London: Cambridge University Rede Lectures, 1959, p. 1.
[53] *Ibid.*, p. 4.   [54] *Ibid.*, p. 15.
[55] On the norm of humility in science, see Merton, "Priorities in Scientific Discovery: A Chapter in the Sociology of Science," *American Sociological Review*,

this does seem far removed from the portrait of uncertainty and confusion among scientists painted by Sorokin. In any case, it would be instructive to have him restate the place occupied by the fact of the accumulation of scientific knowledge in his macrosociological theory of science.

VII. *Themes of the Dialogue*

And here we must stop putting questions in detail. Not that other questions fail to make their appearance as we continue to study Sorokin's macrosociology of science. We encounter the question, for example, of Sorokin's appraisal of the current condition of social science. Is it in a thoroughly parlous state, as he suggests in his *Dynamics*,[56] or is it, as he suggests later in *Society, Culture and Personality*, "entering the stage of a new synthesis and a further clarification of its logical structure"?[57] Or again, we meet the question: How does Sorokin see the relations between science and other social institutions, in particular, the institution of religion? Are the relations between the two confined, as he suggests, to those of active combat or of absorption of one by the other, with "rarely, if ever, close cooperation between them"? The matter appears more complex than that. At least, the work of Whitehead and others finds that some religions have inadvertently lent support to the pursuit of science and that, apart from the times of conspicuous conflict between them, the institutions of science and religion have not infrequently been mutually supporting.

And so we might continue to raise further questions for Sorokin to re-examine. But like those we have just mentioned, these would touch only the surface of Sorokin's sociological theory of science. It might therefore be more useful to wind up our discussion by recapitulating the puzzles and questions that seem to us unresolved in that theory. This would afford Professor Sorokin an occasion, in his comment on our paper, to give us the benefit of his current

XXII (1957), 635-59, esp. 646-47. The most famous expression of this norm by Newton can perhaps bear still another repetition: "I do not know what I may appear to the world, but to myself I seem to have been only like a boy playing on the seashore, and diverting myself in now and then finding a smoother pebble or a prettier shell than ordinary, whilst the great ocean of truth lay all undiscovered before me."

[56] II, 304.   [57] P. 30.

thinking on these issues and even, perhaps, to divest himself of ideas which once had a definite place in his evolving theory but which now, in the light of further inquiry and reflection, he no longer sees any need for retaining.

In short summary, then, these are the major questions that puzzled us as we reworked our way through Sorokin's sociology of science.

1. Does the theory really adopt an emanationist position which assumes that the principal features of science and knowledge in a particular culture merely emanate from the culture-mentality that underlies it? And since the culture-mentality seems to include, in its definition, what are later said to be expressions of that mentality, must we not take this as rather an implied definition than an empirically testable hypothesis?

2. What is there in the theory to account for the variability of thought and science *within* each of the societies and cultures that are generally characterized as being of one or another type: as ideational, idealistic, or sensate?

3. Since integrated subsystems in a culture are said to have a margin of autonomy, a degree of independence of their social and cultural environment, how does the theory account for the margins of autonomy exhibited by the various subsystems? By way of example, does the theory lead us to expect the same or differing margins of autonomy for science and politics, for religion, law, and the economy?

4. What place is assigned, in this theory, to the connections between social differentiation and knowledge? How does the theory deal with the possibility that differences in the social location of men of knowledge, in their statuses and group affiliations, affect the character of what they take as authentic knowledge and what they produce as new claims to knowledge?

5. In view of his variously expressed ambivalence toward social and cultural statistics, what is Sorokin's current position on the place of such statistics in the sociology of science and, by implication, in other branches of sociology as well? Does he consider cultural statistics of the kind employed in the *Dynamics* as only a means of communicating with his sensate compeers or as also a basis for testing and developing his theory? And since the very stringent criteria of sound quantitative analysis he advocates in *Fads and*

Foibles do not seem fully met even by his own cultural statistics in the *Dynamics,* would we do better to take his precepts or his practice as guidelines to quantitative inquiries in sociology?

6. Which criteria of scientific truth are utilized in Sorokin's own theory? How does it escape from the relativistic impasse of making scientific truth only a matter of taste, in which each type of culture prescribes its own criteria? Does Sorokin consider each system of truth just as compelling or just as arbitrary as the next?

7. How does the theory take account of the accumulation of scientific knowledge? Does this accumulation make our sensate period different from the sensate cultures that have gone before?

If we are right in supposing that the foregoing questions direct us to gaps in this macrosociological theory of science, then perhaps the gaps will be bridged as we listen to the rest of this dialogue.

Part Three

Reply to My Critics

Pitirim A. Sorokin

I. Introductory Remarks

I have just finished my reading of the manuscripts of the remarkable essays of this volume. I am deeply impressed and pleasantly surprised by the fact of its preparation and eventual publication. I did not expect that there would be an eminent scholar, like Professor Philip J. Allen, personally unknown to me before, who would take upon himself the enormous burden of organizing such a volume, or that a group of distinguished scholars of various countries would be willing to spend their precious time and energy in writing these essays about my theories. Still less did I expect their analysis and criticism of my ideas to be done with such admirable understanding, objectivity, and elegance, which are rare, at least in the fairly vast literature about my works. Even more: though written apropos of my studies, these essays throw a far-reaching light upon several basic problems of philosophy and psychosocial sciences. In this sense the essays are real contributions to these fields of human knowledge.

I am deeply grateful to Philip J. Allen and to all the eminent contributors to the volume for their thoughtful dissection of my views. While their generous appraisal of some of my contributions needs no discussion on my part, their penetrating criticisms require from me a most careful examination. If they are correct, my respective theories must evidently be abandoned and replaced by more adequate conceptions. If the critique is logically or factually defective, however, then my propositions may remain unimpaired in their scientific validity. Finally, if the criticisms are partly correct and partly faulty, then my views need correction of their shortcomings. In all three cases we all profit by getting rid of errors and by obtaining a better understanding of the basic problems discussed.

I shall examine the main criticisms topically: first, the objections against the philosophical foundations and most general principles of my theories; then, the criticisms of my propositions concerning the important but more limited problems of the psychosocial sciences; finally, the critiques of specific, detailed points of my studies.

In this reply I shall examine only the criticisms of the contributors to this volume. The limited space of the reply does not allow an examination of many other reactions to my theories published by various authors in books about my books, Ph.D. theses, and numerous articles. Perhaps in the future I may have a chance to reply to their interpretations, evaluations, and criticisms. For the present, however, I shall limit my task by answering the thoughtful questions and objections of the distinguished participants in this volume.

II. An Outline of My Integral Philosophy

Perhaps I can begin my answers to the criticisms of various points of my philosophy by quoting a few lines from the beginning and the end of my two articles in which I concisely sketched my philosophy and religion.

Integralism is its name. It views total reality as the infinite X of numberless qualities and quantities: spiritual and material, ever-changing and unchangeable, personal and superpersonal, temporal and timeless, spatial and spaceless, one and many. . . . In this sense it is the veritable *mysterium tremendum et fascinosum* and the *coincidentia oppositorum* (reconciliation of opposites). Its highest center—the summum bonum— is the Infinite Creative X that passes all human understanding. . . .[1]

I agree with all true mystics and great logicians of all great cultures that our language cannot define adequately the ultimate (total) reality and/or the supreme value. All our words, concepts, and definitions, and all our signs and symbols have evolved for indication, denotation, description, and definition of only the finite, the limited, the specific differentiations of the all-embracing, undifferentiated, and quantitatively and qualitatively infinite total reality. . . . They are unfit for definition or

[1] P. A. Sorokin, "Integralism Is My Philosophy," in Whit Burnett, ed., *This Is My Philosophy* (New York: Harper, 1957), p. 180.

conception of the total reality in its infinite manifoldness. By our words and symbols we can define any of the bounded, specific ripples of an infinite ocean of reality, but we cannot adequately describe the ocean itself: it contains all the ripples and at the same time is not identical to any and all of them. The same is true of the *summum bonum*. . . . This explains why many a mystic called it "the Unutterable," "the Unexpressible," "the Divine Nothing," "into which fade all things and differentiations," to use St. Thomas' expression.[2]

Such, in a rough outline, is my "integral religion" and philosophy. I realize its inadequacy. I do not claim any superiority for it over any and all the other religions and philosophies. I *do not have even any missionary zeal to convert to it followers*. At the same time, it is the result of my humble observations, thoughts, experiences, and actions carried on for many years of my life. As such, this integral philosophy-religion fairly well satisfies my needs, quests, and inquiries concerning the *mysterium tremendum et fascinosum*.[3]

My ontology represents a mere variation of the ancient, powerful, and perennial stream of philosophical thought represented by Taoism, the Upanishads, and Bhagavad-Gita, brilliantly analyzed by the Hindu and the Mahayana Buddhist logicians, like great Nagarjuna, Asanga, Vasubandhu, Gotama, Dignaga, Dharmakirti (all of whom lived between the first and seventh centuries A.D.),[4] shared by all branches of Buddhism, including the Zen Buddhist thinkers, and reiterated by the great Muslim thinkers and poets, like Al Hallaj, Al Ghazzali, Rumi, and Abu Said. In the Greco-Roman world this philosophy was developed by Heraclitus and Plato (especially after 385 B.C.), it was partly supported by Aristotle, and with variations it was reiterated by Plotinus, Porphyry, and other thinkers of the Neo-Platonic, the Hermetic, the Orphic, and other currents of thought. In Christianity it was expressed by many Church Fathers, like Clement of Alexandria, Basil the Great, Gregory of Nyssa, Origen, St. Augustine, Pseudo-Dionysius, Maximus Confessor, John Scotus Erigena, St. John of Damascus, and later on by Hugh of St. Victor, St. Thomas Aquinas (in his later period of life), Nicolas of Cusa, and by many Christian mystics like St. John of the Cross, St. Teresa of Ávila, Meister Eckhart, Ruys-

[2] P. A. Sorokin, "This Is My Faith," in S. G. Cole, ed., *This Is My Faith* (New York: Harper, 1956), pp. 212-13.

[3] *Ibid.*, p. 227.

[4] See on this the excellent two-volume work *Buddhist Logic*, by Theodosius Stcherbatsky (Leningrad, 1932).

broeck, Jakob Böhme, and others. Even such rationalist philosophers as Descartes, Spinoza, and Giordano Bruno, and such great scientists as Pascal, Kepler, and Isaac Newton (in his theological works) supported several tenets of this philosophy. It has continued to flow as one of the major streams of philosophical thought up to the present time,[5] in the Western as well as the Eastern world.

My personal reasons for preferring this sort of ontology to those of materialism or other types of ontological metaphysics are integral, that is, based upon a concordant—empirical, logical, and intuitive—body of evidence. Empirically, the inexhaustible manifoldness of total reality and "the reconciliation of opposites" in it are clearly confirmed by our direct, daily experience, as well as by the total evidence of science.

Even in the very limited world of our existence we daily observe the coexistence of the opposite phenomena of motion and the state of rest, of light and darkness, of fulness and emptiness, of health and sickness, of ugliness and beauty, of the true and the false, of A's and non-A's, to mention only a few of the uncountable, contrasting, or opposite sensory phenomena. Our own life is woven of the coexistence of joys and sorrows, hopes and despairs, tensions and relaxations, knowledge and ignorance, achievements and failures, rational and non-rational elements, life and death, conflicts and solidarities, and of thousands of other opposite experiences. Furthermore, the whole life of any of us represents a coexistence of the unchangeable Being—the identity and sameness of our self— and ever-changing Becoming. In this sense we are ever old and ever new, ever the same and ever different at any moment of our existence.

Our direct experience and observations show that the same is true of the life-history of any group, the whole of mankind, and the entire physical and vital universe known to us. Their incessant Becoming or Change coexists with their continuous unchangeable Being: in any change *something in that which changes*—be it physical or chemical or biological or psychosocial phenomenon—preserves its sameness or identity and must remain unchangeable; otherwise we can neither think nor talk of a change of either physi-

[5] See the detailed list of the representatives of this philosophy of mysticism in the Greco-Roman and the Western world from 600 B.C. to A.D. 1920 in *Social and Cultural Dynamics*, II, pp. 639-42.

co-chemical phenomenon A, or biological phenomenon B, or psy-cosocial phenomenon C, or of the whole cosmos X, or of any phenomenon Y that changes. Without the persistence of identity of these A, B, C, X, Y, in their transformations, the very term of change becomes meaningless and empty. To sum up: empirically, our direct observation and experience testify that not only total reality but even its infinitesimal fragment—the limited world of our existence—represents a perennial coexistence of Heraclitus' "every-thing incessantly changes" with Parmenides-Zeno's denial of the reality of change and assertion of the reality of the unchangeable total Being. Empirical reality appears, indeed, as a reconciliation of opposites.

Our daily experience shows, further, that our own continuous change and that of the surrounding world incessantly unfolds *something new* in this reality and that there are no limits to the *new* objects, aspects, events, properties, relationships, uniformities, qualities, and quantities of this reality. In other words, our sensory or empirical experience shows this reality as *infinitely rich and in-exhaustible* in the forms of its Being and Becoming.

This conclusion of the inexhaustibility and infinite manifoldness of total reality is well corroborated by today's science. A rapid increase in discoveries hardly decreases the realm of the undis-covered enigmas of this reality. Each deciphered enigma opens several new undeciphered ones, whether in the field of the in-finitesimally small or macrocosmically big forms of the total Being-Becoming. As science has forged ahead, the smallest units of physi-cal reality have progressed to atoms and from atoms to the "cryptic, arcane, and inscrutable elementary particles" whose discovery opened a set of new enigmas as to their nature, behavior, and re-lationships and as to the still smaller particles or waves of these supposedly ultimate "elementary particles-waves."

Similarly, with the progress of biology an organism was "broken" into organs, the organ into cells, the cell into its parts (for instance, chromosomes), and each of these parts was broken further into its own parts (chromosomes into genes), while genes are now being broken into their component molecules. There seems to be no limit in this progression from the smallest units of living forms to par-ticles smaller still. And again, each new discovery, here, brings with it a set of new undeciphered enigmas to be studied and accounted for. In this sense total reality is "the smallest of the small." Similarly, with the progress of science, the macrocosmic aspect of total reality proved to be "the biggest of the big." From a small, bounded cosmos of the "flat" earth covered by the limited firmament, the macrocosmos has progressively expanded into an ever-bigger and eventually limitless universe with an uncountable number of galaxies and other "heavenly bodies," with cosmic rays, radiations, magnetic fields, and other still little-known and unknown forms of Being and Becoming. Here again each new discovery opened a set of new undiscovered "mysteries."

Despite the ever-increasing discoveries of science, it can hardly exhaust all the enigmas of total reality, nor can it ever reach the point when it can say: "Everything and all is discovered; we fully know the whole plenitude of total reality, and now nothing remains to be discovered." To possess this absolute knowledge, man must become the omniscient God.

These examples of a vast body of *empirical* evidence support the outlined conception of total reality as an infinite X and as a *coincidentia oppositorum*.

Still more clearly, this conception is supported by *logical evidence*. The partisans of hylozoistic or mechanistic or dialectical materialism insist that total reality is Matter while the partisans of objective or subjective idealism claim that ultimate reality is Mind, Spirit, *Geist*, God, or ideal Forms. Claiming such, the partisans of both currents of philosophical thought commit several logical errors in attempting to substantiate their contention. They start their argument with the meaning of *Matter as something radically different from Mind, Spirit, Geist, etc.* (or with the meaning of these as different from Matter). In this confrontation and differentiation, the terms Matter and Spirit have the meaning of two different forms of total reality. Then, when they begin to claim that Spirit or Mind is nothing but Matter in its dialectically developed form, or that Matter is but Spirit or *Geist* in "its otherness," they make these hitherto different categories or different forms of reality identical with each other. By this operation they make each of these categories meaningless and each of these forms of being perfectly empty: If Matter is identical with *Geist* or Spirit, or *Geist*-Spirit is identical with Matter, then, the difference between the partisans of idealism and materialism becomes purely terminological: materialists call the same total reality "Matter" while idealists call it "Spirit" or "*Geist*." Concretely, this can be seen from confrontation of Marx-Lenin materialistic ontology with that of Hegelian objective idealism.

In Lenin's *Materialism and Empiriocriticism,* matter is defined in such a way that if you replace matter in this definition by the Hegelian *Geist,* the definition will fit this *Geist* about as well as matter. "Matter is a philosophical category for a designation of the objective reality given to man in his sensations and perceptions. This reality exists independently from, and is copied, photographed, and reproduced by, our sensations-perceptions." Spontaneous, continuous motion or change is an inherent and inalienable property of this reality. "The World is the eternally moving and self-developing matter." "Its higher form is represented by organic matter." "It contains the potentials of sensations, reflexes, and conscious thought which are actualized in its dialectic development."[6]

This conception of matter differs little from the Hegelian conception of the incessantly and dialectically self-developing objective *Geist* realizing itself in the dialectic process of the *Geist* "in itself," "in its otherness," and "in itself and the otherness" (thesis, antithesis, and synthesis). Since Marx and Lenin accepted practically the whole framework of Hegel's philosophy, we must not be surprised at finding that the difference between the Hegelian "objective idealism" and the Marx-Lenin "dialectical materialism" is mainly terminological. By the different terms "*Geist*" and "Matter," Hegel, Marx, and Lenin designate an essentially identical reality and ascribe to it almost identical properties and a dialectic process of self-realization.

Doing so they and other partisans of materialism or idealism commit the following logical errors: (1) the *contradiction of two propositions*: first, they start with the proposition "Matter is different from *Geist* or Mind" and, second, they replace it with: "Matter is not different from *Geist* or Mind; these are but the same matter in its self-developed realization" (the same contradiction is given in similar propositions of the partisans of idealism); (2) the *confusion of part with whole*: in the first proposition, matter and *Geist* are thought of as a *part or differentiation* of total reality; in the second proposition, they are *identified with total reality*. This contradic-

[6] See V. Lenin, *Sobranyie Sochineniy,* XIV (Moscow, 1928), 117-24.

tion engenders an additional error of the *pars pro toto* in the second proposition. (3) The identification of these two categories in the second proposition makes the terms of matter and *Geist* or Spirit *meaningless*: each of these terms has a meaning only as a category different from the other. When they are identified as the same category ("Matter is Spirit" or "*Geist* (Spirit) is Matter") both terms become meaningless and empty, devoid of any specificity. As any pair of correlative terms, like "father" and "son," they can have meaning only in confrontation or in correlation with each other, when each category maintains its correlative difference from the other. If this difference is eliminated and each category is merged into, or identified with the other, their meaning vanishes and each term becomes completely indetermined and empty of significance. (4) Starting with matter as opposed to and devoid of mind, thought, and spirit, they subsequently "bootleg" in by the back door "life, sensation, reflexes, and conscious thought," asserting that these immaterial forms of being in some miraculous way are developed by matter in its evolution. By this operation the materialists commit again the error of self-contradiction, of "miraculous conception" of "conscious thought" by thoughtless matter, and they make other logical blunders. The same errors are committed by the idealists in their own way.

The conception of total reality as the infinite manifold X is free from these contradictions and errors. Since X has innumerable forms of being, among these it has also material, vital, and immaterial (spiritual) forms with all the immense variety of their manifestations as physico-chemical, biological, and mental (immaterial) phenomena and energies. The immaterial (mental) phenomena and energies are also manifold and manifest themselves in such differentiations as "the bio-unconscious," "the conscious," "the consciously-rational," and "the supraconscious and the supra-rational" energies and forms of being. All these—material, vital, and mental (or spiritual)—forms of being coexist in boundless total reality, interact, and, within certain limits, even transform into each other (as physico-chemical matter transforms into physico-chemical energy, and the latter condenses into matter). The immaterial energy of creative thought "materializes" itself in all the innumerable creations of the human mind—in all the technological gadgets and machines, in all the simple and magnificent buildings, in all the instruments of science, in ritual objects of religion, in all the masterpieces of the fine arts, in brief, in the vast, man-created realm of so-called material culture. And vice versa, the physico-chemical (material) and vital "things" and energies as the means of subsistence (like food) for creative persons and their mental activities are transformed into Beethoven's symphonies, Dante's *Divine Comedy*, Newton's *Principia*, and in thousands of forms which favor and hinder, engender and destroy, effect and transform the whole realm of "material and immaterial culture," the functioning of the mental energies in the human universe, and the life and creativity of human beings.

This integral view of total reality is free from the logical errors of materialistic or idealistic or other ontologies: contradictions, *pars pro toto*, eventual meaninglessness, and a back-door bootlegging of the other category into their matter or spirit. The integral view contains in itself "the principle of complementarity" rediscovered by modern physicists.

Finally, this integral conception of total reality is in agreement with our *primordial* (*"supraconscious"*) intuitions. In its plenitude, total reality is axiomatically thought of as: spatial and spaceless, eternal and temporal, inexhaustible qualitatively, limitless and infinitely divisible quantitatively, in brief, as the infinitude of infinitudes. Its parts and differentiations are finite, but its whole can hardly be thought of as limited, finite, and exhaustible. In one way or another, practically all cosmologies—theological, philosophical, scientific, and poetic—express these views. Some of them ascribe these characteristics to the omniscient, omnipresent, omnipotent, eternal, infinite God or Deity whom they regard as the true reality; others—the materialists—ascribe them to matter; still others to some other "primordial stuff"; but nearly all of the ontologies and cosmologies assume the manifold infinitude of total reality.

This cursory sketch gives an idea of the integral—empirical, logical, and intuitive—reasons underlying my preference for this kind of ontology or metaphysics of total reality. The sketch also gives an illustration of the integral method of concordant testimony of empirical, rational, and intuitive evidence. My preference for this kind of ontology may not, however, be shared by others. For various reasons they may prefer to take its material or spiritual or any other differentiation of total reality for its whole. In doing so they are partly correct so far as their matter or spirit is a real part or differentiation of the whole reality. As I mentioned at the outset, their ontology may suit them better than the outlined ontology of mine. For this reason I do not have any desire to convert them to my metaphysics. Here, as in many other complex fields, everyone has a right to be wise or foolish in his or her own way.

So much for my ontology of total reality.

III. The Integral Cognition and System of Truth

In close connection with the outlined integral ontology stands my integral theory of cognition and of sensate, ideational, and integral systems of truth. Here, again, my theories are not a new discovery but a mere variation of classical theories of this type formulated by great thinkers of China, India, Persia, Greece, Rome, Moslem countries, and those of the medieval and modern West. In black and white the gist of these theories can be summed up as follows: Being ourselves an important part of total reality, we can grasp some of its basic differentiations. Of its innumerable modes of being, three basic forms appear to be essential: (1) empirical-sensory, (2) rational-mindful, and (3) "suprarational-suprasensory," that is, the deepest and highest forms of reality different from sensory and rational forms and directly inaccessible to sensory and rational cognition. This conception does not deny the sensory-empirical form of total reality, but it makes it only one of its three main aspects. Though this "three-dimensional" or integral conception of total reality is only a rough approximation to its innumerable aspects, nevertheless, it is a more adequate approximation than any of the philosophies that reduce total reality either to purely sensory-empirical or consciously-rational or "superrational" modes of being.

In accordance with this three-dimensional cognizable reality stands the three-channeled integral theory of cognition of this reality. In contrast to one-sided theories of cognition which claim that we cognize reality (a) only through sense-perception and observation, or (b) only through rational, logico-mathematical reasoning, or (c) only through "superrational" intuition, the integral theory of cognition contends that we have not one but many ways of cognition and, among these, three basic channels of acquiring knowledge of total reality: sensory, rational, and "supersensory-superrational." The empirical aspect of total reality is perceived by us through our sense organs and their extensions: microscopes, telescopes, radars, masors, etc. The rational aspect or differentiation of reality is comprehended by us mainly through our reason: mathematical and logical thought in all its rational forms. Finally, glimpses of the "superrational-supersensory" modes of being are given to us by the true "supersensory-superrational" "intuition," "insight," "inspiration," or "flash of enlightenment" of all creative geniuses: founders of great religions, sages and giants of philosophy and ethics, great scientists, artists and other pre-eminent creators in all fields of culture. This supraconscious "intuition" or "insight" is different from the sensory and rational ways of cognition. It should not be mixed with Freud's or Jung's or von Hartmann's "unconscious," "subconscious," or "racial memory" as is usually done. While the "supraconscious" lies above the conscious, the unconscious is below the conscious level of mental activity. Though the supraconscious-intuitional mode of cognition and creativity is still doubted by many sensate psychologists and epistemologists, at the present we have a sufficient body of empirical and logical evidence ascertaining its existence and functionings.[7] Its main function is that of a revealer, starter, and supreme guide in the great discoveries, inventions, and creative achievements (small ones are achieved by co-operation of sensory and rational cognition). In this capacity it co-operates with sensory and rational ways of cognition and creation, whose main functions seem to consist in developing and empirically testing the illuminating idea flashed by the supraconscious intuition. All great achievements and discoveries

[7] See an analysis, evidence, and literature on this in my *The Ways and Power of Love*, chaps. v, vi; *Social and Cultural Dynamics*, IV, chap. xvi; under the term of "spiritual insight" it is discussed by E. W. Sinnott in *Two Roads to Truth* (New York: The Viking Press, 1953); as "intuition" in F. S. C. Northrop's *The Meeting of East and West* (New York: Macmillan, 1946); as "inductive leap" in H. Margenau's *Open Vistas* (New Haven, Conn.: Yale University Press, 1961); as the supreme form of mental activity by Björn Sjöval in his *Höjdpsykologi* (Stockholm, 1959); as the Taoist "no knowledge" by R. G. H. Siu in his *The Tao of the Sciences* (New York: John Wiley and Sons, 1957); as "mystical experience" in R. G. Johnson's *Watcher on the Hills* (London: Hodder and Stoughton, 1959). Under different terms the supraconscious is acknowledged by V. Frankl, G. Allport, St.-John Perse, C. Gattegno, R. Assagioli, and many other investigators of human personality, human mind, and methods of cognition and creativity.

are always the result of the unified work of all three ways of cognition and creativity. The truth obtained through the integral use of all three modes of cognition is fuller and greater than that achieved through one of the three channels alone. The history of human knowledge and creativity is a cemetery filled with wrong empirical observations, false reasonings, and cockeyed pseudo-intuitions. In the integral use of all three ways, they supplement, correct, and balance one another. Integral cognition means that we learn about total reality not only from empirical scientists, logicians and mathematicians, but also from great religious and ethical leaders like Buddha, Lao-Tse, Jesus, and from the creative geniuses like Beethoven and Mozart, Phidias and Michelangelo, Homer and Shakespeare.

IV. The Integral Theory of Man and of the Sociocultural World

Integral cognition is particularly necessary in man's cognition of psychosocial and cultural phenomena because the superorganic human world is made up not only of physico-chemical and biological forms of being but especially of the immaterial-unconscious, conscious-rational, and supraconscious-suprarational forms and energies of total reality. An integral view of human personality sees man as an integral being; he is not only a physical object and biological organism but above this he is a rational thinker and doer, and particularly a "supersensory and superrational" being, an active and important creator, an eminent participant in the creative processes of the cosmos. So also is the sociocultural, human universe, created by man. It is the rational and the superconscious in man that give the answer to the ancient question: "What is man, that thou shouldst magnify him?" Franz Kafka's "des Menschen Tiefe ist seine Höhe" ("the deepest in man is his highest") beautifully sums up this point.

Now, we can take, one by one, the questions and criticisms of the philosophical issues raised by the various distinguished contributors to this volume.

V. Reply to Criticisms of My Integral System of Knowledge by Professor Joseph B. Ford and Dr. Daya Krishna

The first and crucial criticism questions the *very possibility of the integral system of truth and the validity of the truth of "suprasensory-suprarational intuition."* Professor Ford and especially Dr. Daya Krishna raise these questions and tend to answer them negatively. Let us glance at their thoughtful analysis and chain of reasoning. Krishna's admirably developed argument is as follows.[8] He accepts the intuitional channel of cognition of empirical and rational realities, and the fact of historical rise and decline of ideational, sensate, and idealistic (integral) systems of truth as well as several other consequences of fluctuation of these systems developed and demonstrated in my *Dynamics*.[9] But he finds the following crucial flaws in my conception of systems of knowledge: (1) He states: "As for the integral cognition, which combines intuitional, sensate and rational elements in a synthesis, he has given no examples of it." (2) He says that my conception of the suprasensory-suprarational intuition and of the ideational system of truth is ambiguous; that it has

. . . two different, if not incompatible, things under the term "intuitive." It may designate the way of cognition that leads to the knowledge of entities of a *particular* sort; *i.e.*, those which are supra-sensory and supra-rational or the way which, while itself being non-sensory and non-rational, may lead to the knowledge of *any* sort of entities whether sensory, rational or supra-rational in their nature. There is a radical difference between the sensory-rational objects of intuitive knowledge and those that are supra-sensory and supra-rational. The intuitive or revelatory knowledge that the world was created five thousand years ago is essentially different in its nature from the intuitive knowledge that there is a supra-sensory, supra-rational reality called God or Brahman or Tao. The

[8] See Daya Krishna, "Pitirim Sorokin and the Problem of Knowledge," *The Indian Journal of Philosophy*, I, No. 3 (April 1960), 175-84.

[9] "P. A. Sorokin's *Social and Cultural Dynamics* seems to be such a definitive work, both in its data and methodology, that most thinkers seem to be afraid of coming to terms with it. Instead of discussion, there is a general evasion of the issues raised by this outstanding work which combines the encyclopaedic exhaustiveness of the data with a self-consciousness about methodology that is rarely met with among sociological thinkers. . . . Sorokin has conclusively shown that over large tracts of time (Ideational) belief was regarded as natural and normal and that there has been no continuous movement from the one [system of truth] to the other but only an alternative fluctuation between them."

object of knowledge in the first case is an empirical state of affairs and has, thus, a *possibility* of being verified through other sources of knowledge. In the second case, however, the *very possibility* of an independent verification is excluded by the designation of the object of knowledge as supra-rational and supra-sensory. The refusal to make any distinction between the two would only lead to great confusion, since the former can be accepted by any scientist with impunity while the latter would *always be irrelevant* for his purposes. . . .

The unitary category of ideational culture should, therefore, be broken into two parts: one part is concerned with truths that are suprasensory and supra-rational; the other, that which is concerned with things empirical and rational. . . . [These] two radically different kinds of objects of intuitive cognition are so incommensurate that they cannot form a logico-meaningfully unified system in any sense of the term.

(3) The intuitional cognition of *empirical and rational* phenomena can be integrated with the sensory and rational knowledge of such phenomena and "modern science with its hypothetico-deductive-verificational method seems, *par excellence*, to be the integral system of knowledge which Sorokin is talking about." But the intuitive cognition of the suprasensory and the suprarational objects can hardly be integrated with the sensory and rational knowledge because the intuitive cognition of the suprasensory and suprarational objects cannot be verified—neither proved nor disproved—by the rational and sensory ways of validation. " 'The triple epistemic correlation' cannot be established between these." Therefore, "the so-called integral cognition is either already achieved in the methods of present-day science or impossible of achievement." (4) From these analyses Dr. Krishna concludes that only "the empirical-rational field of knowledge crosses the classificatory categories of ideational and sensate cultures and that it is *only* with respect to it that a cross-cultural, developmental, integral system of cognition is even possible." Though a system of truth can be built upon the mystic experience, that is, upon the suprasensory and suprarational intuition of suprasensory and suprarational objects, such a system cannot be verified and therefore cannot become a cross-cultural, integral system of cognition.

Such is the essence of the criticisms of my theory of integral cognition admirably formulated by Dr. Krishna and reiterated by Dr. Ford. I can begin my reply to the criticisms by an easy removal of their first objection, namely, that I did not give any example of integral cognition. As a matter of fact, the first two chapters of Volume II of my *Dynamics* give quantitative as well as qualitative analysis of all the main theories of integral cognition from the pre-Socratic period of Greek thought to the period of A.D. 1920, with a fairly detailed analysis of Plato's, Aristotle's, St. Thomas Aquinas', and other important theories of knowledge of the integral type. Then in the Appendices to these chapters (pp. 635-643) there are listed all the names of the Greco-Roman and Western thinkers from 500 B.C to A.D. 1920 who in various forms adhered and contributed to the development of the theory of integral cognition. In the light of these purely factual indications, the statement of the critics that I did not give any example of the integral theory of cognition is obviously incorrect.

As to the subsequent and most important criticisms of Krishna and Ford, they are based upon a somewhat incorrect interpretation of what I mean by suprasensory and suprarational intuition, cognition, and reality. This incorrect interpretation is given by Krishna in the following statement: "The distinction between these different [sensory, rational, and intuitive] ways of cognition thus seems to be based on the different sources of knowledge, *viz.*, sense-perception, deductive reasoning, and intuition, revelation or inspiration. But Sorokin also seems to define, at least ideational culture, by its content rather than by its *organon* of knowledge. The fact, for example, that intuition is 'at the initial phase of creativeness' of a scientific hypothesis would not make it *ideational* for Sorokin's purposes. It is only if the intuition, revelation or inspiration gives a knowledge of supra-sensory and supra-rational kind, such as God, Brahman or Tao, that it is to be called ideational. He seems to have put two different, if not incompatible, things under the term 'intuitive.' "[10]

Perhaps a poor wording of some of my statements gave a foundation for this interpretation of the meaning of the term "intuitive" as covering "two different, if not incompatible, things." Intentionally, however, I meant and mean by the suprasensory and suprarational intuition a specific *way of cognition and creativity* essentially different from the ways of sensory and rational (mathematico-logical) cognition and creativity.[11] The terms "suprasensory and supra-

[10] Krishna, *op. cit.*, p. 178.

[11] "We must not forget that any genuine creation is a real cognition, just as any real discovery is a creation. When Beethoven or Shakespeare or Buddha or Newton

rational" applied to intuition do not mean something "supranatural" or "esoteric" or "mysteriously-mystic," but they simply mean ways of cognition and creativity quite different from ways of sensory perception and mathematico-logical reasoning in all their forms. By "suprasensory and suprarational" forms of reality I mean those forms of it which are either completely or essentially inaccessible for cognition or creative realization through sensory and rational methods alone.

Any idea or pattern of a masterpiece, flashed by intuition, would be intuitive knowledge or creative achievement *regardless of its content.* The *content* of the intuitive flash is not a necessary defining characteristic of intuition. For this reason my understanding of intuition does not cover "two different, if not incompatible, things." Not being one of the *differentia specifica* of intuition, *the content* of cognition or creativity, however, attaches itself to intuitional, sensory, and rational cognition and creativity as a "fellow traveler" typical for each of these kinds of cognizing and creative activity.

Our senses perceive mainly concrete, sensory phenomena and do not perceive abstract relationships, uniformities, and discreet unities. Our rational, mathematico-logical thought, on the contrary, successfully grasps and analyzes these abstract relationships, uniformities, and discreet entities and can hardly perceive the concrete sensory phenomena. The *intuition intuits those forms of being, relationships, and uniformities which are inaccessible or only partly accessible to our sensory and rational apparatus of cognition or creativity.* Being such, the intuited forms and relationships can be called the deepest and highest aspects of total reality (in Kafka's sense, "the deepest in man is his highest"). They seem to be opened to and are grasped only by men of genius, that is, those persons endowed with the grace of intuition at its purest and best.

Illuminated by a flash of intuition, these men of genius conceive —usually "in the twinkling of an eye" and in unexpected condi-

---

or Plato created their artistic or religious or philosophical or scientific systems, they actualized the hidden potentiality existing in reality; they discovered it and disclosed to us what we had not yet seen, heard or known. In this sense any creation is a cognition and discovery just as any scientific discovery is a creation in the sense of actualizing the hidden potentiality in reality, bringing it to light, and thus enriching our knowledge. From this standpoint Newton *created* his law of gravitation, Robert Mayer his law of conservation of energy and so on." P. Sorokin, *Crisis of Our Age* (New York: E. P. Dutton Co., 1941), pp. 106-7.

tions—with a sense of certainty, the first essential idea of their great scientific discovery or important technological invention; of their great religious, philosophical, ethical, political, or social system; and of the pattern of their literary, musical, or other artistic masterpiece so illuminated. Then, through use of their sensory and rational methods, they develop, test, and realize their great intuitional idea or pattern or plan. Any *great* discovery, invention, system, or creative masterpiece is usually started by the illuminating flash of intuition and then developed, tested, and accomplished through co-operation with the sensory and rational methods of cognition and creativity. *Small, pedestrian discoveries and petty creative achievements can be and have been accomplished through a patient and careful use of merely sensory and rational methods;* but these methods are inadequate for accomplishment of truly great discoveries and immortal masterpieces, which open to us the deepest and highest forms of being and becoming.[12]

Besides revealing the deepest and highest forms of being, either in empirical or rational or in still deeper realms of reality, the *primordial* intuitions give to us the ultimate, self-evident verities upon which the whole superstructure of our empirical and rational knowledge (and creativity) is built, including the methods of sensory, mathematical, and logical verification. Such are, for example, the intuitional self-evident truths as: that there is objective reality; that within certain limits it is cognizable; that there are connections, relationships, and uniformities of "coexistence, co-variation, and correlation" among the parts of this reality; that the canons of deductive, inductive, and "seductive" procedures, used in scientific research, can deliver to us a valid knowledge of the properties and relationships of the studied parts of reality, and so on. The primordial intuitions are also responsible for the basic differences between the categories and respective aspects of the reality which we designate by the terms "true and false, right and wrong, beautiful and ugly," and for such concepts as number, time, and space. The concrete contents of these categories, postulates, and axioms may vary but the categories themselves remain the perennial "forms of our mind," the foundations of the whole logico-empirical super-

[12] See the details, the evidence, and the literature about these problems in P. Sorokin, *The Ways and Power of Love*, chaps. v, vi, vii, viii; *Social and Cultural Dynamics*, IV, chap. xvi.

structure of cognition and verification. It is these "primordial" intuitions (many of which concern non-empirical and non-rational forms of being and becoming) that insure and guarantee the validity of all mathematico-logical and empirical methods of cognition and verification, and it is not these methods that precondition the truthfulness of the primordial intuitions. Only retroactively, after being sponsored by primordial intuitions, can these methods be used for testing and finding out which of a legion of various intuitions, daily claimed by a multitude of men and women, are genuine and which are false. Just as there are correct and incorrect empirical observations, true and false mathematical and logical reasonings, so also are there genuine and false intuitions. The methods of logico-empirical verification often help in diagnosing which of numerous intuitions claimed are genuine and which are not.[13]

These considerations about intuitional cognition, creativity, and forms of reality, cognized and created through its grace, answer the main criticisms of Krishna and Ford.

Since the *content* is not the necessary characteristic of intuitional cognition and creativity; since intuitional "enlightenment" has initiated great discoveries and creative achievements in empirical, rational, and "suprasensory and suprarational" realms of reality; and since the terms, "suprasensory and suprarational" mean not something "supernatural" but simply the deepest and highest forms of being, inaccessible to our sense-perception and rational thought, all the objections and criticisms, based upon somewhat incorrect interpretation of my conception of intuition, become disarmed and neutralized, and among these, first of all, is the criticism that I "put two different, if not incompatible, things under the term 'intuitive.' "

I do not think, moreover, that my conception of ideational culture, when properly understood, gives a basis for this criticism. Ideational culture is based upon the intuitional belief that true reality is suprasensory and the suprarational *ens realissimum* called God, Brahman, Tao, the World Soul, Spirit-Mind, and so on. This

---

[13] Generally, we still know little about the intuitional way of cognition and creativity, as well as of the main forms of the intuition. Despite this meager knowledge, we can distinguish between genuine and false intuitions, and among the genuine intuitions we can discern the primordial intuitions with which most normal human beings are endowed, and then the non-primordial ones of various degrees of cognitive illumination and creative inspiration. Men of genius, great discoverers, inventors, and creators seem to be graced by the highest forms of intuition at its purest and best.

belief is accepted by the society of such a culture as absolute truth revealed by the grace of divine intuition, which post-factum can, however, be confirmed but cannot be denied by sensory and rational arguments. The main characteristic of this system of truth and type of culture is exactly the society's belief that the *ens realissimum* can be revealed only through divine intuition, but not through sensory and rational methods of cognition. As to the *content* of this intuitional postulate that the *ens realissimum* is God, Brahman, etc., it is a logical by-product or consequence of this postulate, rather than the specific characteristic of intuitional or ideational truth.

Similarly, from the main postulate of a sensate system of truth and culture that true reality can be cognized only through sense-perception (now and then assisted by rational thought) its logical by-product follows: that the *ens realissimum* and *ens reale* are sensory and largely material. In both systems of truth (and culture) *their contents* are *typical* and logically consistent with their postulates, but the *contents are not the necessary differentia specifica* of each of these systems of truth and culture.[14]

Theoretically, any discovery of an empirical nature, obtained through intuition, makes it intuitional or ideational knowledge and any discovery concerning God, Brahman, and other "supersensory entities," if it is achieved through sensory methods, is sensory truth. Actually, intuitional propositions concerning empirical reality are found in ideational (religious, metaphysical, and theological) systems of truth[15] and culture, although they occupy a *minor* place in them. Conversely, propositions and theories concerning God, Tao, and other "supersensory entities" comprise a *minor* part of sensate (including scientific) systems of truth and culture. Such propositions as comprise a *minor and peripheral part* of each system of truth are *not typical* for the respective systems of knowledge and culture, nor are the contents of their theories.

[14] See the detailed analysis and specifications of ideational, sensate, idealistic, and eclectic systems of truth, culture, and types of mentality, personality, and society in the *Dynamics*, I, chaps. ii, iii, and *passim* throughout all four volumes.

[15] Dr. Krishna acknowledges this by stating that one of three parts of ideational systems of knowledge "consists of those truths which are concerned with empirical-rational states of affairs in the world" (*op. cit.*, p. 181). Still less questionable is the presence of many sensory-rational theories concerning God, the World-Mind, and other "supersensory entities" in scientific *and* sensate systems of truth. Such theories *are* often called by the terms, "philosophy of science," "religion of science," "metaphysics of science," or "first principles of science."

These comments, I hope, absolve me from the sin of putting "two different, if not incompatible, things under the term 'intuitive' "!

The above considerations entitle me also to disagree with the critical conclusions derived by my learned colleagues from their faulty interpretation of my concept of intuition, ideational system of truth, and the terms "suprasensory and suprarational." These critical conclusions are as follows: (1) that no logico-meaningful integration of the intuitional cognition of suprasensory and suprarational entities with the sensory-rational cognition is possible; (2) that intuitional insights concerning suprarational and suprasensory reality are unverifiable by logico-empirical methods; (3) that today's science has already achieved the integration of sensory-rational knowledge with intuitional knowledge of sensory-rational phenomena, and that this integral system of science is the only "cross-cultural, developmental, integral system of cognition ... possible."

Despite their logical elegance, these conclusions are questionable in their validity: first, because Dr. Krishna does not give any convincing—intuitional, logical, or empirical—evidence to support them, and second, because his claim of the impossibility of integration of intuitional knowledge concerning the "suprasensory and suprarational" forms of being with sensory-rational knowledge into one integrated system of truth is sharply contradicted by logical as well as *empirical* evidence. If the integration of sensory cognition with *mathematico-logical and intuitive* cognition concerning the empirical states of reality is possible, why is the integration of these forms of knowledge with intuitional knowledge concerning the "suprasensory" and "suprarational"—that is, the deepest and highest aspects of the reality—impossible?

If their reasons for this impossibility are: (*a*) a profound difference between these forms of cognition, and (*b*) inaccessibility of the "suprarational and suprasensory" realms of reality to sensory perception or to the comprehension of rational thought, these reasons are decisively repudiated by the following relevant facts and reasons.

Perceptions of an empirical object through *different* sense organs (seeing it, hearing it, smelling it, touching it, and tasting it) are quite different from each other and give very different perceptional knowledge of the object. And yet these differences do not hinder unification of the different perceptions into a fuller and more adequate sensory knowledge of the object than that received through only one of the sense organs. This unified knowledge is possible despite profound differences in the perceptions through different senses. Likewise, there is a profound difference between sensory cognition (for instance, sense-perception of "water" or "blue") and rational cognition (for instance, the chemical formula of water, H_2O, or the physico-mathematical formula of the wave length of "blue"). And yet this enormous difference between sensory and logico-mathematical knowledge does not hinder their integration into a fuller sensory-rational knowledge of these phenomena. Nobody as yet has proved that the difference between sensory-rational and intuitional cognition of either empirico-rational or still deeper and higher ("suprasensory and suprarational") aspects of reality is greater than the differences in perception through different sense organs or those between sensory and rational cognitions. If the differences between the diverse sense-perceptions or between sensory and rational knowledge do not hinder the integration of different sense perceptions and sensory-rational knowledge into a fuller unified knowledge of the cognized forms of reality, there is no reason whatsoever for denial of a possibility of integration of sensory, rational, and intuitional knowledge of deeper dimensions of reality into a fuller and more adequate integral system of truth.

The same can be said about the inaccessibility of deeper and higher forms of being to sensory and rational cognition, as an obstacle to the integration of this form of intuitive knowledge with sensory-rational forms into a unified system of truth. An innumerable variety of qualitative aspects of phenomena, perceived through our sense organs, are inaccessible to logico-mathematical cognition of these phenomena. One with the best logico-mathematical mind can compute the exact quantitative formulae of the colors of a "dark-green lawn," of Raphael's "Madonna," and of a "beautiful sunset," or of the wave lengths of the sounds of a "terrible thunder," "soothing lullaby," or of Beethoven's *Missa Solemnis,* or of the bodily changes in the state of "passionate love" or "deadly hatred," but if such a person, being blind, has never seen the dark-green lawn, the "Madonna," or the infinitely rich world of colors and forms, and if, being deaf, one never heard thunder, a lullaby, the *Missa Solemnis,* or others of an innumerable variety of the sensory world's sounds, or if he never experienced "passionate love" or "hatred," he would remain essentially ignorant of the infinitely rich perceptual world of sensory reality. His formulae would give him only quantitative, "dry and lifeless," conceptual knowledge of these multidimensional sensory phenomena. In their sensory form they would remain inaccessible to his logico-mathematical cognition. Conversely, for creatures endowed with most sensitive organs of perception (like rats, bats, dogs, and other animals whose organs of seeing, hearing, or smelling are better than human) but who are devoid of a rational, logico-mathematical mind, the whole rational realm of reality—its *ens reale*, its connections, relationships, uniformities, and values, as well as the whole conceptual, abstract, logico-mathematical knowledge of rational forms of being—would remain inaccessible and unknown. The creatures' senses simply cannot catch this abstractly rational aspect of reality.

Despite this inaccessibility of many forms of sensory phenomena to rational, logico-mathematical cognition, on the one hand, and of many forms of the rational aspects of reality to sense perception, on the other, sensory and rational types of knowledge have nevertheless been successfully unified into a sensory-rational system of knowledge. Why, then, must "suprasensory and suprarational" forms of being, inaccessible to sensory-rational cognition, comprise an insurmountable obstacle to the integration of this sort of intuitional "enlightenment" with sensory-rational knowledge, into one integral system of truth? Until such a demonstration is convincingly given, the objection of my critics remains void. Nobody as yet has demonstrated this impossibility.

So much for the *logical* reasons underlying my rejection of the critical conclusions of Krishna and Ford. Their conclusions are still more clearly contradicted by the *relevant, empirical evidence,* which may be pointed up as follows: First, they are contradicted by the fact of the integration of primordial intuitional knowledge (mentioned above) with the whole superstructure of sensory-rational knowledge built upon these intuitions. Many, if not all, of these primordial intuitions concern suprasensory and suprarational forms of reality. If integration is possible in this truly basic case, it is still more possible in cases of non-primordial intuitions.

Second, the Krishna-Ford conclusions are also contradicted by the fact that the greatest integral epistemologists, like Lao-tze, Plato, Aristotle, and St. Thomas Aquinas, not to mention hundreds of other eminent partisans of the integral system of truth, did not have any difficulty in integrating into their systems all three forms of cognition—sensory, rational, and intuitional—concerning "the suprasensory and suprarational" forms of being. We may accept or reject their integral systems of truth, but even the rejectors have to acknowledge the supremely logical elegance and unity of their systems of knowledge. Contrary to the claims of critics, the very empirical fact that such systems have remained for millennia the greatest epistemological systems in the history of philosophical and even, in part, scientific thought demonstrates—empirically and logically—the possibility and achievement of a logico-meaningful integration of all three forms of cognition into one unified system.

Third, equally questionable is the claim that intuitional propositions concerning suprasensory and suprarational forms of being (differentiated or undifferentiated) are unverifiable by logico-empirical methods. We must remember, again, according to nearly all epistemologists, logicians, and science methodologists, including those who employ methods of logical, mathematical, and empirical verification, that all these methods themselves are based ultimately upon primordial intuitions as the ultimate, self-evident truths.

Since rational and empirical methods of verification are, so to speak, the children of these primordial intuitional "parents," this relationship gives a solid basis for mutual verification of the children by the parents, as well as a retroactive verification of the intuitional parents and relatives by the grown-up sensory-rational children. The relationship also permits the learning of whether the testimony of intuitional parents and children is concordant or discordant. Primordial intuition axiomatically informs me that "I exist" (*sum*); on this intuitional axiom I can build Descartes' logical evidence ("Cogito ergo sum") as well as empirical evidence testifying to my existence. All three reasons concordantly confirm the truth of my existence and mutually reaffirm each other's testimony. If, hypothetically, instead of Cartesian reasoning we would reason that "doubting *everything* I must doubt also the fact of doubting itself; if I doubt the doubt I can hardly be sure that I either think or exist."

This hypothetical reasoning clearly contradicts the primordial intuition of my existence; but the very fact of its contradiction shows, again, that these intuitions can be either confirmed or denied by logical (or empirical) evidence. This means that the intuitional truths can be either in concordant or discordant relationship with the logical methods of verification.

Similarly the genuineness and validity of any intuitional idea concerning sensory or supersensory reality can be verified in many cases by *empirical means of verification*. From time to time I receive letters, articles, or books claiming that their authors have had a mystic union with God or that every word of the article or pamphlet was inspired and dictated by God. In nearly all such cases I do not have the slightest difficulty in seeing the baselessness of the claims of these self-deluded authors. Compared with the essential empirical characteristics and psychosocial "fruits" of a genuine "mystic experience," or with the significance of the idea flashed by a genuine intuition, all the pseudo-genuine "revelations," "mystic experiences," "enlightenments," "discoveries," and "inventions" show themselves devoid of all important characteristics, creativity, and fruitfulness of the genuine experience of this sort. On *purely empirical* grounds, a basic difference can be established between the genuine intuitional "flash of enlightenment," "illumination," "mystic experience," "transfiguration," "conversion," or "revelation"—concerned either with empirical or superempirical aspects of reality—on the one hand, and the simulacra of these real experiences, on the other, including the pseudo-mystic experience induced by psychedelic drugs like mescalin, lysergic acid diethylamide, etc., or by hypnosis, or superficial "transfigurations and mass conversions" occurring after one hour of eloquent preaching, and other "counterfeits" of the real "supersensory and superrational" experiences, discoveries, and creations of founders of great religions and moral systems, of great scientific discoverers and technological inventors, of great philosophers, writers, musicians and artists, up to the eminent inventors of new and constructive forms of social, political, and economic organizations. By their rational significance and empirical fruits the genuine and false intuitional insights show a profound empirical and logical difference from one another.

Fourth, elsewhere I have given a vast body of purely empirical evidence showing that nearly all *great* discoveries and creative achievements in all fields of culture have been started, generated, or "flashed," first, by "the suprasensory and suprarational" intuition and, then, subsequently, have been developed and verified by the logico-empirical methods of verification.[16] A careful empirical study of how *great* scientific discoveries and inventions have been made clearly shows that nearly all such discoveries and inventions, "revealed" first by intuition, have been accomplished through subsequent co-operation of intuitional, logical, and empirical methods of cognition and creativity. The same is true with the creation of the *great* religious, philosophical, and ethical systems, the outstanding social-science theories[17] and masterpieces of literature, music, painting, sculpture, and architecture. All such great achievements have been accomplished, to use Thomas Edison's expression, through "ten per cent of (*intuitional*) *inspiration*" combined with "ninety per cent of [rational-empirical] perspiration." These well ascertained facts of the conception, development, and verification of the great achievements in all fields of culture convincingly demonstrate not only a possibility but an actual integration of all three ways of cognition and creativity incessantly repeated in practically all *great* scientific discoveries and inventions.

Fifth, if we turn from great scientific discoveries to the creation of great philosophical systems, the whole history of philosophy, in its ontological and epistemological parts, testifies to the same fact of integration of—right or wrong—intuitional postulates concerning the nature of "suprasensory" and "suprarational" ultimate reality, the *ens realissimum* and *ens reale*, with logical and empirical evidence confirming the intuitional postulate. Just now it is unimportant to determine whether the intuitional postulate of either idealistic or materialistic or integral ontological system is genuine and adequate; what is important for our argument is the basic intuitional postulate taken as self-evident truth by the respective great philosophers and the fact of buttressing its validity by a long series of logical and empirical proofs. Do not all the partisans of materialism, beginning with Parmenides and Democritus and ending

[16] Cf. my *The Ways and Power of Love*, chaps. v, vi, and my *Dynamics*, IV, chap. xvi.

[17] See on that my "How Are Sociological Theories Conceived, Developed, and Validated," *Social Science*, XXXV (April 1960), 78-91.

with Marx and Lenin, marshal a vast body of rational-empirical arguments to support their "suprasensory and suprarational" entity-matter as the *ens realissimum*? Is not the same true in regard to all idealistic or integral metaphysics, beginning with Plato's, passing through St. Thomas Aquinas' most ingenious "five arguments of natural reason" proving the existence of God, and ending with the contemporary idealistic or integral or even agnostic and skeptical ontological philosophies?

We may disagree with their intuitional postulate about the *ens realissimum* but we cannot deny the fact of integration by all great philosophers of their basic intuitional postulates about the "suprasensory-suprarational" entity with rational and empirical knowledge. Moreover, if their intuitional postulate is accepted, their logical and empirical arguments are very elegant, consistent, and excellently blended with their basic assumption. This integration's steadily going on through the whole history of philosophy, including the history of "philosophical backgrounds of science" or "philosophy of science" or "first principles of science," is convincing evidence that the integration discussed is not only possible but it has been continuously accomplished by practically all great philosophers and many great scientists of the past and of the present.

As for the statement that only "modern science seems, *par excellence,* to be the integral system of knowledge Sorokin is talking about" and that only such a science can be "a cross-cultural, developmental, integral system of cognition," the statement is partly correct, although for its fuller adequacy it needs a few qualifications and supplementations. If we realize that modern science incorporates into its system of knowledge not only logico-empirical but also intuitional verities concerning sensory-rational as well as the deepest and highest "suprasensory and suprarational" aspects of reality, as it certainly does, to some degree; if its methods of verification embrace all three methods, intuitional, logical, and empirical (the method of "the triple epistemic correlation," to use Professor Northrop's terms); and if this modern science endeavors to cognize the deepest and highest realms of being as much as the rational-sensory aspects of total reality, then, indeed, it can become the integral system of knowledge and, as such, can grow into the cross-cultural, universal, developmental system of truth. If, however, it limits its tasks to the cognition of only rational-sensory forms of reality, studied and verified only through rational sensory methods, then, it becomes *not* the integral, but only a partial, somewhat truncated, logico-empirical system of truth.   In that case, religion, philosophy, ethics, and fine arts, cultivating intuitional methods and not dodging the cognition of deeper and higher aspects of reality (inaccessible to logico-sensory cognition), will continue to give a supplementary, intuitional knowledge neglected by a purely logico-empirical science.   In that case intuitional verities of great religions, philosophical and ethical systems, and of fine art masterpieces ("the merry form of science," in Nietzsche's felicitous terms) will continue to be the supplementary cross-cultural systems of truth running parallel with the logico-sensory system of science.

Factually, up to the present time, science, religion, philosophy, and fine arts have occupied a somewhat intermediary position in this respect.   Science now and then has grudgingly admitted the presence of primordial and other intuitional verities in its system of knowledge and has now and then attempted to cognize the "suprasensory and suprarational" forms of reality (in the "first principles of science," "philosophical foundations of science," and "philosophy of science"), but, side by side with this grudging acknowledgment, science has often intentionally denied the validity of intuitional cognition; it has deliberately dodged the task of cognition of the deeper and higher aspects of reality; fairly frequently it has denied the very existence of such aspects, and it has prided itself upon its logico-empirical knowledge, "free of metaphysics."

On the other hand, religion, philosophy, and the fine arts have often neglected to test which of their intuitional insights have been genuine and which have been false; they have frequently failed to verify their "illuminations and revelations" through logico-empirical methods and now and then categorically denied any value of sensory-rational knowledge.   (Recall, for example, St. Paul's "The wisdom of this world is foolishness with God," Tertullian's "Credo quia absurdum," St. Augustine's "Deum et animam scire cupio. Nihilne plus? Nihil omnino," or Hegel's famous reply "the worse for the facts").[18]   This ambivalent state of science, philosophy, religion, ethics, and the fine arts still persists.   For this reason none of these branches of human cognition and creativity in their present state can be regarded as the fully realized three-dimensional integral

[18] See on this *Dynamics*, I, 78-95.

system of truth, nor can any of them claim a monopoly for being the only "cross-cultural, developmental, integral system of cognition," nor that its corpus of knowledge incorporates "the whole truth and nothing but the truth" about total reality.

Each of these disciplines contains and conveys to us some real knowledge and understanding of various aspects of reality and, at the same time, some pseudo-knowledge mistakenly taken for truth at a given moment. This observation is empirically confirmed by three series of relevant facts: first, by the existence of discordant and mutually contradictory philosophical, scientific, religious, ethical, and artistic theories within each of these disciplines; second, by continuous change of the theories, beliefs, postulates, hypotheses, and basic principles in each of these branches of knowledge and creativity; and third, by the fact of our learning about various forms of reality, not from one but from all of these disciplines.

If we carefully examine the total system of science we easily discover in it, side by side with more or less generally accepted propositions, many discordant, even contradictory theories, assumptions, hypotheses, principles, "constructions," and "models," far from universally accepted, concerning the general as well as the special problems of physical, biological, and, particularly, psychosocial sciences. Such a discordance and contradiction *are a sure sign of inadequate scientific knowledge* of the respective phenomena.

Similar discordance and contradiction are found in the fields of philosophy, ethics, psychosocial disciplines, and fine arts. Furthermore, in all these fields many scientific theories, philosophical principles, religious beliefs, and ethical precepts do not remain valid forever but continuously change in the course of time. A scientific theory, or philosophical system, or a religious dogma, for the time being regarded as true, eventually is found to be inadequate and it is replaced by another, supposedly more accurate, theory, philosophy, or belief, which in its turn often undergoes the same cycle of replacement by its successors.[19] If these theories, philosophies, and beliefs were entirely true, such a change would have hardly oc-

[19] See a survey of such change of physical theories of the atom and of the nature of light, biological theories of vitalism, mechanism, abiogenesis, and of evolution, of the changes in the categories of time, space, causality, and number in my *Dynamics*, II, chaps. x, xi, xii; also my *Sociocultural Causality, Space, Time.* See also there the fluctuation of domination of ideational, sensate, and idealistic systems of truth and knowledge. Cf. also on a logic of alternation Kalidas Bhattacharia's *Alternative Standpoints in Philosophy.*

curred; if it has been continuously occurring, these theories, philosophies, and beliefs must have been inadequate and must not have contained the whole truth and nothing but the truth.

Finally, that not only science, but also religion, philosophy, and the fine arts contain and convey to us some real knowledge and understanding of specific forms of reality more easily grasped by each of these disciplines is confirmed by our daily experience. We learn about human personality, psychology, and behavior not only from the textbooks of psychology or sociology, but no less from the tragedies of Sophocles or Shakespeare, from great novels and poems, from philosophical and religious treatises, not to mention our direct experience in self-understanding and understanding of others. We obtain our comprehension of the deepest and highest aspects of reality (or, to use Wagner's expression, of the *universalia ante rem*) not only and, perhaps not so much, from scientific texts as from musical masterpieces of Bach and Mozart and Beethoven, from paintings and sculptures of great artists, from religious and philosophical treatises, from the testimony of genuine mystics, yogi, and saints, and from our direct intuitional encounters with these forms of being. Imagine, for a moment, that our total knowledge is limited exclusively by what we learn from the best textbooks of physical, biological, and psychosocial sciences, and that we remain completely ignorant of all philosophical, religious, and ethical systems and of all fine art masterpieces. Imagine how utterly impoverished our knowledge and understanding of reality would be in such conditions! Think of how completely castrated such a purely scientific culture would be in its cognitive, as well as in its aesthetic, ethical, and other great values!

It is high time to realize that the terms knowledge, cognition, and understanding mean much more than the purely logico-empirical knowledge of logico-empirical forms of being, and that this fuller and greater knowledge means a cognition and understanding of all possibly cognizable forms of total reality, and particularly of its deepest and highest forms, through all channels of cognition and from all sources of knowledge available to man from science, philosophy, religion, ethics, fine arts, and other fields of man's creative and cognitive achievements. At the present time none of these fields incorporates the whole truth and nothing but the truth, and none of them has a fully developed integral system of knowledge at its best.

A systematic development of such an adequate integral system of cognition is an urgent need of our time. Such a system would include in it not only rational, sensory, and intuitive knowledge of rational-sensory realities but also the cognition of "suprasensory and suprarational" forms of reality—the knowledge called "no-knowledge" by the Taoist sages, *prajna* and *jnana* by the Hindu and the Buddhist thinkers, and *docta ignorantia* by Nicolas of Cusa. Development of such a genuine integral system of truth and cognition can greatly help mankind in enriching, deepening, and enlarging human knowledge of total reality, in eliminating the mutually conflicting claims of science, religion, philosophy, and ethics through reconciliation and unification of their real knowledge into one integral system of truth, in stimulating man's creativity in all fields of culture and social life, and in the ennoblement and transfiguration of man himself.

VI. Summary Answers to Other Philosophical Issues

On the basis of the preceding replies to the central philosophical issues of the critics I can now answer briefly the specific points raised by Professor Ford.

First, there is no contradiction between my statement that total reality is inexhaustible and can hardly ever be known in its infinite plenitude and the statement that, nevertheless, many forms of it are cognizable, and human knowledge in its various aspects can increase if the cognitive-creative efforts of man are relentlessly continued. Both statements are quite reconcilable logically as well as empirically. I repeat: it is improbable that the totality of human knowledge will ever reach a point when the best minds can say: "Total reality is now fully known; there remains nothing to be discovered or created." Besides the improbability of reaching such a point, the absolutely full knowledge of total reality carries with it the grave danger of its misuse and abuse by morally imperfect man. Ancient sages symbolically pointed out such a danger. Consider, for example, the significant myth in the Bible, concerning "the tree of knowledge of good and evil" (Genesis, chaps. 1-3), and the story in Greek mythology about Semele's desire to be loved by Jupiter not only in the form of man but in the form of God in his full divine status. The result of such a desire was that Semele was consumed by God's fire. At the present time, when human knowledge is still very far from such omniscience, we already witness this danger of abuse and misuse of knowledge in spectacular forms of the bombing of Hiroshima and Nagasaki and in the gigantic arsenal of nuclear, bacteriological, and chemical weapons for man's extermination of man. In view of the uncertainty of man's reaching absolute moral perfection it is, perhaps, well that absolute omniscience never be achieved by man. Of course, it will remain the supreme ideal goal of man's cognitive efforts and, as such, it will continue to inspire him to acquire a fuller and richer knowledge; but in man's own interest some forms of reality may remain undiscovered and hidden from him forever. It is not often wise to give a child a bomb with instructions to explode it.

Second, there is no contradiction in my statements that total reality has its metarational and metasensory aspects; that some of these aspects can be cognized by intuition; that through the three channels of cognition we can cognize it more adequately than through one of these channels; that intuitional, logical, and sensory cognitions can be integrated into one system; and, finally, that there may be some forms of reality inaccessible to all three channels. As I explained above, the terms "suprasensory" or "metarational" mean not something "supernatural" but simply those forms of reality which are inaccessible to sensory perception and rational cognition, though they are largely open to intuitional insights. These statements are based upon the well-ascertained facts that each of our channels of knowledge can cognize only one of the main forms of reality, but not all its three forms, and that the knowledge derived from each of these channels can be mutually checked and unified into one "three-dimensional" knowledge. As to the statement that there may be aspects of reality which are inaccessible to all three channels of cognition, such a hypothesis is, at least, as probable as the opposite hypothesis of the accessibility of all forms of reality to these three ways of cognition. If we admit the infinite manifoldness of total reality, it is very probable that some of its forms are "closed" to all channels of human cognition.

Nobody has ever proved that man is endowed with an apparatus of cognition that can perceive, rationally grasp, intuit, or learn in other ways all forms of total reality. It is only in regard to those forms inaccessible to and unverifiable by all three ways of verification and in regard to the yet unknown, though potentially discoverable and verifiable realities, that faith appears as a substitute for knowledge. Man has always been speculating and inventing all sorts of beliefs about such realities. But since such beliefs of faith, by definition, cannot be or are not yet verified by the three ways of verification, they cannot be identified with real knowledge and should be regarded as a class of beliefs different from the class of an ascertained knowledge. As such a class, the beliefs have been and will continue to be largely subjective and private possessions of individuals and groups. They have played a most important role in the life, culture, and creativity of persons and groups, but they have little chance to become "a cross-cultural and universal system of knowledge."

Each of us, including the most eminent scientists, has in his mental equipment a notable place occupied by diverse, unverified beliefs based upon faith only. As long as these beliefs are morally, socially, and aesthetically beneficial, as they often are; as long as they do not contradict the verified corpus of knowledge; and as long as they are not coercively imposed by us upon our fellow men, they are one of the great values of human life and culture.

These remarks show that I do not mix knowledge and beliefs based upon faith only, that my system of integral cognition has little to do with ideas and opinions based upon unverified beliefs, and that the proper place for all constructive beliefs is the realm of the "unknowable" and yet undiscovered—though potentially knowable—realities. So much about these questions or objections.

Third, as to "the problem of incompatibility of the consequents as a necessary entailment of the opposition of the premises" (of cultural supersystems) and the ensuing question—"How can we hope for a successful integration (of these incompatibilities) on the level of sociocultural events?"—my answer is as follows: The incompatibility of the postulates and ideas is a symptom of their one-sidedness, of their containing only a part of truth, but not the whole truth. Their incompatibility can be removed by discovery and formulation of more adequate, more true postulates or ideas, that absorb and embrace the true part of each of the hitherto incompatible competitors in a truer, fuller, and larger synthesis. Now and then this task has been achieved by a logico-mathematical and dialectic demonstration that each of the incompatible postulates (thesis) potentially contains in itself its incompatible competitor (antithesis) or for its own adequacy requires the opposite postulate-theory as its "complementary principle." These ways of replacing incompatible "little truths" by a "fuller truth" have always served and will continue to be used for removal of all small—and great—incompatible postulates, ideas, and theories in science, philosophy, and other cognitive fields.

They can also serve the task of replacing the one-sided, incompatible postulates and systems of truth of ideational and sensate cultural supersystems, by a more adequate postulate and system of truth. The integral postulate and system of truth humbly endeavors to serve exactly this task. By embracing the partial truths of ideational, as well as of sensate postulates, giving to each his own, the integral system unifies them into a fuller and more adequate synthesis and thereby removes their incompatibility. The same operation can be used for overcoming all other incompatibilities of sociological ideas and theories. To sum up, if a more adequate theory is not created—empirically, such a failure frequently happens and we cannot logically assume that a more adequate theory can be created at any moment when needed—then the incompatibility of postulates and ideas will continue and result in not only a social struggle of their partisans, but also in fluctuating or alternating domination of competing theories or values which are paralleled, in time, by fluctuating victories of the proponents of varied irreconcilable postulate-theories in their social struggle. "Historical logic of alternation" of one-sided postulate-theories and the argument by coercive means, inevitably, then, take the place of rational resolution of contradictory ideas, postulates, and values.

Assuming that the integral or another, more adequate, postulate and system of truth resolve the incompatibilities of ideational and sensate postulates and systems of knowledge, the removal of the basic theoretical incompatibilities resolves also the incompatibilities of all the secondary theories, ideologies, and values on which the practical incompatibilities on the level of sociocultural events are based. By removing such theoretical incompatibilities, the ground is prepared for actual resolution of corresponding practical incompatibilities. What appeared to be incompatible before become, in the light of a more adequate system of truth and theory, quite compatible and complementary. Thus, for instance, from the standpoint of the integral system of truth, value, and culture the truths of science and religion considered as incompatible from the sensate and ideational standpoints, are quite compatible and complementary, within the cognitively legitimate limits of each of these disciplines; compatible and harmoniously coexistent become also sensate and ideational values and forms of culture as components of the integral system of values and culture, each component occupying its proper place.

From a more adequate—deeper and larger—standpoint, mutually compatible and complementary become also the *main* truths and values (moral precepts and "the feeling of the presence" in the terms of Brother Lawrence) of all great religions while their secondary dogmas, rituals, and mythologies can coexist as mutually neutral appendices to each of these religions.

In the light of a fuller knowledge mutually compatible and complementary become also such seemingly incompatible systems as communism and capitalism,[20] materialism and idealism, religion and atheism, and a legion of other cultural and social movements, systems, and values. From a one-sided, inadequate, narrow, fanatical standpoint, all of these seemingly opposite phenomena have appeared to be incompatible and their apparent conflicts have often led to religious, philosophical, political, and social conflicts and wars. From a more adequate, integral viewpoint, all these bloody crusades and wars have been unnecessary and incapable of solving their superficial incompatibilities. The only resolution of all theoretical—scientific, philosophical, religious, political, economic, and other—incompatibilities is by way of a discovery and formulation of a more adequate and correct theory that overcomes the contradiction of little truths and values by a greater truth and value. The resolution of theoretical incompatibilities serves as the first decisive step for elimination of the corresponding practical incom-

[20] See on that my "Mutual Convergence of the United States and Soviet Russia," *International Journal of Comparative Sociology*, Vol. I, No. 11; in German translation: "Soziologische und Kulturelle Annäherungen zwischen den Vereinigten Staaten und der Sowjetunion," *Zeitschrift für Politik*, 1960, Heft 4.

patibilities based upon the conflicts of the theoretical semi-verities and values.

The next step in the elimination of these practical irreconcilabilities consists in mitigation and elimination of emotional and interest factors involved in the maintenance of the one-sided theories, ideologies, and values. Their theoretical foundation made untenable by a more adequate unifying theory, and their practical effects increasingly becoming disserviceable and harmful for their partisans, these emotional and other irrational forces are bound to be progressively abandoned in favor of the new and more beneficial practices and values dictated by the new and more adequate "truth-value-culture." Such is the general schema of how theoretical and practical incompatibilities have been removed and reconciled in innumerable *rational* solutions of small and great conflicts of postulates, theories, dogmas, ideologies, values, and their social and behavioral practices by individuals and groups. This schema covers also the theoretical and practical incompatibilities of sensate and ideational systems of truth-value-culture and social and personal life.

If the outlined *rational* resolution of the incompatibilities is not available at a given moment—and factually it is often unavailable because a more adequate theory or system of value cannot always be discovered and produced at a moment's notice—then, the unresolved incompatibilities may lead to social conflicts and wars between their partisans. Instead of a rational resolution of their incompatibilities, they try to suppress and destroy their opponents and their "truth-value-culture" by non-rational coercive means, beginning with verbal denunciations and various pressures and ending with bloody wars and revolutions. With a victory of each faction its "truth-value-culture" becomes temporarily dominant and leads, with change of victors, to fluctuation of domination of the competing "truths-values-cultures." For some time each of these factional "truth-value-cultures" can serve the needs of the victors and their societies by the limited creative fund they possess. But eventually this fund is exhausted and the victorious "truth-value-culture" becomes increasingly non-creative and disserviceable for the entire victorious society, including the leaders themselves. Under the increasing attack of its opponents this sterile "truth-value-culture" and its supporters eventually lose their domination and are replaced by the competing "truth-value-culture" and its partisans. And so this struggle and fluctuation of these partial "truths-values-cultures" can go on until either they destroy each other and their partisans or until a truly rational resolution of the incompatibilities is found and implemented in the mentality and behavior of the members of the respective societies and in their cultures.

Such is the schema of the non-rational pseudo-resolutions of the little and great, short-time and long-time, theoretical and practical incompatibilities. In the past, this non-rational method has been continuously practiced and has cost mankind countless millions of human lives, an unbounded ocean of suffering, and a gigantic destruction of all kinds of values and resources. At the present time it is still used on a global scale for elimination of a legion of mostly unimportant interpersonal, intergroup, and international incompatibilities. Its unlimited practice today begins to threaten the very existence of mankind. Observing this dangerous folly of an allegedly "civilized humanity," one can only hope that it will be abandoned before its catastrophic consequences explode over us, and that it will be replaced by the rational method of resolving all sorts of incompatibilities through discovery and creation of a greater system of truth, a nobler system of values, and a better way of social and cultural life in the whole human universe. Such in brief is my answer to the questions or objections of Professor Ford.

Fourth and finally, as to "why an idealistic (integral) system of truth has proved, according to Sorokin's own studies, the least stable of the three main systems of truth," the main reason for this is the same which we observe in such daily phenomena as a comparative instability and poorer survival of fine grass and beautiful flowers *when they are not cared for*, in comparison with crab grass and coarse weeds. The same reason is operative in the so-called Gresham's Law, according to which in the conditions of free circulation the inferior currency tends to drive out of circulation the better currency; or, more generally, the vulgar, inferior values—aesthetic, religious, philosophical, and others—tend to drive out the finer values, *if and when the cultivation of these finer values is neglected.*

The more "refined" and complex is the nature of the value, the more special qualification and training is needed for its use and enjoyment, the less is its spread (diffusion and demand for it) within a limited time in comparison with a value of the same class and cost but much less refined, simpler and demanding fewer qualifications and much less training for its use and enjoyment.[21]

Elementary arithmetic, physics, biology, and psychology are more accessible and known to a much larger part of the population than advanced mathematics, physics, biology, and sociology. The same is true of practically any class of ideas and values. Any fine cultural value, be it a beautiful flower, an important scientific theory, an outstanding invention, a religious or philosophical system, or an art masterpiece, does not fall from the sky like manna, nor does it emerge and appear spontaneously by a mere play of natural forces. Each such value is created by men of genius and talent. Nor can it live and blossom for a long time without continuous cultivation and competent care in contrast to "cultural crab grass and weeds" that can live and spread without any care by the "cultural gardeners." A continuous, creative effort is necessary to insure a long life and luxurious blossoming of practically all great and fine cultural values, theories, and systems.

Meanwhile, in any long-living culture the great creators are not always available to perpetuate its creative growth and to maintain, fertilize, and successfully cultivate its fine garden for an indefinitely long time. As soon as there appears a lack or scarcity of the great creative gardeners and as soon as the careful and competent cultivation of the great gardens of culture ceases, the garden is bound to decline and to revert to the wilderness of cultural crab grass and weeds.[22] By its nature, the integral system of culture is more complex, more refined, and richer in truth-goodness-beauty than the eclectic, sensate, or ideational cultures. For its long life, as *the dominant culture,* it continuously needs the availability of creative integral gardeners and relentless cultivation; and it needs these gardeners and care more urgently than the simpler and less refined eclectic, ideational, or sensate gardens of culture. For this reason the periods of domination of the integral system of culture are liable to be shorter than those of eclectic, or ideational, or sensate cultural systems.

[21] *Social and Cultural Mobility,* p. 622. See on this and related uniformities pp. 620-40.

[22] Something like this is happening in today's "mass-culture": There is a manufacturing of numerous varieties of "intellectual chewing gum and cultural crab grass."

To this reason Professor Ford adds two additional reasons for the comparatively shorter periods of blossoming of the integral system of culture: first, that "the integral systems of the Golden Age in Greece and of the thirteenth century in Europe were imperfect efforts to approximate an integral system"; and, second, that "the conflicting tendencies in them may have led to an early decline and fall, whereas, the one-sided ideational and sensate systems prevailed for longer periods." These three reasons seem to explain satisfactorily the problem discussed.

On the other hand, as regularly happens with great values in all fields of culture, despite shorter periods of domination of the integral system, its great values secure to it an indefinitely long life, virtual immortality, and a most important place among all unified systems of culture. For a period of some 2,500 years, from 580 B.C. to A.D. 1920, in the history of the Greco-Roman and the Western systems of truth, the continuity and influence of the *integral* system of truth are represented by an indicator of 1292 while the indicators for *ideational* and *sensate* systems of truth are respectively 1650 and 1338, and for *skepticism* and *fideism* only 476.[23] Like other great values the integral system of culture may have somewhat shorter periods of its blossoming, but even during the domination of other cultural systems it still continues to live a most vigorous life, only slightly less vigorous than the dominant—sensate or ideational—systems. This means that its creative and vivifying functions are continuously needed by any great culture and by any great society to guard these against extreme one-sidedness and rapid disintegration. Viewed so, the immortality and continuous importance of this system of culture confirm the maxim: *Die Weltgeschichte ist das Weltgericht.*

The above considerations neutralize, to some extent, the critical issues raised by Krishna, Ford, and other scholars in their penetrating analysis of my theory of the integral system of truth and culture. I am grateful to them for bringing to light the ambivalent implications and doubtful points of my theory. I hope, however, that my brief comments will help somewhat to clarify and support the validity of the integral theories discussed. So much for philosophical issues.

---

[23] *Social and Cultural Dynamics,* abridged edition, 1957, p. 255. See there quantitative and qualitative analysis of the movement of different systems of truth in chaps. xiii and xiv.

VII. Civilizations and Cultural and Social Systems

Having replied to the questions and objections concerning my integral system of philosophy, I can now turn to the central issue of integral sociology, cultural morphology, and theory of history. These issues are thoughtfully raised by Arnold J. Toynbee and Othmar F. Anderle in their admirable papers. From the outset it is to be said that there is an essential concordance between some of our philosophical premises (especially those which are formulated by A. J. Toynbee in his *Reconsiderations,* volume twelve of his *Study of History*), between topics of our study, several basic principles and generalized conclusions. Already, in my *Social Philosophies of an Age of Crisis,* I indicated several "areas of agreement" among the theories of Danilevsky-Spengler-Toynbee-Northrop-Kroeber-Berdyaev-Schubart-Sorokin. To these names the names of José Ortega y Gasset and F. R. Cowell should be added.[24]

The first basic agreement of these theories is that in the boundless ocean of socio-cultural phenomena there exists a kind of vast cultural entity, or cultural system, or civilization which lives and functions as a real unity. It is not identical with the state or the nation or any other social group.

The second important agreement in regard to the vastest cultural entities is that their total number has in the whole history of human culture been very small.

The third point of agreement is that *each of these basic types of cultural prototypes is different from the others.*

The fourth similarity consists in that *each of the vast cultural systems is based upon some "major premise" or "philosophical presupposition" or "prime symbol" or "ultimate value" which the supersystem or civilization articulates, develops, realizes in all its main compartments, or parts, in the process of its life-career.* Correspondingly, each of the great cultural unities is either logically or aesthetically consistent in the meaningful aspects of its parts and compartments.

The fifth concordance is that each of these supersystems grounded in empirical reality is either a *meaningful-causal* [or holistic] *unity.*

The sixth point of agreement concerns the *general characteristics of the supersystem or civilization,* namely: (a) its *reality,* different from that of its parts, (b) *individuality,* (c) *general and differential dependence* of its parts upon one another, upon the whole, and of the

[24] See especially Ortega's *Man and Crisis* and *Man and People* (New York: W. W. Norton Co., 1958); F. R. Cowell, *Culture in Private and Public Life* (London: Thames and Hudson, 1959).

whole upon its parts, (d) *preservation of its individuality or its "sameness"* in spite of a change of its parts, (e) *change in togetherness,* (f) *self-directing (immanent) change and self-determination of its life-career* with external forces either accelerating or slowing up, facilitating or hindering the unfolding of the potentialities of the supersystem or civilization, sometimes even destroying it, (g) *selectivity of the supersystem* or civilization, which takes in what is congenial to it and rejects what is uncongenial, (h) *limited variability of each supersystem* or civilization.[25]

Additional similarities of all these theories are: (1) rejection of the linear conception of historical processes as a universal pattern for all historical changes and replacement of such a conception by a multiform one, "cyclical," "alternating," "trendlessly fluctuating," and linear but only for a limited period for some historical processes;[26] (2) concentration of attention upon the repeated uniformities, rhythms, and "cycles" in sociocultural processes instead of a concentrated hunting for various, especially perennial, linear trends of sociocultural "evolution and progress" as it was done in the eighteenth and nineteenth centuries; (3) similarities in the main "phases" in the life-history of "civilizations," "historical prototypes," "high cultures," and "cultural supersystems," and several other concordant conclusions.[27]

[These] agreements are significant and are likely to be valid—for otherwise their authors, so radically different in their basic premises, methodologies, and factual material, as well as in personal mentalities and temperaments, could hardly have arrived at concordant conclusions.[28]

The *differences* between Toynbee's theory of history and Anderle's cultural morphology, on the one hand, and my integral-structural and dynamic system of sociology, on the other, are mainly due to the *difference between the vast sociocultural entities* we deal with, the difference between their "civilizations" and my "cultural supersystems." While at the outset Toynbee and "cultural morphologists" set out to investigate a vast "particular species of society," as an "intelligible field of study," as "a common ground be-

---

[25] P. Sorokin, *Social Philosophies of an Age of Crisis,* pp. 275-79.

[26] It is highly significant that Toynbee in the latest, twelfth, volume of his *Study of History, Reconsiderations* (New York: Oxford University Press, 1961), pp. 144-222, accepts *three* models of the life-course of civilizations: Hellenic, Chinese (alternating), and Jewish, instead of one "cyclical" (Hellenic) model stressed in his previous volumes.

[27] See the details in *Social Philosophies of an Age of Crisis,* pp. 279-322.

[28] *Ibid.,* p. 275.

tween the respective individual fields of action of a number of different people,"[29] I set out to deal with structures and changes of social systems (organized, unorganized, and disorganized social groups), of cultural systems and congeries, and particularly with the vastest cultural supersystems.

In order to deal fruitfully with these exceedingly complex phenomena, I had to construct a systematic and fairly precise theory of the componential structure of sociocultural phenomena generally; then I had to distinguish clearly five main forms of relationships of sociocultural phenomena to each other: (1) mere spatial or time adjacency, (2) indirect causal relationship, (3) direct causal-functional relationship, (4) pure meaningful relationship, and (5) meaningful-causal relationship. In so doing, I defined as social or cultural systems only those groups or cultural configurations which are either causal or consistent-meaningful or causal-meaningful unities with tangible interdependence of important parts upon one another, parts upon the whole, and of the whole system upon its parts. Thus, by definition, all social and cultural phenomena which are merely adjacent to each other or loosely connected by indirect causal relationships with one another were excluded from the class of the *real* social or cultural systems. This point reached, I proceeded further to study in detail the necessary characteristics of all causal-meaningful organized social groups, in contrast to the unorganized and disorganized ones, and of all cultural *systems* in contrast to cultural *congeries*. The result of such a study was the following definition of an organized social group (system): "A social group, as a totality of interacting individuals, is organized when its central set of meanings and values, as the reason for their interaction, is somewhat consistent within itself and assumes the form of the law-norms precisely defining all the relevant actions-reactions of the interacting individuals in their relationship toward one another, the outsiders, and the world at large; and when these norms are effective, obligatory, and enforced in the conduct of the interacting persons." Unfolding this definition I enumerated fairly precisely six empirical characteristics of all organized social systems or groups.[30]

In a similar manner a cultural *system* is defined as a logically

[29] A. J. Toynbee, *Reconsiderations*, pp. 284 ff.
[30] *Society, Culture and Personality*, pp. 70-92.

or aesthetically consistent set of meanings-values-norms in contrast to cultural *congeries* as a pile of meanings-values-norms either neutral or contradictory to one another. Beginning with the simplest propositions like "A is B" or "Two and two make four," and passing through the vast systems of language, of science, of religion, of philosophy, of ethical and law codes, of fine arts, and of a consistent style, and ending with the vastest cultural supersystems that articulate in all compartments of culture their ultimate premise concerning the nature of true reality, such—small and vast—cultural *systems* differ sharply from cultural *congeries*. Cultural systems or sets of consistent meanings-values-norms exist either in purely *ideological forms,* not rooted in overt behavior, social institutions, and material vehicles of persons or groups, or in *behavioral-material forms* which are manifested in overt actions-reactions of individuals and groups and are objectified in material forms of buildings, books, laboratories, instruments, pictures, sculptures, cult objects, and so on.

On the basis of these concepts I developed a systematic "structural anatomy," "taxonomy," "physiology," and typology of life-courses of the main social and cultural systems and especially of the vastest cultural supersystems.[31]

I have allowed myself to bore the reader with this brief outline for two reasons: first, to make clear that my study of the supersystems is an organic part and logical consequence of my systematic theory of sociocultural phenomena, generally, and of social and cultural systems in their structural and dynamic aspects, particularly; and second, to make comprehensible why I had difficulty in placing "civilizations" among the main classes of sociocultural unities: Is civilization an indirect causal or direct causal-functional or meaningful or meaningful-causal unity? If it is none of these unities, then, what sort of unity is it? Is it, in my terms, an organized vast social system (group), or is it a vast cultural system or a unity of both? After a careful analysis of the concept of "civilization," brilliantly sketched by Danilevsky and Spengler and magnificently developed by Toynbee, not to mention other "cultural morpholo-

[31] This systematic development of my integral system of sociology is given in my *Society, Culture and Personality, passim,* and a most detailed analysis and life-history of the supersystems is presented in four volumes of my *Social and Cultural Dynamics.*

gists," I made the following diagnosis of it in terms of my categories:

i. Most of these "civilizations" seem to represent, primarily,
important *social groups* with a central set of cultural meanings-
values-norms because of which, for the sake of which, and around
which these groups are organized and function. (Any organized
group has such a central cultural set or system.)

ii. In my classification of organized groups, some of these "civilizations" seemingly are *language or ethnic groups* whose members
are united into a real collectivity by a community of language,
territory, and ethnic culture resulting from living together on the
same territory and often having common ancestors (real or mytho-
logical); other "civilizations" are *territorial-state groups* united by
belonging to the same state within its territory and by a respective
set of cultural meanings-values-norms-interests resulting from membership in the same territorial-state group; still other "civilizations"
are mainly *religious-state-language groups;* and there are even other
"civilizations" that represent a still more complex *"multibonded"*
group with its complex central set of cultural meanings-values-in-
terests or configurations. In other words, "civilizations" represent
not the same class but different kinds of organized social groups that
have played an important part in human history and in the socio-
cultural world.

iii. Each of such organized groups with its culture makes up
the core of each of the "civilizations." Besides this main group,
each "civilization" contains one or more "alien groups" with their
own "group-culture" different from the central culture of the main
group. These "alien groups" live in the given "civilization" but they
are not an organic part of it, nor is their group-culture necessarily
consistent with the central culture of the main group. Then, each
"civilization" is connected mainly through indirect causal relationships with several "outside groups" and their "group-cultures" which
enter the total culture of "civilization" as congeries.

iv. Considering the fact that the *total* culture of practically every
social group comprises not one cultural system uniting into one
consistent whole millions of meanings-values-norms-interests of its

members, but a multitude of ideas-values-interests-aspirations-precepts that are partly neutral, and partly even contradictory to one another, it is fairly certain that the *total culture* of each civilization contains, side by side with the central cultural system of its main group, a multitude of different, partly neutral, partly contradictory, cultural systems and congeries.

v. On the basis of this diagnosis I made certain criticisms of a number of specific points in the theory of civilizations of Danilevsky-Spengler-Toynbee.[32] Since their "civilizations" and my "cultural supersystems" happen to be fairly different "entities," it is understandable why our views disagree at a number of points. The really surprising thing is, however, not the presence of these disagreements but the presence of far more numerous agreements concerning essential problems of our study.

vi. My criticisms of Danilevsky-Spengler-Toynbee are answered by Dr. Anderle's counter-criticisms. Let us begin with the main points of Anderle's counter-criticism:

a. His first defense of the unified, "holistic" structures, "civilizations," comprises a reference to supposedly modern theory of *Ganzheiten* (wholes) as it is developed in psychology by von Ehrenfels, Köhler, Sanders-Volkelt, Wellek, Netzger, Wertheimer, Koffka, Katz, and Lewin; in biology by Driesch, Bertalanffy, Troll, Portmann, and others; and in philosophy and sociology by Spann, Friedmann, and Burkamp. I do not have any quarrel with the method of the holistic morphologists of grasping and understanding each of the *Ganzheiten* first as a whole, in its totality, with its holistic characteristics. But I find it difficult, practically impossible, to apply their diagnostic criteria of the concrete and compact *Ganzheiten* to the discontiguous, discrete, non-compact cultural com-

---

[32] See for this criticism my *Social Philosophies of an Age of Crisis*, chaps. iii, iv, v, and xii; my *Society, Culture and Personality*, pp. 638-44. My criticisms in no way prevented me from a very high estimation of their works, expressed in these terms: "a brilliant treatise on the philosophy of history and cultural sociology and an unusually shrewd and correct piece of prognostication and prophecy" (about Danilevsky's work); "extraordinary rich and idea-laden masterpiece" (of Spengler's *Decline of the West*); "he clothes his theory in a rich and full-blooded body of facts. . . . The main theses are painstakingly tested by the known empirical facts of the history of the twenty-one civilizations studied. The work as a whole is a real contribution to the field of historical synthesis" (of Toynbee's *Study of History*), *Social Philosophies of an Age of Crisis*, pp. 71, 112, 120.

plexes and social groups. Some of these characteristics such as "systematic unity," "logical and ontological articulation," "super-summativity," and "independence" of the *Ganzheiten* are really not diagnostic criteria of the *Ganzheiten* that can help to distinguish the *Ganzheiten* from the non-*Ganzheiten* but mere synonyms for that word. As such they cannot help in finding out which con-glomerations of various sociocultural phenomena are *Ganzheiten* and which are not. Other diagnostic traits, such as distinguisha-bility of *Ganzheiten* from their environment, transposability, and non-interchangeability of parts, are either inapplicable to dis-contiguous, discrete, and largely "immaterial" cultural systems and congeries, social groups and conglomerates of populations, or they are wrong criteria of the *Ganzheiten*. How, for instance, can mathematics, or an idealistic system of philosophy, or Romantic music, or communist and capitalist ideologies, be "distinguishable from environment" (and what kind of environment) or, how can they be "transposed" (and in what kind of space)? And if these operations can be carried out in some way, they can be carried out even more easily with a heap of numbers, or an eclectic philosophy, or cacophony of musical sounds, or an incoherent pile of various ideas and notions. How, on the basis of these criteria, can we iden-tify in the ocean of human population such non-territorial discon-tiguous groups as the International Sociological Society, or the Roman Catholic church, or the British Empire, whose members are scattered all over the world? And if in some way we found these organizations, would not these criteria induce us to take as real *Ganzheiten* such pseudo-unities as the adjacent populations living on the boundary of two or more different states, or the population of a big apartment house, though their members do not belong to the same state or the same social groups? These simple questions show that these criteria of the *Ganzheiten* do not help us much to distinguish a multitude of real cultural and social systems from the unintegrated cultural and social congeries.

Finally, the characteristic of non-interchangeability of parts is largely a wrong characteristic of *Ganzheiten*. In most of the mechanical *Ganzheiten*, like automobiles, all parts are interchange-able and replaceable by new ones; and even in biological organisms experienced surgeons are replacing and transplanting some parts from one organism to another. Similar interchangeability (in the form of "substitutes," imitations, borrowings, and acculturations) within certain limits, takes place not only in congeries but also in many social and cultural systems.

The moral of these remarks is that these diagnostic criteria for distinguishing the *Ganzheiten* from the non-*Ganzheiten* are rather useless in the field of sociocultural phenomena. My own system of finding, identifying, and distinguishing the real social and cultural unities from nominal social groups and cultural congeries, through analysis of their meanings-vehicles-human members, through "meaningful induction" and additional characteristics of organized social groups and cultural systems (ideological, behavioral, and material),[33] appears to be simpler, more precise and adequate for this purpose than the Ehrenfels-Kohler-Volkelt criteria, which were devised not for the sociocultural but for the psychological field.

To sum up: Dr. Anderle's defense of the *total* unity of "civilization" by reference to these (not modern at all) "morphological criteria" of *Ganzheiten* does not prove his point.

b. Neither do his remaining arguments substantially disarm and neutralize my other criticisms. Despite his valiant defense of the unifying role of Spengler's "prime symbols" of civilizations, Anderle does not give any proof that the prime symbol of stone unifies into one consistent whole the total culture, that is millions of ideological, behavioral, and material cultural systems and congeries of the Egyptian civilization; nor that the *Ursymbol* of "the sensuous individual body" does this in regard to the Greek ("Apollonian") civilization; nor that "pure limitless space and voluntarism" does it in

---

[33] This "meaningful induction" comprises a method suggested by the following questions: (1) Is a given complex of meanings-values-norms logically or aesthetically consistent? (2) Is it objectified in material vehicles and, if so, what are they? (3) Does it have its human agents who profess it ideologically, practice-enjoy-use it in their behavior and life and incorporate it in their "material culture"? (4) If so, exactly in what forms and activities?

For finding out whether a given group of individuals is an organized group (social system), or an "as if organized," or "unorganized," or "disorganized" nominal plurel, the presence or absence of a consistent set of meanings-values for whose realization the group is organized, and especially presence or absence of law-norms regulating the behavior and relationships of its members, are the main keys answering the problem. Additional criteria indicated in my work make the solution of the problem clear and decisive. Here, again, these "keys and criteria" are much more precise, serviceable, and reliable than the criteria of cultural morphologists. See a detailed analysis of these problems in my *Sociocultural Causality, Space, Time*, pp. 79-90 and chaps. i, ii; *Society, Culture and Personality*, chaps. vii-xv and pp. 638-39; *Dynamics*, IV, 423-39; and *Fads and Foibles in Modern Sociology*, pp. 268-78.

regard to the Western (Faustian); nor that "the cavernous, vaulted eternal space and the cavern-feeling" does it in regard to the Magian civilization. Any one of these prime symbols is chosen arbitrarily and a few impressionistic associations that Spengler tries to build around them neither logically nor meaningfully are necessarily connected with these prime symbols. Instead of stone one can, perhaps, with greater reason take the sun, boat, Apis, or dozens of other symbols which played an important role in the Egyptian religion, morality, mythology, and fine arts. And why is Greek civilization called Apollonian but not Zeusian or Dionysian, or Athenian, while the Western is called Faustian, a symbol which, if anything, does not fit the medieval Western culture at all and represents the modern culture of the West in no way better than the symbols of Don Quixote or Macbeth or Hamlet or dozens of other literary types? Likewise, why cannot Platonic "ideal forms" serve as the prime symbol of Greek civilization, or "the sensuous individual body" for the sensate period of Western civilization so strongly stamped in all compartments exactly by the sensuous body, libido, materialism, sensuality, hedonism, and other characteristics related to it? These and many other "prime symbols" can be chosen with as much intuitive, logical, or empirical foundations as any of the Spenglerian "prime symbols." I am reasonably certain that no logician or historian can demonstrate meaningful or causal relatedness of millions of cultural phenomena of the *total* culture of each of the civilizations to Spengler's prime symbols and, still less, show a real unification of these phenomena into one consistent whole.

c. The same is true in regard to the meaningful or causal-functional interdependence of all the millions of sociocultural phenomena found in each of these civilizations. Stating this, I do not mean a strictly "mechanical causality" but a much more embracing and "elastic" "meaningful causality" that includes also *causa efficiens* and most of the six Aristotelian forms of cause-effect relationship.

In several of my works I repeatedly indicated the insufficiency and often inapplicability of "mechanical causality" in a study of sociocultural phenomena. J. S. Mill's inductive rules must, it seems, be modified considerably in their application to the study of causal relationships between sociocultural phenomena. The meaningful character of these often permits one to establish with reasonable certainty the existence of a causal relationship by a "short-cut" method of ascertaining meaningful relatedness between two or more phenomena, and then of factual contact between them. On the other hand, a strict application of either method of identity or difference, or of concomitant variation, is rarely possible in sociocultural phenomena because in their appearance they are radically different and rarely give the necessary number of identical repetitions of the same variables. If we had not known what the Catholic Church was meaningfully, we should never have been able to connect causally all the manifestations of the Catholic sociocultural system: from the phenomenon of a missionary activity in China to the support of the Polish London government, creation of five new American cardinals, and thousands of other—externally quite different—manifestations of the Catholic system. . . . No Mill's method would be able to disclose to us this relationship. Many of the social scientists seem to be still unaware of this and of other differences in the discovery and establishment of causal relationships between the purely biophysical phenomena, devoid of component of meaning, and sociocultural phenomena.[34]

None of the eminent theorizers of civilizations has demonstrated how the causal interdependence in this larger sense of causality of all the millions of sociocultural phenomena of the total culture of each civilization is made up, and I doubt that any "morphologist" can do that. As mentioned above, meaningful-causal interdependence can be found among the main parts of what I called "the core" of each civilization and direct causal and indirect causal ties among several peripheral parts of it. But the core and these parts make up only a portion of the total civilization. Its other portion consists of a multitude of mutually neutral or even contradictory systems and congeries.

d. The lack of unity of the *total* culture of each civilization and heterogeneity of the social groups covered by this term do not give a clear, objective foundation for finding out which of the innumerable social and cultural systems in the ocean of human population are "civilizations" and which are not. This explains why the identifications, classifications, and number of "civilizations" by Danilevsky, Spengler, Toynbee, and other morphologists are quite different. What for Danilevsky is one (Assyro-Babylonian-Phoenician-Chaldean-Semitic) civilization, Toynbee treats as three or four different (the Babylonic, the Hittite, the Sumeric, and possibly the Syriac)

[34] *Society, Culture and Personality,* p. 638; see a development of this in my *Dynamics,* IV, chaps. iv, vi, vii; *Sociocultural Causality, Space, Time,* chaps. ii, iv; *Fads and Foibles,* chap. xi.

civilizations, while Spengler divides it into two civilizations. What for Spengler is one civilization—the Magian—Danilevsky considers as two and Toynbee as four different civilizations. Even more, as a great scholar, Toynbee did not hesitate to revise substantially his own list of civilizations as it was given in the previous volumes of his *Study of History* and to replace it, in his latest volume, by a notably different list of civilizations—different in number, in name, and in the classes of civilizations.[35]

Faced with this discord among the theorizers of civilizations, Anderle admits that some arbitrariness is inevitable in this matter; but in spite of his valiant efforts to persuade us and insist upon the unity of civilizations, he hardly succeeds in this task; a mere complaint about its difficulty is not a valid argument proving his point. If "civilizations," except their "core," are not meaningful-causal unities, and if their central social groups are different in different civilizations, then arbitrariness and discord in identification and classification are expected to continue.

e. No more convincing is Anderle's next argument against my position that civilizations of the Danilevsky-Spengler-Toynbee varieties represent social groups rather than cultural systems and that the social groups, covered by the same name of "civilization," are really heterogeneous in various civilizations (now ethnic, now state, now religious group, now nation, now various "multibonded" groups). For this reason, they should not be put into the same identical class of "civilizations." The argument of Dr. Anderle consists in a somewhat vague statement that "the social groups corresponding to the 'cyclical' cultural systems (civilizations) are by no means heterogeneous. We only lack a common name for them. It is our categories (classifications of social groups) which are insufficient and misleading." This statement applies, indeed, to "cultural morphologists": they have hardly any systematic "structural anatomy" and "taxonomy" of social groups. The same cannot be said about several sociologists, including me. Some two hundred pages of my *Society, Culture and Personality* are devoted exactly to this problem. There I have given a systematic analysis and "taxonomy" of all powerful "unibonded" and "multibonded" groups,

[35] Toynbee, *Reconsiderations*, pp. 540-61. Generally in that volume Toynbee revises a number of important points of his theory as it has been developed in preceding volumes of his monumental work.

including such "multibonded" groups as "clan," "tribe," "nation," "caste," "feudal order," and social class.[36] In the light of this classification, we can see with glaring clarity, the lack of analysis by the "civilizational morphologists" of the kind of social groups that make up a human substratum of civilizations, as well as a heterogeneity of social groups they cover by the term "civilizations." For this reason, this argument of Anderle does not really answer my criticism.

f. Moreover, I do not think that Anderle has successfully disposed of my other criticisms of morphological theories of civilizations, namely: (i) that they inexcusably mix cultural and social systems; (ii) that with their unwarranted assumption of the total integration of civilization, Danilevsky and Spengler wrongly contend that there is a total disintegration and death of all civilizations; and (iii) that the Danilevsky-Spenglerian life-cycle of civilization, with its phases of birth-maturity-senility-death, is in no way a universal model of the life-courses of all organized groups and cultural systems.[37]

Anderle admits, to some extent, the validity of these criticisms, but he still tries to salvage the unity of civilizations. Unfortunately, he does not give us any convincing and significant empirical, logical, or intuitional evidence to support his contentions. Nearly all of his arguments consist in purely dogmatic assertions, suggestive analogies with the unity of personality, and in references to a few neither very authoritative nor "modern" books in psychology and political science. In addition, some of his arguments are based upon a somewhat incorrect interpretation of my views and lack consideration of fairly precise generalized conclusions in these fields.

Instead of taking up, point by point, Anderle's counter-propositions concerning these problems, I shall simply sum up my views in these matters by quoting a few paragraphs from my works. The quotations give—directly or by inference—my answers to the problems discussed.

One of Anderle's main arguments consists in ascribing to me not only a rigorous distinction between cultural and social systems (which is correct) but also an exaggeration of this distinction to a

---

[36] See chaps. ix-xiv, inclusive, in my *Society, Culture and Personality*.
[37] See these criticisms in my *Social Philosophies of an Age of Crisis*, chap. xii.

degree that "Sorokin . . . does not even wish to admit their over-lapping." After assuming the validity of his judgment which in-correctly alleges this exaggeration, Anderle tries to demolish my criticisms of the unity of civilizations. But anyone who wishes to get my actual views on this point need only go to my *Society, Culture and Personality*, where I have stated:

. . . an integrated cultural system in each and all three (ideological, behavioral, and material) levels, and an organized social group, are not identical unities. *Only in part do they coincide and overlap, namely, insofar as any organized group has a set of meanings, values, and norms as the raison d'etre of its existence; and this set must be and usually is integrated in the bulk of its meanings, especially in its law-norms, and in the respective actions and vehicles of the group enforced by it.* Except for this set . . . an organized group and cultural system are different unities, having different boundaries, even within the same population.[38]

In the light of this quotation nearly all of Anderle's counter-criticisms become largely void. On the one hand, there is not the slightest doubt that each organized group, and still more such vast sociocultural fields as "civilizations" have, besides their cultural system which is the *raison d'etre* of their existence and activity as an organized group, a multitude of other cultural systems and con-geries, partly neutral and partly contradictory to each other and to the "core systems." On the other hand, nearly all great cultural systems (like mathematics and other sciences), languages (like English), great religions or philosophical systems, great technologi-cal inventions (domestication of fire and animals, elements of agri-culture up to the steam engine, electricity, the airplane and nuclear gadgets), great law codes (like the *Corpus Juris Civilis*), art masterpieces, and even such cultural objects as whiskey, lipstick, television or radio, spread over, are taken in, and become an integral part of the total cultures of numerous and heterogeneous social groups. From this difference several other differences in the life spans and life careers of cultural and social systems follow.[39]

Contrary to the Danilevsky-Spengler-Anderle statement that each civilization is a closed system whose culture cannot be trans-mitted to other kindred systems, a multitude of cultural systems

[38] P. 335. See there also the development of, and evidence for, these statements, pp. 335-41, and *passim*.

[39] See on difference of life spans and life careers of social groups and cultural systems my *Society, Culture and Personality*, chaps. xxxiv, xlvii.

can and do migrate and get transplanted from the culture of the group or person that created them to the cultures of many other groups and persons. Again, contrary to their claim that with the disintegration or death of the creator-group or person their cultural system dies also, great cultural systems as a rule do not die with their creators, but with or without some modification they continue to live a vigorous life in many total cultures of numerous heterogeneous social groups.

I happened even to formulate several generalized propositions which fairly precisely and correctly define under what conditions any cultural system can be transmitted from group to group, person to person, and "civilization to civilization," and how much such a system may be expected to change in the process of this transmission and in rooting itself as an integral part in the culture of its immigration.

Here are two main uniformities:

When a cultural object or value—be it a simple element or a cultural complex or system—moves from one cultural center to another, (a) it may remain essentially unchanged if the culture of its immigration is similar to the culture from which it departed; (b) it changes if the cultures of immigration and departure are different; and the greater the contrasts between these, the greater the transformation of the migrating cultural value or system in the process of its migration and incorporation into the culture which it enters; (c) if the cultures of departure and of arrival are profoundly different, certain cultural systems of the first cannot penetrate and be rooted in the second culture at all. Even cultural congeries absolutely uncongenial to the culture of immigration find enormous difficulty in rooting themselves in a new culture.

If we hold the difference between two cultures constant, then the magnitude or profundity of the transformation of the migratory cultural phenomenon depends upon its nature, especially in cultural systems and particularly upon the degree of its complexity, delicacy and intricacy. Other conditions being equal, the more complex, refined, and intricate the cultural system is and the greater ability, qualification and training it requires for its adequate understanding and use, the more profoundly it transforms in the process of its passage from culture (or person) A to culture (or person) B, and in that of its infiltration and incorporation into B.

These propositions are applicable to and valid for migration of cultural phenomena from person to person and from group to group, as well as from civilization to civilization, in both horizontal and vertical migration of cultural congeries, complexes, and systems.[40] These propositions seem to define the problems discussed more precisely and adequately than Danilevsky-Spengler-Anderle do.

g. As to their "universal" model of the life-cycle of civilizations with its analogical organismic phases of birth-maturity-senility-death, it is correct only in regard to minor portions of organized social groups and cultural systems. Life courses of social groups and cultural systems are exceedingly multiform and their life spans fluctuate between the durations of a few minutes, days-months-years, up to the durations measured by centuries, millennia, and virtual immortality.[41]

In regard to different life courses of civilizations, I now have a powerful ally in the great scholar of civilizations, Arnold J. Toynbee himself. As I mentioned earlier, in his latest, twelfth, volume of *A Study of History: Reconsiderations*, he admits and excellently documents, not one, but *at least three* different models of life courses of civilizations.[42]

h. The final argument of Anderle for the unity of civilization is his reference to the holistic psychology which "describes personality" as "a well-integrated whole, . . . distinct from its surrounding, unified into a system, articulate, interdependent, supersummative, . . . self-regulative, . . . 'stylistically' determined, 'a form, die-cast but alive and developing'. . . . Individuals are integrated holistically in their psychic-spiritual makeup, insofar as they are normal."

As *biological organisms*, endowed with integrative functions of their nervous system, human individuals are certainly causal-functional unities in which any important part of the organism depends upon other important parts, each part depends upon the whole organism, and the latter depends upon its important parts. Quite different things, however, are human individuals in their "psychic-spiritual makeup," and in the structure and content of their total mentality. In the total mentality-structure of normal individuals we can distinguish at least four different forms of mental energy and levels of activities: "(1) the biologically unconscious (subcon-

---

[40] See details, analysis, and evidence for these and other uniformities in the field of mobility, diffusion, and transformation of cultural phenomena in my *Dynamics*, IV, 252-53, and chap. v, reproduced in my *Social and Cultural Mobility*, pp. 549-640.

[41] See an analysis and typical durations in *Society, Culture and Personality*, chaps. xxxiv, xlvii; *Social Philosophies*, chap. xii.

[42] A. J. Toynbee, *Reconsiderations*, pp. 170-222.

scious); (2) the biologically conscious; (3) the socioculturally conscious; and (4) the supraconscious. Figuratively speaking, man appears to be a sort of four-story building, instead of the two- or one-story structure depicted by the prevalent psychological theories."

In nearly all normal individuals there is some conflict between and among these forms of mental energies, their urges and imperatives, their drives and activities. Only individuals whose supraconscious and socioculturally conscious centers are in mutual harmony and together completely control the unconscious and biologically conscious parts of their mentality and behavior can be regarded as completely integrated persons. The majority of ordinary human beings do not reach this high degree of integration and therefore are subject, in different degrees, to inner conflicts due to the conflicts or urges, drives, wishes, and imperatives of these four forms of mental energy incorporated in the human individual. Even more, different urges of the same level or form of energy (for instance, sex and hunger of the biologically unconscious and conscious) are often conflicting with each other. The same is even more true of the socioculturally conscious level of mentality. Here, every individual has as many and as different "egos" or "roles" as there are groups of which he is a member. And if these groups are mutually antagonistic, then respective sociocultural egos in the individual also become antagonistic, resulting in a corresponding inner conflict in the individual. Only when all sociocultural and biologically conscious egos (or roles) in the individual are mutually harmonious and urge him to the same actions and line of conduct, and only when all these egos are subordinated to the supraconscious, only then is the individual at peace with himself, with all his egos, conscious and unconscious biological drives. Such a "peace that passes all understanding" or such a complete integration is achieved as a permanent state of mind only by very few individuals and only for comparatively short moments by most of us.[43]

If from the mental structure of individuals we pass to *the total*

[43] See a development of this theory of mental structure and evidence for it in *The Ways and Power of Love*, chaps. v and vi. See in this present volume the essay of A. Vexliard that gives a comprehensive analysis of it. At the present time, with some variation, this theory of mental structure of individuals is becoming increasingly accepted by post-Freudian psychologists. Björn Sjövall calls it the "height-psychology" in contrast to the flat Freudian and other "depth-psychologies." See B. Sjövall's *Höjdpsykologi* (Stockholm: Svenska Kyrkans, 1959), pp. 43-81.

content of their mentality, there is not the slightest doubt that it represents a coexistence of a large number of mental, moral, aesthetic, and other systems and congeries, partly consistent, partly neutral, and partly antagonistic with one another. There are very few, if any, individuals whose sum total of ideas, values, standards, drives, aspirations, emotions, tastes, and imperatives are all logically or aesthetically consistent with one another. The outlined structural conflicts of different levels of mentality, of different egos or roles of an individual, plus a membership of most individuals in several different groups (the family, the state, the occupational, economic, religious, political, ethnic, cultural, sport, neighborhood, and other groups) make such a complete integration impossible. As long as—voluntarily or not—the individual belongs to different, and often mutually antagonistic, groups, he has to give his "pound of flesh" to each of these groups, to fulfil his duties and to obey the requirements of each of his groups. And these duties, requirements, and respective systems of ideas-values-norms required by each of these groups are mostly either neutral or frequently even contradictory to each other. The state often imposes upon us duties, values, and ideologies which contradict those required from us by our family, religious organization, occupation, or political party. And each of these groups often demands from us what is disapproved by some other group of which we are members. This multigroup membership thus introduces into our total mentality not only mutually neutral but often quite contradictory cultural systems and congeries. In addition, many such systems and congeries get into it by way of incidental, unsought contact and communication, via reading, radio, television, advertising, and so on. Like most of my fellow men, I do not wish to be informed through thousands of advertisements about the virtues of cigarettes, deodorants, bras, or detergents, but I cannot help having these bits of pseudo-information slipped into my mentality. Similarly thousands of other bits of ideas, values, norms, or cultural systems and congeries have slipped through my defenses into my mentality.

For these reasons, the total content of the "psychic and spiritual makeup" of individuals rarely, if ever, comprises the happy, completely integrated "holistic unity," so beautifully described by Dr. Anderle. If, indeed, his picture of a "holistic man" were true, then we should have to conclude that all normal human beings are perfectly rational and happy persons, invariably at peace with themselves and the world, and free from any non-rationality and irrationality, inner conflicts, emotional upheavals, and so on. Unfortunately, the stubborn, ugly facts do not allow us to accept this wonderful picture of man.

With these remarks I can end my defense against the penetrating criticisms of Dr. Anderle and leave him with his valiant defense of the morphological theories of civilizations. Our disagreement in a number of points does not prevent our agreement in a number of most essential problems discussed. The reason for this agreement consists in the fact that the eminent theorizers of civilizations have dealt with and studied, under the mistaken entity of civilizations, some important social group and the central "core" of its culture. Since this group is organized and its central cultural system is notably integrated these investigators did not fail to observe, to grasp, and to interpret correctly a series of the most significant—structural and dynamic—characteristics of such social and cultural systems. Hence, the essential concordance between many of their conclusions and my own.

VIII. Arnold J. Toynbee's Critical Inquiries

In his masterful and magnanimous essay, Toynbee asks for my comments on a number of very hard questions or objections he raises with utmost elegance of thought and style. The first of his criticisms is directed against my own assessment of "the dichotomic theories" of Bacon, Marx, Coste, Tugan-Baranovsky, Louis Weber, Veblen, Alfred Weber, McIver, Ogburn, F. S. Chapin, and others. With variations, these dichotomic theories contend that a "material," technological-economic culture or civilization-system leads in sociocultural change and, in the course of time, changes occur along a linear trend of accumulation and progressive improvement, diffusing and being adopted *urbi et orbi* in all kinds of culture and society while a "non-material," "ideological" culture-system lags in change, is not accumulative, has no linear trend to become better in the course of time, and is not universal in its diffusion.

In my *Dynamics*[44] I seriously questioned the validity of the

[44] *Dynamics*, IV, 154-96, 303-88.

dichotomic theories and tentatively concluded that nearly all of their claims are quite doubtful and that both—material and non-material—cultures, "civilization-systems" and "culture-systems," are accumulative, selective, diffuse over many and different kinds of societies, and, if we introduce a somewhat arbitrary and subjective criterion of "improvement," both parts, with serious relapses, show a trend of progressive improvement in the course of time; finally, both change together in the integrated culture and neither one *uniformly* leads or lags in the change. At least one of these conclusions is pointedly challenged by Toynbee. Instead of a confrontation of "material to non-material" culture, he tellingly points out a profound difference between a continuous accumulation and progressive improvement of scientific discoveries and an absence of such a linear progress in poetry in the course of their change. Says he:

The present-day physicist's work will have superseded the sixteenth-century physicist's work and will have made it obsolete and out of date, because a physicist begins where his predecessor left off, and stands upon his predecessor's shoulders. On the other hand, a poet's relation to his predecessor is not the same. . . . Unlike the physicist the poet is not able to start where his predecessor left off; he has to start all over again from the ground up, and therefore he is not bound to surpass his predecessor. . . . Sheer posteriority does not give to the poet the decisive superiority that it does give to the physicist.

By this master stroke, Toynbee seems to have irreparably punctured this point in my theory. However, after a careful examination of the puncture, I feel I can fix it, if not fully, then, at least, to the extent of allowing a further riding on this theory until a more adequate new "theoretical tire" can be produced. Toynbee's statement has three shortcomings: it exaggerates the difference between the modes of change-evolution-progress of physics and poetry (or natural science and fine arts); it elevates this difference into a universal and perennial rule while, in fact, it is merely "local" and "temporal" occurring only in some cultures and at some periods; finally, especially in its part concerning "superiority," it is somewhat ambiguous and arbitrary.

Yes, if we have in view the state of physics or any natural science in the West in the sixteenth and the twentieth centuries, then, with some reservation, "sheer posteriority . . . does give to the physicist" of the twentieth century "the decisive superiority." But our eminent historian, sociologist, and philosopher well knows that this rule is in no way universal. In ancient Greece the total number of scientific discoveries and inventions—important ones—declined sharply after the fourth century B.C. A similar decline occurred with scientific discoveries and inventions in Rome after the third century A.D., in Arabia after the eleventh century and, so far as Western culture was an inheritor of the Greco-Roman culture and science, for some eight centuries, from the fifth to the twelfth A.D. Western physics and natural science made far fewer discoveries and inventions and hardly any single more important discovery than Greek or Roman or Arabic science did. And during the subsequent centuries, from the twelfth to the twentieth, some European countries, like Spain and Portugal, made the greatest number of their discoveries and inventions in the fifteenth and sixteenth centuries, but not in subsequent centuries. If the number of discoveries and their importance in these—and several other countries—have been decreasing in the later period of their history, and sometimes dwindled to a zero line, this signifies that the physicists and scientists of these later periods could have hardly been superior, or even equal, to their more inventive and more creative predecessors of the preceding centuries of a comparative blossoming of physics or natural science in these cultures.[45] This means also that "sheer posteriority does not give the decisive superiority . . . to the physicist" at all periods and in all cultures.

Toynbee's statement that "the present-day physicist's work will have superseded the sixteenth-century physicist's work and will have made it obsolete and out of date" needs a further limitation even in this exceptional case of extraordinary progress of the Western natural sciences for the last four centuries. The present-day physicist's work does not make obsolete and out of date everything from the great discoveries of the physicists or natural scientists of the preceding centuries: macro-physics and macro-mechanics are still largely based upon the discoveries of Galileo, Kepler, Pascal, and Newton, to mention just a few names. The same is true of the great discoveries of other natural scientists of the preceding centuries. The true part of their discovery is not obsolete; it still

[45] See the detailed statistics of the movement of scientific discoveries and inventions in my *Dynamics*, II, chap. iii, IV, chaps. iv, vi, vii.

serves as a foundation for the work of later scientists. These, at best, as Toynbee himself says correctly, stand upon their predecessors' shoulders and add their own—now small, now great—contributions to it. And among these contributions, not all new additions are necessarily more valid and correct than the respective formulae, theories, and discoveries of their predecessors.

The history of science informs us about many cases when a posterior physical or biological theory, fashionable for some period, eventually seemed to be less valid than the respective preceding theory. Not infrequently, the posterior theory was abandoned in favor of the preceding theory without or with some modifications. And subsequently, the—earlier and later—theories often fluctuated in their domination, now one, now the other getting the upper hand. Such fluctuation of domination has been taking place with many "first principles" and "basic theories" of science like atomistic theories in physics, vitalistic and mechanistic theories in biology, the theory of abiogenesis and of the nature of light, principles of determinism and indeterminism (including their latest variation— Heisenberg's "principle of uncertainty"), Niels Bohr's "principle of complementarity" (which is the modern variation of the old Taoist principle), and many other principles and theories.[46]

There is hardly any doubt that, as far as mere oscillation is concerned, there probably has been no scientific theory which has not undergone it, and, like a fashion, now has been heralded as the last word of science and now has fallen into disrepute. At least, for me it is exceedingly difficult to indicate any single comparatively broad theory in the whole field of natural sciences which has been free from such a vicissitude.[47]

Moreover, now and then, succeeding natural science and technology are incapable of keeping up to their preceding levels and undergo a process of regression and decay. And none other than Toynbee himself gives a long and excellent series of such regressions in technology and partly in science, like the cases of the previously splendid Roman roads, of the excellent irrigation system of the Tigris-Euphrates, of water storage in Ceylon, of Chinese river conservation, and so on; these went to pieces in the later periods of

[46] See a concise outline of the fluctuations of these "first principles" and basic theories of physical, mathematical, biological, and social sciences in *Dynamics*, II, chaps. iv-xii, especially xii.

[47] *Dynamics*, II, 467.

these countries.[48]   And Toynbee, Spengler, and other historians of civilizations give overwhelming evidence of regression of science and technology in the decaying phase of practically all the disintegrated civilizations.

All these facts fairly clearly contradict the unreserved statement of Toynbee that "sheer posteriority does . . . give . . . the decisive superiority . . . to the physicist."

On purely logical grounds, the statement also appears to be doubtful; if accepted at its face value, it amounts to an assumption that any posterior formula, theory, technique and state of the natural sciences is more true, more valid, and more precise than the preceding ones.   Our eminent historian-sociologist-philosopher would hardly insist on this variation of Voltairean Candide's optimistic philosophy that everything in the natural sciences continuously becomes bigger and better in the course of time.

These observations largely disarm the puncturing power of Toynbee's argument so far as it concerns the relationship between the works of the earlier and later physicists or natural scientists in general.

Unduly exaggerated and generalized also is that part of his statement which outlines the relationship between the works of the earlier and later poets or, generally, the fine-arts creators: novelists, musicians, painters, sculptors, architects, actors, and so on.   With a very rare exception, most of the poets and fine-arts creators hardly ever "start all over again from the ground up," although they are "not able to start where [their] predecessors left off."   As a rule, like scientists, all competent art-creators start after absorbing the essential "discoveries" of their predecessors, at least, the style, character, and topics of one of the important currents of their time or— more rarely—of one of the preceding currents that happens to appeal to a given poet or fine-arts creator.   Is it not true that in all fine arts (just as in science) there always has been, in one form or another, a short or long apprenticeship during which the apprentice learned the ABC's of his art and its technique, either from his master or from the art school?   Is not this training in the essential discoveries-inventions of all the preceding masters of a given art the main function of our schools of music, painting, architecture, drama, and literature?   Is it not true also that after an important discovery-

[48] See A. J. Toynbee, *A Study of History*, IV, 40 ff.

invention, like the rules of polyphony, counterpoint, harmony, modulations, rhythms, "vertical and horizontal" writing in music, all the posterior important composers have been obliged to learn and to follow these rules and in this sense to "stand upon their predecessors' shoulders"? Is not the same true in regard to important discoveries or creations of masterpieces in painting and literature, sculpture and architecture, and in other fine arts? As in science, the outstanding creators may modify and even deviate from these rules, and create their own style or hypothesis or theory, but to do it successfully even such creators must know a great deal about the previous achievements of their great predecessors. Without a Bach, Stamitz, Mozart, Haydn, Handel, there could hardly have emerged a Beethoven; just as without their predecessors could hardly appear a Dante or Shakespeare, Raphael or Michelangelo, or any other great fine-arts creator? As to the small creators, they "stand upon their great predecessors' shoulders" to an extent of being mere imitators and followers of their great master(s). As a result of this "standing upon the predecessors' shoulders" in poetry, as well as in all fine arts, we have had the appearance of various "schools," currents or movements like "classic and romantic," "impressionist," "expressionist," "cubist," "pointilist," "surrealist," and "seven- and twelve-tone music," while in literature, we have had periods of domination of religious literature in the Middle Ages, of heroic epics, or "naturalistic and realistic" novels and poetry, of great tragedies and drama, and so on.[49] If poets and fine-arts creators were indeed "starting all over again from the ground up," none of the foregoing could have taken place. Under such conditions neither long apprenticeship and training in schools of fine arts, nor knowledge of discoveries, techniques, and masterpieces of their predecessors, would be necessary for poets and fine-arts creators; nor would there have been intentional or non-intentional imitators and followers of great creators, nor distinct currents and movements among the poets and artists belonging to the same "aesthetic denomination," nor the phenomena of art-creators learning the secrets of creativity from their predecessors. These relevant facts limit greatly the validity of Toynbee's statement concerning the poets

[49] For a succession of main styles and currents in Greco-Roman and Western painting, sculpture, architecture, music, and literature see my *Dynamics*, I, chaps. v-xiii.

"starting all over again from the ground up." In exceptionally rare cases, perhaps, such a thing happens, just as it happens in science, but it is in no way a general rule.

Finally, to the extent that from a long-range view there seems to be some real progress in science, comparable progress can be said to be taking place in the fine arts, including poetry, religion, philosophy, and in other compartments of culture. In regard to religion, Toynbee himself testifies to it by classifying religions into the classes: "primitive," "rudimentary higher," "higher," and "secondary higher," and by asserting that "the movement of the chariot of religion was continuous in its rise and constant in its direction."[50] The same can be said of the fine arts.

Certainly, after the mathematics and physics of the twentieth century we do not return to the mathematics and physics of the Greek Eleatic school. But similarly, after the great religions of the world we do not return to the "primitive" totemic, animistic, and fetishistic forms of worship. After Bach, Mozart, and Beethoven we can hardly return to the mere plain chant or to the elementary polyphonic music of the early Middle Ages. After Raphael, Michelangelo, Rembrandt, and the later great masters in painting and sculpture, we do not go back to the drawings of primitive geometric or even the visual style in these arts. After the great classics of literature of the last few centuries, we can hardly revert to the literature of a "primitive" people. After Mommsen, Gibbon, and other great historians, we do not return to the fantastic mythology of earlier history. In brief, so far as not returning to previous forms is a criterion of progressive perfection, such a non-return takes place in all compartments of culture.

I hope that these brief comments[51] repair Toynbee's puncture in my theory, at least to an extent of allowing us to drive upon it until a more adequate theory in these matters is produced.

Of other friendly—and invariably thoughtful—criticisms of Toynbee's, some have been answered in my reply to Anderle's criticisms, while some can be replied to briefly because of a considerable concordance of our views on these points. I did not and do not deny "the distinctive individualities," the local *Physiognomik*, even "the

[50] Toynbee, *A Study of History*, VII, 444, Table IV, and pp. 381-568.
[51] See for the detailed analysis of this and related problems in my *Dynamics*, II, chap. iii, IV, chaps. iv, vi, vii, and *passim* in all four volumes.

prime symbols" of various cultures, not even local coloring and variations of ideational or sensate supersystems in different cultures.

"In the case of some civilizations Spengler's prime symbol serves well as a premise for the meaningful integration of several systems and congeries. But this unified system is only one among many systems and congeries present in the *total* Apollonian, Magian, Faustian, Egyptian, or any other 'civilization.' "[52] Still less do I deny "the distinctive individualities" of cultures in fields of their fine arts. I do deny, however, that *most of the distinctive character-istics* of the fine arts of a great culture remain unchanged in the course of time and I humbly claim that the fine arts of different cultures clearly exhibit essential similarities in style and content if and when these cultures are in the same—ideational, or sensate, or idealistic—dominant phase, or, according to W. Deonna, in the same "archaic," "classical," or "decadent" phase. In Volume I of my *Dynamics* I endeavored to prove these points through quantita-tive and qualitative analysis of enormous samples of pictures, sculptures (more than 100,000), architectural buildings, musical compositions, and more limited samples of literature of the Greco-Roman and the Western world throughout the whole historical existence of these cultures. So far nobody yet has even attempted to prove that either my samples were non-representative or my analysis and statistics (more correctly, simple arithmetic) were wrong. On his part, Deonna (and other historians of fine arts), analyzing the Paleolithic, the Neolithic, the Greco-Roman, and the Christian sculpture and painting, convincingly shows even in photo-graphic reproductions in his work that the traits and style of all four types of art are strikingly homogeneous.

The similarity is so great that the statues of early medieval Europe (be-fore the twelfth century A.D.) can easily be mistaken for those of archaic Greece (before the sixth century B.C.), and vice versa. Likewise, com-paring the Aurora of Michelangelo with the Niobe of Rome; the Nymphs of the Fountain by Jean Goujon (sixteenth century A.D.) with the Danc-ing Woman figure of Pergamum (third-second century B.C), geometric statues of the archaic Paleolithic with those of the Neolithic, and with Greek, archaic medieval, and so on, one cannot fail to see a striking similarity between them, although they be separated from one another by centuries, even by thousands of years.[53]

[52] *Social Philosophies of an Age of Crisis*, p. 211.
[53] *Ibid.*, p. 30. See, there, an outline of several other theories with similar

Some of the statues of the Acropolis are remarkably similar to the works of Mino da Fiesole, Francia, and Desiderio da Settignano, some of the sculptures of the Scopa School in Greece (fourth century B.C.) to the sculptures of Francia, some of the Greek and Pompeian vase paintings to the paintings of Mantegna, R. Van Weyden, and Titian and so on.[54]

I do not claim that the similarities of the fine arts of various cultures in the same phase of their development are necessarily greater than the similarities of the fine arts of the same culture at different stages of its development; we hardly have an objective measuring stick for clear decision of this problem. But I contend that the essential similarity of the fine arts of different cultures being in the same predominantly ideational or sensate or idealistic phase cannot be denied and this contention is in no way "paradoxical." So conceding to Spengler, Toynbee, and "cultural morphologists" a part of truth which their claims contain, and hoping that on their part they also may make a similar concession in favor of my points, we can peacefully agree in these matters.

As to the subsequent gracious comments of Toynbee, I do not find any essential disagreement between his views, as they are expressed in his essay and in the truly monumental *Study of History* (especially in his latest volume, *Reconsiderations*) and my own. The difference in our standpoints concerns secondary points, "shadings," "manner of expression," and details rather than the substantial theses and propositions. I am glad to find a real concordance and congeniality of our conclusions in the following problems touched upon in Toynbee's essay and in his *Study of History*:

i. Toynbee does not deny the principle of immanent change in social and cultural systems; his explanation of the genesis, development, and subsequent disintegration or "life in death," or fluctuation of civilizations is predominantly "immanent" in its character, especially in his verdict that civilizations perish by suicide but not by murder.

On my part, I do not deny the role of external factors which

---

claims. For a detailed documentation of Deonna's thesis, see his *L'archeologie, sa valour, ses methods* (3 vols.; Paris: H. Laurens, 1912).

[54] *Social Philosophies of an Age of Crisis*, p. 31.

through their challenge may accelerate or retard, facilitate or inhibit the unfolding and development of the inherent potentials of
a sociocultural system; in exceptional cases, they can even destroy
a system. Viewed thus, our theories are not only reconcilable but
quite congenial to each other.

ii. The same is true in regard to Toynbee's three "models" (the
Hellenic, the Chinese, and the Jewish) of life courses of civilizations
(or vast supersystems) admirably developed by him in his *Reconsiderations*. The only difference, here, is that if we have in view
not only "civilizations" and "the supersystems" but all—vast and
small—social and cultural systems, then there would be not only
three but a much larger number of "models" or "patterns" of life
courses of all these systems.

iii. Quite concordant too, are our views in regard to such problems as this: Is a too great and too easy success fatal for the continuity of creative blossoming of sociocultural systems and civilizations? Toynbee has given us a most penetrating analysis of deleterious effects of an intoxicating and unmerited success in the forms
of development in the victors of the proclivities of "resting on
their oars," of idolization of relative values as absolute, of progressive replacement of their charismatic creativity by coercive and
uncreative policies, and so on.[55]

Very similar to this theory is my hypothesis of decline of ideational, idealistic, and sensate supersystems and practically many
other systems: when each of these exhausts the creative fund of
cognitive, moral, aesthetic, political, and other values, and continues to dominate not through its creative grace but mainly by
inertia, fraud, coercion, tricks, and pseudo-values, such a system is
bound to decline as sterile, often poisonous, and disserviceable to
its members and humanity at large.

iv. My basic definition of the class of sociocultural phenomena
has the meaningfully interacting human beings as one of the three
components of these phenomena (side by side with the components
of meanings and vehicles). From this very definition the reciprocal
influence of individuals upon the social and cultural system, created,

[55] See Toynbee's *Study of History*, Vols., IV, V, VI.

activated and controlled by them, and the influence of the systems upon its human members follow. As far as I can see, the position of Toynbee in this matter is similar to mine.

v. Similar concordance marks our views on many other problems,[56] such as: determinism-indeterminism, predictability or unpredictability of certain sociocultural phenomena in their historical development, our ontologies, our super-denominational religious standpoint, our emphasis upon the paramount value of unselfish, creative love, up to our attitude toward too narrow-minded "fact-finders" and "too shortsighted chronicler-historians," engrossed completely, in the satirical description of Herbert Spencer, with "the genealogies of kings, and the fates of dynasties, and the quarrels of courts" and with such problems as to "whether or not the plot for the murder of Amy Robsart was contrived by Leicester himself . . . and whether or not the account of the Gowrie Conspiracy, as given by King James, was true," and whether the stepmother of Frederick I of Prussia tried to poison him, and so on. Both of us probably would agree with Herbert Spencer's conclusions in this matter that "still, after due attention has been paid to those indispensable matters, a little time might, perhaps, with advantage be devoted to the natural history of societies,"[57] or civilizations, or sociocultural systems and supersystems.

Personally I am glad that in the mentioned basic problems there is much more concordance than discordance between my humble ideas and the ideas of the eminent thinker and scholar of our age.

IX. *Sociology in General and Homosociology in Particular*

There is similar concordance between my integral system of sociology and the neo-organic sociological system of another eminent scholar of our time, Corrado Gini. Despite my readiness to plead "guilty" in regard to several defects of my works pointed out

[56] See on these problems particularly Toynbee's *Reconsiderations*, quoted; and besides my *Dynamics* consult my *Fads and Foibles in Modern Sociology* and *The Ways and Power of Love.*

[57] H. Spencer, *The Study of Sociology* (London: Williams and Norgate, 1880), pp. 68-70.

in the otherwise very gracious essay of Gini, this concordance shows itself even in the points criticized by this outstanding sociologist, demographer, and statistician.

i. Besides some general shortcomings of my theories and correctly observed characteristics of my personality, like my "lone wolf's stubbornness," the first specific criticism of Gini's consists in finding my conception of society and sociology too restricted, not covering animal and preliterate societies and sociologies. To this specific charge I plead "not guilty." After establishment of the Department of Sociology at Harvard, I asked the foremost authority on the social life of ants and wasps, Professor W. M. Wheeler, to organize a course in animal sociology to be given by the most eminent specialists in the field of social life of fish, bees, ants, wasps, monkeys, and other animal species. And for a number of years such a course was successfully given at Harvard, not by homosociologists but mainly by biologists and animal psychologists who devoted themselves to the study of the behavior and social life of one of the animal species. In my Russian *Sistema soziologii,* I deal concisely not only with animal but also with plant societies studied by plant ecologists. Then, in my *Contemporary Sociological Theories,* I devote some 238 pages to "Biological Interpretations of Social Phenomena," and in my *Society, Culture and Personality,* I give an outline of "cosmosociology," and "biosociology," referring to a number of works in these fields dealing with animal and plant societies. These facts clearly show that I did not and do not deny the scientific fruitfulness of such branches of sociology. If I did not do any research in these fields the reason is that not being able to cultivate thoroughly the animal and the plant sociologies, I intentionally chose to specialize in *homosociology.* Accordingly, my definition of sociology is made for *homosociology* and my sociological studies have been confined to this field. From this homosociological standpoint, physical and biological sciences, including animal and plant sociologies, are "presociology" or "presocial science." "The task of sociology and the social sciences begins where the physical and biological study of man and his world ends." "Social scientists, to be sure, must know the conclusions of the physical and biological sciences concerning man; but these conclusions do not form an integral part of sociology or of the social sciences."[58]

These comments show that on this point there is no real disagreement between Gini's stand and mine. The same is still more true about the sociology of preliterate and preindustrialized societies.

Contrary to Gini's statement, in my younger days I did considerable field work in a study of the Komi and the Samoyed peoples in Northern Russia.[59] Then subsequently I made a few strictly experimental studies on the efficiency of work and the influence of suggestion,[60] not to mention my studies of rural societies published in the form of four substantial volumes.[61]

These facts testify that I did some field-work, some experimental research, and quite a considerable study if not exactly of preliterate societies, then, at least, preindustrial, pastoral, agricultural societies. Then, in nearly all my volumes, I have paid constant attention to anthropological or ethnographic works concerning preliterate societies. For these reasons I plead "not guilty" to this charge of my eminent critic and friend.

ii. "Not guilty" also do I plead to his subsequent charge of my ignoring the role of physical, physiological, and geographic factors in conditioning social phenomena. Don't I devote to an examination of these factors and respective literature several long chapters in my *Contemporary Sociological Theories* and a concise survey of the cosmosociological, mechanistic, biosociological, and demographic factors in my *Society, Culture and Personality* and other works? Does not my very definition of sociology explicitly say that it studies "first, the relationship and correlations between various

[58] *Society, Culture and Personality*, p. 3. Quite consistent with this stand, I deliberately asked that the course in animal sociology at Harvard be organized and given, not by homosociologists who know little about societies and social life of animal and plant species, but mainly by biologists—lifelong investigators of these phenomena in the species of their specialization.

[59] These field studies were published as a monograph, *Istoriko-Statistichesky Ocherk Zyrian* (St. Petersburg, 1910), and in a series of articles: "Perejitki animisma u Zyrian," "Kvoprosu ob evoluzii semiy i braka u Zyrian," "Sovremennyie Zyriane," in *Isvestia Archangelskago Obschestva Izuchenia Russkago Severa*, 1910 and 1911.

[60] Published in the form of two papers, Nos. 33 and 34 in the "Article" section of the bibliography of my publications listed at the end of this volume.

[61] Nos. 15 and 16 in the bibliography of my books in this volume.

classes of social phenomena; second, those *between the social and the non-social (geographic, biological, etc.,) phenomena;* and third, the general characteristics common to all classes of social phenomena?"[62] Those references are sufficient to explain why to this charge, I plead "not guilty" and find that Gini's views and mine are again in essential agreement.

iii. "Not guilty" is also my plea to Gini's charge of "the lack of comprehension of the concept of equilibration." Since I delivered one of the main addresses on this topic at the Thirteenth International Congress of Sociology and since I devoted some sixteen pages to a survey of the vast literature, analysis, and criticism of the principle of equilibrium in its application to sociocultural phenomena,[63] I can hardly be accused of a "lack of comprehension" of this concept; the more so since nobody has shown as yet that my detailed analysis and criticism of all five main meanings of equilibrium is wrong. Gini is entitled to disagree with my conclusions, but he is not entitled to accuse me of ignorance or of noncomprehension of this term, so widely used but hardly ever clearly defined in the social sciences. On this point our views seem to be different.

iv. I never objected to a study of the functions and effects of this or that specific factor—geographic, climatic, biological, economic, demographic, or any other—upon the structure, processes, and evolution of sociocultural systems and congeries. As I mentioned above, long chapters in several of my volumes deal with this sort of theories and the facts underlying them. My conclusions in regard to such specific-factor theories are almost identical with those which Gini gives in his essay.

Taken as a whole all these varieties of investigation into the relationship of [physical], biological, [psychological] and sociocultural phenomena have amassed a prodigious amount of impressive facts and have disclosed a series of important uniformities and correlations between these classes of phenomena. They have thrown light upon many problems, both general and special. [The fact that each of these schools studies primarily its specific aspect does not necessarily mean that these theories are contradictory.] Rather it signifies a specific standpoint from which the manifold sociocultural universe is studied. . . . The net out-

[62] *Contemporary Sociological Theories,* p. 760.
[63] Cf. my "Le concept d'equilibre est-il nécessaire aux sciences sociales," *Revue Intern. de Sociologie,* 1936; *Dynamics,* IV, 677-93.

come of such a divergence is a more adequate and many-sided knowledge of the manifold sociocultural universe. [On the other hand, most of
these investigations have exaggerated the influence of their specific
factor; some of their findings have proved fallacious. Generally, these
mistakes have been discovered and corrected by the criticism of other
sociologists.][64]

The meaning of these lines hardly differs from the meaning of
Gini's lines treating this subject in his essay. My criticism of some
of these specific-factor theories is aimed exactly at the unproved ex-
aggerations, extrapolation, misapplication, and errors but not at
their character and real contributions. This means again that I
plead "not guilty" to this charge.

v. Finally, Gini is correct in his statement that there is a considerable congeniality between his neo-organicistic and my integral
system of sociology. Already, in my *Contemporary Sociological
Theories* and then in *Society, Culture and Personality*, this congeniality was mentioned and stressed. As a personal matter, I was
much impressed with Gini's excellent monograph, *I fattori demografici dell' evoluzione delle nazioni*, already in my undergraduate
senior year (1914). Since that time I have tried to follow his main
works as much as I could. My study of these works has invariably
deepened and expanded my knowledge. With this note of my
indebtedness to the eminent maestro and personal friend I can close
my reply to his thoughtful and gracious critical remarks.

X. Problems of Sociological Measurement

Most of the shortcomings and inadequacies of my procedures
and techniques of study, indicated in the insightful and competent
paper of Matilda White Riley and Mary E. Moore, do not need any
defense on my part: repeatedly, I stress and overstress them in my
works. Whether because of lack of exact and adequate data, or because the phenomena studied do not have clear-cut units for precise
measurement, or because only a very rough quantification is possible under several arbitrary assumptions, I seldom fail to stress explicitly such defects, uncertainties and assumptions, and to warn the

[64] *Society, Culture and Personality*, p. 24. See also *Contemporary Sociological
Theories*, pp. 757-61, and *passim*.

reader of a possibility that my subsequent conclusions may be uncertain, and even erroneous.

A detailed indication of a series of uncertainties, inadequacies, difficulties, and assumptions involved in my study of wars and internal disturbances—the cases in the Riley-Moore essay—can serve as a typical example of this regular procedure of mine. In introductory parts of such studies, I carefully point out such difficulties, as I do, for example, in my *Dynamics*:

A. *Factual Difficulties.* (1) In many cases the *necessary data are lacking.* . . . (2) The next factual difficulty is the *unreliability and inaccuracy of many of the existing data.* . . . (3) The third factual difficulty is with the *wars that lasted for a number of years.* (4) Differences in sustained continuity in wars of *"long duration,"* such as World War I (four years, uninterrupted) and the "Hundred Years' War" (a series of battles occurring at long intervals of time). (5) There is the difficulty of estimating the proportion of each nation's total army engaged in a given battle or war. (6) There is the difficulty of comparing naval and territorial wars. (7) There is also a lack of data about the exact size of the population of each country studied, etc.

B. *Methodological Difficulty.* The main methodological difficulty, added to all the factual difficulties, is the impossibility of making a "perfect translation" into purely *quantitative* language of any phenomenon that is *qualitative-quantitative.* Most sociocultural phenomena, including the phenomena of war and revolution, are of this nature. [In addition to such difficultly of "translation," or quantifying the partly qualitative phenomena of wars and revolutions, several arbitrary assumptions in ranking, scaling, and measuring are unavoidable. An evaluation of the magnitude of each disturbance (revolution) on such assumed scales involves an element of subjectivity; and here is a source of probable error.]

["In these conditions" a choice is forced upon the investigator.] *Either he must pass the problem by, however important it be, in order not to take chances of making too many, or too great blunders, or he must go ahead and take these chances. In this latter case the study would be of value if he would try to be as careful and unbiased as possible. . . . The relevant facts he collects must be at least as complete as or more complete than [those] in any other study hitherto made. He should not claim the privilege of infallibility or validity of his results, but should simply say, "Let us study the relevant facts as well as possible and then see what the results will be without certainty . . . but with confidence that they are more reliable than purely inspirational theories or theories based upon only fragments of the existing data." He must put "all his cards on the table," in the sense of stating his assumptions explicitly and making the nature of his procedure perfectly clear to the reader. Finally, he must be ready to bear most vicious, and for the most part, incompetent, criticism of a crowd of waiting critics, from ignorant journalistic "snipers" and politicians . . . up to the finicky and meticulous scholar accustomed only to a study of narrow topics and the art of "straining at gnats."* . . . Of these alternatives I chose the second, with all its conditions, especially the last. . . . The tentative results based upon the available body of data are better than results based upon mere wishes or upon fragments of these data. No exactness in detail can be claimed for such a venture; but I can at least urge in its favor that it has a more complete and more solid factual basis than [inspirational and fragmentary studies].[65]

As the above lines indicate, I have been fully aware of various difficulties, uncertainties, doubtful assumptions, and other impediments confronting me in my major studies, but I repeatedly stressed them, warning my readers of such pitfalls. Realizing such dangers, I tried to take all available precautions to minimize their influence in every possible way.

True, I did not use several allegedly "modern" techniques of quantitative research, such as those of modern sampling, data processing, content analysis, interviewing, and others (which in their essentials were already developed when I published my *Dynamics*). I refrained from using them intentionally for several reasons: (*a*) partly because they were hardly applicable to the kind of studies I was carrying on; (*b*) partly because some of these techniques, such as sampling, were superfluous, since I used the entire universe of facts studied, instead of mere samples of it; (*c*) partly because I questioned their infallibility and doubted their ability to deliver correct and valid results, especially when mechanically applied; (*d*) partly because some of the theories upon which such techniques are based appeared to me to be vulnerable (e.g., theories of "intervening opportunities," "scalogram methods," "latent classes," and others mentioned in the Riley-Moore essay);[66] and (*e*) partly because I am less interested in "techniqueways" than in "substantive" studies. But my main reason was that I used other kinds of precautionary procedures that appeared to me more effective in minimizing elements of error found in the above-mentioned factual shortcomings of the empirical material, methodological difficulties of measurement of multi-dimensional, qualitative-quantitative phe-

---

[65] *Dynamics*, III, 265 ff. and 390 ff.

[66] See my criticism of these techniques and underlying theories in *Fads and Foibles in Modern Sociology and Related Sciences*.

nomena, and in the arbitrary assumptions involved in such measurements.

A concrete example to justify my non-use of modern sampling techniques may be given. In *Dynamics* particularly, I ignored sampling, since the long-time series of the phenomena studied included the *complete, known series or the total universe of such phenomena:* not mere samples, but *all known* scientific discoveries and inventions, *all* Greco-Roman and Western philosophers, mentioned in the fullest histories of philosophy, all ethical thinkers, *almost all* known European pictures and sculptures (more than 100,000), *almost all* French, Germanic, and Russian codes of criminal law beginning with the barbaric codes of the fifth-sixth centuries and extending to the Soviet, Nazi, and Fascist codes, *all* Greco-Roman and Western wars and internal disturbances recorded in historical annals, etc. Needless to say, a study and measurement of *a complete universe* or *the total class* of the phenomena investigated gives a fuller and more adequate knowledge of such phenomena than a study and measurement of *a fraction or mere sample* of them. Sampling, here, would be superfluous. For these axiomatic reasons, I bring no apology to devotees of sampling methods for my having ignored such methods.

It is true, as Riley and Moore point out, that a study of the total class requires much greater effort and time than an investigation of its representative samples. But despite some progress in sampling techniques, there is an absence of a precise definition of what sort of sample is an adequate or truly representative sample in a study of numerous, many-dimensional, complex, abstract, and discrete sociocultural phenomena. Moreover, even in studies through sampling methods of such comparatively simple, concrete, and "unidimensional" phenomena as "yes-no-undecided" replies in public opinion polls, or in diagnosing and predicting "depression-prosperity" of business conditions, etc., the supposedly representative samples now and then happen to be unrepresentative and inadequate. When applied to a study of "many-dimensional," discrete, and somewhat abstract phenomena, especially in historical investigations of long-time, continuous trends and fluctuations in science, philosophy, fine arts, ethics, law, and other sociocultural phenomena, sampling techniques are particularly liable to yield but fragmentary, inadequate results, often merely illustrative cases incidentally or biasedly selected.

For these reasons, I have preferred to use, whenever possible, especially in my *Dynamics*, the *total known* series of each class of phenomena, instead of their samples, and I have regarded my procedure more reliable scientifically than any sampling methods.[67]

The reasons I have given for ignoring "modern sampling techniques" can, with slight modifications, apply to other "modern techniques of social research." Just as I replaced the "sampling method" by a more reliable method of study of the total class investigated, I similarly substituted for most of these techniques several other procedures which appeared to me more effective in minimizing the mentioned possibility of errors involved in a study of the main problems of my *Dynamics* and of some other works.

Thus, for instance, to reduce the elements of subjectivity and incompetence in the early but important phase of any empirical research, namely, in the collection of the relevant empirical data for substantiation and verification of a respective theory, I intentionally eliminated myself from this task in practically all quantitative series published in *Dynamics* and arranged this enormous spadework to be done *by the internationally known specialists in the field of each series without telling them the purpose or hypothesis for which each of the factual series was needed.* This simple procedure virtu-

---

[67] This is confirmed by even vitriolic critics of my *Dynamics* who acknowledged the fact that "In general, Mr. Sorokin appears to have been most conscientious about his facts" (Crane Brinton, "Socio-Astrology," *The Southern Review*, Autumn, 1937, p. 252), while several eminent historians like M. I. Rostovzeff and sociologists like L. von Wiese found "the factual framework of *Dynamics* so solidly built that its essentials are unlikely to be changed by future investigators; they certainly will correct here and there some sidewalks and secondary streets of the city of *Dynamics* but its main features are likely to remain unchanged." Another notable sociologist remarked that "despite Sorokin's criticism of empirical methods his *Dynamics* gives a fuller and more systematic empirical verification of his hypotheses and conclusions than any other sociological work I know of." When some of the *Dynamics'* studies, such as the movement and fluctuation of wars, were repeated along somewhat similar lines by Quincy Wright in his monumental work, *A Study of War* (Chicago: University of Chicago Press, 1942), his results happened to be in essential agreement with my results, indexes, and curves of war movement. The same is true of Prof. Urlani's studies of the wars of the 17th, 18th, 19th, and 20th centuries: despite his criticism of my procedures his curve of the movement of the wars of these centuries is similar to mine. I am deeply gratified also with confirmation of most of my main conclusions, formulated in *Social Mobility* and other works, by subsequent investigators of these phenomena. Even most of my prediction-guesses, made in the 1920's and '30's and summed up in my *Dynamics* (III, chap. xvi, and IV, chap. xvii), happened to be "lucky" and have come to pass, despite their having been dubbed as "crazy" by some critics when they were first published.

ally eliminated the element of subjectivity and, at the same time, secured a more competent handling of this decisive phase of any empirical research than could have been done by routine application of the "modern techniques" mentioned by Riley and Moore. The danger of subjective biases and incompetence in collecting empirical facts studied (for substantive and verificatory purposes) is not eliminated by "modern data collecting and processing techniques"—neither by techniques of sampling or item analysis or paired comparisons and others. In many allegedly empirical studies using "modern techniques" this phase of research is often done without taking serious measures to insure accuracy and relevancy of the collected material. The collection itself is frequently intrusted to incidental and hardly competent agents without an effective control over the competence of their operations. The material presented by them to the researcher-scholar is often "processed" without sufficient testing of its adequacy, etc. The whole situation resembles an archeological excavation in which the workers digging are simply told to dig, without continuous instruction and watchful supervision of their digging by archeologists themselves. In this way many research projects are already vitiated at the outset, during the early phase of collection of their empirical facts.

Moreover, in order to provide a complete possibility of verification of every detail of our procedures and summary tables, in many long appendices to each volume of *Dynamics* I have given the detailed lists of all wars, internal disturbances, philosophers, ethical thinkers, scientists, painters, sculptors, etc., on which all the summary tables are based with all details of quantitative evaluation of each person or event. Any interested, competent scholar, therefore, is given a full opportunity to check each detail of our series and of our quantification procedures for factual adequacy and correctness.

Another precautionary measure in my quantification of the many-dimensional qualitative-quantitative phenomena has been my preference, when possible, for the *simplest quantitative procedures with an absence or a minimum of arbitrary assumptions, ranking, scaling, complex formulae, and other intricate manipulations of figures and facts.* There are two main reasons why I preferred the simplest quantitative procedures to "the more sophisticated" ones: the first is the nearly axiomatic scientific rule that *the fewer the arbitrary assumptions, rankings, scalings, estimates, and other arbitrary elements contained in a measurement or quantification device, the more reliable and correct the results of the quantification are likely to be;* and the second concerns *the shortcomings of the factual material, as well as the many-dimensional and somewhat vaguely discrete nature of the phenomena measured, which precluded precise quantitative results and hence made superfluous and misleading any attempt at precision.* In this type of research, my efforts at measurement and my cognitive ambitions have seldom aimed at results that were more than only *roughly valid.*

Both of these reasons and respective procedures appear to me perfectly sound. In accordance with the first reason, for example, referring to my own studies in *Dynamics,* I regard the tables giving the movements of scientific discoveries and inventions, fluctuations of materialism, idealism, realism, nominalism, conceptualism, universalism, singularism, determinism, indeterminism, ethics of absolutism and those of relativism, fluctuations of various characteristics of ideational-idealistic-sensate paintings, sculptures, music, and other fine arts as giving more correct results than, say, the tables giving movements of magnitudes of internal disturbances. The first type of table is essentially free from arbitrary assumptions and procedures. Such tables give the actual number and percentage of *counted, known* discoveries and inventions, of materialistic and idealistic philosophers, of paintings and sculptures with religious and secular topics or representing paysage-genre-nature-mort-portraits, etc., summed up by decades, quarter-centuries, and centuries, in Greece, Italy, and other major European countries. The total measurement operations consist, there, in a mere counting of the respective phenomena, a summation of the results by periods mentioned, and then a conversion of the actual numbers into percentages. The entire process of quantification does not go beyond the simplest arithmetic and involves practically no arbitrary assumptions, rankings, and estimates (with the exception of one verificatory operation of supplementing several tables computed with the value of *one* given to each thinker in tables where different values—on a 1 to 12 scale—are assigned to each thinker).

In contrast to these simple "arithmetic" measurements, the measurement of the magnitude of internal disturbances and tables giving their movement contains several arbitrary assumptions: selection of four main dimensions out of many dimensions of each disturbance, assignment of different values to each of the four dimensions of each disturbance on scales from 1 to 5 or from 1 to 100, then computation of the total magnitude of each disturbance, now as a product and now as a geometric average, and several other arbitrary manipulations aimed at a roughly correct appraisal of the real magnitude of each internal disturbance. The complex and somewhat elusive nature of this phenomenon does not easily lend itself to even roughly accurate measurement free from a host of arbitrary assumptions and procedures. As a result of such arbitrary assumptions and procedures, the quantitative tables giving movements of internal disturbances are likely to be less reliable than the tables giving results of simple arithmetic computation of respective phenomena.

Even in comparison with the *Dynamics'* indices of movements of wars (computed with some but not with so many arbitrary assumptions and estimates as those of internal disturbances) the tables of internal disturbances probably contain more errors than those of wars. On this point, I fully agree with the remarks of Riley and Moore.

My distrust of quantifying operations that are loaded with *arbitrary* assumptions, rankings, scalings, estimates, and manipulations explains my cautious attitude toward, and my reluctance to use, many of "the midcentury modern techniques" in measuring complex and many-dimensional sociocultural phenomena. On this point I am less enthusiastic than Riley and Moore over such techniques as those exemplified by Guttman's "scalogram" method, Suchman's "scalogram-board" procedure, Lazarsfeld's theory and technique of the "latent classes," the technique of content or item analysis, and others, not to mention a legion of various mechanical tests. While I do not deny their cognitive value and usefulness in quantifying relatively simple, concrete, and "unidimensional" phenomena, I seriously question their applicability and infallibility in efforts to quantify many-dimensional, complex, and discrete sociocultural phenomena. One of their main weaknesses is exactly their contamination with arbitrary assumptions, scalings, estimates, and subjective elements. I welcome their use when they can be fruitfully applied—as they have been so applied by some who have thoughtfully mastered such techniques—with all the necessary caution and warning of their possible shortcomings and uncertainties.

But I distrust their mechanical application and an implicit faith in their magical infallibility which, unfortunately, has often characterized the behavior and beliefs of their enthusiastic practitioners and devotees. My criticism of these techniques and of various psychological, psychiatric, and sociological tests has been directed, not against their sound core, but against their skill-less, automatic application and an exaggeration of their "truth-delivering" and "lie-detecting" capacity. I did not and still do not believe that there is any technique which automatically insures correct results in the hands of everyone who uses it.

We seem to forget that, after all, technique is a mere means—not the end of creative work (in the arts or sciences). We must remember, also, that genius creates its own technique. In the hands of a moron, the best technique can produce nothing but what is moronic. In the hands of a master, any will yield a masterpiece. . . . Technique is mechanical in its nature. Many can learn the mechanical operations. But they do not result automatically in a chef-d'oeuvre.[68]

As a matter of fact, the history of science contains a number of important discoveries made with what the "orthodox technicians of science," contemporaries of the discoverers-scientists, regarded as wrong techniques. Conversely, a host of researchers faithfully using the allegedly most "modern techniques" rarely, if ever, have made a significant discovery or invention. To achieve this, something else is needed: a spark of creative genius and a rigorous—inductive, deductive-dialectical, and mathematical—logic to develop the intuitively inspired idea and to verify it empirically.[69] A scientist graced by the spark of creative genius who follows the fundamental rules or logic can and often does make fruitful use of a most "unorthodox" technique he finds best for his studies.

I make no claims to being such a genius. Far from it, I regard myself as one of the ordinary scholars. But this does not prevent my seeing the paramount importance of creative élan and logic and my insistence upon a subordination to them of the much less significant, specific, "pedestrian" techniques of handling minor operations in important scientific research. Recently the social sciences, including sociology, have been too busy elaborating various

[68] *The Crisis of Our Age*, p. 73.
[69] See my "How Are Sociological Theories Conceived, Developed, and Validated?" *Social Science*, XXXV (April 1960), 78-91.

"techniques of research" and too little occupied with "substantive" studies of basic sociocultural phenomena, which promise to enrich our knowledge of the "what, how, and why" of such phenomena. Being much more interested in the "what, how, and why" of the fundamental realities of the human universe, I have focused upon these and tried to study them as well as I could. No doubt these studies, as I have pointed out, contain many defects and probably a number of errors. These shortcomings, however, are due, not so much to my use of wrong techniques, as to that common weakness of human nature, found also in scholars, which is expressed by the ancient dictum: *humanum est errare*.

I hope that these remarks have answered, at least in part, some of the questions and points found in the able essay by Riley and Moore. Their constructive and somewhat complimentary comments do not require any reply, other than a simple expression of my thanks for their considerate appraisal of some of my research methods and procedures.

XI. *Problems of Social Mobility and Stratification*

Professor Carlsson's fair and competent appraisal of my *Social Mobility* contains a number of prudent criticisms of several conclusions given in this volume. The distinguished author of *Social Mobility and Class Structure* sets these criticisms in the form of questioning rather than rejecting my views as wrong. Agreeing with him, in that a large number of problems in the field of mobility, stratification, and social classes are still insufficiently studied and need a great deal of additional research, I here give brief replies to his specific criticisms.

i. To Carlsson's question: "How far can valid inferences be drawn from past to present or future social conditions?" the best answer is given by the formula of probability: the greater the number of observed recurrences of the event or process studied and the lesser the number of exceptions from the uniformity observed, the more valid our inferences are likely to be, with reservations for the creative factor in history and social life, which can upset the probability prediction. In the case discussed, the number of ob-

served *organized* groups that are stratified is enormous, the number
of *organized* but unstratified groups is exceedingly small, practically
nonexistent; therefore, with a high probability we can expect that
in the foreseeable future stratification of *organized* groups will continue. The same reasoning applies to the fluctuation of stratification in the future. Its forms, height, and profile may change; for
instance, largely compulsory forms of stratification may give way to
freely accepted forms, and the sharp forms of inequality may be
increasingly replaced by milder ones; but on the basis of the observed fluctuations in the past, it is more probable that the fluctuations will continue in the future than that they will stop, leaving
stratification (or equality) forever frozen on a certain level, height,
and profile. If stratification and its fluctuations have been continuously occurring in the past, such facts do not give any ground
for the prediction of their disappearance in the future.

ii. These conclusions are directly challenged by Carlsson's contention that in modern, industrialized, Western society there seems
to have prevailed the trend of economic, political, and occupational
("prestige") equality or destratification, tied together with the trend
of ascending economic and social well-being. Unfortunately, the
distinguished scholar hardly gives convincing evidence for corroboration of his statement. Since, with the help of several historians, I happened to deal substantially with short-time and especially long-time fluctuations of economic, political, and occupational
conditions throughout the history of Greece, Rome, France, and
Germany in my later works,[70] on the basis of this study my answer
to Carlsson's challenge may be summed up as follows:

a. If we pay attention only to short-time fluctuations, then in the
life-history of Greece, Rome, France, Germany, and other countries,
as well as in the life-history of almost all social systems, one can
pick up a period of equalization—economic, political, and social.
In the history of Western society, considered apart from hundreds
of millions of its colonial populations, the period from (roughly)
the seventeenth to the beginning of the twentieth century was to
some extent the period of decreasing and softening stratification. If,
however, we examine the whole life-history of these and other
countries, as well as that of any long-living organized social group,

[70] See my *Dynamics,* III, chaps. ii-viii.

then, we find in it only fairly trendless fluctuations of all forms of stratification. And the later periods in the history of Greece, Rome, ancient Egypt, ancient Persia, Babylonia, the Inca or the Aztec empires, ancient China and India were marked not by a decrease but rather by a conspicuous increase of economic or political or social or occupational stratification. Even a decrease of some inequalities in the modern Western world for the last three or so centuries was followed by an enormous expansion and heightening of stratification in many times larger colonial populations—conquered, exterminated, enslaved, and heartlessly exploited by the West during this period of industrialization. The whole Western "equalitarian" and "democratic" population represented just a privileged oligarchic minority superimposed upon hundreds of millions of disfranchised colonial populations. This means that Carlsson's statement is incorrect even in regard to this "equalitarian" period of Western society. His thesis becomes one-sided even for Western society in the twentieth century.

While important equalitarian tendencies have continued to develop in this century, several opposite trends have also emerged and have grown within Western society itself. In the *field of political stratification,* after 1914, we witnessed a replacement of several democratic regimes by a multitude of totalitarian and dictatorial regimes of Communist, Nazi, Fascist, military, plutocratic, and other forms of Caesarism so brilliantly analyzed by Spengler. Has not this century witnessed an enormous growth of limitation and abrogation of liberties and inalienable rights of millions of citizens not only in "totalitarian" but also in democratic countries? Has not this century, in connection with its world wars and revolutions, transformed almost the total population of the West into Spencer's "militant society," or a vast armed camp with the sharpest forms of an army's regimentation and hierarchical stratification? Do we not observe also, side by side with liquidation of many forms of colonial, racial, and ethnic stratification, the emergence and growth of the *Apartheid*-type of inequalities, and of various forms of Caesarism even among "the liberated" colonial peoples?

b. As to *economic stratification,* don't we have even in Western countries enormous differences in incomes, capital, and standard of living between our multimillionaires and "power elite" and those of the millions of the unemployed, semi-employed, and peasant-labor classes? Are there not large differences in income between our upper and middle strata, on the one hand, and that of millions in so-called backward countries, on the other? Are there not enormous differences in totalitarian countries between the plane of living of Communist and totalitarian elite, on the one hand, and that of the toiling masses, on the other?

By these remarks—which can be multiplied and well substantiated—I merely want to point out that even in the industrialized West of this century, the factual situation is much more complex than it is depicted by Carlsson. Side by side with several equalitarian trends, a number of other trends are working in the opposite direction, and which of these trends will prevail in the future nobody can tell at the present. My guess is that, if mankind avoids a new world war, the fluctuation of stratification will continue, incessantly changing its forms, configurations, height, and profile.[71] The reason for the guess is that the three fundamental, perennial, and universal factors of stratification, namely, "living together," innate differences of individuals, and environmental differences in which individuals are placed from the moment of their conception, are going to stay with the human race as long as it lives and creates.[72] The reason for a trendless fluctuation of stratification in the future is that its "primary factors," demographic factors of fertility of the upper classes, dissimilarity of parents and children, incessant change of especially anthropo-social environment and the defective social distribution of individuals within social layers,[73]

[71] For a more detailed analysis of today's stratification, see my *Power and Morality*, chaps. v-xi; my *Society, Culture and Personality*, chap. xv, where all main forms of stratification are analyzed; and my "War and Post-War Changes in Social Stratification," *American Sociological Review*, X (April, 1945), 294-303. As symptomatic of a vigorous existence of stratification, today's intensive discussion of the problem of "status" and hierarchical arrangements of various strata on a "superior-inferior" scale in almost all sociological investigations can be mentioned, side by side with the enormously intensified "struggle for superior positions," glorification and stimulation of all sorts of successful climbing, and "cult of success." Together with many more important processes these "syndromes" can hardly be interpreted as symptoms of acceleration of leveling processes in today's Western society. If and when they are replaced by "the cult of and competition in humility" then we can seriously take the hypothesis of withering of inequalities. So far the cult of and competition for humility has only a handful of followers completely lost in the world of ferocious adepts at "superiority and success" among individuals as well as among social groups.

[72] See on these factors my *Social and Cultural Mobility*, chap. xiv.

[73] For a discussion of these primary and secondary factors of fluctuation of stratification, see *ibid.*, chap. xv.

are likely to continue to oscillate or to vary in the future. With their variation, the forms, height, and profile of stratification are bound to vary also as the consequence of these primary factors. For support of his challenge Dr. Carlsson should have shown that these perennial and primary factors are either not the real factors of these phenomena or that in the future these factors will cease to operate. As long as he did not do this, my theory and guess stand.

c. My theory of the factors of stratification and of its fluctuation has very little to do with so-called functionalism in sociology and has no teleological elements in it, contrary to the assertion of my eminent critic. For this reason I do not need to answer his criticisms of functional and teleological theories repeatedly criticized by me. In this criticism our standpoints are essentially similar.

d. They are similar, too, in regard to the availability of much fuller data on various forms of mobility at the present time in comparison with the data available when I was writing my book and also in regard to the best formulae for the measurement of mobility. Concerning the first point I have, however, a sort of objection to Carlsson's statement that my data "do not meet modern standards" and "are not representative of the general population." If these statements imply that my conclusions, based upon more limited data, are fallacious, then I must point out that I have not yet seen any of the ampler data available in any way disproving my main conclusions. So far as I have studied the new data and the recent works in this field, I have found that they confirm rather than deny my generalizations. As to the second point, out of several measurements of mobility I still definitely prefer the simplest, the most straightforward, to the complex ones involving several arbitrary assumptions and doubtful manipulations of figures and facts.[74]

e. Though in Social Mobility I studied mainly "the distributive mobility," I did not ignore the "demand and supply," "individual" and "collective," orderly and "catastrophic" forms of it. Chapters 2, 3, 4, 5, 6, and 7 deal with all these forms. In my Dynamics, "the

[74] See my criticism of these assumptions and manipulations in supposedly "refined" statistical procedures in my Fads and Foibles in Modern Sociology, chaps. vii, viii, and passim.

demand and supply" mobility "of society moving as a whole along the income, power and prestige" gradient is studied quite substantially in the whole life-history of ancient Greece, Rome, France, Germany, and the whole of Europe.[75] This substantial study, made with the help of competent historians, corroborated fully the conclusions reached in *Social Mobility*.

f. Finally, I fully share Carlsson's realistic "speculations" about the relationships between stratification and mobility, about his "utopian or nightmarish" society, and about the need for further study of many problems of mobility by narrow specialists and experts. Welcoming such detailed research, at the same time I wholeheartedly share Dr. Carlsson's apprehensions that in the too narrow studies "the essential unity of the subject may get lost in the process, so that no one is any longer able to see how the various pieces can be fitted together to form a meaningful picture." This danger has already manifested itself in a number of recent studies of some specific points of mobility and stratification. However, as long as this sort of research is paralleled and supplemented by work like Carlsson's *Social Mobility and Class Structure*, this danger will be counteracted and the net result of both kinds of research is going to be a more adequate knowledge of these phenomena in their general as well as special aspects.

XII. Problems of Law, Revolution, War, and Calamities

Before answering the criticisms of my distinguished friend, Professor N. S. Timasheff, I want to thank him for the footnote "showing to what extent the gathering of facts" for my *Dynamics* "was free of influence by any preconceived idea." Several of my critics have accused me that the whole process of gathering an enormous body of empirical facts for the *Dynamics* was, as F. R. Cowell aptly remarks, "framed in advance," and that I found "what I first injected into the inquiry and then tried to palm off the results as more 'scientific' than anything achieved by my predecessors."[76] As a matter of fact, none of the distinguished collaborators who actually gathered and summarized statistically the systematic series

---

[75] See *Dynamics*, III, chaps. ii-viii.
[76] See F. R. Cowell's "How Cowell of England Assesses Sorokin" in this volume.

of empirical facts concerning painting, sculpture, architecture, music, literature, scientific discoveries and inventions, philosophical systems, ethics, law, revolutions, wars, economic and political conditions, historical persons, and so on, none of them was told exactly for what purpose or theory I asked them to do the difficult spadework in the field in which each of them was an outstanding expert. Their statistical tables and other results were reproduced in my *Dynamics* without any correction or change. If they happened to fit and to support my main hypotheses, as they actually did, this fortunate result occurred without any "preconception," "presuggestion," or "framing" on my part. Moreover, each of the distinguished collaborators did not know who the other collaborators were and what sort of research they were doing for my *Dynamics*. These facts decisively repudiate the accusations of all those unduly suspicious critics who accused me and the collaborators in the plot of "framing in advance," and in "doctoring" the empirical facts, as well as the conclusions, of my *Dynamics*. This explains my excitement each time when I received the reports of the collaborators. "Would or would not their results confirm my hypotheses?" That was the question. Fortunately in practically all cases the results supported my expectations.

Turning now to the criticisms of Timasheff's, it seems that his objections to my conception of law, its place in culture, and its role in individual and group behavior concern specific details rather than the essentials of my theory, which represents a slight variation of the theory of law and morality of my great teacher, Leon Petrazhitsky. In essentials Timasheff's and my own views in this field are similar and congenial to each other. Both of us have been greatly influenced by Petrazhitsky and with personal modification (which is greater in Timasheff's theory of law than in mine)[77] both of us have accepted most of the main theses of Petrazhitsky's "psychological" (and sociological) theory of law and morality. With the background of an essential congeniality of our views, Timasheff's criticism of secondary points of Petrazhitsky's concept of law and of my modifications of it may be passed by without a

[77] See N. S. Timasheff, *An Introduction to the Sociology of Law* (Cambridge, Mass.: Harvard University Press, 1939); also Timasheff's Introduction to Leon Petrazhitsky's *Law and Morality* (Cambridge, Mass.: Harvard University Press, 1955).

detailed reply on my part. Some of his criticisms appear to be correct, while others are questionable.

More substantial are Timasheff's observations concerning my theories of revolution, war, and social calamities. In his admirable sketch, he correctly points at a tangible change of my views on revolution as they were given in my early work, *The Sociology of Revolution,* and in my later works. Indeed, in my later studies I largely abandoned the "instinctive-reflexological" theory of causation of revolution and some of its processes.

He is correct also: (*a*) in singling out my central theory of causation of revolution from "the peripheral, temporary, and local" circumstances of its explosion (like crowding of revolutions in some of the periods of blossoming or decay of a given society), and (*b*) in his assumption that some of the uniformities in revolutionary processes noted by me are observable and occur only in the great fully developed revolutions but not in small social disturbances or "palace revolutions."

Confirming these observations of Timasheff's, at the same time I want to say a few words in defense of my statement about more frequent explosions of revolutions in periods of blossoming and decay of a given society. This supplementary observation in no way contradicts my thesis about the main and necessary cause of revolution. Some periods of blossoming and decay are periods of rapid transformation of the basic values and social relationships of one part of a given society, while the other part does not undergo it; for this reason such blossoming (or decaying) periods as the fourth century B.C. in Greece, or the first century B.C. in Rome, or the eighth, the twelfth, and the thirteenth centuries in France, or the period of the early Renaissance in Italy, have been a "good breeding ground" for revolutionary disturbances. If my statement is applied only to this sort of blossoming and decaying periods, as it is meant to be applied, then the statement giving a supplementary knowledge about the circumstances favorable or unfavorable for explosion of revolution has considerable cognitive value. It also corrects a widely accepted opinion that revolutions explode only in periods of decay and never in those of prosperity, rapid progress, and blossoming of a society.

As to my main uniformities observed and occurring only in the fully developed revolutions, in describing these uniformities I simply followed the sound Aristotelian precept: if you want to study the properties of an oak, you should study them on a fully developed oak, not the acorn. If interpreted as fairly frequently but not invariably repeated uniformities in many revolutions these uniformities again give us a significant knowledge of a series of important processes taking place in many fully developed revolutions.

In the sociocultural world we rarely, if ever, observe strictly universal, perennial, and unexceptional uniformities. We should feel satisfied if and when we can discover merely roughly valid uniformities applicable to a large portion of revolutions or any other phenomena studied. Thus viewed, the uniformities of the two—destructive and constructive—phases in the cycle of revolution, of "the law of polarization," appear to occur in *nearly all* fully developed revolutions. The other uniformities, outlined in my studies, take place possibly not in all but still in a large portion of great social upheavals.[78]

In a slightly modified form these considerations answer Timasheff's and Martin's criticisms of my theory of war-and-peace causation. Their contention that I have given two or three incompatible hypotheses in this matter may be correct "formally" but it is not correct "substantially." As a matter of fact, all these allegedly incompatible theories are but variations of one and the same theory of war-peace causation, slightly modified in accordance with the circumstances and conditions of specific wars discussed.

International peace is promoted: (*a*) when there is present in each of the interacting societies a well-integrated system of ultimate values and the corresponding norms of conduct, (*b*) when these

---

[78] For empirical verification of the movement, causation, and uniformities of revolutions and wars in the history of Greece, Rome, and other major European countries, I give not just representative samples of these phenomena but historical series of *all* the wars and *all* the important internal disturbances recorded in the history of these countries. For this reason, my empirical verification is more systematic and fuller than that found practically in any other work in the world literature dealing with such problems. This explains why my indices of the main fluctuations of wars were confirmed by a subsequent study of the movement of wars by Quincy Wright and his collaborators, published in Wright's *Study of War*, Vol. I. I am reasonably certain that, side by side with corrections of secondary points, my main indices of the movement of internal disturbances—factually compiled by Timasheff and Oldenburg—will also be confirmed if such a study is repeated by other competent scholars. (So far our study remains unique in the world literature on revolutions.) The same can be said about my series of historical corroborations of the "law of polarization" and of some other uniformities formulated in my works.

systems are mutually compatible, (c) when they glorify, urge, and inculcate the value of peace but not of war, the values of reverence for life and dignity of man but not the values of lustful extermination, destruction, and subjugation of "the enemies" for this or that highfalutin purpose, and (d) when these compatible systems efficiently curb greediness, lust for power, plain human wickedness, and similar irrational drives and selfish propensities of human individuals and groups.

Conversely, the main factors underlying war are: (a) the absence of these conditions in the universe of interacting societies, and (b) the presence of either anomic congeries of values and norms amounting to a real moral anarchy and selfish cynicism in all or in particularly powerful interacting societies, or (c) the presence of mutually incompatible systems of values and norms, (d) the extolling of the values of war but not of peace, glorifying subjugation and extermination of the "enemies" but not, to use Schweitzer's expression, "ethical affirmation of life" and dignity of human beings, and (e) under the cover of highfalutin ideologies, "liberating in man or a group the worst of the beasts," instead of curbing "beastly" passions, lusts, greediness, cruelty, cussedness, and similar proclivities still remaining virulent in individuals and human groups.

In the light of these "formulas,"[79] all my allegedly incompatible hypotheses of war-peace causation become mere variations or shadings of one and the same hypothesis. Yes, wars tend to explode frequently in periods of political, economic, or cultural blossoming of powerful nations because such blossomings often occur, either in the conditions of moral anarchy and anomy, or when the system of values and norms of the politically and economically prospering nation educates it in glorification of its wars, its superiority, subjugation to it of its "enemies" and competitors, and in similar "virtues."

For the same reason, wars tend to explode in periods of great transitions from one basic system of values-norms-relationships to

[79] These "formulas" are notably developed and specified in my *Dynamics; Society, Culture and Personality;* British edition of my *Russia and the United States;* and in "Mutual Convergence of the United States and the U. S. S. R. to the Mixed Sociocultural Type," in the *Mémoire du XIXᵉ Congrés International de Sociologie,* Vol. III, Mexico, D.F., 1961; also published in the *International Journal of Comparative Sociology,* September 1960, and in German translation in the *Zeitschrift fur Politik,* Heft 4, 1960.

different ones, particularly from ideational to idealistic or to sensate order, or vice versa. In such transitional periods the old, crumbled system ceases to control groups and individuals, while a new system of social control has yet to emerge. The result of such a situation is the utter confusion, relativization, and atomization of all values, utter anomy and moral anarchy, and ensuing "liberation" in man of "the worst of the beasts," with rude coercion coupled with fraud as the supreme arbiter and controlling force of individual and collective policies. These features of transitional periods tend to become more devastating in the transition from a decaying sensate culture to an idealistic or ideational one than from the declining ideational to an idealistic or sensate one. While an individual or group passing from fading ideational values to noble sensate or idealistic values still is controlled to a notable extent by the surviving ideational and emerging sensate values at their noblest and best, the decadent sensate man and society become a prey to their own demoralization, confusion, anomy, and to an unleashed fury of rude force and fraud.

The same reason accounts for a tangible increase of wars in at least two idealistic periods studied, the fifth and the fourth centuries B.C. in Greece and the thirteenth up to the seventeenth centuries in Europe ("up to the seventeenth" because in several sections of the whole European culture the transition from the ideational to the well-established dominant sensate culture was non-synchronous and stretched throughout all these centuries).

Finally, the same reason explains why already at the end of the 1920's I ventured to predict the coming gigantic explosions of wars, bloody revolutions, orgy of destructiveness, bestiality, and an emergence on the historical stage of Man-the-Killer. Having diagnosed the real state of Western culture and society as the state of disintegration of a sensate order, I did not hesitate to make my prognoses. Despite the severest criticism of these by my fellow-scholars, my general as well as specific prognoses have come to pass even sooner than I expected.

The twentieth century has already become the most turbulent in regard to revolutions and the bloodiest century in regard to wars of all twenty-five centuries of Greco-Roman and Western history. In this case the reason for such a record is not so much an incompatibility of systems of values and norms of various countries as it is the extraordinary anomy, atomization of values, demoralization, extreme inflation of individual and collective egos, emergence of rude force and fraud as the supreme controlling arbiters of persons and societies, and other consequences of the crumbling sensate order in the West and decaying pseudo-ideational and eclectic orders in the East.

Mankind has entered possibly the greatest and most dangerous transition from these dying orders to a new—largely unknown and unbuilt as yet—order. Shall we wonder that this great transition has made this century possibly the most belligerent and the most turbulent, so far as revolutions and wars are concerned, in all of recorded human history?

The same formula explains why the postwar cold war has centered between the United States and Soviet Russia: since rude force and fraud are the only "effective" arbiters of our age, and since the decadent sensate man, or sensate group "understands only the argument from the position of strength, massive retaliation and deterrence" (as contemporary politicians say), it has been inevitable that the international conflict centered between the two most powerful Leviathans of our time.[80]

Finally, Timasheff's two main criticisms of some of the tentative uniformities formulated in my study of calamities are partly correct: some of these uniformities take place only in the fully developed calamities, and do not appear in a clearly observable form in all minor calamities. However, most of the uniform—personal, social, and cultural—consequences of great famines (and of sharp economic depressions), of revolutions, wars, and plagues, described in my study, seem to occur even in a large portion of purely local, temporary, and small calamities, like a local flood, tornado, volcanic eruption, landslide, fire, earthquake, and so on.

After publication of my volume, several of my previous students and readers of the book reported to me their observations of some of the local calamities which they witnessed. Their reports definitely confirmed the uniform effects of the specific form of calamity described in my study. I also continued to test my uniformities by studying for several years many special and press reports about this or that calamity visited upon a village or town or a local group.

[80] See a development of this in the British edition of my *Russia and the United States* (1950), chaps. x and xi.

Such repeated tests also confirmed the essential correctness of my uniformities. If these are taken as very approximate, not necessarily unexceptional or universal but as frequently occurring in most of the great catastrophes and in a large part of minor calamities, they are likely to be correct generalizations. As such they can be expected to occur in many future calamities. As such they have a significant cognitive value, even a considerable predictive value. My distinguished critic-friend seems to be inclined to a large extent to grant these virtues to my limited and approximate uniformities. With my thanks to him for his most valuable collaboration in the past years and for his excellent analysis of my theories of law, revolution, war, and calamities I can end my reply to his criticisms.

XIII. Problems of American-Russian Relationships

Dr. Inkeles' excellent essay shows many points of agreement in our views of the comparative structures of, and relationship between, the United States and Soviet Russia. The main disagreements can be reduced to four substantial points: (*a*) that "the mere number of similarities and differences, however important, is unlikely to be decisive" in determining friendly or inimical relationships between the two nations; (*b*) that "the most important are the differences in the freedom of political activity, the share people have in deciding their future, the opportunities for free expression of the spirit in art and religion," that "it is very difficult to believe" that "in the judgment of history the differences in the political structure of the Soviet Union and the United States, and in their role in the period following World War II, will be seen as inconsequential"; (*c*) that it is uncertain at all that the social, economic, and political system of each country "is moving away from its polarized position toward some common middle ground"; (*d*) that my prognosis of good relationships between the two nations has not been borne out by the facts and consequently my theory as well as my assessment of the degree of congeniality between Soviet and American social structures is incorrect.

As to the first point of dissent, there is hardly any real disagreement. In my *Society, Culture and Personality*,[81] the role of simi-

[81] Chaps. v, vi, vii.

larity and dissimilarity in social solidarity and antagonism is quite thoroughly discussed and a series of fairly precise generalizing conclusions are formulated. The main ones of these conclusions state:

1. *An important sociocultural similarity can generate both solidarity and antagonism of the parties.* It generates solidarity (*a*) when the values equally important for the parties are abundant and sufficient for all. . . , (*b*) if and when the egos of the interacting parties are fused together in one "we" . . . , (*c*) if the norms of the parties governing their relationship in the field of similarity are concordant.
2. An important sociocultural similarity generates antagonism of the parties (*a*) when the important values are scarce, when their norms are permeated by egotistic competition and are discordant and (*b*) when the nature of the important value does not permit its sharing between the parties. . . .
3. An important sociocultural dissimilarity can generate both solidarity and antagonism between the socioculturally dissimilar parties.[82]

Further on I specify under what conditions dissimilarity produces either solidarity or neutrality or antagonism of the interested individuals and groups.

These lines show that "the mere number of similarities and differences, however important, is unlikely to be decisive" in determining a friendly or inimical relationship between interacting parties—in our case, between the United States and Soviet Russia. In my *Russia and the United States* I outlined a number of similarities of the two nations, not so much for the sake of using these similarities as an explanation of the peaceful relationship (until the recent conflict) between the two countries, as for pointing out the similarities as important comparative characteristics of both countries. Only those similarities which meet the conditions specified in the preceding quotation were used as a modicum of explanation of why throughout the whole history of the United States its relations with Russia were peaceful, largely solidary, undisturbed by any war, even by any serious conflict. (My book was written in 1942 when both countries were fighting the common enemy and when no conflict marred their relationships.)

These comments explain why, in the first point of an apparent dissent, there really is no disagreement in our views.

As to the next two points, (*b*) and (*c*), there certainly is a tangible discordance between the view of Dr. Inkeles and my own.

[82] *Ibid.*, p. 142.

For the sake of economy, both points can be discussed together. Dr. Inkeles seems to think that for some forty-four years of the existence of the Soviet Revolution there have hardly been tangible changes in Russian sociocultural life and particularly in the political and economic regimes of Soviet Russia, and that for the same period the social, political, and economic systems of the United States have undergone scarcely any serious modifications and, finally, that there has been hardly any mutual convergence of social institutions, culture, and system of values of both nations to a mixed intermediary type. My theses in these matters have been that both countries have notably changed in their culture (social, political, and economic institutions and values) during these forty-four years and that, contrary to the noisy claims of politicians, in this change they have been converging to an intermediary type, becoming more and more similar in their sociocultural structure and their systems of values. I expressed this hypothesis in the American and British editions of my *Russia and the United States* and reiterated it in my address given at the plenary session of the 19th International Congress of Sociology, in September 1960, at Mexico City.[83]

In these problems I am inclined to disagree with Dr. Inkeles and to contend that my conclusions are more correct than his. My first reason for this is that Dr. Inkeles' stand implies a very dubious assumption that in our feverishly changing age no substantial change has taken place in the sociocultural order of Soviet Russia and the United States for almost half a century. This assumption appears doubly questionable for a Russian nation in the state of greatest revolution. If for purposes of comparison we take England forty-four years after the beginning of the Cromwellian revolution or France forty-four years after 1789, or the United States forty-four years after the beginning of the American Revolution, or practically any revolutionary country half a century after the explosion of its revolution, we know well how greatly each of such countries changed in such a period, including most important changes of its politico-economic regime. These observations alone make Dr. Inkeles' hypotheses very doubtful in their correctness.

This conclusion is well supported by a study of the actual

[83] It was published in German, English, and Spanish editions. Its English title: "Mutual Convergence of the United States and the U. S. S. R. to the Mixed Sociocultural Type."

changes in all compartments of culture, in major social institutions, the system of values, and the way of life that have occurred in both nations for these forty-four years. In my previously mentioned address, "Mutual Convergence," these changes, concisely but systematically outlined, show indeed that both countries, especially Soviet Russia, have undergone notable transformations and that in these changes both societies have been mutually converging to a third intermediary type and thereby have been becoming more and more similar to each other. In some compartments of culture, like natural science and technology, their positions are now nearly identical, while in most of the other compartments—of the social sciences and the humanities, philosophy, ethics and criminal law, education, sport and recreation, fine arts, and even religion—their present position is much more similar than it was at the beginning of the revolution.

In the fields of marriage and the family Soviet Russia has passed from the initial phase of a conspicuous disintegration of the monogamic family and marriage to the re-establishment of these institutions to a level more stable, and even more "Victorian" and monogamic than in any other country of the West. Likewise, their economic systems are much more similar at the present time than they were at the beginning of the revolution. In this field, during this period, this greater similarity has been reached mainly by great changes in the economic system of the United States in the form of an enormous expansion of governmentally managed sectors of the American economy, in rapid dwindling of "small business" as the only real form of the free enterprise, and in increasing governmental control of agriculture and the corporate economy. When the economic realities of both nations are studied in their real forms, and not in the form of highfalutin written and vocal propaganda, slogans, and formulae, they appear to be much more similar—even in peacetime—than the propagandists of both countries depict them.

Finally, even in the field of freedom and political regimes, both countries have been converging toward an intermediary position, through a mitigation and decrease of totalitarian features of the early Soviet regime and through "creeping" totalitarian tendencies in the political system and activities of the government of the United States. Even in such features as planning or the party system, both countries are now more similar than Inkeles claims.

Planning has been rapidly growing in the sectors of governmentally managed and corporate economy in the United States (up to such details as a progressive replacement of free market prices by "the administered prices" of the government and corporations and so on). Our nominally "two-party system" is factually but a "one-party system" functioning under two different names: Democratic and Republican. The difference between these parties is so intangible that even their leaders find it very difficult to formulate it in a clear-cut form, as was strikingly demonstrated during the Kennedy-Nixon presidential campaign, and as is daily shown by the greater difference between "the left and right wings" of the same party than the difference between the two parties. The same can be said of freedom and inalienable rights. In Soviet Russia, especially after Stalin, these liberties and rights have been slowly expanding, while in this country they have tended to contract in various—overt and covert—ways.

This does not mean that in all these respects Soviet Russia and the United States are already in an identical position and that no important differences exist in their sociocultural (including economic and political) orders.[84] It means, however, that the differences now are notably lesser and the similarities tangibly greater than they were in 1917-1924.

The outlined political changes as well as their future trends are largely explained by Herbert Spencer's and F. LePlay's formula, generalized by myself. The essence of this formula is as follows: Each time when in a given society there appears an important emergency in the form of war or threat of war, or great famine, or great economic depression, or devastating epidemic, or earthquake, or flood, or anarchy, unrest, and revolution, or some other major emergency, the amount and severity of governmental regimentation invariably increase and the society's economy, political regime, way of life, and ideologies experience a totalitarian conversion; and the greater the emergency the greater the totalitarian transformation. Conversely, each time a society's major emergency decreases, the

[84] I can "measure" the existing difference in the field of freedom by my "personal yardstick." While for my "political non-conformism" I was imprisoned three times under the Tsarist regime and three times under the Soviet regime, was condemned to death, and finally banished, in the United States for some forty years of living in this country as its naturalized citizen I have never been imprisoned or arrested, despite my nonconformity with, and criticism of, policies of the American government and of ruling groups.

amount and severity of its governmental regimentation begins to decrease and the society's economic, political, ideological, and cultural systems undergo a de-totalitarian reconversion toward less regimented and more free ways of life; and the greater the decrease of the emergency, the greater the reconversion to freedom.[85]

This formula accounts for the very emergence and growth of the Communist totalitarian regime in Russia (in the conditions of the greatest emergency of World War I and of the gigantic revolution with all their disasters and catastrophes in Russia in 1917-1918). The formula explains also the later trend of de-totalitarianization in Russia in recent years when the previous tremendous emergencies had greatly subsided. The formula explains also the creeping increase of totalitarian tendencies in the United States after the post-armistice de-totalitarian reconversion. With the protective safety of ocean neutralized by modern arms, the threats of a new world war, cold war, some hot wars, the armament race, economic depressions, and other emergencies have forced this country to increase the amount and severity of its federal and state governments' regimentation and control of economic and political activities of the nation and fostered its totalitarian conversion. It has been reinforced also by a rapid elevation of the United States to the position of the most powerful nation, which position inevitably fosters development of governmental centralization, control, and planning to a substantial extent. If, in the future, these emergencies continue to increase in one or in both nations, then we can expect a growth of totalitarianism in both countries which will reach its possible maximum if a new world war explodes.

This formula and my comments give a concise, clear-cut answer to these points of disagreement between the stand of Inkeles and my own in these matters. The coming years will decide who is right or wrong in this controversy.

Finally, as to my allegedly wrong prognosis and assessment of American-Russian relationships as they were given in the American edition of my *Russia and the United States*, I do not think that they are wrong or, at least, as wrong as Inkeles states. Here are the essential lines of the prognosis and assessment, written at the time

[85] See the development and corroboration of this fairly general uniformity in my *Dynamics*, III, chaps. vi and vii; *Man and Society in Calamity*, chaps. vii and viii.

of the closest military co-operation of both nations against the common enemy (in 1941):

Our attitude toward Russia presents a peculiar contradiction. We are highly enthusiastic about the Russian army; . . . we feel grateful to it for saving us and all the United Nations from utter catastrophe. At the same time many of us entertain serious suspicions and vague apprehensions respecting Russian Communism, atheism, "imperialism" and "barbarism." Some go so far as to find fault with Russia for *whatever* she does. If her armies retreat under the pressure of the German hordes, such detractors condemn her for her inability to defeat singlehanded the common enemy. . . . On the other hand, when the Red Army forces the German legions to retreat, such critics warn us gravely about the danger of a Muscovite invasion of Europe—the dire menace to civilization which would result from the victory of these twentieth century "Scythians!" Their fundamental purpose is to see Russia's population and culture utterly exterminated and the earth freed from "such scum." . . . The prevalence of this attitude naturally raises the questions: To what extent is it justified? . . . Is it to be seriously reckoned with in constructive planning for the postwar order? Should this country in particular strive for a close alliance with Russia, or should it avoid such intimate co-operation in its own interest as well as for the sake of the well-being of mankind?

These questions are highly important and must be clearly answered. *Throughout the entire history of the United States Russia has been its best friend. If the respective governments do not commit the stupidest blunders, Russia will constitute in the future our best and most important ally. In the interest of both nations and of humanity at large, the most wholehearted co-operation is not only possible and desirable but essential. The chances for co-operation between Russia and the United States are better, and those of . . . armed conflict are slighter, than the respective chances in the relations of either of these countries and any other great power. Without the co-operation of these two nations no lasting peace is possible. If a new and nobler social order is to emerge from this tragic war, the United States and Russia must play a leading role in the work of reconstruction.* . . . Such is my answer to the problem. It is clear.[86]

It is obvious that the second part of this prognosis has been perfectly correct and has been confirmed by history. As to the first part of the prognosis concerned with the chances of postwar co-operation of the two nations, it has not been borne out by history. But this fact does not make the prognosis wrong, since the clearly specified condition of a possibility of such a co-operation has not

---

[86] *Russia and the United States,* 1944, pp. 13, 14.

been met by the governments. As a grave matter of fact "the respective governments" *did commit the stupidest blunders in determining their mutual policies.* Neither the Truman-Churchill fatal declaration of war against Communism—that is against Russia and the Russian people—at their fatal meeting at Westminster College, Fulton, Mo., nor subsequent belligerent reaction to it on the part of the Stalin government, was necessary or wise or far-sighted. They were, in fact, the most unfortunate and stupidest blunders. Since that time subsequent policies of both governments have been truly catastrophic for both nations and for humanity at large. As I have written elsewhere:

Although more than fourteen years have elapsed since the armistice, there is no real peace, no mitigation of the cold war, and no decrease in the danger of the Third World War. Instead, both blocks have been . . . increasing their . . . military bases, intensifying the armament race, recruiting allies for wholesale murder, and conducting short-sighted military, economic and political maneuvers, which result in the deterioration of freedom and the alienation of the inalienable rights of citizens of both alliances. . . . The post-armistice governments of both blocks . . . have already exploded the Korean, the Indo-Chinese, the Middle East and other "police actions" in which a larger number of victims were killed and mutilated than in all Napoleonic wars and the wars of the nineteenth century put together. . . . Today's governments have also dismally failed to maintain internal order in their own empires or populations by civilized and humanitarian means. . . . The policies of the French government in Algeria, of the English government in Malaya, Cyprus, Yemen, and elsewhere, of the Soviet government in Hungary, the policies of the Formosan and the Chinese governments [and of the American government in Cuba and in America's satellite countries] are the examples of this bestial method of maintenance of order. . . . The ruling groups have uselessly wasted a cosmic amount of the world's natural resources and have not only squandered the accumulated wealth of mankind, but have piled up trillions in "national debts" to be paid by future generations. . . . The governments have also succeeded well in cultivating fear, distrust, and hatred by poisoning the neighborly relations of various nations and groups. By intensive training of millions of draftees and civil populations in the art of killing, by glorifying the "patriotic" extermination of all those who are not with us and those who are our opponents, the contemporary [rulers of both blocks of nations] have demoralized mankind, especially its young generations, more than any other agency. The increase in juvenile delinquency is partially due to these policies. The governments have also contributed to the disintegration of the greatest values, beginning with science and ending with religion, and of the greatest social institutions, beginning with the family and ending with the government itself. By these policies, the present rulers have caused the death of millions of victims of their "police actions" and "brush-wars," notably harmed the physical and mental health of additional millions, . . . and planted the radioactive seeds of a potential degeneration of the human species on this planet. These blind and irresponsible actions of those in power have robbed mankind of security, peace of mind, happiness and creativity.[87]

My prognosis has only one wrong point: I did not foresee that the postwar governments could be so blind, so irresponsible, so cynical, and so destructive. In regard to this point I plead guilty. In regard to all other points my prognosis happened to be quite correct.

In the British edition of *Russia and the United States* (1950), a detailed explanation is given of what are the apparent and the real causes of the Russian-American conflict and why the postwar conflict centered between the two nations. So far my hypothesis has not been repudiated by history, nor have any relevant facts appeared which necessitate either an abandonment or revision of this explanation.

In terms of the above propositions concerning the role of *similarities and dissimilarities* in social solidarity and antagonism, the American-Russian conflict falls into the categories 2 and 3 specifying the conditions of when similarities and dissimilarities generate antagonism and conflict. So much for this dissent between Dr. Inkeles' and my views on this point. Despite these disagreements, fortunately, there is a great deal of basic congeniality in our approaches to the study of these vital problems and in our conclusions regarding a number of the features of and trends in Russian-American structures and relationships. Inkeles' essay, his book on *Public Opinion in Soviet Russia,* and subsequent studies have notably contributed to our knowledge of several aspects of the Soviet Leviathan.

XIV. Sex Problems and Theories

Since there is a fundamental similarity (almost identity) between the views of Dr. David R. Mace, admirably expressed in his

[87] *Power and Morality*, pp. 100-103.

brilliant essay, and my tentative conclusions in the field of sex problems, I can promptly proceed with my replies to his critical comments and questions.

I plead guilty to his initial three criticisms. I hope, however, that my sins may be somewhat mitigated by my confession of my motives and intentions involved in committing these sins. My *American Sex Revolution* does not have a bibliography and references because I wrote it as a popular essay for intelligent lay readers, and not as a monograph for scholars and specialists. Popular pamphlets hardly need extended bibliography, footnotes, and references. So much for my first "sin." The intentional popular character of the essay accounts also for my second sin—"pressing a convincing case too far." In our age of blatant advertising, deafening propaganda, and Gargantuan exaggeration of everything to be sold to the public, one has to hammer his points as hard as he can to be heard by the public, especially if his points are "unpopular" and run against the prevalent fads and opinions. This is my excuse for the second and, in part, for the third sins. In this third sin, however, I plead not guilty to that part of Dr. Mace's indictment which accuses me of attacking not only the theories criticized but also their authors. At least I did not intend such an argument *ad hominem*, or the transference of my criticisms of Freudian and other theories to their authors. On the contrary, my criticism of their theories in no way has reduced my profound respect and admiration for Sigmund Freud and other criticized authors. In my *Contemporary Sociological Theories* I clearly stated: "The author wants to stress the fact that his criticism of a theory does not mean at all that he does not appreciate it, or does not have respect for its author. The opposite conclusion is true. This should be borne in mind to understand the writer's real attitude."[88] This attitude explains why I plead not guilty to this part of Mace's indictment.

Having dispensed with these sins, I can briefly reply to other criticisms of Mace's. I do not think there is a contradiction between my two statements about the Bohemians: in the first statement I talk about ordinary Bohemians who are obsessed by sex pursuits, spend an enormous portion of their time and energy in these pursuits, and otherwise are not graced by an outstanding creativity. In my second statement I talk about eminent creators in the field of

[88] *Contemporary Sociological Theories*, p. xxiii.

the fine arts who are often accused of conspicuous licentiousness. My statement contends that most of these accusations are either untrue or enormously exaggerated; and for this reason the fashionable theory of "sex freedom" as the necessary factor of creativity is fallacious. I do not see any contradiction between these statements, nor between different consequences of different sex activities of two dissimilar types of personality with different main pursuits in their life and activities. Creators live to create and in this supreme pursuit they may, now and then, indulge in sex activities. Ordinary licentious Bohemians live to copulate and in this pursuit they neither care nor can create any real values. It would be incomprehensible if the results in both cases were similar.

I do not retract, moreover, my statement about the deleterious consequences of excessive overindulgence in sex activities, particularly in their illicit form. Dr. Mace somehow overlooked the fact that I am talking not about normal sex activity but about *excesses and overindulgence* in such activities and particularly when they assume *illicit* forms. *Overindulgence* in eating or drinking or in any other kind of activity is found to be harmful; overindulgence in sex is not an exception to this general rule. Or does Dr. Mace think that overindulgence in this sort of activity is impossible? I am afraid he can hardly prove such a thesis. And talking about the deleterious consequences of sex excesses, I mean not so much or even not at all an anatomical or physiological "damage to sex capacity through use" (which may or may not result from promiscuity and excesses, though in various forms, like contracting venereal disease and so on, such damage fairly frequently happens) as much as several—tangible and intangible, physical, mental, moral, and social—transformations, deteriorations, and disintegrations of the sick sex addicts, especially devoted to illicit forms of sex pursuits. In these pursuits they are in states of perennial conflicts and often violent clashes with persons and groups whose interests they violate; they become habitual transgressors of moral and legal norms of their society; they provoke hatred and dislike on the part of their victims and neighbors, lead a life of constant tension and fear, and lose self-control over their passions and lust. Now and then they are killed or seriously harmed by some of their many enemies. In these and hundreds of other ways their vitality, health, integrity, and safety are incessantly undermined by direct and indirect consequences of their sex excesses. No wonder, therefore, that the life span of such sex addicts or sexually sick Don Juans and Messalinas is notably shortened; the rate of their death by violence is tangibly higher; and they age earlier than other persons. Interpreted so, my statement seems to be supported by Dr. Mace himself, in the later part of his essay, and by the third volume of Dr. Kinsey's studies. On this note of concordance I can end my reply to this criticism.

With reservations, I concur with Mace's hypothesis that in some cases asceticism and continence may also be harmful and among other effects they may generate aggressiveness, war, and bloody conflicts. Yes, complete continence is hardly possible and hardly desirable for the overwhelming majority of human beings (with the exception of the few saints and moral heroes). In some cases it leads to warping human personality and to impoverishment of the joy of living for the rank and file. I am not sure that it contributes to aggressive wars and bloody conflicts. The cases mentioned by Mace are unconvincing and can be countered by many opposite cases. Admitting the possible harmfulness of imposed non-voluntary asceticism, at the same time, I believe this harmfulness is much less dangerous and less serious than the sex excesses; there has hardly ever been and there certainly is not now any scarcity of normal and excessive sex activities, while complete continence has always been very scarce in all societies and at all times. Even involuntary ascetics have been an insignificant minority. There never has been nor is there now a real danger of inundation of the human universe by asceticism and by its possible harmful consequences. In its voluntary form it is very rare and beneficial rather than harmful. In its involuntary form it is still a mere rivulet in comparison with a big river of normal, abnormal, and excessive sex satisfaction of an overwhelming majority of men and women. If this rivulet contains some unhealthy elements, they can harm only an insignificant fraction of humanity.

I am glad to know that Dr. Mace's studies and personal observations of sexual realities, marriage, and family in Russia and in this country led him to the conclusions very similar to mine. As to the chances of overcoming today's sexual anarchy in the United States, I am reasonably certain that *if mankind avoids the explosion of a new world war and if the present cold and brush wars are replaced by a more or less peaceful coexistence of all nations,* the American and Western sexual anarchy will be overcome, as it was largely overcome in Soviet Russia. This change will probably be proceeding as part and parcel of a much more basic replacement of today's disintegrated sensate order by a new, probably integral (or idealistic), sociocultural and personal order.

The paramount trend of our time consists exactly in a gigantic struggle between the dying sensate and the emerging integral orders. Elsewhere I have shown that this tremendous struggle is going on at the present time in all compartments of Western and Eastern cultures, in all social institutions, and in all basic systems of values.[89] If there is no new world war or other major wars, there is hardly any doubt concerning the coming victory of the new integral order over the moribund sensate one. Its victory implies also the replacement of today's sexual anarchy by harmonious, sound, and noble sexual mores, marriage, and the family. It is true that at the present time the new integral order or "positive polarization" is just emerging, but its first fresh blades have already appeared and are slowly growing in science, philosophy, religion, ethics, fine arts, law, and even in politics and economics, as well as in other basic social institutions. To be sure, the great transition from a sensate to an integral order will take a long time (in the past similar basic transitions have required roughly one hundred and fifty years), but if mankind can avoid suicidal wars, the transition will surely be made and mankind's creative history will enter a magnificent new era, including a new sex order. Despite today's leadership of decadently sensate "hucksters" and uncreative "smart alecks" in this country, and despite a permeation of the American way of life by semi-rotten sensate values, this great nation still has *a tremendous reservoir of creative forces fully capable of building this new order.*

Just now these forces are hardly visible on the surface of a glittering, sensate American scene. But in the deep currents of American life, and in the undertows of the American mind and soul, they are already on the move in their reconstructive work. Given the

[89] See my "Three Basic Trends of Our Time," in *Main Currents in Modern Thought,* Jan.-March 1960, reprinted in *Estudios Sociologicos Internaciónales,* Vol. II, Instituto "Balmes" de Sociologia, Madrid, 1961, and in several other journals and publications. It is also recorded by the Campus Library, Campus World, Inc., Los Angeles.

necessary time, they will successfully accomplish their paramount task. Such is my answer to (and prognosis of) the momentous questions of Dr. Mace.

XV. Problems of the Wissen-und-Kultursoziologie

A. Pro Domo Sua. Like many elderly teachers I feel deeply gratified by the fact that numerous students who have taken some of my courses and seminars, or have co-operated with me as instructors and research associates, have grown into distinguished leaders of the younger generation of sociologists, scholars, and educators. If I did not contribute much to their growth, at least I did not hinder the development of their creative potential. Neither at Leningrad, nor at Minnesota, nor at Harvard did I ever press them to accept my personal theories uncritically. I repeatedly advised them to follow the path of independent investigation and formulation of their own views, regardless of their agreement or disagreement with my own or any other conceptual schemes, methods, and conclusions. This attitude and policy have been well justified by subsequent growth of these students, research associates, and instructors into notable leaders of today's sociology, psychosocial sciences, education, and other areas of creative endeavor.

The following represent a *partial* list of these scholars: Professors C. A. Anderson, B. Barber, C. Q. Berger, R. Chamblis, A. Davis, K. Davis, N. Demerath, N. DeNood, O. D. Duncan, J. B. Ford, J. Fichter, W. Firey, F. Frey, H. Hitt, G. Homans, C. Joslyn, H. Johnston, F. Kluckhohn, P. Landis, M. Levy, E. Lott, Charles Loomis, W. Lunden, R. Merton, E. Monachesi, W. Moore, T. Parsons, V. Parenton, A. Pierce, J. and M. Riley, E. Schuler, T. Lynn Smith, C. and I. Taeuber, E. A. Tiryakian, N. Whetten, R. Williams, Logan Wilson, and C. C. Zimmerman.

For some forty years of my professorial activities in this country, I have observed their growth with deep satisfaction, as each developed in his own way, free from pressures of *magister dixit*. (It is not unlike the enjoyment I have derived from the luxuriant growth of my plants into an outstanding flower garden—which has been starred in national magazines and granted a gold medal—

though some of these plants have taken an unexpected turn in their rapid growth.) Planted in good soil and supplied with good fertilizer of seminal ideas, such strong plants—human and horticultural —have freely grown into amazing gardens of notable beauty and creative achievement.

As one of the "hands" laboring in the garden of human talent, I feel particularly gratified when some of these younger leaders among my previous students and collaborators devote their time to a thoughtful analysis and competent criticism of my own theories. The Merton-Barber paper in this volume is an excellent example of such analysis and criticism. With the skill of topnotch surgeons, the authors artfully dissect my views in the field of the sociology of science and—what is more important—they set forth most searching questions which are basic for any brand of *Wissensoziologie*. Their analysis, queries, and criticism have so clearly focused upon the basic problems of the "sociology of mental productions" that they require carefully formulated answers, and such answers I shall try to provide.

But first I wish to acknowledge that it was Robert Merton who did most of the spadework for those parts of Volume II of my *Dynamics* which deal with scientific discoveries and inventions and with the fluctuation of various scientific theories given in chapters 3, 11, and 12 of that volume.—Now, to the Merton-Barber questions.

i. *Is my Kultur-und-Wissensoziologie tautological and idealistic?* The first—and possibly most important—weakness of my sociology of science, mental life and culture consists, according to Merton-Barber and several other critics, in its somewhat tautological character.

For it would appear tautological to say, as Sorokin does, that ". . . in a Sensate Society and culture the Sensate truth based upon the testimony of the organs of senses has to be dominant." . . . For, sensate mentality . . . has already been *defined* as one conceiving of "reality as only that which is presented to the sense organs." . . . In this case, as in other comparable cases, Sorokin seems to vacillate between treating this type of culture-mentality as a defined concept and as an empirically testable hypothesis.

My answer to this criticism is emphatic: "Not guilty!" Since Kant's distinction of "analytical" (tautological) and "synthetic" propositions, all truly tautological propositions have been expressed by the formula, A *is* A. In such propositions (or theories) the *predicate,* A, neither adds, nor unfolds, nor indicates anything new or different from the *subject,* A; their tautology, as well as their cognitive sterility, is quite obvious. All propositions of the type A *is* A can be called sterile tautologies.

All propositions of the type A *is* B differ radically from these real tautologies. In all such statements the predicate B unfolds or points out something not obviously given in A. If logically and empirically correct, the propositions (and theories) of the type A *is* B enrich our knowledge. This sort of proposition makes up the stuff of theories, equations, and formulae of all sciences and of all consistent systems of philosophy, religion, ethics, and law.

In a much broader sense, as E. Meyerson has indicated,[90] these propositions may also be viewed as tautological, identifying A and B, or 2 plus 2, as identical to 4. But all such propositions become tautological in this sense only after discovery that A *is* B—a discovery which sometimes requires years, decades, and even centuries of cognitive effort to accomplish. Before the discovery, the identity of A and B is neither obvious, nor known, nor easily discernible. All scientific propositions, inferences, formulae, and equations consist exactly of the statements of the type A *is* B.[91] Propositions, inferences, and generalizations comprising my *Wissen-und-Kultursoziologie* belong to this type. For it is obvious that the following propositions in the two columns below are not of the type A *is* A, but rather of the type A *is* B.

Basic Propositions:	*Inferred (and empirically verified) Propositions:*
1. "True and total reality is sensory."	1. In cultures based upon this sort of propositions: (*a*) "Scientific discoveries and inventions proliferate much more than in ideational cultures." (*b*) "Testimony of senses becomes the main criterion of the true and the false."

[90] In his *Identité et realité* (Paris, 1924), and *Du Cheminement de la pensée* (3 vols., Paris: F. Alcan, 1931).

[91] See on this my *Dynamics,* IV, 27 ff., and *passim.*

(c) "Topics of painting and sculpture are empirical phenomena."

(d) "Their style is visual and illusionistic."

(e) "The dominant ethics is utilitarian and hedonistic."

(f) "The dominant philosophies are materialistic, empiricistic, deterministic, nominalistic, and positivistic."

(g) "Social life is very dynamic in character: there is rapid change."

(h) "Secular power dominates over the spiritual one."

Hundreds of other propositions similar to those above may be found in my *Dynamics*.

2. "True and total reality is supersensory and superrational."

2. In cultures based upon this sort of proposition:

(a) "Scientific discoveries and inventions are comparatively few."

(b) "Supersensory and superrational revelation" prevails; "enlightenment" and "intuition" become the main "criteria of truth."

(c) "Theology becomes the 'queen of the sciences.'"

(d) "The topics of fine arts are the supersensory and superrational forms of being and mysteries of becoming, and their style is symbolic."

(e) "The dominant ethics is absolutistic: unconditional imperatives given by God."

(f) "The predominant philosophies are idealism, mysticism, indeterminism, and transcendental rationalism."

(g) "Government tends to be theocratic."

(h) "Social life is relatively static
in character: change is
slow."

Hundreds of other propositions
—still more specific and concrete
—may be found in my *Dynamics*.

Comparison of the propositions at the left, above, with those at the
right will certainly show that they belong not to the type *A is A*,
but to the type *A is B*.

Additional proof of this may be seen in the fact that: (a) most
of the "inferences" in the right column, as well as hundreds of other
—very specific and concrete—propositions of the *Dynamics* had hardly ever been made before; (b) several of these "inferences" have
been contested in their correctness (which could not happen if they
represented propositions of the type *A is A*); (c) each of the propo-
sitions-inferences of the *Dynamics* was subjected to empirical verification—more systematic and more complete (given in hundreds of
statistical tables and other forms of evidence) than any found in the
large majority of sociological works dealing with big problems and
variables; and (d) when all the "variables" of either an ideational,
or idealistic, or sensate supersystem, based upon their ontological
postulates, were "intercorrelated," these "variables" did not give
a coefficient of correlation of 1.00 (which they should have given
if they belonged to the type *A is A*), but they gave instead a coefficient r between 0.40 and 0.80.

These considerations decisively demonstrate the non-tautologi-
cal character of practically all those propositions, as well as others
of my entire sociology of knowledge and system of culture built
from such propositions and found in my *Dynamics*.

The propositions and the whole system were derived not from
tautological pseudologic, but from scientifically accepted empirical
procedures of investigation that yield verifiable knowledge, plus a
vigorous use of the deductive-inductive method.

These propositions and the whole theory may have many defects, but they are free from the mortal sin of sterile tautologies.[92]

[92] In passing, I should say that if my theory were infected by tautological disease,
no less infected by it would be all "structural" and other sociologies of knowledge,
because they also start with various postulates of "class structure," "group structure,"
"economic" or "technological" structure of a given society as the main determining
factor of that society's science and its whole "ideological" superstructure, and then

As to the "emanationist" character of my theory, I do not think the term is fortunate, nor does it accurately describe my *Wissensoziologie*. The term has so many different connotations that unless Merton and Barber specify the one they mean, the query cannot be answered intelligently. Its purported inquiry, however, may be clearly answered by the following theses of my sociology of knowledge.

First, in their mental activities human beings (as *homines sapientes*) fairly continuously conceive a great variety of meanings, ideas, beliefs, images, concepts, values, and norms of conduct. They often combine a part of these meanings into logically or aesthetically consistent systems of meanings, which less frequently some of them unify into progressively vaster meaningful systems, while still less frequently a few others unify the vast systems into the vastest supersystems of meanings: sensate, ideational, and idealistic. Side by side with meaningful systems, nearly all human beings have a portion of their total meanings in the form of the un-unified and inconsistent pile of meanings ("congeries").

Second, human beings (as *homines fabri*) fairly continuously "objectify" and "materialize" their systems and congeries of meanings through various physical and biological media and through their own verbal and overt actions ("vehicles").

Third, human beings (as *homines socii*) tend and often do succeed in socializing their objectified systems and congeries of meanings by making them known to, as well as accepted and practiced by, other human beings.

Fourth, in the way of the three stages (of conception-objectification-socialization) the superorganic or sociocultural realm of empirical reality—quite distinct from the inorganic and the organic classes of reality—has been built and superimposed by man upon the physical and biological forms of being and becoming.

Fifth, throughout the historical existence of human species,

---

they make a series of inferences from a postulate which they subsequently try to verify empirically. This is equally true of Marxian, Mannheimian, Schelerian, Weberian, Freudian, and other brands of *Wissensoziologie*. The same reasons which absolve my theory of the sin of tautology also absolve all these other theories from it. In my opinion their weaknesses consist not in tautology but in a vague formulation of their postulates, in the haphazard and fragmentary character of inferences drawn from their postulates, and in the incidental, inadequate, and merely illustrative character of empirical verification of their inferences and postulates.

billions of various congeries, small and vast systems, and a few supersystems of meanings have been conceived, objectified, and socialized. In their totality, they comprise the whole sociocultural stratum of empirical reality in its ideological, material, and behavioral forms.

Sixth, the total ideological, material, and behavioral cultures of different individuals and social groups differ greatly in the degree of their integration or unification into consistent systems and supersystems. Nearly all human beings and all social groups have a portion of their total culture in the form of an un-unified and inconsistent pile of ideological, behavioral, and material cultural congeries. Only a comparatively few individuals and groups succeed in unifying a greater part of their total culture into vast systems and into a supersystem. In the total culture of even such highly integrated individuals and groups there coexist, side by side with the dominant supersystem, the other two supersystems as minor currents, as well as a multitude of systems and congeries which are neutral or even contradictory to the dominant supersystem and to each other. The total culture of less integrated individuals and groups represents a sort of dumping place of heterogeneous systems and congeries without any dominant supersystem.

Seventh, the basic postulates of the sensate, ideational, and idealistic supersystems were conceived long ago and have been objectified and socialized several times in the total cultures of many "preliterate" tribes (like the Zuni or Dobu), as well as "historical" peoples of Ancient Egypt, Babylonia, China, Iran, India, Creto-Mycenaea, Greece, Rome, Europe, and others.

Eighth, my thesis that the three supersystems of culture are based upon and articulate in their compartments the basic—sensate, ideational, and idealistic—postulates is congenial to the theories of Danilevsky, Spengler, Toynbee, Northrop, Kroeber, and other scholars of the "Holistic School" of Germany and elsewhere who maintain that all high cultures (HochKulturen) are based upon and articulate in all their compartments their basic postulates: the "primary symbols" of Spengler, the "basic philosophical premises" of Northrop, the "master-patterns" of Kroeber, and so on.

These theses of my Wissensoziologie can hardly be questioned in their scientific accuracy. They hardly contain any of the "mystical" element implied in the term "emanationist." Such a term, therefore, can hardly be applied to my theory.

As to the "idealistic" (or, as I now prefer to call it, "integral") character of my theory, it can be called such in the following senses: first, in the sense I specify in the preface to the first volume of *Dynamics* (p. x) where I explicitly state that I deliberately assume the idealistic (integral) standpoint in my studies of structures and dynamics of sociocultural phenomena because methodologically this standpoint allows one to observe, study, and understand both sensate and ideational types of culture, while the sensate or ideational standpoint not only imposes limits upon one studying this one-sided type of culture itself, but it hinders his adequate understanding of all other types of culture. It inescapably yields a somewhat "cross-eyed," one-sided perspective and interpretation of the whole cultural universe.

Second, my position is idealistic or integral because my ontology or theory of reality, as outlined earlier, is integral. My sociological theories are a consistent continuation of this integral philosophy and methods of cognition into my studies of sociocultural and psychological phenomena.

Third, my standpoint may be called idealistic or integral also because all cultural phenomena—systems and congeries—according to my theory are first conceived as meanings (ideas, images, patterns, plans, models, blueprints, norms, values) in the "mind" of their inventor (discoverer, thinker, experiencer) and only after their mental conception are they "objectified," "materialized," "incarnated," or "externalized" in various physical, chemical, biological, and behavioral media, and are then diffused, socialized, and adopted by other individuals and groups. Neither in inorganic nor in organic reality does there exist any material spade or bomb or automobile or any "superorganic" or sociocultural phenomenon which could later produce their corresponding ideas or meanings in the mind of man. The idea or model of spade, automobile, or atomic bomb was first conceived in the mind of its inventor and then it was constructed in the form of a "material" spade, automobile, or bomb.

The same thing is true of science, technology, philosophy, religion, ethics, fine arts, politics, and economics: their "objectified" and materialized forms (such as books on scientific, philosophical, religious, aesthetic, legal, political, and economic matters, as well as instruments, laboratories, university buildings, temples, factories, markets, court buildings, museums, pictures, sculpture, and music scores, no less than overt activities of a scientific, religious, legal, political, or economic character) emerge only after these forms are thought of or are conceived as pure ideas, patterns, models, images, and other forms of meaning. Nearly the entire sociocultural reality has been created by man in this way: by subsequent objectification and socialization of meanings previously conceived in the minds of human beings. Nearly the entire superorganic world represents, besides the already conceived but not yet objectified and socialized meanings, the totality of materialized, "congealed" and "incarnated" meanings. Such a theory of structure, emergence, accumulation, and change of cultural phenomena can be called an idealistic or integral theory (or "law of three stages").[93]

This term does not prevent this theory from being more scientific than many other "materialistic" or "eclectic" theories. Such theories often seem to claim that it is not from previously visualized ideas, images, and meanings of automobiles, sculptures, or rituals that their material or behavioral forms are born, but rather from the non-existing material automobiles, statues, and rituals in the inorganic and the organic worlds, that the ideas, "blueprints," or images of these phenomena are generated in the human mind. This theory of the birth of ideas, images, models, and meanings of automobiles or other cultural phenomena from their non-existing in nature material models—is obviously absurd. Hardly any cultural object or phenomenon has ever been born and grounded in the empirical sociocultural world in this manner. The uniform way of emergence and growth of all meaningful sociocultural phenomena is from their mental conception to their materialization and socialization, but *not the reverse*.

ii. *Social and cultural factors in the Wissen-und-Kultursoziologie.* Of the two interdependent variables, cultural and social, I chose the cultural factor as the more fruitful or more important one that accounts for a given state of science, as well as of philosophy, religion, ethics, law, fine arts, polity, economy, and social theories. This means that each of these cultural systems is more decisively de-

---

[93] See on this my *Society, Culture and Personality,* chap. xxxv.

termined by the rest of the *cultural* systems and supersystems than by the *social structures* of the respective groups having these cultural systems and supersystems. Barber and Merton quite correctly point out my position in this matter.

I made this choice quite deliberately and for several reasons: First, *because the Marx-Mannheim-Stark-Gurvitch variable* (of the "social position of an individual" or the "structure of the social group") *cannot account for a large series of fundamental phenomena in the field of Wissen-und-Kultursoziologie.* For how can individuals occupying different social positions, as well as groups having heterogeneous structures, be said to have different cultural systems, supersystems, and congeries in the face of the unquestionable facts of *diffusion, acceptance, and practice of numerous cultural systems and supersystems—in their ideological, behavioral, and material forms—by millions of individuals occupying quite different social positions and by a multitude of social groups with radically diverse structures?* Millions of such individuals and hundreds of such heterogeneous groups speak the same English or Russian language (language cultural system), profess and use the same table of multiplication, algebra, geometry, arithmetic, or other system of science; hundreds of millions of individuals and thousands of groups with enormous differences in their social positions and structures belong to the same Taoist, Confucianist, Hindu, Buddhist, or Christian religion; they have similar ethical convictions on the Golden Rule, or on the Mosaic rule of "an eye for an eye," and similar aesthetic tastes, ideas, beliefs, and preferences, including the postulates of sensate, ideational, and idealistic supersytems.

"Like an ocean current, washing many shores and islands, such cultural systems—in their ideological, behavioral, and material forms —spread and root themselves in various occupational, nationality, territorial, economic, political, racial, and sex-age groups, as well as in various social classes, families, tribes, castes, and states."[94]

If the social position of an individual, or the structure of a social group, where the main determining factor in their total culture, or in adoption of any cultural system—beginning with science and ending with jazz and religion—the "planetary" diffusion of this sort of cultural system and supersystem over a multitude of different social

[94] *Society, Culture and Personality*, p. 336. A detailed analysis of the relationship between cultural and social systems may be found there.

groups and millions of individuals occupying most diverse social positions would have been impossible. If such diffusion has been taking place—and who can say that it has not?—then the emergence, diffusion, and acceptance of all such cultural systems have not been primarily determined by the social position of individuals, nor by the social structure and position of groups.

Second, "the social factor hypothesis" is contradicted also by the basic fact that *individuals in similar social positions, as well as groups with similar structures, often have quite different scientific, religious, philosophical, artistic, political, economic, and ethical cultural systems in their ideological, behavioral, and material forms.* Among rich captains of industry and finance, in this and other countries, there have been liberal, conservative, socialist, and even a few communist ones, affiliated with different religions, espousing different philosophies and ethical systems, and having acquired contrasting aesthetic tastes, scientific education, and economic policies. The same is true of kings in similar monarchial regimes, as well as dictators and their corresponding dictatorial regimes, not to mention the "proletarian" class voting for different parties, and so on. Such a cultural diversity of individuals whose positions are similar, and of groups whose structures are similar, clearly contradicts "the social factor hypothesis."

Third, this hypothesis is further contradicted by the fact that a given group may remain unchanged in its formal, structural constitution while at the same time, it may notably change its cultural systems and policies. The formal structure or constitution of many states, religious organizations, political parties, and other groups remains essentially unchanged for decades, while their cultural systems and policies undergo substantial transformation every few years, or even every few months.

This is also true of the formal structure of universities and research institutions: while in essentials their structure remains little changed for decades in its differentiation and stratification into president (rector), deans, full, associate, and assistant professors and senior to freshmen students, their scientific, philosophical, religious, artistic, legal, ethical, political, and economic theories and ideologies almost incessantly change.

Such obvious facts of daily occurrence as these clearly refute the hypothesis which holds to a decisive determination of science and other cultural systems by the social factor, position of individuals, and structure of social groups.

My fourth reason for assigning a preponderant role to the cultural factor is that in its specific form it is a *logical* and *factual precondition* for the very emergence, structuralization, and functioning of an organized social group itself. There is no organized social group which does not have its system of meanings, values, purposes, and norms of conduct around which and for whose realization and utilization the group emerges and functions. As a matter of fact, before their incorporation or actual establishment, most organized groups formulate in advance in their constitution their specific, meaningful objectives-values-functions, for whose realization-development-use the group is going to be organized and established. Whether the specific cultural system of the group is economic (as in all economic organizations), or religious (as in all religious organizations), or scientific, or artistic, or political, or occupational, or another *meaningful* system, it is the most important component of any organized group. Without this cultural component any group becomes a mere collection of interacting human organisms, "faceless" and devoid of individuality, a proper object of study by biologists and not by sociologists.

In all deliberately planned organizations, the conception of their constitution and their system of values-meanings-objectives, including their structure, precedes its "objectification," socialization (incorporation), and transformation into overt activities in the empirical social world. In spontaneously emerging social systems, the same process takes place but in a less clear and more intermittent way, with less lag occurring between conception and establishment of cultural phenomena.[95] Since no organized group (social system) can be without its cultural component (system of meanings-values-norms-objectives) and since this cultural component often is conceived before the "objectified" and "socialized" group is established, *the cultural system may be viewed as the logical and factual precondition of the very emergence and existence of the social group itself*, as a *social* group. For this reason, in the interdependent relationship of cultural and social factors, *it is the cul-*

[95] See my *Society, Culture and Personality*, chaps. xxi and xxii on "how groups originate and become organized," and chaps. iv, viii, and ix on specific characteristics of organized groups.

tural factor which predominantly determines the emergence, existence, and structure of social groups (systems), *rather than the latter determining the former.*

If we exclude the role of cosmic and biological factors in conditioning scientific or other cultural systems—since a study of these factors properly belongs not to the *Wissensoziologie* but to the *Wissenphysik* and the *Wissenbiologie*—then the preceding statement, applied to science and knowledge, means that their ideological, behavioral, and material forms (including structures of scientific organizations) are conditioned, first of all, by the preceding state of science itself; second, by the state of other cultural systems and supersystems; and third, by the structural forms of scientific organizations and agencies.

These reasons explain why in my *Wissensoziologie* I took the cultural and not the social factor as "the basic independent variable." The cultural factor, beginning with the ultimate postulates of the supersystems and the narrower premises of vast cultural systems, has permitted much more numerous, more substantial, and more specific deductions, as well as more systematic and definitive verification of each deduction by the relevant empirical facts, than the social factor—"the position of the individual" and the "structure of social group" or their constellations—would have allowed. My choice of the "cultural factor" enabled me to investigate and to clear up not only the kind and closeness of the interrelationships among a multitude of—often very specific—cultural variables (science, philosophy, religion, ethics, law, fine arts, etc.), but also the relationships of these *cultural variables,* and especially cultural supersystems, to such basic *social phenomena* as "familistic-contractual-coercive" social relationships, theocratic-secular, and totalitarian-democratic forms of government, the movement of wars and revolutions and fluctuation of economic standards of living, plus such specific social facts as the fluctuation of percentages of royalty-aristocracy-bourgeoisie-labor classes, as well as of men and women in the portraiture of European countries in the centuries from the tenth to the twentieth, and the role of cultural and social factors in determining what kind of cultural values become "best" or "poor" sellers and why.

In all these respects the hypothesis of the cultural factor taken by me as the "independent variable" proved itself more fruitful in a cognitive sense than has the hypothesis of the social factor in practically all the extant studies in the field of the *Wissen-und-Kultursoziologie*.

This does not mean that I deny the cognitive fruitfulness of the *Wissensoziologie* starting from, and based upon, the social factors of the position of an individual and group structure. Certainly such a *Wissensoziologie* has its own place and these social factors have to be considered in any *Wissensoziologie*. An already defined social position of an individual, e.g., of a scientist, in the differentiated and stratified body of all social groups to which he belongs, certainly conditions his mentality and behavior; and an already crystallized structure of a given social group, e.g., university or research institution, tangibly affects scientific and other activities of such a social system. But considering the above given four reasons, particularly the fact of preconditioning by cultural factors of the very social position of individuals and social structure of groups— that is the entering and workings of these cultural factors through and from within the very media of social positions and structures— the total role of the social factors in the field of *Wissen-und-Kultursoziologie* appears to me to be secondary compared to cultural factors. *The social Wissensoziologie can account for a lesser number and less basic classes and characteristics of social and cultural phenomena, including scientific phenomena, than the cultural Wissensoziologie.*

This conclusion is well supported by the existing works of the "social *Wissensoziologie*" type. Soberly appraised, the *Wissensoziologie* of Marx, Mannheim, and other leaders of this type of *Wissensoziologie* has yielded, so far, mainly vague generalizations and fairly indefinite formulae of uniformities as to precisely what kind of social position of individuals determines their acceptance or rejection of precisely what kind of ideological-behavioral-material cultures, and what kind of group-structures definitely conditions acceptance or rejection of what kind of their "cultural superstructures." Even such a fundamental claim of Marx as to the uniform predilection of proletarian and labor classes to Communism has proved itself to be neither universal, nor general, nor of perennial uniformity. Many causal formulae and generalizations of other partisans of this type of *Wissensoziologie* have turned out to be even less correct. Some of their conclusions seem to be correct, but they happen to be of a purely "local" and "temporary" character and not universal and general. Several other contentions may be correct, but so far their authors have given us only fragmentary and inadequate proof for their propositions.

Summing up, I can say that *co-operation of the cultural and the social types of Wissensoziologie is necessary for adequate cognition of sociocultural reality, but of these two types the cultural Wissensoziologie is more important and more fruitful than the social Wissensoziologie.*

With this background of propositions set forth in this section, I can now briefly answer the pointed questions of Merton and Barber, numbers 2, 3, 4, 5, 6, and 7, summed up at the end of their essay.

i. They are quite correct in naming my theory "macrosociological." Being such, it does not pay sufficient attention to many "microsociological" problems of the *Wissen-und-Kultursoziologie*. But is my preoccupation with macrosociological problems really a defect or shortcoming of my theory? Are these problems not basic enough, not important and complex enough to be the object of study, not only by one but by many generations of scientists and scholars? If I made a contribution to the cognition of these basic problems I am quite satisfied with such a modest achievement, even if my theory completely passed by all microsociological problems. But did it, in fact, pass these by? It did not, as shown below.

ii. Like any basic theory, systematically documented by the long-time series of empirical relevant data, my macrosociological studies give, at the same time, a detailed and most systematic qualitative and quantitative "microsociological" account of the state or spectrum of each of many social and cultural systems and processes in their coexistence and covariation for each year, decade, half-century, or century over some twenty-five centuries of the existence and change of these structures and processes. Could such eminent scholars as von Wiese and Znaniecki, not to mention many others, be entirely wrong? Said von Wiese: "Comtes, Spencers, Paretos und Spenglers Versuch etwa erscheinen willkurlicher, im Vergleich zu Sorokins Werk."[96] Said Znaniecki:

[96] Leopold von Wiese, "Ideekultur und Sinnenkultur," *Archiv für Rechts-und Sozialphilosophie*, XXXI, 371.

As yet the only thorough and consistent effort to integrate *all* specialized nomothetic cultural science into a general theory of culture is that of Sorokin. Sorokin is the first cultural scientist to apply the same approach to every compartment of culture and to relationships between cultural phenomena and different compartments. . . . The number and diversity of particular cultural systems he includes in his investigation are unequalled. Moreover, his study covers systems ranging from the very simple to the very complex. He takes into account differences in their integration ranging from congeries to highly organized systems and compares their relative duration and the range of their extension. . . . As a philosophy of culture Sorokin's theory is certainly superior to all philosophies of culture developed by his predecessors.[97]

iii. My macrosociological theory accounts also for many variations of thought and science *within* each of the societies and cultures dominated by the same cultural supersystem. The coexistence of different currents of thought and different theories in science in the same society is due, first (especially when differences are great as, for example, when there coexist in a society persons—including scientists—and groups with an atheistic and a religious *Weltanschauung*), to the coexistence of the dominant supersystem with the other two supersystems which, as minor currents, nearly always coexist with the dominant supersystem in the total culture of a given integrated society or of persons. I never contended that the *total* culture of either a person or a group is completely integrated into one of the supersystems, and I have repeatedly stressed that each of the supersystems unifies only a major part of the total culture. The coexistence of atheistic and religious scientists means that the atheistic ones are "infected" mainly by the sensate, while religious scientists are notably influenced by the minor ideational or idealistic supersystems.

Second, such variations may be understood in terms of the many-sidedness of the total sensate or ideational or idealistic reality. None of us, including scientists, grasps and interiorizes *all* aspects of each of these classes of sociocultural reality, and each of us "imbibes" or "inhales" only some of its aspects, which vary greatly with different individuals; hence, the variations found in sensate or ideational beliefs, ideas, and tastes within the same dominant supersystem.

[97] Florian Znaniecki, *Cultural Sciences* (Urbana, Ill.: University of Illinois Press, 1952), pp. 377-78.

Third, some variations may be due to the immanent, often *dialectic,* development of tensions and problems inherently present in any system of thought, including the system of science, and to the fact that none of the various theories and beliefs, including scientific ones, incorporates in itself "The whole truth and nothing but the truth," giving us absolute knowledge of total reality in its infinitely manifold plenitude.[98]

In cognizing any form of being, be it sensate, idealistic, or ideational, there is always an opportunity for creative thought to discover a hitherto unknown aspect of such reality and to produce a theory or ideology essentially different from any other. And this creative process of discovering new aspects and resolving unresolved tensions and contradictions goes on, with different degrees of intensity and interruptions, almost incessantly throughout the history of human thought and creativity.[99]

Fourth and finally, the variations may be due to differences in existential conditions and group affiliations, as well as position in each of such groups, plus probable differences in biological equipment of respective scientists, creative individuals, and groups. These three cultural factors, plus the fourth—social and biological factors—can account for the coexistence of the differences discussed in the same society dominated by the same supersystem.

iv. As to whether the margin of autonomy of various cultural and social systems is the same or different for various systems, I answer this question in some detail in my *Dynamics.*

The amount of self-determination of their own destiny or the amount of dependence upon external conditions is not constant for various sociocultural (and personal) systems. . . . First, it depends upon the kind of social or cultural (or personal) system. . . . Second, upon the kind of milieu. . . . Third, upon the total and the specific immunity of the system from its environment, in the molding of its own destiny. . . . Fourth, other conditions being equal (including the milieu) in the social, cultural (and personal) systems of the *same kind,* the greater and better is their integration, the greater is their self-determination and autonomy from the environment in molding their own destiny: . . . the least amount of self-determination is found in unorganized social groups and in cultural congeries, while the greatest margin of autonomy is found in the per-

[98] See on this my ontology which I outlined earlier in this reply.

[99] I discuss this in an article, "The Factor of Creativity in Human History," *Main Currents in Modern Thought,* XVIII (1962), 99-104.

fectly-causally and meaningfully-integrated social, cultural and personal systems.[100]

Several other more specific conditions affecting the margin of autonomy of systems are enumerated and analyzed in the above-cited volume.

Many tables of my *Dynamics* and especially the graphs and coefficients of correlation of the interrelated movements of the main systems of sensate and ideational supersystems throughout some twenty centuries given in Chapter 15 of Volume III clearly support the above conclusions. All eight variables (systems) of sensate, as well as ideational, supersystems move in a tangible togetherness, or correlation with each other, throughout these centuries, but the degree of simultaneity differs among the variables, as indicated by the fluctuation of the coefficients of correlation between .40 and .80. None of these variables moves along trajectories identically with others and, as a detail, the curve of economic conditions fluctuates in the most deviating manner from the curves of other sensate or ideational variables. The movements of these eight variables indicate that all eight systems in each—sensate or ideational—supersystem function and change interdependently; but each of these systems seems to have a notable and different margin of autonomy in its movement; and seven of the eight variables show a comparatively great independence from the eighth—the economic variable (or conversely, the economic system changes more independently from the other seven than any of the latter do from each other).

This means that Karl Marx and partisans of the economic interpretation of the "ideological superstructures" are grossly exaggerating the role of the economic factor in the determination of ideological systems. (In passing, I should note that Merton and Barber quite correctly point out an essential similarity between Marx and Engels and my standpoints: both theories operate mainly with the sociocultural systems and not so much with the congeries; both assume and start with the basic—though different—postulates; both acknowledge the marginal autonomy in different systems; and both stress the immanent dialectic change of the systems. While

[100] *Dynamics*, IV, 608-20. See also chaps. xii, xiii, and xiv. Incidentally, in these chapters the theory of the "inner-directed" and "other-directed" types of persons, later developed by David Riesman in his book, *The Lonely Crowd*, is clearly outlined in a nutshell.

differing radically from the "materialistic" aspects of the Marx-Engels ontologies, my views and theirs are congenial in the above respects.)

v. I have already answered Merton's and Barber's question 5. Microsociological investigations, especially those dealing with why and how a given scientist or any other individual happened to formulate, accept, or acquire his theories, ideologies, beliefs, tastes, moral convictions, etc., must take into account his social position in and degree of affiliation with all groups of which he is a part, as well as all the cultural influences exerted over him by numerous agencies, including the cultures of the groups with which he has been interacting. In addition, his biological properties should also be considered. (In the short autobiographical microsociology of my mental life at the beginning of this volume, I concretely show the relevancy of certain social and biological factors in accounting for several significant traits of, and changes in, my mentality and behavior.)

If we exclude the cultural influences exerted upon him by the cultural components of his groups, the influence of one's social position among the various "cultureless" groups becomes comparatively insignificant.

vi. As to my position on quantitative methods (including the statistical one) in a study of sociocultural and psychological phenomena, I have always regarded such methods as necessary and most fruitful if and when they have been shown to be applicable and competently and expertly used. In my *Fads and Foibles* I reiterated this view, stating that "mathematical reasoning has played a royal role in the development of science and rational thought itself. Mathematical analysis has been largely responsible for a good share of scientific discoveries and inventions. With the development of mathematics the quantitative approach to a study of psychosocial problems has also grown and immensely contributed to our knowledge of the psychosocial world."[101] If in the same work I criticize many seemingly statistical and quantitative procedures, it is because such procedures are pseudo-mathematical, quasi-statistical, and "quantophrenic," representing misuse and abuse of true quantitative methods.

[101] *Fads and Foibles*, pp. 102-3.

vii. The answer to Merton's and Barber's question 6 is that I have been trying to use the integral criterion of truth and method of cognition as they are outlined in the earlier "philosophical" part of this reply. In a much better form, the integral method of unified—"intuitional," logico-mathematical-sensory—cognition has been used in making all *great* scientific discoveries and inventions, as well as in *great achievements* in various fields of social and cultural life: *great* religious, philosophical, ethical, and legal systems, no less than the masterpieces in the fine arts. *Small* discoveries and achievements have been made by combining mainly the logico-mathematical and sensory ways of cognition, without the grace of genius or "suprasensory-suprarational intuition" at its purest and best.

With the continued decay of the sensate supersystem and with the emergence of the first spring grass of the coming new—possibly integral—sociocultural order, contemporary science may be expected progressively to move toward the integral system of truth and knowledge by becoming in its basic principles less and less sensate and more and more integral.

This double process has manifested itself on the one hand in: (*a*) an increasing destructiveness of the morally irresponsible, Sensate scientific achievements like the nuclear means of warfare invented and perfected by the Sensate scientists; on the other, in (*b*) an increasing number of scientists who refuse to cooperate in this destructive misuse of science; and, finally, in a transformation of the basic theories of science in a morally responsible, Integral direction. This change has already made today's science less materialistic, mechanistic and deterministic—or less Sensate—than it was during the preceding two centuries. For this modern science, matter has become but a condensed form of energy which dematerializes into radiation. The material atom is already dissolved into more than thirty "non-material," "cryptic, arcane, perplexing, enigmatic, and inscrutable" elementary particles: the electron and the antielectron, the proton, the photon, the mesons, etc., or into "the image" of waves which turn into waves of probability, waves of consciousness which our thought projects afar. Around a bend of quantum mechanics and at the foot of the electron ladder the basic notions of "materialistic and mechanistic science"—such as matter, objective reality, time, space, and causality—are no longer applicable and the *testimony of our senses largely loses its* significance. The deterministic causality is already replaced in the subatomic world by Heisenberg's principle of uncertainty, by fanciful "quanta jumps," and by a mere chance relationship, while in psychosocial phenomena it is replaced by "voluntaristic," "freewilling" law of direction, or by immanent self-determination largely free from causality and chance. This last point is stressed by such leaders of physical sciences as Max Planck, A. Einstein, A. Eddington, E. Schrö-dinger, W. Heisenberg, H. Margenau, P. Dirac, and many others.[102]

If human folly, assisted by destructive sensate science, does not destroy the human universe, including science itself, then the new sociocultural order and its science seem to be progressively shaping into what I define as integral order and science in which science and truth will again be reunited with goodness and beauty (in philosophy, religion, fine arts, ethics, law, politics, and economics), re-establishing, in St. Simon's terms, a new "organic" order in the human world.

viii. Finally, my answer to Merton's and Barber's question 7 is already given in my reply to Arnold Toynbee's criticism. I never denied the accumulative character of scientific discoveries and inventions. What I have stressed is that, in the long run, creative achievements in philosophy and religion, the fine arts and ethics, as well as in all other fields of cultural and social life, are also accumulative. I have also stressed the point that these processes, being on the whole accumulative, are also somewhat intermittent, having temporary arrests and even regressions.[103]

The total fund of discoveries, inventions, and other creative achievements of mankind at the present time is certainly richer in science and in other systems of culture than it has been in the past. It is already so immense that no single man can know and use it in its plenitude. A large part of mankind fails so much as to grasp even its most notable parts, let alone appreciate its greatest values.

Just as contemporary sensate science is richer and more mature than that of preceding sensate periods, so also is the totality of other cultural systems in comparison with previous totalities. If mankind does not destroy the human world in a new apocalyptic war, each of the future sensate or integral or ideational periods will be adding their own contributions to the extant, truly immense, fund of socio-cultural values. The continued shift of human culture from one of the dominant types to the others is not a sign of regression. On the contrary, it represents a striking manifestation of indefatigable hu-

[102] See my "Three Basic Trends of Our Time."
[103] See my *Dynamics*, IV, chaps. vi and vii.

man creativity which, having exhausted for the time being the creative potential of a given supersystem, shifts and continues its creative *élan* in the form of other supersystems, each opening ever-new aspects of the inexhaustible total reality undiscovered by the other two supersystems. Each subsequent sensate or integral or ideational order is not a monotonous replica of its preceding recurrences, but an ever-new—and ever-original—variation of its main theme. And there is hardly any limit to this creative *élan* of man-creator in the discharge of his main mission on this planet and beyond it, in the infinite outer space and the cosmos.

With these remarks I bring to a close my reply to the thoughtful criticisms and searching questions of Robert Merton and Bernard Barber, my distinguished companions in the search for a fuller understanding of the enigmas of the superorganic, human universe.

XVI. Reply of Profound Gratitude to T. Lynn Smith, F. R. Cowell, Alexandre Vexliard, Lucio Mendieta y Núñez, and K. M. Munshi for Their Magnanimous Evaluations of My Contributions

Since the most generous essays of these eminent scholars and cultural leaders contain virtually no criticism of my ideas, my reply to their papers is naturally reduced to an expression of my heartfelt thanks for their most friendly assessment of my contributions to the fields of rural sociology, the philosophy of history, psychology, ethics, and religion. To these thanks, with their permission, I should like to add a few short comments.

First, their outlines and analyses of my theories are quite correct and admirable in all respects. Second, in their magnanimity, they greatly overestimate my modest contributions to these fields. Third, their few criticisms, like Dr. Vexliard's tempered remarks concerning my untempered criticisms of various psychological tests and Freudian theories, are quite accurate. In my reply to Dr. Mace's criticisms I have already confessed to this sin. The same is to be said about my other shortcomings mentioned in other papers. Fourth, Dr. Cowell's eloquent defense of my theories from the attacks and misinterpretations of their critics is perfectly correct in his interpretation of my real views and quite convincing in Cowell's powerful counterattack on the views of the critics themselves. In addition, his paper gives a remarkably competent and clear picture of the state of "philosophy of history" and sociology in contemporary England. My only "criticism" of his essay is that he did not give in it a more comprehensive outline of his own theory of culture as it is developed in his significant volume, *Culture in Private and Public Life,* and that he did not mention at all his own theory of history that served him as a foundation for his remarkable volume *Cicero and the Roman Republic.* Fifth, Dr. Munshi's penetrating observation of a congeniality of my views with the prevalent currents of Indian philosophical, ethical, and psychological thought well agrees with my own experience in this matter. Beginning with the philosophy and ethics of the Upanishads, the Bhagavad-Gita, Patanjali's yoga, the works of the great Buddhist logicians like Nagarjuna, Asanga, Vasubandhu, Gotama, Dignaga, Dharmakirti, various Brahmanas and Puranas, and ending with the recent philosophies and moral teachings of Ramakrishna, Vivekananda, Gandhi, Vinoba, Sri Aurobindo, S. Radhakrishnan, and Dr. Munshi himself, all these works have notably enriched, deepened, and enlarged my mental and moral horizon and have quite tangibly influenced my ontological, epistemological, and ethical views.

Finally, as to the essays of Dr. Alexandre Vexliard, Dr. T. Lynn Smith, and Dr. Lucio Mendieta y Núñez, I can only say that I am very grateful to these eminent scholars and outstanding leaders from France, North America, and Latin America for their magnanimous assessments of my humble contributions to psychology, rural sociology, and Latin-American sociology, to which each of them has contributed much more than I. I am proud of having among many of my students such an outstanding rural sociologist, demographer, and expert in Latin-American problems as Professor T. Lynn Smith; of having among my colleagues and friends such an international leader in sociology and most eminent Latin-American sociologist as Dr. Lucio Mendieta y Núñez, and such a young but already distinguished French psychologist as Dr. Alexandre Vexliard.

With my warmest thanks to Dr. Philip J. Allen and to all the contributors to this volume I can close my reply to their penetrating and most thoughtful analyses, evaluations, and criticisms of my contributions.

Publications of Pitirim A. Sorokin

(Listed Chronologically)

I. Books

1. *Prestuplenie i kara, podvig i nagrada* (Crime and Punishment, Service and Reward). St. Petersburg: isdatelstvo Dolbysheva, 1913.
2. *L. N. Tolstoi, kak filosof* (Leo Tolstoi as a Philosopher). Moscow: isdatelstvo Posrednik, 1915.
3. *Problema sozialnago ravenstva* (The Problem of Social Equality). St. Petersburg: isdatelstvo Revoluzionnaia Mysl, 1917.
4. *Pracheshnaia Tchelovecheskikh dush* (Laundry of Human Souls, science fiction). St. Petersburg: Ejemesiachnyi Journal, 1917.
5. *Uchebnik obschey teorii prava* (General Theory of Law). Iaroslavl: isdatelstvo Iaroslavskago Soyuza Kooperativov: 1919.
6. *Obschedostupnuy uchebnik soziologii* (Elements of Sociology). Iaroslavl: isdatelstvo Iaroslavskago Soyuza Kooperativov, 1920.
7. *Sistema soziologii*, 2 vols. (A System of Sociology). St. Petersburg: isdatelstvo Kolos, 1920.
8. *Golod kak factor* (Hunger as a Factor). St. Petersburg: isdatelstvo Kolos, 1921 (destroyed by the Soviet government).
9. *Sovremennoie sostoianie Rossii* (Contemporary Situation of Russia). Praga: Kooperativnoie isdatelstvo, 1922.
10. *Popularnuye ocherki sozialnoi pedagogiki i politiki* (Popular Essays in Social Pedagogics and Politics). Ujgorod: isdanie Komiteta delovodchikov i narodnoprosvetitelnukh rad Podkarpatskoi Rusi, 1923.
11. *Leaves from a Russian Diary*. New York: E. P. Dutton & Co., 1924; Boston: Beacon Press, 1950.

12. *Sociology of Revolution.* Philadelphia and London: J. B. Lippincott Co., 1925.
    Translations:
      Die Soziologie der Revolution. Munchen: Lehmanns Verlag, 1928.
      Latvian edition. Riga: 1934.
13. *Social Mobility.* New York: Harper & Brothers, 1927; *Social and Cultural Mobility.* Glencoe, Ill.: The Free Press, 1959.
    Translations:
      Chinese edition. Shanghai: Shanghai World Publishing Co., 1933.
      Estratificacion y Movilidad Social. Mexico: Institute de Investigaciones Sociales de la Universidad Nacional, 1956.
      Japanese edition (in part). 1928.
      Italian edition (expected to be published in 1963).
14. *Contemporary Sociological Theories.* New York: Harper & Brothers, 1928.
    Translations:
      Soziologische Theorien. Munchen: C. H. Beck Verlag, 1931.
      Les Theories sociologiques contemporaines. Paris: Payot, 1938.
      Soziologija. Beograd: isd. Geze Kona, 1932-33.
      Sociologicke nauky. Prague: Jan Laichter, 1936.
      Chinese edition, 1932.
      Chinese edition (another), 1936.
      Yüzyilimizin Sosyoloji Nazariyeleri. Istanbul: Husnubiat Basimevi, 1949.
      Another Turkish edition, 1950.
      Teorias sociologicas contemporaneas. Buenos Aires: Editorial Depalma, 1951.
      Hindi edition. Agza: Prasad & Sons, 1963.
      Japanese edition (in part). 1930.
15. *Principles of Rural-Urban Sociology* (with C. C. Zimmerman). New York: Henry Holt & Co., 1929.
    Translation:
    Japanese (in part). 1931-32.
16. *A Systematic Source Book in Rural Sociology* (with C. C. Zim-

merman and C. J. Galpin). 3 vols. Minneapolis: University of Minnesota Press, 1930-32.

17. *Social and Cultural Dynamics.* 4 vols. New York: American Book Co., 1937-41; New York: Bedminster Press, 1962.

Abridged, one-volume edition. Boston: Porter Sargent, 1957.

Translations: *Dinamica social y cultural.* Madrid: Instituto de Estudios Politicos, 1962. Several others in preparation.

18. *Time-Budgets of Human Behavior* (with C. Q. Berger), Cambridge, Mass.: Harvard University Press, 1939.

19. *Crisis of Our Age.* New York: E. P. Dutton & Co., 1941.

Translations:

A Crise do nosso tempo. Sao Paulo: Editora Universitaria, 1945.

La Crisis de nuestra era. Buenos Aires: Espasa-Calpe, 1948.

De Crisis onser Eeuw. Deventer: N. Kluwer, 1950.

Aikamme Kriisi. Porvoo-Helsinki: Werner Söderström Osakeyhtiö, 1952.

Die Krise Unserer Zeit. Frankfurt am Main: Joachim Henrich-Verlag, 1950.

Japanese edition. Tokyo: Kitaro Sekine, 1952.

Norwegian edition. Oslo: Statistisk Sentralbyra, 1948.

20. *Man and Society in Calamity.* New York: E. P. Dutton & Co., 1942.

21. *Sociocultural Causality, Space, Time.* Durham, N. C.: Duke University Press, 1943.

22. *Russia and the United States.* New York: E. P. Dutton & Co., 1944.

Revised English edition. London: Stevens & Sons, 1950.

Translations:

Russia e Estados Unidos. Sao Paulo: Editora Universitaria, 1944.

Japanese edition. Tokyo: Toyo Keizai Shimpo Sha, 1953.

23. *Society, Culture and Personality.* New York: Harper & Brothers, 1947; New York: Cooper Square Publishers, 1962.

Translations:

Sociedad, cultura y personalidad. Madrid: Aguilar, 1960.

Portuguese edition. Rio de Janeiro: El Globo Co., 1963.

Japanese edition. Tokyo, 1962.

Hindi edition. Beawar: Rawat Brothers, 1963.
24. *Reconstruction of Humanity*. Boston: Beacon Press, 1948.
   Translations:
   Menneskehetens gjenreisning. Oslo: Olaf Norlis, 1950.
   Japanese edition. Tokyo: Bungei-Shunju-Shinsha, 1951.
   Die Wiederherstellung der Menschenwurde. Frankfurt
      am Main: Joachim Henrich-Verlag, 1952.
   Indian edition. Bombay: Bharatiya Vidya Bhavan, 1958.
   Hindi edition. Rajghat: Akhil Bharat, 1961.
25. *Altruistic Love: A Study of American Good Neighbors and
   Christian Saints*. Boston: Beacon Press, 1950.
26. *Social Philosophies of an Age of Crisis*. Boston: Beacon Press,
   1950. New York: Dover Publications, 1963.
   Translations:
   Kulturkrise und gesellschaftsphilosophie, Stuttgart-Wien:
      Humboldt Verlag: 1953.
   Las Filosofias sociales de nuestra epoca de crisis. Ma-
      drid: Aguilar, 1954.
   Hindi edition. 1964.
27. *Explorations in Altruistic Love and Behavior* (symposium).
   Boston: Beacon Press, 1950.
28. *S. O. S.: The Meaning of Our Crisis*. Boston: Beacon Press, 1951.
29. *Estructura Mental y Energias del Hombre*. Mexico: Instituto
   de Investigaciones Sociales, Universidad Nacional, 1952.
30. *The Ways and Power of Love*. Boston: Beacon Press, 1954.
31. *Forms and Techniques of Altruistic and Spiritual Growth* (symposium). Boston: Beacon Press, 1954.
32. *Fads and Foibles in Modern Sociology and Related Sciences*.
   Chicago: Henry Regnery, 1956.
   Translations:
   *Achaques y manias de la sociologia moderna y ciencias
      afines*. Madrid: Aguilar, 1957.
   Tendences et déboires de la sociologie americaine. Paris:
      Aubier, 1959.
   Japanese and German translations of several chapters
      of the book.
33. *The American Sex Revolution*. Boston: Porter Sargent, 1957.
   Translations:

La Revolution sexual en los Estados Unidos de America.
Mexico: Instituto de Investigaciones Sociales, Universidad Nacional, 1958.

Sex-Besatt Vasterland. Stockholm: Tidningarnas Artikelvorlag, 1959.

Japanese edition. Tokyo: Gigi Tsushinsha, 1957.

Indian edition under the title *Sane Sex Order.* Bombay: Bharatiya Vidya Bhaven, 1960.

Portuguese edition. Rio de Janeiro: Editora Fundo de Cultura, 1961.

34. *Power and Morality* (with Walter A. Lunden). Boston: Porter Sargent, 1959.

Indian edition. Bombay: Bharatiya Vidya Bhavan, 1960.

35. *A Long Journey: An Autobiography.* New Haven: College and University Press Services, 1963.

II. Articles

Of several hundred editorials and essays published in such papers as *Delo Naroda, Volia Naroda,* and other popular periodicals, and of some 200 papers published in the scientific journals of various countries, here are given only a few articles typical of the kind of problems discussed in these papers.

1. Granitzy i predmet soziologii *Novyie Idei v Soziologii,* No. 1, "Obsor teoriy i osnovnykh problem progressa," in *Novyie Idei v Soziologii,* No. 3.

2. "E. Durkheim ob religii," *Novyie Idei v Soziologii,* No. 4.

3. "Sakony rasvitia nakazaniy s tochky zrenia psychologicheskoi teorii prava L. I. Petrajitzkago," *Novyie Idei v Pravovedenii,* No. 3.

4. "K voprosu ob evoluzii i progresse," *Vestnik Psykhologii i Kriminalnoi Antropologii,* September, 1911.

5. "Glavneishia teorii progressa," *Vestnik Znania,* September, 1911.

6. "K. Hamsun i E. Verhaern," *Vseobschiy Journal,* September, 1911.

7. "Istoriko-Statistichesky Ocherk Zyrian" (with K. Jakov). *Trudy expedizii po isledovaniu semli Pechorskago kraia,* St. Petersburg, 1910.

8. "Perejitki animisma u Zyrian," *Isvestia Archangelskago Obschestva Isuchenia Russkago Severa*, 1910.

9. "K voprocu ob evoluzii semiy i braka u Zyrian," *Isvestia Archangelskago Obschestva Isuchenia Russkago Severa*, 1911.

10. "Sovremmennyie Zyriane," *Isvestia Archangelskago Obschestva Isuchenia Russkago Severa*, 1912.

11. " 'Tretia' shkola i spor 'klassikov' s 'soziologami' u ugolovenom prave," *Iuridicheski Vestnik*, 1915, No. XI.

12. "Kategoria 'doljnago' i eia primenimost k izucheniu sozialnykh iavleniy," *Iuridicheski Vestnik*, 1916.

13. "Struktura sovremennoi dogmatiki ugolovango prava," *Vestnik Psikhologii, Kriminalnoi Antropologii i Pedagogiki*, Vol. XIII, 1917, Nos. 1-5.

14. "Osnovnuie problemy soziologii P. L. Lavrova," *Sbornik Pamiaty Lavrova*, Petrograd: Kolos, 1920.

15. "Vliyanie professii na povedenie liudey i refexologia professionalnykh group," *Journal Psychologii, Nevrologii i Reflexologii*, 1921.

16. "Golod i ideologia obschestva," *Ekonomist*, 1922, Nos. 4, 5.

17. "The New Soviet Codes and Soviet Justice," *Michigan Law Review*, November, 1924.

18. "American Millionaires and Multimillionaires," *Social Forces*, May, 1925.

19. "Monarchs and Rulers," *Social Forces*, September, 1925; March, 1926.

20. "Changes in Occupations and Economic Status of American Families During Four Generations," *Publications of American Sociological Society*, Vol. XXXII, 1926.

21. "Die Russische Soziologie in Swanzigsten Jahrhundert," *Jahrbuch f. Soziologie*, Vol. II, 1926.

22. "Impoverishment and the Expansion of Governmental Control," *American Journal of Sociology*, September, 1926.

23. "Sociology and Ethics," in W. Ogburn and A. Goldenweiser, *The Social Sciences*. Boston: Houghton Mifflin Co., 1927.

24. "A Survey of the Cyclical Conceptions of Social and Historical Process," *Social Forces*, September, 1927.

25. "Leaders of Labor and Radical Movements in the United States and Foreign Countries," *American Journal of Sociology*, November, 1927.

26. "Stratification sociale et intelligence," *Revue Intern de Sociologie*, 1927, Nos. 9-10.
27. "Russian Sociology in the Twentieth Century," *Publications of American Sociological Society*, Vol. XXXI, 1927.
28. "Farmer Leaders in the United States," *Social Forces*, September, 1928.
29. "Experimente zur Soziologie," *Zeitschrift f. Völkerpsychologie und Soziologie*, March, 1928.
30. "Die Politische Einstellung der Farmer und Bauern," *Zeitschrift f. Völkerpsychologie und Soziologie*, March, 1929.
31. "Some Contrasts of Contemporary European and American Sociology," *Social Forces*, September, 1929.
32. "Die Soziologie als Spezialwissenschaft," *Zeitschrift f. Völkerpsychologie und Soziologie*, March, 1930.
33. "An Experimental Study of Efficiency of Work Under Various Specified Conditions," *American Journal of Sociology*, March, 1930.
34. "An Experimental Study of the Influence of Suggestion on the Discrimination and Valuation of People," *American Journal of Sociology*, March, 1932.
35. "Metabolism of the Different Strata of Social Institutions and Institutional Continuity," *Metron*, 1932, Nos. 1, 2.
36. "Soziale Bewegungsvorgänge," *Kölner Vierteljahrshefte f. Soziologie*, Jahrgang VI, Heft 2, n.d.
37. "Arbeitsleistung und Entlohnung," *Kölner Vierteljahrshefte f. Soziologie*, Jahrgang VII, Heft 2, n.d.
38. "Life-Span, Age-Composition, and Mortality of Social Organizations," *Mensch en Maatschappij*, 9e Jaargagn, Nos. 1, 2, n.d.
39. "Studien zur Soziologie der Kunst," *Sociologus*, March, 1933.
40. "Recent Social Trends: A Criticism," *Journal of Political Economy*, April/June, 1933.
41. "The Course of Arabian Intellectual Development, 700-1300 A.D.," *Isis*, February, 1935.
42. "The Fluctuation of Idealism and Materialism, From 600 B.C. to 1920 A.D.," *Reine und Angewandte Soziologie, Eine Festgabe f. F. Tönnies*, Leipzig, H. Buske-Verlage, 1936.
43. "Forms and Problems of Culture Integration and Methods of Their Study," *Rural Sociology*, September, 1936.

44. "Le concept d'équilibre est-il necessaire aux sciences sociales?" *Revue Intern. de Sociologie,* vol. 44, 1937.

45. "Social Time: Methodological and Functional Analysis," *American Journal of Sociology,* March, 1937.

46. "Pseudo-Sociologos," *Journal of Social Philosophy,* July, 1938.

47. "Histrionics," *The Southern Review,* Winter, 1938.

48. "A Neglected Factor of War," *American Sociological Review,* August, 1938.

49. "Les Phases socio-culturelles dans la culture Euro-Americaine," *Melanges offerts a Emile Witmeur.* Paris: Sirey, 1939.

50. "Arnold J. Toynbee's Philosophy of History," *Journal of Modern History,* September, 1940.

51. "La Influencia de las calamidades sobre organizacion politica, economica y social," *Revista Mexicana de Sociologia,* 1942, No. 3.

52. "Dinamica socio cultural y evolucionismo," *Revista Mexicana de Sociologia,* 1944, No. 2.

53. "The Cause and Factors of War," *Annual Report of the American Historical Association, for 1942,* Washington, 1944.

54. "The Conditions and Prospects for a World without War," *American Journal of Sociology,* March, 1944.

55. "Sociocultural Dynamics and Evolutionism," in G. Gurvitch and W. E. Moore, *Twentieth Century Sociology.* New York: Philosophical Library, 1945.

56. "War and Post-War Changes in Social Stratification," *American Sociological Review,* April, 1945.

57. "O Papel da Semelhanca e Dessemelhanca na Solidariedade e Antagonismo Sociais," *Service Social,* March, 1945.

58. "Qu'est-ce qu'une classe sociale?" *Cahiers International de Sociologie,* 1947, No. 2.

59. "Concept, Tests, and Energy of Spontaneity-Creativity," *Sociometry,* 1949, Nos. 1-3.

60. "The Real Causes of the Russian-American Conflict," *World Affairs,* April, 1949.

61. "Lasting and Dying Factors in the World's Cultures," in F.S.C. Northrop, editor, *Ideological Differences and World Order.* New Haven: Yale University Press, 1949.

62. "Notes on the Interdependence of Philosophy and Sociology," *Revue International de Philosophie,* July, 1950.

63. "Amitology as Applied Science of Amity and Unselfish Love," *Soziologische Forschung in unsere Zeit*, Ein Sammelwerk L. von Wiese zum 75. Geburstag, Köln, 1951.

64. "Polarizacion en la frustracion y en las crisis," *Revista Internacionale de Sociologia*, July-September, 1951.

65. "El Supraconsciente," *Revista Internationale de Sociologia*, January-March, 1953.

66. "Les Travaux du Centre de Recherches de Harvard sur l'altruisme crèateur," *Cahiers International de Sociologie*, 1954.

67. "Remarks on J. L. Moreno's Theory of Spontaneity-Creativity," *Sociometry and the Science of Man*, December, 1955.

68. "Testomania," *Harvard Educational Review*, Fall, 1955.

69. "This Is My Faith," in *This Is My Faith*, ed. S. G. Cole. New York: Harper & Brothers, 1956.

70. "Leon Petrazycki's Law and Morality," *Harvard Law Review*, April, 1956.

71. "Fifty Years of Change in Sociology," *Sociology and Social Research*, July-August, 1956.

72. "Integralism Is My Philosophy," in *This Is My Philosophy*, ed. Whit Burnett. New York: Harper & Brothers, 1957.

73. "The Fine Arts in the College Curriculum," *Bulletin of Association of American Colleges*, March, 1957.

74. "Physicalist and Mechanistic School in Sociology," in *Contemporary Sociology*, ed. J. S. Roucek. New York: Philosophical Library, 1958.

75. *Sociology and the Advances of Natural Science.* The National Academy of Economics and Political Science, Special Publications Series No. 13, Washington, 1957.

76. "The Integral Theory of Values," in *New Knowledge in Human Values*, ed. A. Maslow. New York: Harper & Brothers, 1959.

77. "Theses on Moral Transformation of Mankind," *Indian Sociologist*, March, 1959.

78. *Studies of Harvard Research Center in Creative Altruism.* Cambridge, Mass.: Harvard University Press, 1959.

79. "How Are Sociological Theories Conceived, Developed, and Validated?" *Social Science*, April, 1960.

80. "Three Basic Trends of Our Times," *Main Currents in Modern Thought*, 1960, Nos. 3, 4.

81. "The Mysterious Energy of Love," *Akten des XVIII. Kongresses des Institut Intern, de Sociologies,* Vol. I. Meisenheim/Glan: Verlag Anton Hain K. G., 1960.

82. "A Quest for an Integral System of Sociology," *Mémoire du XIXe Congrès Intern. de Sociologie,* Vol. I. Mexico Comité Organisateur du XIXe Congrès, 1960.

83. "Mutual Convergence of the United States and Soviet Russia towards a Third Intermediary Type," *Mémoire du XIXe Congrès,* Vol. I. Mexico, 1960.

84. "Theses on Creativity," *Syracuse University Symposium on Creativity,* 1960.

85. "Soziologische und kulturelle Annäherungen zwischen den Vereinigten Staaten und der Sowjetunion," *Zeitschrift fur Politik,* Jahrgang 7, Heft 4, 1960.

86. "Mutual Convergence of the United States and the U.S.S.R.," *International Journal of Comparative Sociology,* September, 1960.

87. "Variations on Spencerian Theme of Militant and Industrial Types of Society," *Social Science,* April, 1961.

88. "The Factor of Creativity in Human History," *Main Currents in Modern Thought,* May-June, 1962.

89. "Theses on the Role of Historical Method in the Social Sciences," *Transactions of the Fifth World Congress of Sociology,* Vol. I, 1962.

90. "Practical Influence of Impractical Sociological Theories," *Sociology and Social Research,* October, 1962.

Name Index

Subject Index

Abortion in United States, 156
Absolute, 175; love for, 303
Absolute monogamy: and aggressiveness, 152; and cultural expansion, 141
Accuracy, of Sorokin's statistical tables, 447
Achievement, cumulative and non-cumulative, 72
Acropolis, 434
Active-ideational mentality, 169
Active-ideationalism, 170-171
Active-sensate mentality, 171
Adharma, 302
Adumbrationism, 363
Advertising, television, 425
Aggressiveness: in sexually restrained cultures, 152; Soviet and American, 238
Agriculture, collectivism in Russian, 233-234
Alcoholism Sorokin's father's, 5, 6
Allah, 175
Altruists, 175, 176-177
American Academy of Arts and Sciences, 9
American and Russian systems: differences in, 242-246; similarities in, 242
American Association of Marriage Counselors, vii
American-Russian relations, 244, 245, 461-469; causes of conflict in, 469
American society, "cultural decline" of, 158
American Sociological Association, viii, xviii
American Sociological Forum: aims of, xi; origins of, xiii
American Sociological Society, vii, xvii, 203
American studies, 117
American universities, 9
Americans, present and past, 145, 146
Amnesia, psychologists', 180
Analysis, biological, 375
Anarchists, 21

Animal sociology, Harvard course on, 437
Ankara, University of, x
Anomy and anarchy during cultural "blossoming," 458, 459, 460
Antagonism and solidarity, sources of, 462
Ants and wasps, social life of, 437
Apartheid-type inequalities, 451
Apollonian civilization, 416, 417, 433
Apostles of irrelevancy, 61, 62
Aptitude tests, assessment of, 182
Arabia, inventions in, 428
Archangel, Russia, 8
Archimedean point, 358
Aristotelian theories: of "effective" cause, 34; of forms of cause-effect relationships, 417; of Metathesis Criterion, 100; precept of acorn and oak, 457
Armies, increasing destructiveness of, 211
Art, 83, 86-87, 206, 289-290, 433
"Asabiyah" or "social solidarity," 85
Ascetic-ideational mentality, 169
Ascetic ideationalism, 170
Asceticism and aggressiveness, linkage of, 472
Ascetics, early Christian, 151
Assumptions: arbitrary in Sorokin's research, 446-447; testing of, 208; underlying measurement of, 440, 443
Astronauts Gagarin and Glenn, 362
Atman, 175
Atom, change in theories of, 398
Atomic Age, xi
Atomic explosions forecast, 364
Atomic theory and ancient Greeks, 363
Atomistic theories, fluctuation of, 429
Austerity and religious persecutions, 151
Australia, vii
Autonomy: cultural, 75; principle of, 346; varying degrees of, 490-491

Babylonia, 108, 480
Babylonian studies, 117
Balliol College, ix
Banishment, Sorokin's, 8